REGULATING GLOBAL CORPORATE CAPITALISM

This analysis of how multilevel networked governance has superseded the liberal system of interdependent states focuses on the role of law in mediating power and shows how lawyers have shaped the main features of capitalism, especially the transnational corporation. It covers the main institutions regulating the world economy, including the World Bank, the IMF, the WTO and a myriad of other bodies. The book introduces the reader to key regulatory arenas: corporate governance; competition policy; investment protection; anti-corruption rules; corporate codes and corporate liability; international taxation, tax avoidance–evasion and the campaign to combat them; the offshore finance system; international financial regulation and its contribution to the financial crisis; trade rules and their interaction with standards, especially for food safety and environmental protection; the regulation of key services (telecommunications and finance); intellectual property; and the tensions between exclusive private rights and emergent forms of common and collective property in knowledge.

SOL PICCIOTTO is Emeritus Professor of Law at Lancaster University Law School.

INTERNATIONAL CORPORATE LAW AND FINANCIAL MARKET REGULATION

Corporate law and financial market regulation matter. The Global Financial Crisis has challenged many of the fundamental concepts underlying corporate law and financial regulation; but crisis and reform has long been a feature of these fields. A burgeoning and sophisticated scholarship now challenges and contextualizes the contested relationship between law, markets and companies, domestically and internationally. This Series informs and leads the scholarly and policy debate by publishing cutting-edge, timely and critical examinations of the most pressing and important questions in the field.

Series Editors
Professor Eilis Ferran, *University of Cambridge.*
Professor Niamh Moloney, *London School of Economics and Political Science.*
Professor Howell Jackson, *Harvard Law School.*

Editorial Board
Professor Marco Becht, Professor of Finance and Economics at Université Libre de Bruxelles and Executive Director of the European Corporate Governance Institute (ECGI).

Professor Brian Cheffins, S.J. Berwin Professor of Corporate Law at the Faculty of Law, University of Cambridge.

Professor Paul Davies, Allen & Overy Professor of Corporate Law and Professorial Fellow of Jesus College, University of Oxford.

Professor Luca Enriques, Professor of Business Law in the Faculty of Law at the University of Bologna.

Professor Guido Ferrarini, Professor of Business Law at the University of Genoa and Fellow of the European Corporate Governance Institute (ECGI).

Professor Jennifer Hill, Professor of Corporate Law at Sydney Law School.

Professor Klaus J. Hopt, Director of the Max Planck Institute of Comparative and International Private Law, Hamburg, Germany.

Professor Hideki Kanda, Professor of Law at the University of Tokyo.

Professor Colin Mayer, Peter Moores Professor of Management Studies at the Saïd Business School and Director of the Oxford Financial Research Centre.

James Palmer, Partner of Herbert Smith, London.

Professor Michel Tison, Professor at the Financial Law Institute of the University of Ghent, Belgium.

Andrew Whittaker, General Counsel to the Board at the UK Financial Services Authority.

Professor Eddy Wymeersch, former Chairman of the Committee of European Securities Regulators (CESR); former chairman of the IOSCO European Regional Committee, and Professor of Commercial Law, University of Ghent, Belgium.

REGULATING GLOBAL
CORPORATE CAPITALISM

SOL PICCIOTTO

CAMBRIDGE
UNIVERSITY PRESS

CAMBRIDGE UNIVERSITY PRESS
Cambridge, New York, Melbourne, Madrid, Cape Town,
Singapore, São Paulo, Delhi, Tokyo, Mexico City

Cambridge University Press
The Edinburgh Building, Cambridge CB2 8RU, UK

Published in the United States of America by Cambridge University Press, New York

www.cambridge.org
Information on this title: www.cambridge.org/9780521181969

First published 2011

Printed in the United Kingdom at the University Press, Cambridge

A catalogue record for this publication is available from the British Library

Library of Congress Cataloguing in Publication data
Picciotto, Sol.
Regulating global corporate capitalism / Sol Picciotto.
p.   cm. – (International corporate law and financial market regulation)
Includes bibliographical references and index.
ISBN 978-1-107-00501-3 – ISBN 978-0-521-18196-9 (pbk.)
1. International economic relations.   2. International business enterprises.   3. Globalization.
4. Corporate governance.   5. Capitalism.   I. Title.   II. Series.
HF1359.P534   2011
337 – dc22   2011008367

ISBN 978-1-107-00501-3 Hardback
ISBN 978-0-521-18196-9 Paperback

CONTENTS

PREFACE

I will not attempt to provide an extensive introduction to this book, but I hope the detailed outline and chapter and section headings provide the reader with a map of the topics covered. However, some explanation of the structure, format and approach may be helpful here. The book attempts to provide an account and analysis of some of the main conceptual and institutional forms which have shaped the development of international corporate capitalism over the past century and a half. The focus is on the legal, institutional and regulatory forms, although the analysis is in terms of their development as a historical social process and within a political and economic framework. I focus on law not only because it is my main field, but also because law mediates power in capitalist society. Examining actual legal rules and institutions, providing this is done in their socio-economic context and in historical perspective, enables analysis to go beyond the abstract generalizations of some versions of social and political theory, and indeed helps to contextualize and evaluate those various theories. My aim is to give sufficient detail for an adequate understanding, and at the same time to locate the various theories and viewpoints, including my own, which have tried to rationalize these developments.

Indeed, my main method has been to immerse myself in the detail, while using as a guide some initial perspectives, which have been developed, revised and refined as the work proceeded. In that sense, the methodology was one of immanent critique. Although this sounds deliberate and strategic, in practice I have been in many ways moving through a dimly lit landscape, which only gradually became more clearly illuminated. Yet, to my surprise, most of my initial intuitions have taken increasingly solid form in this process, even some ideas of which I had been doubtful, or which were only semi-formulated. Perhaps this is because, although I have long had an interest in social theory, I have also been highly sceptical about abstract theorizing. The attempt to impose one's ideas on the world is a pointless and sometimes dangerous exercise, whether conducted by the armchair academic or the political activist, or a combination of the two.

Thus, although the book is presented as a logical sequence, its writing did not unfold in that way. The first chapter, providing a general overview of what I understand to be the main contours and dynamics of contemporary global economic governance, resulted from earlier work on the main substantive topics, and has been continually revised. The next two chapters trace the historical development of the international system, over the past two centuries in particular, including a discussion of the main ideas about internationalism and international law and the key institutions in that historical context. I hope that they will be helpful to those without a background in international law, as well as to international law and international relations students and specialists. Their aim is to go beyond generalizations about globalization and deterritorialization, and examine in more detail the shift from the system of interdependent states of classical liberalism, to the more complex and fragmented system of interacting jurisdictions described today as multilevel or networked governance.

The six succeeding and substantive chapters give an account, again in historical perspective, of the shaping of the main legal and institutional forms of corporate capitalism, and of their internationalization, and of current issues and controversies. They are written to be substantially free-standing, so that readers can decide which (if any) of the specific areas are of interest, although there are of course interrelationships, which are indicated by cross-referencing. Chapter 4 examines the large corporation, the key institution which fundamentally changed the capitalist economy and society from the market economy of the nineteenth century to the corporatist capitalism of the twentieth, and its transnationalization and further transformation into the corporate networks of post-industrial capitalism. It also deals with antitrust and competition regulation, which emerged in the USA as a populist reaction to oligopoly, but became a means to manage and legitimize it, and with the internationalization of competition regulation in the second half of the twentieth century, and its current international coordination through informal expert communities. Chapter 5 discusses the dual processes of business regulation: the facilitation of corporate transnationalization through liberalization of capital controls and protection of international investment, counterpointed by growing regulation by both home and host states and the emergence of regulatory networks. It includes discussion of the international spread of anti-corruption measures, transnational liability litigation against corporations, regional frameworks, the rapid emergence of international investment adjudication, and also of corporate codes and the corporate social responsibility movement.

Chapter 6 deals with taxation, which both constitutes and defines the state and its separation from the private economy, especially the income tax which has been central to the legitimization of the increasingly high levels of taxation and state expenditure in the main capitalist states, while the much lower levels of tax revenues in colonial and post-colonial countries have contributed to their dependency. The bulk of the chapter examines the emergence of international coordination of business taxation and of avoidance and evasion, the important roles of tax havens and the offshore system, and the more recent attempts to reassert more effective international tax cooperation. Chapter 7 considers the key sphere of finance and especially its international liberalization, which contrary to common belief was accompanied by an enormous growth of formalized regulation, loosely coordinated internationally. However, this regulation has taken forms which have stimulated and supported financialization, including the emergence of extraordinary levels of trading in complex instruments, and increasing financial fragility and banking failures, culminating in the 2007–8 crisis. The chapter explains the main forms of regulation and its complex coordination through public–private networks, shows how they contributed to the crisis, and analyses the main proposals for regulatory reform and ideas for a more radical reorganization of finance.

Chapter 8 examines the World Trade Organization (WTO), beginning with an account of its emergence from the General Agreement on Tariffs and Trade (GATT), and then an analysis both of the WTO itself and of its role as a central node in international regulatory networks. This includes discussion of the tensions between politics and science in setting and applying technical standards for food, the interactions of trade rules with national and international environmental protection regulation, the impact of the Services agreement especially in relation to the key areas of telecommunications and finance, and the debates about the 'right to regulate'. The last part of the chapter considers the debates about the 'constitutionalization' of the WTO and its relationships with human rights norms, and surveys the operation of its important system of adjudication. Chapter 9 analyses the international expansion of the private-property paradigm of intellectual property rights due largely to pressures from key industries, but also traces the emergence of alternative models of shared or common property such as 'open source', and forms of collective property such as ethical brands, and geographical indications.

The final chapter draws the material together and uses it to put forward my own perspectives on the role of law and lawyers in global economic governance, in the context of an evaluation and critique of some of the main viewpoints of others which I consider important. I suggest that lawyers have played a key part in creating the key institutions of corporatist capitalism, as they work at the interface of the public and private in mediating social action and conflict, and because their techniques and practices of formulating and interpreting concepts and norms which are inherently malleable and indeterminate provide the flexibility to manage these complex interactions. These techniques have also been central both to the construction of the classical liberal system of interdependent states, and its gradual fragmentation and the transition to networked regulation and global governance. Some readers may prefer to jump straight to this concluding chapter, which again supplies cross-references to relevant material in the earlier chapters.

Thus, the book is both broad and relatively detailed, even though the substantive chapters offer only an overview of what are in my view the main issues of each field, which some specialists may find insufficient. Inevitably, some topics are only briefly mentioned or not dealt with at all. Perhaps the most significant omission is the lack of a chapter on environmental regulation, especially the climate change emissions-trading regime, which raises central questions about regulation of the high-energy economy.

To make it easier for readers to follow the general argument, detailed accounts of a number of specific points and issues are given in footnotes, some of which are in consequence quite long. I hope that readers will find this helpful rather than irritating, and the presentation of these detailed 'asides' as footnotes rather than endnotes should make it easier to decide how much detail to read. For the growing number of students, researchers and others interested in international business and economic regulation and governance, I hope I have provided an overview account and analysis that is both interesting and challenging.

Parts of some of these chapters draw on previously published work of mine, which has been cited where appropriate. An earlier version of Chapter 1 was delivered as a paper at the Hart Workshop in June 2006, then at a workshop at Oñati, and was published in an edited collection of papers from that workshop as 'Regulatory Networks and Multi-Level Global Governance', in Olaf Dilling, Martin Herberg and Gerd Winter (eds.), *Responsible Business: Self-Governance and the Law in Transnational Economic Transactions* (Oxford: Hart, 2008), pp. 315–41.

ACKNOWLEDGEMENTS

This book has had a long gestation period. I first sketched it out in the mid-1980s, but what was intended to be one chapter turned into a book of its own, *International Business Taxation* (1992). My move to Lancaster University meant new challenges and less time for research, although in the mid-1990s I benefited from a grant from the Leverhulme Foundation to conduct some research into financial market regulation, in which I was greatly assisted by Jason Haines. My teaching and research shifted towards the tensions between the rights being granted to corporations, in bilateral investment treaties and the proposed Multilateral Agreement on Investment (MAI), and the revived movement for codes of corporate social responsibility, in connection with which I benefited from working with Ruth Mayne and her colleagues in the Oxfam–GB Policy and Research department, Nick Mabey and others. I subsequently became involved with the Tax Justice Network, in which John Christensen was instrumental; and I have learned much from working as an adviser on international tax issues with him and others, notably Bruno Gurtner, Jim Henry, Richard Murphy, Nick Shaxson, Prem Sikka and David Spencer. I also ventured into the fascinating field of intellectual property rights (IPRs), and examined aspects of the considerable impact of the creation of the WTO. A kind of connecting thread between all these developments was provided by the fashionable debates about globalization, and the role in it of law and of lawyers. Then the publication of the challenging and influential book by John Braithwaite and Peter Drahos, *Global Business Regulation* (2000), showed that it was possible to write a synthesis and overview which could also deal with substantive aspects in sufficient depth.

The opportunity to make my own attempt at such a synthesis came when I was fortunate enough to be awarded a research fellowship by the Economic and Social Research Council (ESRC) for a research programme on Regulatory Networks and Global Governance (Award RES-000-27-0117) for three years from 2004. I owe a great debt especially to those who were willing to accept that the purpose of these fellowships of 'career development' could include allowing me to try to bring up to date my knowledge and understanding of the diverse fields I had studied over the years, and try to pull them all together. I hope that the efforts I have made to bring the project to conclusion after my formal retirement will encourage them to take similar chances with other researchers. I have also been very fortunate in finding almost the perfect place in which to complete the final chapters: the Oñati International Institute for the Sociology of Law. I would like particularly to thank the staff of the Institute for their indefatigable efficiency which made it possible for me to continue writing while also acting as scientific director, and the warmth which makes being here such a pleasure.

Both the ESRC fellowship and my earlier research grants have enabled me to carry out considerable empirical research, mainly consisting of interviews with practitioners of various sorts. Without the insights these have provided, my writing would have remained at the level of vacuous speculation or dogmatic assertion, which is unfortunately all too common in both academic and popular writing. Over one hundred interviews were conducted in the 2004–8 period, and a similar number in the earlier periods of research. The interviews were conducted on a non-attributable basis; mainly for this reason I will not list here the names or positions of individuals. I am nevertheless extremely grateful to all those who gave their time and shared their experience with me.

Along the way I have benefited enormously from interaction with many others. It is probably invidious to mention individual names, since there will inevitably be some omissions, but I feel that some specific debts should be acknowledged. Probably the greatest influence on the succeeding pages has been that of David Campbell, although our discussions have included often vehement disagreements, they have equally often been conducted in the most pleasant of contexts, usually country walks or memorable meals. Equally challenging to my thinking have been my discussions, from a different perspective but with a similar Marxist heritage, with Jane Kelsey, who is perhaps unusual in combining vehement conviction with strict technical rigour. I greatly benefited from a month's stay in early 2004 at RegNet in Canberra, specifically in the Centre for Tax System Integrity directed by Valerie Braithwaite, and where John Braithwaite, Peter Drahos, Peter Grabosky and their colleagues, as well as others such as Neil Gunningham, have created an unparalleled centre of socio-legal research. A visit to Dar es Salaam and Nairobi provided an opportunity to see again many former students, friends and colleagues, particularly Marjorie and Simon Mbilinyi, Issa Shivji and the late Haroub Othman, and meet new ones, especially Florens Luoga. Other memorable and fruitful visits have been to Wisconsin Law School, thanks to David Trubek and Heinz Klug, and the American Bar Foundation, thanks to Bryant Garth, where I began discussions with Terry Halliday about globalized business regulation which have resumed at various places and times since. Yves Dezalay and Bérénice Cleeve have provided hospitality on a more personal basis, and Yves has tolerated my sometimes sharp criticisms of his work with Bryant Garth, which has nevertheless greatly influenced me. My collaboration with Joe McCahery and Colin Scott, as well as Bill Bratton, on conferences which led to two edited books, also shaped my thinking, as have subsequent interactions with Colin in his work on regulation.

Many colleagues and friends have been generous in sharing with me some of their research material, and reading and commenting on draft chapters, notably Michael Littlewood, Ronen Palan, Greg Rawlings and Jason Sharman on international tax and the offshore system; Paddy Ireland on the corporate form and property; Peter Muchlinski, David Schneiderman and Gus van Harten on investment regulation; Imelda Maher on competition regulation; Daniel Drache, Joanne Scott, Andrew Lang and Greg Shaffer on the WTO; Julian Cockbain, Jakrit Kuanpoth, Chris May, Dwijen Rangnekar and Alan Story on IPRs.

I have been fortunate enough to have found institutional locations which have provided fruitful intellectual interactions with both colleagues and students, first in Dar es Salaam, which was very formative; then at Warwick, where I learned much from colleagues in both law and sociology, and then Lancaster, which also in its own way offered an interesting social science context. Students, especially those whom I have been lucky enough to supervise in their research, have always been a source of stimulation; and in this book I have particularly benefited from the research of Louise Davies, Marika Toumi, Attiya Waris and Yun-Jung Yi. Others have kept in touch, and some have given me a warm welcome and help with contacts on research visits, especially Christine Agimba, Yao Graham, Patricia Kameri, Chin-Tarn Lee and Terence McDonald.

Needless to say, while I have learned much from all of these, and I am sure that this book has greatly benefited from these interactions, none of them bears any responsibility for the content of this book. My greatest debt is to Catherine Hoskyns, for more years of love and companionship than either of us cares to remember, also to our wonderful daughter Anna, to Ed who also appreciates her, and to Freddie, Alice and Lily who give us hope for the future.

Oñati, July 2010

TABLE OF CASES

ABBREVIATIONS AND ACRONYMS

AB	Appellate Body (of the WTO)
ABS	access and benefit sharing
ABT	Agreement on Basic Telecommunications
ACJ	Andean Court of Justice
ACP	African, Caribbean and Pacific
ACTA	Anti-Counterfeiting Trade Agreement
AML	anti-money laundering
AoA	Agreement on Agriculture
APA	Advanced Pricing Agreement
ASCAP	American Society of Composers, Authors and Publishers
ASEAN	Association of Southeast Asian Nations
ATCA	Alien Tort Claims Act
BCBS	Basel Committee on Banking Supervision
BCCI	Bank for Credit and Commerce International
BIS	Bank for International Settlements
BIT	bilateral investment treaty
CAFC	Court of Appeal for the Federal Circuit
CAP	Common Agricultural Policy
CARICOM	Caribbean Community
CDO	Collateralized Debt Obligation
CDS	credit default swap
CEO	chief executive officer
CERDS	Charter of Economic Rights and Duties of States
CFA	Committee on Fiscal Affairs (of the OECD)
CFC	Controlled Foreign Corporation
CFIUS	Committee on Foreign Investment in the United States
CFT	countering financing of terrorism
CGIAR	Consultative Group on International Agricultural Research
CIA	Central Intelligence Agency
CIIME	Committee on International Investment and Multinational Enterprise
CITES	Convention on International Trade in Endangered Species

Codex	Codex Alimentarius Commission
CRA	credit-rating agency
CRO	collective rights organization
CSR	corporate social responsibility
CUTS	Consumer Unity & Trust Society
DG	Directorate-General
DGComp	Directorate-General for Competition
DMCA	Digital Millennium Copyright Act
DRM	digital rights management
DSB	Dispute Settlement Body
DSU	Dispute Settlement Understanding
EAC	East African Community
EC	European Community
ECAI	external credit assessment institution
ECJ	European Court of Justice
ECN	European Competition Network
ECOSOC	Economic and Social Council
ECOWAS	Economic Community of West African States
ECSC	European Coal and Steel Community
ECT	Energy Charter Treaty
EEC	European Economic Community
EPC	European Patent Convention
EPO	European Patent Office
EPZ	Export Processing Zone
EST	expressed sequence tag
ETUC	European Trade Union Confederation
EU	European Union
FAO	Food and Agriculture Organization
FATF	Financial Action Task Force
FCPA	Foreign Corrupt Practices Act
FDI	foreign direct investment
FIU	Financial Intelligence Unit
FLOSS	free *libre* open-source software
FoC	flags of convenience
FSA	Financial Services Authority
FSF	Financial Stability Forum
FTC	Fair Trade Commission
GAAP	Generally Accepted Accounting Principles
GAO	General Accounting Office
GATS	General Agreement on Trade in Services
GATT	General Agreement on Tariffs and Trade
GDP	gross domestic product

GI	geographical indication
GM	genetically modified
GPL	General Public Licence
GSP	generalized system of preferences
HGP	human genome project
HNWI	high net worth individual
IAIS	International Association of Insurance Supervisors
IARC	International Agricultural Research Centre
IASB	International Accounting Standards Board
IASC	International Accounting Standards Committee
IATA	International Air Transport Association
ICANN	Internet Corporation for Assigned Names and Numbers
ICC	International Chamber of Commerce
ICJ	International Court of Justice
ICN	International Competition Network
ICSID	International Centre for the Settlement of Investment Disputes
IDA	International Development Association
IETF	Internet Engineering Task Force
IFI	international financial institution
IGO	intergovernmental organization
IIA	international investment agreement
ILO	International Labour Organization
IMF	International Monetary Fund
INGO	international non-governmental organization
IO	international organization
IOSCO	International Organization of Securities Commissions
IP	intellectual property
IPIC	(Treaty on) Intellectual Property in Integrated Circuits
IPPC	International Plant Protection Convention
IPR	intellectual property right
IRS	Internal Revenue Service
ISDA	International Swaps and Derivatives Association
ISO	International Standards Organization
ISP	internet service provider
ITF	International Transport Federation
ITO	International Trade Organization
IT–PGRFA	International Treaty on Plant Genetic Resources for Food and Agriculture
ITU	International Telecommunications Union
LLR	lender of last resort
LTCM	Long-Term Credit Management

MA	Market Access
M&A	merger and acquisition
MAI	multilateral agreement on investment
MAP	mutual agreement procedure
MEA	multilateral environmental agreement
MERCOSUR	Mercado Común del Sur (Southern Common Market)
MFA	Multi-Fibre Agreement
MFN	most-favoured-nation (treatment)
MLAT	mutual legal assistance treaty
MNE	multinational enterprise
MOU	memorandum of understanding
NAAEC	North American Agreement on Environmental Cooperation
NAALC	North American Agreement on Labor Cooperation
NAFTA	North American Free Trade Agreement
NATO	North Atlantic Treaty Organization
NCI	National Cancer Institute
NGO	non-governmental organization
NIC	newly industrializing country
NIEO	New International Economic Order
NIH	National Institutes of Health
NLFT	no-less-favourable treatment
NT	National Treatment
NTB	non-tariff barrier
OECD	Organization for Economic Cooperation and Development
OFC	offshore financial centre
OGBS	Offshore Group of Banking Supervisors
OHCHR	Office of the High Commissioner for Human Rights
OTC	over the counter
PBR	plant breeders' right
PCT	Patent Cooperation Treaty
PE	permanent establishment
PPMs	processes and production methods
PRO	Public Records Office
PTA	preferential trade agreement
R&D	research and development
RBP	restrictive business practices
ROSC	Report on Observance of Standards and Codes
SCM	Subsidies and Countervailing Measures
SEC	Securities and Exchange Commission
SEZ	special economic zone

SMTA	Standard Material Transfer Agreement
SPS	(agreement on) Sanitary and Phytosanitary Measures
SPV	special purpose vehicle
TBT	(agreement on) Technical Barriers to Trade
TI	Transparency International
TIEA	tax information exchange agreement
TNC	transnational corporation
TPM	technological protection measure
TRIMs	(agreement on) Trade-Related Investment Measures
TRIPs	(agreement on) Trade-Related Intellectual Property Rights
TUAC	Trade Union Advisory Committee
UN	United Nations
UNCITRAL	United Nations Commission on International Trade Law
UNCLOS	United Nations Convention on the Law of the Sea
UNCTAD	United Nations Conference on Trade and Development
UNDP	United Nations Development Programme
UNEP	United Nations Environment Programme
UNGA	United Nations General Assembly
United Nations HCHR	United Nations High Commissioner for Human Rights
UNIDO	United Nations Industrial Development Organization
United Nations ODC	United Nations Office on Drugs and Crime
UPOV	Union internationale pour la protection des obtentions végétales (Union for the Protection of New Varieties of Plants)
UR	Uruguay Round
US	United States
USA	United States of America
USPTO	United States Patent and Trademark Office
USSR	Union of Soviet Socialist Republics
USTR	United States Trade Representative
VaR	value at risk
VCLT	Vienna Convention on the Law of Treaties
WB	World Bank
WIPO	World Intellectual Property Organization
WIR	World Investment Report
WTO	World Trade Organization

Transformations of global governance

The past few decades have seen major changes in the patterns and forms of international economic activity, and in their political, legal and institutional setting. The aim of this chapter is to outline the contours of these changes, to analyse and discuss the main concepts through which they might be grasped, and in that way to provide a basis for the more detailed studies in the succeeding chapters.

1.1 Globalization, regulation, legalization

1.1.1 Globalization or economic imperialism?

The transformations in global governance, and their contentious nature, have been debated through the concept of globalization, which became current especially in the 1990s. The controversies were partly due to the confusing character of the term. Perhaps inevitably for an abstract analytical concept, it was applied both descriptively and prescriptively. As description, the term globalization is unhelpful, since it implies a process of global unification, yet the world remains divided. Its use seemed to result from an abrupt awareness by some scholars and politicians that their assumptions and theories were too narrowly focused on the national state and economy, while failing to inquire whether such perspectives had ever been valid.[1] While the critics of globalization were right to argue that the trends of the 1990s were part of a much longer history and that capitalism has always been global, too often such arguments led them to overlook or minimize the real changes taking place.

---

1 Thus, economics has focused on the national economy, reinforced by the perspective of Keynesianism (Radice 1984), and found it hard to cope with phenomena such as the transnational corporation (see Chapter 4, at 4.2); and international politics has been dominated by a 'realist' perspective which reifies national states, while other theories just dissolve it (Rosenberg 1994).

The term globalization misleadingly suggests a trend towards global homogeneity, rather than an increased awareness of the variety and inter-connectedness of the world's diverse and interacting societies, states and legal systems. Partly for that reason, the term was hotly debated, came under increasing criticism, and seemed to fall from favour, especially after the dramatic events of 11 September 2001 cast a pall over the generally favourable use of the concept (Rosenberg 2005). The concept of glob-alization should be distinguished from the issue of global governance. The sharp conflicts over many aspects of the emerging contours of this form of rule perhaps suggests that we are seeing struggles around a new form of imperial rule (Hardt and Negri 2000, 2005), or a renewal of the 'spirit of capitalism' in which power is based on new forms of commod-ification and on mobility through networks (Boltanski and Chiapello 1999).

The term globalization could more defensibly be said to refer to closer international economic integration. Yet even here things are not quite as they seem. It is generally thought to involve an increasing volume or velocity of international flows: in economic terms, of trade, investment and finance; in cultural terms, of artefacts, signs and symbols. Certainly, globalization could be said to have 'given a cosmopolitan character to production and consumption in every country', so that 'in place of the old local and national seclusion and self-sufficiency, we have intercourse in every direction'. Yet those are quotations from the description of the creation of industrial capitalism given in 1848 by Karl Marx and Friedrich Engels in *The Manifesto of the Communist Party*. While the nature of the world economy has greatly changed since then, it is not obvious that there has been any substantial increase in the degree of what they already at that time described as 'the universal interdependence of nations'. Attempts to quantify the growth of international transactions over the past century or more, when calculated in proportion to local or national transactions, do not generally show a significant *relative* increase.[2]

---

2 It has been frequently pointed out that although trade and international investment have grown faster than gross domestic product (GDP) in the 1970s and 1980s, the degree of openness and integration in the world economy has merely returned, in quantitative terms, to the pre-1913 period (e.g. Krugman 1994b: 258ff.; Bairoch 1996; Hirst and Thompson 1996: 26ff.); and this applies also to international communication (Thomson and Krasner 1989). There are quantitative counter-arguments (see Held *et al.* 1999), but the more cogent issue is the qualitative changes in the nature of social and cultural interactions (e.g. Featherstone 1990). The broader point, in my view, is that social change is neither linear nor circular, but dialectical.

What has been more important has been the increased potential for such flows. This results from what is generally referred to as *liberalization*: the reduction or elimination of national and local restrictions on cross-border economic and social flows and transactions. The gradual reduction of tariff barriers and elimination of exchange controls during the 1960s and 1970s widened in the 1980s into a more generalized drive to reduce other administrative, legal and even cultural barriers to economic access, opening up all kinds of economic activities to participation by outsiders, and facilitating access to foreign goods and services, as well as culture and ideas. This has resulted in a heightened awareness of the *differences* among the many regional, national and local arrangements or institutions within which economic activity is embedded, and the influence of such differences on international flows. Thus, globalization has often been seen as a primarily economic process, generally with negative impacts on local culture and institutions.

Liberalization also involved an important change in the nature of competition. Not only firms but also national governments came to feel under the pressure of competition (Porter 1998). Very often, a government's response to social demands from its citizens has been to point to the constraints of international competition and the need for economic discipline. It has also led to debate about 'regulatory competition': competition between states to attract business investment by providing the most favourable conditions. Much of this has focused on whether and in what circumstances such competition leads to improvement or deterioration of public provision – a 'race to the bottom' or 'to the top' (Vogel 1995; Murphy 2004). However, this depends on many unrealistic assumptions, and the debate tends to overlook in particular the more important question of how regulatory competition is structured by international coordination (see further Chapter 3, at 3.2.1).

Much of the debate about globalization has been about whether these trends are inevitable or desirable, and hence about the prescriptive implications of the term. Globalization is generally taken to imply a drive for free markets and economic efficiency. Looked at more closely, however, it can be seen that liberalization was as much a political as an economic process (Helleiner 1995). Furthermore, far from resulting in markets free from political intervention, economic activity has actually become more highly and explicitly governed by rules (Vogel 1996).

In fact, liberalization has been accompanied and facilitated by the emergence of *regulation*, and indeed what some have called a new 'regulatory state' (Majone 1993; Loughlin and Scott 1997; Braithwaite 2000;

Moran 2003), and even 'regulatory capitalism' (Levi-Faur and Jordana 2005; Braithwaite 2008). This has deep roots in processes of juridification by which 'the political system takes control of social processes', producing 'a new type of law, regulatory law' (Teubner 1987: 18). This trend to legalization gathered momentum in the 1970s and continued to accelerate in the 1980s and 1990s, even as central governments were privatizing state assets, subcontracting many activities and delegating a wide range of public functions to relatively autonomous bodies. Thus there has not been a retreat of the state but various processes of state *transformation*.

The shift towards more formalized regulation results from both internal and external pressures. The intrusion of newcomers into a previously closed economic and social space often generates an impetus to introduce or reform regulation, especially if it involves some dramatic event or crisis. Frequently this has occurred when groups cemented by traditional customary practices have come under pressure from outsiders. In such cases the impact of external economic forces has been mediated by the introduction of regulation, although often only following a crisis or conflict. Thus, the redefinition of the City of London as a global financial centre entailed its transformation from the closed world of a gentleman's club through a long series of regulatory reforms, initially sparked off when an influx of credit mainly through foreign bank branches triggered the secondary bank crisis of 1974.[3] Another example is the transformation of traditional agricultural practices with the growth of factory farming and agribusiness, and the way that these processes have been mediated by an enormous growth of regulation in relation to both the production and consumption of food.

Ideas and models of regulation have been devised and diffused internationally, mediated by competition within and between different groups of professionals such as lawyers, economists and accountants (Dezalay and Garth 2001, 2002), recycled through global arenas and imported, with more or less adaptation, into national systems. An awareness of the need for new forms of international cooperation and global governance often stems from pressures for reform of regulation at local or national level, and models or prescriptions from the international arena are used as catalysts or weapons locally. These new forms of regulation tend to displace closed and informal modes of supervision or management at national

---

3 Moran 1984, 1991; a similar pattern in the Asian financial crisis of 1997 involved talk of 'crony capitalism'.

level, so this process can perhaps be more accurately described as international re-regulation (Majone 1990; S. Vogel 1996). A dramatic example is provided by financial markets, where the breaking-down of relatively closed national systems of credit and finance in many countries around the world has been accompanied and facilitated by elaborate new regulatory arrangements, developed through complex international political processes, producing a raft of Brussels directives and Basel guidelines. These have introduced formalized rules and professionalized supervision in place of informal oversight by central banks and finance ministries (see Chapter 7).

This has involved some intriguing shifts in the *character* of rules and law, away from top-down direct instruments of control by central state bodies, and towards more complex decentralized modes of governance involving technical specialists and based on the construction of new professional regulatory cultures. These experts – economists, accountants, lawyers, scientists and managers – in many ways constitute a new 'cadre class' (van der Pijl 1998: ch. 5) of technical specialists.

1.1.2 The shift to post-industrial capitalism

These changes have been part of a prolonged process of social and economic restructuring of both the 'private' sphere of economic activity, and the 'public' realm of politics and the state, and of their interaction.

The reasons or causes have been equally diverse, but they are deep-rooted and have involved a mixture of political and economic factors. Importantly, these changes have generally been driven by social pressures from below. Since the 1960s, there have been widespread revolts against autocratic power in the family and the factory, the classroom and the boardroom, in the metropolitan centres and the dependent peripheries. In general terms, these entail a rejection of authoritarian domination and the power to control truth embodied in tradition, involving demands for increased personal autonomy and dignity, equality (notably, between women and men), the ending of coercion, and economic justice. Rather than the desire for economic liberalization bringing about political democratization, it has been the struggles against autocracy that have created an opening for economic liberalization.[4] While undermining

---

4 Political studies have found that domestic factors have had the strongest influence in democratic transitions, although the international context plays an important part through processes of emulation and influence (Whitehead 1996). However, as Philippe Schmitter

patriarchy and hierarchy, these anti-authoritarian movements have also paved the way to post-industrial capitalism, with its emphasis on flexible production and working systems, information management and a global outlook.[5]

Most visibly, there have been significant changes in the form and functions of the state, resulting from widespread experiences of state failure. This was most stark in the collapse of state socialism, which clearly experienced a systemic social breakdown, both of political autocracy and economic centralization (Kornai 1992). Indeed, all states have experienced major shocks and crises requiring radical reforms. However, there has been as much experimentation and failure as real success: this has been so for US-regulated corporatism, European-style social–democratic welfare states, the developmental states of Japan and the Asian 'tigers' and the post-colonial bureaucratized states of underdeveloped countries. Although the relationships between the political and economic processes have been less clear than in the case of state socialism, the connection has often been expressed as a fiscal crisis, the increased difficulty of legitimizing public expenditures from general taxes, in particular direct taxes on income (see Chapter 6, at 6.1). This not only affected social or welfare spending, but also led to privatization of state-owned infrastructure and utilities, as it became harder to raise taxes to fund renewal and development to keep pace with new needs and technologies, in areas such as transportation and telecommunications.

In the developed capitalist countries, political systems found it increasingly difficult to respond to demands for improvements and to resolve conflicting claims in relation to public services, as well as employment and wage policies. However, despite much political talk of 'rolling back the state', and the extensive divestments of state-owned assets, the process has largely consisted of remodelling the 'public' sphere of politics and its relationship to the 'private' sphere of economic activity. The role of the state has not diminished, as shown even by crude measures such as tax revenue as a proportion of gross domestic product (GDP), which strikingly has continued to increase in developed countries despite

---

indicates, the transmission belt for democratization has been the international communication outside government controls of images and information across borders (1996); he also points out that the hypothesis that economic freedom leads to political democracy is an inversion of Kant's view in his famous 'Perpetual Peace' essay, that republics would be more likely to engage in international commerce and renounce war ([1795] 1966).

5 What Manuel Castells has called the Information Age (1996, 1998).

extensive privatization.[6] However, there has been political pressure to reduce the tax burden on citizens, especially from general income taxes, and governments have resorted to sales taxes and other kinds of duties and charges, often aiming to reconnect the cost and benefit for the citizen (see Chapter 6). Also, new mechanisms have been devised to decentralize decision-making and introduce 'market' principles to public sector resource allocation. Although this was often presented as a devolution of power, this characterization was in many respects misleading, as the power devolved was generally limited to micro-management of limited resources within centrally defined parameters.

The former colonized or dependent countries, often dominated by patrimonial autocracies, experienced a crisis of state-centred 'developmentalism', the symptom of which was the debt crises that began to emerge in the 1980s (McMichael 1996). States which had carried out extensive nationalizations, especially of natural resources, had to bear the risk of fluctuating world prices for these commodities while repaying the former owners for the assets (Faundez and Picciotto 1978; Shafer 1983). Although state ownership sometimes succeeded in ensuring exploitation of resources in the public interest, nationalized industries were often dependent on foreign specialists hired to run the operations under management contracts, or stultified by corruption and top-down central planning (Bolton 1985). In many cases, the ballooning debt repayments and the bloated state bureaucracies could not be sustained by the revenues generated by primary commodity exports and import-substitution industrialization on which many former colonies have had to rely. This resulted in a crippling dependence on foreign investment and aid, which was inevitably subject to policy 'conditionalities' supervised by the World Bank and the International Monetary Fund (IMF). Greater success was achieved from the 1980s by China, India and Brazil, as well as the Asian 'tigers', which adopted new kinds of public–private mix, combining significant state direction with a controlled inflow of foreign investment for export-oriented industrialization (World Bank 1993; Wade 1994, 1996).

6 In developed countries the weighted average rose from 23% in 1965 to 33% in 1999, although in the USA it levelled out at some 28% while in a number of European countries it rose above 40% (OECD 2001a: 10). However, in developing countries the tax revenue/GDP ratio has been about half that of OECD countries in recent years (Zee 1996), and they have been unable to make collectively funded provision of social services, even those as basic as free primary education. See further Chapter. 6.

At the same time, major transformations have also been occurring in the so-called 'private' sphere of the market and the firm. Private enterprise or the business economy in reality is dominated by large corporations,[7] and these also have changed. Large-scale mass manufacturing has been reorganized, and the centralized bureaucratic firm has become the 'lean and mean' corporation, concentrating on its 'core competences', but operating within a web of strategic alliances, supplier chains, and financial and governmental networks.[8] In parallel, the public sphere has become much more fragmented, as many activities have been divested from direct state management through privatization and subcontracting, and operational responsibility for an increasing range of public functions has been delegated to bodies which are substantially autonomous from central government. In this 'network society' the public and the private, which were never truly separate social spheres, have become harder to distinguish, and their interactions and permutations have become more complex.

These changes have undoubtedly been very liberating for some, who in many ways constitute a new global elite, but the benefits have been limited, partial and exclusionary. Certainly, most people in Western Europe and North America enjoy higher living standards, and many in Asia and Latin America, and even some in Africa, have felt the benefits of economic development. At the same time, there has been an increased polarization both within and between states: the gap between rich and poor states has continued to widen, and income inequality has increased even in developed countries. Marginalization, poverty and social exclusion affect both the underclass in developed countries and wide regions of underdevelopment, especially in Africa.[9] Also, many of those who have benefited materially have nevertheless experienced greater insecurity and alienation.

The disintegration of traditional social bonds has also led to new assertions of identity, sometimes destructively based on ethnic or cultural exclusivity. The widespread outbreaks of ethnic, racial and religious conflicts, ranging from Northern Ireland to Rwanda, are not simply the

---

7 A cogent demolition of the 'myth of the market economy' has been provided by Lazonick 1991; see further Chapter 4.

8 See further Chapter 4. Bennett Harrison (1994) stresses that this has not been a matter of small-firm dynamism, but a reorganization of big business, adapting to an era of rapid technological change, shorter product life cycles, and specialized but globalized markets. See also DiMaggio 2001.

9 The data are evaluated by Manuel Castells 1998: ch. 2. A comprehensive database developed by the UN University is now available at www.wider.unu.edu/research/Database.

revival of ancient tensions but result from the disintegration of the 'imagined communities' of the liberal nation-states (Anderson 1991). In general terms, this is largely due to the failure not only of these states, but more crucially of the international system as a whole, to deliver economic as well as social justice.

1.2 The emergence of multilevel governance

The term governance has come into increased use, generally to describe changes in governing processes from hierarchy to polyarchy, or decentring. In international relations theory, it denotes the management of world affairs in the absence of a global government (Rosenau and Czempiel 1992), hence the term 'global governance' has become commonplace. For theorists of the state it refers to the 'hollowing out' of the unitary state, or the decentring of government, and the shift to 'governing without government' (Rhodes 1997).

As argued in the previous section, this has involved transformations of both the political or 'public' sphere of the state and the 'private' sphere of economic and social life, as well as in the relationships between the two. Most evident has been the extensive privatization of state-owned firms and assets, accompanied by the introduction of contracting into public arenas and the delegation of a range of activities (from waste disposal to the running of prisons) to service providers. Conversely, however, there has been a parallel and complementary trend, much less discussed, in which the apparently 'private' sphere of business and economic activity has become more public. The corporations and business networks which dominate the so-called 'market', even as they urged a reduction in intrusive state controls, found their activities governed by an increasing plethora of various types of regulation. Indeed, the biggest paradox has been the growth of industry and corporate codes of conduct, the private sector adopting public standards for itself, although this has generally been in response to pressures from their customers, workers and suppliers, and sometimes in order to forestall the imposition of legal obligations (discussed in Chapter 5, at 5.2.2). This has generated a 'moralization of markets', driven by practices of responsibilization involving new techniques of governance (Shamir 2008).

The second and interrelated process has entailed transformations in the international coordination of governance. The classical liberal international system of interdependent states relied on coordination through governments, operating on the international plane through public international law; while they had exclusive legitimate powers internally, and considerable scope to decide how to fulfil their international obligations through domestic law. On the domestic axis, national law governed individuals and legal persons, and governments could insulate their internal management of the national economy from external forces and shocks by controlling cross-border flows of money and commodities. However, as the demands on government have become greater, national economic management has become more difficult and complex. At the same time, there has been a movement towards deeper international economic and social integration, facilitated by international economic liberalization through the substantial removal of border barriers to economic flows (tariffs and currency controls), and greatly improved communications.

This shift towards more 'open' national economies did not create a unified and free world market but, like an outgoing tide, it revealed a craggy landscape of diverse national and local regulations. Trying to deal with these differences has generated an exponential growth of networks of regulatory cooperation, coordination and harmonization. These are no longer primarily of an international character, but also supranational and infranational, frequently bypassing central government. They also reflect and reinforce changing public–private forms, since these regulatory networks are very often neither clearly state nor private but of a hybrid nature. Indeed, a major reason for the growth of corporate and industry codes has been concerns that state-based regulation is ineffective and leaves too many gaps (Haufler 2001: 114–15).

Thus, there has been a movement from the classical liberal international state system, towards one that is often denounced as neo-liberal, but is perhaps better described as post-liberal.[10] The remainder of this chapter will sketch out some of the main elements of these changes, and then analyse three main problematic features of the new landscape: the destabilization of normative hierarchies; the blurring of distinctions between normative forms; and the political problems caused by the fragmentation of statehood accompanied by the growth of technocratic governance.

1.2.1 Changing public–private forms and relations

Privatization appeared to be part of a wider move away from a state-centred direction of the economy, especially as it was powered by

---

10 The term 'post-national' is also sometimes used (Habermas 2001), although this is also in many ways inappropriate in a period of increased nationalism and particularism. A more detailed account and analysis of this process is given in Chapters 2 and 3.

anti-statist ideas and accompanied by much talk of deregulation and free markets. In fact, this movement was not initially ideologically driven, but generally began as pragmatic reforms (by political parties of the right and sometimes also the left), and only subsequently became articulated as broader systemic projects to 'roll back the state' (Feigenbaum *et al.* 1998; see Chapter 3, at 3.1.1). The outcome generally has been the decentralization of operational responsibility for a wide range of activities to cadres of managers. Although privatization is often justified in terms of shifting of risk, the importance of collective and infrastructural services in practice has meant a continuing role for the state in providing subsidies and acting as lender of last resort. Thus, privatization did not substantially reduce the importance of the state, but instead entailed changes in its form, with a shift to corporate provision of public services within a regulatory framework (S. Vogel 1996; Feigenbaum *et al.* 1998; Prosser 2000).

It has been the increased demands made on the state which have resulted in its fragmentation, as regulatory functions have increasingly been delegated to public bodies or agencies with a status semi-autonomous from central government. Such agencies are generally not formally part of the government, and may be constituted as private organizations, with a mandate either laid down by public law or by private legal forms such as contract, or a mixture of the two. These bodies themselves may deploy a greater variety of forms and techniques of regulation. In the USA, which had almost no state ownership and a long tradition of regulation by independent agencies, there was some criticism of 'command and control' forms of regulation for being excessively legalistic and adversarial (Bardach and Kagan 1982), leading to new debates and theories about regulation and its design (e.g. Noll 1985). This has spread to other countries (notably Australia), and generated debates about new approaches to 'smart regulation' (Gunningham and Grabosky 1998). These build on the seminal work of Ayres and Braithwaite (1992) who argued that business regulation should be viewed as an interactive process, involving both firms themselves and civil society actors, with the 'big stick' of the state being a last resort.

Hence, the character of regulation has significantly changed, away from the top-down hierarchical model of state command, towards more fluid, often fragmented, and interactive or 'reflexive' processes. This involves a mixture of legal forms, both public and private, and an interplay between state and private ordering. Thus, a private legal form such as contract can be used as a tool to achieve both managerial and policy objectives, either when private firms are entrusted to deliver public services, such as refuse collection or hospital cleaning, or even entirely within the public sector if quasi-markets are introduced (Vincent-Jones 1999). This is not to say that such adaptations are always successful. Contracts provide flexibility, but private contract law does not easily accommodate and may undermine the public interest safeguards developed by public or administrative law (Freeman 2000). On the other hand, public bureaucracies find it hard to achieve genuine responsiveness to individual citizens, although they have tried to do so by adopting a managerial culture of service delivery (corporate plans, customer charters, performance targets, etc.). Hence, some authors have argued that traditional administrative law approaches should be modified and find new ways of applying public norms to private actors (Aman 2002; Freeman 2003).

Indeed, from this broader perspective of regulation it can be seen that 'private' economic actors also may take on a regulatory role. This may occur if the state adopts a policy of 'deregulation', leaving a void which may be filled by a non-state actor. Thus, private bodies may themselves assume tasks which are of a public character, or entail provision of 'public goods'. The role of private entities may even extend to controlling public as well as private activities (Scott 2002), for example bond-rating agencies and technical standards compliance certification institutions, both of which assess public as well as private entities (discussed in Chapters 7 and 8). There has also been considerable delegation of public functions, especially in developing countries, to civil society or non-governmental organizations (NGOs: see Chapter 3, at 3.1.1).

1.2.2 State transformations

Thus, the so-called 'retreat of the state' left a gap which was quickly filled by new corporatist institutions and techniques of regulation. In place of administration based on close social ties within closed corporate–state bureaucracies, new types of formalized regulation have emerged. But state restructuring has stumbled through an often bewildering variety of experiments, with many dramatic failures and few clear successes.[11] These developments have been seen as a shift from the Keynesian welfare state to a 'new regulatory state' better able to deal with the 'risk society' (Braithwaite 2000). Influential ideologists have argued for a redefinition of the role of government, to separate 'steering' from 'rowing': politicians should define aims and targets but subcontract delivery, which should be competitive and aim to meet the needs of customers (Osborne and Gaebler

---

11 See further Chapter 3.

1992). Thus, the state having failed to deliver on expectations raised by state-centric models, now has a new role of trying to maintain coherence via steering, since roles previously considered as those of government have been recast as societal problems concerning a variety of actors (Kooiman 1993; Pierre 2000).

More critically, followers of Foucault have argued that the state is a 'mythical abstraction', without either the unity or functionality attributed to it, and suggested a broader understanding of 'governmentality' as involving 'a proliferation of a whole range of apparatuses pertaining to government and a complex body of knowledges and "know-how" about government' (Rose and Miller 1992: 175). In this light, the shift from welfarism to neo-liberalism means, according to Rose and Miller, that 'private enterprise is opened, in so many ways, to the action at a distance mechanisms that have proliferated in advanced liberal democracies, with the rise of managers as an intermediary between expert knowledge, economic policy and business decisions' (1992: 200). The disintegration of hierarchical bureaucratic structures in both the public and private sectors can be seen as a shift in modes of social control towards more dispersed organizational and internalized disciplinary forms, 'from the cage to the gaze' (Reed 1999).

From a more Marxist perspective, the shift towards new forms of governance may be seen as rooted in the transition from the Fordist model of industrial capitalism based on the mass worker, to a late-capitalist high-technology economy and knowledge society. In many ways this entails new processes of socialization of economic activity and de-commodification, as production is increasingly 'immaterial' and much more directly social (Hardt and Negri 2000: 285ff., 2005), and valorization involves far more than the sale of physical commodities. Thus, there has been a shift to 'lifestyle' products and the 'services' economy. At the same time, this has entailed pressures towards re-commodification, as seen in the very concept of the sale of 'services', as well as the increased emphasis on intangible property, or intellectual property rights (IPRs), ranging through trade marks, copyright, patents and proprietary information. While this re-commodification and re-individualization may re-establish the conditions for production and circulation based on exchange, it also requires institutional networks to manage the flows of information and remuneration. These institutions and networks are generally of a hybrid public–private character, for example the collective rights organizations (CROs) that license activities such as the public playing of music, or the educational use of copyright works (see Chapter 9).

These changes have led to increasingly formalized regulatory arrangements, often based on a fragmented but loosely coordinated 'epistemic community' of regulators, whose mainly private negotiations with corporate managers are periodically brought to public attention by a drama or crisis. Public debate of key issues, such as the extent of public service obligations and the proper scope of competition, is severely restricted by the substantial reliance on technocratic legitimation. Examples from the UK include telecommunications, where the public regulator has been criticized for slowness in requiring the privatized telephone company BT to give its competitors access to its fixed-line network. In the case of the railways, the public regulator–private operator split broke down due to the crisis over safety standards dramatized by successive rail crashes in 2000 to 2001, leading to the establishment of a new type of body in Network Rail. This is a 'public interest company' supposed to 'operate on a sound commercial basis', with instead of shareholders, members representing both the rail industry and the public interest.

The difficulties facing the transformation of national states have been exacerbated since they also resulted from the pressures of renewed globalization. In the UK, the very machine which was used to push through the drastic restructurings, the strong parliamentary central government, was itself becoming 'hollowed out', with the transfer of significant powers upwards to Brussels, and downwards to Edinburgh and Cardiff (Moran 2003). Similarly in other countries, various types of national corporate–state arrangements have also been undermined, although they have followed different trajectories. The relatively formal neo-corporatist institutions which in some countries, especially in continental Europe, tied governments, business and trade unions together in bargaining over wage rates and macroeconomic policy could not easily be maintained in a more competitive and fluid world economy.

The attempt to recreate institutions to represent 'organized interests' at the regional level in Europe also failed (Schmitter and Streeck 1991). Instead, the EU has evolved into a paradigm of networked governance (Castells 1998: ch. 5; Kohler-Koch and Eising 1999). From the 1980s, the earlier impetus to supranationalism and integration gave way to the 'new approach' to harmonization of technical regulations (Joerges 1990; Dehousse 1992; Woolcock 1996). This was sparked off by the development by the European Court of Justice (ECJ) of the principles of mutual recognition and equivalence of standards, to prevent national regulations from acting as a barrier to imports (see Chapter 3, at 3.1.4). The 'new approach' broadly aimed to reduce the role of European legislation to the setting of minimum essential requirements, often using framework Directives, leaving it to technical organizations (public, private or hybrid, but in any case usually dominated by industry experts) to specify detailed standards. Implementation was through various kinds of networks, generally consisting of experts and often dominated by business. The result was a tension between regulatory competition and loose coordination through a maze of political and technical regulatory agencies and 'comitology' (Vos 1999). Furthermore, the expansion of EU membership and the extension of issues needing coordination to politically sensitive areas such as direct taxation has led to even more flexible and informal or 'open' methods of coordination (European Commission 2001a; Mosher and Trubek 2003; Radaelli 2003). These EU techniques and patterns of regulatory networking have inevitably had a wider influence, through the various forms of association of the EU with other states and regional bodies, and its involvement with global networks, especially through the WTO (to be discussed in Chapter 8).

Hence, as outlined at the beginning of this section, the changes in the public and private spheres and in their interaction also have an international dimension. Economic liberalization has further exacerbated the pressures on the political sphere, which have led to its increased fragmentation and the growth of new regulatory forms. The new types of hybrid public–private regulatory networks often develop in response to the need to govern economic activities that are increasingly internationally integrated and yet take place in very dispersed and diverse geographic and cultural contexts.

Indeed, public functions may more easily be provided in the global sphere by private bodies. They nevertheless face the dual difficulties of partiality towards specific private interests and power–political interference by governments. Two paradigmatic instances may serve as illustrations: international financial markets, and the internet.

The liberalization of financial flows has certainly created an internationally integrated financial system, but it consists of a maze of networks involving banks and other financial firms, organizations such as exchanges and clearing houses, specialist traders of many kinds, and professionals such as lawyers, with both private associations and public bodies playing regulatory and supervisory roles. Financial markets and transactions are in fact highly regulated, but a large amount of this regulation is generated by and among market participants themselves (Abolafia 1985). Of course, such private regulation is not autonomous, but intersects with more public forms of supervision and control. However, as Tony Porter has argued, international public institutional arrangements have generally been developed only when private governance is absent or weak (1993), the converse of the movement we have seen at the national level where the retreat of the state has led to the formalization and privatization of regulation. Generally, however, it has become harder to distinguish between public and private bodies, many indeed are hybrid, and their interactions are complex. Regulatory networks for finance will be discussed further in Chapter 7.

Like financial markets, the internet, although highly decentralized and apparently anarchic, is in fact a highly ordered system. Also in somewhat similar fashion to finance, the development of the internet has been substantially driven by the formulation of norms and standards by non-official groups, networks and institutions.[12] Probably most successful has been the Internet Engineering Task Force (IETF), which has been responsible for developing the technical standards that enable the internet to function and grow. The IETF itself developed in an entirely unplanned way, as a network of specialists, who evolved very non-bureaucratic methods of cooperation, based on principles which later became clarified as: open process, volunteer participation, technical competence, consensual and practical decision-making, and responsibility.[13]

Of course, this work has been greatly facilitated because its subject matter is specialist and the participants may be said to share a common commitment and understanding and hence form an 'epistemic community' (Haas 1992). However, as Michael Froomkin points out in his fascinating analysis of the IETF and internet regulation (2003), the commitment of the IETF community is not to a closed apolitical technicist task, but to the much broader normative value of ubiquitous global communication (2003: 810–81). He contrasts the IETF with another key body, ICANN (Internet Corporation for Assigned Names and Numbers). ICANN was also set up as a private entity, although at the suggestion of the US government, to take over from the IETF the task of managing internet domain names, and it claimed to model its procedures on those of the IETF. However, Froomkin demonstrates that in practice ICANN's methods have been closed and secretive rather than open, and its decisions made by fiat rather than consensus (2003: 838ff., esp. 852–3), resulting

---

12 Although of course the internet began as a US defence project: for further details see Leiner *et al.* 2003.

13 See 'A Mission Statement for the IETF', Request for Comments 3935, October 2004 (available from www.ietf.org/rfc/rfc3935.txt).

in severe legitimation problems. This he attributes to the greater political and especially economic contentiousness of the subject matter, as well as ICANN's institutional design failures.

1.3 Characteristics of networked governance

The previous section has sketched out the tensions in the classical liberal state system which has led to its fragmentation, involving both changes in the nature and interaction of the private and public, and the shift towards networked international coordination. This section will look more closely at three major features of these international regulatory networks.

1.3.1 The destabilization of normative hierarchy

The 'network' metaphor attempts to capture this central feature of governance which distinguishes the post-liberal from the classical liberal system. In the latter, legal rules fell into relatively clear categories and hierarchies, with international law binding states, and national or local law governing legal persons. This made it possible, at least in principle, to determine the validity of rules and to decide which should apply to a particular transaction or activity. In networked governance, normative systems overlap and inter-penetrate each other, and the determination of the legitimacy of an activity under any one system of norms is rarely definitive, since powerful actors are usually able to challenge it by reference to another system. Also, the fragmentation of the public sphere sometimes involves the creation of largely private arenas to which only the more privileged or powerful economic actors have access, resulting in a kind of privatization of justice.[14]

Thus, international law now includes supranational law, which may have direct applicability to legal persons (see Chapter 2, at 2.3.1). However, this possibility is not definitive, since the interaction is often indeterminate or problematic. The most developed supranational law is EC law, which was greatly expanded by the ECJ's development of the jurisprudence of 'direct effect' of some treaty provisions and Directives (which formally are addressed to states not legal persons). Yet managing these interactions depends on accommodations between the national-level authorities and

---

14 A good example is the way US waste management firm S. D. Myers manoeuvred through regulatory networks to obtain approval for cross-border shipment of hazardous waste between Canada and the USA, discussed in Chapter 5, at 5.2.1.3.

courts and those at the EU level, as shown for example in the German Constitutional Court's reservation of Kompetenz–Kompetenz in its famous *Maastrichturteil* (MacCormick 1995; Weiler 1995). Importantly, the supranational character of EC law gives private parties a legal basis to challenge national laws and administrative practices which might limit the market freedoms enshrined in EC law. This mainly benefits large firms, which have the resources to take advantage of these opportunities.

Supranational law is much less developed globally, at least from the formal viewpoint. Notably, states have taken care to insist that WTO law does not have direct applicability as part of national law. Nevertheless, the WTO's rules impose sweeping obligations (or in WTO-speak 'disciplines') with which national measures must comply. This compliance is ensured both by elaborate monitoring procedures through the WTO's Committees, and in the final resort by binding adjudication through the WTO's powerful Dispute-Settlement procedure (discussed in Chapter 8, at 8.3). Although this is formally a state–state procedure, the two most powerful trade blocs have established procedures to give (some) private entities procedural rights to invoke WTO law at national level: in the USA under s. 301 of the Trade Act, and in the EC under the Trade Barrier Regulation. These create what has been described as a system of public–private partnerships, so that 'WTO law, while formally a domain of *public* international law, profits and prejudices *private* parties' (Shaffer 2003: 3, emphasis in original).

An even starker example of the carving out of a specific and privileged jurisdictional arena is provided by international investment or market liberalization agreements (discussed in Chapter 5, at 5.2.1). These give 'investors' (essentially transnational corporations (TNCs)) a direct right of access to international arbitration if they consider that national laws or administration have contravened the broad non-discrimination and property-protection provisions of the treaty. This basically enables the private rights of a legal person to be used to challenge the public policy decisions of government and state bodies, using secretive procedures modelled on private commercial arbitration. The effect is to destabilize the legitimacy of national laws, even if the outcomes of such arbitrations rarely override national law in any definitive way. The threat of such a claim, which could lead to an award which may run to hundreds of millions of dollars, as well as the cost of defending it, gives foreign investors a powerful weapon especially against poor states. This grant by states to private parties of a right to international arbitration acts in effect as a governance mechanism, in which private rights, enforced by an extension of the private procedure of commercial arbitration, may override formal state law (van Harten 2007).

There has also been a growth of what may be called infra-state regulation: legal and quasi-legal regulatory arrangements, involving both public and private, as well as hybrid, bodies. For example, tax authorities in the main Organization for Economic Cooperation and Development (OECD) countries have developed procedures for the coordination of taxation of related members of corporate groups (see further Chapter 6, at 6.3.4). These operate under provisions in bilateral tax treaties which authorize information exchange, as well as consultations between the 'competent authorities', for the purposes of ensuring that taxation is in accordance with the treaty. These procedures enable international consultations between the two (or sometimes more) tax authorities and the TNC (or its advisers, usually the large accountancy firms), in particular to debate and negotiate the methodology each firm uses for setting transfer prices for goods and services supplied between its constituent parts. Agreements between the competent authorities, which may relate to individual cases or to more general issues of interpretation of the treaty, have an ambiguous legal status: they may be treated as no more than a statement of intent by and between administrative authorities. Although a good argument can be made that they are binding international agreements, they are not treated as such, so are not usually published.[15] They clearly have a very hybrid character, with elements of public and private, national and international law.

A major destabilizing factor is the creation of jurisdictions of convenience or 'havens'. These entail a kind of privatization of sovereignty (Palan 2002), in which a legal enclave offering privileges for certain types of private business is created, often designed by lawyers acting as intermediaries between government and private interests. These aim to provide the beneficiaries with a legal refuge or protection from the laws of other states, often without needing to relocate in any real sense since they can use the legal fictions of corporations or trusts (discussed further in Chapters 3 and 6, at 3.2.3 and 6.3).

At the same time, there has been an enormous growth of international regulation of various kinds. A number of areas of international law

---

15 An interesting anomaly was the agreement in 2009 between Switzerland and the USA regarding obtaining information about clients of the Swiss bank UBS, which took the form of an intergovernmental agreement, signed on the US side by a senior tax official, the Competent Authority, and was published (Switzerland–USA 2009; see further Chapter 6, at 6.4).

have become extensively elaborated, such as international human rights, the law of the sea, trade law, environmental law and the law of armed conflict, on the basis of both formal international agreement and informal norms. Further, more specific arrangements or regimes have been developed, often involving a variety of state and non-state participants, as well as diverse legal forms, covering issues from fisheries to finance. The increasing complexity of interactions between various international normative systems has given rise to concerns about the 'fragmentation' of international law, debates about whether and how such interactions can be managed, and concerns that this fragmentation and incoherence benefits only the powerful.[16]

As these examples show, networked governance disrupts the channels of democratic accountability, which in the classical liberal system are through national constitutional structures, ideally parliamentary representative democracy.

1.3.2 The blurring of distinctions between normative forms

A corollary of the erosion of the hierarchical norm structure of classical liberalism has been both the erosion of the public–private law distinction (discussed already above), and a shift from formal law to quasi-legal forms of regulation in global arenas. These are generally referred to as 'soft law', as opposed to formal 'hard law' (see Chapter 2, at 2.3.2).

Soft law is generally considered to be weak, but as with any normative system, its impact greatly depends on the effectiveness of the procedures for encouraging and monitoring compliance. These may be relatively rigorous, at least compared to the generally liberal arrangements in public international law. For example the implementation of the Recommendations of the Financial Action Task Force (FATF) has been closely monitored, through 'peer-review' procedures, and 'naming and shaming' jurisdictions which fail to meet the standards. The efforts to reform the 'international financial architecture', following financial crises both of states and financial institutions in the 1990s, led to the formation of the Financial Stability Forum, which identified a Compendium of Standards, and since 1999 compliance of national regulation with these has been monitored by the Standards and Codes programme of the IMF and the World Bank, supported by the FATF (see Chapter 7, at 7.2.2).

---

16 See ILC 2006; Fischer-Lescano and Teubner 2004; Benvenisti and Downs 2007; Young 2011; see further Chapter 10.

Second, Codes and Guidelines have been developed since the late 1960s to establish standards at the international level addressed directly to firms. Here again, a non-binding form is often deliberately chosen, yet the implementation in practice could be rigorous (though often has not been), and could involve adoption or transformation of the soft law norms into hard law. For example, the Baby-Milk Marketing Code adopted as a Recommendation by the World Health Organization (WHO) in 1981 has been used as a basis for national legislation in a number of countries, although the main pressure for compliance has come from a sustained and vigorous international campaign (see Chapter 5, at 5.2.2.1). In the 1990s, following a decade or more of pressures by business on states to reduce regulation and dismantle barriers to market access, TNCs themselves began to introduce corporate codes of conduct in order to reassure customers and other stakeholders of their adherence to international standards of social and environmental responsibility (Haufler 2001; Jenkins *et al.* 2002). Firms have generally preferred 'voluntary' codes, stressing the need for flexibility to adapt the norms to the specific characteristics of the business, and the desirability of raising standards by encouragement and self-generated commitment, as opposed to the rigidity and instrumentalism of externally imposed and bureaucratically enforced law. Corporate critics and sceptics have countered by challenging the effectiveness of self-selected and self-monitored standards, and have argued that competitive equality requires generally applicable rules rather than self-selected codes. However, on closer examination it becomes clear that the sharp distinction between voluntary codes and binding law is inaccurate: codes entail a degree of formalization of normative expectations and practices, and may be linked to formal law, both public and private, in various complex ways which may be described as a 'tangled web' (Webb and Morrison 2004), so the question is how they should be articulated (see Chapter 5, at 5.2.2).

Finally, the growth of international regulatory networks linking public bodies at 'sub-state' level has involved the use of novel forms of agreement, especially the 'memorandum of understanding' (MOU). These are often very specific and establish detailed arrangements: for example there is a network of MOUs between regulators of financial markets and exchanges for cooperation in information exchange and other enforcement activities.[17] They also are sometimes stated to be 'non-binding'

---

17 These grew on a bilateral basis in the 1980s, but became coordinated through the International Organization of Securities Commissions (IOSCO), in which the public supervisory authorities agreed the Boca Declaration of 1996, which is intended to augment the MOUs

although in practice compliance may be quite effective. There may in any case be doubts about whether they can be formally binding because it is often not clear whether they fall under national or international, public or private law. Under international law, sub-state or non-state bodies are not considered to have the capacity to bind the state or government concerned. In some cases they may be regarded simply as 'private' contracts, if the parties are legal persons: for example, agreements between stock exchanges or futures markets to enable reciprocal trading of products or cooperate in market monitoring and enforcement. Yet they may have a very hybrid character, as with the international tax 'competent authority agreements' discussed above.

Generally, the growth of soft law and the blurring of the public–private law divide indicates that the range and depth of international normative coordination no longer fits within the classical liberal model of agreements negotiated by central governments on behalf of states (Reinicke and Witte 2000). Soft law allows regulatory regimes to be developed and applied directly by the body involved, rather than through a foreign ministry, and for them to involve a wider range of participants regardless of their formal status as state, public or private entities. Soft law is not necessarily fuzzy or vague, it is often specialized and detailed;[18] but it does provide greater flexibility for adaptation to change. Equally, it may be ad hoc or particularistic, and lack independent mechanisms for ensuring and monitoring compliance.

1.3.3 Functional fragmentation, technicization and legitimacy

The fragmentation of statehood and the transfer of specific functions to relatively autonomous public bodies is also a further extension of the process of technicization in the modern state. In the traditional Weberian perspective, technocracy is seen as a means merely of implementing policies which have been formulated through political processes. From this viewpoint, the growth of delegation to specialist regulators is a response to the problems of governing increasingly complex societies, by giving

agreed between the (private) exchanges themselves; the Boca Declaration and the lists of MOUs between supervisory authorities are available on the IOSCO website at www.iosco. org/library/index.cfm?section=mou.

18 I disagree on this point with Abbott and Snidal (2000), who suggest that soft law tends to be less detailed; this rests on their initial definition of 'legalization' with which I also disagree (see further Chapter 10).

greater autonomy to technocratic decision-makers within a policy framework set by government. However, the new forms of governance are more
decentralized and interactive, which further exacerbates the problems
which Weber already identified with controlling the irresistible advance
of bureaucracy to safeguard individual freedom and democracy (Weber
et al. 1978: 1403).

Indeed, functional fragmentation may also be seen as reflecting the
broader changes in the nature and relationship of the 'public' and the
'private' sphere which we have been discussing. The transfer of specific
public functions to what have been described as 'non-majoritarian' regulators (Coen and Thatcher 2005) is often justified in terms of the need
to insulate some areas of decision-making from influence by private special interests and the short-term considerations which dominate electoral
politics. Hence, it also reflects changes in political processes, with the
breakdown of representative government, which 'public choice' theorists
have argued is prone to capture by private interests (Buchanan and Tollison 1984). In place of party democracy there has been the emergence
of what Bernard Manin has called 'audience democracy' (Manin 1997),
increasingly based on populist forms of political mobilization. This in
turn poses the question of whether the decentralization or fragmentation
of hierarchical government based on formal or instrumental rationality,
and the shift to networked governance requiring reflexive interactions
and based on communicative rationality, may offer a basis for new forms
of deliberative or discursive democracy (Dryzek 1990, 1999). The changes
in public–private interactions discussed above make it vital to find ways
to remodel the sphere of political debate and decision-making. Central
to this are questions about the nature of technocratic governance and the
basis of its legitimacy.

This is especially relevant to global governance, since much of the activity of international regulatory networks has been generated by technical
specialists, sometimes described as 'epistemic communities'. There is certainly evidence that global expert action networks have been extremely
effective in mobilizing and sustaining global governance regimes. Far
from being depoliticized, however, such networks often include activists
as well as technical specialists; and even if the issues are specialized, the
participants share common social values. This seems to be the case, for
example, with the computer scientists of the IETF who have developed
and maintained internet standards, discussed above. The contribution
of technical specialists to international diplomacy is often to help gain

acceptance for proposals which are put forward as objective and scientific, although actually carefully calibrated for political acceptability.

In this context, the importance of expertise suggests that the dangers of technicism must be addressed. This is especially the case since so many decisions now entail inputs often from different specialist or expert fields, as well as an evaluation from the general public perspective. Indeed, Mikulecky, one of the pioneers of the new approach to science based on relational systems theory, defines complexity as 'the property of a real world system that is manifest in the inability of any one formalism being adequate to capture all its properties' (2001: 344). Technical rationality can operate in an autocratic way, if it seeks to claim a spurious authority. This can be counter-productive, as has occurred in the frequent episodes when it has resulted in a spiral of public mistrust of science, and scientists' despair at public ignorance. To avoid technicism, specialists need to acknowledge the ways in which their techniques rest on formal models based on assumptions which allow them to abstract the specific aspects of an issue or the data with which they are concerned from the entirety and complexity of the issue in the real world. Since the conclusions they can reach based on such assumptions can only have a partial or conditional validity, they should not be treated as determinative of the issue as a whole, but as important contributions towards more general public debates. Scientific responsibility should therefore include cognitive openness and reflexivity (Dryzek 1990, 1999).[19]

These issues will be explored in the detailed studies in the ensuing chapters, while the final chapter will conclude with a discussion focusing especially on legitimacy and the role of law in global governance.

---

19 Michael Froomkin's interesting account and analysis of the governance of the internet (mentioned already above), suggested that the success of the Internet Engineering Task Force (IETF) in terms of both efficacy and legitimacy was due largely to its essentially democratic participative procedures, which he argues is an exemplar of Habermasian practical discourse ethics; in contrast, the Internet Corporation for Assigned Names and Numbers (ICANN) suffered a legitimation crisis, because its operations were secretive and claimed legitimacy from a rigid corporatist representation system (Froomkin 2003).

2

Liberal internationalism: strengths and limits

The modern nation-state was born and has developed within an international system that can be described as liberal internationalism. However, the social and political pressures outlined in the previous chapter have resulted in a fragmentation[1] of the liberal state, and a transformation of the international state system. In place of centralized government primarily through national-states, within relatively loose forms of international coordination, there has been a shift towards what has been described as multilevel governance. State fragmentation entails the performance of public or state functions by an increasing and bewildering plethora of bodies, public, private and hybrid. It also involves a dual process of decentring of the state: a delegation downwards by central governments to the infra-state level, and a transfer upwards to the international or supra-state level.

Not surprisingly, this has created acute concerns and conflicts, since it is seen as undermining the institutions of liberal democracy based on the nation-state. This has often been cast in terms of the weakening or decline of state sovereignty. However, public authorities in general have been doing more, not less. Indeed, the delegation of many regulatory functions to specialist public bodies relatively independent of central government in many ways results from the increased range and complexity of governance activities. Although the main influences moulding institutional change in each state have been internal, state transformation has been an international process of interrelated responses to global change. Although this is often said to have undermined national states, greater global interconnectedness may also increase national capacity to govern,

---

1 Picciotto 1997a. This concept has some similarities to what others have described as the 'hollowing-out' of the British state (e.g. Rhodes 1997); however, I prefer the term fragmentation, which avoids the implication that the state has been weakened, and I think better captures the growth of regulatory networks (although this is also an important part of Rhodes's thesis).

albeit often in new ways (Weiss 2003). Thus, we have seen not the demise but the transformation of the nation-state.

To understand these changes it is important to look inside the black box of state sovereignty. Certainly, the key institution of the international system of liberal capitalism is the national state, yet its character is too often taken for granted. Especially enigmatic is the simultaneously national and international form of the modern state. A better understanding of current debates about the contradictions and limits of the present-day process of reconstruction of the international system can be gained from a broader historical perspective. To help present this in schematic terms, I suggest that there has been a transition from the classical liberal international system to an emergent model, which may be described as neo-liberal or perhaps better post-liberal. This chapter will outline the classical liberal system and the tensions which have led to its fragmentation. The next will look more closely at the contradictory dynamics of the contemporary period.

2.1 Classical liberal internationalism

2.1.1 State sovereignty and interdependence

The ideal of a state based on an impersonal sovereignty, the 'rule of law, not of men', was conceived by enlightenment political philosophy, born in the French and American revolutions, and grew to puberty during the nineteenth-century period of modern state-formation.[2] The liberalism

---

2 The standard view in international relations and international law which dates the origins of the international state system to the treaty of Westphalia in 1648 is unhelpful, since it is not based on an understanding of the changing forms of statehood and social relations, or of how international law has been able to reimagine them. Dating the birth of the modern system from Westphalia suggests a sharp break from the previous period, sometimes thought of as 'medieval', and continuity from the absolutist and mercantilist state systems of the seventeenth and eighteenth centuries into that of liberal capitalism which emerged in the nineteenth century, resulting in an ahistorical view of state sovereignty (Rosenberg 1994; Krasner 2001). The idea of modern international law emerged much earlier than Westphalia, as Pablo Zapatero argues, in the imagination of Francisco Vitoria, who devised the concept of the *jus gentium* (law of peoples), which was later elaborated by Hugo Grotius. Vitoria was concerned with the issues posed by the contacts of Europeans with other peoples and cultures, and he aimed to provide Charles V with theological guidance in the encounter with the 'new world', and both the theory of the state and of internationalism, based on natural law, which he offered were in many ways far-sighted. Grotius developed this further, writing on behalf of the Dutch East India Company, so that 'two of the first key documents of international law as a discipline were written under the shadow of great global players of that age: an Emperor and a corporation' (Zapatero 2009: 230). The

which emerged from the eighteenth-century enlightenment viewed society as consisting of autonomous and equal individuals interacting on the basis of their free choices. Classical liberalism aimed to break down the old absolutist authoritarianism based on rigid social hierarchies and loyalty to personal sovereigns.[3] The impersonal sovereignty of the liberal state was based on the emergence of capitalist social relations, in which overt coercion was removed from social and economic relations and vested in autonomized institutions with a public character. Hence, the capitalist state asserts a monopoly of the legitimate use of force. The state is seen as existing outside and above the realm of 'civil society' where the 'private' exchanges between free and equal citizens take place, and its power, exercised through law, must be limited to defining and enforcing the terms of those transactions.

Thus, the sovereignty of the state consists of an impersonal power, wielded by public authorities. Importantly, however, in the liberal state force is a last resort, power depends substantially on ideology, enabling government to rest on consent, even if this is mainly passive consent. State power exercised through law should not be viewed in instrumental terms, it is mediated by abstract concepts. These concepts are fluid and

classical liberal international order which emerged in the nineteenth century was based on a positivistic view of law as based on certain institutions, which as Anghie argues 'facilitated the racialization of law by delimiting the notion of law to very specific European institutions' (1999: 25), and hence could exclude 'uncivilized' entities from the category of sovereign states and the 'family of nations'. However, positivism also found it hard to conceptualize international law as positive law, since sovereign states could only be bound with their consent. The importance of these transitions is easy to overlook because of the ways in which international law has been able to reintegrate its earlier intellectual heritage. State-centred international law was able to draw on some of the statist doctrines both of absolutism and of the post-Westphalia period of mercantilism. However, the liberal internationalism which emerged in the last third of the nineteenth century, emphasizing cooperation between states within an overarching normative framework (Koskenniemi 2002), developed into a growing universalism during the twentieth century, and could hark back to the *jus gentium* tradition (Kennedy 1986). The strength of international law still lies in the flexibility which enables its practitioners to accommodate the tensions and contradictions between utopian visions of universalism and the realities of the political power of states and the economic power of corporations, or in Koskenniemi's striking phrase between utopia and apology (Koskenniemi 1988).

3 The term liberalism has somewhat different connotations in the USA, where the end of the eighteenth century was the moment of creation of a republic, emphasizing values held in common, and republicanism as a political philosophy stresses the commitment and obligations of all citizens to those values. Since the 1930s the term liberalism has been used in the USA (in contrast to its origins in European political philosophy) to refer to a belief in government action to manage the economy; the European and US versions of liberalism converge in agreeing that state intervention may be justified to remedy inequalities.

subject to interpretation, so that the exercise of state power is adaptable and contestable, through interpretive practices, which help to legitimize that power. Central to those legitimizing interpretive practices is law.

Classical liberalism did not dream of a single world society, nor even a global market. The counterpart to the national state and its free and equal citizens was seen as an international society of autonomous states, politically independent of one another, but interacting through free international trade, rather than the coerced or unequal exchange of mercantilism.[4] Hence, the classical liberal international system was envisaged as a community of equal, sovereign states, loosely coordinated by consensual rules and agreements based on broad general principles, and an allocation of jurisdictional competence between them based primarily on territoriality.

In the modern, post-Napoleonic state system, state sovereignty has two aspects, internal and external. Since the state asserts a monopoly on coercive force, internally each state claims the monopoly of legitimate power over its own subjects. Other normative orders can be tolerated, or even encouraged by delegation to self-regulating associations or institutions; but they are subject to the overriding authority of state law, which alone can validate coercive sanctions. State sovereignty can be, and often is, authoritarian; but within the liberal state it is legitimized by the rule of law. Government through the rule of law claims to guarantee the formal equality and freedom of all legal subjects and to facilitate free economic exchange, through institutions, processes and concepts based on abstract and universalist principles of fairness and justice. The personal political freedom and equality of citizens corresponds to their economic freedom to conduct transactions based on private property and the exchange of apparent equivalents. However, from a Marxist perspective, both are predicated on a society in which social relations are very largely mediated by the exchange of commodities. The generalization of commodity production is predicated on the creation of private property, entailing the dispossession of workers from the land and other means of subsistence and production. Hence, even human labour, although no longer directly

---

4 The model international society put forward by Kant in his famous paper 'Toward Perpetual Peace' was based on national republican states founded on freedom and equality of citizens and representative governments; he considered that such states would not be permitted by their people to wage war, but would coexist through the mutual self-interest of commerce, so that the essential cosmopolitan right is that of hospitality – the right of the foreigner to be admitted (Kant [1795] 1966).

coerced (as in serfdom or slavery), is commoditized in the form of labour–power, and thus subject to the 'silent compulsion of economic relations' (Marx [1867] 1976: 899). From this viewpoint, the claims of liberalism are hollow, and inequality and coercion are inscribed in the social structure, although hidden by the illusory separations of the economic and the political, the private and the public spheres.

Externally, liberalism considers that it is states themselves that are free and equal legal subjects, forming a 'community' which in many ways replicates the internal realm of the state. Thus, just as the poorest citizen is formally equal to the richest, the smallest and weakest state is formally equal to the most powerful. However, just as the formal equality of individuals was the result of the dispossession of labouring people from the land and other means of subsistence to create an economic compulsion to wage–labour, so the formal equality of states resulted from a long process of colonialism and dependency, which produced a world economy with a highly unequal division of labour. Thus, the creation of a single global geopolitical system based on apparently equal nation-states resulted from a social process of capitalist industrialization, involving both forcible urbanization and large-scale international migrations and colonizations (Rosenberg 1994). Indeed, although the post-colonial states resulted from autochthonous nationalist movements, the elites which led them were often transnational; their state forms and institutions were generally imported or imposed, while national ruling groups sought to emulate their more powerful rivals or patrons and obtain legitimacy in their eyes (Badie 2000).

However, the external aspect of sovereignty means that states themselves are not subject to any higher authority, so they interact formally as equals in a community of a different order and on a higher plane than the national. For some, this creates serious doubt as to whether there can be any international law worth the name. Others can agree that it is law, but of a different kind, based on principles and obligations freely accepted as binding by its sovereign state subjects. Thus, obligations of international law are grounded in the mutual self-interest of states, each pursuing what it considers to be its *national interest*, but bound together within an overarching normative order. The lack of centralized institutions with overriding coercive powers is said by some to indicate the primitive or anarchic nature of the international legal system. Others assert that on the contrary the relatively orderly interaction of states without the need for a higher authority shows the effectiveness of international law as a self-regulating system (Franck 1990; Kratochwil 1989).

While the state is clearly an important focus of identity and locus of power, it is the reification of the state as an abstract entity that results in its personification. This turns it into the 'subject' of international law, and conceptualizes the international state system as a 'community of states'. By ignoring the social relations underlying statehood, this makes it hard to understand either the internal or the external role of states.

Instead, sovereignty should be seen as a particular way of distributing political power, within and between states. The fiction of unlimited internal sovereignty is complemented and sustained by its corollary, the sovereign equality of states. The exercise of power is legitimated within the liberal state by the generation of consensus around the national common interest. Internationally, formally equal sovereigns bargain on the basis of the national interest of each for reciprocal benefits or to secure mutual or common interests.

Hence, the modern state is an abstract form of political power, a kind of fiction, the substantive content of which can be reimagined, although never on a fresh canvas. As regards their substantive functions and modes of exercising them, states are historically specific and contingent, even though formally the state appears to be timeless. This means not only that specific states can be constructed, flourish, and then disintegrate and be restructured; more crucially, it means that the forms and functions of statehood can change, as indeed they have.

The debates about the decline of the nation-state and sovereignty tend to obscure the more important question: how is statehood changing? Although the principle of state sovereignty appears to establish a clear structure or order in the international system, it rests on a shifting foundation, which continually produces fault lines. The existence and continued dynamic of international economic activity continually reshapes the interdependent or interconnected character of social and economic activities. At the same time, the uneven and unequal patterns of accumulation create substantive political and economic inequalities which undermine the formal principle of sovereign equality. Thus, state sovereignty is not an impermeable barrier but a fluid point of articulation between the international and the domestic sphere. Furthermore, its character shifts and is contested.

2.1.2 International law and organization

Classical liberal internationalism was formally based on a bifurcated hierarchy of law, with the state's government acting as the hinge. The horizontal plane was governed by international law, created by and binding only on states, represented by their governments. The vertical dimension was that of the internal law of states, applied to individual legal persons. Governments manage the interface between internal and international law and ensure that domestic law is kept in line with the state's international obligations, by making any necessary changes. Classical liberalism implies a dualist view, which sees international and internal law as two different orders. Thus, international legal obligations on the state must be implemented in national law by specific governmental measures. Only states, represented by their governments, can be 'subjects' of international law. Conversely, national law is expected to give immunity to a foreign state, as well as its representatives (head of state, ministers and diplomats acting ex officio).

Thus, the classical liberal system was based on state-centred law, but international trade and investment could be facilitated through cooperation, based on agreements and rules developed between states. However, economic and political interactions resulted in various processes of emulation, imposition and importation of legal institutions, especially those governing commerce. General private-law principles and procedures (private property, contract and delict or tort) which developed to reflect and facilitate the spread of capitalism in late eighteenth- and nineteenth-century Europe, had some commonalities due to the Roman law heritage and the codifications which spread during the Napoleonic period. European legal principles and ideas were then exported to much of the rest of the world, through both formal and informal empire.[5]

In the important formative period of corporate capitalism from 1860 to 1914, many of its key institutions were developed as part of an

---

5 Some countries that were not formally colonized (e.g. Japan, Turkey, Thailand, Ethiopia) chose to import foreign laws both to facilitate their modernization and to strengthen their political independence. Paradoxically, the imperialist European powers tended to prefer 'indirect rule' and created modified forms of local customary law for family and personal matters, while European laws dominated the commercial economy and the key areas of labour relations and land ownership. The result was a hybrid system of colonial state law, which was generally accepted with little change by the post-colonial rulers, except that ironically they generally preferred to phase out 'customary' law (Mommsen and de Moor 1992), since it was often viewed as traditionalist by modernizing elites. The study of diverse legal traditions has only relatively recently come to consider the interactions between them (Glenn 2000). During the colonial period, anthropologists began to study 'primitive' or 'traditional' law, or 'folkways'; this gave rise in the post-colonial period to the concept of legal pluralism (Snyder 1981), extending also to analyses of interactions between normative systems more generally, which Merry has described as the 'new legal pluralism' (1988). In this period also, comparative lawyers became increasingly interested in legal 'transplants' (Watson 1974, 1993), especially as a tool of law reform (Kahn-Freund 1974).

international process of debate, emulation and coordination, although with significant national differences.[6] The institutions which spread through the main capitalist countries included the legal framework for incorporation of limited liability companies, the protection of intellectual property, a general tax on income as the central source of state finance, and the regulation of competition through cartels and corporate concentration. The maturing of industrial capitalism also involved social transformations, notably large-scale labour movements and the recognition of trade unionism, and struggles to recognize women's rights, extend popular education, broaden the franchise, and establish social welfare provision. These institutions were established by and helped to consolidate national states, and there were often significant national differences; but they nevertheless established a loosely coordinated framework for international corporate capitalism.[7]

International coordination could result from unilateral state action, joint arrangements agreed between states, or the establishment of an international institutional framework. In practice, these methods could be combined. Thus, some states might unilaterally decide to enforce foreign court judgments, or grant a foreign tax credit, but more extended and explicit coordination developed through agreements negotiated internationally. In many fields cooperation was facilitated by the growth of international organizations, both intergovernmental (IGOs) and non-governmental or 'private' (INGOs). It has been estimated that by 1914, 466 INGOs and 191 IGOs had been established (Lyons 1963: 14). There was a clear distinction in formal legal terms between IGOs and INGOs, since only states could by international treaty establish an IGO, but in practice the two interacted. Initiatives often came from private groups, such as the pressures from the International Literary Association which led to the Berne Copyright Convention of 1886, or the activism of individuals such as David Lubin, who was instrumental in the establishment of the International Institute of Agriculture in 1908 (Lyons 1963: 91–102). Private organizations often continued to play a key role: for example the

---

6 Horn and Kocka 1979; Freedeman 1993. Koskenniemi argues that this period of European liberal retrenchment laid the foundations of modern international law, aiming to temper Europe's awakening nationalism by *l'esprit d'internationalité* (2002: 15–16).

7 The period after 1870 has some parallels with recent history: nationalism and the formation of new states (Italy, Germany) was counterpointed by liberal internationalism and the creation of international organizations (as well as formal imperialism); we may hope not to repeat the earlier pattern of a turn to virulent nationalism and descent into worldwide warfare.

international conventions on humanitarian law, which largely resulted from private initiatives (especially from the two Swiss, Henri Dunant and Gustave Moynier), give a specific role to the national Red Cross Societies in armed conflicts, which is coordinated through the (non-governmental) International Committee of the Red Cross. Similarly, the International Chamber of Commerce (ICC) grew out of international congresses of national business organizations starting in 1869, and became an advocate of economic liberal internationalism; for over a century it has both lobbied on behalf of international business, as well as itself establishing some key institutions, especially for international commercial contracting and arbitration (Ridgeway [1938] 1959).

By 1914, these initiatives had resulted in multilateral agreements, often establishing international organizations or Unions, coordinating state functions ranging from transport (rivers, railways, roads and shipping) and communications (the post, telegraph and radio-telegraph), to weights and measures and intellectual property protection (Murphy 1994). Some had a more specific focus: for instance, following earlier efforts dating back to 1869, in 1902 a Sugar Union was established which lasted up to 1913. This was in effect the first international commodity agreement, aiming to equalize the conditions of competition between cane and beet sugar, by liberalizing trade between non-subsidized production and requiring countervailing duties against subsidized exports (Lyons 1963: 103–10).

In the carnage of the First World War, some argued that a renewal and strengthening of such international cooperation offered the only prospect for avoiding future conflicts.[8] The League of Nations attempted to establish a more comprehensive institutional basis for cooperation, which

8 Notably, John A. Hobson argued that such conflicts are caused by inter-imperialist rivalries; he therefore proposed an 'international government' combining compulsory arbitration of disputes and an executive power to apply both economic sanctions and in the last resort international force, with a strengthening of cooperation on 'non-political' matters of government, such as the post and telegraph, transport, prevention of disease, and money and finance; although he stressed that such a government should 'seek to remove all commercial restrictions which impair the freedom of economic intercourse between nations', this should be left to education and 'the common sense and goodwill of the several nations' (1915: 135). The choice between 'military domination and the reign of war, or internationalism and the reign of law' could not be left to diplomats and politicians, but he rested his hopes on the growing 'internationalism of commerce, finance, and labour' (Hobson 1915: 195). See also Woolf 1916. There are both similarities and significant differences between these proposals and those of David Mitrany put forward in 1943, after the experience of fascism (see 2.3.3 below), although both were liberal internationalist.

included granting observer status to some selected non-governmental organizations (NGOs) such as the ICC. However, internationalism weakened during the period of autarchy of the 1930s, although some of the economic work of the League provided a basis for future international cooperation. Notably, the International Labour Organization (ILO), established as a bulwark against communist internationalism, created a framework for developing global minimum standards for labour, based on a unique tripartite structure which gave representation rights to employers' and workers' organizations as well as governments.

2.2 Re-embedding classical liberalism

The establishment of a more comprehensive system of international organizations after 1945 centring on the United Nations and its specialized agencies further reinforced international cooperation. This was still firmly based on the classical liberal model of intergovernmentalism, in which each state had a single vote. However, there were two significant exceptions: for the legitimation of the international use of force a veto was given to the five permanent members of the Security Council; while a weighted voting scheme reflecting states' economic power in the International Monetary Fund (IMF) and the World Bank (WB) gave a dominant role to the USA and Europe in monetary and financial affairs. By the beginning of the twenty-first century shifts in political and economic strength of states made these structures obsolete, but they were hard to change.[9]

2.2.1 Territoriality and jurisdiction

The elasticity of state sovereignty is especially evident when we look more closely at the legitimate scope for the exercise of its power, referred to as its *jurisdiction*.[10] This is generally considered to be limited to its territory, since in formal terms, the sovereignty of the state consists of an impersonal power, wielded by public authorities exercising their functions over a

---

9 However, the weighted voting systems of the IMF and WB can be adjusted, as they are linked to countries' economic weight. Thus, in April 2010 the WB announced a general capital increase of $86bn, linked to an increase in the voting power of developing and transition countries of over 3%, bringing it to over 47%.

10 Some of the loose talk of 'deterritorialization' of the state comes from neglecting jurisdiction, which is why it will be analysed in some detail here.

defined territory.[11] The exclusive rights of a state are supported by the prohibition in international law for any state to exercise any such power in the territory of another state. This territorial boundedness creates a 'billiard ball' view of states and their interactions (Burton 1972: ch. 4).

Certainly, the reification of 'the state' as an objective entity, beyond and outside social relations, means that, whereas earlier forms of state were defined in terms of communities based on kinship, the modern state is defined in terms of its territory. Paradoxically, however, this entails a *loosening* of the close links of social communities to land that characterized pre-modern societies, whether nomadic or settled, hunter-gatherers or pastoralists. Because states are territorially defined, social relations can be freed from any roots in land or locality. Since a geographical area does not constitute either a society or a polity, each actual state is formed around the 'imagined community' of nationhood (Anderson 1991), constituted and continually recreated through a variety of cultural practices and rituals.

However, liberal internationalism entails a high degree of interdependence, which makes it seriously misleading to see states as autonomous and compartmentalized units. Private economic and social relations often involve contacts with two or more states, and hence may come within the scope of several overlapping *jurisdictions*. The effective exercise of states' powers is not mutually exclusive. As defined by their jurisdiction, which is the substance of sovereignty, the power of states is flexible, overlapping and negotiable. The existence of a world market generates private economic and social relations which transcend state boundaries, so that claims to the exercise of powers and functions by different states inevitably intersect and overlap. Concurrent, and sometimes conflicting, claims to jurisdiction inevitably result when an international transaction or activity is subject to the regulatory requirements of more than one state, and often two or more states may have effective powers of enforcement against some of the persons or property involved. Conversely also, transnational mobility of persons or assets means that a state may need assistance from another to ensure effective enforcement of its claims to jurisdiction.

Thus, the 'interdependence' of states is central not only to their external interactions but, most importantly, in the internal exercise of 'sovereignty'. This creates a competitive and interactive tension between states in the

---

11 The classic definition in international law is: 'the right to exercise (in regard to a portion of the globe) to the exclusion of any other state the functions of a state' (Judge Huber, *Island of Palmas case* (1928): 92).

exercise of the functions of statehood, which increases as cross-border movements and transactions are facilitated and intensify.

The territorial jurisdiction of a state can apply to all activities taking place within its borders, even only partially, and to persons with any presence there, even temporary. While states have generally imposed obligations on all within their borders, the privileges of citizenship have usually been bestowed on a more restricted category, nationals. The bonds of allegiance between its nationals and the state have also been used to extend both the state's requirements and its protection to their conduct outside its borders.[12] This may apply not only to individuals but also artificial legal persons, especially corporations, which may be treated as nationals if they are headquartered in the state or incorporated under its laws. Nevertheless, other states are under no obligation to recognize such grants of nationality.[13] Thus, the potential scope of a state's claim to

12 The classic statement of this principle in international law was the *Lotus* case (1927): 20, in which the international court found no basis to prevent Turkey from prosecuting under its domestic law an officer of the French ship involved in a collision with a Turkish vessel; although the collision took place outside Turkish territorial waters, the French officer was arrested after his ship entered a Turkish port, giving Turkey enforcement power. Most states claim the right to apply their laws even to conduct outside the territory *by* their own nationals (the nationality principle of jurisdiction); this may extend further, for example the UK's Bribery Act 2010 applies in respect of conduct outside the UK by persons with a 'close connection' to the UK, including individuals ordinarily resident in the UK. Some states go further and assert their jurisdiction in relation to acts by foreigners *against* their nationals (the passive personality principle), and some also where national interests are affected (the protective principle), although other states reject some or all of these principles (Akehurst 1972–3). International law textbooks also refer to universal jurisdiction for acts considered crimes under international law, but the only generally accepted example of this is piracy (UNCLOS, art. 105). Far from representing a universal revulsion at this offence, it was largely due to the common concern of states to repress unauthorized brigandage, in favour of licensed 'privateering' (Kontorovich 2004). See further n. 48 below.

13 The ICJ's decision in the well-known *Nottebohm* case (1955) appears to establish a normative limit on states' freedom to grant nationality by suggesting that there must be a 'genuine link' for that nationality to be recognized by other states. However, this was in the context of a claim by Liechtenstein on behalf of Nottebohm against Guatemala, which had frozen his assets there since it considered that he was German and hence an enemy alien (for which there was considerable evidence: Seidl-Hohenveldern 1987: 11); the ICJ decision meant that Guatemala had no responsibility to Liechtenstein for its treatment of Nottebohm, since it was not obliged to recognize Liechtenstein's grant of nationality due to the lack of a genuine link. If the claim had been by Guatemala, requesting that Nottebohm's assets in Liechtenstein be frozen, Liechtenstein's grant of its nationality would no doubt have been upheld, entitling it to reject the request. Hence, although state sovereignty means that each is in principle free to bestow its nationality regardless of any 'genuine link' (for example, on ships, or companies), other states are

jurisdiction is very broad, especially if its nationals are involved in extensive activities abroad; but such prescriptive claims will only be effective if the state is powerful enough to be able to enforce them.

Inevitably, claims to jurisdiction will overlap. For example, if states claim to tax residents on their income from all sources, as well as non-residents on income generated from activities within the territory (which many do), there will be complaints that the same income is being taxed twice. Accusations that a state is asserting 'extraterritorial jurisdiction' usually refer to situations of overlapping jurisdiction, so the term is at best misleading.[14] However, it is generally the strong states, with significant international interests, which have the concern and the power to make extensive jurisdictional claims. Hence, it is not surprising that it was the USA, in the second half of the twentieth century, that made most use of 'long-arm laws' and has most often been accused of making extraterritorial assertions of jurisdiction.

However, extensive claims to prescriptive jurisdiction depend on the availability of effective enforcement, either by state officials within its territory, or by cooperation with other states within their territory. The voluntarist and permissive nature of liberal international law meant that even if no objection was made to extensive prescriptive claims, their practical impact would be limited since the state has legitimate enforcement powers only within its own territory, unless it can secure assistance from others. Cooperation of this kind, for example to obtain information or evidence, extradite suspects or enforce judgments, depends on an acceptance by other states of the requesting state's claim to jurisdiction, and the patterns of reciprocal accommodation could provide a normative basis to evaluate prescriptive claims to jurisdiction (Brilmayer 1989). Yet, even if the power to enforce is essentially territorial, it can be asserted against all persons and property with even a partial or temporary presence in the territory. Hence, persons or firms with activities in more than one state are likely to be subject to overlapping jurisdictional claims.

As regards penal or public law, courts have generally deferred to the authority of the legislature or executive to express public policy. This has had two consequences: courts have felt disqualified from applying foreign

---

not obliged to recognize the validity of such a grant, still less to refrain from applying their laws to such persons. This is important in relation to laws combating tax or other regulatory avoidance.

14 For a critique of the pejorative connotations of the term see Lowenfeld 1996: 15–16, and see further the discussion of the 'effects' doctrine at 2.2.2 below and in Chapter 4, at 4.3.2.

penal or public law;[15] but they might try, where possible, to avoid conflicts by restricting the scope of their own. Commonly, therefore, a presumption has been accepted that sanctions should not normally be imposed on acts committed outside the territory. The legislature might nevertheless assert a broader jurisdiction, and in some countries did so, to assert claims either to impose obligations on or to protect the state's nationals abroad. However, in criminal cases other states have been generally unwilling to cooperate to facilitate such enforcement (through procedures such as extradition) unless the actions complained of took place within or had a close connection with the requesting state. Thus, penal or public law jurisdiction could only be effectively asserted by a state against persons with a close connection to its territory, i.e. residents, nationals, or those doing business or having assets within it. This could of course still produce substantial overlapping of jurisdiction, which becomes greater the more persons have substantial contacts with more than one state.

In relation to private-law matters,[16] territoriality gives the effective power to adjudicate on disputes to the court of the state or district where the defendant has a significant presence, since it can compel an appearance and enforce a judgment against the defendant's person or assets. This gives the state of residence or home state a very broad personal jurisdiction over persons engaged in foreign business activities.[17] However, liberal internationalism developed principles of conflicts of law, or private international law, under which the court hearing the case could apply or refer to the appropriate foreign law in making its decision. The basis for such reference to foreign law has long been debated: while some maintained that such reference was a matter for each sovereign state, others argued that it was an obligation derived from international law and rooted in the territoriality of law.[18] Nevertheless, national courts or

---

15 However, the origins of the 'public law taboo' are obscure and its scope uncertain (Tracht-man 1994: 997). The gap was filled to some extent by interstate cooperation in criminal matters, especially extradition. See further n. 26 below.

16 I use the term private law in the traditional sense of the law governing relations between private parties.

17 The issue of which law should be applied is often described as subject-matter jurisdiction.

18 This ambivalence has been expressed in the chequered history of the concept of 'comity', developed in the nineteenth century by Story in the USA, Savigny in Germany and Dicey in Britain, on the basis of principles first formulated by the Dutch jurist Huber at the end of the seventeenth century 'to mediate between the pretensions of territorial sovereignty and the needs of international commerce' (Yntema 1966: 9; see also Yntema 1953). Huber enunciated three principles: that each state had sovereignty within its territory; that it had the right but also the duty 'to administer good law and justice to foreigners

tribunals could be generous in accepting jurisdiction to adjudicate on private disputes, while trying to avoid conflicts by applying conflicts of law rules in deciding the substantive issues presented. Such rules could allow considerable scope to the parties to private transactions to decide for themselves on the applicable law, through choice-of-law provisions in contracts.

The liberal state was also able to tolerate and even encourage private normative systems, or 'self-regulation', although they are ultimately dependent on state power for compulsory enforcement. Thus, businesses engaged in international commerce may choose and be permitted to regulate their relationships under their own rules, often governed by trade associations or chambers of commerce, which may provide for arbitration of disputes. This gave substantial scope for those engaged in international commerce to regulate themselves privately, providing considerable continuity with the *lex mercatoria* of the Middle Ages (see further at 2.3.3 below). However, state courts have the final say if compulsion is required, whether to compel a party to produce evidence, enter an appearance, or comply with a decision or an arbitral award.

2.2.2 Jurisdictional coordination and conflicts

Hence, in the classical liberal system, the tension between the territorial definition of the state and the often extensive scope of international (especially economic) activities entailed various techniques for dealing with jurisdictional interaction. No state was autonomous, but the forms of coordination generally respected and indeed reinforced national sovereignty, in the sense that the *substance* of regulation was generally left

and citizens alike', and that state rulers arrange by comity that the laws of each state enforced within its boundaries maintain their validity everywhere. Although the concept of comity was adapted by Lord Mansfield in Britain, it fell into disuse there as well as in continental Europe, understandably in the period of classical liberalism which considered that each state administered only its own law. There nevertheless remained disagreements in both Britain and Europe as to whether deference to foreign law in appropriate cases was entirely within the discretion of national courts and based on the importance of doing justice between private parties, or whether it expressed a link between private and public international law and a unity in diversity of legal systems. In the USA the comity concept was revived in the 1960s as part of the emergence of 'transnational law', but as a discretionary principle with an ambiguous status between law and policy (Paul 1991; see Chapter 3, at 3.2.5). Anne-Marie Slaughter expresses the more favourable view that the comity principle reflects the mutual respect of courts and 'is thus the lubricant of transjudicial relations' (1998: 708).

to national processes of legitimation, while its *scope* was defined internationally. Coordination was ensured either by the unilateral acceptance by states of international obligations, or by the negotiation of mutual arrangements for jurisdictional cooperation, such as extradition for major crimes (Bassiouni 1974; Nadelmann 1993), and in civil matters the service of process, taking of evidence and enforcement of judgments.[19] To coordinate the application of substantive law, the principle of 'national treatment' was developed, allowing each state to decide the details of its own rules, while attempting to ensure that it gave the benefit of those rules to foreigners and to foreign-owned firms or property within its territory. More recently, this has extended to the creation of compatible or harmonized legal frameworks for important areas of commercial and corporate law, notably through the United Nations Commission on International Trade Law (UNCITRAL).[20]

19 The Hague Conference on Private International Law was convened by the government of the Netherlands in 1893, and held four sessions up to 1905, leading to agreement on six Conventions under its auspices by 1905, mainly on family law matters, but also the important civil procedure agreement, providing for service of process and taking of evidence. A couple of sessions were held in the inter-war period but no new conventions agreed. It was refounded as an intergovernmental organization in 1951, holding plenary sessions every four years, and now thirty-nine conventions have been agreed. In 1994 it launched a negotiation on international jurisdiction in civil and commercial matters, but this was controversial and resulted only in a convention agreed in 2005 to enforce judgments based on choice-of-court agreements, so far ratified only by Mexico and signed by the EU and the USA, and not in force. The International Institute for the Unification of Private Law (known as UNIDROIT) was set up in 1926 as an auxiliary organ of the League of Nations, and re-established in 1940 on the basis of a multilateral agreement establishing its statute. Most European and Latin American states joined in 1940 or 1948; the USA joined both UNIDROIT and the Hague Conference in 1964, and the former now has sixty-three members, while the latter has seventy-two.

20 Established in 1966 with the aim of facilitating trade by furthering the harmonization of relevant laws. This has been done not only by the traditional method of Conventions (notably the 1980 Convention on Contracts for the International Sale of Goods), but increasingly by developing texts for Model Laws (notably for Electronic Commerce, 1996, and Electronic Signatures, 2001), and for other types of soft-law instruments. A significant success for UNCITRAL was the rapid completion of first a Model Law on Cross-Border Insolvency, and then a Legislative Guide for national corporate insolvency laws (Halliday and Carruthers 2009: ch. 4). UNIDROIT also develops both Conventions, such as the Cape Town Convention on International Interests in Mobile Equipment of 2001, and soft-law instruments, notably its Principles of International Commercial Contracts of 2004. An interesting and complex interaction has developed between these various instruments, and their embodiment both in national law and in contractual and other legal relations between private parties, as well as increasingly with public law and even public international law, such as the WTO Agreements (Kronke 2005–6).

The main emphasis in the period of classical liberalism was on regulation to facilitate private economic activity through laws of general application. Far from 'laissez-faire', it required state intervention especially to define and protect property rights and institutions, such as the right to create business corporations with limited liability by registration, and the protection of monopolies over technical innovations and creative works through patents and a system of general copyright protection. Provided there was no explicit discriminatory prohibition against foreigners, cross-national ownership of assets and protection of property could be facilitated. Indeed, national barriers to interstate commerce, such as high tariffs, stimulated transnational forms of business ownership, and the period 1880 to 1914 was the initial period of emergence of the transnational corporation (TNC). This was quite compatible with, and even stimulated by, the existence of a degree of national diversity in regulatory forms, provided the international framework was broadly liberal. Thus, the main conflicts over business regulation were about restrictions on foreign ownership and involved pressures to secure non-discriminatory treatment.

Problems of jurisdictional overlap and conflict were more acute in the case of more interventionist forms of regulation. Thus, the development of direct taxation of income in the main developed capitalist states in the first two decades of the twentieth century very quickly sparked demands from internationally operating business for some jurisdictional restraint or coordination, in order to prevent what was identified as 'international double taxation'. As will be shown in more detail in Chapter 6, discussions and negotiations were initiated through the League of Nations, eventually leading to an international network of treaties, helping to facilitate the growth of international direct investment after 1952. Tax treaties leave each state free to decide the scope and incidence of its taxation of income, and they merely classify and assign between states rights to tax according to types of tax and the relationship of the state to the taxpayer. Similarly, in relation to patents, the Paris Convention of 1883 leaves states free to decide the scope, content and procedures for protection, but seeks to ensure equal access for foreign claimants through the principle of national treatment.

These examples show that problems caused by the interaction of nationally based forms of business regulation became apparent quite early. While in some cases various arrangements for coordination, such as those briefly indicated here, were quickly developed, in others this did not occur, either because national diversity was too great, or interaction did not cause significant conflicts, for one reason or another. Thus, the USA was alone in introducing antitrust or competition laws early in the twentieth century, due to the different political impacts of corporate concentration. Although the potential for conflict if US antitrust provisions should be applied to international business was apparent from an early date, states generally supported the carve-up of world markets by business cartels in the period 1890 to 1939, and only after 1937 did the USA begin to wield its antitrust laws to open up international markets (see Chapter 4, at 4.3.1).

The post-war period saw an international spread of competition laws, as the US antitrust gospel was spread through wartime planning for the post-war international economic order (Freyer 1992: 223ff.), and then through the partial dismantling by the occupation authorities of the German and Japanese industrial cartels and the implantation of competition and 'fair trade' laws. Although these transplants did take root, the very different national soils in which they were established produced different approaches and policies towards regulation of competition (see Chapter 4, at 4.3.1). The more aggressive approach of the USA in applying its antitrust laws soon led to conflicts with other countries, resulting in the enactment of blocking and retaliatory legislation. Hence, disputes over 'extraterritorial' assertions of jurisdiction originated with the application of US antitrust laws to international business structures.

Much concern was caused by the so-called 'effects' doctrine,[21] which was subsequently qualified by reference to 'direct, substantial and reasonably foreseeable' effects, and by a 'balancing test' to determine which jurisdiction was primarily concerned. In practice the US authorities and courts would not hold back on the application of US law to conduct

---

21 This originated in a rather sweeping statement by Judge Learned Hand: 'it is settled law that any state may impose liabilities, even upon persons not within its allegiance, for conduct outside its borders which the state reprehends; and these liabilities other states will ordinarily recognise' (*US* v. *Alcoa* (1945)). However, the case concerned the world aluminium cartel, in which the US giant Alcoa participated through its Canadian subsidiary, and Judge Hand held that US law would not apply if it could be shown that there was no actual effect on imports into the USA (Neale and Stephens 1988: 44–9). A more important reason than the effects doctrine for the more frequent conflicts caused by assertions of jurisdiction by the US authorities was their greater willingness to disregard the separate legal personality of US-owned foreign subsidiaries, and make them directly subject to US legal requirements. Since the USA has been the home of a large proportion of the world's TNCs, and relied more on legal regulation than other forms of implementing business policy, it is not surprising that the complaints of excessive jurisdictional claims were aimed mainly at the USA.

affecting the US economy merely because such conduct was permissible elsewhere, but only if it were required under the other state's law. To help firms to seek shelter under the laws of their home state, most OECD states enacted 'blocking statutes' allowing the government to issue such prohibitions, and hence provide protection against foreign (in practice, US) legal orders. For their part, the US courts found various means to disregard or override claims of conflict with foreign law.

This created an arena of complex regulatory interaction, as non-US firms resorted to their national laws for protection. Thus, ICI succeeded in delaying the enforcement of a US court order to dismantle its cartel with Du Pont based on patent pooling, when the British courts refused to invalidate ICI's sub-licence of a patent to its own subsidiary (*BNS* v. *ICI* (1953)). When Westinghouse brought a private antitrust suit alleging that a producers' cartel had increased the prices it had to pay under the long-term uranium supply contracts on which its sales of nuclear power stations were based (*In Re Uranium Antitrust Litigation* (1980)), the British courts refused to assist in gathering evidence (*RTZ* v. *Westinghouse* (1978)).

This litigation led the UK government to enact the Protection of Trading Interests Act 1980, extending the Shipping Contracts and Commercial Documents Act 1964, which had aimed to block US investigations of shipping liner conferences; similar legislation was enacted by many other OECD countries (Rosenthal and Knighton 1982; Picciotto 1983; Lowe 1983). However, the powers in the 1980 Act were discretionary, and they were not invoked in the 1992–3 conflict over the cases against UK insurance firm members of Lloyd's in relation to the conditions for reinsurance of potentially huge US liabilities for disposal of hazardous waste.[22] The result was often a cat-and-mouse game, in which the US courts would either override the foreign compulsion defence, for example on the grounds that it had been 'deliberately courted', or use their powers to disadvantage a defendant, for example by making an adverse factual finding.

Complaints about 'long-arm laws' became more generalized to other types of regulation, notably the application of US trade and technology export controls,[23] and taxation by US states such as California of

---

22 Upheld by a 5:4 decision of the Supreme Court, on the grounds that although Lloyd's is regulated in the UK, its contractual terms are not mandated by UK law (*Hartford Fire Insurance* (1993)).

23 This was dramatized in 1964 when the US Treasury ordered the Fruehauf Corporation to cancel a contract of its majority-owned French subsidiary to supply semi-trailers to

transnational corporations on a worldwide formula apportionment basis (Picciotto 1992: ch. 9). The issue became sufficiently politicized to be discussed at summit meetings of G7 leaders, and some attempts were made to avoid them by developing a legal doctrine of 'moderation and restraint' in the exercise of concurrent jurisdiction.[24] However, these efforts proved of limited utility as the number and range of issues creating problems of jurisdictional conflicts grew. These included a wide range of matters relating to corporate governance and finance, including financial disclosure requirements, cross-border insolvency, and the regulation of banks and other financial intermediaries. At the same time, US firms also found themselves subject to foreign regulatory requirements, especially by the European Commission's assertion of its competition law powers over both foreign cartels and mergers affecting EU markets.[25]

the French truck firm Berliet, for sale to China, resulting in diplomatic protests from the French government that this action was contrary to international law; the French minority directors obtained an order from the French courts appointing an administrator to carry out the contract, leading the US Treasury to beat a retreat by ruling that the US export control laws would not apply since in those circumstances the subsidiary was not under the effective control of its parent (Lowenfeld 1979: 338–43). In contrast, the French and other European governments raised no objections to the application by the USA of economic sanctions against Iran in 1979 which extended to Eurodollar deposits in US bank branches abroad; but there were more acute conflicts over the application of the US embargo laws to the supply to the Soviet Union for its European-funded gas pipeline project of turbines made by European companies using patents licensed from US firms (Rosenthal and Knighton 1982; Picciotto 1983: 28–34; de Mestral and Gruchalla-Wesierski 1990). Further strains arose in the 1980s over the US application of its technology export controls to computers, which entailed an obligation on purchasers of US computers to obtain permission from the US authorities before reselling or even moving them (Cahill 1986). However, there was also coordination of technology export controls, and some countries, such as the UK, even allowed inspections by the US authorities of the premises of firms which were purchasers or licensees of such high-tech items. See further Chapter 5, at 5.1.3.

24 Initially developed in US case law, and then in the American Law Institute's Restatement of the Foreign Relations Law of the United States (where the issue caused considerable controversy in the negotiation of the Third Restatement of 1987); the principle then received some international endorsement through the OECD (OECD 1987a). Sovereign immunity prevented legal actions against foreign state entities, e.g. against the OPEC oil cartel (*IAM* v. *OPEC* (1981)).

25 The Commission was happy to assert the 'effects' doctrine, for example in relation to a cartel of non-European firms, but the ECJ took the more cautious view that jurisdiction was justified because the cartel agreement was 'implemented' within the market (*Wood Pulp* (1988)). This bore out the view expressed earlier by F. A. Mann that 'the difference between a "constituent elements" approach [to jurisdiction] and the "effects" approach is non-existent' (1964: 196; see also Mann 1984).

It is important to note that these increasing strains on the classical liberal principles for allocating jurisdiction arose as much from the growth of national state regulation as from the internationalization of business. Furthermore, this regulation took forms which obscured the old division between public and private law, which was never easy to maintain, and became more elusive with the development of regulatory law.[26] Competition laws, for example, may be enforced with penal sanctions, or give rise to a private action for damages by an injured party; and the US antitrust laws further confuse matters by allowing the award of penal damages to triple the amount. Many other areas of business regulation have a similarly hybrid character,[27] or may be regarded as public but not penal or criminal law (notably, taxation). The allocation of jurisdiction on the basis that the 'constituent elements' of a criminal offence were committed within the state's territory became harder to apply, especially to economic offences such as fraud, and was even more nebulous when applied to regulatory requirements for economic activities with an international character.

Equally, private civil actions could also have regulatory effects, especially if a firm's activities affected many people and procedural rules could be developed to facilitate mass litigation. Large TNCs became embroiled in multi-jurisdictional litigation, and pressed lawyers and legislators for protection from the traditionally broad approach to civil jurisdiction, which began to be considered 'exorbitant' in creating problems of concurrent jurisdiction (Bell 2003). The US courts, regarded as a favourable forum for plaintiffs especially in personal injury suits, reacted by creating a presumption against foreign plaintiffs suing in US courts, which in effect gave the choice of forum to defendants.[28] At the same time there has been a growing willingness to grant 'antisuit injunctions' to restrain litigants from pursuing a counter-claim abroad, if the courts considered the foreign proceedings 'vexatious'. Thus, the willingness of a court to

---

26 This led jurists to reconsider the 'public law taboo' (see n. 15 above), and to call for the application of conflicts-of-law principles to public law (Lowenfeld 1979: 311), some went so far as to argue that all law should be considered public law, and conflicts should be approached from the policy perspective of allocation of governmental responsibility between states (Trachtman 1994: 985).

27 E.g. regulation of financial markets and institutions, such as the prohibition of insider dealing; corporate law such as directors' duties; consumer and environmental protection laws. All these may give rise to private actions as well as enforcement by public bodies.

28 Notably in the *Bhopal* case, see further Chapter 5, at 5.1.3.2.

accept or refuse jurisdiction came to be seen as an act of judicial power (Farrow 2003: 690).

2.2.3 Extension and limits

From the 1960s the classical liberal international system came under increasing strain. The greater needs and demands for regulation of economic activities, combined with a renewed and extended internationalization of those activities, made international coordination of economic regulation ever more difficult. This was further exacerbated by the exponential increase in the number of states resulting from decolonization. In many ways this reinforced the classical liberal system. In the international sphere, the former colonies and dependent territories, on attaining constitutional independence, mostly became fully-fledged states, in formal international law.[29] Internally, they generally accepted the inheritance of most of the internal laws, as well as participation in international agreements and arrangements, which had been extended to them by the colonial powers.

At the same time, the process of decolonization led to an assertion of national economic sovereignty, expressed in the attempt by developing countries to articulate a New International Economic Order (NIEO). In particular the Charter of Economic Rights and Duties of States (CERDS), adopted in 1974 by the UN General Assembly, affirmed the right of every state to:

> full permanent sovereignty...over all its wealth and natural resources...to regulate and exercise authority over foreign investment within its national jurisdiction in accordance with its laws and regulations and...to nationalize, expropriate or transfer ownership of foreign property, in which case appropriate compensation shall be paid...taking into account...all circumstances that the State considers pertinent.

The Charter was approved at the height of the assertion of economic nationalism by developing countries, and especially the wave of nationalizations of oil, mining and other natural resources. While these entailed a forced divestment of ownership rights, foreign companies generally received substantial compensation, and often maintained or regained an

---

29 Many remained dependent territories of some sort; however, they were often given a wide degree of autonomy especially in internal affairs, and this anomalous status could be exploited to create 'offshore' jurisdictions: see Chapter 3, at 3.2.3.

extensive role in managing the same operations (Faundez and Picciotto 1978; Lipson 1985: 121–2; Ghai and Choong 1988).

However, nationalizations did not reduce the economic dependence of the producer countries on world markets;[30] indeed they often found themselves prey to falling or fluctuating prices for their products. The NIEO aimed to tackle this, at least in relation to producers of primary products, through international commodity agreements.[31] Agreements for five commodities (cocoa, coffee, rubber, sugar and tin) operated with mixed success for some years until they lapsed or collapsed (which was the fate of the Tin Agreement in 1985). They seem to have had little impact on reducing price volatility, which was the hope of consumers, and the producers' aim of achieving 'more equitable' prices was achieved only by the Coffee Agreement, which was based on export controls, but this broke down due to 'an unevenness and perceived unfairness of the distribution of the benefits among and within the producing countries' (Gilbert 1996: 16).

By comparison, agricultural and primary product price support mechanisms are much more stable within large countries or common markets, notably the USA and the EU. Although these subsidies are generally regarded as distorting world production, often creating a barrier against developing country exports of primary products such as cotton, they have resisted attempts at international liberalization through the WTO (see Chapter 8). However, the breakdown of the commodity agreements[32] re-energized attempts to provide fair prices directly to producers in poor countries through fair-trade movements, focusing mainly on consumer

---

30 In 1987 to 1988 41 developing countries were acutely dependent on one or a few commodities for export revenues, e.g. Uganda 92% on coffee, Guinea 82% bauxite, Dominica 73% bananas, Zambia 83% copper, Cuba 74% sugar (Raffaelli 1995: 212).

31 These were in a sense successors to the arrangements for bulk purchase of raw materials through long-term arrangements with colonies operated by the UK in the Second World War and after (Leubuscher 1956). The new commodity agreements included as members both consumer and producer countries, inevitably creating tensions, e.g. over whether the minimum intervention price should reflect existing costs or create a disincentive to over-production. However, even a producers' cartel such as OPEC has only been relatively successful by relying on Saudi Arabia's ability to provide price leadership, in effect aligning itself with the major consumers (the USA), and preferring to discourage alternative energy sources by keeping prices low (in constant 1990 prices oil was $23 per barrel in 1975, peaked at nearly $50 in 1981 and then fell back, averaging $18 in 1986 to 1990: Raffaelli 1995: 210). OPEC has frequently found it as hard to enforce production quotas as did the commodity agreements.

32 Some, such as the International Coffee Agreement, remain in existence in attenuated form, mainly to provide information and research.

products such as coffee and tea, and based on labelling and certification systems, operating internationally but also to some extent in competition (see further Chapters 5 and 9, at 5.2.2.1 and 9.3.3.2).

The rapid increase in the number of states also had the effect of diluting substantive national sovereignty. The UN had 51 Member States at its foundation in 1945, but 160 by 1990 and 191 by 2002, many of which would not have met the economic viability standard understood to be necessary for statehood in the high liberal period (Hobsbawm 1990). This includes many 'micro-states' which have little basis for economic independence, leading some international relations theorists to suggest that the growth in the number of 'quasi-states' results in a minimalist 'negative sovereignty', a right to be free from interference (Jackson 1990). The growth of doctrines of 'humanitarian intervention' has eroded even this (Chandler 2000). Yet both the concept and the practice of state sovereignty can remain a stubborn reality, for example when micro-states have used their regulatory power to create 'offshore' tax havens and financial centres (see further Chapter 6).

In the international sphere, the increased number of states made it even more difficult to negotiate new multilateral agreements of any substance, unless common interests or universalist sentiments were very strong. This was especially so in economic affairs, given the disparity between the great numbers and the economic weakness of the 'less-developed-countries', which not surprisingly pressed that international arrangements should be adapted to their special developmental needs. Thus, while stressing the 'sovereign equality' of states, they also pressed for 'special and differentiated treatment' in international arrangements such as the General Agreement on Tariffs and Trade (GATT; see Chapter 8), a contradictory position, at least from the formalist standpoint.

Certainly, the liberal system could be developed and refined. One of the most extensive examples of this was the negotiation of the 1982 UN Convention on the Law of the Sea (UNCLOS), which took nine arduous years, although a further twelve were needed to find a basis on which a sufficient number of states were willing to ratify and bring it into force. Yet the Convention itself could be said to provide only a loose framework of general rules, the detailed implementation of which must be worked through in disparate forums.[33] UNCLOS also illustrates how

---

33 Critics have pointed to the indeterminacy of most of its central concepts: Koskenniemi (1990: 28) argues that UNCLOS has no 'real' rules but allocates decision-making power elsewhere by the use of equitable principles. For some of these concepts this indeterminacy

the international treaty system can at best produce a patchwork quilt of international coordination, since it is based on voluntary adherence by states. Acceptance of a treaty may be qualified by reservations, albeit within limits.[34] Once a multilateral treaty is agreed, it becomes extremely difficult to modify, since in principle any change must be accepted by all parties. A different approach, which produces results which are not very dissimilar, is to sidestep the negotiation of a multilateral agreement, but to formulate a model treaty, which can be used as the basis for bilateral agreements between states. This technique originated with the League of Nations tax treaty models (discussed in Chapter 6), and it was later used for investment treaties (see Chapter 5, at 5.1.1).

Perhaps the greatest limitation of the classical liberal system, certainly in relation to the regulation of economic activities, is that the enforcement of rules against individuals and legal persons (such as firms) can only be done by national authorities and under national law. Hence, even if agreement can be reached at the international level establishing common norms, for example for the protection of copyright (as in the Berne Convention), they must be implemented in national law by each state party, and all

is chronic, such as the reliance on 'equitable principles' in the delimitation of maritime boundaries; for some it is shared with other global regimes notably the principle of 'sustainable development' in environmental protection; and for some it has been introduced by the Agreement negotiated to obtain the adherence primarily of the USA and other OECD states (Annex to UN General Assembly resolution 48/263 of 28 July 1994); this includes provisions such as the requirement that deep-seabed mining operations by the Enterprise set up under Part XI should be conducted in accordance with 'sound commercial principles', or that the transfer of technology to it should be on 'fair and reasonable commercial terms'. Thus, the actual content of a principle such as the conservation of fish stocks by reference to the 'maximum sustainable yield' (UNCLOS, art. 61) depends on related texts and agreements (e.g. the Convention on Straddling Fish Stocks concluded in August 1995) which in turn depend on bargaining between the main coastal and fishing states to set and enforce specific catch limits. This bargaining is in turn mediated through networks of specialists such as marine scientists as well as lawyers, diplomats and political representatives.

34 A treaty may specify how far reservations are permitted, and multilateral economic agreements often greatly restrict or entirely prohibit them: e.g. the WTO Agreement (in art. XVI), which was deliberately structured as a package deal. However, the general obligations in a convention such as the WTO differ from the specific commitments made by each country, e.g. tariff concessions, which are often subject to different rules about withdrawal and renegotiation. Where specific commitments take the form of exceptions to a general obligation, they are country-specific exceptions rather than reservations: a reservation operates reciprocally by modifying the terms of a treaty also for the party making it; under a multilateral economic treaty such as the WTO the parties attempt to negotiate a package that contains an acceptable 'balance of commitments'. See further Chapter 8.

these national laws are applied and interpreted independently by the relevant national authorities. If there is a significant divergence as to how the norms are applied, the only remedy is a complaint by a state which considers that another state is failing adequately to comply with its international obligations. Even if most states generally make a good-faith effort to comply with their international obligations, there could still be very significant divergences in the ways in which they each in practice implement internationally agreed principles intended to be applied as rules governing private persons.

2.3 New legal forms

2.3.1 Supranational and transnational law

Various techniques have been developed, however, to give direct applicability to internationally agreed rules so that they can immediately create rights and (less often) duties for firms and individuals.

Under the constitutional law of some countries (for example, the USA and Germany) an international treaty is considered part of national law, and can therefore in some circumstances create law directly applying to individual legal persons. This is limited to those treaty provisions which may be regarded as 'self-executing', which means rules which are intended to be and capable of being applied as law without further legislation. Thus, for example, bilateral tax treaties generally give immediate benefits to international investors, notably a reduction of withholding tax rates; in the USA these immediately become part of the tax code, since a treaty approved by the Senate becomes US law. However, this also makes it harder for the USA to conclude international economic agreements; hence, US participation in multilateral trade negotiations has been facilitated by congressional legislation granting a mandate to the executive, on the basis that the resulting deal must be accepted or rejected as a whole by Congress.

In countries, such as the UK, where treaties are not regarded as part of domestic law, automatic internal implementation can be produced by legislation: for example, in the case of tax treaties, a general provision in the tax code enables each bilateral treaty to take effect directly as subsidiary legislation. More generally, courts can try to ensure harmony between national and international law by introducing a presumption that legislation should be interpreted as far as possible compatibly with the state's international agreements.

Where rights or obligations, are created in this way for individual legal persons by international legal agreements, they can be said to create 'supranational' law. This can be reconciled with formal national sovereignty, since rights created by a treaty can in principle be overridden by subsequent national legislation, although courts generally require this to be done in clear and explicit language. In practice, once a state is locked into a binding multilateral convention, or a network of bilateral treaties, changes to national law may be very difficult to reconcile with international obligations. For example, the major US tax reform of 1986 resulted in complaints from several states that it entailed breaches of their tax treaties with the USA, leading to complex renegotiations and several later modifications of the US legislation. The limitation of substantive sovereignty is even greater in the case of a complex package of agreements such as those involved with membership of the World Trade Organization (WTO), even though most states regard these as obligations on governments and not self-executing provisions which could be directly applicable to persons. Nevertheless, the extensive nature of WTO commitments have led both its proponents and critics to describe it as a world trade 'constitution', imposing wide restrictions on how states can regulate (see further Chapter 8).

The most developed system of supranational law is that of the European Union (EU), membership of which carries an obligation to implement EU law. Each Member State has therefore entrenched EU law internally, so that it overrides inconsistent national laws even those enacted later. This makes EU law supreme over national law, a status which is enforced by the European Court of Justice (ECJ), which has actively developed the doctrines of supranationality and direct effect of some treaty provisions (although formally these are addressed to states and not legal persons). Yet managing these interactions depends on accommodations between national-level authorities and courts and those at EU level, which has been actively fostered by the development of a community or network of litigants and lawyers (academics and practitioners) involved with the Community legal system.[35] The ECJ's activism has been made relatively acceptable politically by balancing the rights of business to market access

---

35 Stein 1981; Burley and Mattli 1993; de Búrca and Weiler 2001. This has also occurred around other areas of law which are not EU law, e.g. the European Patent Convention (EPC), which has been implemented in the UK by the Patents Act using different language; nevertheless, the UK courts have preferred to work directly from the EPC text, in order to try to ensure uniformity of interpretation with both the European Patent Office and other national courts (see e.g. *Re Macrossan* (2006)). The development of a European intellectual property community, especially in relation to patents, has nevertheless not prevented some divergences in decisions of national courts.

with some individual social rights (notably, equal pay for women), and then with a Charter of Fundamental Rights of Workers (1989). Interestingly, however, the proposed Convention for a Constitution for Europe, attempting to enshrine a balance of economic and social rights, failed although due to conflicting views: some argued that it would entail the abandonment of national sovereignty, while others that it failed to provide a sufficiently integrative vision.

At the global level, the WTO's Appellate Body (AB) now constitutes a full-blown court in all but name, with an extensive jurisdiction going well beyond trade (see further Chapter 8). However, as already mentioned, WTO law is not yet generally regarded as directly applicable to individuals or firms; nor do they have a direct right to bring claims under its procedures, although both the USA and the EU have institutionalized procedures giving firms rights to initiate complaints (Shaffer 2003). A direct right to bring claims for international arbitration has, however, been given to international 'investors' (which generally means firms) in many bilateral investment treaties (BITs), and under the investment provisions (chapter XI) of the North American Free Trade Agreement (NAFTA). These have become controversial, since firms have been given rights, but not obligations, which are guaranteed under international law, backed by direct access to international arbitration. This gives TNCs a means of effectively blocking or overruling national laws, giving a key role to the lawyers appointed as arbitrators (see further Chapter 5, at 5.2.1.2).

In parallel with the growth of supranational law, the term 'transnational law' was coined. This aimed to describe the combination of public and private international law, together with the various elements of national public and private law, which govern transnational (especially business) transactions.[36] Combining these elements gave a new perspective which

---

36 The term was originated by Philip C. Jessup in his Storrs Lectures at Yale (1956); the casebook subsequently developed at Harvard by Henry Steiner and Detlev Vagts (1968) was more modestly called *Transnational Legal Problems*, since they did not purport to identify anything so systematic as a transnational legal system. Although they included material on aspects of personal law, such as the applicability of constitutional rights to non-nationals, their main focus was on transnational business, in particular the setting up of foreign operations through foreign direct investment, which had become important in the post-war period (see Chapter 4, at 4.2.3). Although in the 1950s public international law was a marginal subject in US law schools, within a decade courses on transnational law and business became widespread and increasingly popular, reflected also in the proliferation of law reviews in this field.

emphasized their interactions,[37] in contrast to the traditional approach in the study of foreign or comparative law, which looked at the similarities and differences between national legal principles and systems. Hence, the transnational law perspective also brought into sharper focus the issues created by the increase in jurisdictional overlaps and conflicts, especially in regulatory matters, discussed above.

2.3.2 Soft law: codes and guidelines

Perhaps the clearest symptom of the strains generated in the classic liberal international system by the trends discussed above has been the shift from formal law to quasi-legal forms. These are generally referred to as 'soft law', as opposed to formal 'hard law', and include a wide range of types, such as codes, guidelines, declarations, sets of principles and memorandums of understanding (MOUs).[38] Although they serve various purposes, their emergence and increased use generally reflect the breakdown of the formal system with its hierarchical relationship between national and international law. They also pose a conceptual challenge for formalist understandings of international law. Although not binding law, in practice they often have considerable normative force, as much or more than does 'hard' international law, which in any case mainly relies on consensual rather than coerced compliance. Indeed, it is often hard even for experts to distinguish the two.[39]

First, the increased difficulty of reaching formal multilateral agreement between large numbers of states on matters of significant substance[40] has led to the use of forms such as Declarations. This is frequent in the practice of the UN and other IGOs, especially since the 1970s with the great

37 Later described by Trachtman as the 'international economic law revolution', a perspective which he suggested allows us 'to recognize and manage the complex and subtle relationships between different countries' laws, and between different areas of public policy' (1996: 36).

38 A comprehensive set of studies and analyses is provided in Shelton 2000.

39 A hard-law instrument may contain weak obligations: for example Christine Chinkin compares the rather weak obligation in article 2 of the International Covenant on Economic, Social and Cultural Rights (ICESCR), to 'take steps . . . with a view to progressively achieving the full realization of rights', with the stricter requirement in the International Covenant on Civil and Political Rights to 'respect and ensure' the rights it specifies, describing the former as 'soft treaty law', although it has become harder (Chinkin 2000: 33); nevertheless, both Covenants are formally hard-law instruments.

40 Thus, Abbott and Snidal (2000) suggest that soft law is preferred where there are high 'transaction costs' of negotiating agreements among many states especially on complex or detailed matters, whereas hard law is necessary for 'credible commitments'.

increase in numbers of states following decolonization. This was seen most notably in the adoption by the UN General Assembly of the Charter of Economic Rights and Duties of States (CERDS) of 1974 (mentioned at 2.2.3 above) supported by developing countries, but with the opposition or abstention of most developed countries.[41] A greater consensus has been achieved in the 'proclamations' of the principles of sustainable development at the conclusion of major international conferences from Stockholm in 1972, to Rio in 1992 and Johannesburg in 2002. From a formal lawyer's viewpoint they may seem to consist of no more than fine-sounding rhetoric. However, they are linked to action programmes (in particular 'Agenda 21' adopted at Rio), and their principles may be given substantive effect,[42] or become embodied in more specific hard-law instruments.[43] Sometimes, this type of instrument is chosen to emphasize the aspirational character of the norms, as with the ILO's 1998 Declaration on Fundamental Principles and Rights at Work, the adoption of which was strongly resisted by the governments of some developing countries. Its impact therefore greatly depends on the effectiveness of the procedures for encouraging and monitoring compliance. These may be quite rigorous, for example the implementation of the Recommendations of the Financial Action Task Force (FATF) has been very closely monitored (see Chapter 7, at 7.2.2).

Second, Codes and Guidelines have been developed since the late 1960s to establish standards at the international level addressed directly to firms. Here again, a non-binding form was often deliberately chosen, yet the implementation in practice could be rigorous (though often has not been), and could involve adoption or transformation of the soft-law norms into hard law. In the 1990s, following a decade or more of demands on states to reduce regulation of business and dismantle barriers to market access, TNCs found themselves under pressure to introduce corporate codes of

41 Seidl-Hohenveldern (1979) attributed the emergence of international economic soft law largely to the desire of the newly decolonized developing countries to lay down new rules for the international economy more favourable to them, and points out that the CERDS was adopted by states with 70 per cent of the world's population but accounting for only one-third of trade.

42 Thus, the Appellate Body of the WTO, in its important decision in the *US–Shrimp* case (1998), in interpreting the provisions of the WTO agreements, took account of the reference to the principle of sustainable development and to the Rio Declaration and Agenda 21 in the WTO Agreement and the WTO Council's Decision on Trade and Environment.

43 For example, the Montreal Protocol on Substances Depleting the Ozone Layer, and the Convention on Biological Diversity (discussed in Chapter 9, at 9.2.5.2).

conduct to reassure customers and other stakeholders of their adherence to international standards of social and environmental responsibility (see Chapter 5, at 5.2.2).

Finally, the growth of international regulatory networks linking public bodies at 'sub-state' level (discussed further below) has involved the use of novel forms of agreement, especially the MOU (discussed in Chapter 1, at 1.3.2). These are often very specific and establish detailed arrangements, for example for cooperation in information exchange and other enforcement activities. These also may be stated to be 'non-binding' although in practice compliance may be very effective. In this case, the formally non-binding character is because it is often not clear whether they fall under national or international, public or private law. Under international law, sub-state or non-state bodies are considered to have no capacity to bind the state or government concerned.[44] In some cases they may be regarded simply as 'private' contracts, if the parties are legal persons: for example, agreements between stock exchanges or futures markets to enable reciprocal trading of products or cooperate in market monitoring and enforcement. Yet they may have a very hybrid character and have elements of public and private, national and international law. For example an Advanced Pricing Agreement (APA) concluded by a TNC with the tax authorities of two (or more) states entails commitments by each authority to accept the agreed transfer-pricing methodology which may be binding under their national administrative law, as well as constituting an international agreement between the two authorities.[45]

Generally, the growth of soft law indicates that the range and depth of international coordination no longer fits within the classical liberal model of agreements negotiated by central governments on behalf of states. It facilitates the growth of normative arrangements and institutions directly between regulatory communities, rather than through diplomatic channels.[46]

---

44 As noted in a leading text on the law of treaties (McNair 1961: 21), the proliferation of agreements between subordinate state agencies, and the great variation in the relationship of such bodies to the central government, makes it hard to determine when such an agreement could be considered to be internationally binding.

45 Such 'competent authority agreements' are authorized under tax treaties, but have an ambivalent status under international and even domestic law: see Picciotto 1992: 297–9.

46 A study from a practitioner's perspective first published in 2000 dealt with the need for soft law such as MOUs to provide a less formal and more flexible means of dealing with detailed and technical matters, or perhaps to provide confidentiality, for example in defence matters; the second edition included a more extended treatment, including the invocation of MOUs in litigation (Aust 2008: ch. 3).

Finally, and most importantly, it should be stressed that there is no sharp separation between 'binding' hard law and 'voluntary' soft law in the global arena. Instead, the two interact in often complex ways, and soft-law standards are often given binding effect through hard-law obligations (see Chapter 5, at 5.2.2.2). An important example of this is the way in which some of the provisions in the WTO agreements create obligations on WTO Member States to comply with soft-law standards developed by other organizations (discussed in Chapter 8).

2.3.3 Towards world law?

Thus, classical liberalism has shown considerable flexibility and adaptability in the face of the dual pressures of increased legalization and internationalization. There is now a much more fluid interaction between national and international norms, so that they no longer operate entirely on different planes.

Dualism has given way to monism, accepting a more seamless continuity between international and national law. National courts are not only authoritative in their own sphere, but also contribute to the development of international legal principles. National courts and lawyers have also become more directly involved in many issues previously dealt with by interstate diplomacy, for example by narrowing the principle of state immunity to bring the commercial activities of states into the ambit of national law, thus allowing claims in national courts against foreign state or public bodies.[47] Conversely, rights and obligations under international law can be invoked in cases under national law, and national courts have become more willing to apply international legal principles as appropriate.

Equally, legislatures have found new ways to incorporate international agreements more directly into national law, and to authorize international administrative cooperation by government departments and other public bodies. There has been a broadening of jurisdiction over acts considered 'international crimes', although falling significantly short of international

---

47 This inevitably leaves much room for interpretation of what constitutes commercial activities and commercial property: for example, in *Af-Cap* v. *Congo* (2004) an attempt was made to enforce a debt due under a bank loan for highway construction, for which the government had waived immunity, against tax and royalty payments due to the government from oil companies; see generally Fox 2002.

acceptance of full universal jurisdiction.[48] An increasing number of international tribunals have been given powers to hear complaints from or apply international law directly to legal persons, both individuals and firms.[49] State laws have relaxed their conditions for enforcing private arbitration agreements, procedures and awards, giving rise to what some have called a 'new *lex mercatoria*'.[50]

48 There does not yet seem to be a general international law principle of universal jurisdiction, despite the efforts of activist lawyers and prosecutors. A series of treaties identify internationally recognized crimes and establish obligations to ensure offenders will be prosecuted, most of which fall short of true universal jurisdiction, which would require all states to criminalize an act regardless of where or by whom it is committed (Bantekas and Nash 2003: 156–60; see now Bantekas and Nash 2010). A number of international agreements relating to acts such as hijacking, drug-trafficking and torture create an obligation on the state parties either to extradite offenders to another state claiming jurisdiction, or to put them on trial (*aut dedere aut judicare*). Some commentators view this as an assertion of the universality principle (e.g. Randall 1988: 819); however, such treaties only explicitly *require* state parties to criminalize acts committed in their territory, or by their own nationals. This is also the case for economic offences such as bribery under the OECD Convention on the Bribery of Foreign Public Officials of 1997, and the UN Convention Against Corruption of 2005 (see Chapter 5, at 5.1.3.1), though the latter Convention also requires the criminalization of the laundering of the proceeds of specified crimes even if the offences themselves are not within the state's jurisdiction (art. 23.2). Some conventions *permit* states to assert jurisdiction based on objective territoriality: thus, the 1979 Hostages Convention (art. 5.1), and the 1985 Torture Convention (art. 5.1) allow jurisdiction to be based on the nationality of the victim, and the 1999 Convention on the Financing of Terrorism allows parties to criminalize the collection of funds for terrorist acts aimed against the state (art. 7.2). The 1948 Genocide Convention provides for trial by the state where the alleged offence was committed, or by an international tribunal set up by agreement. However, universal jurisdiction has been agreed in relation to 'grave breaches' of the laws of war under the 1949 Geneva Conventions, which *require* parties to assert jurisdiction regardless of nationality or location. These include crimes against humanity, and it has been argued that in some circumstances grave economic crimes such as corruption could come into this category (Bantekas 2006). However, even the jurisdiction of international tribunals is not universal. Notably, that of the International Criminal Court is strictly defined: under its Rome Statute it has jurisdiction only if the conduct occurred on the territory, or the accused is a national, of a state party to the Statute (art. 12), and only if a state does not itself investigate or prosecute (art. 17).
49 Notably, as mentioned above, investor–state arbitration under investment treaties (Chapter 5); also, some tax treaties provide for arbitration of claims of double taxation (Chapter 6).
50 The chief legal proponent of this concept has been Berthold Goldmann, but it has been criticized by others (see e.g. Delaume 1989; Carbonneau 1990; Reisman 1992; see also the differing views of De Ly and Dasser in Applebaum *et al.* 2001); Guenther Teubner has argued strongly from a social–theoretical viewpoint that the new *lex mercatoria* represents an abandonment of the traditional hierarchical system of law for a new heterarchical one (1997, 2002); Yves Dezalay and Bryant Garth have studied in sociological detail the competition between arbitrators, and between different national centres and styles of

These trends were given considerable ideological support by the emergence of a new universalism in international law, in opposition to the 'realist' or state-centred perspectives which predominated during the Cold War. Hersch Lauterpacht, an influential figure in the mid-twentieth century, had combined some of the universalist ideals of the Grotian tradition (Bull *et al.* 1990) with a cosmopolitan high liberalism that seemed apt again in the late twentieth century (Koskenniemi 2002: ch. 5). A bolder universal vision was put forward by Wilfred Jenks, arguing that:

> international law has outgrown the limitations of a system consisting essentially, or perhaps even primarily, of rules governing the mutual relations of states and must now be regarded as the common law of mankind in an early phase of its development... [This should be seen as] the law of an organized world community, constituted on the basis of States, but discharging its community functions increasingly through a complex of international and regional institutions, guaranteeing rights to and placing obligations upon the citizen, and confronted with a wide range of economic, social and technological problems calling for uniform regulation on an international basis which represents a growing proportion of the subject-matter of this law.
>
> (1958: 8ff.)

Even this, however, only restated the central liberal dilemma: how can a 'common law of mankind' be constituted 'on the basis of states'?

From the perspective of international relations theorists, talk of a world community seemed merely utopian, especially during the Cold War era, when this discipline was dominated by realism and its emphasis on great power politics. Their liberal internationalism took a different tack, with 'functionalist' views of international organization, which favoured strengthened technical cooperation between states based on the joint organization of specific state functions. Thus, David Mitrany, writing originally in 1943, argued that post-war international cooperation should be based on 'a practical line of action that might overcome the deep-seated division between the needs of material unity

---

arbitration (including attitudes to *lex mercatoria*) that have transformed the field of international commercial arbitration into what they describe as 'a sort of offshore justice' (Dezalay and Garth 1995: 54, 1996); while Claire Cutler has argued that the recreation of the law merchant by a new emphasis on liberal values free from state regulation has contributed to the 'disembedding' of liberalism (1995, 2003). See further Chapter 10, at 10.1.

and stubborn national loyalties' ([1943] 1966: 28). Such piecemeal transfers to international authorities of specific tasks or 'slices' of sovereignty could be regarded, in his words, as a 'sharing' or 'pooling' of sovereignty, rather than its 'surrender' ([1943] 1966: 31–2). This was developed further by those who saw the administrators of such organizations as a nascent 'international civil service', built on bureaucratic interpenetration (Haas 1964; Jordan 1971). With the revival of theories of interdependence from the 1960s, neofunctionalist views argued that growing functional cooperation, especially within a strong international institutional framework, as in the EU, would generate a 'spillover' effect leading to supranationalism. These provided the basis for a new rapprochement of international relations and international law, for example in regime studies.[51]

A functionalist perspective certainly seems to have underpinned the practice of political elites, who preferred to see the post-war growth of international institutions as a matter of technical cooperation, even when the scope of these institutions was greatly extended. The main example of this has been European integration, with its transformation from the European Coal and Steel Community and the Common Market into the European Community and finally the European Union. Although the European project is sometimes viewed, by both some supporters and opponents, as aiming at a European super-state, even its founders saw it as a means of strengthening rather than undermining the national states (Milward 1992). Clearly, such forms of technocratic cooperation have not provided a basis for the growth of international solidarity, as Mitrany and others hoped. Instead, such institutions have suffered from a lack of political legitimacy, since they are not easily made accountable through the classical liberal form of representative democracy within the national state. However, the extension of representative democracy to regional or global institutions does not seem plausible, and this type of

---

51 Groom and Taylor 1990; Slaughter-Burley 1993. The weakening of the classical liberal system created a reconciliation not only between the two disciplines, but also within them, between neo-realism and neofunctionalism: see Baldwin 1993, a collection which shows that within IR theory these two perspectives now differ essentially over their degree of optimism as to the possibilities of international cooperation in a world still characterized by anarchy in the sense of an absence of world government. Andrew Hurrell (in Rittberger 1993) has also pointed out that much less divides those working within the Hobbesian, Grotian and Kantian perspectives on world politics than is sometimes thought. Similarly, the tension between what Koskenniemi (1988) has called 'apology and utopia' is evident in most writers on international law, although they may tend to one or the other pole.

democracy is in any case proving increasingly inadequate and undergoing changes within national states (see further Chapter 10). Yet, although political leaders today repeat as a mantra that the growth of international institutions does not mean the surrender of sovereignty, this rings hollow in view of the transformations of statehood that have occurred over the past half-century.

3

From interdependence to fragmentation

The previous chapter has discussed the tensions within classical liberal internationalism, and some of the attempts that have been made to resolve them while maintaining its basic features. I have argued in Chapter 1 that the strains of these tensions have resulted in a fragmentation of the state, and the emergence of new forms of networked governance. This chapter will examine some of the dynamics of the transformation of statehood, including an overview of the various ideologies which have helped to drive and tried to rationalize this process.

3.1 The firm, the state and regulation

By a strange paradox, in the closing period of the twentieth century the world economy was generally considered as dominated by unrestrained and anarchic 'market forces', although in fact social and economic activities have generally become more explicitly and formally *governed*. A clear understanding of the changes taking place has been greatly hampered by both the aggressive promotion of a fundamentalist version of liberalism proclaiming the virtues of 'the market', and the often ill-judged reactions to this neo-liberalism by its opponents. This was remarkable, since liberalism's central assumption that social and economic relations consist of transactions between autonomous individuals, seems very hard to reconcile with the highly corporatized and regulated social and economic structures that were everywhere evident. Furthermore, much of the political debate in this period centred on the false dichotomy between the 'free' market and state intervention. The concept of 'the market' is unhelpful, since extensive exchange has existed in many societies in some form, so the term obscures the changing character of social structures and institutions which mediate production and exchange. Also, the term 'market' prioritizes exchange, which is assumed to be a sphere of virtually spontaneous and essentially private relationships. It is therefore especially inappropriate in trying to understand the changes wrought during the twentieth century by the emergence of corporate big business, in various forms (Lazonick 1991).

3.1.1 The public and the private

Surprisingly, also, many on the political left and the right seemed to share the essentially liberal conception that social relations are divided between a private sphere governed by the pursuit of individual self-interest, and a public realm through which collective concerns are identified which may justify action or intervention by the state. The disagreements have been between a 'left' perspective that only state intervention can restrict private greed, whereas the 'right' considers that unrestricted private choices provide decentralized decision-making which is most likely to produce outcomes beneficial to all. However, the right's preference for a return to a minimalist state is contradicted by its predilection for strong state intervention to create and protect private-property rights and privileges, and for the maintenance of order even at the expense of individual civil liberties. The left's ambitions for social transformation have generally modified into arguments for more extensive state intervention especially to remedy social inequalities through redistribution, although this comes up against the limits of expanding state expenditure.

Thus, in practice, demands on and expectations of the state have increased from all sides. Existing ideologies of both the right and the left have tended to treat with suspicion the fragmentation of the centralized state and the emergence of new forms of regulation and more complex public–private interactions. On the other hand much of the research and writing on the regulatory state has become caught up in a technicist and often apolitical perspective.

In contrast, the social movements which emerged anew since the 1970s could be said to express a new politics of expertise, articulating with the 'lived world', in both rich and poor countries, involving contests of values and cultures based on access to knowledge (Morris-Suzuki 2000). The wide range of civil society organizations now also include so-called non-governmental organizations (NGOs) which often play a role in governance, especially in developing countries, generally financed from external sources both private and public. International or transnational political activism of course has a long history, but in the recent period has become dominated by various types of international 'advocacy networks' (Keck and Sikkink 1998).

State restructuring has stumbled through an often bewildering variety of experiments, with many dramatic failures and few clear successes.[1] Generally, especially in developed countries, private providers of public services are often highly subsidized, and their price structures closely regulated; they are also generally subject to regimes which require them to deliver specified standards of service and safety, and to comply with public need requirements such as universal service obligations. Their interaction with consumers and related firms, both suppliers and competitors, is regulated either on a specific industry basis (such as postal services, telecommunications, power), or under general competition law, or indeed both.

Privatization was taken up internationally, first in the 'structural adjustment programmes' applied by the IMF and World Bank in developing countries in the 1980s, and then in the radical transformations of the 'transition' countries of Eastern Europe. Both of these were easy targets, since the failures both of nationalist developmentalism and state socialism were evident, especially in the bloated, autocratic and bureaucratic state structures they spawned. However, the 'market-oriented' reforms[2] have generally failed to produce either effective public institutions or stable and successful business growth, but fostered crony capitalism, corruption and organized crime.

Much less noticed than the privatization of the public sector has been the parallel and complementary trend, in which the apparently 'private' sphere of economic activity has become more public. The corporations and business networks which dominate the so-called 'market', even as

---

1 The New Zealand experiments were for a time put forward as a paradigm for others to follow, for a strong critique see Kelsey 1995. Michael Moran has provided a detailed study of the emergence of the new British regulatory state (2003), as a sharp transition from the stagnating traditional British system of government by 'club rule', which had legitimized a high degree of independence from state control throughout corporate business, finance and the professions, from 1880 to 1980. The class compromises which underpinned this system were weakened by the end of empire and the collapse of social cultures of deference to authority in the 1960s, and its transformation was precipitated by the economic crisis of the 1970s and the ensuing renewed burst of globalization, which revealed the exhaustion of both the traditional modes of public operation and of the regulation of private corporations, neither of which provided adequate accountability of managers. However, the shift from closed communities of self-regulation to the formalization and codification of regulation resulted in what he describes as a roller-coaster ride of hyper-innovation and policy disasters, 'from stagnation to fiasco' (Moran 2003: 155ff.).

2 The World Bank's World Development Report of 1980 signalled the end of the developmentalist regime by redefining development as 'participation in the world market' (McMichael 1996).

they urged a reduction in intrusive state controls, have found their activities governed by an increasing plethora of various types of regulation. Indeed, the biggest paradox has been the growth of industry and corporate codes of conduct, the private sector adopting public standards for itself, although this has generally been in response to pressures from their customers, workers and suppliers, and sometimes in order to forestall the imposition of legal obligations (see further Chapter 5, at 5.2.2). Indeed, this contrapuntal process of liberalization and corporate concentration was also an international one, which the next section will outline.

3.1.2 Economic liberalization and global corporate integration

The neo-liberal turn emerged from the breakdown during the 1970s of the national and international state institutions established after the Second World War, which were essentially of a social–democratic or 'welfarist' character. The strengthened institutional framework established after 1945 for the world economy aimed to restart international trade, while leaving to national states the main tasks of socio-economic management. This delicate compromise, described by Ruggie (1982) as 'embedded liberalism', can be seen in the design of the international financial institutions which emerged initially from the Anglo-American negotiations in 1941 to 1943. The proposals put forward for the Bretton Woods conference of 1944 by Keynes and White, the leading Treasury officials for the UK and the USA respectively, had liberal–welfarist aims. The experience of the New Deal in the 1930s had convinced the US negotiators of the need for a multilateral institutional framework both to facilitate international trade and to protect monetary management from private market pressures; while the British planning for a post-war full-employment welfare state based on Keynesian principles depended on freedom from the tyranny of the gold standard.[3]

The key institution was the International Monetary Fund (IMF), initially based on a system of fixed but adjustable exchange rates, backed by drawing rights to provide liquidity and to help states protect their exchange rates from pressures due to perturbations in payment flows

---

3 See Gardner, who cites several statements by Henry Morgenthau, the US Secretary of the Treasury, including one from his speech at Bretton Woods, that the aim was 'to drive... the usurious money-lenders from the temple of international finance' ([1956] 1980: 76). Although this was clearly hyperbolic rhetoric, such a statement from such a source is hardly imaginable today, even after the financial crash.

and speculative short-term capital movements. The prime aim of facilitating international trade entailed an obligation to introduce currency convertibility for current account transactions, but states were permitted to retain controls on capital movements. However, US reluctance to commit substantial funds led to the attenuation of Keynes's ambitious plans for a Clearing Union;[4] and British opposition to external interference in national economic policy-making blunted the US proposals to give the Fund powers to impose conditions on governments, although loan conditionality quickly became its de facto practice.

The second of the Bretton Woods institutions, the International Bank for Reconstruction and Development, familiarly known as the World Bank (WB), was something of an afterthought. Its grand title belied its limited power, as it was largely reliant on borrowing from private capital markets. Its efforts became mainly focused on the developing countries, using its subscribed capital from states to raise funds from private capital markets, where it is a major borrower. These funds have been used to finance projects and programmes on relatively favourable but commercial terms, guaranteed by the borrower state's government, the procurement for which offers a massive and lucrative market for the large firms able to succeed under its competitive bidding processes.[5] The broader remit of lending under the Structural Adjustment Programme launched in 1980 also entailed more stringent 'conditionalities', mainly aimed at economic liberalization.[6] The increased concern with 'good governance' from the

---

4 Although the IMF was able to introduce a reserve asset (Special Drawing Rights, or SDRs) in 1968, it was of limited utility especially after the shift to floating currencies in 1973.

5 Its affiliate the International Finance Corporation was set up in 1956 to lend to private companies without host government guarantees (or oversight). Another affiliate, the International Development Association, was established in 1960 (to deflect pressure for a soft-loan agency under UN auspices: Payer 1982: 33), and provides interest-free loans and some grants to the poorest countries, although its reliance on funds from donor countries means it has often been under-resourced, and makes both the Bank and the borrowers susceptible to donor pressures. The Bank also established the International Centre for the Settlement of Investment Disputes (ICSID), again to help facilitate private investment, by providing an external legal framework to help protect investors (see Chapter 5). For an insightful evaluation of the Bank and the Fund, see Woods 2006, and for current critical perspectives on the international financial institutions (IFIs), see the Bretton Woods Project website at www.brettonwoodsproject.org.

6 Pressures from the IFIs have resulted in many developing countries reducing tariff rates much more quickly than they needed to under the GATT, and such pressures are not necessarily visible as formal loan conditionality. For example, in the 1980s Ghana reduced its average import tariffs from 150% to 25%; in 2003, when chicken farmers complained of being hit by dumping of frozen chicken parts from Europe, the parliament increased the tariff to 40%; but on a visit to Washington the Minister of Finance was told that this

mid-1990s resulted in the wider use of implicit or explicit conditionality, to induce states to introduce a range of legal and institutional reforms (Faundez *et al.* 2000).

The US was able to exert the strongest influence on these organizations, financially due to the strength of the dollar and culturally due to their location in Washington, DC, but this was far from a total hegemony. Indeed, the IMF and WB have been subject to continued criticism in the USA, and kept relatively feeble, so that their supervisory powers have been directed at the weaker developing countries.[7] Their lack of effective power[8] over the rich developed countries leads them to focus on the domestic policies of the poorer countries, neglecting the causal factors of threats to the world economy and even the international effects of their own policy advice.[9] Thus, they failed to establish a perspective for the management of international monetary, financial and economic matters, and instead became facilitators of private finance and corporate expansion, and channels for the diffusion of the current orthodoxies of national economic management. Although nominally specialized agencies of the UN, they have preferred to keep aloof and maintain their patrician positions in the growing international institutional networks.

The third leg of this institutional triptych came into being in stunted form as the General Agreement on Tariffs and Trade (GATT), since the plans for a fully-fledged International Trade Organization were put into abeyance because neither the USA nor the UK could make the political

---

infringed the terms of the Poverty Reduction Facility, so the president sent a notice to the customs authority rescinding the increase; the IMF action was confirmed in a letter by an official to Christian Aid dated 7/1/2004 (interview with D. Ayine, 28/11/2005).

7 Gardner [1956] 1980; Padoa-Schioppa and Saccomanni 1994; Pauly 1997. For contrasting views of the extent of US post-war hegemony, see Brett 1985 and Burnham 1990. The inadequacy of the resources available to both the IMF and the Bank made them unable to respond to the massive deficits that hit the European countries in 1947, so that it was left to the USA to provide funds for reconstruction through the Marshall Plan, offering generous financial terms, but with the explicit political objective of blocking the spread of communism. But the USA was obliged to accommodate its international economic objectives to the reconstruction policies of the European states, and it did not dominate the main channel for Marshall aid, the Organization for European Economic Cooperation, which later became the OECD.

8 Although the Fund does have the formal power to declare a currency scarce (art. VII(3) of the Fund Agreement), this has never been invoked, since it would permit other countries to impose controls over transactions in such currencies, which would target the dollar, and hence would conflict directly with US policy (Woods 2006: 42).

9 A frequently mentioned example is the propensity of the Bank to encourage countries to develop production of export crops such as cocoa and coffee, with no consideration that the result is to bring down world prices.

commitment to phase out trade preferences (Odell and Eichengreen 1998; Goldstein 1993). However, the GATT in the long run proved perhaps the most effective of the three, by providing an unobtrusive framework for a series of tariff negotiating rounds which, greatly facilitated by the three-decade-long period of economic growth, cut the world average tariffs on manufactured goods from 40% in 1947 to 5% by 1995. Ironically, the rebirth of the GATT in 1995 as a fully-fledged World Trade Organization (WTO), placing it at the centre of the new arrangements for global economic governance, also made it the prime target for popular disaffection with those arrangements (see Chapter 8).

The aim of the international financial institutions (IFIs) was international liberalization: the gradual removal of border barriers to international exchange, especially trade in manufactured goods. The IMF's task of ensuring currency convertibility was limited to the *current account*, defined as payments to non-residents for goods and services, which did not include flows of investment capital.[10] OECD states began to liberalize current account payments from 1958, although developing countries did not generally do so until later. However, controls on capital movements were not relaxed until the 1980s, and some have been retained by many states.[11]

---

10 White, the US negotiator, would have preferred to include liberalization of capital flows, and subsequently Joseph Gold, the IMF General Counsel, argued for a reinterpretation of its articles, on the grounds that IMF practice had allowed members to use its resources to meet pressures resulting also from large outflows of capital (Lichtenstein 1997). The IMF Agreement (art. VI.3) still has no formal obligation for members to liberalize capital movements. Although the organization imposes investment liberalization as one of the conditionalities on those, mainly developing countries, which need to use its resources, proposals to extend its formal obligations to capital market liberalization have so far been rejected (Kalderimis 2004).

11 Lowenfeld 2002: 509–10. The OECD countries began to negotiate mutual commitments using a process of 'standstill and rollback' under the Code of Liberalization of Capital Movements, from 1961 (see Chapter 5, at 5.1.1). The IMF formalized its surveillance of capital movement controls in 1977, and has generally encouraged capital account liberalization, which was often included in the package of economic policy commitments in the 'letters of intent' embodying the conditions for IMF assistance, even though it could not formally be imposed as a condition (IMF–IEO 2005). The encouragement of private lending has caused the massive build-up of developing country debt, and the failure to control short-term capital flows has resulted in a number of major crises: that of 1982–3 beginning in Mexico, due to large-scale bank lending to developing countries as part of the recycling of petrodollars; in 1994–5 again in Mexico; in 1997–8 in East Asia, followed by Russia in 1998 (see Lowenfeld 2002: ch. 18). The East Asian crisis resulted in loss of support for proposals to extend the IMF's jurisdiction to capital movements, and to a shift in IMF staff policy advice towards a so-called 'integrated' approach placing capital account liberalization as part of a programme of reforms of macroeconomic policy, the

International investment was not stifled by national capital controls, but from the 1950s it mainly took the form of foreign direct investment (FDI) by transnational corporations (TNCs), rather than portfolio investment, such as international bank lending or the purchase of foreign shares or bonds. The first modern TNCs had emerged in the 1880–1914 period, with some further growth in the 1920s (see Chapter 4). Their renewed expansion after 1950 was possible because they could reinvest their foreign earnings and raise loans abroad through their foreign subsidiaries, thus avoiding capital movement restrictions. Despite occasional doubts, national authorities generally accepted and indeed encouraged both outflows and inflows of FDI. However, its growth eventually helped to undermine the Bretton Woods system.

The rapid growth especially of US-based TNCs in the 1950s and 1960s produced a very significant qualitative change in the world economy, since it involved *the international integration of economic activity internalized within firms.* Despite the improvements in international communications, and contrary to common assumptions, the organization of businesses on a global scale is not easy, indeed its history is littered with disasters as well as successes (see Chapter 4, at 4.2). Hence, the increasing dominance of TNCs was far from inevitable. The competitive advantages of TNCs were not due to closer international political integration, but the converse: it was their ability to take advantage of and manage *differences* in the social, political and economic conditions between countries which powered their rapid growth.[12] For example, from the early days of TNCs (before 1914), an important motive for the establishment of foreign production was to get behind tariff walls. Clearly, some obstacles are too difficult to surmount, such as discrimination against foreign ownership, or severe volatility in conditions between countries. However, the institutional framework developed after 1945 was very propitious for

domestic financial system, and prudential regulation of financial institutions. A Report by the IMF's Independent Evaluations Office in 2005 found that its encouragement of international capital flows had led to the neglect of the risks of volatility, and that greater attention should be given to the supervision of capital outflows from major global financial markets (IMF–IEO 2005). In that period also, IMF economic policies came under attack from Joseph Stiglitz, even while he was chief economist at its sibling institution, the World Bank (Stiglitz and Chang 2001).

12 J. H. Dunning, a leading theorist of TNCs, explains their growth in terms of ownership-specific and location-specific advantages, deriving from their 'privileged ownership of, or access to, a set of income-generating assets, or from their ability to co-ordinate these assets with other assets across national boundaries' (2001a: 176); see further Chapter 4, at 4.2.

FDI, precisely because it involved a strong but limited form of economic coordination. TNCs learned to select and combine the most appropriate locations for their operations, based not only on social and economic conditions (such as skilled but relatively low-cost labour), but also political and regulatory factors. Eventually, the increasing success of giant TNCs at coordinating activities across the globe drew along with them a wider range of smaller and medium-sized firms, and resulted in deeper international integration, undermining some of the mechanisms of national state economic management.

The resumption of growth of TNCs, at first in the 1950s in raw materials and manufacturing, was followed in the 1960s by banking and financial firms, mainly to follow their domestic clients abroad to provide them with investment banking and other wholesale financial services. This also was due to national regulatory differences, since by developing international lending and establishing foreign branches they could avoid the fiscal and monetary controls introduced by governments to manage the balance of payments.[13] Hence, by exploiting interest rate differences, ambiguities in regulations (especially on reserve requirements) and the ambivalence of governments (Hawley 1987; Schenk 1998), the transnational firms and banks between them created a low-cost source of international finance. This was termed the Eurodollar market,[14] and it quickly grew to an enormous size.[15] Combined with the ability of TNCs to move liquid funds between their affiliates by adjusting payment terms for intra-firm transfers, this internationalization of finance made it increasingly difficult

13 Thus, the major expansion of US banks abroad after 1960 was mainly because the Federal Reserve's Regulation Q imposing a capital reserve requirement did not apply outside the USA; while in London the Bank of England's credit and interest rate controls did not apply to foreign banks in the UK or to non-sterling deposits (Jones 1990; Padoa-Schioppa and Saccomanni 1994).

14 Because it consisted (at least initially) of dollars deposited outside the USA (mainly in Europe), which banks could on-lend. The acceptance of foreign currency deposits from non-residents has a long history, and resumed in the 1940s, but by the mid-1950s the relaxation of exchange controls for non-residents led banks in London to bid for funds in the USA to on-lend, thus taking advantage of interest rate differentials (Schenk 1998). Initially, the lack of reserve requirements mentioned above enabled banks to charge lower interest rates for Eurodollar loans. Eurobonds benefited from additional tax advantages: since they were issued by 'special purpose vehicles' in tax havens, they could be free from withholding tax at source, and as bearer bonds, tax could be avoided or evaded in the owner's country of residence (see Chapters 6 and 7, at 6.3.5 and 7.1.2).

15 It was estimated at $7bn in 1963 by the BIS, and had grown to over $90bn by the end of 1972, by which time net euro-currency deposits were estimated at 35% of the US narrow money supply and 17% of its broad money supply (Padoa-Schioppa and Saccomanni 1994: 239).

for central banks to defend their currencies against enormous 'hot money' flows.[16] The position of the dollar as a world currency enabled the USA to run large payments deficits, but the large volume of dollars held outside the USA in the 'offshore' system eventually made it impossible for the US authorities formally to guarantee the substantive value of the dollar against gold (Ingham 1994). Tariff reductions on manufactured goods negotiated through the GATT, combined with the strong dollar, sucked imports into the USA, resulting in a US deficit in merchandise trade in 1971. The USA was obliged to end its guarantee of the dollar against gold in 1971, and the withdrawal of this lynchpin led to the general abandonment of fixed exchange rates in 1973. Thus, the dissolution of the Bretton Woods system resulted from the growth of TNCs which it had helped to stimulate.

By the late 1960s, the impact of TNCs became increasingly evident. First, their sheer size entailed a significant *concentration* of capital, since they could exercise combined control under a unified decision-making framework over enormous socio-economic resources, including large workforces. Second, their control over activities located in different states clearly posed a challenge to national states and to existing methods of international economic coordination, although the nature of this challenge was not always clear. The size and importance of TNCs made them a prime target for regulation, in both home and host states, exposing them to multiple and sometimes conflicting regulatory requirements.[17]

This led to bold proposals that a supranational citizenship for TNCs should be provided by treaty, to deal with the 'inherent conflict of interest between corporate managements that operate in the world economy and governments whose points of view are confined to the narrow national scene' (Ball 1967: 28).[18] However, TNCs themselves generally preferred the policy of being a 'good citizen' in each country where they did business. This certainly maximized their competitive advantage: the ability to exploit the interaction of national rules and regulatory differences, or the internalization of the management of national differences. Governments in any case did not find it easy to reach international agreement

---

16 As shown in the 1967 sterling crisis, attributed to TNCs by the Governor of the Bank of England (Governor of the Bank of England 1973).

17 Thus, they were often the focus of problems of overlapping jurisdiction, discussed in Chapter 2, at 2.2.2.

18 This came from George Ball, formerly a US under-secretary of state and UN representative and then the Chairman of Lehman Brothers International (Ball 1967, 1975), and was taken up by the economist Charles Kindleberger (1980).

on rules to be applied to TNCs. Indeed, under the classical liberal system, as we have seen, it was difficult to apply binding international rules to firms, since they are considered private legal persons, and not subjects of international law.[19] Hence, the main outcome of attempts to regulate international business was a series of soft law codes or guidelines, which were generally weak (discussed in Chapters 2 and 5, at 2.3.2 and 5.2.2).

Instead of a regulatory framework, international measures promoting economic integration gave priority to liberalization. This, as we have seen, was already the primary aim of the Bretton Woods institutions, but in the 1970s it began to take on new dimensions. The removal of barriers impeding access to national economies had initially focused on border barriers – tariffs and quotas on trade in goods, and currency controls – and significant progress had been made in reducing or eliminating these by the 1970s. However, this in turn drew attention to the ways in which regulatory differences also created obstacles to international trade and investment. This was perhaps most evident in the GATT, where by the mid-1970s attention was shifting to 'non-tariff barriers', and a little later to 'trade in services'. Conflicts between trade liberalization obligations and national regulations became increasingly acute during the 1980s, and ranged over issues as diverse as food safety standards, the taxation of business income from export sales, the sanctions for infringement of intellectual property rights, and import restrictions on environmental protection grounds (see Chapter 8, at 8.2). Hence, both at global and regional level, liberalization raised the question of linkages between trade rules and other kinds of regulation.

3.1.3 Theories of state, market and globalization

The increasing power and influence of TNCs and the growth of FDI during the 1960s led to questions about the continued role of the state. This was expressed most pointedly in Charles Kindleberger's assertion that 'the national state is just about through as an economic unit' (1969: 207). From a Marxist perspective, Robin Murray suggested that the international

---

19 Seidl-Hohenveldern made a valiant attempt to accommodate classical liberal international law to TNCs, including discussion of a proposal to bring them under UN supervision (1987: 22–6), and a rather ambivalent analysis of the status of joint enterprises created by states, which he concludes must come under national law if they are commercial in character, but be treated as international organizations under international law if they fulfil public functions. The difficulty of applying this distinction was shown in the litigation following the collapse of the International Tin Council.

economy should be seen 'not as an aggregation of national economies, but as a total system in which nations are subordinate structures' (1971: 85). He argued that the international expansion of TNCs did not necessarily undermine the nation-state, since firms are 'politically opportunist', and that increased international integration of production, growing economic interdependence, and decreasing national powers of economic management pointed to a need for new forms for the exercise of international state functions, including stronger international coordination. Indeed, increased economic liberalization has not been a matter of international economic pressures overwhelming national state autonomy, but has been facilitated by state action, and by policies and arrangements encouraged or imposed internationally. However, the subordination of states to capital has been exacerbated, as they have increasingly competed among themselves both to attract investment and to promote the interests of 'their' TNCs.

Despite the complex nature of the transformations of both the political and the economic spheres and of their interactions, mainstream accounts since the 1970s have remained confined within simple concepts of the state and the market. Most visible have been the failures and limits of states. The notion of state action as being generally in the public interest, which underpinned both functionalist social theory and welfare economics, has been undermined by both theoretical and empirical studies, from the left and right. Thus, Stigler's influential economistic analysis argued that regulation is usually 'acquired' by the industry concerned and 'designed and operated primarily for its benefit' (1971: 3), while several political and sociological studies showed that even if state regulation resulted from wider political pressures, business had generally been able to turn it to advantage through regulatory 'capture' (Bernstein 1955; Kolko 1963). Critiques were also advanced in many leftist analyses in the 1970s arguing that the forms and functions of the state are part of the overall socio-economic power structures (Gough 1979; LEWRG 1980; Jessop 1982; Offe and Keane 1984; Clarke 1991). In the case of nationalized industries, although state ownership in many countries did much to enable the establishment of extensive infrastructures operated by bureaucracies with a public service ethos, the institutional framework of nationalized industries usually provided little or no public accountability. Hence, governments were poorly equipped to evaluate the increasingly large-scale and complex investment decisions demanded by social changes and new technologies in many public services. The increased difficulty of getting public support for higher general taxation to finance the rising public expenditures generated by the socialization of the economy created a 'fiscal crisis', to which governments of all political hues had to respond.

On the other hand, the concept of the market has been used much less critically, by theorists of both the left and the right. Indeed, the 'market' perspective has pervaded many areas of social theory, especially with the extensive application of economic theories to social behaviour, pioneered notably by Gary Becker (1976). Despite the obvious limitations of the drastically simplifying assumptions of neoclassical economics that society is made up of rational, utility-maximizing individuals, this economistic perspective has been very widely used, especially in the 1980s, to promote market-based social theories and policy prescriptions of every kind. Indeed, it virtually conquered entire fields of thought, notably economic law, as exemplified by the dominance of the work of Richard Posner, which is often considered to be based on the work of Ronald Coase. However, Coase developed his analysis of transaction costs as much to demonstrate that the market is a social institution as to provide economic criteria to evaluate state intervention (Campbell and Picciotto 1998; see also Chapter 4, at 4.1.1.3). Furthermore, some sociologists such as Peter Blau and James Coleman themselves developed theories of social action and structure based on exchange and rational choice, and these were taken up by some political scientists.

However, more broadly based economic perspectives were put forward by 'institutionalist' approaches of various kinds, which modified some of the epistemological assumptions of neoclassical economics, especially that exchange takes place between individuals with perfect and equal information. Institutionalist economists have explored the implications of 'bounded rationality', linking up with behavioural psychology (Simon 1982); they have discussed justifications of state intervention in cases of 'market failure' (North 1990); they have analysed the circumstances in which institutions (including firms) might be more efficient than markets, especially due to coordination or transaction costs (Williamson 1985); and have discussed the importance of 'social capital'.[20] Nevertheless, these perspectives still tend to consider economic activity from the viewpoint of exchange, although trying to view exchange in terms of a fuller understanding of human relationships and social institutions.

20 A helpful analysis and critique of this concept is provided by Fine 1999.

Alternative approaches emerged from economic sociologists who rejected the elegant models based on unrealistic assumptions of neo-classical economics (Hirsch *et al.* 1990). They have emphasized the 'embeddedness' of economic action in social structure (Granovetter and Swedberg 1992), and the 'cognitive, cultural, social and political [factors] that neoclassical economics tends to ignore' (Zukin and DiMaggio 1990: 3). They lack the influence on policy-makers of economic theories based on universalistic concepts of efficiency.[21] These approaches helped to understand business relationships as networks, which seems more appropriate in a world where long-term and relational contracting and a variety of types of inter-corporate as well as public–private linkages provide the sinews of economic life. More recent approaches to social studies of markets have drawn on social studies of science and technology and anthropological methods to delve more deeply into the development of forms of knowledge and techniques that help to construct and trans-form markets (Callon 1998; MacKenzie 2006; MacKenzie *et al.* 2007; see Chapter 7, at 7.2.3).

Some approaches in political theory have also contributed to rethinking the role of social institutions. In particular, there has been a revival of the concept of 'civil society', to provide a political theory which might preserve the possibilities of political mobilization aiming at radical social improve-ment or utopian projects in the face of the crisis of the welfare state, and to resolve the conflicts both between elitist and participatory models of democracy, and between rights-based and communitarian views of justice (Cohen and Arato 1992). Yet, while civil society as a concept is appealing in indicating that society does not consist of atomized individuals but a variety of social structures and institutions, it is less helpful when it becomes reified into a separate 'sphere', between social relations and the political realm of the state. As such, it is commonly visualized as filled with a motley collection of NGOs. These range from pressure groups and associations with clearly sectional and partisan objectives such as indus-try groups and trade unions, to self-selected advocacy groups and other organizations with social and political objectives, which generally have various links to both the state and economic activity.

Nevertheless, the dominant ideologies during the 1980s were neo-liberal, and this trend was reinforced by the collapse of the Soviet system, which led to a triumphalism about the virtues of 'free markets', and a

---

21 See Fligstein 2001: 9; his attempt to remedy this deficiency in that book is less convincing than his earlier detailed study of the rise of the US corporate form.

return to ideologies of fundamentalist liberalism or 'laissez-faire'. This asserts that the efficient allocation of economic resources, and even social harmony, are best assured by unrestricted interactions and exchanges between individuals, so the role of the state should as far as possible be limited to enforcing contracts and protecting rights in private property. Other kinds of regulation are seen as 'interventions' by the state and generally regarded as unnecessary and harmful. This has been reinforced by the increased popularity of economic theories of politics, as mentioned above.[22]

From this perspective, collective action amounts to self-interested attempts by organized groups to secure their special interests (Olson 1965), often described as 'rent-seeking'.[23] Founded on this, 'public choice' theories of the state have argued that constitutional principles should limit what they regard as the discretionary powers of government, and so prevent states from being captured by organized interests (Buchanan and Tollison 1984). This viewpoint leads to support for international economic agreements which lock in national states to binding obligations to liberalize their markets, aiming to prevent organized interest groups from securing national regulations which are viewed by definition as protectionist. The restrictions on the powers of national states resulting from such agreements is not only acknowledged but seen as desirable, and indeed as enhancing individual freedom and even democracy, since national states are considered to be prey to the 'tyranny of the majority'.[24] Yet this conveniently overlooks the strong influence wielded by international business and TNCs in global arenas, which they are in many ways able to 'capture'. International arrangements for positive regulatory cooperation, for example to agree harmonized or common standards

22 These often entered common discourse in ways which disregarded the specificities of the assumptions on which they were based, as with Tiebout (1956), discussed below; and sometimes in ways quite contrary to the original author's argument, as with Hardin's 'Tragedy of the Commons' (1968), which argued for restrictions on unlimited individual freedom, but is usually taken to be an argument for private property (see Chapter 9, at 9.2.5).

23 Elinor Ostrom developed a kind of immanent critique of Olson, especially in Ostrom 1990.

24 This view is supported also by European continental ordo-liberalism, which advocates legal and constitutional provisions to institutionalize market frameworks; this perspective has been influential in the international trade community, for example in the thinking of Jan Tumlir, who headed the GATT research department until his death in 1985 (Sally 1998: 153ff.), and Ernst-Ulrich Petersmann, who was appointed as the GATT's first Legal Officer in 1981; it is still put forward as a rationale for the WTO (McGinnis and Movesian 2000), although as discussed in Chapter 8, the WTO agreements go well beyond liberalization.

for products or services, or to cooperate in enforcement of matters such as taxation or competition policy, tend to be viewed with suspicion as 'mercantilist' deals or state cartels. The preferred neo-liberal alternative is regulatory competition, which is seen as offering the possibility of 'exit' to asset owners from the high costs of inefficient and protectionist regulations, as well as constraining states to resist domestic pressures for regulation.

It is this type of free-market or fundamentalist neo-liberalism that has underpinned much of the rhetoric about globalization, sparking opposition from 'anti-globalization' protesters. Yet, while it certainly provides an explanation and justification for the impetus to national deregulation resulting from international liberalization, it offers little basis for understanding the growth of regulation and of networks of international cooperation and coordination that have in fact accompanied liberalization and played a part in shaping global change. Despite this, much of the anti-globalization movement mainly targeted this free-market neo-liberalism, so that many of the debates had an air of shadow-boxing. Subsequently, some critics refocused on the forms and contents of international institutions and rules (Monbiot 2003), and the protest movements rejected the 'anti-globalization' label in favour of the slogan 'another world is possible' (Fisher and Ponniah 2003; Mertes and Bello 2004; George 2004), or even 'globalization from below' (Brecher et al. 2000).

The dominance of 'market fundamentalism' in the 1980s was reflected especially in international economic organizations,[25] and came to be labelled the 'Washington consensus'.[26] However, it began to come under criticism during the 1990s, when the World Bank in particular began to recognize the importance of social and even state institutions, as well as

---

25 Dezalay and Garth (1998) have provided a sociological account of the professional competitive strategies (especially the investment in mathematical economics) that enabled Chicago economics to conquer the Washington institutions (the IMF and the WB); this enabled those institutions to overcome their relative marginalization from the real centres of economic power in Wall Street, by providing the ideological underpinnings for dealing with the debt crises of developing countries such as Mexico through massive bail-outs, which imposed monetarist macroeconomic policies while benefiting mainly creditor banks.

26 A paper by John Williamson in 1990 outlined the 'intelligent convergence' in Washington around ten conditions for 'policy reform' in debtor countries. These were castigated by the next wave of WB economists, led by Stiglitz, who advocated a less rigidly monetarist set of prescriptions termed the 'post-Washington consensus' (1998), which Williamson rejoindered were essentially compatible with his earlier formulation (1999). The 'post-Washington consensus' is also sometimes used to refer to the 'governance turn' taken by the WB after the mid-1990s (see below).

'social capital', in providing strong foundations for capitalist economies, leading to its 'governance turn'.[27] The newer policies relied more on institutionalist theories and were more favourable to state action, but they still begin from a presumption that political intervention is only justified where 'market failure' can be identified, and they generally favour a 'market-friendly state'. Market failure is generally said to arise from 'externalities' (costs or benefits of a transaction which are external to the parties themselves), inadequate information, or imperfect competition. Such situations may justify some form of state 'intervention', although the general presumption is that it should be a minimalist correction, to restore the free flow of private transactions, for example by providing an appropriately defined legal remedy or property right.

Going somewhat further, the concept of 'public goods' has been used to suggest that some goods or services should be freely available rather than bought, due to their natural qualities. Public goods are said to have either or both of two characteristics: they are (a) non-rival in consumption (enjoyment by one person does not detract from enjoyment by another); and (b) non-excludable (it is inherently difficult or impossible to restrict their use or consumption). Ensuring the production of public goods is said to justify state action, although this need not involve direct state provision, but could be by market-friendly solutions, i.e. granting rights or imposing obligations on private actors. Thus, scientific discoveries, technological innovations and cultural products or activities, are often regarded as public goods, production of which may be stimulated either by state subsidies or by state-granted property rights (patents and copyright). In practice there is often a combination of the two, and state power is necessary to create or legitimize excludability and enforce property rights, while states also subsidize activities deemed to have a public benefit, such as research and infrastructure or prestige projects. A concept different

27 After a decade of structural adjustment policies which were heavily criticized as undermining public provision, in 1989 the Bank identified a 'crisis of governance' in sub-Saharan Africa, and published a more general report entitled *Governance and Development* in 1992; its study of the East Asian 'miracle' published in 1993 gave some recognition to the important role of the state (although watered down for political reasons: Wade 1996); this trend culminated in the 1997 World Development Report, *The State in a Changing World* (Faundez 1997; Tshuma 1999). The increased attention to the social aspects of economic development was also reflected in the Bank's increasing emphasis on 'social capital'; a vigorous critique by Ben Fine (1999) traces the development of the concept from its origins in new microeconomic analysis, through the work of US sociologists (Coleman, Granovetter and Putnam), which he distinguishes from the use of the concept of social capital in the more contextualized and grounded sociology of Bourdieu.

from public goods, although also sometimes used to justify state action, is that of 'natural monopolies', for example infrastructure such as rail or road networks: these also may be provided by the state either directly or by licensing private firms.

Theorizing state action through the lens of public goods retains an economistic perspective, although it accepts the possibility of collective provision. A more critical perspective suggests that whether goods are private or public does not simply result from their essential or natural characteristics, but that these qualities are themselves socially constructed.[28] The question of what is a public good is not a technical one, but a public and political matter, depending on social values, and often requiring state action to create excludability. It is the expectations and understandings embedded in social relations and underpinned by social norms and law that determine whether costs or benefits are 'externalized', and whether access to particular goods or services is non-rival or excludable. For example, radio or TV broadcasts may be free to air or subscription only, so whether a cultural or sporting event such as football's World Cup is treated as a public good is not inherent in the technology. Access to natural resources such as water can be controlled, so they are not inherently either public or private. Asserting that something is a public good is often intended to mean that access, especially to the essentials of life, should be egalitarian and hence not determined only by price, but this should be recognized as a normative question.

The revival of market-based perspectives generally resulted from the failures of statist economic management, and the reorientation to world markets. This gave a new impetus to the liberalization of international trade and investment, especially after the economic crisis sparked by the 'oil shock' of the mid-1970s. Liberalization reached its apogee with the successful conclusion of the decade-long Uruguay Round of trade negotiations, resulting in the establishment in 1995 of the WTO.[29] However,

28 For a cogent demolition of the concept of public goods, see Malkin and Wildavsky 1991, and for an attempt to refine it Kaul *et al.* 1999. The concept is an excellent example of what Marxists call commodity fetishism: viewing the characteristics of a social system of economic activity which is based on exchange as determined by the natural properties of the goods which are exchanged, and hence accepting that social relations and institutions are dominated by an impersonal dynamic instead of material human relationships.

29 It took some four years to reach agreement on the negotiating guidelines, adopted in a Ministerial Declaration at Punta del Este, Uruguay, in September 1986; the negotiations were finally concluded in December 1993, and the package of agreements named the Final Act of the Uruguay Round was signed at Marrakech in April 1994 (see generally Stewart 1993).

far from creating a 'free' world market, the WTO established a complex framework for coordinating the regulation of international economic transactions. The package of agreements comprising the WTO go well beyond trade, and effectively create requirements for a wide range of national measures to comply with international standards, many of them set by other organizations. This placed the WTO at the intersection of a variety of international regulatory networks. These kinds of networks had grown up gradually since the 1970s, as part of the process of internationalization of both business and of its regulation. The creation of the WTO established an important nodal point of intersection for many of these networks, which will be discussed in detail in Chapter 8.

Hence, it was perhaps not surprising that the WTO became the target for vigorous social protests about the damaging social effects of economic liberalization, also reflecting concerns about the undemocratic nature of the emerging forms of global economic governance. This culminated in December 1999, at the close of the twentieth century, with the 'battle for Seattle', the political crisis at the Seattle meeting of the WTO's Ministerial Council, when determined protests in the streets contrasted sharply with the indecision and political deadlock in the conference rooms. This cast a new spotlight on the wide-ranging policy debates about both the effectiveness and legitimacy of the emerging systems of global governance.

Unfortunately, these debates have too often been conducted in the simplistic terms of a state–market dyad, and only slowly have they begun to come to terms with the more complex realities of the twenty-first century. The 2007–8 financial and economic crisis provided a rude awakening, resulting in much talk of the need for more effective regulation, and even of the need for morality in markets (Sandel 2009). However, the detailed design and practical implementation of regulation is still largely left to technical specialists, and strongly influenced by business interests.

3.1.4 From negative integration to regulatory interaction

Economic integration through liberalization, the removal of direct barriers to international trade and investment, has been referred to as 'negative' integration, and contrasted with 'positive' integration, which entails greater coordination or harmonization of standards and regulation. It is relatively easy to agree on facilitating international flows by removing border restrictions, at least in periods of economic expansion. However, the reduction of such barriers removed important instruments on which governments had relied to insulate their domestic economies from external shocks. At the same time, demands on government had become much greater, so that socio-economic management had become more complex. Hence, liberalization brought into sharper focus the differences between national regulations. Trying to deal with these differences has generated an exponential growth of new types of regulatory cooperation, coordination and harmonization.

Harmonization does not mean globally unified regulation,[30] which is difficult or impossible to achieve. However, even effective coordination has proved difficult. Instead what has emerged is a complex process of regulatory interaction, involving both supra-state and sub-state arrangements, linking and intersecting in various ways, and forming a maze of regulatory networks.

The limitations of 'negative' integration (Pinder 1968) became apparent by the late 1960s in the European Economic Community (EEC),[31] where the construction of the Common Market came up against the difficulty of reaching agreement on regulations affecting trade in goods, such as labelling and other consumer protection rules.[32] Even among the European countries with a common history and similar levels of economic development, it proved extremely difficult to agree on matters as apparently trivial as the description and labelling of products such as sausages, ice cream or alcoholic drinks. A means of breaking the logjam was eventually provided by the European Court of Justice, in the landmark *Cassis de Dijon* decision in 1979, holding that a Member State could not use its domestic regulatory requirements to prohibit imports unless it could show that such a restriction was necessary and proportional to a legitimate public purpose.[33]

---

30 For a contrary view, see Chimni 2004: 7.
31 Renamed the European Community on the creation of the European Union (EU) by the Maastricht Treaty of 1992.
32 Art. 100 of the Treaty of Rome gave the Community competence to harmonize rules which would impede the functioning of the Common Market, but it required unanimity among the states; the Single European Act (1986) ameliorated this by allowing qualified majority voting for measures necessary to complete the Single European Market.
33 In *Cassis de Dijon* (1979), the German Alcoholic Liquor Authority had refused importation of the French blackcurrant liqueur *cassis*, on the grounds that its alcohol content fell below the minimum for fruit liquors prescribed by German law; national rules still applied because a proposal tabled in 1976 for a common European regulation for the production and marketing of alcoholic drinks had not yet been agreed; however, the ECJ held that to refuse importation of goods which did not meet domestic regulatory standards had an effect equivalent to a quantitative restriction, so was prohibited as an obstacle to the

This created a 'competition among rules' (Nicolaïdis 1992) since, as long as common rules had not been agreed, a state could be obliged to admit products made under other states' rules, although it could choose to maintain its own regulations for local producers. Within the EC, however, the threat of regulatory competition acted as a spur to states to agree upon at least a floor of basic rules, and in practice the opening up of the European market provided an impetus towards more integrated regulation (Dehousse 1992). The principle of mutual recognition was extended to the service sector, especially financial services, in the shape of home-state regulation (the 'single passport') for service providers, such as banks. This entailed often quite detailed common rules, for example capital adequacy rules for financial firms. However, it was also accepted that the host state, although obliged to allow access to foreign goods and services whose quality was regulated by their home state, could nevertheless maintain its own rules to protect the 'general good' (e.g. general contract law, taxation and consumer protection rules).

Building on this, the 'new approach' to harmonization which was the basis for the Single Market programme adopted in 1985 (Dehousse 1989) attempted to minimize rule harmonization by adopting a performance-oriented approach under which the harmonized legal rules could be confined to broad regulatory objectives. These could be met by compliance with technical specifications formulated by specialized institutions, thus permitting a high degree of diversity in both national regulations and detailed technical standards set up by industry or professional bodies (Woolcock 1996: 292–5). Reconciling closer European policy alignment with local diversity also led to greater use of a variety of soft-law methods, which became known as the 'open method of coordination'. For this and other reasons, the EU system came to be recognized as one of complex multilevel governance (Kohler-Koch and Eising 1999).

These developments in Europe often had wider international repercussions and in many ways European regulatory initiatives acted as a catalyst for wider international processes.[34] The closer and more detailed

---

free movement of goods, unless it could be shown to be necessary for 'the effectiveness of fiscal supervision, the protection of public health, the fairness of commercial transactions and the defence of the consumer'.

34 For example, the efforts to integrate the European market for financial services interacted with the development of international standards in matters such as banking supervision (Davies and Green 2008: ch. 4; see Chapter 7); the harmonization of EU product standards has often involved considerable friction with international trade rules, and attempts to reconcile regional with global standardization processes (Joerges 2001; Princen 2002;

regulatory coordination this entailed went beyond the classical liberal model of interdependence, and involved important obligations on states requiring significant changes to their internal laws. This meant in effect a shift from international to supranational law, although governments were often reluctant to accept or admit to this shift. New supranational regimes could result especially from the efforts and determination of social networks of policy specialists and activists, identifying an issue of global concern or resonance. This has been especially strong in relation to environmental issues. For example, the Vienna Convention for the Protection of the Ozone Layer (1985) and its Montreal Protocol (1987) established a comprehensive programme to reduce the global production of ozone-depleting substances. This included measures to ban imports of controlled substances from non-parties, and special provisions for developing countries, notably for technology transfer and for financial transfers through a Multilateral Fund. Most importantly, it established an 'adaptive regime' (Canan and Reichman 2002: 184), with procedures for continuously monitoring progress, and for revision of the phase-out schedules, on the basis of scientific assessments, and involving a wide range of stakeholders.

However, such initiatives frequently failed or stalled due to the difficulty of reaching policy consensus and agreement among sufficient states. This might be due to a divergence of interests or of views between groups of states, or to objections from one or more important or powerful states. For example, in the field of intellectual property (IP), negotiations to amend multilateral treaties through the World Intellectual Property Organization (WIPO) failed, due to wide divergences between states, but these were overcome by the strategic decision by mainly US IP-intensive TNCs to shift the issue to the GATT (see Chapter 9, at 9.1.2).

As a counterpoint to supranational initiatives, a plethora of sub-national coordination arrangements mushroomed, to deal with a wide variety of issues. Often, they have grown from direct contacts between national officials or regulators with specific functional responsibilities. Thus, officials whose powers and policies have been developed within the hierarchy of the national state, have increasingly developed horizontal cross-border contacts with their counterparts in other states, bypassing the coordination of national levels of government and the mediation of

Schepel 2005; see Chapter 8); the debates and conflicts over the EU directive for intellectual property protection for biotechnology intersected with the global negotiations resulting in the TRIPs agreement and were reflected in its art. 27 (see Chapter 9, at 9.2.3).

diplomatic channels and Foreign Offices. The growth of these links has also resulted from the strategic interplay among regulators, and the need to try to resolve jurisdictional conflicts discussed above. The creation of an international procedure for cooperation may be seen by the more assertive regulators as an opportunity to extend their influence, while others may hope that it could restrain unilateral assertions of jurisdiction by powerful states, especially the USA.

In the eyes of the specialists involved in them, such links are seen as a necessary functional response to both the increasing complexity of the problems with which they are concerned, and their international scope. The formation of such networks has been given a greater impetus by the more general shift within states from 'government' to 'governance', involving the delegation or transfer of public functions from central government to specialist bodies, operating on the basis of professional or scientific expertise (discussed in Chapter 1). Thus, central bankers, tax collectors, antitrust or competition law enforcers, financial market regulators, and many more, have asserted or been given increasing autonomy and a 'depoliticization' of their functions. This facilitates new forms of international coordination which are more decentralized, involving direct contacts between national regulators responsible for specific functions, generally bypassing central governments. Indeed, sometimes the dense interactions of transnational regulatory communities can result in the importation or 'migration' of regulation, through what Joanne Scott has called a 'chemistry of regulatory attraction', even countering official government policies.[35] At the same time, these regulatory networks have developed within a wider culture of policy discussion involving business representatives, professional advisers and specialists in the relevant regulatory field, so they are as much corporatist as governmental networks.

This type of sub-state coordination has generally used 'soft law' rather than formal international treaties or agreements. In addition to the reasons discussed already (Chapter 2, at 2.3.2), the use of soft law helps to maintain the view that such regulatory coordination does not entail political commitments but merely technical cooperation. In practice, however, although the issues dealt with are indeed specific and specialized, they

---

35 Thus, Joanne Scott shows how despite the active opposition of the US federal government, which pressed for a deregulatory agenda acting in tandem with a powerful industry association, US NGOs and other advocates of regulatory change acted as a bridge for the importation of much of the substance of the EU regulation on chemicals, while also 'creating opportunities for reciprocally beneficial regulatory learning and for an on-going exchange of ideas about chemicals and about how to regulate them' (2009: 85).

inevitably may involve broader policy issues. Thus, matters such as the patentability of genetic fragments (see Chapter 9, at 9.2.4), intra-firm pricing within TNCs and its impact on tax liability (Chapter 6, at 6.3.4), or the weighting of different tiers of capital in calculating bank reserves (Chapter 7, at 7.2.1), although now coordinated between specialist regulators, entail decisions of major importance to global governance.

3.2 Managing regulatory interactions

Globalized regulation is far from being an orderly system which produces a clear allocation of jurisdiction to regulate. As has already been stressed in the previous chapter, jurisdiction to regulate economic actors, issues, activities and transactions may be asserted by various bodies and forums, in ways which overlap and intersect. The multiplication of these layers of regulation means that a decision taken in one forum often does not finally dispose of an issue, and ways can often be found to counteract or countermand it by raising the same or a related issue in another forum. This offers considerable opportunities for strategic management of regulatory interactions.

3.2.1 Competition and coordination

Regulatory interaction is often discussed in terms of the concept of regulatory competition. A favourable view of such competition is based on theories which assert that it will produce an optimal level of regulation, since each business will choose the jurisdiction which offers the regulatory arrangements it considers most suitable for its purposes.

However, these theories involve rather simplistic assumptions. To begin with, choosing a location for a business activity is not like buying a single product (in this case, regulation) on the basis of evaluating its quality in relation to price, since a variety of factors will affect a decision on where to invest. Indeed, an investment decision is likely to depend more on factors such as the availability of skilled workers, good infrastructure and access to markets than on regulatory concerns. Nevertheless, an investor such as a TNC may well identify several potential locations which all satisfy its main requirements, for example in deciding on a site for a new factory, and then bargain with the regulatory authorities, even playing one off against another, especially to obtain the best financial terms – for example generous investment incentives or tax relief. A firm may also threaten to close or relocate an activity to try to deter regulatory authorities from taking a potentially adverse decision. Indeed, such threats have become a regular or even routine reaction by business sectors to regulatory proposals which they dislike. However, foreign direct investment entails a relatively long-term commitment,[36] as abandoning an existing investment can have considerable costs, both financial and personal, although this has been made easier by the trend to contractual outsourcing (see Chapter 4, at 4.2).

Nevertheless, even the possibility that a firm may choose an alternative location creates competitive pressure on regulatory authorities, and increased awareness of regulatory alternatives has certainly created a competitive tension. Due to the concern to attract inward investment, the main result has been that many countries have offered special investment incentives, sometimes as individual packages (UNCTAD 1996b, 2000; see Chapter 6, at 6.4.1). The competition to attract investment may create pressure either to relax regulatory standards, or to adopt what may be regarded as international best practice in various fields of regulation – a regulatory race to the bottom, or to the top.

However, economistic analyses of regulatory competition are usually based on the assumption that a person or activity is entirely free to move from one jurisdiction to another, and that each jurisdiction is fully autonomous.[37] Much of the discussion of regulatory competition assumes a relatively simple situation, when a person or activity can genuinely be located in and therefore regulated by one jurisdiction rather than another. However, as was pointed out in Chapter 2, at 2.2.2, there is often concurrent or overlapping jurisdiction, because people, firms and activities may have contacts with more than one territory. Also, regulations adopted by one jurisdiction will affect others, both for good and ill. This is referred to in regulatory competition debates by the concept of positive and negative 'externalities': for example a jurisdiction which adopts

---

36 In more arcane terminology, it is a transaction with high asset-specificity: Murphy (2004: 16) has identified asset-specificity as a key factor affecting regulatory competition.

37 The starting point is usually Tiebout's 'pure theory' which suggested that the optimum level of provision of public goods by local communities can result if consumer-voters have a choice among a number of communities in which to reside, which offer different levels of public goods and hence tax rates; the model assumed that residents are entirely free to move (they have income from investment not employment), and decide purely on the basis of their tax-expenditure preferences; in addition, they are assumed to reside entirely within one community which supplies all their public services, with no external economies or diseconomies between communities (Tiebout 1956: 419; see also Bratton *et al.* 1996: 11–15).

lax environmental emissions standards may reduce costs for local firms, but creates an 'externality' by exporting the problem to its neighbours (Revesz 1992). Tiebout himself accepted that, for example, inadequate law enforcement by one community may affect another, by attracting residents who are criminals and can prey on the residents of its neighbours, and that in such cases 'some form of integration may be indicated' (1956: 423).

Thus, unlike the relatively simple and often static picture presented by economistic theories of regulatory competition, the process of regulatory interaction is much more complex. Neither corporations nor individuals are subject only to the laws of their country of nationality or home state. Unless an activity takes place entirely within a single territory, a firm may be subject to regulation in any or every jurisdiction with which it has contacts, and the various regulators have no presumptive obligation to respect the regulations of other jurisdictions. For private law, principles of conflicts of law help to allocate jurisdiction according to which legal system may be considered most appropriate (see Chapter 2, at 2.2). These do not generally apply to regulatory law, indeed even private law is subject to a 'public policy exception', under which a court may decline to apply a foreign law which might otherwise be considered appropriate.[38]

Regulatory competition analysis has focused on the 'Delaware effect': the strong preference of most US companies to incorporate under the laws of the small state of Delaware. This can be attributed to the quality of Delaware's company law rules, which some regard as superior and others as lax.[39] However, the application of Delaware's corporate laws to corporations which do business in other states depends on the US federal

---

38 A number of legal authors argue for the use of conflicts rules to manage regulatory competition, but such rules are themselves very flexible. An analysis favouring conflicts principles which defer to parties' choice of law is proposed by Ribstein and O'Hara (2009), arguing in favour of the 'market for law' based on standard arguments in law-and-economics of the need to constrain state regulatory excesses and regulatory capture. Joel Trachtman (1994) develops a more sophisticated perspective, recognizing that allocation of jurisdiction is about community not just individual interest, and necessarily entails negotiated accommodations between jurisdictions, and argues that it should aim for stable and predictable outcomes. Christian Joerges (2007) proposes that transnational constitutionalism should be based on a conflicts-of-law approach, to provide a stronger social embeddedness for multilevel governance.
39 The concept 'race to the bottom' derives from the famous dictum of Justice Brandeis, who described the competition to attract incorporations as 'one not of diligence but of laxity' (*Ligget* v. *Lee* (1933: 559)).

legal principle that firms should be governed internally by the laws of whichever state they choose for incorporation, without the need for any connection with that state.[40] Internationally, there is no obligation on states to accept such a principle. While some countries do accept the place-of-incorporation rule, many civil law countries follow the 'real seat' principle, according to which a corporation is governed under the law of the jurisdiction where it has its main place of business. Furthermore, different criteria are applied to define the 'real seat', which makes it hard to harmonize this principle internationally.[41] It may be undermined by international obligations to admit foreign firms, such as the 'right of establishment' under EU law.

Whatever way the 'home' state of a corporation is defined, it is nevertheless accepted that host states are entitled to protect their legitimate interests. Thus, despite the US recognition rule, US states still apply qualification requirements and 'outreach' statutes to out-of-state corporations.[42] This possibility of non-recognition or counteracting regulation by host states creates pressures on home states to ensure that their regulatory standards for corporations are internationally acceptable.

Even if companies were subject to only one corporate law, this applies only to the governance of the company itself, and not to its transactions or activities. The choice of place of incorporation does not allow a company to avoid the obligation to comply, in each jurisdiction where it does business, with other local law such as tax, employment or consumer protection regulation. Local rules may even require the firm to be incorporated locally, or in an approved jurisdiction, to defeat the

---

40 Sometimes referred to as the 'internal affairs doctrine' (Ribstein and O'Hara 2009: 107). The obligation to recognize out-of-state corporations and admit them to do business only became accepted relatively late in the nineteenth century, based on a strong notion of corporate citizenship, and the constitutional protection of the rights of corporations to participate in the growing interstate markets (Buxbaum and Hopt 1988: 38–40).

41 A Hague Convention of 1956 on recognition of the legal personality of foreign entities was ratified by only three states and failed to enter into force.

42 Charny 1991; Rock 2002; Xanthaki 2001; Kersting (2002) points out that the 'seat' rule originated as a means of dealing with 'pseudo-foreign' corporations, and suggests that the EU should coordinate host-state protection rules by a suitable EC Directive. The ECJ gave a push in that direction by its 1999 decision in *Centros*, interpreting the right of establishment in EU law as entitling a firm to choose where to incorporate, provided the choice does not amount to an abuse; this appears to require some economic link to the state of incorporation, but falling short of the *siège réel* principle. For a comparison of the 'constitutional' approaches of the USA and the EU to the obligation to recognize incorporation, see Buxbaum 2000.

choice of jurisdictions of convenience. For example, a host state banking regulator may refuse a licence to conduct banking business to a foreign bank unless it is incorporated in an approved jurisdiction (i.e. one with acceptable banking regulations). Stock exchanges' disclosure obligations traditionally required that listed securities must be issued by locally incorporated companies. This created a major limitation on a firm's freedom to choose where to incorporate, but it has been considerably relaxed recently due to competition between exchanges to attract listings from foreign companies.[43]

Nevertheless, it is possible for firms to use the fiction of corporate personality both to choose favourable rules, as well as to try to avoid the application of regulations it considers unfavourable. This type of strategy may take advantage of special provisions offered by some jurisdictions which actively seek to attract the formation of companies owned by non-residents, often described as havens (discussed further in the next two sections). However, such strategies also depend on the reluctance of legislatures, courts and regulators in other countries to challenge the fiction of corporate legal personality, or to 'lift the corporate veil'. Sometimes, however, anti-avoidance legislation can and does disregard corporate personality if it is regarded as fictitious or spurious, although this can be hard to define: for example, the taxation of 'controlled foreign corporations' (see Chapter 6, at 6.3.3).

---

43 Generally, public companies have been listed on the stock exchange of their home state, although the major capital markets such as London and New York have also conducted an often highly liquid secondary market in foreign company shares. Competition between exchanges has led to various methods of facilitating listings by foreign firms. The main method is by listing 'depositary receipts' issued by banks with which the firm deposits some of its shares. In the 1990s there was a significant increase in cross-listing. The number of foreign firms listed on the two main US exchanges, the New York Stock Exchange (NYSE) and the Nasdaq, increased from 170 in 1990 to over 750 in 2000; a majority went to the NYSE on which the proportion of foreign firms listed grew from 5% to 15%, continuing to increase although domestic listings declined after 1998, which has been attributed to the high disclosure and transparency standards of the NYSE (Coffee 2002: 1770–2). As a result, there was a massive shift in the trading of shares of companies from developing country and emergent markets (especially middle-income countries) to the leading stock exchanges, making it harder for such countries to sustain their own exchanges (Claessens *et al.* 2002). Some companies have decided to 'migrate' by seeking their primary listing on one of the large exchanges, usually by incorporating in the relevant state (Rock 2002). Others have sought 'dual listings', and this has been facilitated by rule changes by the exchanges and securities market regulators: for example, the London Stock Exchange has created a market for international securities, which includes securities of a company registered for trading on any approved exchange.

3.2.2 Regulatory arbitrage and forum-shopping

An entity with international operations such as a TNC will experience jurisdictional overlap as creating a problem of coping with multiple and perhaps conflicting regulatory requirements. Complying with a variety of regulatory requirements may impose extra costs on firms, and they are likely to seek to minimize their regulatory exposure, and to learn to take advantage of regulatory differences between jurisdictions, a tactic sometimes referred to as regulatory arbitrage.[44]

From the viewpoint of the authorities, the regulations of different jurisdictions may often be inconsistent, but are rarely conflicting, in the strict sense that it is impossible to comply with one requirement without being in breach of another. In response to regulatory avoidance strategies of firms, regulators have also honed their tactics. For example, a firm may attempt to counter the demands of one jurisdiction by seeking a blocking order from another regulator, for example using commercial secrecy or confidentiality laws to resist requests to provide information, for purposes such as tax or competition law enforcement. This tactic has been used especially as a defence against US 'long-arm' laws, but in response, the US courts and other authorities have countered blocking orders by devices such as requiring firms to show they have made reasonable and bona fide efforts to be released from secrecy obligations in the other jurisdiction.[45]

The strategic use of regulatory networks is sometimes referred to as forum-shopping. This originated with the tactics adopted by resourceful litigants in seeking to have a dispute decided by the court they considered most favourable for them. The increased salience of international concurrent jurisdiction, discussed above, has led both plaintiffs and defendants to develop techniques to try to secure their favoured venue for adjudication. For example, the Russian oil giant Yukos in early 2005 filed for protective bankruptcy in a Texas court, to try to prevent the auction by the Russian authorities of its main assets in order to satisfy a tax claim.[46]

---

44 An arbitrageur buys and sells simultaneously in two markets, to take advantage of price differences.

45 Lowenfeld (1996: ch. 7) analyses this in full and sometimes fascinating detail; see also Picciotto (1992: 262–72) for a discussion of problems of tax authorities and other regulators obtaining information abroad from banks, accountants and lawyers.

46 A US bankruptcy court for the Southern District of Texas initially held that it had jurisdiction to grant an application for voluntary bankruptcy on the grounds that Yukos had some property (a bank account) in Texas, and it saw no reason to refuse jurisdiction on the grounds of *forum non conveniens*, comity or the act of state doctrine. However, the court later accepted a motion by one of the creditors (Deutsche Bank) to dismiss the

In response, court decisions on whether to hear cases, or to refuse to do so on the grounds of *forum non conveniens* (inconvenient forum), have become influenced by policy considerations (see Chapters 2 and 5, at 2.2.2 and 5.1.3.2).

Forum-selection strategies have spread from choice of adjudicators to selecting other kinds of regulators. For example, pharmaceutical companies might seek out suitable jurisdictions for the initial testing and approval of new drugs (Braithwaite 1993). Other jurisdictions are not obliged to recognize the first regulator's decision, but its existence may still put them under pressure to accommodate to it or adhere to the same standard. The converse may also apply, of course: the refusal by one authority to approve a new drug will prejudice its chances in other jurisdictions.

Hence, forum selection must be seen as a complex and interactive game with several players, both regulated entities and regulators. Also, it occurs both in the application and the formulation of regulation. Thus, Braithwaite and Drahos have analysed the strategies of forum-shifting and forum-blocking used, especially by powerful governments and firms, in choosing the most favourable arena in which to negotiate new international rules (2000: ch. 24). Increased opportunities for such strategies have resulted from the growing linkages between regulatory regimes for which different organizations are responsible. In particular, as mentioned above, trade rules have increasingly come into interaction with other types of economic regulation, especially with the birth of the WTO (see

application under chapter 11 of the US Bankruptcy Code, since the vast majority of the business activity of Yukos was in Russia, where it accounted for about 20 per cent of oil production so that 'the sheer size of Yukos, and correspondingly, its impact on the entirety of the Russian economy, weighs heavily in favor of allowing resolution in a forum in which participation of the Russian government is assured' (*Yukos, In Re* (2005: 40)). The Russian state had begun investigating Yukos for tax evasion and financial crimes in 2003, and in 2005 the firm was forced into bankruptcy for non-payment of a $27bn tax claim and its assets acquired mainly by the state-owned oil giant Rosneft, while Mikhail Khodorkovsky and Platon Lebedev, who controlled Yukos through the Menatep Bank, were prosecuted and jailed in Siberia. Meanwhile, legal cases were initiated on behalf of Yukos shareholders in many other jurisdictions, including a claim submitted to the European Court of Human Rights in 2004, which was declared admissible in January 2009 (*Yukos* v. *Russia* (2009)); jurisdiction was accepted in the Permanent Court for Arbitration over major claims against the Russian Federation for expropriation brought by Yukos shareholders under the Energy Charter Treaty (*Yukos claims* (2010)); and there were reports of claims by Spanish investment funds under the Russia–Spain bilateral investment treaty (Peterson 2006). In March 2010 a UK court froze £425m. held by Rosneft in the UK to enforce a Dutch court judgment obtained on behalf of Yukos.

Chapter 8). However, as Braithwaite and Drahos cogently point out, this shift resulted from strategic actions, especially of powerful business lobbies and the US trade negotiators, adroitly transferring onto the agenda of the WTO many of the topics previously dealt with by bodies such as UNCTAD (the United Nations Conference on Trade and Development), which had prioritized the concerns of developing countries. Subsequently, the multilateral negotiations in the WTO have been outflanked and put under pressure by bilateral negotiations begun by the USA, the EU and others with selected trading partners (discussed in Chapter 8, at 8.1.3).

An important role in the management of regulatory interactions is played by creative ideologists, especially lawyers. Yves Dezalay (1996) has pointed out that, since they work as professionals for private clients or public bodies (and often both), lawyers are accustomed to working at the interface between the public and private spheres. Furthermore, although law deals with universal principles of justice, it is also rooted in particular national cultures. Indeed, there is a long history of legal interaction, mediated by techniques of international private and comparative law (discussed in Chapter 2, at 2.2). Now lawyers, like other professionals, are active in the markets for the international production and circulation of ideologies and techniques of corporate and business management, and of modes of governance.

Indeed, as will be shown in some detail in subsequent chapters, lawyers have played a major part in devising and creating regulatory forms, regimes and jurisdictional arrangements, as well as strategies for managing their interactions. The new-style transnational lawyers' techniques importantly include strategies of counteracting or forestalling undesirable regulatory burdens, as well as seeking optimal outcomes, for their clients. These techniques were initially refined in the arenas of transnational private litigation, for example the high-profile mass liability claims such as Bhopal, the Dalkon Shield and Cape Asbestos (Baxi 1999). However, they have spread well beyond international private law, and increasingly involve the interactions of both public and private regulation and hard and soft law, at different levels (local, national, regional, global).

3.2.3 Regulatory avoidance and havens

A key element in the strategies of management of regulatory interactions has been the resort to 'havens' or 'offshore' centres, which act as jurisdictions of convenience for regulatory avoidance. Their main use has been for avoidance of tax, although this has been linked with and has spread to avoidance of other types of regulation, especially of financial regulation.

International regulatory avoidance strategies essentially entail choosing a convenient jurisdiction in which to create a legal entity, such as a corporation, partnership or trust, which can be used as a vehicle to own assets or through which to channel transactions. This is in a sense a type of forum-shopping, since the aim generally is to relocate activities (at least nominally) to a jurisdiction which not only offers more favourable rules, but more importantly can provide a shelter from the regulations of other jurisdictions. This type of shelter, which originated with the desire to avoid taxation, is generally referred to as a haven.[47]

Tax avoidance, in various forms, has no doubt existed as long as taxation. In the mercantile period, when states relied heavily on customs duties, it took the form of smuggling,[48] and this still continues where high-value items such as cigarettes are subject to different levels of duty by different states. However, the modern tax haven was born after the First World War, when an increasing number of states had come to depend on taxation of income or profits, sometimes applied at very high rates on higher income. This led some wealthy families and firms with international investments or business to try to find ways of reducing their tax liability, if possible legitimately. They began to exploit the fiction of legal personality, and to use legal creativity to manoeuvre within the space allowed by abstract legal concepts, in particular 'income' which is in many ways an arbitrary one (Prebble 1998), and residence.

The basic principles of tax avoidance through a haven are relatively straightforward. It simply consists of establishing one or more legal entities (company, trust or partnership) in convenient jurisdictions, through

---

47 This is a relatively neutral term, although sometimes regarded as pejorative, it also has positive connotations (a refuge from storms); the French term 'paradis fiscal' is unequivocally favourable, and the English equivalent 'heaven' is sometimes substituted for the more normal 'haven'.

48 Some havens have made the transition from facilitating smuggling to more modern forms of avoidance. For example, the Isle of Man, which was ruled by the Dukes of Atholl, was forced by the British Parliament to agree a price for the purchase of the rights to 'the legalities and customs of the Island' by the Isle of Man Purchase Act, due to the problems of smuggling of goods into England. In the 1840s the island was accused of 'literary smuggling', as radicals and other activists printed their publications there to avoid stamp duty while continuing to benefit from free postage throughout the UK (Belchem 1992; I am grateful to Terence McDonald for this reference). With the decline of tourism in the 1960s, it took advantage of its fiscal independence from the UK to reinvent itself as a tax haven and offshore finance centre.

which to channel an income flow derived from international investment or business activities. Routing income through a network of intermediary companies or other legal entities can reduce or eliminate taxation both at source and in the jurisdiction where the intermediary is resident, while insulating the ultimate beneficiary from tax liability (Picciotto 1992: 135–41; Chapter 6, at 6.3.2). Such low-taxed income can either be reinvested, or used to benefit the ultimate owners, for example by acquiring assets (houses, yachts, aeroplanes) for their use, or dispensing funds to them or to family members in ways that might attract little or no taxation. It is certainly possible for states whose regulations are being avoided in this way to counteract such strategies. However, the development of anti-avoidance measures may be greatly hindered, especially by the tax authority's lack of information due to the use of complex structures and the protection of secrecy by havens.

Other kinds of activities, especially those which could easily be delocalized particularly by taking advantage of new communications technologies, have also made use of the 'offshore' phenomenon. Commercial radio stations mushroomed in the 1960s aiming at breaking the monopoly of state broadcasting (such as Radio Luxembourg and Radio Caroline). They were described as 'pirates', since some of them actually broadcast from ships on the high seas, and this analogy was perhaps the source of the term offshore (Palan 2003: 22). As with tax havens, cross-border radio had originated in the 1930s, in jurisdictions such as Monte Carlo (Monaco).

Similarly, 'flags of convenience' (FoC) in international shipping began to boom, especially after the Second World War, growing from under 4% of world tonnage in 1948 to 26% in 1970 and 34% in 1990 (Kassoulides 1993: 83). This also had a longer history: in the 1920s the US authorities encouraged registration of US-owned ships in Panama, to reduce costs while ensuring availability of the ships in wartime.[49] They were joined by others, notably the Greek Aristotle Onassis and Erling Naess, a Norwegian who had set up a whaling company in London in 1928. He found that by reregistering his ships in Panama and moving the residence of his company to Paris, the company's shipping profits would be tax-free (Naess 1972: 2–3). After the Second World War another group of US lawyer-diplomats developed Liberia as a flag state, with the added advantage that

---

[49] Panama had seceded from Colombia in 1903, with US support, to facilitate construction of the Canal. William Cromwell, of the New York law firm Sullivan and Cromwell, having drafted some of the documents for Panama's independence, became that country's representative in the USA, and also acted for the shipowners; he was succeeded in this role by John Foster Dulles, the future Secretary of State (Carlisle 1981: 16).

its shipping (and later corporate) registry business was subcontracted to a US corporation based near Washington.[50] Thus, the FoC system could combine avoidance of tax and other regulations, including vessel safety rules and labour laws (Murphy 2004: ch. 2). By the 1990s, the growth of the internet opened up new possibilities for 'offshore', such as online gambling, which also was a development of the earlier phenomenon of casinos being located in favourable jurisdictions (once again, Monte Carlo).

3.2.4 'Offshore': sovereignty for sale

'Offshore' became a generalized phenomenon by the 1970s, and acted as a catalyst for a dual process of national deregulation and international re-regulation. The term 'offshore' has generally been used to refer to jurisdictions, often small countries, offering regulatory advantages usually for non-residents. In particular, some jurisdictions built on their advantages

---

50 The Liberian International Ship and Corporate Registry is run from Vienna, Virginia USA. This is a continuation of an arrangement originally devised by a group including former US State Department officials, headed by Edward R. Stettinius, who after working in the corporate sector at General Motors and as chairman of US Steel, had been Roosevelt's Secretary of State. In 1947 he formed Stettinius Associates with other former State Department staff, and established a number of development projects in Liberia on a profit-sharing basis with the government, of which the ship registry became the most long-lasting, indeed it became the leading flag of convenience in 1955. The Stettinius group drafted Liberia's Maritime Code (with contributions from Esso and State Department lawyers), aiming to take over the flags of convenience business from Panama, one of its advantages (from the perspective of shipowners) being that the administration of the ship registry was subcontracted to a private company based in the USA (Carlisle 1981). During the civil war (1990–6) its contribution to the Liberian government budget increased from 10% to 15% to 90%. However, in 1996 Charles Taylor, who had launched a rebellion in 1989 and was at that time a member of a six-person Council of State, initiated challenges to International Registries Inc. of Virginia which was running the registry, and from whom Taylor had been unable to obtain funds during the civil war. Legal proceedings were begun in the US courts alleging that International Registries was diverting shipowners from Liberia to the Marshall Islands registry, and was failing to account properly to Liberia for its receipts. Taylor worked with a US lawyer, Lester Hyman, and on Taylor becoming President of Liberia the Liberian government signed an agreement with Hyman for the establishment of a new company, the Liberian International Shipping and Corporate Registry, which took over the business in 2000 (UN Security Council 2001). It continues to provide a significant proportion of Liberian government revenue, although competition for the ship registry business, as well as the costs of ensuring adequate safety standards for the ships it registers, mean that the Registry makes profits mainly from the corporate registry side of the business (UN Security Council 2001; interview information), which essentially facilitates tax avoidance.

as tax havens to develop offshore financial centres (OFCs; see Chapter 6, at 6.3.5). Consequently, states with generally strict levels of regulation often reacted by carving out special regulatory regimes to attract such business back 'onshore'. Thus, 'offshore' became a system or process of deregulation, with the result that controls over economic activity based on direct state command over 'national' firms often had to be abandoned. However, in many cases new forms of international regulation gradually emerged, based on networks.

In some cases, states decided that the only way to compete with off-shore jurisdictions was to imitate them, by creating onshore enclaves, in the hope of re-establishing some degree of control. For example, the US Federal Reserve created an International Banking Facility in New York in 1981, yielding to domestic pressures and in response to the rebirth of London as an international finance centre. The intention of the US authorities was to pressure the Bank of England into agreeing reserve requirements for international banking (Hawley 1984). They did not succeed until 1988, but gradually the central banks, acting mainly through the Basel Committee on Banking Supervision (BCBS), did evolve coordinated arrangements for prudential supervision of banking and finance, although this has been a painful process marked by dramatic failures (see Chapters 6 and 7, at 6.3 and 7.2.1).

Similarly, a number of developed states reacted to the growth of flags of convenience for international shipping by introducing special 'captive' registries of their own for nationally owned vessels, offering tax breaks and allowing employment of foreign seafarers.[51] This followed the failure of attempts to bring shipping back under national state control, through an international agreement requiring a genuine connection with the flag state.[52] States have also introduced internal special regimes or

---

51 Some of these are through offshore dependencies, such as the Isle of Man, Madeira, the Netherlands Antilles, or the French Kerguelen Islands; while others (such as Denmark, Germany, Luxembourg and Norway) are special facilities, sometimes established in cooperation with other states (Luxembourg, which is landlocked, established its registry as a facility for Belgium).

52 A requirement of a genuine link between a ship and its flag state was included, at the instigation of the Netherlands, in the 1958 Geneva Convention on the High Seas, and repeated in identical terms in art. 91 of the 1982 UNCLOS. However, 'genuine link' was not defined, and the article explicitly states that 'each state shall fix the conditions for the grant of nationality to ships'. Article 94 of UNCLOS requires flag states to administer their fleets and take measures to ensure safety at sea, but only in general terms. Attempts through UNCTAD to negotiate an agreement defining the 'genuine link' produced a 1986 UN Convention which was a weak compromise, effectively legitimizing the FoC

zones to attract investment, sometimes at the expense of other states. Japan followed the US example and created special banking facilities in Tokyo in 1986, by allowing freedom from interest rate controls, bank reserve requirements and tax regulations for yen transactions outside Japan (Adam 1992: ch. 20). Other countries aimed to combine financial deregulation with fiscal benefits linked to specific industrial strategies, such as Singapore's facilities for regional headquarters and research and development centres. Another example is Ireland's combination of tax incentives for foreign investors with its launching of an International Financial Services Centre in Dublin in 1987, taking advantage of its participation in the EC's liberalized market for financial services to attract offshore business such as captive insurance. The dangers of deregulation were shown by the Asian financial crisis of 1997 to 1998,[53] which stimulated an attempt to improve coordination of international financial regulation. However, the limits, and indeed dangers, of this regulatory system were starkly revealed by the eruption of the global financial crisis of 2007 to 2008 (discussed in Chapter 7).

Other countries went further, and aimed to stimulate investment in manufacturing industry, by establishing Export Processing Zones (EPZs), such as Mexico's duty-free *maquiladora* zone, or in other countries Special Economic Zones (SEZs), or Enterprise Zones. Building on the older concept of free ports, which allowed duty-free importation of goods in transit, the EPZs aimed to facilitate the establishment of industries based on assembly or processing of imported inputs for re-export. However, they often went further, and created enclaves in which other measures were relaxed or waived, especially employment protection regulations, turning EPZs into sweatshop zones. The concept was also expanded from that of a geographical enclave to single-industry zones (jewellery in Thailand, leather in Turkey, or coffee in Zimbabwe), while in some countries individual factories could apply for special status, becoming essentially a type of discretionary industry support scheme. While such zones have helped some countries develop new industries and boost exports, the investments they attract often have few links with the local

---

(Kassoulides 1993: 83): it specifies that there must be either 'appropriate' participation in the ownership of ships by nationals of the flag state, or a 'satisfactory' proportion of the crew must be its nationals. The convention received too few ratifications to enter into force.

53 A significant contributory factor was dollar borrowing by Thai banks, assisted by the creation in 1993 of the Bangkok International Banking Facility aiming to promote Bangkok as an international financial centre (BIS 1998: 124).

economy and are highly mobile, leading to continual turnover of firms, and sometimes a swift decline if better opportunities arise elsewhere (ILO 2003a). For example, garment factories were established in a variety of countries such as Sri Lanka and Kenya, to take advantage of import quotas allocated by developed countries,[54] but faced large-scale closures when the quota system was ended in January 2005. Countries are under competitive pressure to keep wages and other costs to investors low in their EPZ/SEZ, making it hard to use this type of inward investment as a basis for more general economic and social improvement.

The offshore phenomenon is not just a matter of a few rogue jurisdictions, but the result of the mutual interactions of states more generally. As we have seen, the jurisdictional interaction inherent in the classical liberal system of interdependence could be exploited by the strategies of jurisdictional selection and regulatory avoidance, designed by transnational lawyers and other specialists. As national regulation became more rigorous, techniques of avoidance became more sophisticated. As one such specialist put it, 'For the professional, "offshore" is now a structural tool in the efficient management of clients' affairs' (Cabral 1995: 24).

Operating at the interface between the private and the public, these specialists were active not only in creating regulatory avoidance devices for private clients, but also in designing favourable regulatory provisions by acting as advisers to governments. As part of attempts to restore confidence and credibility in the financial security of OFCs, some countries have had their laws designed by global professional firms acting as government consultants.[55] Although this role of 'double agent' is a delicate one and therefore confined to a small elite in large developed countries such as the USA (Dezalay 1996: 66), small jurisdictions can be prone to advice of a less scrupulous character.[56] Particularly radical advice was provided by a team of US lawyers in the early 1990s aiming to promote Nepal as an 'offshore' financial centre (though it is entirely landlocked, as is Lichtenstein). They suggested that, rather than developing its own regulatory system (even if based on foreign models), Nepal should directly

---

54 Under the Multifibre Arrangement and its successor the Agreement on Textiles and Clothing, see Chapter 8, at 8.1.1.

55 For example, the Report of Mr Rodney Gallagher of the accounting firm Coopers & Lybrand for the British Government (Gallagher 1990) on offshore finance sectors in Britain's Caribbean dependent territories included draft legislation.

56 Thus the Cayman Islands Trusts Act of 1967 resulted from advice from 'private interests' in the UK, causing great concerns to the UK Inland Revenue (PRO file T295–892).

incorporate the laws of other countries, by allowing foreign firms registering in Nepal to choose the laws under which they and their transactions
would be regulated. This astounding proposal was put forward by lawyers
working at the interface of business, government and the academy.[57]

Although specially designed laws may be found everywhere, some states
or statelets offer a more comprehensive package of arrangements specifically devised for avoidance purposes of one sort or another, so they may be
considered designer jurisdictions. This phenomenon has been described
as the 'commercialization of sovereignty' (Palan 2002, 2003: 59–62). They
often create an extensive package of laws, aimed mainly at non-residents,
so that what Antoine describes as the 'offshore legal subculture' creates
in effect a dual legal system (1999). The competition among such jurisdictions makes it hard to take countermeasures against them, since if one
is targeted another is likely to take its place. This competition also leads
to differentiation. Typically, states which established themselves early as
leaders, such as Liberia for shipping, or Switzerland for private banking,
or the Cayman Islands for offshore bank accounts, are more willing to try
to safeguard their reputations (and hence their market share) by ensuring
high standards in some aspects of regulation, such as maritime safety
or prudential regulation of banks. However, as discussed in Chapter 6,
they generally draw the line at cooperation in tax enforcement. Their later
competitors entering the market are likely to be less scrupulous, and more
willing to relax standards. These 'bad apples' are therefore more likely to
become the targets of international countermeasures, which paradoxically results in the leading offshore states being held up as good examples,
and legitimizing their use for avoidance of other rules, especially taxes.

Generally, the exploitation of jurisdictions of convenience relies on
taking advantage of fictions such as corporate personality, and the indeterminacy of abstract legal concepts such as income and residence. It is
not usually, as is sometimes asserted, a matter of the greater international mobility of 'capital', since this type of avoidance normally involves
little or no genuine economic activity in the haven jurisdiction. Thus,
ships registered under a flag of convenience have little contact with their

---

57 Collins *et al.* 1996; Jackson 1998. The main attraction would be the India–Nepal tax treaty,
which allows exemption from withholding taxes to residents of Nepal, like the India–
Mauritius treaty, which led to a boom of incorporations of intermediary companies in
Mauritius. Although Nepal did introduce some legislation with this aim, its attractiveness
to investors was marred by political instability, notably the massacre of the Royal family by
the Crown Prince in 2001, and a resurgence of Maoist guerrilla activity, which eventually
led to the demise of the monarchy.

state of registry; offshore radio stations will generally broadcast programmes recorded elsewhere; companies formed in tax havens to receive
tax-avoiding income are usually no more than 'brass plate' entities to
which assets have been notionally transferred; and financial transactions
or activities attributed to entities in offshore centres are generally directed
from elsewhere. Thus, a distinction can in principle be made between a
legitimate jurisdictional choice, for example if a person chooses to be a
tax exile by deciding to live in a low-tax state, in contrast to avoiding tax
in their country of residence by accumulating foreign earned income in a
trust or company formed in a haven. However, the distinction can be very
hard to maintain, especially for financial services (e.g. insurance, portfolio investment), and these are therefore the main users of the offshore
system.

Combating the use of havens is certainly possible, but requires closer
international coordination between regulatory authorities, to establish
feasible and optimal regulatory standards, and cooperation in their
enforcement. However, in many cases, havens have been developed with
the tacit or overt encouragement of at least some of the government
departments or public bodies of the states whose regulations they were
helping business firms to avoid.[58] The often ambivalent positions of the
latter states has meant that the countermeasures have generally been at
best half-hearted (see further Chapter 6, at 6.3.3 and 6.3.5). Although
often neglected or treated as interesting but marginal, the offshore system
is an important element in key economic sectors (finance, international
transport, and industries such as oil and clothing), and thus central to the
world economy.

3.2.5 Formal and informal regulatory cooperation

The increasingly complex jurisdictional interactions outlined in the previous sections have also led to attempts to improve cooperation between

---

58 Notably, in the UK attempts to develop a coherent policy towards moves by UK dependent territories to become tax havens from the late 1960s failed, with divergence of views
   between the Revenue (wanting to combat tax avoidance), the Foreign Office (concerned
   both to reduce the territories' dependence on aid and to comply with the UK's international obligations), the Bank of England (interested to boost the business brought to
   the City of London by the Eurodollar and other forms of international finance) and the
   Treasury (treading a fine line between all of these considerations): see exchange of letters
   between White (Foreign Office) and Ward (Treasury), May 1977, in UK Inland Revenue
   1967–77.

states. However, the development of formal international cooperation has been slow, largely due to the continued strength of the traditional liberal principle of state sovereignty. This is essentially a 'negative' notion based on non-intervention by states in each other's affairs. This perspective leads to a reluctance to accept positive obligations for regulatory cooperation, let alone regulatory harmonization.

This difficulty is exacerbated because formal legal arrangements are between governments, and politicians are often sensitive to accusations that sovereignty is surrendered by cooperation with other states or within international organizations. This is paradoxical, since increased economic integration inevitably weakens national state powers of economic regulation unless international cooperation is strengthened. A further factor is the immense growth in the range and scope of economic regulation, and the emergence of specialist regulatory communities, often based on expert technical knowledge. Although in many ways this facilitates international cooperation, this has been at a more informal level, through regulatory networks (as discussed in Chapter 1). These networks have often found ways to operate 'in the shadow' of the formal legal provisions for cooperation. Hence, international regulatory networks have generally used soft law.

Interstate cooperation initially built on a revival of the old international law principle of 'comity' (discussed in Chapter 2, at 2.2.2). This suggested that state bodies such as courts should respect the laws and regulations adopted by other states, although usually subject to local public policy considerations, and provided they felt that the other state's measures did not exceed the acceptable scope of its jurisdiction.[59] However, the comity principle was an ambiguous one, acting (in Joel Paul's description) both as a bridge and as a wall, since courts generally refused to respect an objectionable foreign law, and preferred to treat comity as a matter of courtesy not a legal obligation (Paul 1991). Comity as a judicial principle is essentially a negative one, of non-interference.

Both jurisdictional overlap and cooperation are more extensive in private law matters (as discussed in Chapter 2, at 2.2.1). States have been

---

59 This could create policy tensions, as occurred when the US courts in the 1960s applied the so-called 'act-of-state doctrine' (essentially an application of the comity principle) to recognize the effects of the nationalization decrees enacted by the Cuban government of Fidel Castro. This prompted the US Congress to enact legislation overruling the act of state doctrine in relation to foreign state acts which are contrary to international law (Rabinowitz 1978).

willing to cooperate in providing assistance in civil litigation, and there has been a growth of conventions negotiated especially through the Hague Conference on Private International Law, covering matters ranging from child abduction to recognition of trusts.[60] In contrast, states have been reluctant to provide positive assistance to enforce each other's criminal laws. Arrangements for extradition of fugitive offenders developed from the end of the nineteenth century, and these have been updated and expanded in recent times, to accelerate the process, sometimes by dispensing with the need to prove a prima facie case to the extraditing state. This has been controversial, especially when applied to economic crimes and extended to cases involving overlapping jurisdiction, which in effect gives enforcement agencies the power to decide where cases should be tried.[61] This reluctance extended to other laws considered to be penal, notably taxation, although the historical origins of the so-called 'revenue rule' are dubious and its applications sometimes elastic.[62] In recent years, however, the provisions in tax treaties for information exchange have been extended to include assistance in tax collection.

---

60 www.hcch.net; McClean 2002; Chapter 2, at 2.2.2.
61 In July 2006 three British bankers were extradited to the USA on charges of conspiracy to defraud their former employer, a Natwest affiliate; the evidence had resulted from the US authorities' investigations of Enron, which was a client of the bank, and senior Enron officials were allegedly co-conspirators. Despite the strong links with the UK, the British authorities decided not to proceed with the case, and the extradition became a cause célèbre (Warbrick 2007). Another US extradition request of a senior business executive, Ian Norris, on criminal charges relating to cartel activity, resulted in lengthier proceedings in the UK courts (*Norris* v. *USA* (2007)). Partly as a result of these cases, the UK and US attorneys-general agreed a document entitled *Guidance Notes for Handling Criminal Cases with Concurrent Jurisdiction between the United Kingdom and the United States of America* (available from www.attorneygeneral.gov.uk), establishing a procedure for prosecuting authorities handling cases involving concurrent jurisdiction to exchange information and consult to determine the most effective way to pursue investigations, and where and how prosecutions should be continued, discontinued, or aspects of the case pursued in each jurisdiction.
62 This refers to the principle that states do not assist each other in the enforcement of taxation, which has meant that fiscal matters were normally excluded from general cooperation arrangements. This refusal to extend comity to tax laws (and public law more generally) has often been misleadingly justified by citing Lord Mansfield's dictum that 'no country ever takes notice of the revenue laws of another' (*Holman* v. *Johnson* (1775)); however, Mansfield was concerned with ensuring that private contracts should be enforced even if they entailed breach of a foreign revenue law, to prevent easy escape from contractual obligations in a mercantile era of stringent customs duties and widespread smuggling (Picciotto 1992: 299–304, Rearden 2006). Like many other legal principles, it has been misapplied in the context of global corporate capitalism.

Historically, formal international cooperation arrangements were established for specific issues which became identified as of general concern, such as suppression of the slave trade and currency forgery. Ethan Nadelmann (1990) provides an interesting analysis of the emergence of 'global prohibition regimes', which he shows were due to proselytizing by moral entrepreneurs from a few European states and the USA; and he points out that most of the activities were at first regarded as legitimate, and indeed even supported by governments (e.g. the slave and opium trades).

With the increased political concerns about the growth of international crime and terrorism, similar joint action has developed more recently for new matters such as drug-trafficking,[63] aircraft hijacking and terrorist offences more generally. A broader approach has been adopted through the Council of Europe, beginning with its Convention on Mutual Assistance in Criminal Matters of 1959, which provided for the service of summonses, arranging for attendance of witnesses and the obtaining of evidence (Gilmore 1995). This was significantly extended in 1990 by a convention on money laundering, which was extensively remodelled and extended to the financing of terrorism in 2005.[64] Although they have certainly become more extensive, these formal arrangements are mainly used in relation to judicial proceedings, and represent the tip of the iceberg of cross-border regulatory action and interaction, much of which has developed through semi-formal networks and using soft law.

In practice, both police and regulatory enforcement agencies often proceed informally and rely on their own resources for international investigations. This includes making inquiries abroad, although the legal limits of such activity are unclear.[65] It is formally an infringement of state sovereignty to carry out official acts without permission within the territory of another state. However, what is an official act is open to interpretation, and it may be acceptable for an official of a foreign state to make inquiries which involve no compulsion or breach of local law, since

---

63 A framework for very broad cooperation was established by the 1988 UN Convention against Illicit Traffic in Narcotic Drugs and Psychotropic Substances, which extended to the criminalization of drug-related money laundering, including requiring bank secrecy to be overridden for such purposes (arts. 5(3) and 7(5)).

64 Both available from the Council of Europe Conventions website, http://conventions.coe. int/Default.asp.

65 Hence, the US Internal Revenue Service produced a guide for its officers on Sources of Information from Abroad (US IRS 1984), a multilateral version of which was developed by the OECD's Committee on Fiscal Affairs (OECD–CFA 2002).

this is no more than a private person could do. However, some states have taken the official position that a foreign official may not exercise any acts ex officio in their territory without permission.[66] Despite this, a variety of agencies, especially from the USA, have been active in conducting overseas investigations, extending in some cases (e.g. narcotic drug offences) to abductions of individuals or 'irregular renditions', usually with the tacit or informal support of local authorities, 'based on money, friendship, and professional understandings' (Nadelmann 1993: 444).[67]

Generally, US agencies have pursued a two-pronged approach, acting unilaterally where they consider it necessary (at the risk of generating what Nadelmann describes as 'frictions'), while using more cooperative and formal channels if possible. Thus, the USA has negotiated a network of bilateral mutual legal assistance treaties (MLATs), targeting especially countries which it regarded as being used for concealment of criminal activities or proceeds, beginning with Switzerland in 1973 (Nadelmann 1993).

A significant aspect of the strengthening of cooperation procedures was the provision in both the Council of Europe treaties and in the MLATs for direct contacts between law enforcement authorities, bypassing the traditional diplomatic channels. In fact, practical cooperation at the operational level has gone far beyond the formal requirements of the treaty arrangements. Indeed, Interpol has developed international police cooperation, including information exchange, since 1923, although it had no formal founding statute until 1946. Its informal character as a policemen's club was deliberately cultivated to reduce political interference (Anderson 1989: 61), although the need for legitimacy has led it to adopt a more public and formal profile in recent years. Nevertheless, Interpol is only part of a network of formal and informal international cooperation arrangements between police and other criminal enforcement agencies.

---

66 Akehurst 1972–3: 147. For example, it is an offence under the Swiss Penal Code (art. 271) for anyone without authorization to take in Switzerland any actions which are within the powers of the public authorities, for a foreign state, party or organization.

67 Such actions are likely to be criminal acts under local law, but the agents involved are rarely apprehended; persons kidnapped in this way have generally been denied remedies under US law, on the grounds that US constitutional and other legal protections do not apply to non-US nationals outside the USA: see *Sosa v. Alvarez-Machain* (2004) (kidnapping of a doctor in Mexico instigated by US drug enforcement officers who suspected him of complicity in the torture and killing of a US agent, see Lowenfeld 1990). The decision was also important in relation to the jurisdictional scope of the US law on foreign torts; see Chapter 5, at 5.1.3.2.

In relation to business and economic regulation, the cooperation that has been developed between a wide range of regulatory authorities, especially since the 1980s, has mainly used soft law, for a number of reasons. Economic and social regulation tends to fall between the two stools of civil and criminal law, so may not be covered by the assistance arrangements mentioned above.[68] Also, the traditional more formal legal channels, for example for obtaining evidence abroad in legal proceedings, are far too slow and cumbersome for regulators, who often need specific information quickly. For example, supervisors of financial exchanges trading related products in different jurisdictions must safeguard against manipulation or irregular market movements due to large transactions, which may require them to exchange information immediately. Hence, bodies responsible for financial market regulation have developed mutual assistance arrangements, coordinated by the International Organization of Securities Commissions (IOSCO) since 1986. Tax authorities have used the provisions in tax treaties for information exchange to develop some more extensive coordination, and this has recently been supplemented by more specific and extensive mutual assistance agreements (see Chapter 6, at 6.4.2).

A particular obstacle to cooperation has been the reluctance to accept formal obligations for a state to use its powers to help enforce the public laws of other states. Only recently have the formal provisions for exchange of information extended to an obligation for the requested state not only to supply information which it already has, but also to use its powers to obtain information just as it would to enforce its own laws.[69] In addition, some mutual assistance arrangements provide a basis for joint enforcement. For example, the provisions in tax treaties for information exchange between 'competent authorities' have been used as a

---

68 Hence, for example, cooperation in tax matters has only developed through specific bilateral and multilateral treaty provisions, and only recently have states been willing to provide such assistance even when they themselves had no tax interest; see Chapter 6, at 6.4.2.

69 This is spelled out in the first of the Ten Principles laid down by IOSCO in 1991 for the negotiation of MOUs. This principle has also been extended to information exchange under tax treaties, as spelled out in the amendments adopted in 1995 to para. 2 of art. 26 of the OECD Model Tax treaty: 'types of administrative measures authorised for the purpose of the requested state's tax must be utilised, even though invoked solely to provide information to the other Contracting State' (Commentary para. 14). This was part of a lengthy process of revision of the important art. 26 of the Model Tax treaty by both the OECD and the UN Tax Committee, discussed further in Chapter 6.

basis for simultaneous tax assessments of related companies. Similarly, cooperation agreements between competition authorities (such as those between the EU and the USA and Canada) have been used to coordinate joint actions against international cartels, mergers and abuse of dominant position. However, the main aim is to attempt to avoid conflicts, especially over approval of corporate mergers, and the move towards 'positive comity' has been very tentative (Evenett *et al.* 2000; Budzinski 2003; Chapter 4, at 4.3).

Finally, some trade and investment agreements now include provisions aiming at ensuring that regulatory standards do not provide a competitive advantage or create a disadvantage. Thus, the two 'side-agreements' of the NAFTA, for labour and environmental cooperation, establish procedures aimed at ensuring effective enforcement of each country's laws, including rights for NGOs to make submissions that such laws are not being effectively enforced (see Chapter 5, at 5.2.1.2). The WTO agreements[70] include several provisions aimed at mutual recognition by states of each other's product standards. The WTO's Services agreement (GATS) also includes provisions (art. VII) encouraging states to recognize the qualifications or licences granted by other states to service providers.

3.2.6 Regulatory networks

These agreements and arrangements, even those which take the form of 'soft law', are only the formal sinews of a much more organic development of regulatory cooperation and coordination. This encompasses not only officials both of government and quasi-governmental public bodies, but also a wide range of formally private bodies which are also involved in a variety of ways in the emerging networks of global governance. These have been discussed in general terms in Chapter 1, and the substantive chapters which follow will provide many specific instances. However, to close this chapter we may take up again the example of international shipping, the regulation of which has been bedevilled by the use of flags of convenience, as discussed above.

---

70 The agreement on Sanitary and Phytosanitary Measures (SPS) has an obligation to recognize the equivalence of another state's measures if they can be objectively demonstrated to achieve the same level of protection (SPS art. 4), and the agreement on Technical Barriers to Trade (TBT) has a similar provision (art. 2.7) as well as one encouraging mutual recognition of conformity assessment for product technical standards (art. 6.1): see further Chapter 8, at 8.2.

Networked regulatory arrangements for international shipping have emerged, largely in response to sustained campaigns about the safety standards of the 'open registries', spotlighted especially by the long-running campaign of the International Transport Federation (ITF) of trade unions. A key development has been cooperation between the maritime authorities of port states. These organizations now coordinate their inspection systems, based on checklists of internationally agreed-upon standards, deficiency reporting, a computerized database, and the sanction of detention of vessels found defective.[71] In practice, flag states essentially offer a ship registration service, the administration of which may have little or no physical contact with the state itself since it is subcontracted to private firms, as discussed above.[72] The actual surveys and the issuing of safety certificates for ships are done by recognized private classification societies, including the American Bureau of Shipping and Lloyd's Register of Shipping.[73]

Thus, the seaworthiness and employment conditions of ships are governed by a variety of regulatory bodies, both public and private,

71 The first port state network was established by twenty maritime authorities covering Europe and the North Atlantic, based on the Paris Memorandum of Understanding (www.parismou.org), and it has been followed by Asia-Pacific, Caribbean and Latin American groups. The ITF also maintains an international network of inspectors who liaise with the Port State Control system (ITF 2005; interview information).

72 The International Maritime Organization (IMO), the intergovernmental body with primary responsibility for shipping, was committed to the principle of regulation by the flag state, despite the failure to establish a genuine link requirement. However, the ITF campaigns led to the adoption by the International Labour Organization (ILO), of Convention 147 on Minimum Standards in Merchant Ships in 1976. This requires flag states to exercise effective jurisdiction over their ships and to establish laws and regulations covering a range of safety standards and shipboard employment conditions 'substantially equivalent' to those in a specified list of related ILO conventions. Importantly, however, art. 4 gave jurisdiction for *port states* to enforce these standards, including taking measures necessary to rectify conditions 'clearly hazardous to safety or health', though they must also not 'unreasonably detain or delay the ship'. This provided encouragement and authority for the development of a network of arrangements for inspection to enforce international standards using Port State Control (Kassoulides 1993), beginning with the Paris group of European countries, followed by Asia-Pacific, Caribbean and Latin American groups. In this way, cooperating maritime authorities have established sophisticated inspection systems, based on checklists of internationally agreed standards, deficiency reporting, a computerized database and the ultimate sanction of detention: see material available on www.parismou.org. This has been further strengthened by the IMO's reorientation to accepting that its standards should be internationally enforceable, rather than relying entirely on the flag state.

73 Ten such bodies have formed the International Association of Classification Societies, which in December 2005 adopted a set of Common Structural Rules for ship classification and approval: see www.iacs.org.uk, and www.liscr.com (Liberian Registry).

national and international. None of them have definitive jurisdiction, although port authorities can apply the ultimate sanction of detention. Hence, a form of global governance of shipping has emerged, coordinated through international networks, albeit with some significant gaps and deficiencies.[74]

74 Couper *et al.* 1999: 172–6; Gerstenberger and Welke 2002; Murphy 2004: 45–71; some argue that the central dynamic of 'flagging out' is to avoid regulation, and that even if Port State Control has tightened enforcement by the main flag authorities, it has exacerbated the problem of 'race to the bottom' due to the emergence of new competitors (Alderton and Winchester 2002). The main problem is perhaps rather that regulatory fragmentation creates a lack of lateral coordination between regulatory regimes, notably between ship safety standards (which have improved overall), and taxation and labour standards.

Corporations and competition

The corporation or company is the main form developed under industrial capitalism for carrying on business, and hence it is a key social institution. It provides an institutional framework which enables business to be organized on a large scale, and to coordinate a variety of activities, even across the world. Institutionalized firms can coordinate and plan activities which are both more extensive and potentially long-term than individual or family businesses. Hence, if the basic business unit is referred to as the firm, incorporation allows it to take a form which may be described as the impersonal firm.

Due to these features, the corporation has enabled the radical transformation of capitalism, from laissez-faire to regulated corporate capitalism. The extent of this transformation is often ignored both by capitalism's supporters and its critics. Its impact has been well summarized as follows:

> Capitalism has developed as a system of a limited number of giant corporations working at vast scales to bureaucratic plans administered by professional managers. Accumulation is pursued but in a restrained form compatible with oligopolistic coexistence. In particular, price competition is irrelevant to pricing decisions in the influential sectors of the economy and has been more or less displaced as a form of competition by cost-cutting (whilst holding price constant) and by the sales effort. The smaller firms and consumers in the residual areas of the economy must take the production decisions of the large corporate price makers as the crucially determining boundaries of the relatively unimportant decisions they are left to make. *Laissez faire* no longer exists and the advanced capitalist economy which has replaced it specifically 'is not an exchange economy in which the price mechanism regulates all economic activity', and 'Thus it follows that the invisible hand theorem of classical theory is not applicable to the capitalist economy'.[1]

This is not to say that capitalism is not prone to crisis, or incapable of further transformation, far from it. Indeed, the past three decades have seen

1 Campbell 1996: 243 (footnotes omitted); see also Lazonick 1991.

a further transition to a post-industrial, knowledge society or 'cognitive capitalism', some of the implications of which were discussed in Chapter 1. The predominance of 'Fordist' large-scale mass-manufacturing has given way to networked corporations, operating through a combination of ownership links and long-term contracting. At the same time, the shift to 'services' reflects new forms of socialized production and consumption, which are no longer so readily mediated by the production and circulation of physical commodities. These tendencies to de-commodification are counteracted by struggles to establish immaterial commodified forms, attempting to maintain both the subordination of labour in production and the realization of profits through sales (Hardt and Negri 2000: 280ff., 2005).

Nevertheless, the dominant firms in today's knowledge economy, not only Microsoft and Google, Goldman Sachs and HSBC, but also providers of health care and hospitals, entertainment, education and information, or transport and communications, have very different relationships with both their workers and their customers than did the mass-production manufacturers characteristic of the earlier phase of industrial capitalism. They depend much more on the personal knowledge and skills of their workers, and are not just sellers of discrete commodities to consumers, but suppliers of services to customers, which implies longer-term relationships based on trust and confidence, and puts a premium on reputation. At the same time, manufacturing industry, which remains important, has also in many cases taken on 'service' characteristics, needing to draw on the varied skills of its workers and cultivate the loyalty of its customers through long-term relationships rather than isolated transactions.

In this changing context, alternative institutional forms of 'social' enterprise can demonstrate renewed relevance and strength, even those with a long history such as cooperatives and other types of worker-owned firms (Davies 2009). However, the shareholder-owned corporation has proved sufficiently flexible to adapt to these changes, though not without some strains, as we will see in this chapter. In particular, competition law, although born from a populist impulse to restrict oligopolistic economic power, has largely become a means of legitimating it.

4.1 The power of corporate capitalism

The activities carried out through the corporation are social in scale, but it has developed as a form of private-property ownership, so it has been described as socialized capital.[2] Hence, the corporation is also a central institutional form mediating social relations of power, especially class, since 'the relationships that class describes, such as hiring people to labour, exercising authority over decisions about what to produce or what technologies to adopt, determining how products are sold, are now mediated by the corporation' (Roy 1997: 6). Indeed, as David Campbell has pointed out, the shift from competitive, laissez-faire to corporate capitalism represented a fundamental transformation which, although glimpsed by Marx himself, has not been adequately grasped by most neo-Marxist and other class-based theories (1996).

The corporate legal form has also been developed as an extremely flexible one. This enables it to be used, with adaptations, for small and large businesses,[3] as a building block for often complex corporate groups and alliances, in combination with other legal forms such as trusts and contracts, and with virtually any combination of personal, family, institutional and governmental involvement. At the same time, however, the basic principles which have been developed to govern the corporation have created an entity which has been described as pathological, since it is legally required to focus all its activities on the selfish pursuit of its own profits (Bakan 2004).

2 Roy 1997; this echoes the remarks of Karl Marx in ch. 27, vol. 3 of *Capital* in which he discusses the separation of management from ownership involved in the joint-stock company, which he described as representing 'the abolition of capitalist private industry on the basis of the capitalist private system itself', and involving 'the control of social capital' in which 'social means of production appear as private property' and 'instead of overcoming the antithesis between the character of wealth as social and as private wealth, the stock companies merely develop it in a new form' (text available at www. marxists.org).

3 In some countries different types of company are available; for a comparative and historical account of France, Germany, Japan, the UK and the USA, see Charkham 1994. For example, in Germany there is a choice between the GmbH (*Gesellschaft mit beschränkter Haftung*, or private limited liability company), which is usually small or medium-sized, and the AG (*Aktiengesellschaft* or (publicly quoted) share company). The People's Republic of China recognized only state and collective ownership until its opening to foreign investment in 1979, when it established a special law for Sino-Foreign Equity Joint Ventures (1979), and then Wholly Foreign-Owned Enterprises (1986), and Sino-Foreign Contractual Joint Ventures (1988); the principle of separate legal personality was recognized for domestic enterprises in the General Principles of Civil Law in 1986, but they have also been governed by diverse laws; although the Company Law of 1993 provided a single framework for all types of enterprises, they were slow to organize under its provisions (Xiao 1998).

4.1.1 Rise and development of the corporation

4.1.1.1 Origins

The status of the corporation combines elements of the public and private, which have varied in different historical periods and countries. The corporation was initially as much a political as an economic body, from the medieval to the mercantile period in Europe. Deriving from its predecessor the guild, it was an association of persons with a common purpose, governing themselves and their activities. There were corporations for ecclesiastical purposes, municipal government, charitable purposes such as education, and to govern different types of economic activity and trade. Gradually, the economic and political became separated, first with the split between the merchant guild and the municipal borough, and later the emergence of the merchant company.

These early business organizations were associations of merchants, who initially had individual accounts within the corporation. In the form of the *commenda*, which originated in the Islamic world and spread across Europe from the fourteenth century, the liability of investors was limited to their shares in the enterprise, while the organizers took the risks of failure.[4] In the period of mercantile capitalism of the seventeenth and eighteenth centuries, the trading companies were granted an economic franchise over trade, as a privilege or monopoly granted by the central state, which gave them a public status and state backing by special statute (Cooke 1950). Monarchs and nobles both lent their names to the enterprises and participated in them financially. State power was closely linked to commerce, which was an often ruthless fight for trade advantages, backed by military force if necessary. For the increasingly powerful foreign trading companies such as the British and Dutch East India companies, it meant state support in the assertion of both political and economic power over foreign territories (Coornaert 1967). The chartered companies were essentially the agents for a new type of imperial expansion, vested with governmental authority and powers: whether to open up new trading activities, as with the Levant, Muscovy and

---

4 Cooke 1950; this was the forerunner of the *société en commandite par actions*, a kind of limited liability partnership giving managerial autonomy to its *gérant*; this was the main business form in France under the Commercial Code of 1807, until formation of limited liability companies by registration (*Sociétés Anonymes*, or SAs) was permitted in 1867 (Freedeman 1979).

Hudson's Bay Companies; to establish and govern new settlements, such as the Virginia and Massachusetts Bay Companies; or to open up new lands for the exploitation of gold or other minerals, as with the British South Africa Company. They learned, some with more enthusiasm than others, to combine commerce and politics in a kind of buccaneering mercantile diplomacy.

During the nineteenth century the main features of the modern corporation emerged, in different ways, in the leading capitalist countries. At the beginning of the century they were still bodies carrying out collective public functions, such as education, religion, urban services, or charitable objects. In the leading capitalist countries, the creation of corporations continued to be by special state charter, and mainly to promote economic development through large-scale infrastructure projects, such as railways, highways and canals. In the mid-nineteenth century, arguments for facilitating incorporation were advanced on the basis of promoting investment in socially useful projects (Campbell and Griffin 2006: 61). The privileges of legal personality, especially limited liability, were considered justified for activities benefiting the public, because of the large-scale investments and high risk they entailed. However, the ambivalent status of corporations led to attacks both from those who regarded them as illegitimate usurpers of public power, and those who argued for their 'democratization' by opening to all the right of incorporation for the pursuit of collective purposes. Indeed, the extension of limited liability, in the middle part of the nineteenth century, resulted from a variety of arguments for encouraging economic activity for worthy purposes, including workers' cooperatives.[5]

Indeed, manufacturing industry did not at first use the corporate form: capitalist industrialization was mainly driven by individual and family entrepreneurs, owning their assets directly or through partnerships.[6] Only some time after incorporation by registration was established did the concept of the corporation as a separate entity from its owners become crystallized, with the related principle of limited liability. This was based

5 Saville (1956) discusses the debates leading to the UK Act of 1856, which were initiated by Christian Socialists, who argued for a legal form to facilitate workers' cooperatives; others, notably J. S. Mill, urged the *en commandite* partnership as the best means of allowing investment with limited liability; key arguments for the eventual approval of the Joint Stock Company were that, in the absence of a UK law, companies were being formed in France and the USA; and in the name of freedom of contract and laissez-faire.

6 This was so even in the UK which led the way to providing incorporation by registration in the Companies Acts 1844–62 (Payne 1988; see also Ireland 2008: 3–4, who argues that the creation of limited liability was a response to the desires of rentier investors rather than the needs of industry).

on the notion that the 'shares' owned by its members were not just rights among themselves but rights *in rem* to property, which could be transferred to others, or 'fictitious capital' (Ireland 1996). So it was with the growth of markets in shares or stocks and bonds, that the corporation came to be considered as a legal person in its own right, separate from its members. This fetishized ideological concept remains a major underpinning of corporate power.

The grant by the state of the right to incorporate by simple registration undermined the public accountability of the corporation, which led to its redefinition as a new and peculiar form of private property. The corporation's charter came to be seen no longer as a delegation by the state but a protection from the state. The behaviour of corporations and their economic interactions through exchange came to be viewed as an essentially private sphere. The corporation became accountable no longer to the public but to its private owners. Yet these owners, its shareholders, were protected from the usual responsibilities of property ownership by the state's grant to them of limited liability (Roy 1997: 45).

By 1870, the general principles of incorporation had been outlined in the laws of the main capitalist countries.[7] However, limited liability companies were still little used by industrial capital, which continued to be controlled by individual or family entrepreneurs for some twenty years. Indeed, some of these enterprises accumulated substantial capital and grew quite large without resorting to incorporation, since their owners saw no need to relinquish their dominion, while investors preferred to lend directly to businesses led by entrepreneurs who were risking their own capital. The shift to widespread use of the corporate form resulted from the instabilities generated by capital accumulation and competition.

4.1.1.2 Combinations, cartels and incorporation

In the leading capitalist countries, rapid accumulation between 1860 to 1890 resulted in periods of boom and bust due to overproduction, as a result of which firms tried to control competition (Fligstein 1990: 36–7). The initial preference was either to drive out competitors, or to cooperate with them through different forms of combination or cartel.[8] Such agreements to restrict competition could be regarded as unlawful under

---

7 Horn and Kocka 1979. What is now called regulatory competition played a part, with arguments in both Britain and France that the other was 'poaching' incorporation (Saville 1956, discussed n. 5 above; Freedeman 1993).

8 For an excellent detailed account of the various strategies of one key company, Du Pont, see Wall 1990.

laws against restraints of trade, which remained in force in many countries from the end of the mercantile period. However, courts, no less than governments and even public opinion, were uncertain how to apply such laws to cartels, in the context of the liberal ideologies which had become generally dominant by the end of the nineteenth century. Although cartels organized markets and therefore restricted competition, cartel agreements could also be considered to be manifestations of freedom of contract.[9]

In the USA, lawyers designed several forms of combination: pools, trusts or holding companies. However, doubts as to their legal validity were exacerbated by populist opposition to the big-business 'robber barons' and their 'trusts'.[10] This led to the enactment of the Sherman Act in 1890, which prohibited 'every contract, combination in the form of trust or otherwise, or conspiracy, in restraint of trade or commerce', and made it a criminal offence to 'monopolize, or attempt to monopolize, or to combine or conspire with any other person or persons to monopolize' trade or commerce. The interpretation of the central concepts of 'restraint of trade' and 'monopolize' created a field of contestation and debate, with sharp judicial disagreements especially in the Supreme Court, where initially a majority took the strict view that the Act prohibited all anti-competitive agreements (Weinstein 1968; Sklar 1988). However, this

---

9 This can be seen in the UK, France and Germany, in contrast to the USA (Cornish 1979). In France, the Penal Code provision against interference with markets dating from 1810 was only applied if a combination imposed excessive prices, so most cases were civil disputes, and in 1902 the Cour d'Appel de Nancy upheld the legality of the Comptoir de Longwy, which governed half the steel production of France (Cornish 1979: 295–7; see also Freedeman 1993: 115–19). In the UK, the courts' tolerance for restrictive agreements was dramatically expressed in the House of Lords' decision in the *Mogul Steamship* case (1892), which refused to allow a claim even by a shipowner who had been excluded from membership of a shipping conference, holding that the fairness of competition was not a justiciable question. A similar action in Germany against a booksellers' association was held admissible in principle by the Supreme Court in 1890, but rejected because the exclusion was held justified by public interest concerns; and generally German courts upheld the validity of cartel rules and decisions in the name of freedom of contract, unless there was evidence of abusive behaviour (Cornish 1979: 299–300), or the cartel could be said to be acting against the public interest economically (Gerber 1998: ch. 4).

10 The archetype was the agreement devised by S. C. T. Dodd, counsel for Rockefeller's Standard Oil, under which some 50 oil company owners placed their stock in the hands of 9 trustees, who themselves owned a majority of the assets, giving them the power to run the whole combination; this was revealed by an investigation by the New York Senate in 1888, leading to court action against the Trust; the operations were recounted and Rockefeller himself demonized in the muckraking classic by Ida Tarbell serialized in *McClure's* magazine 1902–4, which fed the popular hostility to the 'trusts' (Tarbell and Chalmers [1904] 1966).

did not prevent an individual firm from creating a dominant position by driving its competitors out of business, or even by swallowing them up through acquisition of their assets or shares (Sklar 1988: 135–6). The Sherman Act became an even more flexible legal tool after 1911, when in the *Standard Oil* and *American Tobacco* cases, the Supreme Court endorsed the 'rule of reason': this accepted that not all agreements restricting competition were necessarily prohibited, but only 'unreasonable' restraints of trade or monopoly, such as those deliberately aimed at driving out competitors who were not party to the agreement.

Thus, the rapid shift to the use of the corporation as the main institutional form for big business after 1890 was primarily due to the drive to overcome market disturbances and crises due to overproduction, in other words to control and limit competition, through industrial planning and coordination. This was especially strong in the USA, due to the paradoxical effect that the anti trust legislation driven by anti-big-business sentiment actually encouraged corporate concentration, especially as it was applied by selective prosecution and judicial interpretation primarily against 'loose' combinations (Sklar 1988: 154–66; Bittlingmayer 1985). Government's powers of prosecution were used to regulate what official opinion regarded as irresponsible corporate behaviour (Weinstein 1968: 67). Hence, the Sherman Act helped to shape the debate about corporate power and to mediate the process of emergence, during the Progressive Era in the USA, of a consensus around a regulated corporatism.[11]

A key role in shaping and legitimating the new forms of corporate capital was played by a new breed of lawyers who emerged in the USA after 1885. They acted as brokers and intermediaries between the corporations and the investment bankers in Wall Street and Europe, as well as with the various levels of government which dispensed franchises and other proprietary rights. Above all, they devised the legal forms and moulded the legal principles which deflected the populist challenge and legitimated corporate power (Gordon 1984: 59–62; Hovenkamp 1991).

In Europe, a similar symbiosis of state and corporation also emerged, although with a greater tolerance, and indeed encouragement, of cartels. Socialist perspectives went further, and advocated nationalization, which it was envisaged would realize the potential for socialized production

---

11 Kolko 1963; Weinstein 1968; Sklar 1988; and for a detailed account of Du Pont, Wall 1990. As David Campbell has shown, many of the leading economists and policy-makers in the USA in the period after 1880 recognized that competition was the source of overproduction and crisis, and proposed as the solution corporate combinations, state regulation and indeed neocolonialism (Campbell 1993: 114–17).

relations embodied in the high degree of development of the means of production through large-scale corporate organizations (Renner 1904; Hilferding 1910).

4.1.1.3 Theories of the firm and financialization

The dominance in the main capitalist economies of large, integrated, oligopolistic corporations which had emerged at the beginning of the twentieth century was confirmed by the consolidation of these firms in the 1920s, and their survival and recovery following the crash of 1929 and the ensuing depression. It was eventually recognized by managerialist theories of the firm. Berle and Means (1932) focused on the implications of the separation of ownership, which especially in the USA was increasingly dispersed among widely held shareholdings, from the control over the operation of the firm exercised essentially by managers.[12] Alfred Chandler's seminal work, produced at the pinnacle of the consolidation and transnational expansion of giant firms in the great boom of 1953 to 1974, argued that the large multidivisional companies were dominated by a new breed of managers, who coordinated mass production with distribution to mass markets, as well as the sourcing of inputs, to exploit the scale economies resulting from size and scope offered by new technologies (Chandler 1962, 1977).

In 'managerial capitalism', argued Chandler, the visible hand of corporate planning had substantially replaced the anarchy of the market. He took a Weberian view of corporate bureaucracies based on hierarchy and rational decision-making, using professionalized techniques including importantly accounting.[13] He suggested that the success of the multidivisional form was due to the separation of responsibility for operations, devolved to division and plant managers, from the monitoring, strategic and policy role of headquarters. However, subsequent research has shown that the pioneer of this method, Alfred P. Sloan, had in fact resisted such a separation at General Motors, and when it was eventually introduced

---

12 Paddy Ireland points out that Berle and Means were also influenced by critiques of financial capitalism on both sides of the Atlantic, such as Brandeis and Ripley in the USA, and Veblen, Tawney and Laski in Europe, although these more radical perspectives became diluted in official policy proposals (Ireland 2010).

13 Professional public accountants have played a central part in the rise of the bureaucratic corporation: a good account of the structure and role up to 1990 of the 'big nine' (now the 'big four'), and critique of the dominant positivist and rationalist ideology of accounting is given by Montagna 1990. On the spread of this rationality into all social organizations in recent years see Power 1997.

the firm began a long decline. Indeed, Chandler himself in 1994 criticized the 'freewheeling diversification' by firms managed by MBA-trained executives and accountants relying on statistical data and divorced from operations (discussed in Kristensen and Zeitlin 2005: 214–18).

Managerialist theories dominated the period of Fordism, and were not challenged until the 1970s. The oil shock of 1974 sparked off extensive investments in new technologies, transformations of labour processes in industry, and widespread social conflicts around deindustrialization. These changes precipitated the emergence of post-industrial, knowledge-based capitalism, which together with the increased importance of financial markets, led to the emergence of the networked firm. This provided the context for new institutionalist theories of the firm, which claimed their origins in Ronald Coase's pre-war essay revising the microeconomic analysis of the firm in terms of the transaction costs of markets versus coordination.[14] This opened up the 'black box' of the firm by considering the interactions of those involved (managers, investors, directors, workers, etc.) in terms of contracts. From the Coasian perspective, the firm exists to the extent that the internalization of these relationships through the firm's administrative arrangements are more efficient (by reducing transaction costs) than managing them by contracts between independent actors. This introduces consideration of the nature of the firm as an institution, since there are also costs involved in managing a bureaucratic organization, which pose limits to its growth (Campbell and Klaes 2005).

An alternative perspective, rooted in a rather different view of the microeconomic analysis of contracting, is the contractual or agency theory, which sees the firm as a legal fiction serving as a nexus for a set

14 In 'The Nature of the Firm', Coase started from the point that the firm is a system of planned coordination, and analysed the production factors which it would be more efficient to coordinate rather than to buy contractually; he argued that this is most likely to be so when the content of a contract is hard to specify in advance, and that this is especially so for labour (1988: 39–40). In emphasizing the power to determine the content of the labour contract by directing the work to be performed, Coase in effect extended the analysis in Marx's writing on the joint-stock company, which as noted above emphasized that the firm is a system of planned coordination of labour. Although Coase has been claimed as a founding father by the law-and-economics school, he himself has criticized as 'highly inaccurate' the version of his views put forward especially by Richard Posner, the dominant figure in law-and-economics (Coase 1993). In the early 1930s, when he wrote 'The Nature of the Firm' (published in 1937), he was politically a socialist, but by the 1960s he was a political libertarian and has been described as a proto neo-liberal (Campbell and Klaes 2005). For my understanding of Coase, as for much else, I am greatly indebted to David Campbell.

of contractual relations linking the managers as agents to the various suppliers of production functions.[15] Rather than viewing the firm as an institution, which allows for consideration of sociological factors such as power, this is a radically economistic view, which simply considers the corporate form as a kind of standard-form contract. Such theories were principally deployed in the 1980s to justify the often large-scale corporate mergers and acquisitions (M&As) of that period as the operation of a 'market for corporate control'. This was said to enable shareholders as principals to exercise discipline over managers as agents, through pressure to generate value for shareholders, although the evidence for this was scant or dubious (McCahery *et al.* 1993: 3–5). Indeed, instead of shareholder value being a discipline on top managers, it has reinforced their position, as their remuneration has been boosted by the grant of stock options, giving them an incentive to pump up the share price by short-run policies. In practice, the expansion of firms via M&A is not infrequently the result of the aggrandizing strategies of dominant managers intent on extending their corporate empires, often leading to disaster. Conversely, acquisitions by predatory financiers such as private equity groups generally aim for short-term gains through asset disposals, although they can sometimes facilitate corporate restructuring.[16] More fundamentally, the contractarian view flies in the face of the fact that incorporation is not a mere contract but a state-protected form of property (Ireland 2003a). Indeed, the corporation was for this reason viewed with strong suspicion by Adam Smith and other nineteenth-century supporters of entrepreneurial, free-market capitalism (Campbell 1990; Glasbeek 2002: 72ff.).

15 This originated in the work of financial economists (Alchian and Demsetz, Jensen and Meckling); it has been elaborated by Easterbrook and Fischel (1991), who concede that limited liability seems to be a privilege bestowed by law on investors, but nonetheless claim that on closer examination this is not so, since most investment in any case involves some limitation of liability, and '[i]f limited liability were not the starting point in corporate law, firms would create it by contract' (Easterbrook and Fischel (1991): 41); such contracts would, of course, still depend on the willingness of state courts to enforce them. Clearly, if the limitation of liability were to be restricted, for example to expose directors and managers to personal liability, there would also have to be regulation to prevent circumvention, for instance by contract (Campbell and Griffin 2006: 70). This does not negate the point that the contracts linking stakeholders to the firm do not *constitute* the corporation, this occurs through the state's grant of the privilege of incorporation and protection of the share as property.

16 For a racy account of the dramatic $25bn leveraged buyout of Nabisco, showing the complex interplay between corporate managers and financiers, see Burrough and Helyar [1990] 2004.

By the 1990s the impact of competition mainly from Asia made apparent the weakness of the 'Fordist' model of the bureaucratic firm disciplined by its shareholder-owners, dominant especially in the USA. A new emphasis on the study of business networks, exercising coordination not only through diverse legal forms (long-term contracts and franchising as well as ownership links such as joint ventures), but also social relationships, called for a richer analysis of corporate organization and strategy, extending to issues of forms of control of time, space and competition, as well as institutional culture (e.g. Schoenberger 1997).

It is nevertheless not surprising that contractual theories of the firm and the primacy of shareholder-value remained dominant, especially in the USA, even through the 1990s. The unprecedented boom of the 1990s in stock market valuations of companies, and even more so in trading of shares, was part of the renewed shift towards financialization. Total capitalization on regulated stock exchanges worldwide shot up from under $3 trillion in 1980 to over $40 trillion in 2006 (Clarke 2007: 240–1). At the same time, shares became much more actively traded: the rate of turnover of stocks in the USA jumped from a norm of 20% in the 1938–76 period, to over 100% in 1998, and well over 200% by 2007 (French 2008: 1552; see Chapter 7, at 7.1.2). Much of this was concentrated in the leading exchanges, especially in the USA: the New York Stock Exchange (NYSE) alone has generally maintained a market capitalization of domestic listed companies amounting to between 30% to 40% of the world total, as well as attracting foreign firm listings.

Financial liberalization in the 1980s led to a rapid growth in cross-border portfolio investment, which has been mainly towards the leading exchanges: about 90% of portfolio capital flows have been to high income countries, just over 4% to middle-income (excluding China), and under 0.01% to low-income countries (Clarke 2007: 237). Generally, companies became more dependent on market-based finance, rather than reinvested earnings, bank loans or long-term investors. These trends further strengthened the incentives for managers to focus more on short-term share prices than on long-term returns.

Financialization raised to new heights the ability of those with privileged access to the channels of finance to accumulate wealth by exploiting the possibilities of appropriation flowing from the share as a property right. The resulting competition and conflicts have produced a growth of a number of areas of corporate and financial market regulation, which there is no space to treat in detail here. As already mentioned, much of the frenzied M&A activity is better understood as driven by private appropriation of wealth by trading corporate assets, than as a rational process of restructuring. Much of the wealth and power of investment banks has come from their move into financing of hostile takeovers and their key role in corporate finance generally. A new form of acquisition especially in the 1990s was opened up by the privatization of state-owned assets, especially in Russia and other former state-socialist countries. This provided unprecedented opportunities, especially for those with good connections to the state, to obtain corporate assets very cheaply, and some such as the so-called oligarchs quickly acquired gigantic corporate empires. Another key area is corporate insolvency, which provides procedures and mechanisms for the revaluation and transfer of assets, in which some are dispossessed, while others can acquire assets cheaply.[17]

More routinely, the enormous growth of trading in stocks and shares, combined with the emergence of financial derivatives, has offered new ways to take advantage of inside information. Financial markets are driven by access to information, so it is no surprise that the trading boom since the 1980s led to continual scandals and crises around the legitimacy of access to privileged information (Stewart 1992). This resulted in recurrent revisions in the regulation of disclosure requirements and insider trading rules. The international reshaping and juridification of financial market regulation can be said in broad terms to have reflected the ascendancy of multinational financial services firms (Moran 1991: 124–35). However, a more dynamic and contingent view should also view the juridification of insider dealing as resulting from the continued reformulation and reinterpretation of rules to mediate the strategic and competitive interactions of the various powerful players (McCahery and Picciotto 1995). Certainly, it was generally brash intruders such as Ivan Boesky who were criminalized, whereas investment banks continued to make enormous profits from their own-account proprietary trading, while dominating information flows through their roles as market-makers and client service providers (Marcial 1995).[18]

17 The two leading decisions by the International Court of Justice concerning expropriation, *Barcelona Traction* (1970), and *ELSI* (*US* v. *Italy*) (1989), concerned foreign shareholders claiming to have been disadvantaged by arrangements for refinancing or liquidation of insolvent firms (Picciotto 1998: fn. 64).

18 The so-called 'Chinese walls' which were supposed to separate a financial conglomerate's proprietary and client account traders are often notional: on a research visit to a large bank in Frankfurt in the mid-1990s I was shown these two sections, which operated on adjacent desks: the proprietary traders could clearly hear orders being executed for clients, and were closely following that activity. When we interviewed the regulator who was monitoring

The contractual view of the corporation, and its deployment to trumpet the merits of shareholder value as the overriding aim of the corporation, were considerably damaged by the bursting of the 1990s US stock market bubble in 2000 to 2002, when market capitalization fell by an estimated 46 per cent. The role of corporate mismanagement in generating the bubble was highlighted by the collapse in 2001 of Enron. Enron's top managers had pursued a high-growth strategy, turning it from a power utility company into a large-scale dealer in energy derivatives, and the seventh largest US company by market value. The extent of its borrowing and leverage, which resulted in an astronomic debt–assets ratio, had been substantially concealed from investors by the use of complex transactions involving partnerships and other off-balance-sheet 'Special Purpose Entities', devised by its Chief Financial Officer, Andrew Fastow, to circumvent or flout accounting rules and avoid or evade tax.[19] At the time the largest corporate bankruptcy in history, Enron was quickly followed by a spate of others, including Worldcom, Tyco, Global Crossing, Parmalat and two score more, precipitated by the crisis. Many of these involved blatant fraud by managers and directors, who generally had enriched themselves while driving the companies to disaster.[20] This gave further impetus to the long-standing debates about corporate governance, which also involve more fundamental questions about ownership and control.

4.1.2 Ownership and control, governance and accountability

The immense economic and social power wielded by the giant corporation makes the control and accountability of these organizations a

this activity, he informed us that his systems identified such a high level of suspicious trading that it was in practice impossible to control. External regulation of exchanges is virtually impossible, as they are dominated by large-volume 'repeat players', who alone are able to prevent traders from 'stealing the customer blind' (Gunningham 1991: 312). The key element in the regulation of exchanges is control of access to information on trading flows; this is built into the very structure of exchanges: in the case of open outcry the design of the 'pits' was negotiated and specified to the centimetre; in electronic trading, obligations on market-makers to display customer limit orders are hard to enforce.

19 See Enron 2002 (the Powers Report); Rosen 2003; Campbell and Griffin 2006: 48–51; Clarke 2007: 315–30; and on the tax aspects Peckron 2002. William Bratton (Bratton 2003a) analyses how these actions of Enron's managers were directly due to the pursuit of shareholder value, resulting from the incentives to focus on stock market valuation instead of fundamental value.

20 A survey by the *Financial Times* conservatively estimated that between 1999 and 2001 the executives and directors of the twenty-five largest US firms which went bankrupt had arrogated to themselves $3.3bn in personal compensation (ignoring other perks and benefits) while destroying hundreds of billions of dollars of shareholder value and almost 100,000 jobs (Cheng 2002).

crucial question. This has become especially important since the enormous growth of social savings in advanced economies, especially for pensions and other contingent personal liabilities such as healthcare costs, which have been channelled into financial markets, generally through banks, insurance companies and institutional investors. This has enabled those who control the large corporations to enrich themselves by managing 'other people's money'.[21] In effect, this has reversed the allocation of risk for which the early corporate forms such as the *commenda* were devised. Instead of the operators of the enterprise bearing the risk while the shareholders are protected, the top managers and other controllers of the corporation have become enabled to enrich themselves by exploiting the social savings invested in the firm.

Berle and Means had rooted their analysis in the dispersal of shareholdings, which not only gave great autonomy to managers, but also meant that the owners of a relatively small block of shares could control the company's board of directors. This echoed, from a different political perspective, Hilferding's analysis of the power of 'finance–capital'. Berle and Means called for a new 'social doctrine' of the corporation, rejecting the prevailing view that left the board free to decide the company's policy, since this would at most leave control with a small group of leading shareholders in conjunction with the managers. They considered that the alternative would be a property concept which would emphasize that corporate powers are held in trust for all shareholders. However, they acknowledged the limitations of such a fiduciary view, and suggested instead an ill-defined notion of the paramount interests of the community.[22] In the same period, the German Corporation Code of 1937 adopted a very similar 'enterprise' view of the corporation, stating that the duties of directors were to guide it 'as the welfare of the productive unit and its membership and the common welfare of the people and the state [Volk und Reich] require' (Raiser 1988: 117).

By the closing decade of the twentieth century, new debates about corporate governance became focused on the divergence between different models of the corporation, due to national variations in factors such as the structures of financial intermediation, the role of the state and the components of the social wage, and on whether the emergence of more globalized financial markets would lead to convergence. This also became a broader debate about 'varieties of capitalism', linking the organizational

---

21 The title of the classic critique of Wall Street by Louis Brandeis (1914).
22 Berle and Means 1932: 309ff.; see Campbell 1990: 196, 1993: 107.

structures and dynamics of firms to the macroeconomic and institutional features of different societies, and seeing the competition between them as concerning not only economic performance but also social well-being (Hall and Soskice 2001). The issue of convergence of corporate governance requirements was sharpened with the growth of foreign companies seeking a listing on the main exchanges, especially in New York and London.[23] Since the rules laid down by stock exchanges and their regulators play a major part in corporate governance standards (OECD 2009), this gave US rules in particular a worldwide impact.

A broad distinction could be made between a dispersed ownership system with highly developed stock markets, characteristic of Anglo-American capitalism, and a concentrated ownership system, found in Germany and other continental European countries as well as Japan, where strong banks with substantial shareholdings have played an important role in industrial corporate strategies (Charkham 1994; Gugler *et al.* 2004). The former could be described as having 'outsider' systems of corporate control and governance, with little long-term commitment by investors in the firm, an emphasis on shareholder value, and much M&A activity; while the latter's 'insider' systems meant that ownership and control are more closely aligned through block shareholdings by banks, resulting in more long-term strategies and organic growth.[24] In many countries 'insider' systems have become institutionalized in law and regulation, notably the two-tier board system of Germany, in which not only substantial long-term investors but also 'stakeholders' especially employees can have strategic influence through representation in the supervisory board.[25]

---

23 The number of foreign companies listed on the two main US exchanges, the NYSE and the Nasdaq, grew from 170 in 1990 to over 750 in 2000 (Coffee 2002: 1770–2; see also Chapter 3, n. 43).

24 Clarke 2007: 10; note however that despite these overall differences, in the UK and US there are also some companies with block shareholdings, usually held by a family group (Clarke 2007: 96); Australia, although it might have been thought to fit the 'Anglo-Saxon' model, has a high proportion of block shareholdings, and exhibits many features of the 'insider' model (Clarke 2007: 144–6).

25 The system of 'co-determination', originating as a concession to the power of workers' organizations after the German Revolution of 1918, contributed to the German concept of the social enterprise, further developed in the post-war period as part of the 'social market' model, although the concept of enterprise law continued to be controversial (Raiser 1988), and could be said to articulate a form of 'enterprise corporatism' (Teubner 1988). The divergence between the German model of employee participation and the British model of independent trade unionism made it impossible to reach agreement on the proposed EU Fifth Directive on company law on employee participation, and impeded other efforts

In the booming stock markets of the 1990s and euphoric talk of the 'new economy' especially in the USA, many thought it plausible to argue that closed systems inhibited growth, and that corporate law should aim to encourage deep financial markets, by strong rules for the protection of investors especially minority shareholders. Some stressed that corporate structures reflected significant historical differences, especially in national financial markets, which had become institutionally and legally embedded in ways that were hard to change, referred to as 'path-dependency' (Bebchuk and Roe 1999; Bratton and McCahery 1999). However, some convergence towards the shareholder-value model did seem to be resulting from the internationalization of financial markets (Coffee 2001; Gugler *et al.* 2004: 152). From the broader viewpoint of the 'varieties of capitalism' perspective, it was pointed out that the changes were incremental rather than fundamental (Vitols 2001), and convergence in corporate governance was neither necessary nor sufficient for adoption of other economic institutions (Gilson 2001).

Nevertheless, some described this convergence as an 'end of history' for corporate law, resulting from a broad normative consensus 'among the academic, business, and governmental elites in leading jurisdictions' (Hansmann and Kraakman 2001: 440), and even as reflecting the 'deep structure' of corporate law (Kraakman 2004; cf. Easterbrook and Fischel 1991). Against this view, there is still much contemporary relevance to the historical analysis which shows that the corporate form was a political construct, mainly intended to shield the *rentier* investor, so that the vaunted protection for investors provided by limited liability institutionalizes corporate irresponsibility (Ireland 2008). For radical critics of the corporation this poses the dilemma of whether to advocate a reduction of the privileges of incorporation, especially limited liability, in order to restore the market (Campbell and Griffin 2006); or to envisage a strengthening of the social responsibilities of corporations based on 'a reconceptualization of the corporation in which its separate existence is taken *more* seriously and the idea of it as a shareholder-owned, private enterprise jettisoned' (Ireland 2008: 14; see also Ireland 2010).

at EU company law harmonization (European Commission 2003). However, a statute for a European Company (Societas Europaea) was finally agreed (Regulation 2157/2001), and since 2004 this provides a means for incorporation of firms operating in more than one European country; a supplementary Directive (2001/86/EC of 8 October 2001) stated very broadly that such companies must make 'arrangements for the involvement of employees', to be reached by agreement following negotiations with employee representatives, on the basis of specified alternative models.

Certainly, even as the proponents of convergence towards the shareholder value model were proclaiming its victory, the eruption of corporate scandals starkly highlighted the model's many shortcomings. The scandals led to various moves for the reform of corporate governance in national laws, as well as to develop international standards. In the UK this began earlier, as the 1980s financial market liberalization and boom resulted in a series of corporate collapses in 1991 (Maxwell, BCCI, Polly Peck) which highlighted corporate governance failures. In typically British fashion, these led to a series of reports from committees chaired by respected City figures,[26] resulting in soft law 'codes', culminating in the Combined Code issued by the Financial Reporting Council in 1998.[27] When it came to the reform of company law itself, the proposals were both contradictory and anodyne.[28] This again demonstrated the difficulty of establishing accountability based on a social form for the corporation while preserving shares as private property. Elsewhere also in this period there were spectacular corporate busts, notably Australia, where a 'raw form of wild capitalism' produced recurrent episodes of corporate scandal 'culminating in the excesses of the 1980s boom with colourful rogues exposed as crooks' (Clarke 2007: 145).

In the USA, the corporate crisis erupted later but more spectacularly, and the Enron affair and the other scandals were regarded as symptomatic of a more general crisis in corporate governance, involving misfeasance and immorality. A particular problem highlighted was excessive executive remuneration. The pace of top executive pay was set by US chief executive officers (CEOs): the top ten received remuneration calculated at between $114m. and $295m. in 2005, dwarfing that for non-US companies which ranged between $3m. and $6m. (Clarke 2007: 19–20). This reflected an enormous growth of inequality, as the ratio of CEO remuneration to the average employee pay in the USA jumped from 50:1 in 1980 to 525:1 in 2000 (Clarke 2007: 158). Aside from the social implications, these remuneration structures had significant implications for corporate control

---

26 In particular, the 1992 Cadbury Committee Report on Financial Aspects of Corporate Governance, which produced a Code of Best Practice, with which companies were required to comply, or explain divergences; this was followed by the Greenbury report and guidelines on directors' remuneration (1995), the Hampel report of 1998 on disclosure, and the Higgs report of 2003 on non-executive directors.

27 Revised in 2003, and reviewed again in 2006: see Clarke 2007: 139–44.

28 Notably, for the reformulation of directors' duties in terms of 'a shareholder oriented, but inclusively framed, duty of loyalty, in the context of significant public policy oriented mandatory provisions on care and skill, and conflict of interest, and extended disclosure' (UK Company Law Review 2000: para. 3.22).

and governance, especially as the extensive use of stock options and other schemes related only to short-term performance came to be criticized for fuelling greed, and creating incentives for manipulation of financial data and other methods of inflating share prices.

These concerns resulted in the enactment of the Sarbanes–Oxley Act,[29] the main thrust of which was to establish strict corporate audit standards, supervised by an audit oversight board, and with specific obligations on the chief corporate officers to certify compliance. Sarbanes–Oxley was resented by non-US companies which were obliged to comply with it if they wanted a stock exchange listing in the USA, as increasingly many had done. It was also controversial for mandating regulators (mainly the Securities and Exchange Commission (SEC), the main US stock market regulator) to adopt a principles-based approach to regulation, since the previous system of more detailed rules was thought to have encouraged opportunistic behaviour by Enron and others (Bratton 2003b). However, the British regulation of corporate accounting, which prided itself on being principles based, has been equally if not more unsuccessful, developing into a cat-and-mouse 'game' between highly inventive mice and a lethargic and toothless cat (McBarnet and Whelan 1999). Any regulatory system should combine general principles (or standards) with more specific rules, but effectiveness depends on its being erected on sound foundations. These cannot be said to exist when senior executives are effectively immune from personal liability unless caught out in clear misfeasance (Campbell and Griffin 2006), while the lucrative franchise of auditing is protected by the strong oligopoly of the 'big four' firms, buttressed by professional solidarity (Bratton 2003b).

Despite their limited effectiveness, such reforms of corporate governance were adopted across the world, with some variations. A degree of coordination and standard-setting was provided by the development by the OECD of a set of Principles of Corporate Governance. These were issued in 1999, and revised in 2004, following the Enron debacle and related events, and were also propagated through other regulatory networks (Clarke 2007: 242–55). Not surprisingly, an 'ambitious action plan' was launched in 2009 to address weaknesses identified by the financial crisis and recommend further improvements.[30]

Thus, the fierce debates at the start of the twentieth century around the implications of the corporate form and financial capitalism, by the

---

29 Public Company Accounting Reform and Investor Protection Act 2002.
30 See www.oecd.org/corporate.

beginning of the twenty-first century had been tamed into meek reforms of governance standards. Indeed, the debates about corporate governance have effectively disarmed and depoliticized more fundamental critiques and debates about corporate power and the corporate form (Soederberg 2009). Despite the evident need for more fundamental rethinking shown by the recurring eruptions of corporate scandals and financial crises, there seems to be no effective driving force for any significant reconsideration of the corporate form.

4.2 Transnational corporations, groups and networks

A good deal of the power of the modern corporation derives from its ability to operate internationally. Modern transnational corporations (TNCs)[31] have been described as an 'ongoing, continuing, evolving grouping of inter- and intra-company relationships', of a primarily proprietary character, and spreading 'business culture, practices, perspectives' worldwide (Wilkins 1998: 103). Although TNCs first emerged in the last third of the nineteenth century, the concept seems to have been coined only in 1960 (Fieldhouse 1986). Indeed, conventional economics has had difficulty understanding the phenomenon and its implications, which have been studied more in business schools and by economic sociologists.

4.2.1 Classification and quantification

From the conventional economic perspective, TNCs involve international flows of investment, classified as *foreign direct investment* (FDI), which is contrasted with *portfolio investment*. The distinction is based on the concept that the direct investor has *control* over the investment in order to manage it, usually as part of a cross-border integration of business activity, whereas portfolio investment merely seeks financial returns. The concept of control is also central to the definition of a TNC, notably in the draft UN Code of Conduct on TNCs (UN 1983):

---

31 I prefer this to other terms, such as multinational enterprise, since it indicates that such firms originate and usually remain primarily based in one country. There are exceptions of a few binational companies, usually involving firms from countries with smaller home markets, notably the long-lived Anglo-Dutch firms Royal Dutch-Shell and Unilever. A more recent example is ABB, discussed below, although this and other attempts to weld together binational firms have had mixed fortunes, e.g. Daimler-Chrysler which ended their eleven-year 'tumultuous relationship' in 2009 (*Financial Times* 28 April 2009), although another auto firm which became binational, Renault-Nissan, fared better.

> The term 'transnational corporation' as used in this Code means an enterprise whether of public, private or mixed ownership, comprising entities in two or more countries, regardless of the legal form and fields of activity of these entities, which operates under a common system of decision-making, permitting coherent policies and a common strategy through one or more decision-making centres, in which the entities are so linked, by ownership or otherwise, that one or more of them may be able to exercise a significant influence over the activities of others, and, in particular, to share knowledge, resources and responsibilities with the others.

The growth and importance of TNCs is usually measured in terms of the flows and stocks of FDI, but such data should be evaluated very carefully. They assume, firstly, that 'control' derives from ownership of a substantial proportion of the equity (or shares) of the entity in which the investment is made. Thus, the influential World Investment Report (WIR), published annually by the United Nations Conference on Trade and Development (UNCTAD), defines FDI as:

> an investment involving a long-term relationship and reflecting a lasting interest and control of a resident entity in one economy (foreign direct investor or parent enterprise) in an enterprise resident in an economy other than that of the foreign direct investor (FDI enterprise or affiliate enterprise or foreign affiliate). FDI implies that the investor exercises a significant degree of influence on the management of the enterprise resident in the other economy. Such investment involves both the initial transaction between the two entities and all subsequent transactions between them and among foreign affiliates, both incorporated and unincorporated. FDI may be undertaken by individuals as well as business enterprises.[32]

As a rule of thumb, the WIR now defines 'control' as a 10 per cent stake in the equity of an incorporated enterprise, 'or its equivalent for an unincorporated enterprise' (WIR 2003: 247). This is well below the majority stake that gives formal legal control, which was traditionally used, although legal definitions of a subsidiary are now often broader.[33] However, the complexities of business networks (based not only on ownership but also contractual relationships), and the variations of degrees of 'control' they

---

32 The WIR's data and definitions are derived from the IMF and the OECD, see e.g. WIR 2003: 247.

33 Notably, the EU's Seventh Company Law Directive (83/349/EEC of 13 June 1983) requires consolidated accounts for a corporate group to include any affiliate for which the parent holds the majority of the voting rights; but also allows Member States to extend consolidation to affiliates if the parent is a shareholder, and either: (a) exercises a dominant influence on the affiliate; or (b) manages it on a unified basis.

involve, which will be discussed further below, make it hard to establish clear definitions on which to base statistical quantifications.

Furthermore, FDI data mainly focus on financial flows and stocks (and the two are sometimes not adequately distinguished). Direct investments take three main forms: equity capital, reinvested earnings, and intra-firm loans and other debt transactions. Such transactions result largely from corporate strategic decisions, and may bear no relationship to the initiation of a new activity or the provision of new finance, which is how a new investment is commonly understood. In fact, from 1987 to 1999 on average over 50% of new FDI flows (and as much as 75% between developed countries) were constituted by cross-border mergers and acquisitions (M&As), which do not in themselves entail any new activity, and may indeed result in the downsizing of the acquired entity (WIR 2000: 16). It should also be borne in mind that investment may take the form of a transfer to the subsidiary of intangible assets, such as know-how, in exchange for equity or debt. Since this is an intra-firm transaction, it may be difficult or impossible to verify the valuation placed upon such a transfer. The more sophisticated justifications of TNCs argue that they transfer know-how rather than financial investment.

Thus, rather than consisting of an international flow of investment, it is more appropriate to consider the expansion of TNCs as constituting a process of international *concentration* of control over capital. This may also entail a *centralization* of control, if fewer and larger corporations control a higher proportion of an economic sector, or indeed of the world economy as a whole.

4.2.2 Control forms and techniques

Corporate control is usually based on ownership, and TNCs take the legal form of a group of related companies or other legal persons, which can best be termed affiliates. They are commonly thought of as consisting of a parent company and a number of subsidiaries, although in practice the ownership links are often extremely complex, involving many intermediaries, holding companies, split shareholdings and jointly owned companies. They also may combine corporate and contractual ties. It is often very difficult to draw a diagram of the legal relationships of complex corporate groups, and even more so to relate the legal to the business structure.[34] This is especially so because the legal structure often develops in a haphazard way, new affiliates may be created for a specific purpose and then become effectively defunct, but they may be kept legally alive, and then resurrected if needed, perhaps for a different purpose (Hadden 1984). Group structures vary for many reasons, including the state in which the TNC originates and those in which it operates, which may have different legal forms and requirements, as well as varying patterns of finance and ownership (Hadden 1993).

These formal structures have been devised by corporate lawyers, using techniques developed and honed over more than a century, taking advantage of the flexibility offered by legal rules and their interpretation. Even the basic principle of corporate affiliation, (one corporation owning some or all the shares in another), which is now taken for granted, was challenged at first, especially in the USA, due to the populist hostility to big business. Its acceptance was greatly facilitated by the competition between US states to attract corporate registrations.[35] New Jersey first held itself out as a base for incorporation, from 1875, but it became especially attractive in the 1890s, after James Dill, then lawyer for Rockefeller's Standard Oil Trust, persuaded the legislature to adopt an amendment allowing a New Jersey corporation to own shares in another company.[36] 'While unsuccessful in attaining its original purpose of allowing corporate combinations to avoid the then-pending Sherman Act, this provision became the cornerstone of inter-corporate partial integration and allowed such phenomena as the utility holding pyramids of the 1920s and even the development of the conglomerate affiliated enterprise systems of today' (Buxbaum and Hopt 1988: 116). Delaware began to compete from 1899, and was able to offer lower incorporation fees and taxes, as it was a smaller state for which attracting a large number of registrations even with low fees could be a boon. Hence, Delaware became the favoured US state of incorporation by offering management-friendly corporate laws (Cary

---

34 For an analysis of the factors affecting the business and legal forms and the relationships between the two see Muchlinski 2007: ch. 2.

35 This was sparked by the judicial shift in constitutional interpretation towards an obligation on states to recognize out-of-state incorporation (Buxbaum and Hopt 1988: 38–40; see Chapter 3, at 3.2.1).

36 Grandy 1989: 681. In the nineteenth century, the US courts generally considered that under common law a corporation could not own the shares of another, and this was not usually permitted under state legislation either, until the New Jersey legislation of the late 1890s: see Blumberg 1993: 52–8; the argument for maintaining this prohibition as a block to corporate concentration was powerfully expressed in the resounding minority opinion of Louis Brandeis in *Liggett* v. *Lee* (1933).

1974; Bratton *et al.* 1996: 16–18). In Europe, by contrast, the permissibility of corporate affiliation seems to have been more readily accepted (Lutter 1990: 954).

Organization of the firm as a group of companies offers significant advantages. A group that is under common control can be managed as a single enterprise, while exploiting the principle that each company is a separate legal entity when that could be advantageous. Thus a TNC may choose to operate in a host country through a branch, as banks often do in order to avoid host country regulatory obligations especially relating to capital requirements. Normally, however, any significant activities would be carried out through a locally incorporated subsidiary (or often several), especially if this enables the firm to avoid regulatory obstacles such as restrictions on foreign ownership of land. In the case of a company whose shares are publicly listed on a stock exchange (commonly referred to as public companies), its affiliates will usually be private, unless there is a good reason for them to have their own listing.

Thus, the stock exchange on which the ultimate parent or holding company is listed will be regarded as the TNC's home jurisdiction.[37] Host country foreign investment laws have frequently imposed restrictions on foreign shareholdings, which may entail a local listing to allow for local shareholders, or may mean that the subsidiary should be a joint venture with local private or public entities. Early in their history, TNCs became adept at making use of complex corporate group structures, including intermediaries formed in convenient jurisdictions, to gain regulatory advantages; a primary motive was tax avoidance, especially where they considered that overlapping claims to tax by states subjected them to double taxation (see Chapters 3 and 6).

Once the possibility of one company owning another was accepted, the powerful legal fiction of separate personality ensured that the related principle of limited liability was also applied without question to corporate groups (Blumberg 1993: 59). Normally, however, TNCs operate with an integrated financial structure, with consolidated accounts, as this gives them greater flexibility in financial planning, including minimization of tax liabilities. Also, raising low-cost capital from investors in both

---

37 In recent years some companies have 'migrated', usually to establish their primary listing on an exchange with a deeper capital market, rather than by means of a secondary listing (as discussed at 4.1.2 above). The motive may also be to reduce taxation by the home country of income from foreign operations, also referred to as 'corporate inversions', by transferring the shares in affiliates and other foreign assets to a new holding company in a convenient jurisdiction, though this is more often threatened than implemented.

equity and corporate bonds is easier with the backing of the assets of the TNC as a whole. In practice, therefore, parent companies usually stand behind the debts of their affiliates. Sometimes, however, specific activities may be pursued independently, especially if they involve a joint venture with others, and this may create ambiguities about the liability of parent companies. Increasingly, also, some firms have taken advantage of new financial techniques of securitization and disintermediation to spin off bundles of debt into special purpose vehicles or entities (SPVs or SPEs), which may be treated as off balance sheet. In many cases, the parent may retain some liability, contingent on 'trigger events', which makes the accounting treatment of such devices subject to interpretation. It also opens the way to obfuscation and fraud, as in cases such as Enron mentioned above (see also Chapters 6 and 7).

Such complex, ambiguous, and often obscure financial structures create lucrative opportunities for lawyers, especially in the event of corporate reorganization and bankruptcy.[38] A special niche has been created by specialized cross-border insolvency practitioners, particularly the large accountancy firms, excavating the entrails of failed business empires such as Maxwell and BCCI. These legal tangles have generally been resolved through normative arrangements which are largely private (Flood and Skordaki 1997), although rooted in national systems for managing bankruptcy which have become increasingly interlinked, and to some extent harmonized (Halliday and Carruthers 2009).

In addition to corporate ownership ties, TNCs can also make use of various forms of contractual relationships. These include some corporate joint ventures, long-term supply contracts and franchising. They may cause difficulties under competition law, especially if they are 'horizontal' agreements between potential competitors. A contractual form may be chosen for opportunistic reasons, for example if direct ownership would cause regulatory problems.[39] There has been surprisingly little empirical research into long-term business contracting, perhaps because mainstream theory views contracts as discrete and non-recurring, rather than as 'relational' instruments of business planning (Macneil et al. 2001), or

---

38 See e.g. *Kleinwort Benson* v. *Malaysian Mining* (1989), and the negotiations around the financial restructuring of Eurodisney recounted in McGrath 1994.

39 An early example was the Gillette safety razor company, which set up a UK subsidiary in 1908; finding that it could be liable to UK tax on its worldwide profits, it first transferred its UK business to a branch of a US affiliate, and then in 1915 licensed the business to a new company set up by its former UK managing director. The UK Revenue still tried to treat the new company as 'under the control' of the US Gillette, but this was rejected by the courts as 'arbitrary taxation gone mad' (*Gillette* v. *CIR* (1920)).

of regulation (Collins 1999). In practice, all firms have many more or less dense business networks based on contracts, and large TNCs can wield considerable power through such relationships.

Vertical contractual links may be upstream (backwards) to sources of supply, or downstream (forwards) towards distribution. Long-term supply contracts can be used to ensure security of supply and price stability, and may include detailed specifications of quality standards and other requirements. However, it should be borne in mind that the legal contracts provide only a formal framework through which the parties manage their business relationships, perhaps to 'sanctify a moral position' (Daintith 1986: 186). Downstream relationships may be distribution agreements or may extend to production under licence. Franchises are more elaborate versions of such agreements, usually entailing the transfer of a complete business format, while the franchisees contribute their own capital (Muchlinski 2007: 53–4). Franchises can involve complex relationships of power and control, although the franchisor is generally dominant, due to both its ownership of proprietary rights (especially the brand name), and its relative size, which makes it hard for disaffected franchisees to rebel unless they can form a common front (Felstead 1993). The archetypical global franchisor is McDonald's (Ritzer 2008), although McDonald's frequently also owns its own outlets, and even for franchises often owns the site. It has used master franchise agreements with local partners to become established in some countries, which led to a notable legal conflict with its French master franchisee (*Dayan* v. *McDonald's* (1984)).

Consortium arrangements based on contracts are used to carry out major projects in some industries, notably oil drilling, construction and heavy engineering. The use of standard-form contracts, for example in the construction industry, essentially creates a transnational regulatory framework, often with complex interactions of elements of private and public law (Perez 2002, 2004). In other circumstances, a consortium may be a stage towards the creation of a corporate joint venture company, as in the case of Airbus, which began as a consortium using the French legal form of a *groupement d'intérêt économique*, before establishing itself as EADS in 2001.

4.2.3 Transformations of the TNC

Large corporations were able from early in their history, to establish foreign operations, both to acquire foreign sources of supply of raw materials, and to set up plants to assemble or manufacture their products close to foreign markets. Despite some superficial similarities, they were qualitatively distinct from their older forerunners, the chartered trading companies; instead, they tended to grow out of nineteenth-century family businesses built by a 'cosmopolitan bourgeoisie' (Jones 1987). They have also undergone many significant transformations in the 150 years or so of their development.

Vertical integration (combining several stages of a production chain such as raw materials supply and manufacturing) was not necessarily an advantage: grandiose projects such as the oil-palm plantations in the Congo established by William Lever (the founder of Lever Brothers, later Unilever), or Henry Ford's rubber plantation in Amazonia, resulted as much from megalomania as business strategy.[40] The exploitation of natural resources was generally done more successfully by specialist firms, which acquired and developed proprietorial rights and concessions for minerals and oil. However, TNCs in manufacturing could be more successful, especially if they were based on systems which could be transplanted: usually innovative and standardized products, which could be produced by semi-skilled workers. This was characteristic of US firms, which had grown by exploiting the large US market and the 'American system of manufacture', using standardized machine-made parts (Lazonick 1991, 27ff.). These production techniques were easier to implant abroad, and the cheap yet technologically innovative products could conquer world markets. A notable pioneer was the Singer sewing-machine company, which in 1863, the year of its incorporation, shifted to standardized machine-manufacturing, enabling it to establish a production plant in Scotland in 1867, using the same production methods as in the USA (despite the cheaper labour in Scotland), to help reassure European consumers that the quality of the products was as good (Hounshell 1985: 91–6).

Although the first TNCs had already emerged by 1914, long-term international investment at that time primarily took the form of loans, in particular the purchase of foreign, especially government, bonds. It has been estimated that of the total $44 billion of world long-term foreign

---

40 Lever's venture in the Congo began in 1914, after the international denunciations of King Leopold's murderous regime of 'private colonialism' and forced labour. Lever's Huileries du Congo Belge were relatively long-lasting, although by the 1920s Unilever found that producing its own raw materials made the company 'schizophrenic' (Fieldhouse 1978: 449–50), in 1959 they produced 9.2 per cent of world trade in palm oil (Fieldhouse 1978: 494). Fordlandia in Brazil was a spectacular failure, for both social and botanical reasons (Grandin 2009).

investment stock in 1914, no more than one-third could be classified as FDI (Dunning 1988: 72). Even this figure includes as investments involving 'control' many which were significantly different from subsequent international direct investments. Thus, syndicated loans were used, for example for British investments in US breweries in the 1890s (Buckley and Roberts 1982: 53–6), and to develop mining, as for example the purchase of the Rio Tinto concession from the Spanish government by the Matheson syndicate in 1873 (Harvey and Press 1990). Similarly, Cecil Rhodes raised syndicated finance to bring much of Kimberley's diamond mining under his control after 1875; and Rhodes and Rudd again raised capital in the City of London for the development of gold mining in 1887 and 1893, based on the mining finance house system dividing control between operational management on the spot and financial decisions taken in London. These were the successes among some 8,400 companies promoted in London between 1870 and 1914 to manage mining investments abroad (Harvey and Press 1990). A high proportion of FDI prior to the First World War was directed to minerals or raw materials production in specific foreign locations, and did not involve internationally integrated activities. These were certainly the major characteristics of British international investments, which were dominant in that period: Britain accounted for three-quarters of all international capital movements up to 1900, and 40 per cent of the long-term investment stock in 1914 (Dunning 1983).

Although the period 1890 to 1913 was one of economic liberal internationalism, conducive to international trade and investment, the rapid growth of large monopolistic firms in many industries in the USA and Europe also led to accommodations among them, frequently formalized as cartels: notably Solvay's alkali cartel for chemicals (Stocking and Watkins 1946: 430), and the agreements between the USA and German electrical engineering giants (GE, AEG, Siemens and Westinghouse) in the 1890s (Glimstedt 2001: 134). Following the First World War, the large corporations consolidated their power, and US firms such as Du Pont and General Motors developed the bureaucratic, integrated but decentralized, multidivisional firm (Chandler 1962). Some firms, notably the US auto giants, were able to continue and develop overseas activities implanted behind national tariff and regulatory barriers.[41] Generally, however, this

---

41 GM acquired Vauxhall Motors in England in 1925, Opel in Germany in 1929, and Holden in Australia in 1931. Ford followed a slightly different track, setting up its own affiliates, first in England and France in 1911, then in other European countries in the 1920s, as well as Australia and Argentina.

was a period of nationalism, reinforced by the crash of 1929, which resulted in government policies favouring autarchic development. Thus, between the wars the international economy was dominated by international cartels, establishing a geopolitical economic governance, allocating territories and cross-licensing technology (Nussbaum 1986). Only from 1937, in the second phase of the Roosevelt administration, did the US authorities led by Thurman Arnold begin to apply the antitrust laws to strike down participation by US firms in these cartels (see 4.3 below). By invalidating the participation of US firms in international cartels, this policy provided a major impetus for their post-war expansion via FDI.

After 1950, the Bretton Woods system established liberalization of trade and current account payments, while states maintained currency exchange controls and restrictions on capital flows. However, TNCs were able to resume the expansion of FDI, by investing mainly retained earnings and, especially after the further relaxation of controls on transfers by non-residents from 1958, helping to create the 'offshore' Eurodollar market, to provide them with access to low-cost international finance (discussed in Chapter 3, at 3.1.2). Thus, the two decades 1953 to 1973 saw a strong expansion of FDI, led mainly by US firms, which accounted for about 50 per cent of FDI stock in this period. They moved mainly into Europe taking advantage of the Marshall Plan and the construction of the European Economic Community (EEC), and then into other parts of the world following decolonization.

This produced a politicized reaction against the 'multinationals' and their impact on host countries, both in Europe (Servan-Schreiber 1967), and elsewhere (Radice 1975). The political aspects were also dramatically highlighted by revelations that the US telecommunications giant ITT had been deeply involved with the US Central Intelligence Agency (CIA) in covert operations to impede the election of, and then overthrow, Salvador Allende as President of Chile (US Congress 1975, the Church report). The UN asked a Group of Eminent Persons to prepare a report on the impact of TNCs on economic development (UN 1974), and it followed up by establishing a UN Commission on TNCs and the UN Centre on TNCs (Dell 1990). Largely due to this politicization, the 1970s and early 1980s saw extensive debates about how to control TNCs, resulting in regulation by both host and home countries, and the formulation of various international codes of conduct (see next chapter). The UN Centre produced a steady stream of research-based reports, but some regarded it as too hostile to international business, especially due to its work on the abortive Code of Conduct on TNCs, and in 1993 it was wound up and its activities transferred to UNCTAD (Sagafi-nejad and Dunning 2008).

These changes have been reflected in the theories about TNCs. These have generally focused on analysing the specific advantages of TNCs compared to national firms, beginning with the early work of Stephen Hymer which emphasized their oligopolistic nature ([1960] 1976, 1972), and that of Raymond Vernon stressing their exploitation of technological innovation (1971). From this, a mainstream perspective emerged which focused on explaining the circumstances in which the internalization of activities within the administrative structure of a single firm would be superior to organizing them by separate firms through market exchange. This 'internalization' perspective chimed in with the revival of the microeconomic theories of the firm based on Coase, mentioned above (Dunning 2001b). This assumes that markets are inherently superior, and locates the reasons for 'internalization' in various kinds of 'market failure', in which conditions the TNC is deemed to be superior. Dunning's influential 'eclectic' paradigm put forward a synthesis, suggesting that the competitive advantages of TNCs result from their ownership of assets, choice of locations and the synergies from internalization (2001a). However, these dominantly economic perspectives have been criticized for taking 'the market' for granted, as well as overlooking the characteristics of TNCs as social institutions, which should be incorporated into a fuller understanding of the dynamics of the internationalization of capital in terms of social relations (Jenkins 1987: 33).

4.2.4 Global corporate networks

Following the 'oil shock' of 1973 and the ensuing extensive restructuring of industrial capital, the growth of TNCs continued, and they became a more extensive phenomenon, in three main ways. First, the TNC universe expanded to include firms originating in a wider diversity of states, diluting the predominance of the USA (as well as the UK and the Netherlands), as German and Japanese firms which had relied on exports shifted more to FDI; and by the 1990s it included also firms from developing countries such as India (Dunning 2001b: 50). Second, the shift to post-industrial capitalism also entailed a drive to transnationalize by firms in the expanding sectors of the knowledge economy and services (WIR 2004). Third, and as a result of these two changes, there was a greater diversity in types of TNCs, in particular the emergence of new forms of corporate networks.

Data on TNCs have been collected by UNCTAD and published in its annual *World Investment Report* (WIR) since 1991, although the report is generally more concerned with data on flows of FDI, which as discussed above can be misleading and unhelpful. In the early 1990s the WIR estimated that there were some 35,000 TNCs with 150,000 affiliates (WIR 1992: 12); a decade later the estimate was 60,000 TNCs with more than 820,000 foreign affiliates (WIR 2001: 9); and by 2009 it reported 82,000 TNCs, with 810,000 foreign affiliates (although this was a conservative estimate, based on national data), employing 77 million people worldwide.

However, the largest TNCs are especially dominant. In the early 1990s the largest hundred non-financial TNCs were estimated to account for about one-third of FDI stock. By the 2006–8 period, the hundred largest non-financial TNCs accounted for 9% of the estimated foreign assets, 16% of sales and 11% of employment of all TNCs, and since 2000 they have accounted for about 4% of world GDP (WIR 2009: 17). FDI inflows have accounted for an average of some 14% of gross fixed capital formation globally, with significant variations between countries and sectors, while FDI stock as a percentage of GDP globally has grown from 9% in 1990 to 25% in 2008 (WIR 2009: 255). TNCs also dominate world trade: it is usually estimated that about one-third of interstate trade consists of internal flows between affiliates of such groups.[42]

These broad-brush data clearly show the continuing and increasing importance of TNCs, the largest especially. However, the wilder predictions of some that the world economy would be dominated by increasingly few corporate behemoths have not been fulfilled, confirming that bureaucratic management also has its limits. Instead there has been an increase in the number and diversity of types of firm, and of oligopolistic competition between them. Corporate empires can go through periods of expansion through acquisition, or contraction through divestment and downsizing, due to the interactions between strategies of top managers and the pressures of the major financial markets. A firm's fortunes can depend on the whims of institutional investors, and its ability to court governments, deal with regulators, and exploit regulatory interactions and arbitrage. Managing a complex TNC with diverse activities often in far-flung locations

---

42 See WIR 1991: 70; WIR 1997: 18; WIR 2009: 16. However, these are based on extrapolations of US data (Zeile 1997); see further Chapter 6, n. 37.

is not a simple matter of exploiting natural synergies, but of mastering the intricate interactions of a complex and changing network, in which managers of its units often also pursue their own strategies.

A frequently cited example, which illustrates both the power and vulnerability of TNCs in recent turbulent times, is ABB, formed by the merger in 1988 of the Swedish engineering firm Asea and the Swiss Brown Boveri (both founded in the early 1890s), although it is not necessarily typical of all TNCs. Following the merger, ABB pursued a chequered path of restructuring and acquisitions (over 60 firms acquired wholly or partly within two years), and quickly became a giant employing 240,000 people with revenues of $35bn annually, in high-technology engineering businesses ranging from tilting trains to power-plant construction and electrical installation. It consisted of some 1,100 local companies, coordinated through a 'global matrix' of national firms organized in 50 Business Areas, by an Executive Committee of 13 people meeting every three weeks, managed by only 100 professional staff in its Zurich headquarters (Taylor 1991). In the words of its then CEO, Percy Barnevik, it had to manage three central contradictions: it was 'global and local, big and small, radically decentralized with centralized reporting and control' (Taylor 1991: 95). A detailed research study focusing on one of its business areas, looking at both managerial strategies and the plant level, confirmed the complex dialectics involved in trying to 'be local worldwide' (Bélanger *et al.* 1999). Unsurprisingly, it faced stormy seas in the ensuing twenty years, and by 2008 had halved its number of employees, and revenues (adjusted for inflation) had fallen at a similar pace.

The changing nature of the TNC was reflected in new typologies of it as a heterarchy (Hedlund 1986), or an integrated network (Bartlett and Ghoshal 1989). More interestingly, such theories were tested by new types of study, approaching the TNC as a form of *social* organization of business. These not only considered the headquarters' coordination strategies, but examined the strategies and interactions of its various business units, including the characteristics of their workforces and the local and national as well as international business and regulatory networks in which they are embedded.

Detailed studies of this type are hard to carry out, but those which have been done cast new light on TNCs. Notably, the fascinating study by Kristensen and Zeitlin of the British-based firm APV, which attempted for a period in the 1990s to knit together a group of producers of food, drink and dairy processing equipment, illuminates the multilevel strategies of the various actors, showing how the often loose networks of a

TNC can teeter between strategic alliances and warring fiefdoms. They argue, based on the evidence of their study, that the potential for TNCs to combine locally rooted capabilities through problem-solving approaches generating mutual learning could benefit both the firms and the 'many local communities which they tap into and interconnect'. Instead, unfortunately, TNC strategies are dictated by the interactions of headquarters' managers with institutional investors in financial markets. Executives can usually expect only short lives at the top, and tend to favour short-term strategies, especially the high-risk, high-payoff M&As peddled by investment banks (Kristensen and Zeitlin 2005: 302–3).

The new and greater variety of types of TNCs, and the newer perspectives on studying them as part of wider corporate networks, were also reflected in the emergence of work on 'global commodity chains'. This perspective was pioneered especially by Gary Gereffi, originating in the broader world-system theories of Wallerstein and others, and focused not on the firm but on the links between globally dispersed production sites involved in the successive processes of manufacturing specific products (Gereffi and Korzeniewicz 1994; Gereffi 2001). The commodity-chain concept was particularly relevant for brand-named goods, which are designed and sometimes assembled by a dominant firm, which subcontracts much or all of the production, often to manufacturers in low-wage countries, especially in industries such as electronics, apparel, toys and some consumer durables. This perspective also introduced consideration of international trade aspects of business networks, and factors such as control of market access (Raikes *et al.* 2000). Although retailers and marketers of designer brand-name consumer goods could derive many advantages from out-sourcing production to low-wage countries, they also proved vulnerable to consumer-based campaigns focusing on abuse of labour and environmental protection standards, as will be discussed in the next chapter.

More broadly, some economic sociologists argued that there had been a shift to a new form, the 'network enterprise', in response to the unpredictability resulting from rapid economic and technological change. This was particularly characteristic of East Asian firms, whose superior ability to manage business networks gave them a competitive advantage, especially in the context of the crisis of the US model of the integrated TNC (Castells 1996: 164ff.; Yeung 1998; Arrighi 2007). Japanese firms had pioneered networked production, especially in sectors such as automobiles, in which Toyota had used its control over labour and its 'just-in-time' management of component supplies from subcontractors to facilitate flexible production and reduce inventory costs. The Japanese economy had also historically developed through networks of business groups, originally the giant *zaibatsu*, with both horizontal linkages and vertical networks (*keiretsu*), often built around a *sogo shosha* trading company. The equivalent in Korea, the *chaebol*, were more hierarchical. Chinese business networks on the other hand, in Taiwan, on the mainland (especially in south China) and among the widespread Chinese diaspora, were based on family firms and kinship and other informal cultural ties.

Some argue also that this reflects a distinct business culture based on social connections involving reciprocal advantage, known as *guanxi*, relying on ethical obligations flowing from personal knowledge and trust, rather than the emphasis on impersonal obligations of formal law (Appelbaum 1998). However, others counter that there is no necessary opposition between reliance on personal relationships and use of formal law, and that indeed they can be and have been effectively combined by adept exponents of formal law such as the great US law firms (Dezalay and Garth 1997).

4.3 Corporatism and the regulation of competition

Competition law and regulation play an important part in legitimizing corporate oligopoly and planning, and mediating between corporate power and state policies. This role emerged in the formative period of the US antitrust laws 1890–1914, as already discussed above at 4.1.1.2. In the second part of the twentieth century, competition laws spread more widely through processes of jurisdictional interaction, emulation and legal transplantation or imperialism. It is noteworthy that, although competition law is on its face neutral, aiming to establish a 'level playing field' between firms, and there has been considerable convergence of perspectives and principles, there remain significant conflicts in the actual application of competition law. Consequently, the regulation of competition has itself become an arena of contention between different policies towards corporate concentration and cartelization, and a potent weapon for firms to wield against each other in their jockeying for competitive advantage.

4.3.1 From cartelization to regulated competition

The historical initiative towards the deployment of competition laws to foster and legitimize regulated corporatism came from the USA, although in recent years the European Commission has become an enthusiastic apostle of the competition law creed. With the possible exception of a short period during the 1970s of debate focusing on the UNCTAD soft-law code on Restrictive Business Practices (RBP Code), a general consensus has reigned that competition law and policy should not challenge the dominance of large firms but only act as a check on their oligopolistic practices. It has nevertheless proved remarkably difficult to develop any hard-law procedures to ensure internationally harmonized application of national laws, or to coordinate competition law with related areas of regulation, notably of trade.

From about 1890 to 1938, international cartels were generally regarded as the most effective means of planning business sectors and managing the world economy. Their main aims were to mitigate the damaging effects of competition, especially the tendencies to overproduction due to vast economies of scale, resulting in violent price fluctuations and the consequent anarchic creation and destruction of capacity. Cartels dominated many leading industries, accounting for some 25 to 40 per cent of world trade, and their activities included imposing common technical standards (for example for electric lamps), technology sharing especially through pooling and cross-licensing of patents, collecting data to inform members, as well as allocating world markets by zones among the large north American and European firms (Stocking and Watkins 1946, 1948; Wells 2003: ch. 1; Kudo and Hara 1992). Governments encouraged, supported and sometimes themselves organized cartel agreements, especially for primary products such as rubber, wheat, nitrates and sugar.

Even the US authorities generally tolerated and sometimes encouraged cartels, notably in the fostering of associations by Herbert Hoover's administration, and during the 'planned economy' phase of Roosevelt's National Recovery Act. Although it was recognized that the application of US antitrust laws to activities partly taking place abroad raised jurisdictional issues, the problem could be managed, as the rules were sufficiently indeterminate to be applied selectively.[43] Thus, in the late 1930s when the

---

43 Famously, the Supreme Court adopted a strong unilateral limit on jurisdictional scope in *American Banana* v. *United Fruit Co.* (1909), when Justice Holmes forthrightly stated that the application of US laws to acts taking place abroad (in Costa Rica) 'not only would be unjust, but would be an interference with the authority of another sovereign'. A fascinating account of the murky mixture of politics, law and corruption, in both the USA and Central America, that led to that case is given by Noonan, who aptly states that the effect of the decision was to make 'the United Fruit Company free to become both the sponsor of Chiquita Banana and *el Pulpo*, the octopus of Latin American revolutionary

policy changed, the US authorities could begin systematically to apply the antitrust laws to international cartels. The cases started at that time led to a more aggressive attitude towards the application of the US antitrust doctrine and law to international business.[44] The effect of the drive against cartels, as mentioned above, was to propel US TNCs after the war to enter foreign markets through FDI.

The application of US laws to international business was counter-pointed by the export of the US antitrust philosophy and laws, as part of a wider assimilation of the US business model. Wartime investigations by

literature and politics' (1976: 65). A more nuanced view of jurisdiction was taken in *USA* v. *Sisal Sales Corp.* (1927), in which the Court held that a conspiracy between US companies to monopolize the exports of sisal from Mexico to the USA was formed in the USA and affected imports, so it could not be protected from the application of US law merely because one element in the conspiracy involved 'inducements' to Mexican officials to discriminate against rival firms. However, only some dozen cases were brought against US firms by the US authorities before 1940 under the Sherman Act relating to international commerce; all these, apart from three cases before 1914 against shipping conferences, concerned monopolization of foreign sources of raw materials in order to push up US import prices. The Webb–Pomerene Act of 1918 legalized export cartels, and in 1924 the Federal Trade Commission (FTC) ruled that it could enable US firms to join foreign cartels, as long as they did not affect the US market, so Webb–Pomerene corporations were used as a vehicle for US firms to join international cartels, even if their impact on the US market was evident (Wells 2003: 33).

44 The climate changed in 1938, with the launching of investigations by the Temporary National Economic Committee into the 'concentration of economic power', and the energization of the Antitrust Division of the Department of Justice by its new head, Thurman Arnold (see generally Hawley 1966; Freyer 1992; Wells 2003). Arnold tripled the staff of the Division, and he and his 'young Turks' launched a vigorous series of cases against international cartels. This shift was due to changing US perceptions about economic efficiency and the international role of US business rather than to Brandeisian appeals to republican values. Arnold's legal realist view of the symbolic role of law may explain both his earlier criticisms in *The Folklore of Capitalism* (1937) of the antitrust laws as functioning 'to promote the growth of great industrial organizations by deflecting the attack on them into purely moral and ceremonial channels' (cited in Wells 2003: 41), and the apparent change of tack to his vigorous enforcement of those same laws to defend free markets (Duxbury 1990: 34). The contradictions of New Deal attitudes towards monopoly are harder to reconcile (Hawley 1966), but it was Arnold who substantially altered antitrust philosophy from anti-big business towards the regulation of oligopoly (Brinkley 1993). During the war, the antitrust cases against cartels involving British firms were suspended after Foreign Office complaints, and they ground to a halt on US entry into the war (PRO file 371/44589; Wells 2003: 69ff.; for the background to the chemicals industry cases, see Reader 1975: chs. 23–4). They eventually led to a large number of consent decrees, and well-known landmark judgments (see Muchlinski 2007: 133–9). These notably established the 'effects' doctrine of jurisdiction, particularly in the *US* v. *Alcoa* case (Picciotto 1983; Chapter 2, at 2.2.2). Details of all antitrust cases initiated by the Justice Department (i.e. excluding private and FTC cases) are given in US *Bluebook* (1949), continued in CCH *Trade Regulation Reporter, Transfer Binder.*

Congress strengthened opinion in the USA of the need to dismantle the cartels. This view was developed in discussions with the British on planning the post-war economic order, which resulted in the Havana Charter (Joelson 1976: 841; discussed below). The UK Board of Trade also investigated international cartels, although the enactment of the Monopolies Act in 1948 was mainly the result of domestic considerations (Freyer 1992). In continental Europe, and especially in France and Germany, a post-war drive for 'modernization' of business practices, strongly influenced by US corporatism, was led by key policy-makers at the interface of the business economy and the state, notably Jean Monnet (Djelic 1998).[45]

In West Germany, the US post-war occupation administration set about both decartelization and deconcentration of industry, which were regarded as having been central to the 'militarist–industrialist clique' at the heart of Germany's war drive.[46] However, the drive for deconcentration became blunted, as a US policy of ensuring German business 'efficiency' overcame the fervour of the antitrust zealots (Wells 2003: 160ff.). The laws eventually implanted in West Germany dealt mainly with cartels and agreements between firms, with only minimal restraints against size or monopoly. Indeed, the antitrust transplant was grafted onto local rootstock, in the form of both Ludwig Erhard and the ordoliberal 'Freiburg School', which produced a special variant of corporatism in the 'social market' philosophy (Djelic 1998: 108ff.; Gerber 1998: ch. 7). This new German model of competition regulation came to wield considerable influence in Europe and beyond.

In Japan also the initial US drive to break up the main *zaibatsu* and some large firms was overridden by the view that economic recovery and industrial rebuilding should be prioritized. Although the anti-cartel and anti-monopoly law which the Diet agreed to pass in 1947 remained on the books, the Fair Trade Commission (FTC) it established waived through mergers re-creating large firms, and allowed the *zaibatsu* to be re-formed as *keiretsu* (Wells 2003: 185). In the 1960s, however, FTC

45 Gerber (1998: ch. 6) has argued that, with the exception of West Germany, most European countries in the post-war period adopted an 'administrative control' model of competition regulation; this overstates the differences, perhaps reflecting a US perspective in the 1990s critical of 'politicized' enforcement of EU competition law. All competition laws give a central place to an administrative agency; while such agencies may, to varying degrees, resist pressures to assume an industrial planning role, their policies and decisions are generally formed in the context of government policies; note for example the strong links between US antitrust and international trade policies.

46 Wells 2003: 139; this analysis was expounded in *Behemoth* (1942) by the neo-Marxist German refugee Franz Neumann, who worked for the US occupation authorities.

enforcement was reactivated in response to economic change, especially an increased concern for consumer protection; the Act was amended in 1977, with new powers against monopoly and concerted pricing; and the USA again pressed for active enforcement due to concerns in the 1980s about trade imbalances and 'structural impediments' to accessing the Japanese market (Matsushita 1993: 81–7). Although competition law had been planted in very different intellectual and institutional soil in Japan compared to Germany, over the next half-century there was considerable convergence between the two, as more active enforcement in Japan was counterpointed by its moderation in Germany (Haley 2001).

In Europe, decartelization was facilitated by the moves to creation of larger regional frameworks, first with the European Coal and Steel Community (ECSC), and then the European Economic Community (EEC). The ECSC was given strong anti-cartel powers, under provisions which were 'written in Washington and adopted as written',[47] and these made more palatable the dismantling of the German steel cartel (Wells 2003: 173–4). The EEC Treaty's provisions against anti-competitive behaviour became the basis for supranational regulation, especially once activated by the adoption of Regulation 17 by the Council of Ministers in 1962, which gave the European Commission direct powers of enforcement against restrictive agreements, subject only to review by the European Court of Justice (ECJ). This gave an impetus to EU law, and created a major new arena of business lawyering, fuelling the growth of transnational law firms, which in turn helped to mould the field (Morgan 2006). The Commission's Directorate-General for Competition (DGComp) became a pivotal institution, both within Europe and internationally. The procedures for prior notification and clearance of restrictive agreements in Regulation 17, although bureaucratically burdensome, gave DGComp extensive knowledge about markets, and powers to shape market structures. Its role also provided a powerful catalyst for the development of national competition laws. The adoption of competition laws was required of aspirants to EU membership, and many associated states also, leading to a lengthy process of international interaction and gradual convergence of principles. By the mid-1980s the system of parallel enforcement of EU and national Member State law began to change, with DGComp seeking a more effective multilayered coordination (Gerber 1998: ch. 10). This culminated in 2003, with a radical shift to decentralized enforcement of EU competition

---

47 According to Corwin Edwards, one of Thurman Arnold's acolytes, who was active in the post-war spread of the antitrust gospel (cited in Wells 2003: 173).

regulation, coordinated through a semi-formal European Competition Network (ECN) of national authorities orchestrated by DGComp.[48]

The creation of the ECN was surprising although perhaps appropriate. From a functionalist perspective, it is surprising that a more formal institutional structure could not be agreed to govern a matter which for over a half-century has been recognized as a central competence for European institutions, which were developed to establish formal multilevel governance precisely for such issues. Yet it seems appropriate that a regulatory arena which has been largely depoliticized, and in which there has been substantial ideological convergence, should be governed by networked regulation through an expert community. Thus, competition regulation is a prominent example of the transformation of the EU to a system of networked governance (Kohler-Koch and Eising 1999; Maher 2008).

4.3.2 Competitive interactions in competition regulation

Indeed, despite the spread of ideas and legal frameworks for regulating competition, and considerable convergence between their perspectives, the actual application of national laws to international business structures has generated conflicts. US antitrust laws became a potent weapon in a recurring series of high-profile politico-legal cases, from the US investigations of shipping conferences in the 1950s, to the attack by US state Attorneys-General in the 1990s on the terms offered for reinsurance by brokers at Lloyd's of London. The US laws are especially potent because they allow actions by private parties for triple damages, and so can be resorted to by firms themselves in their battles over markets. So Westinghouse brought an action in the late 1970s claiming that Rio Tinto and others had colluded over uranium pricing; while Laker Airways pursued its attempt to compete with British Airways by challenging in the US courts the system for allocation of routes by bilateral treaties under the umbrella of the IATA (Neale and Stephens 1988).

---

48 See Kassim and Wright 2009, who analyse the delicate negotiations resulting in this shift, and Ehlermann 2000, for the background to what he describes as a 'legal and cultural revolution'. The new legal provisions were adopted in Regulation 1–2003, which came into force in 2004, giving powers to national authorities to enforce EU law in this field, with provisions for cooperation such as information exchange; the Regulation mentioned the need for an ECN, but it was created by a non-legally-binding Joint Statement by the Commission and the Council, and its procedures established in a Commission Notice.

Denounced as 'antitrust imperialism' (Baker and Ayer 1993), the general issue of 'extraterritoriality' was taken up through the OECD, which attempted to agree general principles for moderation of jurisdictional claims (discussed in Chapter 2, at 2.2.2). The OECD also from 1967 established a specific procedural mechanism aiming to coordinate the application of competition laws to international business, which had limited success, but contributed to a process of creation of a policy community.[49] Conflicts indeed increased, with the spread and increased enforcement of competition laws. The 'effects' doctrine became widely accepted and applied, especially by DGComp and many European national authorities.[50] Indeed, the US Congress further expanded the jurisdictional reach of the Sherman Act to restrictive practices abroad affecting US exporters, in the Foreign Trade Antitrust Improvements Act of 1982, targeted mainly at Japan. Criteria were also stated for limiting these jurisdictional claims, notably the provision in the US law for 'direct, substantial and reasonably foreseeable' effects, which were reflected in the agreement reached in the OECD on the principle of 'moderation and restraint' in exercising concurrent jurisdiction (see Chapter 2, at 2.2.2). Nevertheless, the extensive areas of jurisdictional overlap created a complex arena for legal games, as competition authorities issued, revised and

---

49 Amended in 1979 and 1986, it provided for voluntary procedures for notification, exchange of information and coordination of action in cases when a member undertook an investigation under its competition laws which another member considered involved its 'important interests', and a procedure for consultations in such cases, with the ultimate possibility of conciliation by the relevant OECD Committee. Between 1976 and 1979 there was an average of 37 such contacts per year, which grew to 106 per year between 1980 and 1985, during which period there were 17 consultations, but no case was referred to the Committee (OECD 1987b: 6–8). Although information was exchanged in some cases, this was often impossible due to commercial confidentiality. The OECD instrument was complemented by a number of bilateral agreements, some of them formal treaties: US–Germany 1976; Australia–US 1982; France–Germany 1984; US–Canada MOU 1984.

50 OECD 1977: 37–8; Halverson 1991. The UK for long tried to insist on a stricter jurisdictional test, notably to resist the case brought by DGComp against ICI before the UK joined the EEC for involvement in a cartel of non-EEC firms. DGComp's explicit adoption of the effects principle, notably in the action against the Wood Pulp cartel in 1985, was slightly checked by the more diplomatic view of the ECJ that there must be some implementation within the territory; since this could take the form of sales, the difference was insubstantial (*Wood Pulp* (1988): para. 17; see also *Gencor* v. *Commission* (1999): para. 87; Chapter 2, at 2.2.2). In *Wood Pulp*, the ECJ did not go along with its Advocate-General, whose opinion elaborated and endorsed both the 'effects' principle and the criterion of 'direct and immediate, reasonably foreseeable and substantial effect'.

revoked policy guidelines,[51] and courts handed down differing judgments reinterpreting the jurisdictional criteria.

The potential for conflict and the need for cooperation were felt particularly acutely in the context of M&As, highlighted for example in the attempt by Gillette to acquire the Wilkinson Sword wet-shaving business in 1989 to 1991. Although the deal was carefully structured to try to comply with all applicable laws, it was nevertheless investigated in fourteen different OECD jurisdictions (OECD 1994a: 66–83). The EU attempted to rationalize its procedures by introducing in 1990 a Merger Regulation,[52] to establish a 'one-stop-shop' at least within the EU. The Regulation gave exclusive competence to DGComp over 'concentrations with a Community dimension', above a specified threshold of size and market share, with a requirement for prior notification and a two-stage screening process. Enforcement necessitated coordination even within the EU, by consultations through an Advisory Committee of Member State representatives.[53] The potential for conflict, even between DGComp and EU Member States, arises from the paradox that an enforcement agency is more likely to favour M&As between local firms in order to create 'national champions' in world markets; whereas DGComp tends to favour cross-border acquisitions, which a national authority may wish to resist. The tendency therefore is more often to approve than prohibit, which may help explain the low proportion of M&As blocked by DGComp.[54]

Armed with its new exclusive powers over mergers in the EU, in 1991 the European Commission negotiated an Agreement with the US Government for cooperation in competition law enforcement.[55] This built on

---

51 The Antitrust Enforcement Guidelines issued by the US Department of Justice reflected the twists and turns of US policy, including foreign trade concerns: the 1977 version asserted that US law could be applied against foreign restraints if either US consumers or exporters were affected; although this was confirmed by Congress in the 1982 Act, the 1988 Guidelines contained a footnote excluding enforcement if only exporters were affected; this policy was rescinded in 1992 (reflecting the US stance against Japan's 'structural impediments') as stated in the 1995 Guidelines.

52 Council Regulation 4064/89 of 21 December 1989 on the control of concentrations between undertakings.

53 This is a longstanding body, provided for in the Treaty of Rome since 1958.

54 In the first dozen years, the elite Merger Task Force of DG IV dealt with 2,200 notifications, over 90% were cleared unconditionally, some 7% conditionally, and 2% were prohibited or withdrawn to avoid prohibition; the proportions have been approximately similar in the USA (Levy 2003: 199).

55 The Commission considered that it had the power to conclude this as an 'administrative agreement' since it concerned an area of EU law in which it had sole competence; but the ECJ upheld an objection by the French government that, although the Commission has

the OECD procedures for notification and consultation when enforcement activities by one party may 'affect important interests' of the other, but with much more detail about the procedures, and provisions for regular information exchange, as well as cooperation and coordination of enforcement. It also spelled out principles of 'comity': first, an obligation to consider refraining from enforcement, based on taking specified factors into account, in order to avoid conflict with 'important interests' of the other party ('traditional comity'); and second a procedure by which one party could ask the other to take action against anticompetitive practices occurring within its territory adversely affecting the first party's 'important interests' ('positive comity').[56] Regular reports on the operation of the agreement have lauded the close cooperation established under its aegis, including 'frequent and intense' contacts between working officials, and frequent high-level meetings. There does seem to have been some effective coordination, especially in cases against cartels, generally to the detriment of the firms involved.[57]

Conflicts have remained, however, especially in M&As in some notably high-profile cases: the Boeing acquisition of McDonnell-Douglas in 1998 (cleared in the USA, but subjected to conditions in the EU); the proposed GE–Honeywell merger in 2001 (approved in the USA but blocked by DGComp);[58] and the monopolistic practices of Microsoft (case settled on lenient terms by the Department of Justice in 2002, but heavily fined and kept under continuing scrutiny by DGComp). Such cases led to complaints from US lawyers that the EU procedures give too much power

powers to negotiate international agreements, only the Council may conclude them (Case 327/91, decision of 9 August 1994); consequently, the Agreement was formally recast by an Exchange of Letters in 1995. This was a reminder to the Commission of the limitations on its powers; notably, the ECJ's strict views on confidentiality of information divulged to the Commission would inhibit information exchange, and the procedural requirements of the Merger Regulation mandate the Commission to take a decision according to a strict timetable, making coordination with US authorities difficult.

56 Introduced by a second agreement, negotiated in 1998, which however does not cover merger regulation.

57 Complaints by firms of double jeopardy because the Commission took no account of penalties applied in other jurisdictions when deciding on the level of fines have been rejected by the ECJ, which has pointed out that the positive comity provisions 'are confined to practical procedural questions like the exchange of information and cooperation between competition authorities and are not in the least related to the offsetting or taking into account of penalties imposed by one of the parties to those agreements' (*Showa Denko* (2006): para. 59).

58 To the surprise of the experienced but mainly US-based lawyers acting for the firms (Morgan 2006: 150–7).

to the Commission, and that its decisions were politicized rather than based on economic analysis. The Commission also suffered setbacks due to adverse decisions by the ECJ, and a review resulted in some procedural reforms, and the creation of the post of Chief Competition Economist in DGComp.[59]

These continuing conflicts also proved a catalyst for the formation of the International Competition Network (ICN) in 2001 (Djelic and Kleiner 2006: 297–8). Established as an informal venue for 'dynamic dialogue that serves to build consensus and convergence towards sound competition policy principles across the global antitrust community', it is a paradigm of a global regulatory community. Although its members are public bodies (competition authorities), it encourages participation of all types of expert, private practitioners, academics, representatives of business and consumer lobby groups. Nor is it alone. Also in 2001, the OECD established a Global Forum on Competition, aimed at capacity-building and outreach, and spreading best practices, deploying the OECD's preferred method of peer review. Meantime, professional practitioners had already in 1991 established through the International Bar Association a Global Forum for Competition and Trade Policy, including academics (especially economists), business representatives, practitioners, and former and current officials of competition agencies. Not to be outdone, an International Network of Civil Society Organizations on Competition was founded in 2003, to establish a 'network of stakeholders', on the initiative of the Indian-based NGO, Consumer Unity and Trust Society (CUTS).

4.3.3 Formal and informal coordination

Thus, after a half-century or more of professional proselytizing, there is general global ideological consensus on the broad principles and aims of competition regulation. There has been substantial convergence of the substantive laws (Horlick and Meyer 1995). Large numbers of specialists work in the field, and several semi-formal global forums have been established, for continuing debates and regular meetings of experts. Yet there has been little success in establishing a more formal global institutional framework for competition regulation, despite repeated attempts.

---

59 Morgan 2006: 157. Economic expertise had transformed antitrust policy earlier in the USA, at the Department of Justice (1960–80) and at the FTC (1970–80) (Eisner 1991).

Far-reaching provisions were included as Chapter V of the Havana Charter for an International Trade Organization drawn up in 1947. Chapter V would have obliged members both to enact and enforce domestic legislation, and to cooperate with the Organization, to combat 'business practices affecting international trade which restrain competition, limit access to markets, or foster monopolistic control'. It provided procedures for Member States to bring complaints against specified practices: price-fixing, territorial allocation of markets, discriminating against an enterprise, limiting production or fixing production quotas, agreements to block technological development, abuses of intellectual property rights, and 'any similar practices which the Organization may declare, by a majority of two-thirds of the Members present and voting, to be restrictive business practices'. Complaints would be dealt with by consultations aiming to reach 'mutually satisfactory conclusions', failing which an Investigation Procedure could be invoked, which if justified could result in 'hearings' on the complaint, with the ultimate power for the Organization to require that 'remedial measures' be taken by the Member State concerned.

Although the attempt to establish the ITO failed (as discussed in Chapter 8, at 8.1.1), the gospel of Chapter V continued to be preached. The demand in 1950 of the occupation administration that West Germany enact a competition law was based on its provisions (Djelic 1998: 107). The United Nations, at the urging of the USA, established a committee on Restrictive Business Practices (RBPs) in 1951, which within a couple of years produced a revised version of Chapter V as a basis for a proposed international organization. However, official US policy changed, to the chagrin in particular of the committee's American secretary, another New Deal antitruster, who complained that 'the United States has led a formidable march up the hill only to beat a retreat and leave its foreign associates stranded at the summit of achievement' (Timberg 1955: 411–12).[60] Not for the last time, the USA balked at a multilateral arrangement that it considered would fetter its freedom to act unilaterally, while being inadequate to restrain others.

Some twenty years later, a new impetus was given by the emergence of worldwide political concerns about TNCs. The UN Report of 1974

---

60 Some criticized the weakness of the provisions of the Havana Charter and in this treaty draft, since the US proposals of 1946 had been modified by others to remove the presumption of illegality for practices such as geographical market allocation (Timberg 1955; Dell 1990). Discussions about revisions of the GATT in 1954 to include provisions about RBPs, resulted only in a Decision in 1960 adopting a Consultation procedure if a state complained of RBPs affecting international trade (Joelson 1976: 844).

(mentioned at 4.2.3) referred to the TNCs' concentration of economic power, and abusive practices such as restrictive clauses in technology transfer agreements, and recommended negotiation of an international agreement. The interest of developed countries in regulating competition came together with the criticisms of developing countries of the abusive practices of TNCs, expressed for example in the programme for a New International Economic Order (NIEO) (Joelson 1976: 848ff.). Indeed, the lead was taken by UNCTAD, dominated by developing countries, which formulated the cumbersomely titled Set of Multilaterally Agreed Equitable Principles and Rules for the Control of Restrictive Business Practices (the RBP Principles). They were adopted by an UNCTAD conference, and also by a resolution of the UN General Assembly, in 1980. UNCTAD also formulated a Model Law, aimed at developing countries, based on the Principles and providing for a national competition law agency.

The RBP Principles included provisions that reflected the developing country perspective on TNCs: its definition of RBPs is based on 'abuse of a dominant position of market power', they cover abusive behaviour by a single firm (mergers, restrictive licensing conditions, discriminatory transfer prices), and include exhortations on TNCs to conform to local laws and consult with host states, and on developed countries to take account in the enforcement of their RBP laws of the interests of developing countries, especially in fostering infant industries and establishing regional arrangements. However, they contain nothing incompatible with US antitrust laws, or with their unilateral application 'extraterritorially', and there was sufficient 'balance' to satisfy the USA and other developed states (Davidow 1981). An institutional framework was established, through an UNCTAD committee consisting of an Intergovernmental Group of Experts, with provisions for consultations, studies and research, and making reports and recommendations to states. However, the Principles firmly stated that the committee should not 'act like a tribunal or otherwise pass judgement on the activities or conduct of individual Governments or of individual enterprises in connection with a specific business transaction', and 'should avoid becoming involved when enterprises to a specific business transaction [sic] are in dispute'.

The RBP Principles were a high watermark of the possibility of formulating global antitrust rules aimed at curbing corporate power, and the tide quickly receded. The first review conference, in 1985, was marked by strong disagreements, especially over state-supported restrictions such as export cartels (permitted by the USA under the Webb–Pomerene Act), and over the 'orderly marketing arrangements' by which developed states were restricting the surge of exports from newly industrializing countries (see Chapter 8, at 8.1.1). The conflicts blocked proposals for strengthening of the Principles. Thereafter, the work mainly consisted of encouraging the international spread of RBP laws, which was especially successful after 1989, so that the vast majority of countries enacted their own national competition law (WIR 1997: 189). By the 1990s, the UNCTAD efforts became largely subsumed to the prevailing global consensus, symbolized by the replacement of the term RBPs itself by 'competition', to describe both the Committee and the Principles.

A further attempt to establish a formal international agreement, to deal with the frequent frictions between competition and trade laws and policies, was made in the negotiations leading to the establishment of the World Trade Organization (WTO). Despite, or perhaps because of, the interactions between the two issues and the long lineage of forging a link dating back to the GATT (Fox 2003), it proved a step too far for the Uruguay Round. It was placed on the WTO agenda and raised at its 1996 Ministerial meeting in Singapore, as one of the 'new issues' linked especially to investment rules. Although a Working Group was established, progress was impossible, as not only were developing countries now adamantly opposed to adding more limbs to the WTO octopus, the USA still remained resistant, leaving the European Commission as the sole prominent advocate of a WTO competition agreement. As with the other 'WTO-Plus' issues, competition rules have been included instead in a number of the widening network of bilateral economic agreements (see Chapter 8, at 8.1.3).

4.3.4 Regulatory coordination by expert community

There are several possible explanations for the apparent paradox that, despite a widespread consensus around the broad principles of antitrust or competition law, repeated attempts to establish a more formal and binding 'hard law' framework have failed. National officials, lawyers and other professionals have considerable intellectual and material investments in their own systems, which perhaps they seek to protect; yet a WTO-linkage would not abolish those, and could even create a whole new lucrative field of trade-related competition law. TNCs experience at least inconvenience and expense, and sometimes major upsets, by their exposure to multiple and often overlapping laws; yet on the whole they have preferred to retain their freedom and power of manoeuvre within the legal labyrinths, rather than be the potential target of a global body with powers of investigation and even sanctions.

Surely, however, the creation over the past decades of a very extensive and deep-rooted 'epistemic community' of technical specialists should have laid a strong foundation for a formal interstate agreement, as some international relations theories predict? Yet the opposite seems to be the case. It seems that the technical specialists themselves are on the whole content with a system based on a strong ideological commitment to universalist principles embodied in soft-law instruments, which provide the basis for debate and application in a variety of enforcement arenas. Indeed, for these very reasons a more formal legal framework is unnecessary, and even if it existed, would merely establish more formal rules for the multi-level games played out in this arena. For it is the legal professionals who are the master interpreters, able to advance their client's cause in friendly rivalry with their opponents, mediating between different perspectives and interests and reaching accommodations, on the basis of common understandings forged from their social and intellectual habitus.

5

Corporate rights and responsibilities

The rapid international expansion of corporations in the second half of the twentieth century led to an intriguing double movement in the forms of business regulation. The dominant trend has been to facilitate that expansion, by liberalization of national controls on investment capital flows, accompanied by measures to strengthen international legal protection of the rights of owners of such investments. However, this has been counterpointed by a growth of regulation, both by home and host states, and increasingly through international regulatory networks.

This double movement took place in two phases. In the first, from the early 1950s to 1980, the liberalization of capital controls was gradual. This helped to pave the way for the renewed expansion of TNCs mainly from the USA and a few other capital-exporting states such as the UK, the Netherlands, France and Switzerland, and their home states also sought to strengthen the international legal protection of their foreign assets. However, this expansion quickly produced a reaction, both from host countries fearful of the effects of foreign economic domination, and from their own home countries (especially the USA), extending regulation to their foreign affiliates. Thus, TNCs found themselves subject to regulation by host and also home countries, which sometimes conflicted.

Amid considerable debate about how to treat these new 'world citizens', the main international response was a move to draw up codes of conduct. After 1980, as liberalization gathered pace and the universe of TNCs widened and deepened, there were increased pressures to remove national controls and apply investment protection rules to 'discipline' national regulation. Again there was a reaction, this time resulting in new and more complex forms of interlocking or networked regulation.

5.1 Liberalization, investment protection and national regulation

The 'embedded liberalism' of the Bretton Woods regime set in train a process of gradual liberalization, first of trade and then of capital flows (see Chapter 3, at 3.1.2). The partial liberalization was enough to stimulate renewed internationalization especially of US firms which already had some foreign activities, and this was spurred by factors such as the dismantling of cartels by the USA and the creation of the EEC (discussed in Chapter 4). In addition, TNCs greatly benefited from their low cost of capital, due to their access to 'offshore' finance, taking advantage of low bank reserve requirements and exploiting the opportunities for tax avoidance (discussed in Chapters 6 and 7).

5.1.1 Liberalization and investment protection

Much was done to pave the way for the expansion of FDI through the OECD, which became a grouping of richer capitalist countries, dealing with issues of economic and business governance.[1] The OECD's work on taxation led to the growth of a network of bilateral tax treaties aiming to eliminate international double taxation which was regarded as an obstacle to FDI (see Chapter 6, at 6.2.2). Most importantly, one of the earliest actions following the foundation of the OECD was a Decision by its Council in December 1961 adopting a Code of Liberalization of Capital Movements, and another on Invisible Transactions (i.e. services). These are 'bottom-up' instruments: they commit states to the

---

1 Its predecessor, the Organization for European Economic Cooperation was founded in 1948 to administer Marshall Aid, and also hosted the European Payments Union; it was re-established as the Organization for Economic Cooperation and Development in 1961, adding the USA and Canada to its eighteen West European country members; Japan joined in 1964, and then Finland (1969), Australia (1971) and New Zealand (1973); then Mexico (1994), the Czech Republic (1995), Hungary (1996), Poland (1996), Korea (1996) and the Slovak Republic (2000). In 2007 a further expansion drive saw accession talks begin with Chile, Estonia, Israel, Russia and Slovenia, while 'enhanced engagement' was granted to Brazil, India, China, Indonesia and South Africa; many other countries are also involved, on a selective basis, in its Global Forums, e.g. on competition and on tax cooperation. Decisions taken by the OECD Council, unlike its Recommendations, require unanimity and are regarded as binding, even though they do not take the form of an international treaty. Having no dispute-settlement mechanism, the OECD has developed procedures for monitoring of compliance through 'peer review' or mutual evaluation by teams of specialists from other member countries. The existence of the OECD provides its members with an alternative to the UN for coordinating economic and business regulation, and a means of anticipating action in UN bodies and forming a common front in them.

progressive abolition of restrictions as a general aim, while allowing the retention of existing controls which are declared and listed.[2] This system permitted great variation in the actual commitments by each state, which generally hardened only in the 1980s; notably in 1984 the Capital Movements Code was extended to cover the right of entry for foreign firms.[3] Overall, priority has been given to liberalizing foreign direct investment (FDI) and other long-term flows such as equity-related portfolio investments; many countries retained some controls on non-trade finance, deposits and derivative transactions by non-banks (OECD 2002c). The Codes also included an exhortation to extend liberalization to other IMF Member States. In practice, once gradual liberalization was begun it acquired unstoppable momentum, as the remaining controls could easily be avoided, especially by TNCs.[4]

5.1.1.1 Protection of foreign-owned property

Efforts to strengthen international legal obligations to protect foreign-owned property complemented liberalization. Such protection has been a matter of contention since the early nineteenth century, as investors and speculators, complaining about defaults on government bonds, cancellation of concessions, or nationalization of their businesses, turned to their home governments for political and often military support.[5] In practice,

2 The Capital Movements code exhaustively defines the types of restriction of inward and outward investment flows which are subject to this system of 'standstill and rollback'; in respect of most transactions (those in List A) a state can list an exception only when an item is added, or an obligation is extended or begins to apply to the state; restrictions may only be reintroduced if their withdrawal results in 'serious economic or financial disturbance', or as a temporary measure to deal with a balance of payments crisis. The Code requires non-discriminatory treatment of all non-resident-owned assets (i.e. most-favoured-nation (MFN) treatment), and freedom to liquidate assets and transfer proceeds. The Current Invisibles Code operates a similar system in relation to non-commodity trade, i.e. services.

3 This was done by adding, under Direct Investments, in the List A commitments (subject as usual to declared country-specific exceptions) a note extending it to national treatment (NT) of non-resident investors in respect of the granting of licences, concessions or other authorizations. The Current Invisibles Code also gives a right of establishment for branches and agencies of foreign insurers. For an overview and history of the Codes see OECD 1987c, 2002c.

4 Countries 'found their control systems undermined by increased financial sophistication on the part of firms and institutions' (OECD 2002c: 26); this undermined the fixed exchange rate system (Chapter 3, at 3.1.2).

5 However, such appeals were viewed with some caution, and the British government's policy was expressed in Lord Palmerston's famous statement in 1848 that 'the losses of imprudent

the experience has been that economic and commercial pressures generally provide a more effective remedy than political intervention, since states which are considered to have dealt unfairly with investors find it hard to borrow again on international markets. There could be good reasons for host governments to cancel concessions obtained under dubious circumstances, or to nationalize businesses in key economic sectors.

Latin American governments, in particular, put forward the Calvo doctrine, whereby foreigners were entitled to the same treatment as nationals, no more. This meant that foreign investors should accept that their rights would be governed by local law, and that they were not entitled either to diplomatic or military protection by their home country under international law. On the other hand, capital-exporting countries argued for a minimum standard of treatment under international law for foreign-owned property, which was essentially an attempt to establish the limits of legitimate action by host governments (Lipson 1985: 55).

This conflict came to a head in debates over the right to nationalization, which was asserted in the period of economic nationalism following decolonization. It was expressed especially as the 'right to permanent sovereignty over natural resources', embodied in a UN General Assembly resolution in 1962, and repeated in the CERDS in 1974 (see Chapter 2, at 2.2.3). These normative statements asserted that a state has the right to control all economic activity within its borders, but in the case of nationalization expressed a duty to pay 'appropriate' compensation, as decided by the law of the host state. In contrast, the international minimum standard demanded by the capital-exporting countries was based on the 'Hull formula', which specified that expropriation is lawful under international law only when carried out for a public purpose, without discrimination, and accompanied by 'prompt, adequate, and effective' compensation. In practice, compensation settlements were negotiated by states (most often on a lump-sum basis), which generally conceded some payments, but falling short of 'full' compensation. A number of cases were submitted to arbitration, and the arbitral awards generally reached a similar conclusion.[6]

men who have placed mistaken faith in the good faith of foreign governments would prove a salutary warning to others' (Lipson 1985: 44).

6 See Lillich and Weston 1975; Dolzer 1981; Schachter 1984; Weston et al. 1999. Penrose et al. 1992 show that from an economic perspective there is no absolute standard of the value of assets (especially a business), but it depends on the perspectives, purposes and assumptions of the parties (see also Hu 1980).

Nevertheless, home states pursued a variety of measures to protect the interests of their investors, ranging from overt and covert political interventions to the negotiation of investment protection treaties (Akinsanya 1980, 1987). Attempts to agree a multilateral convention generally produced only unratified drafts: even the OECD, which produced one in 1962, could agree in 1967 only to 'commend' the treaty to its members as a model for bilateral treaties (Muchlinski 1999). This alternative approach of negotiation of bilateral investment treaties (BITs) was initiated in 1959 by Germany, and then taken up by other European countries. These agreements were mainly political documents, attempting to strike a compromise with developing-country governments anxious to attract foreign investments (Guzman 1998: 653, 688).

5.1.1.2 The new Model BITs

The US Model BIT published in 1980, which was more extensively and tightly drafted in legal terms, was a shift towards hyper-liberalism. In particular it included the apparently innocuous obligation of pre-entry NT, which granted far-reaching rights of entry to investors, or the 'open door' principle. Previous BITs accepted the classical liberal international law principle that states are free to control the entry of foreigners. However, even the US BIT allowed each party to list exceptions, which could be substantial; although this required the negotiators to identify domestic regulations which the signatory wished to preserve from challenges.[7]

---

7 For example, the US–Egypt BIT of 1982 provided as follows:

Consistent with Article II paragraph 3, each Party reserves the right to maintain limited exceptions in the sectors it has indicated below:

The United States of America
Air transportation, ocean and coastal shipping; banking; insurance; government grants; government insurance and loan programs; energy and power production; use of land and natural resources; custom house brokers; ownership of real estate; radio and television broadcasting; telephone and telegraph services; submarine cable services; satellite communications.

The Arab Republic of Egypt
Air and sea transportation; maritime agencies; land transportation other than that of tourism; mail, telecommunication, telegraph services and other public services which are state monopolies; banking and insurance; commercial activity such as distribution, wholesaling, retailing, import and export activities; commercial agency and broker activities; ownership of real estate; use of land; natural resources; national loans; radio, television, and the issuance of newspapers and magazines.

Unsurprisingly, few countries signed up to the US model, although acceptance of its terms began to gain some ground in the early 1990s.[8]

That period saw a big rise in the negotiation of BITs generally, as their number jumped from 385 in 1989 to 2,265 in 2003, involving 176 countries, spreading in particular to Central and Eastern European countries, while they and some developing countries also concluded many BITs among themselves.[9] Although the main motive for doing so was the desire to attract foreign investment, studies showed some correlation with increased FDI but no clear causal link.[10]

The initial aim of investment protection treaties was to provide some reassurance to TNCs. Most BITs could be considered compatible with the powers of host states to regulate entry, impose ownership limitations or conditions, and specify performance requirements (Dolzer and Stevens 1995). Indeed, one analyst described them as embodying 'nationalism behind a liberal façade' (Vandevelde 1998b; see also Vandevelde 1998a). This began to change, especially when the USA introduced its more extensive BIT model, with its 'open door' requirement, although the vast majority of the increased number of BITs did not go so far. However, the pre-entry NT requirement raised the question of compatibility of BIT obligations with host state regulation; and this became more acute from the late 1990s with the rapid growth of claims against states by investors, which will be discussed further below.

---

8 By 2010, forty countries had ratified a BIT with the USA, but others which had signed had not ratified, including Russia which signed one in 1992; none of the rapid-growth economies in East Asia and Latin America had ratified a BIT with the USA, with the exception of Argentina (in 1991, entering into force in 1994). The Argentine treaty was a significant break-through, entailing the virtual abandonment of the Calvo doctrine, although as a remaining obeisance the treaty in its article III included a provision unusual for US BITs reserving the right to regulate the admission of investments 'provided, however, that such laws and regulations shall not impair the substance of any of the rights set forth in this Treaty'. Only Canada has followed the USA in including pre-entry NT in its BITs. Some IIAs include a right of establishment, but usually subject to lists of exceptions.

9 WIR 1997: 19; see UNCTAD's very useful database Investment Instruments Online, available at www.unctadxi.org. BITs are now considered to be part of a broader category of international investment agreements (IIAs); see below.

10 Salacuse (1990: 674) argued that BITs were one of several 'confidence-building measures'; quantitative studies have come to divergent conclusions, compare e.g. Neumayer and Spess 2005 and Gallagher and Birch 2006; see Sauvant and Sachs 2009 for a review of the research. An interesting contrast is between Argentina, which has 57 BITs and experienced a growth in FDI, but was surpassed by Brazil, which has never ratified any BIT.

5.1.2 Host-state regulation of foreign-owned business

The expansion of TNCs in the 1960s quickly led to political reactions and calls for controls on foreign ownership. These were strongest in former colonies, where it was felt that political independence should be followed by economic independence. Such claims were underpinned by populist or neo-Marxist theories of 'dependence' or 'underdevelopment' (Kitching 1989). These had considerable political resonance, expressing the view that integration into the world economy through TNCs would further exacerbate the economic imbalances and inequalities created by colonialism. Economic growth and development, it was widely felt, should come mainly from local entrepreneurship with state support, or (especially where a local entrepreneurial bourgeoisie was lacking) through direct state initiatives.

The strongest expression of economic nationalism took the form of nationalization especially in developing countries, which peaked in 1976 and then fell away. In a relatively small group of about ten countries nationalization was extensive, while in many more it was used as a selective policy instrument aimed at gaining control over what were regarded as key economic sectors, especially extractive and plantation industries (mining, petroleum, sugar), and utilities (Kobrin 1984). Many quickly hit serious obstacles, as state bureaucracies generally lacked the capacity, knowledge or skills to improve the management of enterprises acquired, either resulting in mismanagement, or necessitating the reintroduction of corporate managers under management contracts. Also, often having paid compensation for the acquired assets to ensure continued access to world markets, governments found that they had taken on the risks of fluctuations in world commodity prices. Paradoxically, however, as local managerial and technical capabilities improved, assisted by the experience of direct administration of enterprises, states gained increased confidence in their ability to achieve their policy aims through regulatory means rather than simply direct ownership (Kobrin 1984).

Many countries have deployed prohibitions on foreign ownership in specific economic sectors. Even the USA has maintained restrictions on foreign ownership in what are regarded as strategic industries, notably civil and maritime transport, telecommunications and broadcasting. In 1975 a governmental Committee was formed on Foreign Investment in the United States (CFIUS); and in 1988, amid political concern at increased Japanese economic power, Congress enacted the Exon–Florio amendment empowering the executive to suspend or prohibit any foreign acquisition of a US company which could 'impair national security'. Acting in the shadow of these powers, the CFIUS screens transactions especially in 'critical technology' industries, and has blocked or applied conditions to acquisitions of firms in sectors such as aircraft parts and semiconductors (Alvarez 1989). The process can be influenced by chauvinistic pressures, as occurred with the proposed acquisitions in 2005 of the oil firm Unocal by a subsidiary of the state-owned China National Offshore Oil Corporation, and in 2006 of the UK-based Peninsular and Oriental Steam Navigation Company (P&O), which ran terminal operations at six US ports, by Dubai Ports World.

Japan has also maintained both specific laws controlling investments in what were regarded as key industries (such as shipping, telecommunications and natural resources), as well as a general Control Law. Although this was liberalized in 1979, there remained an obligation to notify and powers of control in emergency situations (Matsushita 1993: 241ff.), and semi-formal controls continued. Canada enacted its Foreign Investment Review Act in 1973, establishing a screening process aiming to ensure that new inward investment was 'of significant benefit to Canada', aimed mainly at resisting US economic domination. Australia also screens foreign inward investment, and is now especially wary of Chinese acquisitions in its natural resource firms.

Whereas developed countries aimed to protect local control of what they regarded as key industries, many developing countries aimed to stimulate local ownership in appropriate sectors, often those with low barriers to entry, and to support local participation in foreign-owned firms introducing important technology or know-how. Such controls could be flexible, as with India's introduction in 1973 of the requirement to obtain permission from the Reserve Bank for any firm with over 40 per cent foreign ownership to carry on business in India, backed by general Guidelines for its application. Some states established administrative agencies to screen applications to make investments, and apply conditions when it was considered desirable (Muchlinski 2007: 201–13). Others classified economic sectors and specified the proportion of foreign ownership permitted, as with the Nigerian Enterprises Promotion Acts of the early 1970s (Muchlinski 2007: 185). Some states went further and specified the promotion of specific local groups, as in Malaysia's *bumiputra* policy, based on dubious ethnic criteria (Sornarajah 2004: 120).

While this type of provision aimed to encourage indigenous private ownership, others aimed at sharing control between the host state and the foreign firm, by requiring joint ventures with local state-owned firms (as with China's joint venture laws mentioned in Chapter 4, at 4.1.1). State-socialist countries in eastern Europe adopted similar laws. Many of these laws were relaxed or removed in the early 1990s.

The effects of such controls were generally to contribute to the emergence of a local entrepreneurial class, while legitimating the entry of TNCs during a period of hostility to foreign firms.

Other types of host country regulation have aimed at ensuring that inward investment contributed to national economic development. Many countries have subjected inward investment to 'performance requirements'. These are generally aimed at ensuring that foreign-owned firms establish a significant local presence and generate 'spread effects', for example by requiring that assembly plants such as auto firms use a specified level of local content, and are not limited to 'screwdriver' operations. Such conditions are often linked to and expressed in terms of the impact on the balance of payments or the balance of trade, requiring that foreign-owned firms maintain a balance or surplus on their foreign exchange or trade accounts (Guisinger 1985). Such controls interact with international trade rules, which may have the same effect. For example, anti-dumping rules may be applied to products locally assembled from imported components and sold at marginal cost prices. Rules of origin can be used to refuse a low-tariff rate or preference to goods assembled in a low-wage country (e.g. Malaysia) by a firm exporting components from its home base (e.g. Japan) (Nicolaïdis 1991).

Such host country controls are also complemented by incentives offered to attract foreign investment, if it takes a form considered to contribute to employment or economic development. In this respect richer countries have the advantage of being able to offer upfront benefits, sometimes including public funds to support R&D, or to ensure location of a new plant in a region of high unemployment. Such incentives are particularly criticized because they are often discretionary and secretive. Poorer countries generally have to resort to incentives in the form of 'tax expenditures', i.e. tax advantages such as generous depreciation allowances, or even tax holidays, which do not require an immediate outlay, but reduce future state revenue. Such incentives exist due to the competition to attract inward investment (see Chapter 6, at 6.4.1). Although incentives are sometimes defended, like other forms of regulatory competition it is generally considered that some agreed limits would be highly desirable (Charlton 2003). Within the EU the state aids rules establish some curbs on this competition, but no substantial attempt has been made to develop a multilateral regime.[11] Indeed the wording of BITs prevents them from acting in this way (see below at 5.2.1.2).

5.1.3 Transnationalization of home-state regulation

The international expansion of TNCs also brought with it regulation by their home states, extending to their foreign operations, especially by the USA. The politicization during the 1970s of the activities of TNCs also led to new types of home-state regulation of their foreign operations. Initially, the application by home countries of their regulation to activities taking place abroad brought accusations of 'extraterritoriality', and resulted in jurisdictional conflicts (discussed in Chapter 2, at 2.2.2). However, the result in many cases was the exportation of similar forms of regulation to other countries, and the growth of international regulatory networks. A good example is antitrust or competition regulation, which was discussed in the previous chapter.

Technology export controls, developed especially by the USA, also led to complaints about the application of 'long-arm' laws. Born during the Cold War, and mainly targeted at the USSR, these controls were coordinated between states mainly through an informal committee linked to NATO referred to as Cocom (Adler-Karlsson 1968). Nevertheless, the US controls regularly caused conflicts with allied states due to both their wide scope (they applied to 'dual use' technologies, such as powerful computers), and their extent – they applied to sales by the foreign affiliates of US TNCs, and indirectly even to foreign purchasers or licensees of such technology.[12] Thus, purchasers outside the USA of items such as supercomputers could find themselves subject to visits by US government inspectors.

The post-Cold War concern with proliferation of weapons of mass destruction saw the emergence of four regulatory networks, the Nuclear Supplier's Group, the Wassenaar Arrangement for conventional weapons, the Australia Group concerned with chemical and biological weapons, and the Missile Technology Control Regime. These have each experienced

11 The OECD Declaration and Decision on Multinational Enterprises of 1976, which formulated the Guidelines on MNEs (discussed below), included an 'instrument' on International Investment Incentives and Disincentives, which provides that if a state considers that its interests are adversely affected by another state adopting such measures it can request consultations, to examine the possibility of reducing such effects to a minimum.
12 Jurisdictional conflicts have been discussed in Chapters 2, at 2.2.2 and 4, at 4.3.2. The OECD Declaration and Decisions on MNEs of 1976 also included a Decision establishing a procedure for consultation between states in the event of such conflicting requirements.

considerable difficulties of coordination among the states involved in them, and they also operate largely independently of each other (Joyner 2004).

5.1.3.1 International corruption

The issue of bribery and corruption was dramatized when a scandal erupted in 1975 in the USA about corporate bribery abroad. Investigations into company accounts by the US Securities and Exchange Commission (SEC), in the wake of the 'Watergate' inquiries into President Nixon, resulted in admissions by over 400 US corporations of foreign bribery totalling over $300m. The most striking revelations concerned Lockheed Aircraft, at that time the largest US defence contractor, which was shown to have bribed a wide range of officials, the most eminent being President Giovanni Leone of Italy, Prince Bernhard of the Netherlands and Prime Minister Tanaka of Japan (Schroth 2002).

The global ramifications led to statements condemning bribery by bodies such as the UN General Assembly, but the most concrete action was the enactment by the USA of the Foreign Corrupt Practices Act 1977 (FCPA). This outlawed bribery of foreign government officials, and provided for extensive controls over not only US TNCs (including foreign affiliates), but any company issuing securities in the USA or in some other way under the SEC's jurisdiction. The accounting requirements enable the SEC to require disclosure of corrupt payments made anywhere in the world, providing it with a powerful enforcement tool, even against foreign companies if their shares are listed on a US exchange.[13] The SEC is spurred to use the very broad jurisdictional scope of the US law, because US firms complain that the FCPA makes them lose business to their foreign competitors. However, US efforts to negotiate multilateral arrangements, especially through the OECD, were rebuffed by its European allies, until the mid-1990s when a new wave of international scandals created fresh political pressures. These resulted first in an agreement to deny tax deductibility to such corrupt payments, and then a multilateral convention signed in 1997 (OECD 2000a).

The OECD Convention on Combating the Bribery of Foreign Public Officials leaves considerable leeway for states to decide the scope of

---

13 So, for example, the SEC brought an action in 1996 against the Italian firm Montedison, whose shares traded in New York via depositary receipts, for false accounting in disguising in its accounts $400m. of bribes, all paid outside the USA (Schroth 2002: 599). The SEC also uses its powers to impose extensive compliance procedures in consent decrees (Schroth 2002: 608–9).

the offence. The definition of bribery covers giving an 'undue pecuniary or other advantage' to obtain an 'improper advantage' from a foreign public official. Some states (including the USA) consider that this does not include small 'facilitation payments' made to induce public officials to perform their functions, and this has been accepted in the official Commentary on the Convention.[14] Acts committed abroad by their own nationals must be covered only if the state's jurisdiction can extend that far; and a firm which wins business due to payments made abroad by its foreign affiliates, or by middlemen, would fall within the definition only if 'complicity in, including incitement, aiding and abetting, or authorisation' can be shown. This requires evidence of knowledge by the parent company or its officials, which is much easier to obtain if there are administrative requirements to report payments, such as those in the US law, but the treaty does not require this.

The 'peer review' process developed for this convention, which is regarded in OECD circles as exemplary, involves continuing scrutiny by the Working Group on Bribery of national laws and their enforcement. Nevertheless, the legalization process has proved very slow in many countries, even close allies of the USA which pride themselves for being in the forefront of anti-bribery efforts, notably the UK.[15] To complement these OECD pressures, the US authorities have vigorously enforced their own laws, applying them also to non-US TNCs which came within their scope, notably the German electronics firm Siemens, Mercedes (an affiliate of the US-German firm Daimler-Chrysler) and the UK aerospace and defence

---

14 Para. 9; see the discussion in the UK Law Commission's report, which recommended that in the UK this should be handled through 'sensible use of the discretion not to prosecute' (UK Law Commission 2008: 89).

15 The UK government at first took the view that its existing law was adequate (though dating back to the early twentieth century). This was criticized by the OECD peer review in June 2000; although the Anti-terrorism, Crime and Security Act 2001 extended jurisdiction to acts of bribery committed abroad by UK nationals or firms incorporated under UK law, it did not extend to foreign affiliates or agents. The OECD peer review in 2005 again criticized the UK law as 'characterised by complexity and uncertainty', and again in 2008 detailed the continuing failure to implement the Convention. The UK law was again reviewed (UK Law Commission 2008), leading to more comprehensive reform proposals; evidence on the draft Bill was given in June 2009 to a joint Parliamentary Committee by OECD officials, as well as representatives of civil society organizations (UK Parliament 2009). The legislation finally enacted in 2010 makes it an offence for a UK commercial organization to fail to prevent bribery, even if done on its behalf by an associated person (including an affiliate or agent), unless it can show that it had in place adequate preventive procedures; and it requires the Minister to issue guidance about such procedures. Unsurprisingly, representatives of the large accounting firms were quick to publicize the need for firms to ensure they had such procedures in place (Kenyon 2009).

contractor BAE. The combination of unilateral action and requests for cooperation has begun to lead to some joint enforcement, involving other authorities as well as the USA; this was seen in 2010, when Russian investigators raided the offices of US firm Hewlett-Packard in Moscow at the request of German authorities inquiring into alleged bribery involving computer sales from HP's German operations to the Russian prosecutor general's office.[16]

The UK criminal prosecution authorities also undertook an investigation of BAE, spurred by persistent reports of bribery in connection with the Al-Yamamah arms deal with Saudi Arabia, the UK's biggest-ever export deal, negotiated by Margaret Thatcher, and reported to have earned BAE more than £40bn (O'Connell 2006; Williams 2008). Prosecutors initially resisted pressures that they should put a halt to their inquiries on national interest grounds, citing article 5 of the Convention, which specifies that enforcement 'shall not be influenced by considerations of national economic interest, the potential effect upon relations with another State or the identity of the natural or legal persons involved'.[17] Their objections were overcome by an intervention by Prime Minister Tony Blair invoking national security interests. A legal challenge by civil society organizations resulted in a decision by the Court of Appeal that this intervention was unlawful interference with the rule of law (*Al-Yamamah* (2008a)); but this decision was reversed in the House of Lords, on the grounds that UK national security concerns could overrule the OECD convention (*Al-Yamamah* (2008b)).[18] BAE continued to be pursued on other bribery allegations, but a veil was drawn over it when the case was settled in 2010, with a payment of $400m. to the US Justice Department, and a more modest £30m. to the UK's Serious Fraud Office.[19]

16 Schäfer and Waters 2010; though some sources emphasized Russian reluctance to act on bribery (Kramer 2010).
17 Suggestions that the provisions of art. 5 should be incorporated into the legislation going through parliament at the time were resisted by the Joint Committee, but it recommended that the guidelines on prosecution should refer to the article.
18 The decision was robustly defended in the arms trade press, on the grounds that the separation of powers requires not only judicial independence, but also responsibility of the executive for political matters, and that 'if the British Government comes to the conclusion that it is in the national interest for a British company to be allowed (or, which might well have been the case here, to be instructed) to "bribe" a highly-placed and influential member of the Saudi royal family, which actually is in view of local customs and requirements, then this is and should remain the British Government's decision alone' (Bonsignore 2008: 9).
19 Despite the heavy fine, the dropping of the investigation removed the threat that if indicted BAE would be disqualified from federal government contracts in the USA, and probably

Indeed, revelations of dubious connections between politicians and business have hit headlines around the world, especially since the 1990s. In France, investigations begun in 1994 of the state-owned oil company Elf-Aquitaine (privatized in 1997), eventually resulted in criminal trials of thirty-seven people in 2003, which showed that managers embezzled approximately €400m., both to enrich themselves and to finance campaigns and bribe leading figures in France and Africa. The revelations embroiled many senior politicians, both in France (extending to prime ministers, regardless of party) and abroad (including Presidents Kohl of Germany, Omar Bongo of Gabon and Sassou-Nguesso of the Congo), and cast much light on the dysfunctional aspects of the nested networks linking the various groups of the French policy elite (Heilbrunn 2005). In Italy, the 'Mani Pulite' investigations initiated in 1992 by magistrate Antonio di Pietro laid bare many of the tangled connections between politics, business and crime in that country, extending even to the Vatican. Although this resulted in the demise or transformation of most of the existing political parties, it also provided the catalyst for the entry into politics of Silvio Berlusconi, who personally embodied a powerful combination of business and politics. In Germany, the engineering group Siemens was found to have engaged in illegal practices involving €1.3bn of suspected payments to officials around the world to win contracts, and the scandal cost the firm in excess of €2bn in legal fees and fines paid to the US and German authorities.

Even at the global level, the $64bn oil-for-food programme for Iraq, initiated by the UN Security Council at the behest of the USA in 1995, was dogged by allegations of corruption in several countries, reaching up to Kofi Annan, the UN Secretary-General. Eventually in 2004 the UN set up an Independent Inquiry Committee led by Paul Volcker, which identified extensive illicit payments, in the form of surcharges paid in connection with oil contracts obtained by 139 of the 248 companies, and kickbacks in 2,253 of the 3,614 contracts for humanitarian aid (Volcker *et al.* 2005). These included the Australian Wheat Board, the largest supplier to Iraq with $2.3bn of sales under the programme, which accounted for 14 per cent of the kickbacks (Volcker *et al.* 2005: 262).

---

also in the EU (Williams 2008). The UK investigations included the allegation that a commission of $12m. was paid into a Swiss bank account to secure a $40m. contract for a military radar system for Tanzania, of which Clare Short, a Cabinet Minister at the time of the deal, later said 'It was always obvious that this useless project was corrupt' (Leigh and Evans 2007).

There has nevertheless been considerable resistance from governments to proposals for a formal international convention. No doubt they feared to accept binding obligations which might upset the delicate patterns of patronage and favours linking economic and political power, which maintain the power of elites everywhere. Efforts within the UN, mainly initiated by the USA, resulted in the draft of a treaty on Illicit Payments produced by a committee of the Economic and Social Council (ECOSOC) in 1979, but the initiative ran into the sands. Twenty years later, however, once the pressure became irresistible, a variety of treaties quickly emerged, in addition to that of the OECD already discussed. An Inter-American Convention against Corruption was signed in 1996; the EU, which had been mired in its own corruption allegations and scandals, in 1997 adopted a convention on the fight against corruption involving EU or Member State officials; in 1999 the Council of Europe concluded conventions for both criminal and civil law provisions against corruption, stating in broad terms the measures to be implemented in their domestic laws by states accepting these treaties; and in 2003 the African Union agreed a Convention on Preventing and Combating Corruption. Finally, a new initiative in the UN, under the auspices of its Office on Drugs and Crime (UNODC), in 2003 produced the UN Convention Against Corruption, entering into force in 2005.[20]

Much had been done to prepare the ground for these formal undertakings by the development of a worldwide policy arena, with networks, meetings and conferences. An International Anti-Corruption Conference has assembled biannually since the first meeting in 1983 held in Washington, DC, with US agencies taking the lead. Now, according to the website of its meeting in 2010, the Conference 'brings together royalty, heads of state, civil society and the private sector to tackle the increasingly sophisticated challenges posed by corruption' with over 1,500 participants from 135 countries. Since the 1980s, there has indeed been a spread of national anti-corruption bodies in many countries, of an official character but often substantially independent of the central government, and sometimes at war with high-ranking politicians.

A key role has been played in stimulating, supporting and coordinating this field by Transparency International (TI), founded in 1993 mainly by former World Bank staff led by Peter Eigen, which became a global

---

20 Although five years later it had been ratified by 143 states ranging from Afghanistan to Zimbabwe, a number of leading states had not yet done so, notably Germany, Ireland, Japan, Lichtenstein and New Zealand.

coalition with chapters in over ninety countries. Shortly afterwards, the World Bank itself overcame its previous scruples about respecting national sovereignty, and in 1996 its President, James Wolfensohn, launched a Governance and Anti-Corruption Programme, utilizing what the website describes as 'a multi-disciplinary approach' and 'rigorous empirical diagnostics and analysis'.[21]

The activities of anti-corruption agencies have involved often politically difficult and sometimes personally highly dangerous investigations of murky dealings at the interface of politics and profit. Nevertheless, the legalization of anti-corruption too often seems only to have provided political leaders and factions with new weapons to wield against their opponents, both high and low. New leaders almost routinely come into power vowing to clean up the legacy of sleaze left by their predecessors, but decisions on who is prosecuted for corruption and who remains in power owe as much to political as legal factors.[22] The stark anomaly of countries where bribery is known to be widespread nevertheless being parties to relevant treaties and having a full panoply of anti-corruption laws is alluded to in the anecdote often retold in anti-corruption meetings, of the delegate from such a country saying that he had nothing to report because 'bribery is illegal in my country'.

Policy and research in the field have also rested on weak foundations. Despite the clear evidence that politics and business are entangled in all countries, often in manifestly corrupt ways, attention has mostly been focused on the 'demand side' of bribe-takers, mainly in developing countries. Relatively simplistic diagnoses have viewed the problem as rooted in autocratic political systems and the failures of state-led developmentalism, and have prescribed multi-party liberal democracy and liberalized

---

21 See also Rose-Ackerman 2006; on the Bank's 'governance turn', see Chapter 3, at 3.1.3; some concerns about corruption had been expressed earlier, see World Development Report 1983: ch. 11.

22 For example, French President Sarkozy's prosecution of former Prime Minister Dominique de Villepin and associates in the 'Clearstream' affair; they were acquitted in January 2010, despite Sarkozy's statement on prime-time television that the defendants were 'clearly guilty'. In Russia, Vladimir Putin confirmed his hold on power partly by his ruthless pursuit of some of the former 'oligarchs', notably the prosecution and imprisonment for fraud and tax evasion of Khodorkovsky and Lebedev (see Chapter 3, at 3.2.2). These instances can be multiplied by more modest examples: among my own personal friends and close acquaintances in different countries in Africa, two have been forced from high official posts due to accusations of bribery which, whatever their rights and wrongs, reflected political faction-fighting.

economies (Szeftel 1998). The tendency to overlook often deeply prob-lematic features of liberal democracy in developed countries, especially political party finance arrangements and other ways for business to buy access and influence, invites cynical responses from politicians in devel-oping countries who often regard their own behaviour as on a par with that of their richer country brethren.

Only more recently has attention been redirected towards an analysis which also includes the 'supply side' role of the corporations as the bribe-givers.[23] This shift was reflected also in the stance of TI, which strongly influenced received opinion and research by launching its Corruptions Perception Index in 1996, providing an annual 'league table' of countries where bribery is considered prevalent, which was seized upon by news editors, and for data by researchers. Following criticism of both the focus and the methodology of this Index,[24] TI also began in 1999 to publish a Bribe Payers Index (ranking the home countries of TNCs seen as most likely to bribe abroad), although this has been less well publicized, and is based on similar methodology. For its part, academic analysis has been split between treating the issue as one of business ethics or of criminality. Both perspectives tend to overlook the ways in which structural inter-twining of business and the state dominated by the pursuit of private profit breeds corrupt practices.

5.1.3.2 Transnational corporate liability

The application of home-country laws to TNCs' activities abroad has also occurred through private law, driven mainly by activist or business-seeking lawyers. The US courts in particular have been regarded as a favourable forum for personal injury suits, as US procedures allow lawyers to act on a contingent-fee basis, permit class actions on behalf of often

---

23 See for example Baughn et al. 2010, analysing the propensity to bribe according to the countries of origin of TNCs, including both domestic (their economic development, culture and domestic corruption) and international factors (those countries' patterns of trade and involvement in international accords); and Calderon et al. 2009, who find that the host-state 'investment climate' is not the decisive factor.

24 Constructing quantitative data from subjective perceptions has obvious limitations; the methodology was defended by World Bank researchers who appear to have originated its use in the context of governance and corruption, on the grounds that better data are hard to compile, and that 'subjective perceptions of governance often matter as much as the legal reality' (Kaufman et al. 2005: 17). Despite their limitations, the data have been enthusiastically used in many studies; for an analysis of the politics, and the political impact, of TI's Perceptions Index see Andersson and Heywood 2009.

large groups of similarly situated plaintiffs, grant extensive rights of discovery to obtain evidence, and use juries in such cases which result in high
awards of damages, including punitive damages in some circumstances.
Historically, it was relatively easy for a foreign plaintiff to sue in US courts:
there was a right to sue if the defendant was a US legal person, unless it
could be shown to be an abuse of the court process; and even non-US
persons could be sued if they had sufficient contacts with the jurisdiction.
From the mid-1970s, however, decisions by the higher US courts began
to restrict this wide jurisdictional scope.[25] US TNCs, which themselves
have been adept at exploiting strategies of forum selection (as discussed
in Chapter 3, at 3.2.2), succeeded in persuading judges that the US courts
should not be too welcoming, especially to foreign plaintiffs.

This was dramatized by the *Bhopal* case, resulting from an explosion
and massive gas leak at a Union Carbide pesticide plant in Bhopal (India)
during the night of 2 December 1984. This was the worst single-incident
industrial disaster in history, with the possible exception of the Chernobyl
nuclear plant failure, causing an immediate death toll of 2,500, while the
poisonous gas led to many more deaths, some 30,000 to 40,000 maimed
or seriously injured and hundreds of thousands affected.[26] Within days,
dozens of US lawyers had arrived on the scene, signing retainers with
thousands of victims, and hundreds of legal claims were begun in US
courts, notably a class action for $15bn filed by Melvin Belli, the well-
known personal injury specialist. In India, the morning after the disaster,
five of the plant's managers were arrested and charged with causing death
by negligence, and a police investigation launched. Although a public
inquiry was instituted by the state, the main focus quickly became the
legal cases, especially the compensation claims.

25 As regards claims in US courts against foreign corporations, moves to expand the jurisdiction of state courts (which are the main venue for private litigation) were checked
by decisions of US federal courts, insisting on a stricter application of the constitutional
'due process' principle, so that a foreign legal person could not be liable to suit unless
this could be considered fair in view of the contacts with the jurisdiction (Hay 1986).
The landmark decision was *Worldwide Volkswagen* (1980), in which the Supreme Court
rejected a claim against Volkswagen's German affiliate Audi, for an accident allegedly
caused by explosion of a faulty fuel tank. For foreign plaintiffs, the principle of *forum non
conveniens* was strengthened to deny claims in US courts against US defendants unless a
proposed alternative forum would be clearly inadequate or unsatisfactory (see discussion
of the *Bhopal* case below).

26 Cassels 1993: 5; many articles and books have been written on the subject, I rely here
mainly on the careful and scholarly study by Cassels; an important early analysis was Baxi
1986; see also Baxi 1999.

The Bhopal plant was owned and operated by Union Carbide India Limited, an affiliate of Union Carbide Corporation (UCC) of New York, which owned 50.9 per cent of its shares (due to India's restrictions on foreign ownership). Within months of the event, the Indian central government enacted the Bhopal Gas Leak Disaster Act, aiming to manage the claims equitably and efficiently, by giving the government the exclusive right to represent the victims both within and outside India, while preserving the right of individuals also to retain their own lawyers. The 145 actions in the USA involving some 200,000 claimants were consolidated, and by May 1986 came before Judge Keenan in the Southern District Court of New York.[27] The issue was jurisdiction, with Union Carbide arguing that the action should be transferred to India as the more convenient forum. Keenan's judgment confirmed the shift in US jurisprudence against the right of foreign plaintiffs to sue a US defendant in US courts. He ruled that, provided an adequate alternative forum was available, it was a matter of weighing what contacts the case had with each jurisdiction, and the private and public interest factors involved. He easily concluded that the case should transfer to India, where the 'overwhelming majority of the witnesses and evidence' could be found, but also because of the administrative burden of the litigation on the courts and its excessive cost to US taxpayers.[28]

The heavy ironies of the case were underlined when UCC deployed two eminent Indian lawyers to argue in favour of the Indian legal system, in response to evidence on behalf of the Indian government by a leading US academic, Prof. Marc Galanter, as to its own system's endless delays and inefficiency (see also Galanter 2002). Undeniably, the reaction to the disaster was transformed by the prospect of obtaining relatively high levels of compensation through the highly effective US tort law system. In February 1989 UCC and the government of India reached a settlement for $470m.; although criticized as inadequate (Bhagwati 1989), it was higher than the $370m. offered in New York, which the US lawyers had been willing to accept. However, the bureaucratic process of evaluating

---

27 Judge Keenan stressed that none of the lawyers on the Executive Committee appointed by the court to represent the claimants were among 'those members of the American bar who travelled the 8,200 miles to Bhopal in those months [who] did little to better the American image in the Third World – or anywhere else' (*Bhopal* case (1986): fn. 1).

28 However, the dismissal was conditional on UCC submitting to the jurisdiction of the Indian courts and agreeing to satisfy any judgment there, and accepting US civil procedure rules (including discovery); these conditions were overturned on appeal (*Bhopal* case (1987)).

claims and distributing the money was time-consuming and resulted in payments to victims that were very low, certainly by US standards (Jayaprakash 1990, 1993). Thus, the *Bhopal* case raised the broader debate of whether the legalization of the case offered only what Cassels, echoing the Supreme Court of India, described as law's 'uncertain promise', which was at most only partially fulfilled, or whether transnational lawyering bringing to bear the power of private law could be an important element in achieving some significant compensation for victims and a degree of corporate accountability (Galanter 2002).

Following *Bhopal*, transnational anti-corporate litigation became more politicized, in different ways. In the USA, it became caught up in the debate about the reform of tort law, as exemplified in litigation in Texas on behalf of Central American plaintiffs. A case against chemicals companies Dow and Shell on behalf of farmworkers in Costa Rica exposed to a pesticide banned in the USA (known as DBCP) resulted in a narrow 5:4 decision in the Texas Supreme Court rejecting the *forum non conveniens* principle (*Dow* v. *Alfaro* (1990)). One of the majority judges, Lloyd Doggett, known as both a liberal and a supporter of the personal injury bar (Bloom 2001: 99) delivered a stirring opinion, forthrightly denouncing the principle as a means of 'immunizing multinational corporations from accountability for their alleged torts causing injury abroad':

> The banana plantation workers allegedly injured by DBCP were employed by an American company on American-owned land and grew Dole bananas for export solely to American tables. The chemical allegedly rendering the workers sterile was researched, formulated, tested, manufactured, labelled and shipped by an American company in the United States to another American company. The decision to manufacture DBCP for distribution and use in the third world was made by these two American companies in their corporate offices in the United States. Yet now Shell and Dow argue that the one part of this equation that should not be American is the legal consequences of their actions.
>
> (*Dow* v. *Alfaro* (1990): 681)

However, business pressures overcame the resistance of the personal injury lawyers in the Texas legislature, which restored the *forum non conveniens* principle into Texas law in 1993, although the Costa Rican workers apparently achieved a very substantial settlement (Bloom 2001: 103).

This type of case began a conversion of personal injury litigation into 'cause lawyering' (Bloom 2001), which also occurred outside the USA. In the UK, one London solicitors' firm in particular, Leigh Day & Co., built a substantial reputation for mass tort claims against UK TNCs on behalf of foreign plaintiffs. It waged a number of successful legal campaigns, especially on behalf of workers and communities in South Africa affected by harmful substances, particularly against Thor Chemicals (mercury), and Cape plc (asbestos). The cases involved significant legal creativity. The reluctance of English law to 'pierce the corporate veil' and hold a parent company liable for actions of a subsidiary meant that legal actions became focused on the direct liability of the parent.[29] This creates practical problems of collecting evidence, but it has the added advantage that it helps to overcome the related jurisdictional obstacle, since the legal issues now concern the actions and decisions taken by the parent company in its own jurisdiction.[30] The English courts considered that the appropriate forum should be the one in which the case could be tried more suitably for the interests of all the parties and for the ends of justice. In a key decision, the House of Lords held that the asbestos litigation could proceed in the UK because the claimants would be denied access to justice in South Africa, due to the lack of legal aid there, which was available to them in the UK.[31]

With the shift to cause lawyering, legal cases against TNCs broadened to encompass violations of human rights. In the USA, enterprising lawyers

---

29 In the South African asbestos cases, the claim was reformulated during the first Court of Appeal hearing, to focus on the parent company's direct liability for failing to take proper steps against the dangers of asbestos, of which it already knew (speech of Lord Bingham, *Lubbe* v. *Cape* (2000)).

30 The US courts in the *Bhopal* case did not squarely face the issue of whether the claim concerned UCC's responsibilities for designing the plant or UCIL's for its operation, or indeed whether the firm was so closely integrated that it should be treated as an integrated entity.

31 *Lubbe* v. *Cape* (2000); this built on the decision in *Connelly* v. *RTZ* (1997); see Meeran 1999; Muchlinski 2001. Subsequently, as funding became available in South Africa, cases were also brought there, notably against Anglo American on behalf of miners suffering from silicosis (Meeran 2009: 3). Attempts by business lobbies to block access to UK courts for such cases, on the grounds that it is damaging to British business, have so far failed. Indeed, in 2005 the ECJ held that under the Brussels Convention of 1968 which governs civil and commercial jurisdiction among European states, a court cannot decline to hear a case on the grounds that a non-party state would provide a more convenient forum (*Owusu* (2005)); the court stressed the need for legal certainty, and was influenced by the fact that *forum non conveniens* is not known in civil law countries; the decision has disturbed lawyers in common law countries, and much effort is being given to finding ways to circumvent it. Negotiations over several years in the Hague Conference on Private International Law for a Convention on Jurisdiction resulted in 2005 in a Choice of Court agreement, which only Mexico has so far ratified, though the EU and the USA signed in 2009; its scope is very limited, and it does not apply to personal injury cases. For documents and analysis on the fraught negotiations, see www.cptech.org/ecom/jurisdiction/hague.html.

discovered a 200-year-old dormant statute, the Alien Tort Claims Act (ATCA), and after some success using it against officials of repressive governments, began to wield it also against corporations. The ATCA simply states that the US federal courts 'shall have original jurisdiction of any civil action by an alien for a tort only, committed in violation of the law of nations or a treaty of the United States'.

ATCA was brought to life and has been exploited by activist lawyers, especially at the Center for Constitutional Rights in New York led by Peter Weiss (White 2004: 213ff.). The first breakthrough case was brought on behalf of an opponent of the dictator Alfredo Stroessner of Paraguay, and his daughter, whose 17-year-old son and brother had been kidnapped and tortured to death in 1976 by a group led by police chief Peña-Irala. The Second Circuit Court of Appeal, overturning the decision of the district court, held that the claim could be brought in US courts since 'deliberate torture perpetrated under colour of official authority violates universally accepted norms of the international law of human rights, regardless of the nationality of the parties' (*Filártiga* (1980): 878).

Other courts rejected ATCA claims, taking a more restrictive view of international law, and of the role of domestic courts in its enforcement. Its scope is in any case limited, as states and governments are protected by sovereign immunity, and few international legal obligations give rise to claims for damages in tort. The divergent views in due course led to the decision in *Sosa* (2004), in which a divided Supreme Court both affirmed the availability of jurisdiction under ATCA, and confirmed its limited scope. In the meantime, ATCA was supplemented by the enactment by Congress of the Torture Victim Protection Act 1991, creating a civil liability for extrajudicial killing.

ATCA is regarded by legal activists as a powerful weapon against corporations, both because they have the resources to satisfy high awards of damages and because they can thereby be made accountable for complicity in egregious violations of human rights, especially labour rights.[32] The first case was brought in 1997 against Union Oil Company of California (UNOCAL), on behalf of villagers for alleged use of forced labour in the construction of the Yadana gas pipeline project in Myanmar (Burma). The district court's initial rejection of the claim was overturned by the

---

32 Fuks 2006. The extent to which labour rights may be considered human rights in international law is being tested by a case brought against the Drummond mining company, alleging that Colombian paramilitaries acting as the company's agents brutalized and killed union workers, denying them their fundamental rights to associate and organize: *Rodriguez* v. *Drummond* (2003); cf. *Sinaltrainal* v. *Coca-Cola* (2003).

Court of Appeals, on the grounds that forced labour is 'a modern variant of slavery' and thus does not require state action, so a claim of corporate aiding and abetting could be adjudicable.[33]

Subsequent claims have included actions against Rio Tinto (allegations of slave labour in copper mines in Papua New Guinea), a Boeing subsidiary (extraordinary rendition), Pfizer (non-consensual medical experimentation in Nigeria), major banking, auto and computer companies (for claims related to apartheid in South Africa), and a variety of companies for atrocities committed during the Second World War (see Wuerth 2009). However, the narrow legal bases for ATCA claims pose considerable difficulties for claimants' lawyers, and cases which have come to trial have tended to fail, notably a claim against Talisman Oil for aiding and abetting human rights abuses in southern Sudan.[34] More frequently, the cases are settled, often on undisclosed terms, and without admission of liability. For example, in June 2009 after thirteen years of legal proceedings, Royal Dutch Shell settled for $15.5m., a claim brought by the family of Ken Saro-Wiwa, who was murdered together with other leaders of the Ogoni people in the oil-rich Niger delta (Wuerth 2009).

Although limited in scope, this type of litigation opened up the possibility of seeking effective legal remedies against corporations, at least in very exceptional cases, which could be said to involve major human rights violations. Thus, it could be seen as providing a 'hard law' edge to the wave of campaigns since the 1990s for more effective accountability for the social impact of business, which has mainly resulted in generally weak 'soft law' mechanisms (Shamir 2004). This will be discussed below. Others have argued that the deployment of the ATCA is an example of the creative use of law to establish some corporate accountability, in contrast to the more frequent use of legal creativity to facilitate corporate regulatory avoidance (McBarnet and Schmidt 2007: 176).

5.2 Hyper-liberalization and globalized regulation

In the 1980s pressures built up for further liberalization, especially of financial flows, and many countries relaxed their controls: developing countries as their debt crises obliged them to accept the 'conditionalities'

---

33 *Doe* v. *Unocal* (2002); the case was settled in 2005 on the basis of payment of undisclosed compensation to the fourteen surviving plaintiffs.

34 *Presbyterian Church* v. *Talisman* (2009): the court held that aiding and abetting entails providing practical assistance with the purpose of facilitating the commission of the crime, which was not proved by the evidence.

of the World Bank and IMF, and the 'emerging economies' of Eastern Europe after the collapse of state socialism in 1989. Certainly, there was a need for reform of existing models of state control, which in many cases had been bureaucratic and inefficient (see Chapters 1 and 3, at 1.2.1 and 3.1.1). However, this new wave of hyper-liberalization also tended to undermine national state regulation, sometimes in unpredictable ways. Thus, the interaction of formal liberalization requirements with national systems of regulation sparked off uneven processes of deregulation and re-regulation.

5.2.1 Legalization of investment regulation

The extension of liberalization during the 1980s and early 1990s led to moves to establish more formal legal frameworks to entrench rights of access for, and protection of, international investments. As with many initiatives for global economic governance, attempts to forge a comprehensive framework failed, and what have emerged are complex regulatory networks.

5.2.1.1. Regional agreements

A major feature of this period has been the growth of regional agreements, which generally cover both trade and investment. They also combine, in various ways, measures for internal liberalization and economic integration among the members, with a common regime of external relations.

The most extensive regional system is of course the EU, which from 1986 to 1992 pursued an ambitious programme for increased internal economic integration, focusing especially on freedom of capital movements and expansion of financial markets. However, this was far from establishing a common framework of corporate or economic regulation; what emerged instead was a complex system of multilevel networked governance (see Chapter 3, at 3.1.4). The EU has undoubtedly exerted a powerful influence, especially as its membership grew from the original 6 to 9, then 12 in 1986, 15 in 1995, jumping to 27 by 2007; it also has extensive links to many more states, and indeed other regional groupings, through various types of associate status (see Chapter 8, at 8.1.1). Despite its limitations, the EU's institutional framework remains both more sophisticated and more complex than that of any other grouping. Consequently, it has often had a significant influence on the patterns of development of globalized regulation.

Some early attempts were made to establish regional economic groupings also among developing countries. However, they faced more difficult obstacles in trying to formulate common economic policies both internally, especially equitable allocation of the benefits of integration among the members, and externally, especially regulation of inward investment.

A notable case is the Andean Common Market, formed by the Cartagena Agreement of 1969 and modelled on the EU with supranational institutions (an executive Secretariat, a legislative Commission and a Parliament). Its best-known policy was the Foreign Investment Code adopted in Decision 24 of 1970, with a screening procedure for inward investment focusing especially on technology transfer. However, implementation of the Code by the Member States was patchy, and it was substantially revised and then replaced in 1987 and 1991, relaxing and then effectively abandoning the common policy (Muchlinski 2007: 656–7). It also established in 1982 a statute for Andean Multinational Enterprises, to be formed by investors from the Member States, aimed at encouraging regional industrial development.

Despite the failure of its initial ambitions, the Andean Pact continued, although with a changing membership,[35] and significantly transformed, renamed the Andean Community in 1997. In 1979 an Andean Court of Justice was established, which began work in 1984. Modelled on the ECJ, it also emulated that court's view of the transnational effect of its law. Unlike the ECJ, however, it has not sought to foster economic integration through law, applying a purposive approach to interpretation which has favoured retention of policy autonomy by the Member States.[36] It is nevertheless performing a significant role in moulding a common system of IP law, which has been the source of 90 per cent of its caseload (Helfer *et al.* 2009).

Other regional groupings fared even less well, and were either abandoned or stagnated (Penaherrera 1980). However, there has been a general revival of regional groupings since the mid-1990s, albeit in new forms. Generally, they now combine a free-trade area or customs union with provisions for the liberalization of other economic flows. An important impetus has been the creation of the WTO, which expanded its scope well

35 The founding members were Bolivia, Chile, Colombia, Ecuador and Peru; Venezuela joined in 1973, Chile withdrew from 1976 (the period of the Pinochet regime) rejoining as an associate member in 2006, the year that Venezuela withdrew.

36 Saldias 2007; Helfer *et al.* (2009) suggest that its rulings have not been purposive, because they have not favoured greater integration, but it seems rather that the Court's view of the intended purposes of the treaty is that it should preserve national policy space.

beyond that of its predecessor the GATT, while retaining its permissive approach towards preferential regional groupings, creating an incentive for them to be formed. This has resulted in interlocking networks of such groupings (see Chapter 8, at 8.1.1).

A distinctive initiative was the formation in 1993 of the Organization for the Harmonization of Business Law in Africa, known under its French acronym OHADA, which at present covers francophone African states.[37] Its Uniform Acts, once adopted, are directly applicable as law in each Member State, and by 2010 seven had been drawn up, covering arbitration, general commercial law, securities, company law and business organizations, insolvency and accounting rules. Its Common Court of Justice and Arbitration hears cases on appeal from the courts of the Member States relating to the application of Uniform Acts.

There has indeed been a new trend towards the inclusion of courts or tribunals in the institutional structure of such organizations (Helfer *et al.* 2009: fn. 19). Most, however, deal with disputes between the Member States and the implementation of treaty obligations in national law. A distinctive innovation as regards the legal position of TNCs has been the creation of tribunals enforcing direct rights under international law of international investors, which will be discussed next, in the context of the North American Free Trade Agreement (NAFTA).

5.2.1.2 The NAFTA and the new-wave IIAs

A major landmark is the North American Free Trade Agreement (NAFTA), which came into force in 1994, between the USA, Canada and Mexico.[38] Its creation involved a historic policy shift for both Canada and Mexico, which had both long resisted commitments to opening their borders to free flows of trade and investment with their powerful neighbour. Their resolve was greatly weakened by the 1981–2 economic crisis, the impact of which combined with the growing internal influence of free-trade ideologies in both countries. In Canada, an independent trade policy review initiated by the Trudeau government gave momentum to a group of policy entrepreneurs to generate sufficient support to persuade the Mulroney government, although elected on an anti-free-trade platform,

---

37 www.ohada.com.

38 Significantly, 1 January 1994 was also the day that there erupted on the world stage the Zapatista uprising in Chiapas, Mexico, a movement protesting against the impact of liberalization on indigenous communities. For a discussion of the far-reaching changes NAFTA required, especially to the important art. 27 of the Mexican constitution, see Schneiderman 2008: 116–18.

to negotiate a bilateral free-trade agreement with the USA in 1985 (Golob 2003: 379–82). In Mexico, despite the explicit liberalization conditions attached to the IMF loan needed after its debt crisis, the shift was more gradual, while the new policy advocates clandestinely built their position within the state apparatus, until Carlos Salinas was ready to take the plunge into a full agreement in 1990 (Golob 2003: 382–7). From there it was a relatively short step to the formation of NAFTA between the three states.

The NAFTA deals with much more than trade, in particular through the inclusion in its Chapter 11 of an investment agreement based on the 1980 US Model BIT (mentioned at 5.1.1.1 above). It is based on strong versions of two core principles. First is a broadly worded NT obligation, for each state to grant all investors and investments of the other parties:

> treatment no less favourable than that it accords, in like circumstances, to its own investors with respect to the establishment, acquisition, expansion, management, conduct, operation and sale or other disposition of investments.
>
> (art. 1102)

Imported from trade agreements, the NT obligation has a potentially far-reaching impact on domestic business regulation, favouring foreign investors. First, it gives the right of entry (right of establishment) to foreign firms, by any means including acquisitions. Second, its 'no less favourable treatment' (NLFT) standard requires foreigners to be given *at least as good* treatment as domestic business, not equal treatment. This does nothing to prevent offering *incentives or advantages* to attract foreign investment, or to restrict the competition between states to attract FDI by such means. Third, the right to complain about discriminatory treatment could potentially extend far beyond regulation which explicitly restricts foreign business, to rules which are neutral on their face in formal legal terms but could be considered discriminatory de facto. As the experience with the NT principle in the trade context has shown (see Chapter 8, at 8.2.1), this opens up a Pandora's box.

The second equally simple and also potentially far-reaching provision was the statement of the minimum standard of treatment. The NAFTA requires that investment and investors be accorded 'treatment in accordance with international law, including fair and equitable treatment and full protection and security' (art. 1105). This establishes a very broadly worded criterion which potentially goes well beyond the issue of nationalization which was the traditional concern of investor protection. The stronger language provided a basis to bring into international economic law the constitutional law debate about 'regulatory takings', in which some take an absolutist view of private property, and argue that any regulatory action by the state which affects the value of a business or asset should be compensated.[39] Hence, this provision also could be used to challenge a wide range of domestic regulation. The ways in which both these principles have been interpreted will be discussed in the next section.

These broad substantive provisions were in effect established as corporate rights in international law, by the inclusion in the NAFTA of what is referred to as an investor–state dispute resolution procedure. This gave a foreign investor the right to bring a claim against the host state against any 'measures' which it considers have damaged an investment or enterprise it owns or controls, if an argument can be made that they are in breach of the treaty. This provision was not new in the NAFTA, since it is a fairly standard one in BITs. A similar procedure is also available in the multilateral Energy Charter Treaty (ECT) of 1994, with a membership of over fifty states, mainly OECD members and Eastern European states, including importantly Russia (Wälde 1996; Muchlinski 2007: 713). In this same period, as already mentioned above, there was also a big jump in the negotiation of BITs, now included within the broader category of international investment agreements (IIAs). However, the inclusion of investor–state arbitration in the NAFTA was decisive in the activation of this procedure which occurred from the mid-1990s, as will be discussed in the next section.[40]

The NAFTA also included different and unique procedures in its so-called Side Agreements, on Environmental Cooperation (NAAEC), and on Labor Cooperation (NAALC). These were negotiated after conclusion of the main NAFTA text by President Clinton, to assuage important sectors of domestic opinion, and help to ensure approval of the NAFTA by the Congress. These agreements stress each state's right to set its own labour and environmental protection standards, and they contain only hortatory

---

39 Thus, Richard Epstein states 'All regulations, all taxes, and all modifications of liability rules are takings of private property, and prima facie compensable by the state' (1985: 95); this is cited and used as the starting point of an extended critique of the 'absolute theory of property rights' by Margaret Radin (1993: 98). See Schneiderman 2008: ch. 2 for the elastic interpretations of the 'takings rule' in US jurisprudence and international law.

40 Some other regional agreements also provide for investor–state arbitration, notably ASEAN and MERCOSUR, although it seems that the host-state's consent is required in the case of an investor from non-Member States of MERCOSUR (Muchlinski 2007: 714–15).

language about the high substantive standards and effective compliance procedures to which the states should aspire. Each agreement establishes a Commission to foster cooperation in its sphere, which is also empowered to consider submissions from one state about another, leading to consultations with the eventual possibility of an arbitration. However, the Agreements do not establish any international standards, and complainants may raise only issues relating to each state's enforcement of its own laws. The NAAEC provides for citizen complaints, but '[c]omplainants are confronted with a veritable steeplechase of procedural pre-conditions' (Tollefson 2002: 183). Under the NAALC only governments may make such complaints (although they may result from citizen petitions), and they must concern 'a persistent pattern of failure' to effectively enforce a specified range of labour laws (Stone 1996: 462).

In a dozen years to 2006, some thirty-one NAALC petitions have been filed, and forty-seven under the NAAEC, and Graubart argues that they provide a valuable 'legalized political opportunity structure for activists' (2008: 44). However, many regard these agreements as window-dressing, and there is a stark contrast between their provisions and procedures and the rights granted to investors under NAFTA's Chapter 11. Continued resistance to free-trade agreements among important domestic political constituencies in the USA has resulted in inclusion in subsequent BITs of somewhat stronger provisions for labour and environmental protection, but they still remain relatively vague and ineffective (Cabin 2009).

5.2.1.3 Business litigation against states

International litigation by investors against states started to boom in the late 1990s, when claims began to be initiated under NAFTA's Chapter 11, soon followed by cases under BITs. Provisions for claims against states by investors had been included in BITs negotiated earlier by developing countries, which provided for arbitration if such claims were not resolved by consultation or mediation. Such arbitrations could be treated like private commercial arbitrations, and the resulting awards enforced under the provisions of the New York Convention, in any country party to it.[41]

---

41 The UN Convention on the Recognition and Enforcement of Foreign Arbitral Awards of 1958. A significant number of investor–state arbitrations do not use the ICSID but are held under the auspices of private commercial arbitration arrangements, such as the Court of Arbitration of the International Chamber of Commerce (ICC), or national arbitration centres such as Stockholm; this has been facilitated by the Arbitration Rules agreed by UNCITRAL in 1976, and its Model Law on International Commercial Arbitration of 1985 (Muchlinski 2007: 709–11; Redfern et al. 2004: 55ff.). Such ad hoc arbitrations have a

During the 1980s and 1990s states competed to relax their conditions for supervision and enforcement of private arbitral awards, as part of the shift towards what was described as the new *lex mercatoria* (discussed in Chapter 2, at 2.3.3). These procedures for enforcement intended for consensual resolution of private commercial disputes were also, however, applicable to arbitral awards against states.

An important step was taken in 1965, when an institutional mechanism was established by the World Bank to hear such claims, the International Centre for the Settlement of Investment Disputes (ICSID), devised by the Bank's lawyers (Sutherland 1979: 373–7). The ICSID Convention does not itself confer jurisdiction over disputes, this requires either the specific consent of a state to submit a dispute, or a clause in a concession agreement or other contract, or a general provision in a BIT or other investment agreement, stating that disputes may be submitted to arbitration. However, an arbitration under the auspices of ICSID is 'truly denationalized', since national law is entirely excluded and state parties are obliged to comply with the award of the tribunal, subject only to the provisions for appeal to an Annulment Committee appointed by ICSID itself (Redfern *et al.* 2004: 67).

The combination of the arbitration provision in BITs and the ICSID had the potential for a fundamental transformation in international law, by allowing TNCs to make claims in their own name against states.[42] Thus, business lawyers and diplomats devised a solution to the problem debated in the 1960s of whether TNCs could be subjects of international law or 'world citizens' (discussed in Chapter 3, at 3.1.2). Under these arrangements, TNCs are able to claim international rights, without being subject to obligations.

longer history than those under IIAs and ICSID, notably including the famous awards relating to oil nationalizations of the 1970s.

42 Under traditional international law, states could bring claims under the principles of 'diplomatic protection' on behalf of their citizens, which could include firms, but these were fraught with difficulties. A major obstacle was created by the decision of the ICJ in the *Barcelona Traction* case (1970), which held that a diplomatic protection claim on behalf of a company must be brought by the state where the company was formed or had its main seat, and not that of its shareholders. Since TNCs operate through a network of affiliates, and generally form one or more subsidiaries in the host country, this rule could make it legally impossible for a claim to be made by the home country of the parent, so not surprisingly the decision was much criticized. In addition, international law required the exhaustion of local remedies before an international claim could be made (see generally Muchlinski 2007: 704–7).

Nevertheless, this possibility was little used until the creation of NAFTA and the new wave of IIAs. The first investor claim under a BIT referred to ICSID was in 1987, and by 1998 there had been only 14 such cases. But by 2005 the cumulative total of all known investor claims had jumped to 219, and by 2010 to around 400.[43] Of the 109 concluded cases by the end of 2008, approximately half were decided in favour of the state (51), and half in favour of the investor (48); a total of $2.8bn in damages had been awarded against states, $1.05bn of this against Argentina (UNCTAD 2009).[44] Although high, this was a fraction of the compensation TNCs had claimed (Franck 2009). The formal disputes were also the tip of a much bigger iceberg of conflicts in which investors could use the threat of resort to arbitration to constrain state action.

Lawyers became alerted to the possibility of potentially lucrative legal actions, especially by the NAFTA, which was the first IIA between OECD countries. Following the first few cases there came a deluge of articles in the professional press, conferences, books and websites, mapping out the terrain of this new field of practice.[45] Like disputes in the WTO (discussed in Chapter 8), although the overall numbers are not large, the amounts at stake may involve hundreds of millions of dollars (UNCTAD 2005: 9). Such disputes also offer lawyers access to an important arena of power at

---

43 The exact number is not known, since there is no obligation to publicize them. Of the 219 by 2005, 132 were with the ICSID (UNCTAD 2005: 4); by the end of 2009, ICSID had registered 305 cases: data and official documents on ICSID cases are published on its website at http://icsid.worldbank.org/ICSID; comprehensive listings of known disputes are maintained by UNCTAD (to the end of 2008) at www.unctad.org/iia-dbcases, and at the Investment Treaty Arbitration website at the University of Victoria: http://ita.law.uvic.ca/about.htm. An excellent source of information is *Investment Treaty News* produced by the International Institute for Sustainable Development (IISD) available at www.iisd.org/investment/itn.

44 Just over forty cases were against Argentina, almost all concerning the measures it introduced following its 2001–2 financial crisis, to delink the peso from the dollar. By 2009, over half a dozen of these had resulted in awards against Argentina, which was understandably very reluctant to pay the compensation awarded (Peterson 2009); some tribunals had accepted the state's argument that its actions were justified by necessity, in particular an ICSID Annulment Committee in *Sempra* v. *Argentina* (2010), but it fared less well in attempting to have awards overturned by national courts, which now apply a very strict standard of review (*Argentina* v. *BG Group* (2010)). As Joseph Stiglitz pointed out, Argentina's decision was a financial disaster for millions of people, and to maintain the dollar peg only for foreign investors would have involved a 'vast redistribution of wealth' (2008: 526).

45 Notably, www.naftaclaims.com was established by Todd Weiler, soon after his involvement with the Myers case as a young lawyer working for the Canadian firm of Barry Appleton, and he quickly built a specialism in investment arbitration, also acting as an arbitrator in some disputes.

the intersection of international politics and economics, away from the more humdrum staple of private commercial disputes.

Investment arbitration starkly illustrates the central anomalous features of the new global governance: the blurring of public and private (with subordination of public to private); the disintegration of normative hierarchies; and the technicization of government (discussed in Chapter 1). As van Harten has cogently pointed out, it entails using private systems of dispute resolution to deal with important public questions of regulation. In effect:

> states have enabled privately contracted adjudicators to determine the legality of sovereign acts and to award public funds to businesses that sustain loss as a result of government regulation.
>
> (2007: 5)

These cases deal with often complex and multilevel regulatory issues, but from the perspective of the private rights of an individual property owner.[46]

A good example is the early case brought under the NAFTA by a US-based company S. D. Myers, which owned a specialized plant in Ohio for disposal of toxic waste, PCB (polychlorinated biphenyl). PCB had been banned in the 1970s, and Canada and the USA had each established regulatory regimes for PCB disposal, both also prohibiting export and import of PCB waste, although Canada's 1990 regulations allowed export to the USA with the prior approval of the US authorities. Despite a 1986 US–Canada Transboundary Agreement, which included a mention in its preamble that the long common border might offer opportunities for transboundary shipment of hazardous waste, the prohibitions in both countries' national laws were maintained. Indeed, international dumping of toxic waste became controversial at this time due to some highly publicized incidents, and an international regime was established by the 1989 Basle Convention on Transboundary Shipment of Hazardous Waste, which prohibited such shipment unless the movements are regulated according to standards it lays down (Kummer 1995). Both Canada and the USA signed this treaty, but the USA had not ratified it by the time of the Myers dispute.

---

46 David Schneiderman provides a detailed analysis of tribunal awards showing how they have generally interpreted the investment protection provisions to constrain state action (Schneiderman 2008: esp. ch. 3).

In 1993 Myers, seeking to prolong the life of its Ohio plant, began court-
ing clients in Canada, especially in Ontario and Quebec, the proximity of
which to Ohio would offer significant cost advantages compared to the
only Canadian PCB facility (in Alberta), owned by Canadian firm Chem-
Security. Despite much lobbying on behalf of Myers, Canada maintained
its policy that Canadian PCB waste should be disposed of in Canada.
However, Myers's multilevel manoeuvres paid off when in 1995 the US
authorities issued a two-year permit allowing Myers to import PCB waste
from Canada. However, faced with counteracting pressure from Chem-
Security that this would mean closure of the Alberta plant and consequent
dependence on the USA for PCB disposal, Canada banned all PCB
exports.

The NAFTA opened up another recourse for Myers, to challenge this
decision under Chapter 11, claiming that Canada's ban damaged its investment. From the economic perspective, of course, Myers' main investment
was its US plant, but it had established a Canadian affiliate in 1993, which
had spent money recruiting potential clients and lobbying, which qualified as an 'investment' under the NAFTA. Although Myers Canada was
not owned by the US company but by family members who had shares in
both firms, the tribunal allowed the claim to be brought, holding that the
precise corporate structure was irrelevant, relying on the NAFTA provision allowing claims to be made on behalf of 'a juridical person that the
investor owns or controls directly or indirectly'.

The arbitrators also upheld Myers's two main substantive claims. First,
they agreed that, although the export ban applied equally to all companies in Canada, it was contrary to the NT clause, which requires a state to
accord 'treatment no less favourable than that it accords, *in like circumstances*, to its own investors' (emphasis added). They considered that this
prohibits de facto discrimination, if 'the practical effect of the measure
is to create a disproportionate benefit for nationals over non nationals'
(*Myers* (2001): para. 252). They also held (by majority) that the action
was a breach of the NAFTA obligation on Canada to provide 'fair and
equitable treatment . . . and . . . full protection and security' to investors,
which they considered means that 'an investor has been treated in such
an unjust or arbitrary manner that the treatment rises to the level that
is unacceptable from the international perspective' (*Myers* (2001): para.
263). Myers was awarded some $6m. in damages plus costs, for the net
profits estimated to have been lost due to the export ban. An attempt by
the Canadian government to have the award set aside was rejected by the
Canadian courts.

Many other cases have also involved environmental protection regulations. A Canadian company Methanex lost a $970m. claim against the US government for loss of sales of methanol due to a California ban on the use of a gasoline additive MTBE. In contrast Metalclad, a US firm, was awarded $15.6m. for the refusal by a Mexican municipality of a construction permit for a hazardous waste landfill, which had been approved by the Mexican federal government subject to various environmental requirements. Under the ECT, the Swedish energy utility Vattenfall brought a claim against Germany in 2009 challenging requirements imposed by the city of Hamburg on a €2.6bn coal-fired power plant, relating to its impact on water purity of the River Elbe, which the city claimed were necessary under European law. A new issue was opened up in May 2010, when the tobacco giant Philip Morris challenged, under the Swiss–Uruguay BIT, stringent new cigarette-labelling rules introduced by Uruguay, which the firm claimed forced it to withdraw several of its Marlboro-brand 'light' products.

Under BITs, a highly publicized case resulted from the 'water wars' in Cochabamba, Bolivia, relating to the concession awarded to an international consortium for privatization of the water supply. Popular opposition, including street riots following a price increase, led to the cancellation of the concession. The consortium was structured through a joint venture company formed in Bolivia, Aguas del Tunari, in which the US giant Bechtel had a 55 per cent stake through a Cayman Islands holding company. As public hostility to the privatization had grown, the consortium had been reorganized so that it became jointly owned by Bechtel and the Italian firm Edison, through a Dutch holding company. The arbitration claim was made under the BIT between Bolivia and the Netherlands of 1994. The tribunal decided that it had jurisdiction over the dispute, rejecting (by majority) Bolivia's argument that the Dutch holding company could not be said to 'control' Aguas del Tunari (as the BIT requires) since it was a mere shell company (*Aguas del Tunari* v. *Bolivia* (2005)). The dispute was settled a few months later, with Bechtel withdrawing its claim for compensation and no admission of liability on either side.[47]

---

47 In a similar case also involving a failed water privatization, the tribunal found that some of the actions of the Tanzanian government were in breach of the BIT: notably 'the failure to put in place an independent, impartial regulator, insulated from political influence, constitutes a breach of the fair and equitable treatment standard, in that it represents a departure from [the investor]'s legitimate expectation that an impartial regulator would be established' (*Biwater* v. *Tanzania* (2008): para. 615). However, it did not award

The majority judgment on the jurisdictional issue in this case frankly spelled out its implications:

> This Decision reflects the growing web of treaty-based referrals to arbitration of certain investment disputes. Although titled 'bilateral' investment treaties, this case makes clear that which has been clear to negotiating states for some time, namely, that through the definition of 'national' or 'investor' such treaties serve in many cases more broadly as portals through which investments are structured, organized, and most importantly encouraged, through the availability of a neutral forum.
>
> (*Aguas del Tunari* v. *Bolivia* (2005): para. 332)

This view enables firms to take advantage of treaty-shopping to incorporate an intermediate affiliate in a state with an appropriate BIT through which to route their investment. A similarly broad approach to interpretation of BIT provisions to create an overarching framework of protection was also seen in the *Maffezini* case (2000). This claim was filed too late under the provisions of the Argentina–Spain treaty which governed it, but the tribunal allowed the claimant the benefit of the more advantageous time limit in the Chile–Spain BIT by applying the MFN clause.

However, other tribunals and individual arbitrators have disagreed with both these broad interpretations. Notably, Prosper Weil, chairing the tribunal in the *Tokios Tokéles* case (2004) pointed out that it was an abuse of the BIT to refuse to look to the beneficial ownership of the company through which the investment had been channelled, since that company was owned and controlled by nationals of the state against which the claim was brought. Similarly, although Maffezini has been followed in some decisions, others have taken the view that only where the parties to a BIT have shown a clear and unambiguous intention to incorporate provisions from other treaties can the MFN clause be interpreted to this effect (UNCTAD 2005: 35).

Some academic commentators have elaborated the proposition that BITs have created a multilateralized regime governing international investment (notably Schill 2008, 2009), going so far as to suggest that they form 'part of a governance structure, [that] helps constitute and shape the emerging body of global administrative law' (Kingsbury and Schill 2009; see further Chapter 10). However, these disputes and such sweeping interpretations quickly led to a crisis of legitimacy of the investment arbitration

---

any damages, as it held that the investment had become worthless essentially due to mismanagement. Tanzania's water privatization had been urged by the World Bank and the UK government, which had supervised the contracting process.

system. The early NAFTA decisions generated widespread criticism and government disquiet, leading the state parties in July 2001 to issue a Note of Interpretation on some of the Chapter 11 provisions, encouraging greater transparency by publication of documents and awards, and curbing the expansive interpretation of the 'fair and equitable treatment' standard. In practice, NAFTA tribunals have been more sensitive than some others in acknowledging state policy autonomy, but this deference to more powerful states itself threatens the legitimacy of investment arbitration (van Harten 2007: 146). In 2007, urged on by activist groups, the leaders of Bolivia, Nicaragua and Venezuela made a joint statement of their intention to leave the ICSID, and Bolivia served formal notice of withdrawal (Peredo *et al.* 2007); in 2009 the President of Ecuador, which was facing several claims involving billions of dollars in total, also denounced the institution and threatened departure.

As van Harten cogently argues, the fundamental flaw of the way the system emerged is that it imported into the public arena a private system of dispute settlement. This is at the root of its problematic features: ad hoc arbitrators chosen by the parties; secrecy of proceedings; divergences of interpretation between different tribunals; and above all lawyers who tout for business both to represent clients and for appointment as arbitrators, creating blatant conflicts of interest. The system of course has its staunch defenders, but also reform proposals are being debated. Van Harten evaluates these, and puts forward an eminently sensible argument for formalization of the system by means of an international investment court (2007: 175–84). Despite the clear rationale for this, both politically and legally, there seems no political momentum behind such a proposal (see Chapter 10, at 10.2.2).

5.2.1.4 The failure of the MAI

The drive to establish a framework for liberalization and protection of international investments reached its apogee with the attempt to negotiate a Multilateral Agreement on Investment (MAI) between OECD Member States, but as a 'free-standing' convention open for accession by others. The ambitious intention was for a 'high-standards' agreement, by which was meant one which established strict constraints or 'disciplines' on government intervention. The negotiations began quietly in 1995 after four years of preparatory work, but did not come to public attention until 1997, when a draft of a proposed agreement was leaked. Debate and controversy quickly built up, with a considerable international mobilization by the MAI's opponents and critics. At the same time, the basic flaws and difficulties of the approach adopted became increasingly apparent among the negotiators, and the effort was finally abandoned in December 1998 (Picciotto and Mayne 1999; Henderson 1999).

The draft MAI embodied broad liberalization obligations for all types of business and financial flows, based on very wide definitions of 'investors' (covering nationals and permanent residents) and of 'investments' (including all types of contractual rights and money claims, whether directly or indirectly owned or controlled). It also included the 'open door' obligation, with an NT provision based on the US BIT, subject to country-specific exceptions to be negotiated (hence top-down rather than bottom-up). To these basic obligations were added other 'disciplines' on states, notably regarding transparency (requiring publication of relevant laws, policies and decisions of general application), performance requirements (prohibiting export, domestic content, domestic purchase, trade-balancing or foreign-exchange-balancing requirements), and employment and immigration laws (rights of temporary entry, stay and work of investors and their employees essential to the enterprise). The enforcement provisions envisaged both state–state and investor–state arbitration.

Thus, the MAI went well beyond the existing network of BITs, and as a multilateral convention it aimed to establish in effect a single economic area for the acquisition of assets and rights of all kinds. Its advocates argued that it would provide a predictable and transparent framework of laws and regulations affecting business. However, critics stressed that it gave investors and speculators rights without responsibilities, and imposed sweeping restrictions and limitations on national laws and regulations, and hence on state sovereignty. Its effects would have been deregulatory, and its impact uncertain, since investors could challenge a wide range of existing and proposed national regulations if they could be argued to entail de facto discrimination or indirect expropriation. This became apparent during the negotiations, as reports began to emerge of the first claims under the NAFTA (Picciotto and Mayne 1999).

In many ways, the MAI resembled a GATT for investments, requiring abolition of border barriers on investment inflows, and laying down broad non-discrimination criteria for internal regulations affecting investments. However, the original GATT balanced its broad liberalization obligations with a substantial list of general exemptions in article XX, expressing areas of legitimate host state regulation (see Chapter 8, at 8.1.1). In contrast, the MAI negotiators aimed to keep general exceptions to a minimum, confined to 'essential security interests'. Following criticism of the draft agreement, a proposed clause was put forward on Non-Lowering of Standards, covering both environmental and labour standards; but it was not drafted as an exception. However, it would have precluded any relaxation of such standards only if made to attract a specific investment; this was a merely symbolic addition, since any such privileged treatment of an investor would in any case be contrary to the MFN clause.

As the MAI negotiations proceeded, the text expanded with the addition of a variety of special provisions and 'carve-outs', mainly to deal with the concerns expressed by specialists in particular areas of regulation when they were consulted about the draft. Notably, taxation was carved out (except for the expropriation provisions, although these excluded 'normal' taxation) since it is dealt with by the network of bilateral tax treaties (see Chapter 6, at 6.2.2); provisions to try to accommodate the MAI principles to the complex international intellectual property regime were being drafted; and a special section on financial services exempted prudential measures and laid down specific fair treatment rules for matters such as authorization, membership of exchanges and regulatory bodies, and access to payments systems. In consultation with IMF experts, provisions were included allowing 'temporary safeguards' for serious balance-of-payments or external financial difficulties; but they appeared to exclude medium- or long-term measures to control short-term capital flows.[48] The top-down character of the agreement meant that the negotiators tabled their proposed national exceptions lists, which became the focus of successive bargaining rounds in an effort to reach a 'balance of commitments', in the process of which the initial 'standstill and rollback' obligations appeared to become weakened.

In the end the draft agreement could be criticized as resembling a Swiss cheese, with more holes than cheese (Picciotto 1998), so it was not surprising that the negotiations collapsed. An attempt to shift the arena for the negotiation to the WTO, led by the EU, ran into opposition from developing countries to the addition of 'new issues' to the already substantial scope of that organization.[49] Nevertheless, the WTO does have a significant impact on investment regulation, due to its broad scope, especially in the Services agreement (see Chapter 8, at 8.1.2).

---

48 At the same time, the eruption of the financial crisis in Asia in 1997, which spread to Russia the following year, drew attention to the dangers of rapid liberalization of financial flows.

49 Picciotto 2000; see Chapter 8, at 8.1.3.

5.2.2 *Corporate responsibility and codes*

The slogan 'No Rights without Responsibilities', adopted by campaigners against the MAI, encapsulated the views of many critics of the regulatory framework for international investment as it emerged in the 1990s. They pointed out that international liberalization measures were creating legally binding constraints on state regulatory powers going well beyond the removal of border controls on the admission of investments. The legal rights given to foreign investors under both BITs and the NAFTA enabled them to challenge a wide range of domestic laws by alleging de facto discrimination or the infringement of a property right. The growth of cases demonstrated the willingness of some investors to devote large resources to block or overturn state measures by resorting to international law. The effect was to undermine or destabilize national state regulation, while doing nothing to strengthen or improve international regulatory cooperation or coordination. TNCs in particular could take advantage of their ability to exploit regulatory arbitrage, without being subject to any overarching global responsibilities.

5.2.2.1 Social responsibility campaigns and codes

This revived the debate of the 1970s, when some had raised the issue of 'global citizenship' for TNCs (see Chapter 3, at 3.1.2). In that earlier period, the pressures to adopt global standards of responsibility for TNCs were generally channelled into the formulation of non-binding guidelines or codes by intergovernmental organizations.[50] Some had a broad scope, such as the International Labour Organization (ILO) Tripartite Declaration of 1977, the 1976 Guidelines for Multinational Enterprises of the OECD,[51] and the aborted UN Code of Conduct for TNCs.[52] Others had a more specific regulatory focus, such as the Set of Principles for the Control of Restrictive Business Practices of 1980 (discussed in Chapter 4, at

---

50 Many of these are conveniently gathered together in UNCTAD 1996a, now also available in UNCTAD's online database *Investment Instruments Online*.

51 As mentioned above, these were formulated as part of the Declaration and Decisions on MNEs, to which they are an Annex. The Guidelines have been reissued and amended following reviews in 1979, 1982, 1984, 1991, 2000 and 2010: see OECD Watch 2005; OECD 2001a.

52 Proposed by the Report of the Eminent Persons which led to the establishment of the UN Commission on TNCs (see Chapter 4, at 4.2.3), this proposed Code was controversial from the start, some regarding it as too weak and others as anti-business, while the OECD's formulation of its Guidelines in effect acted as a spoiler (Sagafi-nejad and Dunning 2008: 109–11).

4.3.3), or the International Code of Marketing of Breast-Milk Substitutes agreed by the World Health Organization (WHO) in 1981, which was aimed at specific industry practices.[53]

Not surprisingly, the impetus for the creation of these instruments and the effectiveness of the mechanisms for monitoring and ensuring compliance, greatly depended on the strength of social pressures brought to bear mainly through civil society organizations, such as trade unions and other social movements. Too often the fact that these codes were not legally binding was used to justify failure or even refusal to back them up with adequate procedures for monitoring compliance or dealing with alleged violations.[54] Thus, 'non-binding' was assumed to mean 'aspirational', which is not at all the same thing.

As we have seen in the previous sections, the next two decades saw a contradictory process, with the strengthening of national state regulation of TNCs (by both home and host states), as well as international legal obligations imposing increasing restrictions on state regulation. The impact of the latter on the former was to create an impetus for deregulation. The overall result, however, was the emergence of new and more

---

53 This has been the most long-lasting and effective of the industry codes, thanks largely to the continuing activist pressures organized through the International Babyfood Action Network. The main target of activist pressures, Nestlé, swung this way and that in response: it first sparked enormous harmful publicity by suing the authors of a provocative pamphlet *Nestlé Tötet [Kills] Babys* [sic]; then it tried to absorb the pressures, by funding a research centre on TNCs, and setting up the Nestlé Infant Formula Audit Commission in 1985, an 'independent social audit committee' chaired by former US Secretary of State Edmund Muskie; after a fact-finding mission found violations by Nestlé in Mexico this was disbanded in 1991, having considered only a handful of the complaints submitted by Nestlé's relentless critics. Details on the monitoring of compliance with the Code may be found on www.ibfan.org; see Chetley 1986 for an insider account of its origins, and Richter 1998, and 2001: ch. 4.

54 Despite pressures from its Trade Union Advisory Committee (TUAC), the OECD's Committee on International Investment and Multinational Enterprise (CIIME) insisted that the OECD Guidelines should remain non-binding and that the CIIME should not reach conclusions on the conduct of individual enterprises. The CIIME described the OECD Guidelines as 'an efficient and realistic framework for further encouragement of the contribution which multinational enterprises can make to economic and social progress and for the reduction and resolution of the difficulties to which the operations of multinational enterprises may give rise' (OECD 1979: para. 7). The CIIME wanted to avoid being seen as providing a 'judicial or quasi-judicial forum' (OECD 1979: para. 84). At most, it was willing to use the details of specific cases as illustrations of problems arising under the OECD Guidelines and issue 'clarifications' where appropriate. For an account and discussion of the early operation of the OECD Guidelines see Blanpain 1979, 1983.

complex forms of regulatory networks. An important element in these have been codes of conduct directly governing the activities of TNCs. Many of these have been adopted by TNCs themselves, or by business and industry associations (Haufler 2001; Jenkins *et al.* 2002; Vogel 2005; McBarnet *et al.* 2007).

The sudden emergence of corporate codes in the mid-1990s took many by surprise and raised new questions for both critics and defenders of big business. The mantra of liberalization suggested that if business were left free to pursue profit, then economic growth and social development would follow. Yet now companies were voluntarily committing themselves to a wider range of social and environmental goals. It was quickly apparent, however, that this commitment did not originate from simple altruism on the part of their directors, or a revival of philanthropic traditions, but rather from an awakened awareness of the importance of the firm's image to its customers, workforce and investors.[55] Reputational damage could quickly affect bottom-line profits, while investment in social responsibility could perhaps reap long-term benefits.

Some companies learned this lesson in an abrupt and dramatic manner. A notable case in point is Royal Dutch Shell, which in 1995 suffered a double blow. The company's decision to end the life of its Brent Spar oil platform by sinking it in the North Sea was exposed to the media spotlight after a dramatic stunt by Greenpeace, although denunciation of Shell's environmental irresponsibility by activists was later felt to have been exaggerated (Vogel 2005: 112–14). Further south, a campaign by the Ogoni people in the Niger delta involving criticisms of Shell was repressed by the Nigerian government, culminating in the execution of nine Ogoni leaders, including the writer Ken Saro-Wiwa. This drew world attention to Shell's apparent indifference to the environmental damage and social deprivation that its highly profitable activities seemed to exacerbate rather than alleviate (Manby 1999). By April 1998, the firm produced the pioneering Shell Report 1998, subtitled *Profits and Principles – Does There Have to Be a Choice?*, which stated that the corporation was 'about values. It describes how we, the people, companies and businesses that make up

---

55 Virginia Haufler's study of corporate codes (2001) concludes that their adoption was driven by activist pressure and the risk of government regulation, and that corporate responses were shaped by concerns for reputation, economic competition and learning processes.

the Shell Group, are striving to live up to our responsibilities – financial, social and environmental'. These were the three dimensions of the so-called 'triple bottom line' of sustainable development, against which Shell proclaimed that all companies would soon be expected to account for their activities. Shell went even further in recasting its annual report for 2000 entirely in terms of social responsibility by addressing issues of health, safety and the environment.

Shell's experience showed that it was not enough for a firm, especially a large TNC, to manage its operations simply in compliance with the law and leave it to governments to deal with social issues and the public interest. The decision to sink the Brent Spar complied with all the regulations agreed among the states bordering the North Sea. The failure of oil wealth to benefit ordinary people, especially in the oil-producing regions of Nigeria, could be attributed to the distribution formula which allocated the bulk of revenues to the central government, where it was dissipated in corruption (Frynas 2000: 53; Wheeler *et al.* 2002). Neither of these facts protected the company from consumer boycotts and the loss of employee morale resulting from the damage to its reputation. As one commentator stated, 'close observers of Shell have said the company's reaction to those crises was not that they were temporary pleasantries to be weathered but truly corporate culture-altering events that shook the staid old giant to its core' (Williams 2000: 76).

Shell's experience was replicated by other companies that are sensitive to consumer concerns and reliant on brand-names. For example, in the apparel industry and retailing, high-profile campaigns on US college campuses targeted firms such as Nike and Gap for their use of supply-chain subcontractors employing under-age workers in sweatshop conditions (Klein 2000: 327). Incidents such as the 1993 fire at the Kader toy factory in Thailand, in which nearly 200 workers were killed and hundreds more injured, and videos showing children in Sialkot (Pakistan) stitching footballs with a FIFA label prior to the 1998 World Cup, were used by international trade union organizations to highlight breaches of international labour standards (Justice 2002). Firms found that trusted brand names, which were often their most significant asset, could quickly be endangered by campaigns that revealed the 'labour behind the label' (Klein 2000). The combination of high investments in design and brand names with outsourcing of the physical product to supply-chain sweatshops in poor countries made firms such as Nike and Reebok both highly profitable and very vulnerable to new forms of social activism (Merk 2004).

Within a short time-span, many companies and industry associations adopted voluntary codes for corporate social responsibility (CSR).[56] Concern about the chemicals industry's poor public image due to events such as the Bhopal tragedy and other less widely publicized disasters motivated the US Chemical Manufacturers' Association to develop the Responsible Care programme to raise safety and environmental impact standards in the industry. This became a worldwide system coordinated by the International Council of Chemical Associations (King and Lenox 2000). Activist groups launched 'social labelling' programmes, aiming to harness the power of brand names and consumer ethical concerns to raise standards of environmental protection and especially workers' employment and social conditions. Rugmark focused specifically on carpet manufacturing and the use of child labour. Fair Trade began with a specific focus on coffee (Murray *et al.* 2003), but extended to many products, including bananas, chocolates, flowers, honey and rice. It is now internationally coordinated through a network of two dozen labelling and producer organizations,[57] and backed by increasingly sophisticated research and social activism (Nicholls and Opal 2005; Raynalds *et al.* 2007). The Fairtrade brand experienced rapid growth in some markets, leading also to attempts by firms such as Nestlé and Kraft to launch their own rival ethical brand.

A different combination of activism and business was involved in the Forest Stewardship Council which, after the failure of an attempt at an intergovernmental regime, was founded in 1993 by a group of civil society organizations, small producers and manufacturers, academics and some retailers, to establish a certification system for sustainable forestry backed by a logo (Meidinger 2006). Some companies, notably The Body Shop and Ben & Jerry's, combined ethical concerns and business in the personality of their founders, although this made it hard to sustain the brand when they were eventually swallowed up by larger firms.

In 2000, an OECD study collected 246 codes, about half of which were issued by individual firms, some 40 per cent by associations, and the remainder primarily by stakeholder coalitions and NGOs (OECD 2000b: paras. 10–11). These codes generally dealt with matters of concern to consumers, such as labour and environmental standards, compliance with the law, and issues of potential risk to the firm, such as bribery and

---

56 Much helpful information is available at www.corporate-accountability.org.
57 Fair Trade Labelling Organizations International: www.fairtrade.net; see Chapter 9, at 9.2.6.2.

corruption (OECD 2000b: paras. 14–39). There were, however, considerable variations both of subject matter and of style, especially in the degree of specificity found in the codes' standards (OECD 2000b: para. 22).

This revival of interest in establishing global standards of corporate responsibility once again attracted the interest of intergovernmental organizations. Notably, in 2000 the UN Global Compact was launched, based on nine (later expanded to ten) universal and agreed values and principles derived from UN instruments, which TNCs were invited to adopt and integrate into their business strategy, day-to-day operations and organizational culture (Kell 2003). This was explicitly formulated as a voluntary 'leadership initiative', relying on 'public accountability, transparency and disclosure to complement regulation'.[58] However, it was criticized by activists as no more than an attempt to lend the legitimacy of the UN to corporate public relations hype (TRAC 2000). Others saw the Compact as exemplary of a trend towards UN–business partnerships, and argued for a careful and critical evaluation of issues such as accountability and policy coherence (Zammit and Utting 2006).

A decade after its establishment, some 5,800 businesses of all sizes and types were participating in the Compact, although over 1,000 had been delisted for failure to meet the requirements of the 'Communication on Progress' policy introduced in 2005, which encourages the use of the sustainability reporting framework of the Global Reporting Initiative. The Compact's principles were largely derived from instruments which come under the responsibility of specific UN bodies, and six of these form an Inter-Agency Team which is part of the Compact's 'multicentric governance framework',[59] although they also continued their own work, albeit with some cross-reference to the Compact.

Thus, the ILO has continued to monitor implementation of its Tripartite Declaration. Following on also from the concerns about the impact of trade liberalization on labour rights (see Chapter 8, at 8.1.3), it embarked on an initiative on the 'social dimension of globalization', setting up an independent Commission which reported in 2004 (ILO 2004). In 2008 it adopted by acclamation the ILO Declaration on Social Justice for a Fair Globalization, to be implemented through a Decent Work Agenda, with the four strategic objectives of employment, social protection, social

---

58 From its website www.unglobalcompact.org.
59 They are the Office of the High Commissioner for Human Rights (OHCHR), International Labour Organization (ILO), United Nations Environment Programme (UNEP), United Nations Office on Drugs and Crime (UNODC), United Nations Development Programme (UNDP) and United Nations Industrial Development Organization (UNIDO).

dialogue and international labour standards (ILO 2008). Within this perspective, international trade union organizations resumed attempts to obtain recognition and a formal framework for collective bargaining with TNCs. These had achieved few results in the 1970s (Northrup and Rowan 1979), although involvement with broader social issues could be said to have facilitated a transition from narrow workerism to a new internationalism (Munck 1988; Waterman 1988; Picciotto 1991; Costa 2006). In 1994, political pressure led by the European Trade Union Confederation (ETUC) resulted in the EU Works Council Directive, which had some success, with 828 firms establishing such bodies by 2008 for consultation with worker representatives (usually trade unions) over matters defined as transnational.[60] Campaigns by international trade union bodies to extend this model to TNCs globally have resulted in 'international framework agreements', some seventy being active in 2010 (Stevis 2010).

In 2005 John Ruggie, who had been instrumental in devising the Compact, was appointed the UN Secretary-General's Special Representative on the issue of human rights and business organizations, and following a process of multi-stakeholder consultations and research, in 2008 he submitted a notable Report to the UN Human Rights Council (Ruggie 2008). This ambitiously aimed to overcome the basic limitation that international human rights instruments impose obligations on states and not on private persons such as firms, by proposing a triple framework to 'protect, respect and remedy'.[61] This involves complementary elements: the state's duty to protect against human rights abuses by third parties, including business; the corporate responsibility to respect human rights; and the need for more effective access to remedies (Ruggie 2008). The report cogently analysed the 'governance gaps' of globalization, especially in relation to TNCs, due to the disjuncture between their power as global economic actors, and the legal framework which considers them as groups

---

60 This was about one-third of those covered by the legislation (firms employing over 1,000 people, with at least 150 in more than one Member State), although they included some two-thirds of the workers covered (14.5 million): see www.worker-participation.eu, and www.ewcdb.org. The Directive was revised and extended in 2009 (2009/38/EC; original Directive 1994/45/EC).

61 This to some extent built on an earlier initiative by the Council's predecessor, the Commission on Human Rights, whose Sub-Commission on the Promotion and Protection of Human Rights in 2003 adopted a set of Norms on the Responsibilities of Transnational Corporations and Other Business Enterprises with Regard to Human Rights, spelling out their responsibilities to 'promote, secure the fulfilment of, respect, ensure respect of and protect human rights' (UN Doc. E/CN.4/Sub.2/2003/12/Rev.2).

of separate legal persons, subject to regulation by different states which themselves are weakened by the competition to attract investment.

5.2.2.2 Interactions of soft and hard law

The private and voluntary nature of CSR initiatives raised two central issues: the rather haphazard and selective content of the codes and the lack of effective implementation mechanisms or procedures for monitoring compliance. Both of these factors reflected not so much the preference of business firms for self-regulation, as often argued, but their determination to try to control how far their activities are subject to law, and to choose which laws should apply to them.

Thus, an analysis by the ILO of labour-related content in approximately 215 codes, focusing on enterprise-drafted codes, showed that the majority used self-defined standards (ILO 1998, 1999). Reference to national law was, however, relatively frequent, especially in relation to wage levels. No more than one-third of the codes referred to international labour standards even in general terms, and only 15 per cent (almost exclusively those developed with trade union or NGO involvement) referred to freedom of association or collective bargaining (ILO 1999: paras. 52–6). A similar OECD study found that only 13 per cent of the codes referred to labour issues or mentioned ILO standards, and only 30 per cent mentioned freedom of association (OECD 2000b: paras. 18–19).

As regards implementation, the bulk of corporate codes rely on internal follow-up and monitoring (OECD 2000b: para. 85). Even where there was a provision for external involvement, as in third-party or industry-association codes, critics raised serious doubts as to whether such third parties were genuinely independent (O'Rourke 2002: 196). Lack of effective implementation was the main reason for refusal of trade unions and some NGOs to join the US Fair Labor Association (Jenkins 2002: 24). Of course, private management consultants were quick to offer their services for compliance auditing, but doubt has been cast on both their independence and competence (O'Rourke 2002). On the other hand, NGOs have been wary of being drawn into this role, for fear of becoming co-opted and merely lending their legitimacy to corporate public relations (Kearney 1999). Although the ILO's survey raised the possibility of the ILO adopting a proactive role towards both specification of the content of codes and the verification procedures (ILO 1998: para.138), the organization instead adopted the low-profile alternative of providing advice and information (ILO 2003b).

The self-selected nature of the content and the lack of independent external implementation or monitoring mechanisms inevitably generated scepticism about the value and effectiveness of corporate codes. This was further fuelled by the startling revelations of unscrupulous behaviour by senior managers following the dramatic collapses of corporate giants such as Enron and WorldCom and the stock-market crash which followed the dot-com bubble (discussed in Chapter 4, at 4.1.1). Inquiries into Enron, for example, revealed that a combination of financial engineering and sophisticated tax avoidance enabled the company to declare net income of $2.3bn between 1996 and 1999, while sustaining a tax loss of $3bn (US Congress 2003). Significantly, the OECD study found that only one of the codes it analysed mentioned taxation (OECD 2000b: para. 29).

As research into the effects of corporate codes has developed, it has become clear that their effectiveness involves far more than the assumption that corporate virtue pays. Studies of the relationship between adoption of CSR policies and profitability showed no evidence of a causal link (Vogel 2005: ch. 2). On the other hand, there is evidence that CSR codes have produced beneficial effects in some respects, including improvement of labour standards by firms producing some consumer goods, and enhanced environmental protection (Vogel 2005: 162–3).

The decision for these instruments to take the form of non-binding 'soft law' codes or guidelines, was not, however, simply due to a desire to weaken them. A major advantage of such codes is that they can be expressed in terms of obligations directly applicable to individuals and firms. Also, it is often easier to reach agreement in much more detailed and specific terms when drafting this type of code than an instrument intended to be binding on states, and they are also easier to amend following experience of their operation. The voluntary nature of codes can also be said to give them some advantages over the rigidity and instrumentalism of externally imposed and bureaucratically enforced law. This characteristic gives them the flexibility to be tailored to the characteristics and circumstances of a specific business and to raise standards by encouragement and self-generated commitment. On the other hand, corporate critics and sceptics challenge the effectiveness of self-selected and self-monitored standards, and argue that competitive equality requires generally applicable rules rather than self-selected codes.

On closer examination, it also became clear that it is inaccurate and inappropriate to treat these instruments as existing outside or beyond the law. Codes entail a degree of formalization of normative expectations and practices. They also interact in various ways with formal law, indeed the relationship has aptly been described as a 'tangled web' (Webb and Morrison 2004). The challenge for creative lawyering is to find ways to combine the strengths of corporate codes and formal law. In practice, as already stated, effective compliance inevitably depends on the monitoring and enforcement mechanisms which can be devised, and especially on the strength of social and political pressures.

Codes may have legal effects in a number of ways (Jülich and Falk 1999; Ward and Lee 2003; Picciotto 2003b; Webb and Morrison 2004). First, corporate codes may be enforceable through private law. They may constitute or form part of contractual agreements, such as when a firm formulates a code for its business networks or supply chains. Thus, a brand-name retailer may establish a code for its subcontractors and suppliers, or a major oil company, such as Shell, may establish one for its franchisees. Companies have preferred to avoid contractual effect by specifying that such codes are not intended to be legally binding. However, it is also generally made clear that failure to remedy identified breaches of the code would lead to non-renewal of commercial contracts (Fridd and Sainsbury 1999: 231; OECD 2000b: para. 20). In addition, obligations to facilitate the monitoring of compliance may form part of the formal commercial contract. Associational and third-party codes are also likely to have effect as contractual arrangements under which participating firms may be entitled to certification which can be used in their product and brand-name marketing, provided the agreed-upon monitoring mechanisms verify that the companies comply with the provisions of the code. There are undoubtedly limitations and variations in how vigorous enforcement can or should be (McBarnet and Kurkchiyan 2007: 81–2), but this is the case in any regulatory system. Hence, the non-legal status of supply-chain codes should not in itself be a concern, unless this status is a signal that the code is not intended to be taken seriously.

Codes may also lead to legal enforcement by private parties based on state regulatory law. For example, firms proclaiming their adherence to a code create expectations which may be legally enforceable by their customers or other stakeholders, for example under consumer protection laws (Glinski 2007: 126–8). Thus, the California Supreme Court has allowed an action to be brought against Nike for false advertising and unfair competition (*Kasky* v. *Nike* (2002)). The action challenged the accuracy of the Report commissioned by Nike on compliance with its corporate code by suppliers, and used in Nike's corporate publicity, which had found no evidence of illegal or unsafe working conditions at Nike factories in China, Vietnam and Indonesia.

There are many ways in which state law can strengthen and support codes. A non-binding code may indeed be implemented as law by states: thus, many states have enacted laws based on the Baby-Milk code. Conversely, state acceptance and implementation of formal legal obligations in binding treaties is often ineffective, as shown by the example of the anti-bribery conventions discussed above. Rather than rely only on state criminal law, it may be more effective to create an obligation on firms to put in place their own code backed by effective monitoring, as was done in the UK's Bribery Act passed in 2010. There have been increasing moves to encourage or require adoption of CSR codes by firms under company law, especially disclosure requirements.[62] The EU's Accounts Modernization Directive of 2003 requires corporate annual reports to include a 'business review' extending to non-financial matters, explicitly including 'information relating to environmental and employee matters'. This minimal requirement can be, and indeed has been, strengthened by states and even firms themselves (McBarnet 2007: 33–7).

At the level of international law also, voluntary standards or codes can be given a legally binding status, in many ways. The principle of 'prior informed consent' governing international trade in dangerous chemicals built upon codes formulated by the FAO and UNEP, as well as industry ethical guidelines, when it became embodied in a multilateral treaty signed in 1998 (Mekouar 2000). A more indirect method is used in the World Trade Organization (WTO) agreements which establish an obligation on states to use relevant standards developed by appropriate international organizations 'as a basis for' national regulations affecting internationally traded goods (see Chapter 8, at 8.2). This has the effect of converting standards developed by organizations such as the Codex Alimentarius Commission, which those bodies themselves do not regard as binding, into mandatory obligations for WTO members.

This is similar to the technique of a Framework Convention, which has emerged in recent years, as a means of establishing a set of objectives and principles which are binding on states, together with implementation mechanisms and processes for the formulation of more specific norms. Initiated for the purposes of developing regimes for environmental protection (such as Climate Change), the technique has been adapted by the WHO for its Framework Convention on Tobacco Control (Bodansky 1999). Its advantages are that it can establish an organizational and

---

62 For an analysis of the possibilities and difficulties of building CSR into existing models of the corporation, see Wedderburn 1985.

procedural basis to develop new standards, as far as possible through deliberative processes involving a range of civil society as well as governmental participants, providing a stronger basis for mutual trust. A Framework Convention can also adopt a more flexible approach to combinations of hard- and soft-law codes. For example, it can establish legal requirements on participating states to lay down specifications for corporate codes in general terms, while providing that they should be based on appropriate internationally agreed standards which may be developed subsequently.

Hence, the question is not whether hard and soft law are mutually exclusive, but how they can best be combined to produce effective regulation. Analysis of corporate codes, briefly surveyed above, suggests that they have two main advantages. First, they can be tailored to meet the specific needs of particular businesses, and applied with awareness and sensitivity to their particular circumstances and local context. For example, rigid laws strictly applied may be a harmful way to tackle the problem of child labour in poor communities and countries. A simple prohibition against employing children below a certain age may merely result in their being excluded from relatively better-paid jobs in the formal sector and forced to resort to informal work which is physically and morally much more damaging. Thus, the UK's Ethical Trading Initiative (ETI) Base Code requires adherents to end new recruitment of child labour, but also 'to develop or participate in and contribute to policies and programmes which provide for the transition of any child found to be performing child labour to enable her or him to attend and remain in quality education until no longer a child'.

This suggests that laws should establish minimum acceptable requirements, while codes should be aspirational and aim at significant enhancement, as well as providing constructive arrangements for achieving such improvements. The flip side of flexibility, however, is one of the significant disadvantages of codes, their patchy and uneven content, resulting from self-selection. Hence, an important function for the broader governmental and intergovernmental codes (such as the UN Global Compact) should be to provide a template of basic principles of CSR, which to some extent they are already performing. However, this has not been expressed either in terms of establishing a basic minimum, or as taking the form of binding requirements. Thus, the flexibility and adaptability of the code format may result in firms picking and choosing from among the standards, effectively diluting them, instead of building more specific provisions and targeted programmes onto them. This suggests that formal law could play a helpful role in defining minimum standards or templates for the content of codes. These could be amplified or specified in more detail by firms, to tailor the standards to their own circumstances. In this way, corporate codes could provide real added value, instead of tending to dilute the standards applicable.

The example of the WTO can also be adapted to deal with the criticism that international investment agreements are one sided in granting significant rights to investors without any responsibilities. A Framework Convention could provide an umbrella for a number of related agreements which would deal with both investor rights and responsibilities. The technique of related agreements could be used, first, to clarify the impact of investment protection obligations on national law. As with the TBT and SPS agreements under the WTO, a presumption could be created that national measures based on internationally agreed standards (e.g. of environmental protection, or human rights) would be valid. This would help to prevent or resolve disputes or claims based on indirect discrimination or de facto expropriation.

Second, international agreements and standards could be associated within a multilateral investment framework either on a required or conditional basis. Some international instruments might be considered to embody such core values and standards that they should form an essential part of the package, just as the TRIPs agreement has made acceptance of basic intellectual property rights a requirement of participation in the WTO system (see Chapters 8 and 9). This might be the case, for example, for the ILO Declaration on Fundamental Principles and Rights at Work of 1998. Other issues which might be regarded as an essential part of a multilateral investment framework, and for which multilateral agreements already exist which could be used or adapted for the purpose, include combating bribery, and cooperation in tax enforcement. This model might also be an appropriate way to deal with the difficult problem of tax benefits and incentives, by associating a code on unfair tax competition, along the lines of the codes now being applied within the EU and by the OECD (see Chapter 6, at 6.4.2.1). Association of such agreements within a single framework would help to create public confidence that the benefits extended to investors by globalization would be complemented by a strengthened framework of international cooperation to prevent abuse of the freedoms of the global market.

Both agreements and non-binding standards could also be associated on a basis of reciprocal conditionality, which would provide flexibility. Thus, states could choose to extend investment protection benefits only to investors from states participating in specified agreements. Such conditionality could also be applied to enterprises, through an appropriate Denial of Benefits clause. This would permit a state to deny the benefits of investment protection to enterprises breaching specified or related standards. Thus, for example, a host state could rule out bids for licences or concessions, or cancel them, if the enterprise concerned were found to be in breach of relevant standards. For example, a firm which breached Prior Informed Consent procedures, or provisions of the WHO Infant Formula Code, could be denied the right to bid for public contracts. A firm which was shown to have facilitated an investment by bribery should be denied protection for that investment.[63]

Finally, relevant agreements and standards could be associated within a multilateral framework for investment on an opt-in basis. States and enterprises could be encouraged to sign up to a range of agreements and codes as appropriate to their activities and circumstances. This would help to provide a higher visibility for positive regulatory standards, as well as helping to authenticate both those standards and their monitoring and compliance mechanisms.

---

63 This position was taken by the arbitrators in *World Duty Free* v. *Kenya* (2006), who dismissed a claim for expropriation of a concession 'as a matter of *ordre public international* and public policy' because it was obtained by bribery.

6

International taxation

6.1 Taxation and governance

Taxation is key to the character and functioning of the state, economy and society. As Schumpeter put it 'Taxes not only helped to create the state. They helped to form it' (1918: 108). Clearly, the ability to extract revenue is central to state power, and the way this is done has changed as the state itself has transformed. Fiscal sociologists and historians have analysed the development of 'tax states' according to various schematic stages: from the tribute state, and the domain state, in which taxes were extracted from subjects for the benefit of the ruler; to the tax state, in which they gradually became legitimized as contributions to the costs of activities accepted as necessary and beneficial for society as a whole; and finally the modern fiscal state, in which taxation is integrated into a system of public finance and macroeconomic management (Bonney 1999; Ormrod *et al.* 1999; Daunton 2001, 2002).

Although it always involves some degree of coercion, taxation is more effective to the extent that it is consensual, and certainly its effectiveness has increased as governments have become more successful at persuading citizens of the fairness of taxation and the benefits of collective spending. Historically the emergence of modern 'fiscal states' has depended on two main factors. First has been the legitimacy of taxation, resting on the acceptance of both justice in its extraction and control over its expenditure. Second, the modern fiscal state based on public finance was both facilitated by and enabled the separation of economic activity, considered to be a private sphere, from the public sphere of the state (Schumpeter 1918; Musgrave 1992), which is characteristic of capitalism. Hence, sustainable public finances in the modern state are inextricably linked to macroeconomic management.

When Adam Smith suggested that the four canons of a good tax system are equity, certainty, convenience and economy,[1] he was also expressing an Enlightenment critique of the tax systems of the absolutist monarchies which, although they had been a key element in the formation of centralized states, were experienced as capricious and oppressive. Britain's success in establishing a 'fiscal–military state' in the eighteenth century could be contrasted with the tax revolts and crises of France, where the fiscal crisis eventually sparked the French revolution (Daunton 2001: 7). Economic growth and the absence of major wars during the nineteenth century enabled Peel and Gladstone to fashion a strong 'fiscal constitution', developing a high degree of mutual trust between government and taxpayers, based on restraint and efficiency in public expenditure and a shift to direct taxation of income (Daunton 2001: 26–30).

During the twentieth century, taxation underpinned the development of the welfare–warfare state, following a similar pattern although with significant variations in the major capitalist countries (Steinmo 1993). In these countries, state expenditure rose from some 5 to 10 per cent of gross domestic product (GDP) at the start of the century, to 30 to 50 per cent by its close, rising as high as 60 per cent in some countries (Tarschys 2001). This substantial level of collective spending has been sustained by the acceptance of the legitimacy of equally high levels of taxation. That legitimacy has greatly depended on the centrality of income tax as the key revenue source.[2]

6.1.1 Fairness and income taxation

The income tax began as a tax on the small section of society which was well-off, on individual income, and on the income or profits of legal persons such as companies from business or commercial activities. It enabled state finance to move away from reliance on a multiplicity of charges such as head or habitation taxes, which fell disproportionately on the poor, and specific duties usually on trade. Its legitimacy was based on the principle of proportionality, justified by the concept of ability to pay,

---

1 *Wealth of Nations*, Book IV, Ch. II, Part II.
2 Direct taxation can be said to have a long pre-history, as land and property taxes, and even some types of poll tax were to some extent income related (Harris 2006), but the modern income tax represents a qualitative shift.

which was reinforced by the shift to a progressive, graduated tax (higher tax rates on higher income).[3]

Although the politics of taxation 'looked as though it would become a major battlefront in an emerging class war' (Steinmo 1993: 22), the acceptance of the income tax, and its eventual spread to become a mass tax, was linked to wartime patriotism, as well as the need to finance a growth in welfare spending, with the first introductions of social security programmes early in the twentieth century, and their major expansion in its second half. Since the 1970s, tax revenue as a proportion of GDP has continued to rise in OECD countries, from around 23 per cent in 1965 to a weighted average of 33 per cent in 1999,[4] and despite the impact of privatizations and the drive to 'roll back the state' state expenditures have

---

3 In some countries, such as France, the income tax originally covered only individuals, with separate taxes on various types of revenues from commerce, business and land. In the UK also, the notion of 'general income' at first meant that of the state and not the individual, and the tax was applied at a flat rate on the different types of income identified in the 'schedules'. The liberal idea that tax fairness should be based on an equal burden on all persons in proportion to their entire income emerged only late in the nineteenth century, in the UK with Gladstone. Adam Smith's argument that citizens should contribute 'as nearly as possible in proportion to their abilities, that is in proportion to the revenue which they respectively enjoy under the protection of the state', put as much emphasis on the notion of benefits as on ability to pay. John Stuart Mill, also reluctant to prioritize ability to pay, supported differentiation (between earned and unearned income) but not graduation. The concept of an individual's 'total income' only emerged in twentieth-century legislation, to deal with both graduation and differentiation (Pearce 2007). The trend to integration intensified after 1945. Applying the income tax to corporations, while including dividends in the income of individuals raised the issue of 'double taxation', so corporate taxes were often treated as distinct, and most countries allowed some imputation of corporate taxes paid on dividends as a credit for the shareholders. The interplay between economic theories and tax policy has been discussed by Daunton (2001: 138ff.) and Mehrotra (2005), who both show how marginalist economics went beyond the classical liberal views, to underpin the shift from a proportionate to a graduated income tax; indeed, differentiation was not introduced in the UK until 1907, quickly followed in 1909 by a progressive, graduated income tax (Daunton 2001: 155). Mehrotra's fascinating account and analysis, shows how US economists such as Edwin Seligman, as part of the progressive movement's shift from the emphasis of nineteenth-century liberalism on negative liberty towards a more actively interventionist state, supported the introduction of direct and progressive taxation based on ability to pay, influenced both by German historical and institutional economics and by marginalism.

4 OECD 2001b: 10, 2005a: 68; the unweighted average is a little higher; see also Hobson 2003. The ratio of tax to GDP is generally accepted as the best measure of the level of taxation and the role of the state in the economy. However, it should be remembered that it only provides an approximation, as there are important differences both between countries and over time on matters such as the treatment of transfer payments or imputation credits, and the effects of tax subsidies and tax expenditures (exemptions, allowances and credits): see OECD 2000c: ch. 3; Stewart and Webb 2006: 165–8.

remained in the 35 to 50 per cent range.[5] Taxes on personal and corporate income have continued to be an important component, at around one-third of total tax revenue. However, the overall growth in state expenditure has required their supplementation by other taxes, particularly value-added tax (VAT) on sales, which has spread rapidly, especially in the 1980s (Tanzi 1995: 46; Ebrill *et al.* 2002).

The evolution has been rather different in peripheral capitalist countries. In colonies and dependencies income taxation played a much less significant part, for both economic and political reasons. In the early empires, political domination and economic exploitation were closely linked: conquest meant the extraction of revenues for the benefit of the emperor and other holders of power such as governors. In the Ottoman empire in the eighteenth century '[t]he most lucrative and influential government positions involved tax collection', and the great tax farmers, employing hundreds of servants and dependents, acted both as administrators and adjudicators of disputes, and as money lenders and businessmen (Marcus 1989: 57–8). Far from regarding taxation as a burden to be shared fairly, exemption from taxes was a privilege or mark of patronage and hence a source of prestige and wealth (Marcus 1989: 38, 46). As industrial capitalism developed during the nineteenth century, the main aim of imperialism became the opening up of dependent territories for profitable trade and investment, especially for raw materials. However, governments of imperial countries such as Great Britain considered that the colonies should at least pay their own costs through local taxation, and if possible contribute to the 'costs of empire'.

For subject peoples, imperial taxation was oppressive, as shown by the revolt of Britain's north American colonies spurred by the slogan 'no taxation without representation'. To establish legitimacy and efficiency, the form of taxation needed to take account of both the economic structure and pre-existing patterns of surplus extraction by rulers, while also aiming to change both of these in line with colonial policy. In India, the complex hierarchy of claims to land was converted to a system of land ownership, providing a basis for a land tax; this provided the fiscal mainstay, but it declined from 52 per cent of government revenue in 1861 to 1865 to 28 per cent in 1920 to 1925, and had to be supplemented by

---

5 See Chapter 1, at 1.2. In the UK the ratio of state spending to GDP peaked at nearly 50% in 1975, and was 46% in 1979 (when Mrs Thatcher came to power) rising to 48% (1982–4), falling to 39% (1989), but rising again to 44% (1992) (OECD 2002b: 94).

import duties, salt duties and an income tax (from 1860 to 1873, reintroduced in 1886). Elsewhere, revenues were mainly raised from taxing commodity transactions, especially by duties on imports. In territories where there was little trade, such as African colonies at least initially, there was reliance on hut, head or poll taxes. In addition to raising revenue these created pressures for the able-bodied to move into the money economy, or to supplement forced labour for infrastructure projects such as road building (Shivji 1986: 9, 11–13). Such taxes often led to revolts, yet they continued to be important even after independence, especially for local government, despite their unpopularity (Fjeldstad and Therkildsen 2008). Thus, colonial taxation created a nexus between state power and legitimate economic activity, defining the important zone of contestation over illicit, semi-regulated or unregulated activities in the 'informal sector' (Roitman 2005).

A shift to direct taxation was urged by Frederick Lugard, who in West Africa developed the system of 'indirect rule' through local elites. He saw direct taxation as essential to civilized states, and a means of providing legitimate revenue which could be shared by the imperial government with local rulers 'not as a dole from Government, which would destroy their self-respect, but as their proper dues from their own people in return for their work as Rulers or Judges' (Lugard [1919] 1970: 167). He argued that this form of tax would allow abolition of slavery and forced labour, and encourage economic development. However, direct taxes on income greatly relied on assessment and collection by local chiefs. This meant less revenue for the central administration, so the imperial government persisted with a poll tax, despite its unpopularity (Daunton 2001: 133–5). Reliance on chiefs also prolonged traditional structures and contributed to the clientelist politics of the post-colonial period.

Colonial taxation did establish a link between taxation and citizenship: the 'tax ticket' was used as a form of identification and policing (Shivji 1986: 13), as well as for participation in elections once the suffrage was eventually extended to 'natives' (Hodgkin 1956: 150). However, given the nature of the colonial state and its forms of taxation, taxes were seen as tributes to the colonial power, rather than contributions to the political collectivity entrusted to its rulers.

In the post-colonial period, developing countries, unsurprisingly, have achieved a much lower level of taxation than the OECD countries: government tax revenues have been in the range of 10 to 20 per cent of GDP, the countries with higher per capita incomes generally being at the higher end of the range (Tanzi 1987: 216).[6] Also, income taxes have accounted for a rather lower proportion of these revenues than in OECD countries (20–30 per cent), and a higher share of this has come from corporate rather than personal income taxes.[7] Import duties continued to be very important, averaging 25 per cent of revenue (Tanzi 1987: 217). However, tariff reductions due to trade liberalization have had a significant impact since the 1980s, both directly by reducing revenues from this source, and indirectly due to substitution effects and the adoption of other means of supporting domestic industries which involve tax expenditures (tax allowances or subsidies) (IADB 2004). Partly to plug this gap, bodies such as the International Monetary Fund (IMF) have urged the adoption of a VAT, and many have followed this advice. However, it has been criticized for being inappropriate and indiscriminate (Stewart and Jogarajan 2004); overall the revenue loss from reduced trade taxes has been only partly recovered from other taxes (Baunsgaard and Keen 2005), and reliance on indirect taxes resulting from the reigning tax policy consensus has been blamed for the stagnation of revenues from taxes other than on natural resources (McKinley and Kyrili 2009).

It is significant that 'the capacity to tax grows with the growth of income' (Tanzi 1987: 218), although a number of other factors, both structural and specific, also affect the ability to raise revenue.[8] Poor countries are restricted by their relatively low tax revenues from stimulating their economic development from their own resources, leading to dependence on aid.[9] On the other hand, those which are able to obtain large revenues from 'rents' on natural resources, especially oil, have generally found this to be a curse rather than a blessing, leading to conflict and corruption (Esanov et al. 2001; Jensen and Wantchekon 2004). It has been suggested that post-colonial or developing states generally can be

---

6 The newly industrialized countries of South-East Asia have been an exception to this (Zee 1996).

7 The averages of course conceal considerable variations: in particular, oil-producing states obviously obtain considerable revenues, which since the 1950s have taken the form of a combination of royalties and profits taxes (which the companies can claim as credits against home-country tax liability).

8 An IMF study has examined a variety of factors, in addition to per capita GDP, that appear to affect 'revenue performance' (the effectiveness of taxation), including economic structure (e.g. the GDP share of sectors such as agriculture, which are hard to tax); it also suggests some significant variations between countries as to how well they actually perform in relation to predictions based on such factors (Gupta 2007).

9 In a number of developing countries foreign aid receipts are close to or higher than tax revenues (Fjeldstad and Rakner 2003: 2).

characterized in terms of fiscal sociology as 'rentier states' (Moore 2004), which helps to underline the importance of their mode of taxation for governance, which has begun to be recognized and studied (Bräutigam *et al.* 2008). The view has gained ground that strengthening the tax systems of developing countries, through taxes accepted as legitimate, would make a major contribution both to their prospects for economic development, and to improving their governance, through greater political pressures for accountability of politicians and state officials to citizen taxpayers.[10] However, this is extremely difficult to achieve in countries where the vast majority of the population are very poor, and which often suffer from autocratic and corrupt governance. A shift in the sources of government revenue towards greater reliance on internal taxation would involve a major transformation of what have been described as the 'lame Leviathans', the post-colonial autocratic states in which local elites maintain the deceptions of sovereignty while using clientelist strategies to exploit external patronage and systematize internal patrimonial practices (Badie 2000).

The developed countries also face some fundamental challenges which go to the heart of the nature of the state and society. The decline of social solidarity, and the recent widening of income inequalities, is undermining direct taxation of income and profits, and hence the efficiency and legitimacy of the tax system. The personal income tax began as a tax on the rich, but became a mass tax from 1940, especially with the introduction of collection at source from employment income, and in advance, via pay as you earn (PAYE). In the boom period of the welfare state, the growing tax burden fell increasingly on individuals, and personal income tax peaked at 30 per cent of tax revenues in 1985, but has declined since then to some 25 per cent. This has been compensated for by rising social security contributions, which became the largest component of tax revenues in 2003 at 26 per cent, attributable to higher social spending, especially on pensions and health care (OECD 2005a: 23).

Income tax now falls disproportionately on salary and wage earners, mainly due to the greater opportunities for avoidance in relation to income from capital, business or self-employment.[11] High marginal rates

---

10 Bräutigam 2002; Moore 2007; Owens 2009. This echoes the views of Lugard, cited above.
11 The term avoidance is generally used to mean attempting to reduce tax liability by means which are lawful, although they might be disallowed; the use of unlawful means (usually requiring proof of deliberate or intentional deceit) is termed evasion, unlike in other languages, such as French, where direct unlawfulness is described as fiscal fraud, and everything else is *évasion fiscale*. See further at 6.3 below.

have been reduced in an effort to curb such avoidance and improve the overall effectiveness of collection. However, with rising economic inequality the reduction of progressivity means that taxation impacts even more on the poorer,[12] and hence reduces its legitimacy. Some countries, especially transitional economies facing difficulties with tax compliance by the rich, have introduced 'flat taxes' (essentially, a single rate of income tax). A flat tax set at a high rate but with substantial personal allowances may succeed in maintaining both progressivity and revenue, but countries opting for a low rate generally see a decline in both, which suggests that this approach is not sustainable (Keen *et al.* 2006). Governments have also tried to supplement income taxes by resorting to a variety of special taxes, such as transaction taxes (e.g. on insurance premiums or air tickets), but these are often resented as 'stealth taxation'. They also create often substantial compliance costs for the tax administrations and taxpayers, both individuals and families as well as businesses.[13] While specific taxes may be used for regulatory purposes such as encouraging energy saving or environmental protection measures, they are unlikely to raise significant net revenue. Not surprisingly, therefore, there has been political resistance to higher taxation, which is often stronger from lower earners, although there is popular support for higher income tax rates on top earners (Fabian Society 2000: 46, 52–3).

6.1.2 Tax reform and democracy

Willingness to pay taxes is strongly linked to taxpayers' sense of the effectiveness of government in delivering key services, especially education, health care and infrastructure (Fabian Society 2000: 47–9). This has led to a variety of proposals for 'reconnection' of taxation and expenditure,

---

12 In the UK, 48% of total income tax receipts came from the top 10% of income tax payers in 1998, compared with 25% twenty years earlier; but in the same period the proportion of their gross income paid in tax by the richest 25% of households fell from 37% to 35%, while for the poorest 25% it rose from 31% to 38% (Fabian Society 2000: 74). It should be noted that such data are based on declared income.

13 Attention has been drawn to the administrative costs for business of the plethora of taxes which firms are required to pay or collect, by a report done by the World Bank in conjunction with the accountancy firm Price Waterhouse Coopers (PWC and WB 2006). The point is partly valid, although it ignores the burden also on families of the growth of special taxes and charges; it is also mixed in this report with more sweeping and spurious claims about the 'total tax contribution' of firms, and arguments which generally encourage reducing taxes on business, especially to attract foreign investment.

including methods of making governments more accountable for public expenditures (Fabian Society 2000: ch. 7). More radically, there have
been attempts to democratize decisions about tax expenditure, through
various kinds of participatory budgeting initiatives (Bräutigam 2004),
the foremost example being the experience in Porto Alegre, Brazil (Santos 1998). This has been lauded as an empowering experiment in a new
democratic–participative form of local state (Baiocchi 2001; Novy and
Leubolt 2005), though some have criticized it as a partisan political strategy which brought tax increases and fiscal insecurity and disappointed
the expectations it had raised (Goldfrank and Schneider 2006). Various
versions of participatory budgeting have also been initiated in a number of countries (Shah 2007). One variant of this is the Constituency
Development Fund, such as that launched in Kenya in 2003, which was
also aimed at involving communities to ensure that spending meets local
needs; however, it has been criticized for political manipulation and reinforcing clientelism (Kimenyi 2005; Waris 2009: ch. 6; see generally van
Zyl 2010).

Another approach is to introduce a direct connection between a specific
tax and a specific service. This may take two broad approaches, hypothecated taxes or user charges. Hypothecated or 'earmarked' taxes are those
which use the revenues they raise for specific, designated purposes benefiting the general public. Charges are levies on the users of specific services
as a condition of access to that service, such as road tolls, or fees for
education or health care services. Although both these forms establish a
direct connection between taxation and expenditure, they have a number of disadvantages, such as inflexibility, and the possibility of political
manipulation. In addition, charges are generally flat rate and therefore
regressive, and erect a barrier to access to vital services especially by
the poor. On the other hand some services, such as higher education,
give advantages to particular beneficiaries, and it may be considered
fairer for them to repay at least some of the costs (World Bank 1988: 21
and ch. 6).

Political obstacles to substantive tax reform have led to a focus on
reform of tax administration, generally involving new managerial techniques and professionalization, and a shift to a culture of service delivery
and customer orientation, aiming to improve tax compliance (Hamilton 2003; Aberbach and Christensen 2007). Tax authorities have been
given greater autonomy from government, within a defined remit, with
corporate plans and performance targets. Although this has led to some
improvements in collection rates, they have tended to be short term, and

accompanied by taxpayer complaints of overzealous enforcement, especially in developing countries;[14] while pressures to do more with fewer resources (to achieve 'efficiency gains') have led to talk of a crisis in tax administration (Aaron and Slemrod 2004). Others have argued for a more holistic approach, which should combine simplification of the tax code (based on broad principles supplemented by more specific regulations, rather than a complex mass of detailed rules), with a more responsive form of administration aiming to build trust and hence improve compliance (V. Braithwaite 2003; Picciotto 2007a).

Clearly however, purely technocratic changes to administration are no substitute for a tax system which itself is generally accepted as fair and democratic. The challenge is whether such systems are possible in a world where the structures of social solidarity binding citizens together and to their state have become increasingly fragmented.

6.2 The internationalization of business taxation

6.2.1 Problems of tax jurisdiction

The taxation of income and profits became the centrepiece of the modern fiscal state from the end of the nineteenth century, in a period when the leading capitalist economies were already highly globalized through extensive flows of both trade and investment.[15] The issue of tax jurisdiction throws into sharp relief the contradictions of the national state in the classical liberal internationalist system. From the beginning, the application of national taxes to income from international business raised issues of the scope of national taxation and possibilities for international coordination. Even if tax jurisdiction is territorially based, an income tax may still produce overlapping jurisdictional claims, since it may be applied both to persons within the territory and to income earned within the territory paid to a person outside it. The UK, which pioneered the income tax, applied it to residents on income from all sources, as well as to non-residents on income earned from UK sources. As other states followed suit, this began to raise complaints of 'double taxation'.

When incorporation began to be more widely used in the last part of the nineteenth century, it became necessary to decide when a company should be regarded as 'resident' in the UK, and what income should be

---

14 Interview information.
15 Indeed, income taxation facilitated a shift away from reliance on high tariffs, so encouraging trade.

regarded as attributable to it, as well as how to characterize such income (due to the schedular structure of the UK income tax).[16] The concept of residence has never been defined by statute in the UK, but the courts developed the test of 'central management and control', which they said meant the location of the meetings of the board of directors, who were considered to manage the company on behalf of its shareholders.

Hence, companies financed from London but carrying out operations abroad, of which there were a great many in the heyday of the City of London as the centre of world finance, were taxable in the UK on their worldwide profits. This was starkly illustrated by the decision in the leading case of *De Beers* (1906). The UK's highest court held that the De Beers mining company, which was formed under South African law and had its head office, general meetings and all its mining activities there, was nevertheless a British resident, since 'the directors' meetings in London are the meetings where the real control is always exercized in practically all the important business of the company except the mining operations' (*De Beers* (1906): 213). Some British judges had shown an awareness of the international implications of the question. In 1876 Chief Baron Kelly remarked that the issue involved 'the international law of the world', since many of the shareholders were foreign residents, so that much of the earnings of the company belonged to individuals not living in Britain and therefore 'not within the jurisdiction of its laws'. However, he contented himself with the thought that if such foreigners chose to place their money in British companies, they 'must pay the cost of it' (*Calcutta Jute* (1876): 88).

The issue looked very different from the viewpoint of some of the leaders of British international business. This was expressed clearly by Sir William Vestey, who was to become well known in UK tax law, and who with his brother had built a corporate empire from a grocery firm by importing dried eggs from China and frozen beef from Argentina. He argued for fairness in relation to his international competitors, especially the Chicago Beef Trust, which paid no UK tax by being based abroad and consigning its shipments to independent importers in the UK. He

---

16 Different categories of income were (and still are) taxed differently according the Schedule and Case to which they might be attributed; in particular income or profits of a trade were taxable as they arose, while income from securities or possessions were taxable only when remitted to the UK. Thus, UK shareholders of a foreign-resident company would only be liable for UK tax on dividends remitted to the UK; whereas if the company itself were regarded as UK resident, its worldwide trading profits would be regarded as directly taxable in the UK (Picciotto 1992: 6–8).

proposed a global approach based on the proportion of sales in each country:

> In a business of this nature you cannot say how much is made in one country and how much is made in another. You kill an animal and the product of that animal is sold in 50 different countries. You cannot say how much is made in England and how much is made abroad. That is why I suggest that you should pay a turnover tax on what is brought into this country... It is not my object to escape payment of tax. My object is to get equality of taxation with the foreigner, and nothing else.[17]

Other countries which adopted a broad-based income tax, such as Sweden and the Netherlands, also applied it to all residents, though in the case of companies the preferred test was the location of the 'seat of management', which placed less emphasis on ultimate financial control (Norr 1962). In Germany, the Corporate Tax Law of 1920 applied two tests: the company's 'seat' (which for a company formed under German law had to be in Germany), or its place of top management, which focused on management of the actual business and not just financial decisions (Weber-Fas 1968). When the USA introduced a federal income tax after 1913, it applied to citizens on income from all sources, as well as on US-source income of non-citizens.

These approaches all involved taxation of residents (or citizens) on their worldwide income. However, some countries exempted income earned (or sometimes only if taxed) abroad. In other cases, foreign business income could generally escape taxation at home by incorporating subsidiaries abroad. Foreign incorporation was sufficient to escape US tax. Also, the USA introduced, in 1918, a credit for foreign taxes paid by US corporations, which could be applied to the taxes paid on dividends from subsidiaries, as well as on business profits of foreign branches. For other countries, care had to be taken to ensure that the management of the business, or in the case of the UK 'real control', was abroad,[18] but payments by affiliates such as dividends could be treated as income of the recipients, whether the parent company or individual shareholders.

A different approach emerged in France, where the general income tax introduced in 1914 was a personal tax on individuals, but followed in 1917 by taxes on specific types of revenue, including commercial and industrial

---

17 UK Royal Commission on Income Tax 1920, Evidence, p. 452, Question 9460.
18 For a more detailed discussion of the complexities and ambiguities involved, see Picciotto 1992: 4–11.

profits, which were considered as separate and parallel schedular taxes.[19] These taxes were regarded as having a 'real' rather than a personal character, so that tax liability applied to profits made by an establishment located in France, even if it was owned or operated by a company formed or resident abroad, but a French company was not taxable on profits of its foreign establishments (Court 1985). However, the tax on income from moveable property was applied to interest and dividends on securities of French companies even if foreign owned. Indeed, the French authorities ruled that it should apply also to foreign companies with an establishment in France, calculated on the proportion of their dividend payments represented by their assets in France.

As more states introduced direct taxes, and tax rates became very high after 1914, businesses operating on a global scale became increasingly aware of the impact of taxation on their competitiveness, and complained that overlapping claims to tax by different states created unfair international double taxation. This was felt perhaps most acutely by firms based in the UK, which was the leading capital-exporting country, and because its 'control' test cast a potentially very wide net. There were complaints when an income tax was introduced in India in 1860, and again when other countries in the Empire did so in 1893. Eventually, some relief was introduced in 1916, to allow deduction from UK tax of the rate of Dominion or colonial tax on the same revenue, up to half the UK tax rate. Beyond this the Treasury was not willing to go, at least unilaterally; this position was affirmed by the Royal Commission on Taxation's report in 1920, although it suggested that international arrangements could be negotiated, perhaps through the newly formed League of Nations.

6.2.2 Building the international tax framework

It was indeed through the League that formal arrangements for international coordination of income taxation gradually emerged in the period between the wars (see generally Picciotto 1992: ch. 1). Two reports, first from economists and then tax experts (officials), led to a diplomatic conference in 1928 and the establishment of a Fiscal Committee of the League. The result fell short of the multilateral agreement for which some had hoped, but took the innovative form of model tax treaties, which could be used as a template for bilateral treaties between states, with modifications

---

19 Replaced in 1948 by a company tax.

to suit their tax systems and the capital flows between them. The Committee subsequently commissioned a study on the difficult issue of 'allocation of business income' (later termed transfer pricing), which was carried out by Mitchell B. Carroll, the US representative, who visited thirty-five countries, meeting both officials and business representatives.[20] This study resulted in another model convention, on allocation of business income, which later was incorporated into the basic income tax treaty model.

The model treaty provisions allocate rights to tax income from international investment between the investor's residence or home country, and the host or source country where the profits or income are made, according to the different categories of income. Essentially, the distinction made is between active income from carrying on a business, and passive returns on investment, or income from capital. The treaty allocates the primary right to tax active business income to the source country, where the business is located. This applies also to the profits of a locally incorporated but foreign-owned subsidiary, which in any case is also usually considered resident in the source country. Source taxation also applies to the profits earned through a branch or office, provided it meets the criteria for a Permanent Establishment (PE). The PE remains a key concept in tax treaties. Otherwise, the treaty aims to restrict taxation at source of the returns on investment, so that dividends, interest, royalties and fees should primarily be taxed in the country of residence of the investor.

The tax treaty approach aims to preserve to the maximum the freedom of each state to define its own income tax system, while establishing sufficient coordination to facilitate economic flows between states, by attempting to reconcile the conflicting principles of taxation based on source and residence.[21] However, the form of international cooperation it entails is minimal, and indeed it has reinforced the primacy of national

20 The study was funded by a $90,000 grant by the Rockefeller Foundation. Carroll had been partly educated in Europe, and worked for the Department of Commerce on taxation of US business in Europe; he was instrumental in persuading the USA to participate in the Fiscal Committee, and accompanied Prof. Adams, the Treasury's Economic Adviser, to its 1927–8 meetings. He chaired the Fiscal Committee between 1938 and 1946, during which time it consolidated the model treaties which it bequeathed to the UN and later the OECD, while at the same time taking a leading part in founding the International Fiscal Association, of which he became the long-serving first President (Carroll 1978; Picciotto 1995: 41–3).

21 From an economic perspective, it was argued that the country of residence should tax the returns on capital equally whether invested at home or abroad (referred to as capital–export equity), and politically that it was in a better position to determine ability to pay. Conversely, it could be said that the source country should apply equal taxation to all business within its territory (capital–import equity), and politically that such activities

jurisdiction, since it requires no commitment to an overarching multilateral arrangement, nor even any agreed international principles for defining or allocating the tax base of internationally operating businesses. Thus, it fell significantly short of the approach suggested by William Vestey. In particular, the Carroll report resulted in an emphasis on taxation of the components of a TNC (subsidiaries and branches) on the basis of separate national accounts, treating each component as if it were an independent business, based on the so-called 'arm's length' criterion. By avoiding the need for international agreement on an allocation formula, this left legitimation of taxation to each state, while also creating a competitive tension between them.

This approach raised problems of its own, both political and technical. Countries which were mainly capital importing were reluctant to cede to the investor's country of residence the right to tax the returns on investment. Some, such as France (as we have seen), considered assets such as shares, or patents, to be moveable property, the income from which could be taxed in the country where they were located. Since the owners of such assets would also be likely to be taxed on the income in their country of residence, this would very clearly involve double taxation. However, between countries with comparable two-way flows of investment, such overlapping jurisdictional claims created some incentive for negotiation of a treaty. Since the model treaty gave priority to taxation of returns on investment to the country of residence of the investor, bilateral treaties aimed reciprocally to reduce or eliminate source taxation of returns from portfolio investment.[22]

The reinforcing of the national basis of income taxation runs counter to the international–integrationist economic logic of TNCs. The problem was well understood by the technical specialists, as revealed in the country studies of the Carroll report, several of which showed a preference for a fractional apportionment approach. This would entail taxing the business profits of a TNC in each country on the basis of an appropriate proportion

should contribute to the costs of infrastructure and other facilities which made the profit possible.

22 Treaties generally restrict withholding taxes on dividends, interest, royalties and fees, often to zero between capital-exporting countries, or at levels between 5 and 15 per cent. Dividends paid to parent companies are normally subject to lower withholding rates than those paid to portfolio investors. Primarily capital-importing countries prefer to retain the right to charge higher withholding tax rates, especially on payments such as interest and royalties, which are deductible from business profits.

of the worldwide profits of the firm treated as a whole.[23] The possibility of adopting an international formula apportionment approach to allocation of business profits was addressed in the Carroll report, which recognized that, to the extent that a TNC was operated as an integrated enterprise, there would inevitably be difficulties in attributing and allocating specific items both of income and expenditure to its constituent parts. However, the report considered it to be 'quite inconceivable' that states could agree on a general formula apportionment principle, especially if it would require them to 'permit income earned within their jurisdiction to be reduced by losses sustained elsewhere'.[24]

Hence, the separate accounts and arm's length-pricing approach resulted from the view taken by technical specialists of the difficulty of reaching international political agreement on a global standard. However, they also understood that in practice fractional apportionment would be inevitable, but it would have to be applied on a case-by-case basis. This would entail arrangements for cooperation between the national fiscal authorities, which the German report in particular presciently suggested might provide a basis for development of agreed general principles, perhaps in the form of defined allocation percentages (Picciotto 1992: 35).

The League treaty models also included treaties for cooperation in both assessment and collection of taxes, as the Technical Experts had stressed that prevention of international double taxation should be complemented by measures to combat fiscal evasion, while accepting that international administrative assistance should not amount to 'an extension beyond national frontiers of an organized system of fiscal inquisition'. In practice, however, states were reluctant to establish cooperation between tax administrations, especially for tax collection, and despite various safeguards suggested by the Fiscal Committee, the model treaties eventually included only a minimal provision for exchange of information necessary for implementation of the treaty.

The autarchic political climate of the 1930s was not conducive to the conclusion of international agreements, and even bilateral treaties to prevent double taxation based on the League models were slow to develop, although almost sixty were signed by 1939. It was not until the 1950s that

23 Even the UK report, which advocated separate accounting, stated that alternative approaches such as calculation of profits as a proportion of turnover were applied in nearly half the cases, and its availability was generally important in preventing taxpayers 'taking up an unreasonable attitude' (cited in Picciotto 1992: 30).

24 In the words of Prof. Ralph C. Jones of Yale, who contributed a study on the accounting aspects (cited in Picciotto 1992: 34).

an extensive network of bilateral tax treaties began to grow, and then mainly between the developed OECD countries, due to the stronger basis of reciprocal capital flows between them. Although the United Nations established a Financial and Fiscal Commission, it was riven by Cold War and North–South conflicts, and could not be allowed to rival the Bretton Woods institutions, so it ceased to meet after 1954. The mantle of the League's Fiscal Committee was taken over by the OECD, whose Committee on Fiscal Affairs (CFA) has dominated the scene since its establishment in 1955. The OECD–CFA's Treaty Model and Commentary, as well as periodic reports on specific issues, have provided the formal backbone of the international tax system.[25] In 1967 the UN set up an Ad Hoc Group of Experts, the lowest level of UN body, which essentially concentrated on discussing minor amendments of the OECD model to try to adapt it to the needs of capital-importing developing countries. It was upgraded to a committee in 2004, with efforts being made to expand its role, especially in strengthening the tax capacity of developing countries.

6.2.3 The 'flawed miracle' of the tax treaty system

The skeleton of the international tax system is provided by the network of bilateral tax treaties, which now number some 3,000. Although countries which were mainly capital importing had insufficient incentive to nego-tiate treaties, in the immediate post-war period states such as the UK and the Netherlands extended treaties to their colonies and dependencies. The preference of capital-importing countries for a wider scope for taxation at source had to some extent been met by the formulation of the so-called Mexico draft of the model treaty by the League of Nations,[26] and was used as the basis for the UN model which eventually emerged in 1980. It allows a wider scope for taxation at source, notably by a broader definition of a PE, and for taxation of fees for professional services performed from

25 The seminal report on Transfer Pricing and Multinational Enterprise was published in 1979; subsequently reports have been produced regularly on various topics, and have been conveniently assembled since 1997 in a loose-leaf format issued as vol. II of the Model Tax Convention on Income and Capital, which is regularly updated, together with its Commentary.
26 This resulted from meetings held in Mexico (1942–3), which were dominated by Latin American countries. The League's Fiscal Committee met for the last time in London in 1946; the alternative London draft produced there reasserted the primacy of residence taxation of income from capital, and was used as the basis for the OECD model (Picciotto 1992: 49ff.).

a 'fixed base'.[27] Paradoxically, a bigger obstacle to negotiation of treaties between predominantly capital-importing and capital-exporting states was the issue of tax 'sparing', when the source state chooses to exercise its claim to tax jurisdiction by granting tax holidays, or exemptions for a period of years, from tax on business profits, in order to attract investment. The model treaty permits (but does not require) the source country to tax business profits, and allows the residence country a choice between full exemption of such profits, or providing a credit for taxes paid.[28] Not surprisingly, states which operated a credit system, notably the USA, have been reluctant to give a credit for tax 'spared', which is the main reason for the lack of a treaty between the USA and most Latin American states.[29]

Despite the asymmetric nature of capital flows between developed and developing countries, the treaty network between them has nevertheless expanded, due to the competition between developing countries to attract investment, and the power of the tax treaty model as an international standard (Baistrocchi 2008). Indeed, tax treaties have been viewed by national ministries of finance as much or more as instruments for attracting overseas investment than for establishing international tax coordination. This has damaged their effectiveness as the competition for such investment has grown (see further below). In addition, the treaty network has become a very cumbersome and inflexible structure, since improvements or refinements of the model can only be implemented by renegotiating every treaty, and the interactions of treaties with changes in domestic tax laws can create great uncertainty.

The muscles of the international tax system have been the professional specialists in international taxation, working at the interface between

---

27 These issues continue to divide developed and developing countries, as seen in the debates in the UN Tax Committee in recent years, notably over a proposal to follow the OECD in eliminating art. 14 of the Model on taxation of professional services.

28 Exemption of foreign income in principle provides an incentive to invest abroad in low-tax countries, so major capital-exporting countries such as the UK and US have preferred to tax worldwide income, but grant credits against foreign taxes paid. However, TNCs are able to benefit from 'deferral' of taxes on the business profits of their foreign subsidiaries, provided these are incorporated or resident abroad, until remitted to the parent. In practice, indeed, by exploiting the tax credit rules and other techniques such as aggressive transfer pricing, they can even reduce their home-country tax liability, so that the result is 'worse than exemption' (Fleming et al. 2009).

29 Except for Mexico (1992) and Venezuela (1999), which do not include tax-sparing credits. Those countries which did allow credits for taxes spared re-evaluated such provisions in the 1990s, as they became aware of tax-avoidance schemes taking advantage of such credits, and opinion turned against using tax incentives to attract foreign investment.

public policy and the private interests of business firms. Mitchell Carroll himself kept in close touch with business firms and associations even while working for the government, then went into private practice in 1933, although still acting as consultant to the State Department and serving as the US representative on the League's Fiscal Committee. His tax practice appears to have consisted of helping to resolve major anomalies and difficulties experienced by large TNCs, such as Unilever, Morgan Guaranty Trust and ITT. The cases he recounts generally involved interceding directly with governments, including persuading negotiators to include appropriate provisions in treaties under negotiation (Carroll 1978: 113–15). While he was clearly an old-style 'gentleman-lawyer', he helped to create a regulatory arena which later became dominated by bureaucratized law and accountancy firms, with specialized international tax departments producing complex tax-avoidance 'products' such as double-dip leasing or currency and interest rate swaps (Picciotto 1995).

The tax treaty system has been described as a 'flawed miracle' (Avi-Yonah 1996: 1304). The central flaw is that the treaty principles for allocation of rights to tax between residence and source states were essentially designed for portfolio investment. As we have seen, those principles rest on the central distinction between active business income and passive investment income, and assume that the investor is independent from the enterprise invested in, merely seeking a return on capital. They were unsuitable and have proved ineffective for foreign direct investment (FDI), the form of international investment which became dominant in the second half of the twentieth century. FDI entails control over the investment, and the TNC operates as an internationally integrated firm, oriented towards growth which is financed substantially from internal funds.

The typical TNC has a high degree of discretion over its financial structure, especially the gearing of equity to debt, and the pricing of internal transfers. TNCs are also able to devise optimal routes for internal transactions within the firm through their chains of affiliates, frequently numbering hundreds (as discussed in Chapter 4). Most importantly, they can form intermediary entities in convenient jurisdictions, often specifically for the purpose of reducing their tax liability. TNCs have therefore been able to take advantage of the limitations of the tax treaty system and hence reduce their cost of capital, giving them a substantial competitive advantage. The techniques they developed, which are briefly explained in the next section, have become more generally exploited by others. In particular, the emergence of the 'offshore' finance system, discussed below, has further undermined the international tax system.

6.3 International tax avoidance and evasion

6.3.1 The grey areas and dark sides of tax avoidance

The limitations and flaws in coordination through the tax treaty system helped to spawn extensive international tax avoidance and evasion. Some forms of avoidance could be regarded as legitimate tax 'planning', certainly from the perspective of business. For example, as mentioned above, the very broad jurisdiction claimed by some countries, especially the UK, to tax the worldwide profits of residents, could fairly easily be avoided by setting up a foreign subsidiary to operate the foreign business activities, making sure that it is controlled and managed from outside the UK. Firms could consider this justified in the period before the development of the tax treaty network, when TNCs had to make their own arrangements to ensure they did not suffer international double taxation.[30]

However, the devices which have been developed for reducing tax liability have sometimes been found to be unlawful avoidance or outright evasion. The dividing lines are often blurred, since they depend on legal interpretation. Legal principles are essentially indeterminate, because of the social character and hence context dependence of language, and the necessarily teleological nature of interpretation of norms (Picciotto 2007a). This is especially problematic for taxation of international income, which relies on the abstract principles of income and residence. Liability to income tax can be very contestable due to the indeterminacy of these abstract concepts. Indeed the concept of 'income' itself, especially in relation to income from capital (including business), was constructed through political, social and ideological processes (Daunton 2004).

It is possible to reduce the scope for interpretation by using more specific or 'bright-line' rules, especially with a physical reference. For example, instead of basing company residence on the general principle of central management or control, a more specific rule could be used, such as the place where the board meets, or the country of incorporation.

---

30 One of the arguments made to the British Foreign Office in favour of a tax treaty with the USA during the negotiations in 1944 was that British firms with US subsidiaries had been obliged to use 'unsatisfactory expedients' such as mispricing invoices (PRO file FO371/38588; see Picciotto 1992: 39–40).

However, as this example shows, rules are less flexible and hence may be easier to avoid.[31] Thus, commentators suggest that tax and other forms of regulation should use a combination of principles and rules (Braithwaite 2002). Underlying the variations of interpretation in the struggles to 'control the legal text' (Bourdieu 1987: 818) are disagreements or conflicts over the issues of legitimacy raised by the allocation of jurisdiction to tax international business income.

An excellent example is provided by the history of the Vestey family, mentioned above, who became pioneers of international tax avoidance, or planning. They had already left the UK in 1915 and moved the control of their business to Argentina, to avoid the consequences of the British rule on residence of companies. Indeed, the Royal Commission heard evidence of a number of such company migrations, which it was accepted would continue. It was difficult for the UK to make a legitimate complaint against the transfer of central management and control from the UK to a foreign country where the substantial business of the company was actually carried on, such as the Vesteys' cattle ranching in Argentina. However, the Vesteys went further, and taking legal advice from 1919 to 1921, they established a family trust in Paris. The trustees would receive the income from their worldwide assets (with no tax liability since France exempted foreign-source income), and they were to apply the funds for the benefit of the family members (but not the brothers themselves). But the trust deed also gave the Vesteys power to give directions to the trustees as to the investment of the trust fund, although subject to such directions the trustees were given unrestricted powers (Knightley 1993). This enabled the Vesteys to return to live in the UK while continuing to direct their worldwide business empire through the trustees, and enjoy the income through their families.

Once the Revenue eventually discovered the existence of these and other similar arrangements, in 1936 and 1938 Parliament enacted the first provisions against foreign trusts. These aimed to prevent a UK resident from continuing to enjoy income by transferring assets to a foreign entity and receiving benefits from it. The terms of the statute were extremely widely drafted, especially the notion of 'power to enjoy' income derived by the UK resident as a result of the asset transfer. Trying to deal with any possible circumvention, the provisions aimed to include any beneficiaries

---

31 Similarly, rules on individual residence and domicile may be easier to avoid if based on number of days in the country: a good example is the saga of Robert Gaines-Cooper, see *Gaines-Cooper* v. *HMRC* (2010), and www.robertgainescooper.com.

and to tax the whole of the income sheltered (potentially including all the income of the transferee whether or not derived from the transferred assets), even if not actually paid over to the resident beneficiary. This gave the Revenue very broad powers.[32] The judges were divided on the central legal question of whether the Vesteys' power to give the trustees directions amounted to a 'power to enjoy' the income; only by a majority did the highest court decide in favour of the Vesteys (*Vestey's Executors* (1949)). Thirty years later the Vestey trust gained an even more decisive victory in the House of Lords, when it confined the scope of the anti-avoidance provisions of the statute to the actual transferor and not other beneficiaries (*Vestey* v. *IRC* (1979)). Amendments to the statute reversed these decisions, but the fertile minds of tax advisers have continued to find ways to try to legitimate such avoidance.

6.3.2 *The systematization of international avoidance*

In the succeeding decades, international tax avoidance has become a central feature of international business organization, especially for TNCs. Although the methods are often quite complex, the basic strategies are relatively simple. Avoidance of income tax generally relies on three basic techniques: (a) altering the timing of payments; (b) re-characterizing the nature of payments; and (c) changing the recipient. International avoidance relies mainly on the third of these, usually combined with the second. It is done by creating intermediary entities (companies, trusts, partnerships, etc.) in suitable jurisdictions, through which to channel assets, transactions and income. The basic aim is to minimize taxation based on residence in the home country of the investor or TNC, as well as taxation at source in the country where the business takes place (see Figure 6.1).

In simplified form, international avoidance entails using two types of intermediary entity: a Base entity (B) and a Conduit entity (C). These carry out various tasks of asset administration or the provision of services for the TNC's operating companies (O). A Conduit generally aims to reduce Source taxation, while a Base entity is used to avoid taxation by P's country of residence of that foreign-source income.

---

32 The provisions were later denounced in the standard monograph on the subject by an eminent QC and tax counsel as creating a 'preposterous state of affairs' which could only be made tolerable by the Revenue's exercise of 'discretion as to whom, and how and how much income to assess', a discretion so wide as to amount to a 'suspension of the rule of law' (Sumption 1982: 116, 138).

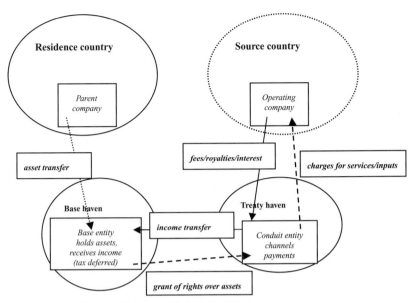

Figure 6.1 Basic tax-avoidance strategies

Base entities are created as residents of countries which do not tax the type of income which they will receive, because either they do not have an income or profits tax, or they exempt income from abroad. The purpose of these is to *defer* taxation of earnings which the TNC wishes to retain for reinvestment, instead of returning it to the Parent (P) for distribution to shareholders. This can be claimed to be legitimate if the income accrues to B as a return on an asset or payment for a service. Hence, Base entities are holding companies, owning either shares in other affiliates in the group, or others assets such as intellectual property rights; or they may operate services, such as shipping, or insurance. Generally, however, this is merely formal: the real decisions are usually taken by another entity, usually in London or New York, which provides 'advice'.[33]

Conduit entities are formed in a country which has a suitable tax treaty with the source country, which reduces or eliminates source taxation. They may obtain the benefit of the treaty even though they are essentially

---

33 See for example *Multinational* v. *Multinational Services* (1983), dealing with complications arising in liquidation of a joint venture, which formed a shipowning affiliate in a tax haven, while the main business of shipbroking was handled through a London-based 'services' company. Similarly, many hedge funds are formed in the Cayman Islands, although their investment advisers are located in London or New York (see below).

passive entities, whose function is merely to channel the income flow. If the income received by C is not taxable, it can be sent on directly. Otherwise, a 'stepping stone' strategy is used, by which C incurs high charges to a related Conduit or Base entity, for example by back-to-back financing, leaving it with no or low taxable profits. Although this may be valid, it is of doubtful legitimacy, since tax treaties are intended to facilitate investment between the countries concerned, on the assumption that the investor is a bona fide resident and normal taxpayer of the treaty partner country. The use of a Conduit intermediary is a form of treaty-shopping, taking advantage of the fictions of legal personality and state jurisdiction (Picciotto 1999). Indeed, even a resident of the source state may be able to use a Conduit for funds to be reinvested at home, sometimes described as 'round-tripping', although this could entail outright tax evasion.

Finally, and perhaps most importantly in terms of total tax liability, the use of a combination of B and C can reduce taxes on the business profits of O, if the payments are deductible as costs: for example patent royalties, interest on loans, or payments for services such as insurance. This helps to explain the data showing that foreign-owned TNCs generally pay less taxes than those locally owned, often indeed no tax at all, although this tends to be attributed to transfer-pricing (US GAO 2008). The use of such techniques has enabled TNCs significantly to reduce the tax they pay especially on retained earnings, and hence reduce the cost of capital to finance their expansion. This ability to manage their international tax exposures has been a significant element of the competitiveness of such firms.

6.3.3 Anti-avoidance measures and their limits

The tax authorities have tried to combat these devices by various means. Since such intermediary entities are set up purely to reduce tax liability, it may be argued that they are a mere sham and should be disregarded, under general anti-avoidance or anti-abuse principles in tax law, either statutory or judicial. Not all countries have such provisions, and in any case they have limitations, as it can be hard to distinguish between genuine and sham arrangements. This depends on some ulterior test of validity, such as economic or business purpose, which requires judges to interpret the purposes of the tax legislation. Political concerns about avoidance, as well as the blatant nature of many tax-avoidance schemes, have made courts more willing to apply or develop general anti-avoidance principles, notably in the UK with the so-called *Ramsay* principle. However, judges have been reluctant to take this too far, expressing concerns about the constitutional implications of usurping the role of the legislature or executive (Simpson 2004). For example, the Indian Supreme Court in 2003 rejected the argument for a general anti-avoidance rule to allow investigation of companies formed in Mauritius for investment into India, to see whether such companies were mere shell entities.[34]

More targeted anti-avoidance provisions have been introduced, especially in OECD countries. Tax deferral is combated by measures against Controlled Foreign Corporations (CFCs), which treat CFC income as directly accruing to the parent P and therefore taxable as part of P's worldwide income. This type of provision was adopted by the home states of TNCs, attempting to claw back into their tax net the retained worldwide earnings of such firms. Since this involves a strengthening of residence taxation of worldwide income, by disregarding the separate legal status of

---

34 *India* v. *Azadi Bachao Andolan* (2003). India concluded a tax treaty with Mauritius in 1983, formally aimed at encouraging genuine Mauritius residents to invest in India; but it became used for conduits, especially after the enactment of the Mauritius Offshore Business Activities Act of 1992 enabled international investors to take advantage of the lack of capital gains taxation in Mauritius. Official data showed that from 1991 to 2002 over 40 per cent of investment into India was through Mauritius. In 2000 some Indian tax offices issued notices to some Mauritius entities with investments in India to show cause why they should not be taxable in India on gains, on the grounds that they were sham entities, controlled from elsewhere. This led to a sharp fall in investment flows, resulting in a statement by the Finance Minister that the tax office actions did not represent government policy; the Central Board of Direct Taxes then issued a Circular stating that a certificate of residence issued by the Mauritian authorities should be accepted as conclusive. The challenge to this was upheld by the High Court, which held *inter alia* that the Circular was *ultra vires*, and applied the earlier Supreme Court decision in *McDowell* allowing tax officers to lift the corporate veil in pursuit of their duty to prevent tax avoidance. The Supreme Court overturned this decision on a number of grounds, holding in particular that the existing tax treaty provisions should be applied by the courts, and it was up to the government, if it thought it desirable, to negotiate with Mauritius provisions against treaty-shopping or modifying the definition of residence in the treaty. Surveying case law on anti-avoidance principles in a number of countries, including the UK, the Supreme Court robustly reaffirmed the legitimacy of tax planning: 'We are unable to agree with the submission that an act which is otherwise valid in law can be treated as non-est [*sic*] merely on the basis of some underlying motive supposedly resulting in some economic detriment or prejudice to the national interests'. The Indian authorities seem content that a tax residency certificate, which requires a company to show that it has adequate commercial presence and operations in Mauritius (Rohatgi 2007: 390), will not be issued if the company is being used for 'round-tripping'. However, a proposal for a statutory anti-avoidance principle was put forward in the comprehensive direct taxation reform of 2010, which was said to be aimed also against tax treaty abuse.

entities formed in another jurisdiction, it can be criticized as 'extraterritorial'. Hence, the formulation of anti-CFC measures was done cautiously,
with sensitivity to the limits of jurisdiction, and to some extent coordinated through the OECD (OECD 1987d, 1996). Thus, such measures
rely on three basic criteria: (a) a 'control' test defining the threshold for
determining that the CFC is controlled by residents of the 'home' state
(and therefore arguably subject to its jurisdiction); (b) a restriction to
'passive' income (which could be said not to have been genuinely earned
in the haven); and (c) that the CFC should be subject to a low tax regime.

All three criteria for CFC rules have become harder to apply following
the latest phase of globalization. Control tests have generally been based
on minimum ownership formulae which were from the start vulnerable to circumvention by taxpayers (OECD 1987d: para. 63); they have
become more problematic as many TNCs have decentralized or regional-
ized, making it harder to identify a single home state. The 'passive income'
test has become harder to apply to a variety of services which are increasingly important to post-industrial, knowledge-based capitalism, such as
professional services (e.g. consultancy), design or intellectual property
licensing, which can relatively easily be 'located' anywhere. Lobbying by
the financial services industry has ensured that most banking, finance
and insurance services income has often been designated as 'non-passive',
despite the ease with which such activities can be performed, at least
on paper, almost anywhere. This has provided a significant boost to the
growth of offshore financial centres (see 6.4.2.1 below). Finally, the competition to reduce corporate tax rates has made it harder to distinguish
low-tax jurisdictions.

Measures have also been introduced to counteract avoidance of source
taxation. Against Conduits, the source state may deny tax treaty benefits
to recipients which it considers are merely passive entities. However, its
ability to do so may be restricted by the treaty, which usually creates rights
for the taxpayer in domestic law. As shown by the Indian Supreme Court
decision discussed above (n. 34), courts may be reluctant to use a general anti-avoidance principle (whether statutory or judicial) to override
specific provisions of a tax treaty. Hence, tax treaties have been refined
to include provisions for denial of benefits to persons considered not to
be genuinely entitled to them.[35] Anti-conduit measures may also need

---

35 Picciotto 1992: 160–4. The OECD–CFA issued a report on The Use of Conduit Com-
    panies in 1986, and another in 2002. The various treaty provisions are discussed in the
    Commentary to the OECD Model Treaty, which is produced in loose-leaf format with

cooperation arrangements between the tax authorities of the two states, both to help the source state to evaluate whether the entity concerned is a Conduit, and to allow that entity to challenge a denial of benefit which it considers unjustified. Although inclusion of a broad anti-abuse principle in tax treaties may be helpful, it is difficult and time-consuming to renegotiate tax treaties, so it may be preferable to rely on a domestic anti-abuse principle, combined with the general international law principle that treaties must be interpreted in good faith.[36]

Generally, avoidance techniques are available to TNCs because they operate as internationally integrated firms, although from a formal legal viewpoint they consist of often highly complex corporate groups with between tens and hundreds of affiliates (as seen in Chapter 4). This allows them to use techniques such as organizing their operating company subsidiaries to reduce taxation of business profits by maximizing their tax-deductible costs: for example, they are often highly geared (a high proportion of debt to equity) since interest is deductible, but dividends are paid from post-tax profits. This may be challenged by the tax authorities under rules against 'thin capitalization', in particular by refusing to allow the deduction and treating the supposed interest payment as a 'deemed dividend'. However, this may raise issues of interpretation of the tax treaty and possibly a conflict with the treaty partner. Hence, many states prefer to treat thin capitalization as a transfer-pricing issue.

6.3.4 The transfer-pricing problem

The term transfer pricing is usually used pejoratively, to refer to the mispricing of cross-border transactions for an illegitimate purpose. Such purposes include not only reducing tax liability, but also evading currency controls, and concealing the origins of funds transferred abroad, especially funds derived from criminal activity or corruption. The mispricing may be deliberate and fraudulent, involving collusion between the exporter and importer. However, the term usually refers to transactions internal to a transnational corporation (TNC), since their complex intra-firm flows are a major component of cross-border transactions. Indeed, it is estimated that intra-firm flows of goods account for 40 to 50 per cent of

updates: see especially in relation to art. 1, paras. 7–22 of the 7th edition of 2008; para. 20 offers a text for a comprehensive limitation-of-benefits provision.

36 See para. 9.3 of the OECD Commentary, and the reports on Improper Use of Tax Treaties produced for the UN Committee of Tax Experts for its 2008 meeting.

world trade. Many other transfer payments within TNCs are made for services and for finance. In addition, TNCs often dominate international supply chains which, although they involve entities in different ownership, also provide opportunities to misprice payments.[37]

Raymond Baker goes so far as to say that 'I have never known a multi-national, multibillion-dollar, multiproduct corporation that did not use fictitious transfer pricing in some parts of its business to shift money between some of its entities' (2005: 30). Statistical studies of US TNCs using trade databases provide strong evidence of very substantial income shifting by means of intra-firm transfer prices.[38]

However, the issue is not just about deliberate fraud: it goes deeper than that. The notion of mispricing implies that there is a clearly correct or normal price. What is the norm for pricing between related parties operating within an integrated firm? Tax authorities have long grappled with this problem, especially in relation to income or profits taxation. For corporate groups operating within a single-tax jurisdiction, the usual approach is to require consolidated accounts, which simply eliminate intra-firm transactions, and include as income the proceeds of sales only once made outside the group. This is difficult for a single tax authority to apply to a TNC, so in the early decades of the twentieth century national tax authorities were given powers to adjust the accounts of companies within their jurisdiction to counteract any 'diversion' of profits to their

---

37 The US Bureau of Economic Analysis from 1977 collected data on intra-firm trade (between related entities) of both US- and foreign-parent multinational corporate groups, and these have occasionally been analysed in articles in the *Survey of Current Business*. The overview by Zeile (1997) showed that the proportions changed very little between 1977 and 1994, being some 32% to 40% of US exports, and 40% to 44% of imports. This covers only trade in goods, and not other transfers such as intra-firm services. It also does not include trade through supply chains, which take place under long-term contracts, but not between affiliates. More recently, the OECD has been attempting to gather comparable data on globalization indicators, which show that intra-firm trade by manufacturing affiliates under foreign control as a proportion of exports ranges between 15% and 60% in OECD countries (OECD 2005b: 11, 2007a).

38 Estimates based on analysing trade databases for abnormal price deviations to show likely levels of income shifting due to under- and over-invoicing between the USA and some other countries indicate mispricing, generally ranging between 2 and 10 per cent of trade volumes, involving billions of dollars per year (Boyrie *et al.* 2004). A study using customs data for all export transactions of US-based TNCs between 1993 and 2000 compared prices charged by the same firm to related and unrelated parties in the same country, in the same month and by the same mode of transport, and found that prices to unrelated firms were on average 43 per cent higher, especially to countries with lower corporate tax rates and higher import tariffs, suggesting a $5.5bn reduction in US corporate tax revenues (Bernard *et al.* 2008: 3).

foreign affiliates (Picciotto 1992: 171ff.). However, conflicting adjustments by different national authorities created a danger of international double taxation. This was the reason for the Carroll report (discussed at 6.2 above), which resulted in adoption of the 'arm's length' principle.

However, the arm's length approach based on separate accounting is inappropriate in principle, since TNCs are by their nature globally integrated. They exist largely due to their competitive advantages in combining the synergies and the economies of scale and scope derived from combining operations located in optimal locations. Hence, treating them as if they were composed of independent entities makes no sense. It has become an especially elusive exercise with the emergence of the knowledge economy since the 1970s, as much added value depends on intangibles, often entailing high fixed costs which are hard to allocate across the firm. The difficulty of applying arm's length has also been shown in practice, since in the clear majority of cases it is not possible to identify comparable transactions. This was indeed known already in the 1930s to the tax authorities, which often used other methods, at least as a backup. These may be based on comparable profits, which are also hard to find in oligopolistic industries, or profit split, which essentially means apportionment. Although the OECD's Committee on Fiscal Affairs (OECD–CFA) continues to maintain that separate accounts based on arm's length pricing of transactions should be the primary transfer-pricing method, it has been obliged to accept alternatives based on profit allocation, which are in practice now often used (UNCTAD 1997).

Transfer-pricing adjustments result in frequent disputes, which may involve many millions of dollars, and drag on for many years. For example, the pharmaceutical company Glaxo was assessed in January 2004 for $5.2bn of back taxes by the US Internal Revenue Service (IRS) for the years 1989 to 1996, in relation to profits from its anti-ulcer drug Zantac. Glaxo counter-claimed that this was 'arbitrary and capricious, and an abuse of... discretion' and unfair treatment, and argued for a refund of $1bn; the dispute was finally settled in 2006 for a payment of $3.4bn (Sullivan 2004a). Although extreme, the Glaxo case is far from unique, especially in globally integrated and knowledge-based industries such as pharmaceuticals.

These adjustments create conflicts not only between firms and tax authorities, but also between different tax authorities, since relatively small differences in transfer prices can shift millions in taxes from one state to another. Tax treaties therefore include provisions for a 'mutual agreement procedure' (MAP) for resolution of such disputes between the 'competent authorities' of the states concerned. Inconsistent transfer-pricing adjustments between different national authorities are said to account for 80 per cent of bilateral double-taxation disputes, although this cannot be verified since the MAP procedure is secret.[39] It can also involve a delay of often many years before the issue is resolved. To help with this, the USA introduced a procedure for Advanced Pricing Agreements (APAs), which has also been adopted by other OECD countries, and APAs can be agreed bilaterally, or even multilaterally. While this can provide firms with some certainty, it can be costly, and means the firm must be willing to open its books in advance to the tax authorities. Neither APAs nor the MAP resolve the problems of arbitrariness or secrecy, since they are essentially private deals with each firm. Indeed, Glaxo's complaint of unfairness, discussed above, was based on a comparison with the APA deal agreed by the IRS with its rival SmithKline, which it only discovered after they merged to form GlaxoSmithKline in 2001.

The indeterminate or arbitrary criteria for transfer pricing inevitably create opportunities and temptations for firms to adjust prices to gain tax advantages. Such practices may often be abusive. Both tax authorities and firms could do much to establish a better basis for preventing such abuse.

Tax authorities could reorient their approach to transfer pricing to abandon the chimera of arm's length, and adopt a unitary or consolidated basis for tax assessment of TNCs, with an allocation of the tax base based on formula apportionment (Hellerstein and McClure 2005; Clausing and Avi-Yonah 2007; Avi-Yonah and Benshalom 2010).[40] This would sidestep the problem of transfer pricing by simply eliminating internal transfers within the firm. It would also greatly help to tackle other thorny problems of international tax evasion and avoidance which (as discussed above and in the next section) generally use intermediary entities formed in convenient jurisdictions or tax havens. Under a unitary approach these would simply be treated as part of the firm as a whole, and the profits attributable to them would be determined by the formula. Of course, it

---

39 For an analysis of the available data see Altman 2005, who supports the introduction of a right to arbitration to resolve tax treaty disputes, which has long been pressed by TNCs; although tax administrations have been reluctant, understandably since they stand only to lose, there has been a move in this direction, especially since the introduction of the European Community Convention for arbitration of transfer-price disputes (90/436/EEC).

40 The European Commission has also been conducting technical studies to develop a Common Consolidated Corporate Tax Base for TNCs within Europe; although sometimes attacked as undermining sovereignty, it would actually help to restore national states' powers of taxing global business, while allowing each country to choose the actual rates of tax (Kellerman et al. 2007; see also Spengel and Wendt 2007; Fuest 2008).

poses its own problems, especially the need for an international agreement on the formula for apportionment. This would not be easy to resolve, since much is stake. However, these issues should be faced and resolved openly, rather than shrouding them in a fog of technical detail, imprecision and uncertainty, as under the present system. Solutions would be facilitated because the approach offers win-win opportunities.[41] Both firms and tax authorities would benefit from greatly reduced compliance costs. This would be especially helpful for developing countries, which do not have the resources to check transfer prices, or to operate complex anti-avoidance rules. Greater effectiveness would mean higher revenues, which would provide the opportunity further to reduce marginal tax rates.

Second, firms should adopt clear and open guidelines for tax compliance. These should include in particular a high degree of transparency about the amounts actually paid by the firm in tax, broken down by jurisdiction. At present, company accounts usually give only a global figure for tax liability, which is also often misleading by showing provisions made for tax, while the amounts actually paid in the end are often lower, due *inter alia* to deferral. A global standard for disclosure by companies of what they pay to each government (as well as by governments of what they receive) has been developed by the Extractive Industries Transparency Initiative, and the Publish What You Pay coalition has campaigned for it to be included in international accounting standards. Also, corporate codes of conduct should include a clear commitment to compliance with both the letter and the spirit of tax rules, and hence rejection of elaborate tax-planning and avoidance schemes. Such a commitment is surprisingly ignored in most corporate codes of conduct.

Such a combined constructive approach could establish a stronger basis of trust between tax authorities and business which would greatly improve tax compliance, and help strengthen the confidence of citizens generally in the legitimacy of taxation.

6.3.5 Tax havens and the 'offshore' finance system

A central element in international tax-avoidance strategies is the use of convenient jurisdictions, or tax havens. It is possible for almost any

---

41 Apportionment is usually based on a three-factor formula: assets, employees and sales; assets should mean physical assets, to prevent the use of havens; employees could be based on payroll costs, but it would be better to use headcount, which would favour low-wage countries, to counterbalance the advantage that richer countries would get by the sales element in the formula.

country's laws to be used to avoid or evade another's taxes. However, a haven is a country which has facilities specially aimed or adapted to enable avoidance or evasion of another country's laws or regulations, such as tax, usually for the benefit of non-residents of the haven.

As we have seen, strategies for avoidance of income tax emerged early in the twentieth century, exploiting the fictions of legal personality and jurisdiction. Thus, in the 1920s and 1930s jurisdictions such as the Channel Islands,[42] the Bahamas and Panama began to be used both for concealment of personal wealth by rich families, and by corporations for the formation of 'holding companies'. The use of havens enabled the wealthy to conceal income from the tax authorities, since it was not easy for state officials to obtain information from abroad, especially if local laws protected the confidentiality of information held by banks and professionals such as lawyers, or did not require publication of company information such as names of shareholders. This secrecy provided a cover for some illegal evasion or tax fraud; but havens could also be used for avoidance, by exploiting the grey areas or loopholes created by the contestability of abstract concepts such as residence, and the fictitious legal personality granted to corporations and trusts.[43]

TNCs in particular began to use such techniques to facilitate their expansion especially after 1950, to avoid home-country taxation of their foreign income, which they considered unjust. The development of sophisticated systems using fictitious affiliates incorporated in convenient jurisdictions secured for them the deferral of home-country tax liability on overseas earnings which they could not always obtain from

---

42 Jersey, Guernsey and Sark which, like the Isle of Man, are British Crown dependencies but not formally part of the UK; they also have special status in the EU, benefiting from some aspects of the Common Market.

43 Thus, in the 1920s the UK Inland Revenue discovered that large numbers of private investment companies had been set up in the Channel Islands which seemed to be controlled by nominees; their beneficiaries could not easily be traced, but many seemed to be British residents. However, an attempt to introduce comprehensive anti-avoidance legislation, including measures to restrict company formation in the Islands to persons carrying on a genuine business there, was unsuccessful. In the USA, since the federal income tax applied only to corporations formed under US law, wealthy Americans transferred assets to companies formed in low-tax or no-tax jurisdictions, such as the Bahamas, Panama and Newfoundland, leading to legislation applying US taxes to 'foreign personal holding companies' of US citizens, enacted in 1934 and extended in 1937 following investigations by a congressional committee set up at the instigation of President Roosevelt.

their governments by persuasion. However, as we have seen above, the system also opened up increasing possibilities for further reducing the overall tax burden on the business profits of internationally integrated firms, by channelling income to their tax haven entities as payments for the use of assets or services. Such payments could be charged as costs to their operating subsidiaries in high-tax countries, and minimize their tax liability.

Some degree of control could be exercised over the use of tax havens in the first half of the twentieth century, through currency exchange controls and rules on transfer of assets or setting up or moving a business abroad.[44] These had limited effects against TNCs which made profits in different countries, and they became even less effective as currency controls were relaxed in the 1960s, and finally abandoned by most countries during the 1980s. This process also gave birth to a new phenomenon, 'offshore' finance, which became closely linked to tax havens (to be discussed in the next chapter).

The range of international financial services, and their tax advantages, were extended by linking them to tax havens, many of which began to develop as financial centres themselves. Since they were often small island countries (e.g. the Bahamas, Cayman Islands, Netherlands Antilles), they came to be called offshore financial centres (OFCs), and bank deposits in such major tax havens are estimated to have grown to $5.3bn by 1968, and to nearly $300bn a decade later (US Treasury 1981: 41). This was largely fictitious, since these deposits were merely entries 'booked' on paper (or electronically), and attributed to 'shell' branches which generally only existed as brass plates, while the beneficiaries of the accounts had no real connection with the havens (Roberts 1994). Hence, tax havens and OFCs are essentially fictitious jurisdictions (Picciotto 1999). Nevertheless, the combination of tax benefits and freedom from banking regulations such as reserve requirements created a segregated financial market offering low-cost capital for the firms able to tap into it. TNCs' use of paper intermediaries for tax avoidance further contributed to the boom in the formation of 'brass plate' companies, partnerships and trusts in haven jurisdictions.

---

44 The UK in particular had extensive rules governing not only transfer of a company's residence but also transfer of any UK business to a non-resident, and even the issuing of debt or equity instruments by a non-resident company controlled by a UK resident; conditional permissions were used to regulate the rate of remittance of overseas profits by British-based TNCs (Picciotto 1992: 102–4).

These countries are perhaps better described as tax and financial havens, or secrecy jurisdictions.[45] They may be defined as jurisdictions which deliberately create regulation for the primary benefit of persons or entities not resident in their territory, which are designed to undermine the regulation of another jurisdiction. The system of 'offshore finance' itself is much more extensive, and much of it operates from the major financial centres 'onshore', such as London and New York (Palan 1999: 22). Tax havens have usually aspired to becoming finance havens as well, though not all have succeeded (e.g. Liberia); but there is no finance haven which does not also offer some tax advantage. Indeed, the major financial centres such as London and New York also offer some tax advantages: notably, they allow payment of interest on deposits and loans such as Eurobonds free of withholding tax, provided that the paying agent or 'qualified intermediary' certifies that the recipient is a non-resident. This turns a blind eye to evasion of other countries' taxes, and supports the offshore system, which undermines all countries' tax enforcement.[46] However, they do not strictly come within the definition of a haven, as they do not provide facilities primarily designed to facilitate avoidance of other countries' laws.

Tax avoidance and offshore finance are closely linked, for several reasons. Tax liability has a direct and significant impact on wealth and on business competitiveness, so that arrangements to avoid other types of regulation are usually combined with tax avoidance (e.g. flags of convenience). This is especially the case for finance, for several reasons.

First, many of the techniques of international tax avoidance, discussed in the previous section, involve managing financial structures and flows. Havens offer services of this type specifically or even exclusively aimed at non-residents. These are mainly financial services: banking (especially

---

45 For a comprehensive analysis and a ranking of secrecy havens based on data, see the Financial Secrecy Index: www.financialsecrecyindex.com.

46 Introduced by the USA and the UK together in 1984, at the same time as the cancellation of their tax treaties with the Netherlands Antilles, which had become the jurisdiction of choice for Eurobond flotations. Although in 2001 the US Treasury issued proposed regulations to require reporting of interest paid to residents of 'designated' countries, these did not enter into force, apparently due to fears that they would lead to an outflow of some of the $1 trillion in US bank deposits held by non-nationals (Sharman 2006: 28–9). The effect is that 'the United States looks the other way when foreign investors avoid home-country tax on U.S. investment income and gain. The QI program effectively preserves bank secrecy, facilitating U.S. investment by nervous foreigners. And . . . it is routinely and rather easily abused by U.S. citizens' (Sheppard 2008: 2; see also US Senate 2008).

private banking for 'high net worth individuals' HNWIs),[47] and insurance (mainly wholesale or reinsurance business);[48] as well as the formation and management of companies and trusts, usually to own assets or channel transactions for tax reasons. Specialist law firms and accountants provide the related services of company formation and management, advice on the structuring of transactions, and litigation if required, and some of these have grown into large, often multi-jurisdictional firms, which can set up and manage complex international structures.

Second, these techniques make use of artificial legal persons (companies, trusts, foundations and partnerships) as intermediary entities. Since the 1970s or earlier, havens have devised legislation for companies or trusts with special features, often designed by finance industry experts themselves, and in recent years havens have competed with and emulated each other in adding refinements. An early development in many havens was the 'international business company', specifically designed for use as a shell entity by non-residents, and benefiting from tax exemption (capital gains as well as corporate income taxes). Hence, such corporate vehicles are convenient for the formation of holding companies, as well as for sales and marketing, and services affiliates. A more recent refinement introduced in several jurisdictions is the 'protected cell company', which is intended to enable segregation of assets within a company, to facilitate its use as a 'rent-a-captive' insurance vehicle, or for collective investment entities.

The ancient common law device of the trust offers the advantage of separating the owner of assets (the settler) and the beneficiary or beneficiaries, by means of an artificial entity managed by supposedly independent trustees, who nevertheless are bound to obey the wishes of the settlor. Lichtenstein's Anstalt has similar characteristics, and other civil law jurisdictions such as Switzerland have introduced laws recognizing trusts.[49] Setting up a trust allows the settlor to avoid tax on

---

47 Wealth held offshore was estimated at $7.4 trillion in 2009, some 8 per cent of the worldwide total of private assets under management (BCG 2010: 5).

48 Proposed legislation was introduced in the US Congress by Congressman Neal in 2009 and 2010 to disallow deductions for reinsurance premiums paid to offshore affiliates; it became the focus for lobbying by conflicting groups, including claims that it would discriminate against foreign firms and violate US obligations, e.g. under WTO agreements.

49 Zaki 2004. So-called international trusts create significant problems of private international law, though they are governed to some extent by the Hague Trusts Convention (in force for states accepting it in 1992: on the interesting process of negotiation of this convention, see Dyer 1999), and the recognition of non-charitable 'purpose trusts' such as the Cayman's STAR, might be challenged: see generally Glasson and Thomas 2006.

the income from the assets, while ensuring that it is used in ways the settlor wishes, such as benefiting family members, or acquiring others assets such as houses or yachts (often using additional intermediary entities). Anti-avoidance measures initially challenged the transfer, as in the *Vesteys'* case, but then sought to ensure that at least the beneficiaries are taxed. However, the trust device has been substantially refined, some would say subverted, to attempt to avoid all taxation of the benefits. The lead was taken by lawyers who devised Cayman Islands STAR regime, allowing trusts for non-charitable purposes rather than specific beneficiaries, although some doubted whether they would be enforceable in other countries.[50] Other artificial entities include foundations. Partnerships can also be a convenient form through which to do business, even in high-tax countries, since their income is usually treated as owned by the partners pro rata.

Third, the central feature of the facilities and techniques used for avoidance of both tax and financial regulation is secrecy. Most national laws provide some degree of commercial, banking and professional confidentiality; but this can be overridden for the purposes of enforcing laws or regulations. Havens have generally strengthened such confidentiality requirements with secrecy obligations, which are often backed by criminal sanctions. The Swiss led the way with their bank secrecy law of 1934,[51] Panama in 1959, Cayman Islands in 1966 and 1976, and others have followed since (Effros 1982; OECD 2006). Banks themselves reinforce the usual client confidentiality by offering facilities such as numbered accounts and nominee ownership of assets. Bank secrecy is backed up by corporate, trust and professional secrecy. Information on the beneficial ownership of legal entities such as companies and trusts is often hard to obtain in any jurisdiction: public records of company details, such as

---

50 Special Trust (Alternative Regime) Law: see Duckworth 1998; Duckworth and Matthews 1999; Huxley 2000; Hayton 2002.

51 Switzerland emerged after 1918 as a financial entrepôt, and Swiss private banking in particular grew substantially by providing facilities based on bank secrecy for tax evasion by wealthy families, especially in France; in 1932 the French police unearthed evidence of systematic facilitation by a Basel bank of evasion of French taxes, resulting in a major political scandal and strong pressures on the bank to reveal details of its French clients. It was this that resulted in the 1934 Swiss law formalizing bank secrecy; only later was the convenient myth constructed that this law was motivated by the humanitarian concern to protect victims of Nazism in Germany, especially Jewish families (Guex 1999, 2007). The 1932 scandal was echoed in 2008 to 2009 when the leading Swiss bank UBS was accused by US authorities of systematic promotion of tax evasion (US Senate 2008); see further below.

names of directors or shareholders, are often unavailable,[52] or may be circumvented by using nominees. However, havens make such information virtually inaccessible, by allowing bearer shares, and dispensing with requirements for information about directors for company formation, or about beneficiaries of trusts. Thus, tax and finance havens are also termed secrecy jurisdictions.

Not surprisingly, these secrecy jurisdictions have increasingly come to be used for a wide variety of nefarious activities, especially since the 1980s (US Senate 1983). Tax avoidance becomes allied to tax evasion with the use of facilities for secrecy. Secrecy also facilitates both the commission and concealment of other criminal activities. For example, shell companies and secret bank accounts can be used to evade financial market regulations, such as those against market manipulation, insider trading or illegal takeover tactics, and such activities became more widespread as financial markets boomed in the 1980s (Stewart 1991). Some of the earliest clients of secrecy havens were the bosses of organized crime, who used Panama, the Bahamas and Switzerland in particular to conceal the funds from illicit activities, as well as to guard against the charges of tax evasion that had brought down Al Capone (Naylor 1994: 20–2). The growth of havens and the ending of exchange controls in the 1980s brought these secrecy facilities within the reach of a wide range of fraudsters and criminals. This includes their use to conceal the proceeds of bribery, sometimes on an enormous scale by corrupt politicians such as Ferdinand Marcos of the Philippines, Sani Abacha of Nigeria[53] and Raul Salinas of Mexico,[54] which has greatly contributed to the capital flight affecting developing countries (Dulin 2007). In 2007, a Stolen Assets Recovery Programme was launched as a joint initiative of the UN Office on Drugs and Crime and the World Bank, citing estimates that international flows of illicit funds are worth more than $1,000bn a year, and that as much as

52 A report to the US Congress pointed out that almost all US states (forty-seven) do not require information on company ownership to be provided either on formation or periodically (US GAO 2006), so that in effect the USA is a secrecy haven for shell companies.

53 It has been estimated that between $2bn and $5bn were looted by Abacha, the higher figure representing about 10 per cent of Nigeria's income from oil during those five years; some $468m. have been recovered from Switzerland, and a further $700m. as a result of proceedings pursued in Jersey, Lichtenstein and Switzerland (see International Center for Asset Recovery www.assetrecovery.org/kc).

54 Brother of the President, he was found to have taken large bribes from drug-traffickers, laundered through Swiss banks; the Swiss authorities eventually froze some $132m. in bank accounts controlled by him (Blum et al. 1998: 44).

25 per cent of the GDP of African states is lost to corruption every year, amounting to \$148bn.[55]

Havens and the service providers in them claim that there are many legitimate reasons for secrecy (which they prefer to describe as privacy), such as concealing assets from oppressive governments, or family members. Nevertheless, when put under political pressure, they have accepted the need to cooperate with multilateral efforts to combat money laundering, as well as arrangements for supervision of financial firms and markets (to be discussed in the next chapter, at 7.2). It is clearly in their interests, especially for those aspiring to the status of fully-fledged centres of international finance, to be seen as respectable and untainted by associations with crime, as well as offering a secure and well-regulated environment. They have, however, tried to draw the line at cooperation in tax matters. They rely on formalistic interpretations of the liberal principles of the international law of jurisdiction, maintaining that there is no obligation for one state to assist another in enforcing its tax laws, although this rests on dubious grounds.[56] Hence, they resist or refuse any responsibility to obtain or supply information to assist other countries' tax authorities to identify potential tax dodgers and argue that it is the users of their services who should declare any income which may be liable to tax to the appropriate authorities. This has greatly exacerbated the difficulties of effective taxation of income from capital, undermining the principles of equity underpinning income taxation to the point of threatening its very basis of legitimacy.

6.4 International tax reform

6.4.1 The crisis of income taxation

The legitimacy of income taxation has become threatened, as the liberal principle of equal taxation of all types of income from all sources has become increasingly difficult to maintain. Overall, tax revenues have not kept pace with the demands on public expenditure, especially for social programmes, leading to higher levels of public debt even in the wealthy

---

55 Callan 2007; a similar estimate came from the research of Kar and Cartwright-Smith 2008.
56 Thus, Richard Hay, a leading specialist and adviser on offshore avoidance, asserts that 'international law is clear: there is no unilateral obligation on any jurisdiction to assist another to collect taxes' (2006: 3); for the dubious legal basis of the 'revenue rule', see Chapter 3, n. 62; for an exposition of how international tax principles should be viewed as part of international law, see Avi-Yonah 2007.

OECD countries, which have only been alleviated in periods of economic growth. Thus, resistance by both capital and labour to tax increases has restricted the ability of governments to reform welfare programmes to meet new challenges from structural shifts in employment and the impact of demographic trends (especially ageing populations), and even to renew basic infrastructure (Genschel 2002; Swank and Steinmo 2002). Since it is much easier for capital to exploit opportunities for avoidance, especially by taking advantage of the weaknesses of international tax coordination, the burden of taxation has fallen increasingly on immobile factors, especially employment income.[57]

Here, a distinction needs to be made between production capital and financial capital. Capital invested in production is generally less mobile, indeed it is sometimes referred to as fixed capital. However, increased global interconnectedness, and the shift to the networked firm and supply chains, have made it easier for firms to pick and choose production locations. At the same time, governments have felt under increased pressure to offer tax incentives to attract investment. Many countries use a variety of tax incentives to attract investment from abroad.[58] Most economists

---

57 Some have challenged the so-called 'globalization thesis', that the tax burden is shifting away from capital, which is mobile, and towards labour, which is not (Hobson 2003; Stewart and Webb 2006). They rely mainly on data which show that overall tax revenues in OECD countries have increased in relation to GDP even since the 1980s, and that revenues from taxes on corporate income or profit have remained steady, as a proportion both of GDP and of government tax revenues (OECD 2001b, 2005a). However, the data on aggregate revenues from corporate tax take no account of the proportion of profits in the overall tax base. A number of factors have tended to increase corporate profit as against individual income, so that the steady level of revenue from corporate taxes as a proportion of GDP conceals a decline due to the increased share of corporate profits in the total tax base. Corporate tax rates have certainly been cut, and this is clearly linked to economic liberalization (Swank and Steinmo 2002: 643; Ganghof 2006). Top marginal rates of personal income tax have also fallen, but the reduction of corporate tax rates to below the top personal rate has increased the incentive for the self-employed and small business to incorporate (Ganghof 2006). Thus, taking account of the increased share of corporate profits in GDP, which averaged across fourteen OECD countries rose by almost 20 per cent between 1980 and 1996, it has been shown that there has been a significant fall in the effective rate of taxation of corporate income (Bretschger and Hettich 2002: 706, 708ff.).

58 For an excellent comparative examination, analysis and evaluation, including proposals on how the design of incentives might be improved, and how they could be restricted to prevent the damaging effects of competition, see Easson 2004. A global survey carried out at the turn of this century found tax incentive regimes in over forty-five countries from all regions of the world. Most targeted specific sectors; while nearly 70 per cent of the countries surveyed offered regional incentives aimed at assisting the economic development of rural or underdeveloped areas; the study found an increasing trend

consider that such incentives are highly undesirable, in effect a beggar-thy-neighbour policy, which is costly in terms of lost revenues, often distortive of investment decisions or ineffective, and hard to administer. Nevertheless, advisers tend to accept them as inevitable, due to politicians' concerns to attract investment for economic growth, and their policy advice is usually limited to ameliorating their harmful effects (Zee *et al.* 2002; Gugl and Zodrow 2006). Yet, as pointed out in Chapter 5, at 5.1.2, neither bilateral nor multilateral investment agreements have even attempted to curb the competition to offer such tax incentives.[59]

Incentives are generally aimed at TNCs, and hence give them a competitive advantage against domestic firms. The ability to locate production facilities in low-tax locations is a competitive advantage for TNCs in a number of industries. For example, it has been pointed out that Intel, the US semiconductor chip designer and manufacturer, has major production facilities in Puerto Rico, China, Malaysia, the Philippines, Ireland and Israel, all of which grant tax holidays (Avi-Yonah 2001: 4). In addition, an increasing trend is for countries to design their international tax regime to try to induce TNCs to locate specific activities there, such as research and development, or global or regional headquarters. Such incentives aimed at TNCs make it easier for them to pit one state against another, as well as providing opportunities for tax avoidance and evasion.

Financial capital, in contrast, is inherently highly mobile, and hence has special advantages in exploiting avoidance and evasion. Indeed its location is essentially fictitious, as money now mostly consists of a bookkeeping entry, which nowadays is electronic. As discussed above, the growth of the 'offshore' system, especially since financial liberalization, has made it much easier for both wealthy individuals and companies to receive income from financial investments free of tax. Thus, the use of 'offshore' vehicles has become a central feature of the complex structures used in international finance, enabling avoidance and evasion of both tax and other regulatory requirements. This enables both the large TNCs and wealthy individuals willing to exploit aggressive tax planning to reduce their effective tax rates, causing enormous social harm, not only through lost public revenues, but the excessive costs of such 'planning', and the distortive effects on capital allocation through the financial system.

---

towards offering full or partial tax holidays or tax rate reductions for specific types of activities, provided by nearly 85 per cent of the countries surveyed (UNCTAD 2000: 3).
59 Nov (2006) makes a proposal for a regime which could constrain their use.

For example, the majority of the world's hedge funds use Cayman Islands companies or partnerships,[60] but these are generally paper entities used for booking the transactions, although some ancillary services such as fund administration are done in Cayman. The main activities of hedge fund management take place in the USA and UK, but they are treated as only provision of advisory services. Income paid from the funds to their investors is not taxed at source, and residence taxation can easily be evaded by using companies formed in secrecy havens to channel and 'park' such income (Sheppard and Sullivan 2008). Similar structures are used to reduce taxation on other kinds of financial speculation, such as credit derivatives, which also entail dubious interpretations of source taxation rules on where financial transactions take place (Weiner 2008). However, the tax authorities in countries with major financial centres, especially the USA and UK, have been reluctant to take action against such extensive blatant avoidance and evasion, apparently due to fears that financial services business such as fund management would move to other centres.

By the 1990s devising and peddling aggressive tax avoidance schemes involving complex financial 'products' had become big business especially for the investment banks and large accountancy firms, and according to one estimate 75 per cent of such schemes were based on international transactions (Braithwaite 2005: 121). Low or zero taxation of financial transactions helped to fuel the growth of speculation, greatly contributing to the 2007–8 financial crash (see next chapter).

Lost tax revenues and distortion of the financial system are far from limited to rich OECD countries. Indeed, developing countries suffer far more from capital flight which is facilitated and encouraged by the off-shore system. Raymond Baker has analysed cross-border flows of 'dirty money', and suggests that two-thirds is due to commercial motives including tax evasion, and the remainder to criminal money laundering (2005). He estimates the total of such flows annually at between US\$1.06 trillion and US\$1.6 trillion, about half of which may come from developing and transitional economies.[61] Studies of individual countries have estimated

---

60 Data collected by the Cayman Islands Monetary Authority for 2006 from 5,052 Cayman-domiciled hedge funds (comprising 81% of the 6,252 active funds in Cayman) showed total net assets of US\$1.38 trillion; by the end of December 2007 the total had grown to 9,413, mostly managed from the USA and UK (CIMA 2008).

61 A report for the Global Financial Integrity project conservatively estimated illicit flows from developing countries in 2006 at \$858bn, having increased at an average annual rate of 18.2% from 2002 (Kar and Cartwright-Smith 2008). A follow-up report (Kar et al. 2010)

annual capital flight as high as an average of 9.2% of GDP for South Africa, 10.2% from China, 6.1% from Chile and 6.7% from Indonesia (Epstein 2005). Although some of this may be reinvested through 'round-tripping', it entails a massive volume of capital outflows, outstripping in aggregate the inflows of foreign aid, as well as considerable losses of public revenues. Indeed, the total losses to developing countries of leakages due to tax evasion and avoidance have been estimated by one commentator at $385bn annually, more than double the level of any potential official aid flows (Cobham 2005).

The availability of these 'offshore' facilities has made it extremely difficult for states to establish effective means to tax the passive investment income of their own residents. This was clearly shown by the attempts by Germany to apply a source deduction on bank interest payments. When this was introduced in January 1989, at the low rate of 10 per cent, it resulted in an outflow of bank deposits estimated at DM60bn, mainly to Luxembourg banks, and was hastily ended after six months (Picciotto 1992: 75; Avi-Yonah 2001: 9). Others also found that their wealthy residents increasingly made use of offshore facilities to evade taxes. At the same time many of the TNCs, who as we have seen above pioneered the development of techniques of international tax avoidance or 'planning', were increasingly using these techniques in an aggressive manner to reduce their effective tax rates.[62] Thus, it is hardly surprising that new initiatives were launched in the mid-1990s to try to counter the problem of tax evasion and avoidance, in conjunction with other harmful effects of the offshore system.

6.4.2 Reforming international tax coordination

6.4.2.1 Initiatives against harmful tax competition

The attempts to reform the international tax system, especially to deal with the problem of tax havens, were given a new impetus in the mid-1990s, and became linked with concerns about the effects of OFCs on financial regulation. The issues were taken up through the G7, which established the Financial Stability Forum (to be discussed in the next

---

estimated that some 56% of the illicit outflows went to banks in developed countries and 44% to OFCs. For further analysis and data, see www.gfip.org.

62 A study by Althshuler and Grubert (2006) using firm-level tax files of US TNCs showed a significant decline of effective tax rates between 1997 and 2002 correlated with a large growth of intra-firm payments and of holding company income.

chapter). However, the tax aspects were referred to the OECD–CFA, with a new political impetus for its work. In 1998 the OECD–CFA issued a report entitled *Harmful Tax Competition – An Emerging Global Issue*, which had a major impact (Sharman 2006). This was supplemented by a parallel initiative by the EU Member States, also aimed at 'harmful tax competition'.

Although the OECD–CFA made a bold start in its campaign against tax havens with its 1998 Report, the flaws in leaving the matter to that body were quickly revealed (Sharman 2006; Sullivan 2007). The rich OECD countries were all too easily depicted as Goliaths taking on the puny tax haven Davids. The initiative could hardly be characterized as a multilateral one to deal with a global systemic problem, as the concerns of the OECD countries were plainly focused on staunching their own tax losses. Instead of holding onto a clear common transparency standard as embodied in the multilateral treaty for information exchange which was initially proposed, the initiative lost its way by leaving it to states separately to negotiate bilateral Tax Information Exchange Agreements (TIEAs). Unsurprisingly, only the USA initially made much headway negotiating these, and even those agreed were slow to enter into force. Ironically, the OECD was forced to adopt a more global approach by the demands of the targeted havens for a 'level playing field'. This led to the formation of the Global Forum on Taxation, which became engaged in a lengthy process of establishing ground rules for a 'level playing field' (OECD 2006, 2008; STEP 2006). Its work quickly burgeoned, so that it was restructured in 2009 with a self-standing Secretariat (based at the OECD), a budget financed by all its members, and a three-year mandate (Spencer 2010a).

Both the OECD and EU initiatives were fatally damaged by starting from the flawed concept of 'harmful tax competition'. This is due to what are regarded as the political difficulties of accepting that international tax cooperation entails a degree of harmonization. Such measures do not need universal acceptance, but coordination among a significant number of leading countries, such as the OECD. Due to the political difficulties, the approach was the rather negative one of trying to identify features which could be agreed to be 'harmful' to others, around the general concept of 'preferential tax regimes' (Radaelli 1997).

The difficulties of this approach became clear from the problems which the 'harmful tax' perspective has encountered. The OECD 1998 report identified as the necessary starting point for defining a tax haven that it:

(a) imposes no or only nominal taxes (generally or in special circumstances) and offers itself, or is perceived to offer itself, as a place to be used by non-residents to escape tax in their country of residence.

This was linked with three subsidiary criteria:

(b) laws or administrative practices which prevent the effective exchange of relevant information with other governments on taxpayers benefiting from the low or no tax jurisdiction;
(c) lack of transparency; and
(d) the absence of a requirement that the activity be substantial, since it would suggest that a jurisdiction may be attempting to attract investment or transactions that are purely tax driven (transactions may be booked there without the requirement of adding value so that there is little real activity, *i.e.* these jurisdictions are essentially 'booking centres'). (1998: 22)

However, the 'no substantial activities' criterion was torpedoed in the volte-face by the USA announced by then Treasury Secretary O'Neill in July 2001, and it was formally withdrawn in the OECD's 2001 Progress report. What amounts to a 'substantial activity', especially as concerns financial services, can certainly be difficult to define, as was acknowledged already in the 1998 report, and this difficulty was again cited as a reason for dropping the test in 2001. As we have seen above, the problem is well known to the OECD tax specialists, since it is central to the operation of anti-CFC rules, which are supposed to be the major weapon against tax avoidance by residents. These have become inordinately complex, yet largely ineffective. The substantive question, which the 'no substantial activity' test avoids, is where *should* financial service businesses, such as hedge funds, reinsurance or futures trading, be regarded as taking place, and therefore be taxable?

Indeed, under pressure from their banks and financial service providers, OECD countries have themselves granted tax exemption for income from offshore financial services business booked in OFCs and tax havens. Notably, the US anti-CFC rules enacted in 1962 (Subpart F) exempted 'active financing income', which allowed financial firms to defer taxation on many types of offshore income; this was eliminated in 1986, but reintroduced in 1997.[63] Hence, other OECD countries also gave way to

---

63 Sicular 2007; Nadal 2008; although the 1997 reintroduction was accompanied by anti-abuse rules aimed at preventing the use of 'brass plate' entities, these can be and have been avoided (Sullivan 2004b); data from 2004 showed that the large US banks booked about

pressures from their financial services providers to be similarly exempt.[64] Thus, while the OECD was waging a campaign against tax havens and OFCs, the tax laws of the main OECD countries enabled or encouraged financial services providers to make use of such havens as 'booking centres'. Thus, it is hardly surprising that for example the Cayman Islands has been the main jurisdiction for creation of vehicles to operate hedge funds. Combined with other devices and making use of the secrecy offered by such havens, this has enabled avoidance or evasion of taxation not only of the profits of hedge funds themselves, and of their managers, but even of investors in them (Sheppard and Sullivan 2008).

With the dropping of the 'no substantial activities' test, the OECD initiative became focused on transparency, especially exchange of information. As Jeffrey Owens of the OECD stated in testimony to the US Senate Finance Committee, 'it is about all countries that lack transparency and are not prepared to cooperate to counter tax abuse' (Owens 2007). However, the effect of this was further to strength the arguments for a 'level playing field' made by the OFCs, or on their behalf by practitioners (STEP 2006). It has turned the spotlight on the extent to which even the leading OECD states themselves lack transparency and provide facilities for both tax avoidance and illicit transactions. Thus, even while a US Senate committee presented a denunciation of the use of 'shell companies' in tax havens for tax evasion (US Senate 2006), other agencies documented the facilities for such companies offered in the USA itself (US GAO 2006; Spencer 2007).

The effort to attain tax transparency was also greatly weakened, first by being limited to information on request, and second by shelving the initial idea of a multilateral treaty. Information on request may help target egregious tax evaders, and may help discourage the fearful (Sullivan 2007). However, only arrangements for automatic provision of information on

---

half their international lending through tax havens; the leader, Citicorp, had a reported reduction of 3.4 per cent in its effective tax rate due to tax deferral (Sullivan 2004b: 1380).

64 In 2004 Australia amended the 'active income' test in its CFC rules to include income derived from the provision of services to non-residents or to the foreign permanent establishments of Australian residents, previously designated 'tainted services income'. The official Explanatory Memorandum for the Bill stated that 'Reducing the scope of tainted services income will improve the competitiveness of Australian companies with offshore operations, and reduce their compliance costs' (Australia Treasury 2004: para. 3.3). New Zealand's International Tax Review of 2006 also recommended a revision of New Zealand's CFC regime to exempt the 'active income' of a CFC, which would exempt income from offshore services including banking.

payments to non-residents, such as provided for in the EU's Savings Directive (although limited to individual interest income), would establish a realistic basis for ending evasion of tax on passive investment income. But, as we have seen, even major OECD financial centres, notably the USA, have not put themselves in a position to provide such information. Limitations on the commitments which OECD countries are themselves able to make may also explain the reluctance to insist on a multilateral tax cooperation treaty. As a result, each OECD country had to embark on the lengthy process of negotiating bilateral TIEAs based on the OECD model.

6.4.3 Towards a new approach

Following the financial crisis, political pressure grew for a more determined effort to end the 'offshore' system. An important component of such a radical reform is a strengthening of international tax cooperation, focusing on a more positive approach to coordination of taxation of both international business (TNCs) and passive investment income. Although some significant steps have been taken, much more remains to be done.

An important first step should be a shift towards taxation of TNCs on a unitary basis (discussed at 6.3.4 above). As we have seen, this idea is far from new, indeed a unitary approach was essentially that suggested by William Vestey in 1920. Today the problem is much starker, but the response is not much different. A major reason for this has been the technicization of these initiatives. Tax specialists, both revenue officials and professional advisers and tax planners, are very aware that in practice the present system leads to often arbitrary allocations of the tax base, and thus creates incentives for aggressive tax planning and avoidance. After several decades of attempting other approaches, the European Commission finally decided that the elimination of 'tax obstacles' to a single market should mean moving away from tax treaty principles of jurisdictional allocation, towards a system based on consolidated accounts (European Commission 2001b). Although this could be done in a way which would retain national taxation and even national tax rates, the Commission anticipated the inevitable negative response from those national state political representatives who have stridently opposed any move to tax harmonization in Europe. Yet state corporate taxation in the USA is already on a unitary basis, and proposals have been made by some specialists for this approach to be adopted internationally (Avi-Yonah and Benshalom 2010).

Nevertheless, the Commission has continued to approach the matter cautiously, in a highly technical way, setting up specialist working parties to work through the arcane details of company accounts and their tax treatment.

The unitary approach would provide a much more effective basis for dealing with the key problems posed by taxation of international business profits, such as transfer pricing and tax deferral. It also would dispense with the need to obtain cooperation from tax havens for these purposes. The thorny problem of distinguishing between active and passive income would be avoided, by basing the allocation of the tax base on 'real' criteria (employees, external sales, physical assets). Perhaps most importantly, it would provide a much more effective basis for taxation of TNCs by developing countries. The present approach, based on treating affiliates of integrated corporate groups as separate entities, can only be applied by deploying a variety of anti-avoidance measures, for example against thin capitalization and transfer pricing, which have been discussed above. Such measures require substantial staff with a high level of expertise, which are not generally available even in the middle-income countries. As an interim measure, greater transparency in the accounts of TNCs would be introduced if the International Accounting Standards Board (IASB) included within its International Financial Reporting Standard on segment reporting a requirement that multinational corporate groups report on a country by country basis on all their transactions, as has been called for by several NGOs, and supported by the European Parliament in October 2009.

Second, there is a clear need for a more comprehensive system for obtaining and exchanging information for the purposes of tax enforcement. Under the pressure of fiscal shortfalls resulting from the financial crisis, the OECD states stepped up their efforts to use their own powers to obtain information, enabling them to begin to crack down on at least the most blatant tax evasion. For example, in 2007 the UK tax authorities managed to obtain a broad order against a number of UK banks obliging them to reveal details of offshore accounts of UK residents, thus identifying 400,000 potential tax evaders (*Application by HMRC* (2005), (2007)). It appears that the legal discovery order became possible only when it was discovered that the banks in the UK had effective control over the data relating to accounts in their offshore branches. Information from international banks could be used much more systematically in this way: for example, the Australian Tax Office has direct access to AUSTRAC, a database containing information from banks which extends to all

Australian-dollar transactions including those passing through offshore banks and branches.

As a result of such inquiries, the numbers of tax cheats revealed have been so great that the tax authorities have resorted to administrative devices such as amnesties to recover the large sums involved.[65] Tax authorities have also used unorthodox methods to obtain information, such as purchasing the data of client accounts from disaffected bank employees. Following up such information, the US IRS in 2009 issued a 'John Doe' summons against the Swiss Bank UBS, seeking information regarding a large number of its US clients suspected of evading taxes based on advice provided to them by UBS staff, for which UBS was charged with defrauding the US government. This resulted in a settlement between the IRS and UBS (which admitted the charges and paid $780m.), as well as an intergovernmental agreement (Switzerland–USA 2009) establishing a procedure under the bilateral tax treaty for examining US requests for information relating to some 4,500 accounts. This followed the revelations of systematic tax evasion through Lichtenstein banks, after raids by German police acting on evidence obtained by the purchase of a data disc from a disgruntled employee (Weiner 2009). The resulting public outrage fuelled renewed attempts by OECD countries to overcome the obstacles bank secrecy poses for cooperation in tax enforcement.[66]

The political pressures gave a strong impetus to the negotiation of bilateral tax information agreements, and even a renewed attempt to establish a multilateral framework (OECD 2010a). The number of TIEAs soared, although many were spurious, and large gaps remained.[67] The bilateral

---

65 The UK amnesty in 2007 offered to cap penalties at 10 per cent, and led to the recovery of some £400m., although the total losses had been estimated at between £1.75bn and £5bn; this was much less than the €840m. collected by the Irish tax amnesty in 2004 on undeclared offshore assets, or the Italian amnesty which resulted in the disclosure of €75bn in assets held offshore (Houlder 2007).

66 The Final Communiqué of the G20 meeting in London in April 2009 laying out a Global Plan for Recovery and Reform included a strong pledge: 'to take action against non-cooperative jurisdictions, including tax havens. We stand ready to deploy sanctions to protect our public finances and financial systems. The era of banking secrecy is over.' However, some of the pressures seem to have dissipated by the time of the next G20 meeting in Toronto in June 2010, which mainly referred to efforts within arenas such as the Global Forum, although it did reaffirm that governments 'stand ready to use countermeasures against tax havens'.

67 Havens rushed to sign the minimum number of twelve which had been stated as necessary to avoid being listed as 'uncooperative': e.g. Monaco signed agreements with Andorra, the Faroe Islands and San Marino; by June 2010, although some OECD countries had concluded over twenty, Japan still had only one TIEA (with Bermuda). Data and texts

approach is not only time-consuming, its fatal flaw is that it leaves many gaps and creates new variations, and so creates new tax-avoidance opportunities based on exploiting such gaps and differences. TIEAs are used mainly with states which do not have tax treaties, so these treaties have had to be revised to implement the strengthened information standard. However, differences remain between them and the TIEA requirements. In particular, the Model TIEA includes an explicit positive obligation to ensure that the competent authorities of the requested state can both obtain and provide information held by banks and other fiduciaries, as well as ownership information on banks and other artificial legal persons, and information on settlors, trustees and beneficiaries of trusts.[68] The standard double tax treaty does not include such a provision, and in fact important OECD Member States, especially the USA and the UK, still do not obtain, and hence cannot readily exchange, information relating to persons who are neither their citizens nor residents. The Foreign Account Tax Compliance Act passed by the US Congress in 2009 extended sweeping obligations to foreign banks to report information about offshore accounts, but only in relation to US persons. As already discussed above (at 6.3.5), the existing US regime for 'qualified intermediaries' does not require information on persons who are neither US citizens nor residents. Hence, the USA is using its power to compel full disclosure from foreign banks about US citizens, while allowing its own banks to provide secrecy to foreigners (Spencer 2010b). What is needed is a more concerted, rather than a competitive approach, perhaps with a joint introduction by OECD countries of a refundable withholding tax on non-residents' accounts, as suggested by Reuven Avi-Yonah (2009).

are available from the website of the OECD Centre for Tax Policy and Administration at www.oecd.org.

68 The explicit obligation is in arts. 5(2) and (4) of the Model TIEA. The OECD Model Tax Treaty's art. 26 on information exchange has been amended to clarify that the requested state must use its powers to obtain information even if it does not have a tax interest itself, and that it cannot decline to obtain information 'solely because the information is held by a bank, other financial institution, nominee or person acting in an agency or fiduciary capacity or because it relates to ownership interests in a person' (art. 26(5)). In addition, a tax treaty is preferable, because it provides for reduction of withholding tax at source, which enables a jurisdiction with such treaties to attract offshore business for conduit companies. Thus, OECD states such as Switzerland are bargaining for such provisions in exchange for agreeing to the broader information exchange clause; while other tax havens are trying to obtain a 'quid pro quo' for agreeing to a TIEA, usually in the form of reduced source withholding taxes.

Moves have also been made to establish a multilateral framework, based on the 1988 Convention on Mutual Administrative Assistance in Tax Matters, agreed by the OECD and the Council of Europe, which is currently in force among fourteen states.[69] This convention was revised by an amending protocol in 2010, to bring it into line with the revised OECD Model Tax Treaty, and opened for adherence by all states (Saint-Amans and Russo 2010). It provides a greatly improved basis for tax cooperation, but it still establishes only a framework which requires development. First, it is important to be more specific about the information which should be provided. This should extend to information needed to penetrate behind the secrecy offered by entities such as shell companies and trusts, such as the names of shareholders, directors, trustees and beneficiaries. Second, the provision in article 6 of the Convention for automatic exchange of information must be activated, by establishing computerized systems, which can inter-communicate, especially for information on cross-border interest and other similar payments. The OECD has been working on this technical problem for over twenty years, but has kept this work shrouded in secrecy; it should be given greater visibility and a higher priority.[70] The Convention contains extensive protections to ensure confidentiality of such information, which should allay reasonable concerns.

This multilateral framework should extend globally, beyond Europe and the OECD countries. Its provisions could become a global standard, if tax authorities treated with suspicion transactions with jurisdictions which refused to accept it, and subjected firms and individuals involved in such transactions to detailed tax audits. Combined with the application of unitary taxation to TNCs, this would greatly reduce the flow of funds to financial centres in jurisdictions lacking transparency for tax enforcement. Reputation is all important for financial markets, and the establishment of a high standard of fiscal transparency should be made a key element for any reputable financial centre.

---

69 CETS no. 127, available from http://conventions.coe.int. The UK finally adhered from May 2008, and parties now are Azerbaijan, Belgium, Denmark, Finland, France, Iceland, Italy, the Netherlands, Norway, Poland, Sweden, the UK, the USA and Ukraine; seven others countries – Canada, Germany, Korea, Mexico, Portugal, Slovenia and Spain – have signed the convention but not yet ratified it.

70 A paper-based format was agreed in 1981, then a Standard Magnetic Format adopted 1992, which was reformulated in 1997, and a Council Decision in July 1997 recommended its use together with standard Taxpayer Identification numbers; this has apparently been replaced by a new Standard Transmission Format based on XML code, which seems to be in line with the FISC 73 standard adopted by the EU in 2008 for the Savings Directive data (see OECD-CFA 2006: Module 3).

These two proposals would go a long way towards an effective reform of international tax cooperation. They would also be greatly facilitated by institutional reforms, which could both establish such cooperation on a sounder basis, and lay the foundation for other initiatives.

It is clearly essential to upgrade the UN Committee into a proper International Tax Organization. As a Committee of Tax Experts, it has minimal resources,[71] and an extremely limited mandate, essentially confined to working on the Model Tax Treaty and its commentary. Although it is supposed to be concerned especially with the problems of developing countries, much of its activity consists of adapting the work already done by the OECD–CFA to the relations between developed and developing countries. Other international institutions, notably the World Bank and the IMF, have taken relatively little interest in international tax. Although this is now changing, they adopt an individual country rather than a system-wide perspective. A loose network for discussion mainly among officials and specialists has been established in the International Tax Dialogue, but it is little more than a professional forum. The attempt by the OECD to convert its 'Global Forum' into such an organization clearly lacks legitimacy. An ITO would establish a much more effective institution to develop the kind of more positive coordination of taxation outlined above, restoring the powers of national states.

---

71 It has the equivalent of 1.5 professional staff; hence, its members (who are usually senior tax officials in their own governments) must provide their own organizational support for the work done between annual meetings in working groups; not surprisingly, members from developing countries do not have such resources, so most of the spadework is done by members from rich countries, sometimes indeed by non-members from business or tax professionals.

Regulation of international finance

Finance provides the lubrication for the economy and society. It is a powerful socialization mechanism, linking savings and investment, allocating resources, funding deferred liabilities such as pensions, and managing risks and contingencies, especially through insurance. Bankers and financiers have historically been discreet but powerful, wielding decisive influence behind the scenes in both business and politics, while facilitating myriad petty transactions as well as structuring large-scale deals. Its central paradox is that although a stable and sound system of money, credit and finance is a key public good, banking and finance have generally been treated as a private sphere. This paradox was starkly dramatized by the great financial crisis of 2007 to 2008, which followed a long period of liberalization and privatization, but required extensive state nationalizations and bailouts of financial firms. While these were regarded as short-term measures, the crisis resulted in protracted debate and further extensive regulatory measures, loosely coordinated internationally. However, without a determined move to set finance on new structural foundations, regulation will not prevent future such crises.

7.1 Transformations of international finance

7.1.1 From banking to financial capitalism

The modern era of financial capitalism emerged in the last part of the nineteenth century, in conjunction with the rise of corporate capitalism (discussed in Chapter 4). Two significant shifts were involved.[1] First was the extension of the function of finance from providing commercial credit

---

1 As argued in the clear analysis put forward early in the twentieth century by Hilferding, following in the footsteps of Marx (Hilferding [1910] 1981).

(for commodity circulation in trade) to investment credit (for production). Second, linked to the growth of corporations, was the creation of markets in corporate financial instruments (mainly company shares, or 'fictitious capital').

Hence, financial capital became a distinct sphere, but closely linked with productive capital. The character both of the financial sphere and of its connection with production has varied in different countries and periods.[2] In some countries, notably the UK and the USA, investment credit was provided by 'wholesale' banks and financial markets, while separate commercial and 'retail' banks concentrated on small business and trade credit and individual savings and lending. In other countries, notably Germany and the Netherlands, there was a growth of 'universal banks', which covered both retail and wholesale banking as well as providing investment credit.[3] In Germany banks have been very closely involved with industrial capital, by owning and controlling a high proportion of share capital.[4] In Japan, banks were the linchpins of the powerful *zaibatsu* cartels, and continued this role when the *zaibatsu* were reformed in the 1950s as bank-centred conglomerate groups, in which the *sogo shosha* (large conglomerate trading companies) also played an important part (Young 1979). In countries such as France, banking was highly segmented by activity, and separated from the corporate finance markets, as well as having substantial state ownership. Indeed, segmentation was common in many countries, often with specific legal frameworks governing small-scale savings and credit institutions.

Historically, banking and finance developed as private activities, and indeed states were often dependent on bank loans for public finance,

---

2 Hilferding considered that the concentration of industry due to the growth of giant firms and cartels, and the parallel concentration in banking, resulted in an interpenetration of the two, through ownership and social links, which he termed 'finance capital' ([1910] 1981: 220, 234–5); this was more accurate for the countries he knew best, Germany and Austria, than e.g. the USA and the UK. However similar views were expressed in the USA, notably Louis D. Brandeis, later elevated to the Supreme Court, wrote a populist classic at that time denouncing the US financial oligarchy, and the power wielded through interlocking directorates (1914). For a more contemporary comparative analysis of the structures of big business and finance from a class perspective, see Scott 1997.

3 However, in Germany today the commercial banks have only some 25 per cent share of the market, only half of which is accounted for by the large corporate banks; the rest is shared by mutuals or cooperatives and the state-owned *Landesbanken* (Busch 2009: 92), which play a big part in lending to local and medium-sized business.

4 The combination of direct shareholding and proxy votes controlled by banks in 32 of the largest 50 companies was estimated at over 70 per cent in the mid-1980s (Story 1997: 252).

and assistance in crises. The 'central bank' was generally just the govern-ment's banker, and many were privately owned until relatively recently.[5] It was usually as a result of banking crises that various forms of bank-ing supervision and regulation came to be established, often through the central banks. In the USA the banking crisis of 1907 led to the creation of the Federal Reserve system in 1913. Investment banking and finance were also very international, especially during the peak period of the gold standard, when the traditional large merchant banks such as Barings and Rothschilds moved into investment banking, and US financiers such as Drexel Morgan accessed European capital markets to finance US railroad and industrial investment (Roy 1997: 133–5). A handful of US banks also developed extensive international networks for both wholesale and retail banking, notably Citibank (Huertas 1990), as did some British banks such as Barclays (Jones 1990).

This came to a halt in the 1930s, following the 1929 Wall Street crash and the ensuing banking crises. The collapse of hundreds of mainly small US banks in 1933 resulted in strict regulation of the financial system, including the Glass–Steagall Act, which imposed a separation between commercial and investment banking, and established the Federal Deposit Insurance Corporation (FDIC). With the abandonment of the gold stan-dard and the introduction of exchange controls, finance came under stricter national control. Under the ideological ascendancy of Keynes, the emphasis was on the need to restrain the autonomy of finance and curb speculation. Indeed, there was unprecedented financial stability from the mid-1930s to 1973, with virtually no banking crises in this whole period (Reinhart and Rogoff 2009: 204). However, during the boom period of the 1950s and 1960s finance began to push at its restraints, and to take advan-tage of the partial liberalization established under the Bretton Woods institutions (see Chapter 3, at 3.1.2).

Liberalization of currency exchange controls from the 1970s[6] led to a 'new world order' of international finance (Underhill 1997), and a form

---

5 The Banque de France was until 1936 a private company, although governed by a statute issued by an imperial decree of Napoleon Bonaparte; the Bank of England became state owned only in 1946. The Reichsbank was also owned by private shareholders, although under the Banking Act of 1875 establishing it the German Chancellor chaired its gov-erning body and was empowered to direct its management, but in practice it was largely autonomous, though firmly within the German power structure (Marsh 1992: ch. 4).

6 These were given an impetus by the OECD Codes of Liberalization (see Chapter 5, at 5.1.1); for a helpful graph of the gradual progress of capital account liberalization among OECD countries (1973–95), see Busch 2009: 29.

of domination which has been described as 'financialization' (Epstein 2005; Krippner 2005; Montgomerie 2008; Erturk *et al.* 2008; Lapavitsas 2009). The cross-border and cross-industry integration promoted by liberalization has involved: (a) a shift in corporate funding from relational banking to market-based finance; (b) a massive expansion of financial systems in relation to the real economy; (c) an unprecedented growth of financial assets and leverage; (d) the emergence of highly complex financial instruments; and (e) extraordinary levels of financial trading. These factors have generated a far greater potential for financial instability, and an enhanced mobility of financial risks (Schinasi 2006: 5–8).

Contrary to many conventional accounts, finance has become highly regulated in many countries and internationally, but in forms favouring private or quasi-public self-regulation (see 7.2.2 below). Also, by focusing on market participants rather than transactions, these forms of regulation in practice stimulated and supported them to turn finance into a self-sustaining sphere of circulation and speculation. These activities were legitimized by ideologies of 'risk management', underpinned by models of financial markets as efficient allocators based on rational decision-making. The new cultures of finance became increasingly hard to challenge as the structures of financial transactions became more complex and opaque, and these cultures were moulded and legitimized by arcane techniques of mathematical modelling based on calculation of relative volatility (MacKenzie 2003, 2006).

Although the main driver for financial regulation ostensibly has been to prevent bank crises and failures, it has clearly failed to do so, as shown most spectacularly by the 2007–8 crisis leading to the economic slump. However, this was only the culmination of a continuing trend of bank crises, contrasting sharply with the experience of the twenty years prior to 1973, during which there was not a single one.[7] Many commentators seem

---

7 Surveys by IMF economists in the mid-1990s showed that since 1980, 133 out of 181 IMF Member States (=73.5%) experienced 'significant' problems in the banking sector, either 'crises' involving bank failures and government rescues (41 instances in 36 countries) or extensive unsoundness (108 cases); the costs ranged from 3% to 6% of GDP in richer countries to 10% to 15% in middle-income countries, and to 25% in developing countries (Caprio and Klingebiel 1996; Lindgren *et al.* 1996; Goldstein and Turner 1996). This of course was prior both to the crises which began in Asia in 1997 and spread to Russia and elsewhere, and to the great financial crash of 2007 to 2008. A study by Reinhart and Rogoff confirms that in a longer historical timescale the period since the mid-1980s has seen a significantly higher incidence of banking crises (hitting alike countries at different levels of development), while 1951–72 saw none (2009: 204–8; see also Reinhart and Rogoff 2008: 8).

still to accept volatility and crisis as an endemic feature, and consider that regulation can at best hope for their mitigation rather than prevention.

The opaque and distorted character of the globalized financial system has also meant that finance has been channelled from poor to rich countries and people. The secrecy and lax regulation provided and promoted by the 'offshore' system[8] have provided powerful incentives for 'capital flight' from developing countries towards the main financial centres (discussed in the previous chapter). It has also helped to sustain the position of the dollar as the de facto global reserve currency, enabling the USA to finance its external deficit by high levels of borrowing, and creating massive international imbalances by which funds especially from Asia both maintained and became hostage to the strength of the dollar.

The sphere of finance became greatly expanded during the economic boom period of the 1950s and 1960s. An unprecedented proportion of individuals and households especially in richer countries became able to generate savings, but also became reliant for deferred expenditures (especially pensions), consumer credit and housing finance on the financial system, which exploited this dependency (Lapavitsas 2009; dos Santos 2009). Money managers and financial specialists could use their inside knowledge of finance to exploit their access to these large pools of institutionalized individual savings, and financial services became an overblown and parasitic sector. While small business continued to be generally reliant on bank loans, large corporations had direct access to capital markets, and to the advantages of low-cost finance through the offshore system. Liberalization of national financial markets tended to result in new exclusionary patterns of financial recycling, as banks and savings institutions were sucked into participating in global financial markets. The poorest in all countries have become particularly dependent on extortionate forms of money lending, unless alternative institutions such as credit unions could be established (Leyshon and Thrift 1995). Micro-finance was much touted as an innovative method of lending to poor people, but became a high-profit business. This has led countries such as Bangladesh (where it took root) and India to introduce regulation, both to protect borrowers from abuses and to prevent collapse due to high levels of default, although experts from the IFIs continue to argue that it should be lightly regulated to minimize costs. On the other hand, high levels of liquidity were the fuel

---

8 As discussed in the previous chapter, this system is not confined to offshore finance centres alone, indeed the major financial centres especially London and New York play a key part in it.

for a consumer credit boom in richer countries, which generated excessive indebtedness, making large sectors of the population very vulnerable when the financial crisis came.

7.1.2 Liberalization and financialization

The new period of international liberalization of finance is usually said to have begun on 15 August 1971, when the USA suspended the dollar's guaranteed convertibility to gold, precipitating the end of the post-war system of fixed exchange rates. However, the process had already started in the late 1950s with the liberalization of current account payments from 1958, gathering momentum between OECD countries in the 1960s. The partial liberalization enabled those engaged in international business, especially TNCs, to vary their holdings of different currencies and switch between them, especially in anticipation of a currency devaluation. These 'hot money' flows greatly contributed to the collapse of the fixed exchange rate system (see Chapter 2, at 2.1.2).

Offshore banking and finance also began to develop in the 1960s, as US banks in particular began to establish foreign branches, to provide mainly wholesale financial services to their TNC clients. This expansion was initially mainly towards London as the City, with Bank of England support, reinvented itself as global financial hub.[9] With the Bank's encouragement, the 'Eurodollar' market grew rapidly from the late 1950s, once limited currency convertibility was introduced by OECD countries.[10] This itself involved regulatory avoidance: US bank reserve requirements did not apply abroad, while other countries' credit and interest rate controls did not apply to foreign banks or dollar deposits. US banks needed little

---

9 Foreign-owned banks were exempt from all credit and interest rate requirements except in transactions with UK residents; after 1971, when a 12.5% reserve assets ratio was introduced for all banks, it applied only to sterling liabilities (Wilson Committee 1980: ch. 4).

10 According to the detailed account by Schenk, the Midland Bank in 1955 began to engage in swaps using dollar deposits by clients, taking advantage of the permissive attitude to exchange controls of the Bank of England, which considered that since banks were allowed to accept dollars, and to buy Treasury bills, they could be allowed to attract foreign exchange deposits from non-residents and convert them to sterling via swaps. Although this was intended for bank clients, this restriction was impossible to police, and banks exploited the permission to arbitrage between interest rates. 'In summary, a combination of Bank of England support, Treasury tolerance, and controls elsewhere created a regulatory environment which gave London a competitive advantage in the Eurodollar market' (1998: 237).

encouragement to set up branches abroad, to serve their clients' expanding overseas operations. Also, by establishing themselves in London, US commercial banks could engage in corporate investment banking which was forbidden to them at home under Glass–Steagall. In 1963 Warburgs, a small British-based investment bank, launched the first Eurodollar bond flotation (Ferguson 2010), carefully designed to attract investors from all over the world by avoiding withholding taxes (as discussed in Chapter 6, at 6.3.5), so that tax avoidance and evasion further fuelled the rapid growth of this globalized market for low-cost corporate finance. At the same time, the traditional barriers which segmented the UK financial markets began to break down from the late 1950s, as the large clearing banks moved into consumer credit finance, investment fund management, merchant banking and financial consultancy (Maycock 1986).

The period since 1973 has seen a major transformation of financial intermediation. Its main features have been: (a) liberalization: the breaking down of internal and international barriers between different sectors and channels to form ever-wider global pools of financial capital; (b) a shift from relational to market-based finance which is described as disintermediation, or marketization; and (c) financialization: the relative growth of the financial sector and its profitability (Krippner 2005), linked to the enormous escalation of financial transactions and speculation (Epstein 2005). These changes have generally been followed and facilitated by the emergence of formalized regulation of financial institutions and financial services provision.

Liberalization has been a double movement, both international and internal. The gradual elimination of controls on currency exchange and capital movements, and the opening of national financial services markets to foreign firms, have interacted with the erosion of the segmentation of financial intermediation which separated activities such as retail banking, mortgage finance, insurance, investment banking, fund management and money-market operations. Much of this was driven by financial firms themselves, which used techniques of regulatory avoidance to break down the barriers. Central to these techniques was the development of the 'offshore' system, based on setting up branches or affiliates in convenient jurisdictions (discussed in the previous chapter). In many ways this was centred on the City of London, which from the 1970s became an 'offshore' centre itself for the US and other foreign banks, and helped to create the wider offshore system using OFCs in UK dependencies and other havens (as discussed in the previous chapter). The internationalization of the City undermined the traditional system of 'club rule' centring on the Bank of England leading to a rapid switch to formalized regulation (Moran 2003), and the 'big bang' in 1986 further stimulated a period of headlong financial innovation and regulatory response (Dale 1996; Vogel 1996: ch. 5). The rebirth of London as a global financial entrepôt, in turn put competitive pressure on other centres and national financial systems.

The US, with its financial system polarized between a few very large banks and a mass of small state-chartered banks and thrifts, and responsibility dispersed between fragmented and competing regulatory bodies, had difficulty in adjusting to the emergence of wider financial markets. Conflicts between sectional interests and turf wars between regulators led to both deregulatory and re-regulatory movements and frequent deadlock in Congress, leaving scope for regulators to relax rules, and for banks to exploit regulatory arbitrage (Busch 2009: ch. 3). When the thrifts[11] came under pressure from money-market funds, controls on their deposit rates were removed in 1980, and in 1982 there was a relaxation of the assets in which they could invest, making them like banks. This led to extensive lending to real estate and other risky sectors, and when the real estate bubble burst at the end of the decade hundreds collapsed, requiring a government bailout of $180bn. Meantime, the banks lost ground to their foreign competitors, and chafed at the obstacle posed by Glass–Steagall; since some could in any case avoid it by using foreign affiliates in London, regulatory agencies were persuaded to erode the restrictions by administrative decisions. Finally, Glass–Steagall was effectively abolished, as limits on affiliations between commercial and investment banks through bank holding companies imposed in 1956 were formally relaxed in 1999, while affiliations with some thrifts were also allowed (US Treasury 2008: 35–7).

Thus, there was a shift away from relationship-based to market-based finance, led by both financial firms and regulators in the UK and the USA, acting in tandem as the dominant centres of global finance. Although often described as a period of deregulation, there was actually an enormous growth of formalized regulation, through which the competitive and dynamic processes of change were mediated and contested. This formalization of regulation was national in focus, but it developed as an international process, through networks of officials and specialists, who developed principles and standards, changing rapidly, usually under the impact of scandals and crises.

---

11 Also known as savings & loan (S&Ls), like the UK building societies they originated as mutuals for small savers and mortgage lending.

7.2 International re-regulation

The emphasis since the 1970s on liberalization has allowed and encouraged financial firms to develop market-based finance, develop and trade in innovative instruments, and engage in trading both for their own account and for clients. Regulation by public authorities with responsibility for stability and security of the financial system (central banks and sectoral regulators) has concentrated on allocating responsibility for supervision of entities and establishing prudential standards for them, mainly in the form of capital reserve requirements. They have generally adopted a hands-off attitude towards financial transactions. Regulation of markets has mainly been done by private industry bodies: exchanges, clearing houses, credit-rating agencies (CRAs) and private associations such as the International Swaps and Derivatives Association (ISDA), although acting under powers granted by public authorities or backed by law.

The focus on firms and not transactions has created incentives for regulatory avoidance and arbitrage, by creating competition for firms to move into markets and jurisdictions with lighter requirements, as well as to devise transactions avoiding such requirements. Financial firms have been stimulated to reduce their cost of capital by using innovative means to circumvent reserve requirements, and to exploit opportunities for international tax avoidance (discussed in the previous chapter). At the same time, private bodies to which regulation of transactions and markets has been delegated have inevitably developed vested interests in encouraging rather than controlling the growth of markets in those instruments. The form of regulation adopted by the public authorities (capital reserve requirements) also had the effect of creating a false sense of security (sometimes referred to as 'moral hazard'). Further encouragement for risk-taking was created by the state's guarantee of lender-of-last-resort (LLR) support in case of bank failure. This was provided explicitly under deposit insurance schemes, but also implicitly, usually by central banks, due to the danger of a run on banks, and the systemic risk posed by major bank failures for the whole economy.

The result was that the new forms of regulation, although increasingly extensive, have tended to encourage rather than control the forces leading to financialization and speculation. The focus on firms rather than markets also exacerbated the difficulties of achieving both international and inter-sectoral coordination between regulators, especially as liberalization broke down barriers between markets and brought different types of firms into competition.

It is therefore hardly surprising that, in a period of rapid liberalization which has created ever wider and more open markets, regulatory failure has been endemic. The response has been to create new regulatory institutions and networks which have grown ever more complex, despite all efforts to improve their coordination. In the face of the best efforts of the regulators, the increasingly globalized financial system has generated new forms of risk and instability with ever-wider effects.

7.2.1 The Basel Committee and the capital adequacy regime

Central banks and other financial supervisors have been mainly concerned for the soundness of banks and the stability of the financial system. The dangers of instability were brought home by bank failures in the early 1970s in the UK (the 'secondary banks'), the USA (Franklin National) and especially Germany (Herstatt). In 1974 central bankers, working through the Bank for International Settlements (BIS), and on the initiative of the Bank of England, established what became known as the Basel Committee on Banking Supervision (BCBS).[12] The BCBS began by attempting to allocate responsibility for the supervision of transnational banks, based on the broad principle of home-country responsibility for solvency, and that of the host for liquidity. However, it was clear that this distinction could only be a loose one, and was hard to apply in many cases (e.g. to subsidiaries, especially joint ventures). Hence close cooperation, including exchange of information between supervisors, would be crucial; while it was noted that a problem would be posed by the 'virtual absence of supervision in some popular "off-shore" banking centres' (Blunden 1977: 327).

These principles were issued as the Basel Concordat in 1975, which has been continually revised and expanded to try to improve coordination between bank supervisors, and to ensure that banks' international operations are monitored in an integrated way. However, recurrent crises have revealed the gaps, especially those created by the 'offshore' system; and

---

12 Known at first as the Committee on Banking Regulations and Supervisory Practices, it consisted of the central banks and banking supervisors of the Group of Ten (G10) countries, plus Luxembourg, Spain and Switzerland. Following the financial crisis of 2008 it was expanded and now includes Argentina, Australia, Belgium, Brazil, Canada, China, France, Germany, Hong Kong SAR, India, Indonesia, Italy, Japan, Korea, Luxembourg, Mexico, the Netherlands, Russia, Saudi Arabia, Singapore, South Africa, Spain, Sweden, Switzerland, Turkey, the UK and the USA, and reports to the Group of Central Bank Governors and Heads of Supervision of those countries.

this fatal flaw has continued despite the creation in 1980 of an Offshore Group of Banking Supervisors (OGBS), which has worked in conjunction with the BCBS. First in 1982 came the developing-country debt crisis triggered by the Mexican default, and the failure of the Ambrosiano bank due to reckless euromarket operations, concealed through a Luxembourg holding company which escaped supervision (Herring and Litan 1995: 101). This led to a revision of the Concordat in 1983, to strengthen the supervision of bank groups on a consolidated basis.

Even as this was being negotiated, a fresh crisis was brewing which showed its inadequacies, with the final collapse in 1991 of the Bank for Credit and Commerce International (BCCI). BCCI had been 'carefully structured... to avoid consolidated supervision in all the countries in which it did business' by using subsidiaries in Luxembourg and the Cayman Islands, though it was run from London and Pakistan (Herring and Litan 1995: 104; see also Alford 1992; Bingham 1992). A new standard issued in 1992 stressed the need to identify a clear home-country authority capable of supervising groups on a consolidated basis, with adequate arrangements for obtaining information from others involved. This was further strengthened in 1996 by a report, issued jointly with the OGBS, setting out twenty-nine recommendations relating to obtaining and sharing information, and procedures for on-site inspection in host countries by home-country supervisors.[13]

This still left open the question of groups engaged in both banking and financial market operations, which was starkly illustrated by the collapse of Barings Bank in 1995, due to inadequately monitored futures market operations based in Singapore (BBS 1995; Singapore 1995; Zhang 1995; Gapper and Denton 1996). The Barings debacle accelerated the attempts at coordination between banking and financial market supervisors, with the formation in 1996 of the Joint Forum, linking the BCBS with the International Organization of Securities Commissions (IOSCO) and the International Association of Insurance Supervisors (IAIS). This has focused mainly on trying to coordinate substantive standards on capital requirements for all types of financial firms, which the BCBS had been working on for banks since the 1980s.

---

13 This has been supplemented by standards for customer identification and due diligence, as well as a report in 2003 on 'shell banks' (defined as those managed in a jurisdiction different from that in which they are licensed, hence escaping supervision). These arose from heightened concerns about money laundering, especially terrorist financing, after September 2001 (see further below).

The substantive standards for capital provisioning developed by the BCBS supplemented the procedures for coordination between supervisors. Actually, the formalization of capital requirements largely *resulted* from the emergence of internationalized financial markets, prior to which central banks generally used more direct means of trying to ensure bank stability, such as requiring them to hold deposits in the central bank, and controlling their borrowing facilities and lending practices. These did not apply to international banking activities, but when the US authorities became concerned at the lack of any reserve requirements for Eurodollar banking by the end of the 1970s, they initially found little support for international convergence of capital requirements (Kapstein 1994: 108). In 1981 they yielded to pressure from large US banks to create an International Banking Facility in New York, but this failed in its intention to apply pressure on the UK to move towards stronger international coordination, and instead brought New York into the offshore banking system (Hawley 1984).[14] The pressure for convergence grew again after US reserve requirements were reviewed following the failure of Continental Illinois Bank in 1984, and convergence was facilitated by the US adoption of risk-based capital requirements similar to those of the UK and others. This led to a bilateral agreement with the Bank of England, extended to Japan, and paving the way for the adoption by the BCBS of an international standard for bank capital, issued as the Basel Accord of 1988 (Kapstein 1994: 106–19; Murphy 2004: ch. 5).

The Accord was eventually combined with the Concordat, following an extensive process of consultation with bank regulators outside the G10, into the Basel Core Principles issued in 1997, which link the minimum procedural requirements for supervision with the substantive capital adequacy standards.

7.2.2 Public–private regulatory networks

The new forms of regulation of internationalized finance have produced a multiplicity of regulatory bodies, interacting through a veritable maze of

---

14 This was consolidated by the joint move of the USA and the UK in 1984 to bring Eurobond flotations 'onshore' by allowing payment of interest gross provided that the paying agent certifies that the recipient is a non-resident (Picciotto 1992: 168); despite proposals to end this, it still continues (see previous chapter).

networks, national, international, infranational and supranational.[15] The interactions between these bodies makes it difficult to attain any degree of functional cooperation, and their specialized character creates new tensions between technocracy and political accountability, with considerable problems of legitimacy. Although the regulatory agencies and their networks are fragmented and often competing, they can be said to form a 'policy community'. However, this has been dominated by the needs and perspectives of the financial firms themselves, expressed through the various industry representatives, think-tanks and lobby groups,[16] and reinforced by the revolving doors which allow senior bankers to move between government advisory positions or Ministries to the City or Wall Street. Given also the 'many possibilities for innovative avoidance of regulatory provisions' this inevitably 'enhances the dependence of the official agencies on the industry' (Underhill 1997: 25).

A significant characteristic has been the importance of regulation by private organizations, or quasi-public bodies often given independent powers, although authorized by the state. For example, a major role is played by exchanges and clearing houses in formulating standard contracts and regulating the terms on which they are traded, including margin requirements and settlement arrangements (Lee 1998). They also try to coordinate their regulation of markets internationally through cooperation agreements (usually in the form of MOUs), which include provisions for information exchange and cooperation, for example in monitoring large trades. Whether they are run as mutual organizations by their members or as independent entities, their main aim is to achieve growth in trading volume and membership, so they have little incentive to crack down on activities which may harm outsiders or damage the financial system.

Bilateral or 'over-the-counter' (OTC) financial instruments, including an infinite variety of complex transactions in derivatives and swaps, which quickly grew to account for the vast bulk of the market,[17] are also governed by private associations, notably through the standard-form contracts of the ISDA. These are backed by its private arbitration procedures, and supported by national legislation and rulings to ensure their enforcement

---

15 Underhill 1997; Picciotto and Haines 1999. An attempt to chart at least the main bodies involved is made in Davies and Green 2008: 33.

16 Particularly influential in banking and finance has been the Group of Thirty (see www.group30.org).

17 Since they are generally transferable and relatively standardized they are traded, although privately, not in an open market or exchange.

(Partnoy 2002: 217). Standard-form agreements such as the ISDA's have serious limitations as regulatory instruments, as they are based on the existing consensus view of the risks entailed. This discourages parties from considering the specifics of the transaction, and puts all market participants in the same boat, although it may be a leaky one (Hudson 2009: para. 32-14). The private and bilateral nature of OTC contracts has also meant a serious lack of transparency, since neither market participants nor regulators have information about the exposures of counterparties.

A key role has also been played by the CRAs, such as Moody's and Standard & Poor's, which evaluate financial instruments and the creditworthiness of their issuers, both firms and governments (Sinclair 2005). These agencies, although private and profit-making companies, have in practice been given an official status, since their ratings have important regulatory consequences.[18] Hence, they form in effect a state-backed oligopoly. However, their private interest in expanding the market for their services meant that, in the words of Frank Partnoy, they became 'more like gate openers than gate-keepers', especially in the development of new forms of structured finance (2006: 60; see also Aguesse 2007). Despite debates in the USA following the Enron affair, no significant moves were made to establish tighter controls on the CRAs, and their failures contributed significantly to the bubble in mortgage finance and the 2007–8 crisis (Mason and Rosner 2007; Davies and Green 2008: 68–71; BIS 2009: 8–9).

Another important issue which has been substantially delegated to a private body has been the development of international accounting standards. The International Accounting Standards Committee (IASC) was formed as a professional body in 1973, following difficulties in reaching political decisions in conflicts over a proposed EU Directive on company accounts. The IASC tried to reconcile different national reporting systems (including the US Generally Accepted Accounting Principles – GAAP) by publishing International Accounting Standards. In the 1980s the IASC skilfully linked up with both international bodies such as the BIS and IOSCO as well as national authorities, aiming mainly to ensure

18 In the USA, since 1975, institutional investors have been required to place their funds in assets which are given a high or investment grade by a recognized rating agency, and for most of the period since then only three such firms have been recognized (White 2009: 392). The Basel II Capital Standards Framework (paras. 90–108) gave responsibility to national regulators for recognising whether an 'external credit assessment institution' (ECAI) meets the criteria which it lays down, and its capital requirements are dependent on the ratings given by recognized ECAIs.

acceptability of its standards to stock exchanges and financial market supervisors (Botzem and Quack 2006). As its work gained importance and visibility, it was reorganized in 2001, to try to balance the involvement of the preparers (large accounting firms) and users (finance and corporate interests) of accounts, by establishing the International Accountancy Standards Board (IASB), operating under a private non-profit Foundation, and aiming to broaden the basis of its funding, and hence accountability. It has also sought to enhance the legitimacy of its standards by using a 'due process' of consultation, modelled on that of the US Financial Accounting Standards Board (Botzem and Quack 2006: 283). Audit standards are still solely set by the accountancy industry for itself, through the International Auditing and Assurance Standards Board, a technical committee of the International Federation of Accountants; and some have suggested that the IASC or an analogous body should take over this role (Davies and Green 2008: 220).

Although it is a private body, the IASB has become an important mediator for contests between national and stakeholder interests over issues which are not merely technical but have important economic and political ramifications (Mattli and Büthe 2005; Botzem and Quack 2006; Perry and Nölke 2006; de Bellis 2006). It achieved a notable success when the European Commission decided not to proceed with its own revisions of EU accounting standards, and instead the IASB's standards have been given formal legal force in the EU under Regulation 1606/2002, establishing a procedure for adoption of those standards and requiring companies listing any security on an EU market to use such adopted standards. The IASB standards have further reinforced the trend to financialization by shifting away from historic cost towards 'fair value' accounting, involving bringing intangibles on to the balance sheet and a 'mark-to-market' basis for valuing financial assets (Perry and Nölke 2006).

The multiplicity of regulatory bodies creates significant problems of coordination. Indeed, supervision of global financial institutions and markets has been beset by conflicts and 'turf battles', both between authorities in different countries and between different kinds of supervisors and regulators. This is especially the case in the USA, where banking has four distinct federal regulators, as well as regulators in every state,[19] while

---

19 Federally chartered banks are supervised by the Office of the Comptroller of the Currency, bank holding companies by the Federal Reserve, other deposit-taking institutions by the Office of Thrift Supervision, and the Federal Deposit Insurance Corporation has some supervisory authority for the deposit-taking institutions which it insures (US GAO 2007:11); state regulators supervise state-chartered banks and thrifts (for an overview, see Busch 2009: 54; and for a critique, see Kotlikoff 2010: esp. 49–51).

financial derivatives are regulated by both the Commodity Futures Trading Commission and the Securities and Exchange Commission (SEC), whose rivalries are legendary (Coffee 1995).[20] In Europe, bank and financial market regulation remains at the national level,[21] although within a coordinated institutional framework and regulatory Directives aiming at market liberalization. Hence, it is based on a stronger version of the BCBS's home-state supervision principle, to provide a 'single passport' for firms to enter markets, although host states may regulate their markets, e.g. to provide consumer protection. Regulation is coordinated through EU 'comitology' networks, involving finance ministry officials, central banks and supervisors of banks and other financial services providers.[22]

The problems of international coordination of regulatory networks are well illustrated by the responses to the issue of tax havens and offshore financial centres. Concern about the use of these jurisdictions for money laundering led to the setting up of the Financial Action Task Force (FATF), which was formed in 1989 as an initiative of the G7, but actually housed

20 Following the financial crisis of 2008, the Dodd–Frank Act of 2010 (discussed below) again extended the number, in particular by creating a Bureau of Consumer Financial Protection; it attempts to deal with the complexity by creating a new coordination body, the Financial Stability Oversight Council.

21 The possibility of a direct role for the European Central Bank in prudential supervision has been largely rejected, although under article 105.6 of the EU Treaty, the EU Council acting unanimously may 'confer upon the ECB specific tasks concerning policies relating to the prudential supervision of credit institutions and other financial institutions with the exception of insurance undertakings'. It has not done so, mainly due to the insistence of German governments that the ECB should remain focused on its primary target of monetary stability in the euro-zone, coordinating with EU states which have not adopted the euro through the European System of Central Banks. Following the 2008 crisis another 'high-level group' again examined the system and reported problems of coordination and recommended more consistency. It confirmed the view that the ECB should not become involved in micro-prudential supervision, but recommended an extension of its role to include macro-prudential supervision, to be coordinated with other agencies through another new body (de Larosière et al. 2009). The result was the setting up in September 2009 of a European Systemic Risk Board (ESRB), and a European System of Financial Supervisors (ESFS), composed of national supervisors and three new European Supervisory Authorities for the banking, securities and insurance and occupational pensions sectors. The Committee of European Banking Supervisors was renamed the European Banking Authority and moved to London by the end of 2010, but remains essentially another coordinating body.

22 Davies and Green (2008: ch. 4) provide a good account and analysis, focusing on the changes following on the financial services action plan launched in 1999 and the Lamfalussy Report of 2002; the 2010 edition includes a revised Introduction updating the story.

at the OECD in Paris.[23] Its work deals with similar issues to that of the OECD–CFA, for instance obstacles to exchange of information such as bank secrecy. Tax authorities would greatly benefit from being able to exchange information with agencies dealing with money laundering, and this is possible at national level in some countries.[24] Joint action might also be helpful in putting pressure on jurisdictions which may be reluctant to accept or enforce regulatory standards. Yet cooperation between the FATF and the OECD–CFA has been minimal, probably because AML regulators consider that they would find it even more difficult to obtain information if it were known that tax authorities could have access to it. Practical cooperation between Financial Intelligence Units (FIUs) takes place through an even more informal (but nevertheless quite effective) body, the Egmont Group, formed in 1995.[25] This in turn intersects with networks dealing with narcotic drugs (the UN Office on Drugs and Crime, UNODC) and corruption.[26]

Financial and monetary regulation is the area of global governance in which the mushroom growth of regulatory networks has been probably the most active. Even when better coordination has been attempted, the

23 It is in fact in the main OECD building, whereas the Fiscal Committee is in an Annex. The FATF established an international standard for anti-money-laundering (AML) regulations in its Forty Recommendations, issued in 1990. Although only 'soft law' they provided a very effective template for AML regulations which spread rapidly all around the world. They were revised in 1996 and especially 2003, following the 9/11 attack, extending AML to countering the financing of terrorism (CFT). The FATF now has thirty-four members, but also works in conjunction with related regional bodies, known as FSRBs, which have some overlapping membership with and are associate members or observers of the FATF. The OGBS is an observer in the FATF and evaluates observance by its members of FATF standards. Monitoring of the effectiveness of national AML–CFT regulation is done through regular 'peer review' visits and reports.

24 Notably, Australian Taxation Office officials have direct access to the extensive Australian Transaction Reports and Analysis Centre (AUSTRAC) database, which is collected under AML legislation, and is more extensive than in most other countries, in that it includes all foreign exchange transactions of any amount anywhere in the world involving the Australian dollar. This enables systematic analyses of currency flows, to identify possible suspicious transactions involving illegitimate tax arrangements (ANAO 2008; interview information).

25 This grew significantly after the increased concerns about terrorist financing, from 69 members in 2002 to 108 by 2008 (Annual Report 2008, available from www.egmontgroup. org). The links between money laundering and tax evasion are illustrated in some of the 'sanitized cases' in a report published by the Egmont Group in 2000 (Egmont 2000).

26 Due to political sensitivities, there is no intergovernmental organization dealing with this, and the NGO Transparency International was set up by former WB staff, largely in reaction to constraints felt by the WB about interference in the internal politics of states. For other international arrangements relating to corruption, see Chapter 5, at 5.1.3.1.

result has been the creation of new bodies or networks. Thus, the initiative to reform the 'international financial architecture', following the financial crisis which started in Asia in 1997, resulted in the creation of the Financial Stability Forum (FSF), once again as a political initiative through the G7. The FSF attempted to improve the international coordination of the plethora of regulatory standards developed by international bodies related to finance, mainly by identifying a Compendium of financial standards and codes. Compliance with these has been monitored by an enhanced form of peer review mainly organized through the IMF, producing Reports on Observance of Standards and Codes (ROSCs).[27] In practice, the creation of the FSF added another node in the complex regulatory networks. The FSF also prompted the creation of new international networks, notably the International Association of Deposit Insurers, established in 2002, also based at the BIS in Basel, which however seems to have had limited success so far in improving harmonization and coordination of LLR support (Davies and Green 2008: 52).

Although international networks have facilitated the diffusion of regulatory forms and practices and their coordination, this has been in the context of competition between financial centres and national economies to maintain or develop their own markets. The complex interactions between regulators multiplied rapidly as the shift to market-based finance broke down structural barriers and created competition between different types of intermediary (retail and investment banks, insurance companies, and other financial services providers), and produced concentration into financial conglomerates.

---

27 The FSF (renamed the Financial Stability Board after the 2008 crisis) brought together regulators responsible for financial stability, led by central bankers, and is housed at the BIS. It reports to the IMF's International Monetary and Financial Committee, and the actual monitoring of the extent to which jurisdictions comply with the standards and codes was taken on by the IMF and WB. Since 1999 IMF and WB staff have conducted regular reviews to produce ROSCs on compliance with the FSF standards. The ROSCs cover the main financial centres, extended in 2000 to all OFCs even if not IMF members. However, they do not include a review of the centres' cooperation in tax enforcement, which was referred to the OECD–CFA. After 9/11 the ROSCs were extended to cover compliance with AML–CFT standards, monitored by the FATF (or its related regional bodies). However, the IMF strongly opposed the use of public name-and-shame methods such as 'blacklisting', and dissuaded the FATF from using them, although there was considerable evidence of their effectiveness, due to the sensitivity of OFCs to reputational damage (Sharman 2006: 101–26, 155–6). This has enabled OFCs to use the ROSCs as a seal of approval of their 'high' standards in financial supervision, while continuing to maintain strict fiscal and financial secrecy, thus facilitating regulatory and tax avoidance (discussed in Chapter 6).

7.2.3 Financial innovation and regulatory arbitrage

The Basel Accord allowed for some flexibility in capital requirements by assigning weightings to different categories of assets. This enabled it to go beyond credit (counterparty) risks to take account of market risks, which became important as banks became heavily involved in market-based finance. However, the capital adequacy regime itself stimulated the development of new financial techniques, involving the 'securitization' of loans, and a shift to disintermediation and market-based finance (Calaby 1989). Following its introduction there was indeed an explosion of innovation in the creation of ever more complex financial instruments, especially techniques for shifting and managing risk.

This in effect created markets in risk. The main methods have been the use of financial derivatives, especially credit derivatives and swaps; and the bundling together of packages of securitized loans,[28] allowing them to be moved off the balance sheet to special investment vehicles or special purpose vehicles (SPVs) and sold off to other investors.

In the early years after the invention of financial derivatives in the 1970s concerns were raised that at least some of these instruments would fuel speculation and lead to 'casino capitalism' (Strange 1986: 113–19), and this debate occasionally surfaced again especially during crises. In the days of commodity derivatives, Keynesian economists pointed out the potential for excessive speculation resulting from the shift from simple forwards contracts to systematic trading of standardized futures on organized exchanges. However, derivatives in physical commodities could be justified by the need to manage and finance stocks or inventories in the face of uncertainties of crops due to the vagaries of nature (Williams

---

28 The initial step for structured credit was the use of securitization to create Asset-Backed Securities, consisting of a package of assets producing a cash flow; these were often loans or bonds, vested in a specially created corporate vehicle and used to back the issuance of notes, known as Collateralized Debt Obligations (CDOs). This technique was then combined with credit derivatives, by bundling together a package of credit default swaps (CDSs), known as synthetic CDOs, pioneered by investment bank JP Morgan in 1997 with its Bistro (Broad Index Secured Trust Offering). This combined the credit risk of a range of corporate bonds, which since they carried varied risks of default, was considered to spread the risk, and could be further 'sliced and diced' into senior, mezzanine and junior tranches. The same technique was then applied to residential or commercial mortgages to create Mortgage Backed Securities, the lowest grade of which were termed subprime. The innovators at JP Morgan decided not to venture into this market, mainly because the lack of historical data on mortgage defaults made it impossible to predict correlation, which was central to the VaR model (Tett 2009: 62–82; MacKenzie 2009), but it grew rapidly from 1999 (for UK data, see Turner 2009: 14).

1986). The lack of any such justification for financial derivatives strongly suggested a need for a much more cautious approach to them, especially as speculation can be greatly magnified by leverage.[29] Nevertheless the blanket justification was accepted that they helped to manage risk and reduce the cost of finance, despite recurrent incidents of major losses attributable to them (Kuprianov 1995).

Furthermore, derivatives trading was allowed to expand exponentially, away from exchanges, which at least provide some transparency, into private, and hence totally opaque OTC markets.[30] Regulation focused on dealing with their potential consequences. This gave free rein, indeed encouragement, to the financial rocket scientists to devise the ever more elaborate instruments, especially synthetic CDOs which, as many only too late realized, became so complex and opaque as to defeat effective valuation. Indeed, socio-economic research suggests that the uncertainty and ambiguity inherent in credit derivatives, whose value depends on the occurrence of a specified event, is the reason that they remained privately traded between a small group of banks, despite the efforts of powerful lobbies and 'cognitive and political communities' led by the ISDA and 'battalions' of legal experts (Huault and Rainelli-Le Montagner 2009).

The 'originate and distribute' model using SPVs was thought to reduce risk by spreading it, but since SPVs directly raised their own debt, financial leverage was greatly increased. Also, although creation of an SPV took the debt off the balance sheet of one firm, since a high proportion of the SPVs' debt was bought by other banks and financial institutions, it was simply being circulated around the system, in effect creating what came to be known as a 'shadow banking' system. This generated incentives for lax practices in providing credit, since the individual debts were wrapped in a securitized package and immediately passed on to others. It also placed great reliance on the bond gradings by CRAs, which however depended on information supplied by the issuers, who also paid the fees for the ratings.[31]

---

29 Campbell and Picciotto 2000; when we delivered this paper at a conference in 1999, the response of a financial economist from the UK's leading and well-funded research centre on financial markets was that financial derivatives were 'not different from baked beans'.

30 The BIS has attempted to quantify OTC derivatives market activity since 1998 by surveys of market participants, on a six-monthly basis; the most recent triennial report of December 2007 estimated that the total amounts outstanding had grown by an average annual rate of 25% since 1998, but by 33% in the 2004–7 period, reaching an estimated $516 trillion (BIS 2007).

31 Although the Basel II standards for approval of an 'external credit assessment institution' included independence from political or economic pressures which may influence the

The Basel capital standards therefore provided further encouragement for financial techniques motivated by avoidance or 'regulatory arbitrage' (US GAO 2007:15), since many of the innovative financial instruments aimed to reduce the capital reserve requirement, which has a direct impact on the firm's profitability. This was indeed the main reason for the use of SPVs (Tett 2009: 114), which could be used to take loans off the balance sheet because the originators of the loans retained only a contingent liability (dependent on the occurrence of specified 'credit events'). The reduction of capital requirements was also a major driver in the development of credit derivatives such as credit default swaps (CDSs), and credit insurance.[32] By these means, capital requirements were greatly reduced or eliminated, enabling banks and other institutions to ramp up the volume of lending sometimes to an enormous extent. This meant that counterparty credit risk had been converted to market risk. Amendments of the Basel standard were therefore proposed in 1994 to 1995 to deal with off-balance sheet items and market risks resulting from trading activities. This began the shift towards allowing banks to use their own internal models to determine capital requirements, based on calculating 'value at risk' (VaR).

In parallel with this, the blurring or breaking of barriers between commercial banks and other financial firms also created concerns about competitive equality. Although a BCBS study argued that many factors other than regulatory differences affected competition (Jackson *et al.* 1999), it must be accepted that regulatory requirements create incentives for regulatory arbitrage unless they apply equally to economically equivalent transactions (Kuritzkes *et al.* 2003: 148–50). Coordination between regulators of banks, financial markets and insurance was taken up through the Joint Forum, where the 'building block' approach of the BCBS created substantial disagreements (Steil 1994). The 'market risks' amendments finally adopted in 1996 therefore offered two options, a standardized method (Basel I) and the internal models approach. The latter emerged fully-fledged as Basel II, entailing a shift from capital standards defined by supervisors to establishing criteria for the approval of risk-management systems of firms themselves. Indeed, approval of the risk

rating, nothing was said at that time about the standard practice that the issuer paid the fee, and the competition between the oligopolistic rating agencies inevitably created pressures to give favourable ratings.

32 Ample evidence is provided in Gillian Tett's detailed account, for example of how the CDS concept was regarded as having 'pulled off a dance around the Basel rules' (2009: 74). See also Huault and Rainelli-Le Montagner 2009: 562.

model and capital provisioning was only one of the three pillars of Basel II, which also specified supervisory procedures, and market disciplines facilitated by transparency requirements.

The consultation process for the Basel II proposals was further extended by the need to improve and refine the standards to cope with the explosive growth of trading of increasingly complex financial derivatives. Although this growth was mainly driven by non-banks such as hedge funds, such entities created risks for the banking system by boosting their own funds with loans from investment banks and further leveraging this capital by using it as margin to take positions in derivatives involving enormous exposures. The dangers involved were brought home with the failure in September 1998 of Long Term Credit Management (LTCM), a hedge fund run by Wall Street's top financial rocket scientists,[33] which triggered a rescue facilitated by the New York Reserve Bank. This showed that central banks might be obliged to provide LLR support to non-banks, due to the systemic risk created by banks' involvement in their activities.

Basel II aimed to resolve the problems of rigidity of formal requirements, which are unresponsive to innovation or indeed tend to encourage regulatory avoidance, by harnessing regulatory standards to the firms' own risk-management tools. This more 'reflexive' approach has some advantages, for example allowing the inclusion of a wider range of risks, not only market but also 'operational' risks (resulting from system or managerial failures such as 'rogue traders').

---

33 Led by Wall Street veteran John Meriwether, LTCM's partners included Robert Merton, the Nobel-prizewinning economist who devised the Black–Scholes model for valuing financial derivatives. Following its collapse, a document leaked from the Swiss bank UBS showed that it had estimated that LTCM was leveraged at least 250 times – 27.2 times on balance sheet but an undisclosed amount off balance sheet; nevertheless, UBS had ignored its own lending guidelines, resulting in a loss of SwFrs950m. (Treanor and Tran 1998). The BCBS report following the affair estimated the size of LTCM's total assets at $125bn, but its notional off-balance-sheet positions at well over $1trillion; its leverage ratio had been 25:1 in early 1998, without taking account of derivatives. While LTCM's size, leverage and secretiveness 'may have made it a unique case', competition had led financial institutions to 'compromise important aspects of the risk-management process', especially by offering generous terms on margins for OTC derivatives (BCBS 1999: 10). Although this extremely high leverage was the source of the problem, the direct causes were more complex: Donald MacKenzie's detailed analysis suggests that the decisive factor was that emulation of LTCM's trading model by others created a 'superportfolio', and that as Russia's default on rouble-denominated bonds caused traders to sell other assets, it created a self-fulfilling spiral which dried up even LTCM's immense resources of liquidity (2006: 218–41).

However, Basel II carried its own dangers, since it involved a reversion to self-regulation. In encouraging firms to adopt sophisticated risk modelling, regulators 'struggled to balance incentives (in the form of permissible capital reductions) for banks that adopt the advanced risk measurement approaches with the objective of broadly maintaining the aggregate level of minimum required capital' (US GAO 2007: 22). Indeed, the introduction of Basel II in the USA was delayed by studies which showed that it would result in substantial reductions in minimum capital requirements (US GAO 2007: 26). This does indeed seem to have been the result in the UK, which was an early adopter, as shown by the case of Northern Rock (see 7.3.1 below).

The use of risk models also runs the danger of creating self-reinforcing practices among firms and practitioners, and their effectiveness greatly depends on the validity of the models used and the mathematical and statistical techniques on which they are based, in particular the reliance on probabilities based on historical data and systems of backtesting.[34] The establishment of detailed parameters for backtesting took international regulators into even more difficult and arcane regions, and indeed some specialists suggested that the risk modelling should be left to the banks (Rochet 2008: 31).

A fundamental objection is that VaR combined two formalist theories in a way that compounds the errors of both. On the one hand it accepts the assumptions of efficient market theory put forward by financial economists (originated by Eugene Fama of Chicago): that prices of traded assets efficiently reflect all relevant information. Although held with fervour by many financial practitioners, it is a justification for financial markets rather than a description of their actual workings.[35] These

---

34 The so-called Value at Risk (VAR) models became publicized in October 1994 when investment bank JP Morgan made available over the internet its RiskMetrics system and the data needed to apply it. Although financial economists argued at the time that such models are consonant with portfolio theory (Dowd 1998), they were strongly criticized, notably by Naseem Taleb, for ignoring the effects of low-probability high-impact events, so-called 'black swans'. For a retrospective re-evaluation of the errors of modern financial theory, concluding that it 'rests on unsound assumptions and should largely be ditched', see Dowd and Hutchinson 2010.

35 In practice, as Donald MacKenzie points out (in an understated way) 'Probably a majority of the finance theorists . . . have had some involvement in practical activity that would make no sense if the efficient-market hypothesis were taken to be an entirely accurate model of markets.' This is true also of other basic building blocks of derivatives, the Capital Asset Pricing Model (CAPM) and the Black–Scholes option pricing model; indeed Black himself 'delighted in pointing out "the holes in Black–Scholes"' (MacKenzie 2006: 248).

assumptions were combined with mathematical techniques using historical data to estimate correlation probabilities (e.g. of default) based on Gaussian statistical modelling which assumes random distributions.

The assumptions of both of these theories have been strongly criticized. Micro-sociological and anthropological studies of financial markets show that traders react to conventional signals,[36] or even rumour and panic, since their main aim is to anticipate market movements. Such observations are consonant with the perceptions of behaviouralist economists and others about market volatility due to herd behaviour, or 'self-reinforcing positive feedback processes'.[37] Statistical techniques based on assumptions of random distributions have been challenged by Benoit Mandelbrot, who has shown that real-world events are not random but tend to cluster, and in particular that financial market movements have a higher probability of reflecting recent behaviour, hence they move in cycles. Thus, VaR risk management models based on a combination of the efficient market hypothesis and random distribution probability theory will be poor predictors of cyclical market movements.[38]

7.3 The crash and its lessons

The period of financialization culminated in the great financial crash of 2007 to 2008. Whereas the crisis of 1929 began in the stock market and only badly hit the banking system after it triggered an economic

MacKenzie examines in detail how these techniques helped to construct financial markets, based on a 'performativity' theory, which he suggests flows from 'the cognitive limitations of human beings', so that 'economic action involves distributed cognition' (MacKenzie 2006: 265). A study based on similar methodology by Huault and Rainelli-Le Montagner (2009) of credit derivatives argues that the efforts of a powerful 'cognitive and political community' failed to produce an open market in these instruments due to their inherent uncertainty, suggesting that there is a limit to the financial theory of risk, and to the ability of technical specialists to create practices through 'performance'.

36 For example, traders on a wide variety of financial markets focus on the release of US non-farm payroll employment data, which is self-reinforcingly assumed to be an indicator of likely market movements.

37 The noted practitioner, George Soros, argues that participants seek both to understand and to influence markets on the basis of their perceptions (which he terms 'reflexivity'); hence markets operate with a prevailing bias which is self-validating but eventually self-defeating, causing booms and busts ([1987] 2003). The ways in which perceptions and the general cultural climate contributed to the 'irrational exuberance' that fed the bubble were also pointed out by Robert Shiller (2000).

38 See Cooper 2008: 143–51. These views have gained increased salience in some official reports following the crisis, see e.g. Turner 2009: 39–42, 44–5; BIS 2009: 9–10.

crisis, in 2008 a generalized financial crash sparked an economic crisis,[39] which affected the whole world, although unequally. Although the crash was triggered by the contagion caused by the popping of the bubble in mortgage-backed CDOs, it revealed many failings in the system of bank and financial regulation and supervision, which had in effect stimulated both financialization and the practices which created the bubble.

The crisis generated general popular feeling that finance must be put on a new footing, which has even been expressed by politicians. This was eloquently articulated in the conference hosted in Paris in January 2009, *Nouveau Monde, Nouveau Capitalisme: éthique, développement, régulation.* The conference called for a restoration of 'trust in capitalism' as 'a humanistic economic, social and organisation [*sic*], able to create and fairly redistribute wealth', by drawing up a more responsible and ethical 'new capitalism', and even a 'new world of solidarity and multilateralism'.[40] Yet there was an enormous gap between such bold words and the actual proposals for regulation put forward, although as the implications of the crisis sank in some influential voices argued for a more radical approach. More seriously, despite growing popular hostility to bankers, there was little sign of any significant change in the culture of finance.

7.3.1 Responses of the regulators to the unfolding crisis

The crash took place just as the Basel II standard was beginning to be implemented. The immediate response of regulators was to affirm that this 'market turmoil' underlined the importance of Basel II, while accepting that it required further amendments (Wellink 2008). In effect, by the end of 2009 the BCBS had put forward a programme to strengthen the regulatory capital framework, involving counter-cyclical capital standards (to promote the build-up of capital buffers during boom periods that can be drawn down in periods of stress); increased capital requirements for

39 Although it can also be said that the financial bubble was rooted in broader global economic imbalances.

40 From the statement on the website of the conference (www.colloquenouveaumonde. fr/home), by Eric Besson, Secretary of State in charge of Strategic Planning, Public Policy Evaluation and Digital Economy Development, who opened the conference. In the way of politicians (and the academic media stars invited to such events), there were counterbalancing statements supporting 'entrepreneurial risk valuation without sharing mistakes', and opposing 'excessive regulation'.

banks' trading books; and to introduce a leverage ratio as a backstop to Basel II.[41]

From the viewpoint of the regulatory authorities, it is understandable and perhaps justifiable to seek to learn the lessons of the crash by pressing on with Basel II, with further improvements. As pointed out above, Basel I created significant incentives for regulatory avoidance in ways which contributed substantially to the eventual crisis, especially the various devices for moving CDOs off balance sheet.[42] These initial responses nevertheless ducked serious questions about Basel II and the existing approach to regulation. It was significant that the UK, which had led the way in introducing the Basel internal models approach, nevertheless experienced its first bank run for 130 years in 2007. In fact, the bank in question, Northern Rock, despite being considered a 'high impact firm', was given a Basel II waiver at the end of June 2007, allowing it greater reliance on its internal risk model, on the grounds that the model had been extensively stress-tested. On 25 July Northern Rock declared a 30 per cent increase in its interim dividend because the waiver and other asset realizations meant that it had an 'anticipated regulatory capital surplus over the next three to four years'. Unfortunately, the scenarios used in the stress tests did not include what was in fact actually happening even as the waiver was granted. Within a couple of weeks Northern Rock faced a collapse of the mortgage-backed securities market and an extended drying up of liquidity in interbank lending, and in mid-August was forced to approach the Bank of England for support. The announcement of a

41 BCBS 2009; these reforms were sometimes referred to as Basel III, though not by the BCBS. Some of the measures required coordination with other standards: notably, the counter-cyclical capital standards would run counter to the mark-to-market approach of the IASB, so the BCBS urged the adoption of an Expected Loss approach to debt provisioning to 'address the deficiencies of the incurred loss approach without introducing an expansion of fair value accounting' (press release of Group of Central Bank Governors and Heads of Supervision 11 January 2010, www.bis.org/press/p100111.htm).

42 Those who have recognized potential problems with risk-based capital requirements, especially due to the additional risk introduced by the risk models themselves, have suggested that they be supplemented, for example by a simple leverage ratio requirement; however, a leverage ratio would be pro-cyclical, and would encourage the use of off-balance-sheet devices (Hildebrand 2008). The US authorities had in any case intended to retain a simple leverage ratio requirement as a complement to the Basel ratios (US GAO 2007). They also propose to allow banks the option of a 'standardized' version of Basel II, which essentially means sticking with Basel I; it is likely that the vast majority (all but a dozen or less) would do so, both because of the complexity and costs of introducing internal risk models, but also because the capital requirement seems likely to be lower, due largely to a different method of quantifying operational risk (Rubin 2008).

rescue on 13 September started a panic which eventually resulted in the nationalization of the bank (UK Treasury Committee 2008a).

What is perhaps most striking about the great financial crash is the extent to which regulators seem to have been working in the dark, despite ample warning of the dangers and their potential systemic effects. The bursting of the housing price bubble took place over some eighteen months, and it took a further twelve months or more for the impact of the crisis to work its way through. Yet such was the degree of opacity of the entire 'shadow banking system' that, as it struck one eminent financial institution after another, the regulatory authorities seemed taken by surprise on each occasion yet again. Delinquencies and repossessions on US sub-prime mortgages had begun to rise in 2005, and by December 2006 the Center for Responsible Lending predicted that 'one out of five sub-prime mortgages originated during the past two years will end in foreclosure' (Schloemer *et al.* 2006: 3). These warnings were amply justified in the first half of 2007, yet in July, after Bear Stearns bailed out two hedge funds specializing in sub-prime mortgages, Fed chairman Ben Bernanke estimated in testimony to Congress that the cost could amount to $100bn. A year later it had risen tenfold.

The onset of the crisis was signalled on 9 August 2007, by two events. First, the European Central Bank made a brief announcement that it was opening an unlimited funding line for banks due to 'tensions in the euro money-markets'. This was followed within hours by a statement revealing that forty-nine banks had taken advantage of this to the unprecedented level of €94bn (Tett 2009: 215). More low key was the second event, the suspension by BNP Paribas of withdrawals from three of its hedge funds that had invested in sub-prime residential mortgage securities, declaring that 'the complete evaporation of liquidity in certain market segments of the US securitization market has made it impossible to value certain assets fairly regardless of their quality or credit rating', and that the 'situation is such that it is no longer possible to value fairly the underlying US ABS [asset-backed securities] assets in the three above-mentioned funds'.

These events forced the CRAs into a long overdue revaluation of CDOs,[43] and banks began hastily to identify their losses and shore up their balance sheets, leading to a freezing up of inter-bank lending. The impact

---

43 Mortgage-backed CDOs had generally been assigned AAA ratings by the agencies, which abruptly began to downgrade them by several notches from August 2007; this resulted in criticism that they had done very well from their role in the CDO boom, since their pricing model had changed from charging the issuer rather than the buyer, and that they had failed adequately to evaluate complex CDOs layered into several tranches with

was immediately felt by institutions most heavily involved in market-based mortgage finance, such as Northern Rock, but like an undersea earthquake a tsunami was unleashed which would eventually overwhelm many more.

It seems that the regulatory authorities had no clear appreciation of the potential repercussions of the puncturing of the bubble in house prices in the USA and other countries, although they had plenty of time to evaluate the extent of the problem. By August 2007 the disastrous impact on the valuation of mortgage-backed CDOs and the knock-on effects on liquidity and inter-bank lending were clearly known. Only in December 2007 was some coordinated action attempted, with a joint announcement by five leading central banks of arrangements to provide liquidity to the banking system and unfreeze inter-bank lending. Yet the crisis rumbled on for a further nine months to its climax.

At the G7 meeting in Tokyo in February 2008 the estimation of write-offs related to the US mortgage crisis had reached $400bn, though by April the IMF's financial stability report estimated losses would come to $945bn. By the time the G7 leaders had reconvened in Washington, DC in October, the USA had been forced into a recapitalization of its entire financial system of some $700bn, following rescues of a half-dozen of its biggest financial institutions (Bear Stearns, Fannie Mae and Freddie Mac, AIG, Merrill Lynch, Wachovia) involving a total of some $245bn of government guarantees, while other major entities (IndyMac Bank, Washington Mutual, Lehman Brothers) had been closed or allowed to fail or be bought up. The climax came in mid-September 2008, when Lehman Brothers was allowed to go bankrupt,[44] while AIG was effectively nationalized; the rationale for the contrasting decisions was hard

different risk levels, relying on unverified data from the issuers and historical mortgage default statistics; their response was to argue that their ratings were only 'opinions' on default risk (editorial (*WSJ*) 2008). In saying this they were attempting to rely on defences which had partially succeeded in the post-Enron litigation (Partnoy 2006: 86–7) to protect themselves from the inevitable investor lawsuits.

44 The collapse of Lehman after 158 years in banking has been largely blamed on the policies of its autocratic CEO, Dick Fuld (Partnoy 2008); it certainly shows the weakness of corporate governance: Lehman's Finance and Risk Committee included a theatre producer who had been on the board for twenty-three years, and a former chief of the American Red Cross and the Girl Scouts, but it was chaired by Henry Kaufman, the former Federal Reserve Bank of New York economist (Macintosh 2008), known as 'Dr Doom' for his bearish forecasts, who had resigned from his research post at Salomon Brothers in 1987 as it accelerated its speculation in high-risk business, and had published repeated warnings of the dangers of derivatives and their inadequate regulation, most recently five weeks before Lehman's collapse (Kaufman 2008).

to understand, since both were known to have significant involvement in credit default swaps or insurance. The tragicomic anticlimax came with the 'Minsky moment' when Bernard Madoff's hedge fund collapsed with losses estimated at $50bn, and was revealed to have been no more than a Ponzi scheme.[45]

The impact in the UK was of a similar scale, with the government rescue package of October 2008 being worth at least £50bn ($88bn) plus up to £200bn ($350bn) in short-term lending support; the £50bn loan book of Bradford & Bingley was nationalized and its banking business sold, and a takeover was facilitated of the biggest mortgage lender HBOS by Lloyds TSB in a £12bn deal creating a banking giant holding close to one-third of the UK's savings and mortgage market. Nevertheless, this new group was forced to accept recapitalization under the £37bn government scheme announced in November, which resulted in the government taking a stake of 43 per cent in this group, as well as 58 per cent in RBS. European institutions also succumbed: banking and insurance giant Fortis was partly nationalized by the Netherlands at a cost of €11.2bn; Dexia was saved by an injection of €6.4bn by the Belgian, French and Luxembourg governments; while several German banks were rescued, and the German authorities engineered a €50bn deal to save Hypo Real Estate. The Netherlands rescued ING to the tune of $13.4bn, while Sweden's government set out its own bank rescue plan, with credit guarantees to banks and mortgage lenders up to a level of 1.5 trillion kroner ($205bn). The Icelandic government was forced to take control of the country's third-largest bank Glitnir, and then of the second largest, Landsbanki, ultimately having recourse itself to an IMF rescue package of $2.1bn.[46]

45 Neo-Keynesian economist Hyman Minsky's theory of financial bubbles and crashes, based on the psychology of financial speculation during a boom, suggested that the final stage of speculative mania is the Ponzi scheme, i.e. the pyramid selling of assets in which investors are paid large returns from the continuing flow of new investments, until the scheme collapses (1992). Minsky's is a post-Keynesian behaviouralist perspective, which suggests that stable financial markets themselves inevitably encourage experimentation, risk-taking, optimism and even euphoria, and hence that finance is inherently fragile and crises inevitable (Nesvetailova 2007: 154).

46 Iceland's financial centre was the subject of an ROSC organized by the IMF in 2001, with an update in 2003; however, its financial sector expanded vertiginously between 2004 and 2007, with bank assets climbing from 100 to 900 per cent of Iceland's GDP. This was noted in the IMF's additional ROSC Update carried out in June 2008; it is hard to tell from the language of that report if the IMF team anticipated the imminent disaster, as by that stage no doubt the need for damage limitation was uppermost, which presumably explains its assurance that 'reported financial indicators are above minimum regulatory requirements and stress tests suggest that the system is resilient'; the Report was eventually

Even Switzerland threw a lifebelt of SwFrs6bn ($5.3bn) to UBS, plus a funding facility for up to $60bn of distressed assets.

The main problem seems to have been the totally opaque nature especially of OTC derivatives, so that the extent of exposure of financial institutions was impossible to estimate. This seems to be the root cause of both the collapse of trust and confidence which paralysed the markets, and the failure of the regulatory authorities to quantify the potential impact with any degree of accuracy. Indeed, despite its extensive recapitalization from public funds, the banking system remained paralysed for some time, requiring continuing life support through further public credit guarantees and asset protection schemes.

The costs of the various types of public support for the financial sector alone, ranging from capital injections and asset purchases to the provision of guarantees, was estimated by February 2009 to amount to 43 per cent of GDP across the advanced economies and 28 per cent for the G20 countries as a whole.[47] Even these estimates were subsequently shown to be based on partial information. Not until early December 2010 did the US government issue data which showed that the $700b Troubled Assets Relief Programme (aptly named the Tarp), enacted after much political wrangling by the Congress, had been dwarfed by the $3,300bn more discreetly made available by the Fed. to a wide range of banks and companies, both US and foreign owned. These included central pillars of Wall Street, such as Goldman Sachs, Morgan Stanley, Blackrock, Fidelity and GE Capital, as well as a range of firms from Verizon Communications and Harley-Davidson to Sumitomo Corporation and the Bank of Nova

published after the crisis broke, in December 2008. The bank collapses resulted in a dispute between the Icelandic government and the UK and the Netherlands, since much of the expansion had been by attracting deposits from those countries, which their governments argued should under EU rules be covered by the home-state's deposit insurance scheme; an agreement between the governments capped Iceland's liability to 4 per cent of its GDP, but was nevertheless politically controversial, due to the enormous burden already imposed by debt service on Iceland's population of some 300,000 (compared to over a half-million foreign depositors in Icelandic banks).

47 IMF 2009: Table 1. However, a high proportion was due to liquidity provisions and guarantees which do not require upfront financing, excluding this, the cost for advanced G20 countries averaged 5.2 per cent of GDP. The actual eventual costs were hard to estimate, the IMF paper suggested they might be about half the upfront costs, but this could be optimistic, and the cost of losses on guarantees would be additional to this. It estimated that government debt would rise to over 100 per cent of GDP in advanced G20 countries by 2014. Nevertheless, the actual bank losses seem to have been relatively concentrated: of the 4,500 banks worldwide monitored by *The Banker*, 196 incurred pre-tax losses of $5m. or more in 2008, totalling around $400bn (OECD 2010b: 12).

Scotia. Thus, less than one-quarter of the rescue funds had been publicly dispensed let alone politically sanctioned, demonstrating both the enormous power of unelected central bankers, and the crucial reliance of the financial system on state support and ultimately the taxpayer (Mallaby 2010). Only gradually did the wider implications begin to emerge, as governments began to restructure public finances to deal with these enormous accumulations of debt, and faced the inevitable social and political consequences. Countries such as Iceland and Ireland, with large financial sectors in relation to their economy, were affected first and worst, followed by southern European euro-zone members. Continuing survival of others depends on their prospects for resumed economic growth, now driven by new emerging economies, especially China, India and Brazil. Even US economic power now hinges on its uneasy symbiosis with China: massive trade imbalances, largely fuelled by the direct investments in China of US TNCs, and a strong dollar propped up by China's purchases of US Treasury bonds. These events bore out the predictions of some commentators, made relatively early, that this was not just a limited 'credit crunch' affecting parts of the home mortgage finance system, mainly in the USA. Notably, Martin Wolf in the *Financial Times*, in December 2007 described it as a turning point for the world economy, and a 'huge blow to the credibility of the Anglo-Saxon model of transactions-orientated financial capitalism' (2007).

7.3.2 A new approach to financial regulation?

There were clearly many aspects and contributory factors to the crisis, and there are many lessons to be learned. These include economic, political, social and moral issues, which go well beyond those of legal regulation. The focus here is specifically on international regulatory standards and coordination.

The crash dramatically brought home how central the financial system is to the world economy. The realm of finance poses more sharply than any the central dilemmas facing economic regulation today. Financial transactions are quintessentially regarded as private, market relationships, yet a stable financial system is an essential public good. This sharp contradiction has been starkly driven home by the extensive state bailouts, yet governments have shunned the word nationalization, and have done all they can to leave firms in private hands. The effect, as many commentators pointed out, was that while enormous private profits were made in the boom years, the losses were socialized, and borne by the public. It is therefore clear that any new approach to the regulation of finance should include a fundamental re-evaluation and rebalancing of the relationship between public authorities and regulators and the finance industry.

Central to a new approach should be a withdrawal of protection and state support for financialization, to restore something closer to efficient functioning of financial markets. As the analysis and account in this chapter have shown, liberalization of financial markets since the 1970s has resulted in hyper-regulation, which in turn has generated regulatory arbitrage and avoidance, spawning further regulation. The root of the problem has been the state protection and support for financial firms, which created perverse incentives and market distortions. These take three main forms. First is the protection of limited liability. This enables the managers of all types of financial vehicles, from investment banks to hedge funds, to engage in speculation without assuming any personal risk. Thus, they bear no losses, but are nevertheless very generously rewarded through profit-sharing and bonus schemes from the profits. In effect, they are able to make bets, using other people's money, from which they cannot lose, which is inevitably a strong incentive for gambling. Second, the safety net of LLR support has been provided for virtually any type of financial firm. Retail financial firms (deposit-taking institutions), for which this type of support is necessary and intended, have been allowed to invest in all kinds of instruments and vehicles. This has provided enormous leverage for hedge funds and other kinds of arbitrageurs and speculators, and hence further incentives to gamble with no downside risk, while the state provides the safety net due to the systemic danger when they fail (e.g. LTCM, discussed above). Third, financial firms and transactions have greatly benefited from access to low-cost capital due to exploitation of the opportunities for tax avoidance and evasion provided by the 'offshore' system (as discussed in the previous chapter). The measures taken to reform the financial system, which will take some time to unfold and become embedded, should be judged in terms of whether these perverse incentives are removed.

A strong case can be made for movement towards new forms of social ownership and accountability for financial institutions. These could build on historic forms such as mutual and cooperative ownership.[48] This would ensure some check on money managers, and more active monitoring

---

[48] Laurence Kotlikoff has gone further and advocated that all financial firms should operate as different kinds of mutual funds (2010; see further below).

should be possible even by shareholders, such as the large institutional investors, especially pension funds (Blackburn 2002: 487–90). This type of structural change would go a long way to putting finance on a new footing, although it should be supplemented by regulation. Such regulation can establish a framework of social objectives, within which managers should be free to take investment decisions based on criteria of efficient resource allocation (Blackburn 2002: 490). Central to such social objectives should be financial stability; but as the financial crisis has shown, several factors contributed to excessive risk-taking. Not the least important were the remuneration structures for financial managers, which have now become a focus for public debate and regulatory concern,[49] although the 'bonus culture' still seems impervious to public opprobrium or regulators' threats and rules.[50]

7.3.2.1 Effective coordination

A key issue, not least for measures to ensure social accountability, is how to ensure effective regulation on a worldwide scale. One response would be to call for a World Financial Authority, however utopian it may seem. Such a suggestion was already made by some commentators following the Asian financial crisis of 1997 to 1998 (Eatwell and Taylor 2000), on the grounds that 'the domain of the regulator should be the same as the domain of the market' (Alexander *et al.* 2006: 15). There are however a number of difficulties with this view. It is certainly the case, as the account in this chapter has made clear, that the fragmented character of financial market regulation has created serious problems both of coordination and of legitimation. However, that fragmentation cannot be wished away; it is essentially a reflection of the diversity of the aspects of money and finance that call for regulation, as well as differences in the forms of finance

---

49 In August 2009 the Attorney-General for the State of New York, Andrew Cuomo, released a report which showed that nine of the largest US banks, which between them had received $175bn of support under the Troubled Assets Relief Program (TARP), had nevertheless paid bonuses in 2008 amounting to $32bn; compensation and benefits remained at the levels set during the bull markets even after the collapse: thus, Citigroup and Merrill Lynch, despite each posting losses of nearly $28bn, paid out bonuses totalling $5.3bn and $3.6bn respectively (Cuomo 2009: 2–5).

50 Thus, in the UK the FSA issued a Code requiring remuneration policies to be 'consistent with effective risk management', and threatened that if necessary incomplete adherence to the Code could result in increased capital requirements (Turner 2009: 79–81). In July 2010 the European Parliament approved a proposed Directive which will impose a cap on cash bonuses and require at least half of bonuses to be paid as a mix of contingent capital and shares; this will apply to EU financial firms' subsidiaries abroad (including offshore) as well as foreign-owned financial entities operating in the EU.

and of financial institutions as they developed historically in different countries.[51] As mentioned above, the response following the Asian crisis was to provide some coordination, by creating another regulatory body, the FSF. The FSF proved if anything less prescient than other regulators in failing to warn of the asset price bubble which precipitated the crisis. A single global regulator would still have problems of coordination, while any error of judgement it made would have enormous repercussions.

Systemic stability can certainly be identified as an overarching global imperative for regulation, if one accepts that international liberalization has gone so far that financial instability in any one part of the financial system can create serious dangers worldwide. The crisis also threw into doubt the policies of encouraging greater financial integration in the form of cross-border financial services. Indeed, one commentator has warned that the European single market in banking is falling apart, as bank rescues have been on a national basis; consequently, supervisors will in future insist on separately capitalized subsidiaries in host countries, unless agreement can be reached either on joint support, or at least a system of burden-sharing for rescues (Schoenmaker 2009), both of which seem out of reach at present.

There are indeed several regulatory functions which potentially affect stability. Monetary policy has important effects, and the loose money policies especially of the US Fed. created the excessive liquidity that fed the house price bubble in the early years of this century, as Alan Greenspan himself acknowledged to the US Congress in October 2008.[52] Another distinct function is supervision of the financial firms, which is often done by several regulators for different types of firm (banking, insurance, brokerage). Even in the UK, which created a single regulatory body covering all market participants when the Financial Services Authority (FSA) was established in 1997, coordination with the Bank of England and the Treasury in the 'tripartite system' was problematic (UK Treasury Committee 2008b).

51 A comprehensive survey for the G30, by a group chaired by Paul Volcker (G30 2008), classified regulatory systems as institutional (based on the legal form of regulated entities), functional (based on type of business), integrated (single regulator), and 'twin peaks' (separating safety-and-soundness and conduct-of-business regulation). It found a trend towards integration and regulation by objective, but also cautioned that coordination problems were also present in integrated regulators, which also sometimes suffered from bureaucratic overload.

52 These were also rooted in international economic imbalances, which led to large foreign holdings of US bonds especially by China, Japan and oil-exporting countries (see Exhibit 1 in Turner 2009: 14; data and analysis in BIS 2009: 5–7).

Problems of coordination would remain even if all aspects of financial regulation were brought together under the umbrella of one enormous global regulator. The challenge is to design regulation appropriately, so that: (a) no significant loopholes are left; and (b) those responsible for each specific aspect also look to the bigger picture and communicate well with each other. Although the detailed accounts of the 2007–8 crisis which have emerged do show some failures of communication, the defects of the regulatory system were due much more to the failure to take a more holistic view, by both regulators and market participants.[53] A major reason of course was that the public regulatory authorities were entirely *unable* to see the whole picture because they had in effect abandoned any attempt even to understand let alone regulate the actual transactions taking place in the marketplaces of finance. Finance had become an increasingly opaque and secretive world, protected by arcane technical practices, regulation of which had largely been delegated to practitioners themselves. This suggests that the three aspects of regulation, of *firms*, *markets* and *instruments*, should be geared towards the overarching issue of systemic risk and should be properly coordinated (BIS 2009: 125).

7.3.2.2 Systemic risks and structural reform

A new approach should therefore go beyond proposals for specific regulatory reform to consider the interactions of the various aspects of regulation and their systemic implications. This is especially challenging because finance has become both interconnected and complex. The rescue of failing firms has created fewer and larger financial conglomerates,[54] and even smaller firms are highly interconnected. Hence, the mega-firms may be too large and complex to be able to manage their own risk adequately, yet too big to be allowed to fail, while the smaller ones may be too interconnected with the system as a whole to let fail (BIS 2009: 120). Integrated finance may have advantages in helping to spread risk, but as the crisis has shown only too starkly, it can also act as a transmission mechanism for risk (Beck *et al.* 2010: 23).

This has raised the question of whether the future financial system should have a clearer separation between firms providing standard forms

---

53 This is the conclusion of Gillian Tett's detailed, insightful and readable account (2009: 298–9).
54 Notably, the completion of the acquisition by Bank of America of Merrill Lynch has combined an enormous retail bank network with the largest brokerage and a major investment banking business, to create the biggest financial institution in the USA.

of financial intermediation as a kind of public utility, referred to as 'utility banking' or 'narrow banking', and those involved in more risky and speculative activities. A significant step in this direction was taken in January 2010, when President Obama (under political pressure) announced the principle, originating with Paul Volcker, that banks should 'no longer be allowed to own, invest or sponsor hedge funds, private equity funds or proprietary trading operations for their own profit unrelated to serving their customers'. Proposals to implement the principle were introduced in the comprehensive legislation which became the focus of struggles in Congress, resulting in the Dodd–Frank Wall Street Reform and Consumer Protection Act enacted in July 2010. This wide-ranging legislation itself comprises some 850 sections, and grants essentially discretionary powers to various regulatory agencies to issue further detailed regulation, so it will undoubtedly create new terrains of negotiation and contestation. Notably, the Volcker Rule was watered down to impose only a limit on a bank's investment in private equity and hedge funds of 3 per cent of its tier-1 capital, and 3 per cent in any one fund. This does not prevent banks from engaging in proprietary trading themselves, nor selling participations in their funds to clients. Proprietary trading is itself a slippery concept, and since the move was not internationally coordinated, US banks will be able to put pressure on regulators for favourable interpretations by threatening to shift dubious transactions abroad. Initial evaluations suggest that the regime opens a new era in the corporatist partnership between the government and the largest financial institutions (Skeel 2010).

Regulators who mainly focus on prudential supervision of firms inevitably emphasize reform of capital requirements. This attempts to learn the lessons of the crisis, in particular to introduce counter-cyclicality and to tighten up the provisioning for market risk and the trading book, which has resulted in proposals for much higher minimum capital ratios. In addition, as was pointed out in the Turner Report, there needs to be a more fundamental evaluation of how the levels of capital provisioning are determined, based on principles rather than pragmatism (Turner 2009: 53–8). International agreement through the BCBS is inevitably taking time, and implementation is also likely to be phased in gradually, to avoid exacerbating the economic recession. It is likely to be very uneven: although the Basel standards are supposed to be *minimum* standards, and some countries avoided the worse of the financial crash due to having adopted higher requirements, such as India and Spain, the economic impact was also variable.[55] Capital standards are only one of the three pillars of Basel, and should be supplemented by rigorous supervisory reviews of firms (the second pillar). The third pillar of Basel, 'market discipline' needs more radical reform, since it is now clear that much more needs to be done to introduce transparency. This relates to the other two aspects of regulation, of markets and instruments.

Ensuring safety of markets centres on a fundamental reform of OTC trading, to introduce transparency in place of the totally opaque and private system which was allowed to mushroom. In principle, this should involve central counterparties and trading on a public platform, although not necessarily a full-blown exchange, which would generate its own momentum and vested interests. Not surprisingly, proposals requiring this especially in the USA quickly ran into determined opposition. The legislation so far enacted, notably in the Dodd–Frank Act, gives regulators considerable discretionary power to exclude some types of bespoke instruments from the transparency obligations, which opens up a new area of regulatory contestation. Nevertheless, transparency is clearly the only way to prevent contagion leading to liquidity crises due to lack of knowledge about exposures. It has also been proposed that the risks arising from interconnected and common exposures should be safeguarded against by introducing a systemic capital charge (BIS 2009: 129).

The greatest regulatory gap revealed by the crisis is in relation to financial instruments, which have been left almost entirely to private regulators. Plugging this gap needs more than the introduction of tighter controls on credit-rating agencies such as the Code of Conduct put forward by IOSCO in 2008, or a system of licensing and supervision of CRAs which has been the favoured direction of regulation on both sides of the Atlantic. Public regulators should have a more direct role in vetting financial instruments, and there should be a reversal of the presumption in favour of financial innovation (Bell and Quiggin 2006: 646). Financial derivatives should be treated like pharmaceutical drugs. No one suggests that all new drugs should be released on the market, leaving it to consumers or even doctors to decide how safe they are and for which uses. The financial crisis starkly demonstrated that financial derivatives can be economically toxic, and

---

55 Ironically, however, Spain's economy was especially badly hit by the collapse of the property bubble, and the bank supervisors were slow to take action to deal with weaker elements in the banking sector, notably the savings banks (*cajas*).

they should be regulated accordingly, through a system of registration and certification. The approvals process should include determination of the tax treatment, as well as conditions of use: how they should be treated on the balance sheet and for capital provisioning, and which categories of investor should be allowed to deal in each.

Regrettably, although some commentators have suggested such an approach,[56] there does not yet seem to be sufficient political pressure behind it. The most radical, and yet simple, proposal has been Laurence Kotlikoff's scheme for 'limited purpose banking'. This would combine prior approval by a single public regulator of all financial instruments, based on full transparency of the risk evaluation, with a conversion of all banks (i.e. financial firms) into pure intermediaries selling shares in different kinds of mutual funds (Kotlikoff 2010). This would have the great merit of greatly *reducing* the extent of regulation, by targeting the crucial point: approval of the financial instruments which may be marketed, and their restriction to mutual investment funds. It also aims to avoid the need for LLR support, by turning banks into cash mutual funds, and hence with 100 per cent capital reserve; while requiring investors in other kinds of funds to take on their risk, on a mutual basis. This shifts much of the responsibility of managing investment risk onto investors, which is desirable and necessary, but inappropriate for most small savers. Such needs could perhaps be catered for by suitable broad-based mutual investment funds. However, the main purposes of social savings are for health care, social security and pensions, which entail a degree of socialization that must surely entail state provision.

The greatest concern has inevitably been about the enormous scale and cost of the bailouts. This has led to two main proposals. One is for a bank tax or levy, to finance a contingency fund which could pay for any eventual rescue. However, national Treasuries are unwilling to have such a potentially large fund sit idle, especially at a time of increasing fiscal crisis. Yet to use the proceeds of a bank tax to help alleviate current fiscal stringency would leave open the question of financing future bailouts. Not surprisingly, it has proved impossible to reach international agreement on such a move. A second proposal is that financial firms should be required to draw up a 'living will', in the form of a 'plan for an orderly

---

56 This was proposed by the BIS (2009: 126–7), and even the Turner report accepted that direct regulation of both retail and wholesale financial products should be considered (Turner 2009: 106–10).

wind down of their activities', suggested among others by the Governor of the Bank of England (King 2009: 7). A somewhat different provision for 'orderly liquidation authority' was included in US legislation in the Dodd–Frank Act of 2010 (ss. 201–217). However, unless such a requirement is linked to some clear reimbursement mechanism, it would still leave taxpayers bearing the ultimate cost of bailouts.[57] Both the bank levy and the living-will requirement have the major failing that they imply that a future crisis is inevitable, and do little to avert it. Perhaps the most important aspect of regulation has however remained little discussed: the circumstances in which state support should be provided for failing firms, and the terms for such support. The authorities should now explicitly identify the firms for which they accept ultimate responsibility, and finally abandon the long-discredited policy of 'calculated ambiguity' about their LLR function.[58] Indeed, LLR support could become a keystone linking together the regulation of firms, markets and instruments. This should be done by making any guarantees of public support for financial firms which are deemed systemically important conditional on strict conditions on the type of financial intermediation in which they may engage.[59] The aim should be to insulate the social financial intermediation system from financial speculation. Since licensed financial entities

57 The Dodd–Frank Act, s. 214 firmly states that 'no taxpayer funds shall be used to prevent' liquidation, and that all funds expended in a liquidation 'shall be recovered from the disposition of assets of such financial company, or shall be the responsibility of the financial sector, through assessments'; but it remains to be seen how this will be implemented in practice. The legislation again gives regulators wide discretion, both in deciding when a firm is put into liquidation, and in allocating losses between creditors: normal bankruptcy procedures are ousted, and the authorities are empowered to regulate 'with respect to the rights, interests, and priorities of creditors, counterparties, security entitlement holders, or other persons with respect to any covered financial company or any assets or other property of or held by such covered financial company' (s. 209).

58 This telling phrase and the proposal are from an analysis made over fifteen years ago (Herring and Litan 1995: 128). Yet the same ambiguity was evident in the statement made in October 2008 by G7 finance ministers and central bank governors, that they 'agree to take decisive action and use all available tools to support systemically important financial institutions and prevent their failure'. Rochet (2008) has argued that the problem is that decisions on when to mount a rescue are over-influenced by political considerations, so the solution should be greater independence and accountability of regulators; but this would not seem to deal adequately with the tension between moral hazard and the need to maintain systemic stability.

59 As the Governor of the Bank of England pointed out 'It is not sensible to allow large banks to combine high street retail banking with risky investment banking or funding strategies, and then provide an implicit state guarantee against failure. Something must give' (King 2009: 7).

would only be permitted to deal in approved instruments, there could be no danger of primary financial markets moving 'offshore'.[60]

A similar approach should be adopted to other forms of speculation, such as hedge funds. Thus, financial firms backed by the public guarantee of LLR support should be prohibited from lending to hedge funds. By greatly contributing to the leverage of hedge funds, such loans facilitate market manipulation and further fuel financial volatility and instability, as well as creating systemic risk in the case of a hedge fund failure such as that of LTCM. There should also be a crackdown on the various methods of tax avoidance and evasion, to which a blind eye has been turned by national finance ministries for fear of losing out in the competition among financial centres, as discussed in the previous chapter. Without the benefit of the significant reduction in the cost of capital due to the public subsidies resulting from these two factors, hedge fund activity would sharply diminish or perhaps even die out. Current proposals for regulation such as those in the EU, based on licensing managers of 'alternative' investment funds, tackle the problem at the wrong end. Hedge fund investors are supposed to be sophisticated, or at least rich, so they may be left to bear their own losses. Indeed, licensing and regulation of such funds could be counter-productive by inducing a false sense of security in investors.

However, an excellent case can be made for devising an incentive structure which would make hedge fund and other money managers bear risks from their trading, rather than the present arrangements which generally allow them to benefit enormously from the upside, and lose nothing from the downside. This could be done by ensuring that they face personal responsibility for losses and failure, instead of being insulated by corporate limited liability (Hudson 2009: 854; Kotlikoff 2010: 178).

7.3.3 Rebalancing the world economy

There would of course be a price to pay for the re-establishing of a truly prudential framework for finance. The ending of the addiction to easy credit would impose a cold-turkey cure on the consumption-led boom growth of late capitalism based on asset-price bubbles. Certainly, radical critics have warned for some time that 'financialization' was the symptom

---

60 A financial group might still use an affiliate formed in an offshore jurisdiction to engage in transactions for which the parent is not licensed, but the affiliate would lose LLR support of the home state.

of deep-rooted contradictions of an unstable growth model which rested on widening income inequalities both within national economies and internationally, in a vain attempt to maintain US hegemony (Brenner 2002, 2006; Arrighi 2007; Turner 2008). A transition to a global financial system no longer addicted to cutting the costs of capital to unrealistic levels by systematic avoidance of taxation and regulatory requirements, as well as engaging in reckless financial speculation, could result in a more efficient allocation of capital to productive uses. Indeed, analyses of the costs of financial trading support the common-sense perception that the financial sector now drains enormous sums from the economy which cannot be justified.[61]

Coupled with a rebalanced international economy based on paying realistic social wages to workers in the new economic growth poles of Asia, Latin America and even Africa, as well as reducing income inequalities in the developed countries, a more sustainable pattern of economic growth could be possible. If one lesson is clear from the great financial crisis, it is that banking and finance cannot be allowed to remain the province of unrestricted pursuit of private profit. It must be recognized as having become highly socialized, the transmission belt between social savings and investment, and its institutional structures should begin to reflect this.

---

61 This has been surprisingly little researched; see now Bogle 2008; French 2008. The Governor of the Bank of England has pointed out that the British banking system was, in proportion to GDP, five times greater than that of the USA, creating correspondingly greater risks to the economy (King 2009).

8

The WTO as a node of global governance

The WTO has been denounced by its critics and lauded by its supporters as a standard-bearer for free trade. In fact, the WTO Agreements
erected a complex framework of rules which delineate the battleground
for struggles over fairness and justice, the right to regulate and the forms
of regulation, in a wide range of international economic issues. Hence,
following its establishment in 1995, the World Trade Organization (WTO)
quickly became the focus of debate about governance of the world economy. Its limitations as an organization reflect the enormity of these global
governance issues, the inadequacy of existing political structures, and the
forms of contemporary economic power.

The package of agreements negotiated through the 'bargain-linkage
diplomacy' of the Uruguay Round (UR) negotiations established the WTO
as a central institutional framework for the international coordination
of economic regulation. This completed the organizational triumvirate
originally designed at Bretton Woods, with the WTO now complementing the IMF's role in monetary management and that of the World Bank
in development finance. However, the WTO is a different animal from
the International Trade Organization (ITO) proposed in 1946, which
was still-born due to fears of opposition from the US Congress.[1] The
Havana Charter envisaged the ITO as an institutional framework through
which a managed relaxation of trade barriers would go hand in hand
with measures to stabilize primary commodity prices, control business

---

1 Discussion began in 1943 when a seminar between US and UK officials produced a detailed
  trade Code to be backed by an organization with powers of enforcement but, unlike
  Treasury negotiators of the IMF and WB proposals, the US government trade negotiators
  kept members of Congress in the dark until 1946, when US proposals to the UN were
  published, and the ECOSOC established a preparatory committee. Although negotiations
  proceeded at meetings in New York, Geneva and finally Havana in 1948, the lack of US
  political resolve was crucial to the loss of impetus, and having failed to prepare the political
  ground, President Truman decided not to seek the approval of Congress (Hudec 1975:
  ch. 2; Odell and Eichengreen 1998).

monopolies and restrictive practices, and ensure respect for internationally agreed labour standards (Dell 1990; Drache 2000).[2]

In contrast, the WTO itself is driven by the imperative to remove barriers to market access, usually described as 'negative integration'. The complex and comprehensive set of agreements to which all WTO members must subscribe are almost entirely concerned with setting limits, or in WTO language 'disciplines', on national state regulation. With the major and significant exception of intellectual property rights, it generally leaves to other organizations the task of developing international standards. Nevertheless, it now plays a key part as a central node in global governance networks (Braithwaite and Drahos 2000; Picciotto 1997b), contributing to what has been described as a new global administrative law (Krisch and Kingsbury 2006). However, as an institution, it is riven by the contradiction between the neo-liberal ideology of liberalization and deregulation which dominated its period of gestation in the 1980s, and the realization that markets depend on regulation.

8.1 From trade agreement to governance node

With the failure to agree the establishment of an ITO, the General Agreement on Tariffs and Trade (GATT) came into force on a 'provisional' basis in 1948.[3] Although the GATT was more modest institutionally and in its scope, as a multilateral trade agreement with obligations expressed as very broad principles, it proved very powerful. The original GATT provisions resulted from a series of compromises between free-trade aims and the need for national autonomy in setting domestic regulations (Goldstein 1993). The dynamic of the GATT is provided by the broad obligations of non-discrimination in articles I and III, as well as the prohibition of quantitative restrictions in article XI. These are counterbalanced by a series of exclusions and exceptions in the rest of the treaty.

Thus, like the Bretton Woods institutions, GATT was based on 'embedded liberalism', since its broad principles favouring liberalization were counterbalanced by exceptions allowing states considerable policy space

2 The Havana Charter's provisions on international investment were in outline only, but envisaged it as a process of international mobilization of 'capital funds, materials, modern equipment and technology and technical and managerial skills', and thus entailing state measures both to assure just and equitable treatment for such assets and to regulate their use in the public interest: see Havana Charter arts. 11 and 12 (in UNCTAD 1996a vol. I: 3).

3 This formula was considered sufficient for the USA to accept it as an 'executive agreement' rather than a treaty, ratification of which would require Senate approval.

to manage the social and economic effects of such liberalization (Ruggie 1982). However, as the ratchet of liberalization was turned, it became increasingly difficult to manage the interactions between the GATT obligations of market-opening and the various internal regulatory arrangements of states. Hence, although the GATT began as just a multilateral trade agreement among twenty-three states, it gradually became the point of interaction or node of a web of legal and regulatory arrangements. The culmination was the conclusion of the complex package of treaties negotiated in the UR which established the WTO. This brought many new issues under the WTO umbrella, but even more importantly, it established the WTO as a central node of international regulatory networks, interacting in various ways.

8.1.1 GATT: broad principles and exceptions

The Most-Favoured-Nation (MFN) principle in Article I obliges states to extend any concession they make (to any state) to all other GATT Member States. Although MFN was a long-standing concept in trade agreements, in the GATT it is much more sweeping because it is both *multilateral* and *unconditional*. GATT members are obliged to extend any trade concession they make to any state immediately, and without any reciprocal benefit, to all other members. This means that all trade negotiations among members are automatically multilateral: each state must bear in mind the potential effects of a concession not only in terms of trade in the affected goods with its current major trading partners, but all *potential* partners. This leads to multilateral linkage-bargaining, because the difficulty of obtaining a reciprocal advantage from all potential beneficiaries in return for a particular concession encourages trade-offs against other items or issues. Issue-linkage reached its apogee with the conclusion of the WTO package of agreements.

Article I of the GATT operates in conjunction with article II, under which parties are bound to the concessions and commitments they make, listed in each country's Schedule, which are all considered annexes of the agreement. These are referred to in WTO-speak as 'bindings',[4] whether they entail an actual concession (such as a tariff reduction) or a commitment (e.g. to maintain current tariff levels). It is important to note that the GATT itself does not impose any *requirement* to reduce tariffs; however,

---

4 The WTO website has a helpful Glossary, as well as a Terminology Database, of WTO-speak, www.wto.org/english/thewto_e/glossary_e/glossary_e.htm.

countries enter into the agreement on the basis of reciprocal obligations, which generally entail some trade concessions. Certainly, when a state applies to become a party, its accession is subject to often quite extensive negotiations aiming to extract a 'price for admission' satisfactory to existing members. In the boom period from 1953 to 1973, multilateral-tariff-negotiating 'rounds' resulted in substantial reductions in tariffs on manufactured goods, especially in the Kennedy Round of 1963 to 1967 which substantially achieved its ambitious target of a 'linear' cut to halve all such tariffs (Preeg 1970). Over the lifetime of the GATT the average tariffs on manufactured goods fell from 40% in 1948 to 5% in 1995, although some tariffs remain significantly higher than this average.

The bindings under article II are complemented by the obligation in article XI to eliminate quantitative restrictions. This aimed to end the use of quotas, so that import restrictions would rather take the form of tariffs (referred to as 'tariffication'), since tariffs are considered to be non-discriminatory between states, and easier to negotiate downwards. Article XI has a strong impact, not only because it imposes an immediate obligation to phase out quotas (although transitional periods were allowed), but also because it applies broadly to 'prohibitions or restrictions' effected not only by quotas but also by 'other measures'.[5] Such restrictions or prohibitions are invalid unless justified under one of the exceptions in article XX.

The second important non-discrimination principle is in article III, which requires imported products to be given National Treatment (NT). Importantly, however this is expressed not as the same or similar treatment, but no-less-favourable treatment (NLFT) than that accorded to 'like domestic products'. Article III has a complex structure, which was later subjected to detailed textual analysis by the WTO's Appellate Body. The obligation applies to both all internal *taxes and charges* on products (para. 2) and all '*laws, regulations and requirements* affecting their internal sale . . . transportation, distribution or use' (para. 4). Like all non-discrimination or equal-treatment principles, it leaves considerable scope

---

5 It has been argued (Pauwelyn 2005) that there is a strict separation between art. XI and art. III, because the Ad Note to Article III says that any 'regulation or requirement' which 'applies to an imported product and to the like domestic product and is collected or enforced in the case of the imported product at the time or point of importation' comes under art. III. Nevertheless, a narrow interpretation of 'likeness' can treat a prohibition of a specific type of product as discriminatory and hence as falling under art. XI and not III; this view was taken in the notorious *Tuna–Dolphin* cases (see below), although Pauwelyn stresses that those Panel decisions were not adopted.

for interpretation, especially of what constitutes 'like' products. The problem became increasingly important in the 1980s, when attention began to shift from tariffs to the 'behind-the-border' barriers created by differences in regulation. This began to raise the issue of the 'right to regulate' (discussed further below).

In the GATT, states were allowed some regulatory space, mainly under the General Exceptions in article XX. This left states free to adopt and enforce internal measures (and to exclude goods which did not comply with those standards), which they considered necessary in a range of areas such as the protection of human, animal or plant life or health, and intellectual property rights. However, the right to set national standards was subject to the important proviso (in the introductory paragraph or 'chapeau' of article XX) that such national regulations should not be applied in an arbitrarily discriminatory manner or constitute a disguised trade restriction. In the early years of the GATT these provisions were not very significant (McRae 2000); but as they became more salient in the 1970s and 1980s, when the growth of public concern over matters such as product safety and environmental protection led to a sharp growth of regulatory requirements, they came to be relied upon more, and also applied more stringently. Furthermore, the requirement that a measure should be 'necessary' to meet the permitted purpose became a strict 'necessity test'. This was famously expressed by the Panel report in the *Thailand – Cigarettes* case (1990), which stated that measures 'could be considered "necessary" . . . only if there were no alternative measure consistent with [the GATT] which Thailand could reasonably be expected to employ to achieve its . . . objectives'. Applying this test, Thailand was obliged to withdraw its higher taxes on imported cigarettes, although there was evidence from the WHO that the 'western-style' cigarettes were a greater public health risk than the more lightly taxed, domestic, coarse tobacco products, which were preferred only by a small and declining proportion of older people.

Other exceptions in the GATT were more important in its first twenty years, when the focus was on border barriers. Thus, the GATT included provisions permitting members to apply trade restrictions (usually quotas) for balance-of-payments reasons, mainly in article XII. This was originally designed to link the GATT to the system of fixed exchange rates in the first period of the Bretton Woods system, since trade fluctuations could undermine the fixed par values of national currencies. Thus, such trade restrictions were allowed, but only if necessary to stop a serious decline in monetary reserves or help rebuild those reserves, and this was to be established in cooperation with the IMF (article XV). However, this exception continued to be used to justify quotas long after the demise of fixed exchange rates. Indeed many developing countries continued to do so even after the establishment of the WTO, despite the inclusion of an additional Understanding on the Balance of Payments provisions, but decisions under the WTO's Dispute-Settlement system acted as a spur to phase them out.[6]

From the start of the GATT, it was seen to be unsuited to the needs of less developed countries. These were generally, and many still remain, at a low level of industrialization and hence largely reliant on exports of primary products. International trade in many primary products had long been regulated by commodity agreements (see Chapter 2, at 2.2.3), which were to have been integrated into the ITO. In the GATT, approved agreements were simply covered by an exception (article XX(h)). The richer countries of Europe and North America protect their domestic agricultural production through domestic support schemes as well as tariffs. The agreements leave these largely unaffected,[7] and agricultural products were largely excluded from the GATT. Thus, it was regarded as a major achievement for the developing countries that the WTO included an Agreement on Agriculture (AoA), although this was also desired by the USA, which had long fretted against the EU's Common Agricultural Policy (CAP). However, the AoA provided essentially a framework for future negotiation of tariff reductions on agricultural products, by requiring quotas and other barriers to be converted to tariffs, and establishing criteria for 'disciplines' on domestic price support systems.[8] Also, the agreement on Subsidies and Countervailing Measures (SCM) could apply to agriculture (except for subsidies permitted by the AoA), but this was subject to a 'peace clause' restraining complaints until the end of 2004.[9]

Recognition of the developing countries' disadvantages in trade led the GATT to commission the Haberler Report in 1958, but little was done until pressure from developing countries led to the United Nations Conference

---

6 Notably the Appellate Body's decision in *India – Quantitative Restrictions* (1999).
7 Article XI(2) permitted restrictions on agricultural and fisheries imports if maintained in conjunction with domestic production or marketing controls.
8 AoA, art. 6 and Annex 2 define permissible subsidies (essentially those which are considered not price related), usually referred to as 'green box' (e.g. research, extension and support, infrastructure) and 'blue box' (direct payments aimed at limiting agricultural production (e.g. 'set-aside'), and developing country subsidies to encourage production); some permissible subsidies are subject to limits, so referred to as 'amber'.
9 AoA, art. 13.

on Trade and Development (UNCTAD), which was established as an organization, in many ways a rival to the GATT, in 1964. In 1965 a new Part IV was added to the GATT urging favourable treatment for developing countries, but its 'commitments' were not binding but hortatory. In 1971 a waiver of MFN allowed developed countries to introduce a Generalized System of Preferences (GSP), and developing countries to grant each other mutual preferences, and this was formalized as a decision in 1979, usually known as the Enabling Clause. This established the principle of 'special and differential treatment' for developing and least developed countries, although it included a 'graduation clause' anticipating that preferences should be phased out as economies developed.

Nevertheless, some developing countries did succeed in establishing export-oriented manufacturing industries, in labour-intensive products, especially the 'newly industrializing countries' (NICs) of South-East Asia. As they did so, they began to face a range of defensive measures erected by developed countries to protect their domestic industries. These took advantage of other exceptions in the GATT agreement, in particular the three types of 'trade remedy rules': anti-dumping or countervailing duties (both under article VI), and safeguards actions (article XIX). Sometimes, however, defensive actions relied on dubious interpretations of these rules. This led to the adoption of codes elaborating the GATT articles, notably the Anti-Dumping Code, adopted in 1967 as part of the Kennedy Round and modified in 1979, which became the WTO Agreement on Article VI. Countervailing duties, which have been used primarily by the USA, are only permitted for the purpose of offsetting the exporting country's production or export subsidies. A Subsidies Code was agreed in the Tokyo Round to try to define impermissible subsidies and hence control the use of countervailing duties, and this subsequently became the WTO's SCM Agreement.

The Safeguards provisions in article XIX were intended to make it easier for states to make trade concessions on a multilateral MFN basis by means of an 'escape clause', allowing temporary protection against an unexpected surge of imports, to give domestic industry time to adapt. Safeguards measures are subject to three conditions: (a) there must have been 'unforeseen developments' as a consequence of obligations incurred under the GATT (e.g. a tariff reduction); (b) resulting in increased imports; and which (c) are in such quantities and under such conditions as to cause or threaten serious injury to domestic producers. In such circumstances, states may suspend, modify or withdraw the concession (e.g. reimpose the tariff) for as long as is necessary to deal with the injury. The other

GATT members must (except in critical circumstances) be notified of such action, to give those affected a chance to make representations; but if the actions go ahead, those affected members have a right to retaliate by withdrawing 'substantially equivalent' concessions. These provisions gave rise to many disputes, especially as to whether safeguards must be non-discriminatory (and therefore applied to all states even those whose exports were not excessive) or could be selective. More detailed and specific rules were established in the Safeguards Agreement negotiated in the Uruguay Round to become part of the WTO package of agreements.

The various conditions of the escape clause in article XIX had the paradoxical result of leading states to prefer to take other kinds of action to protect domestic industry, referred to as grey-area measures. These included 'orderly marketing arrangements' and 'voluntary export restraints', usually negotiated with the specific country responsible for the export surges,[10] sometimes directly with or involving the relevant industry association. Although outside the GATT rules, they could be argued to be legitimate, since they were agreed by the exporters concerned, albeit under coercion. In some circumstances the exporters could benefit, since the restraints on exports could enable a scarcity premium on the price they could charge importers for products such as automobiles. All these measures were eventually prohibited by the WTO Safeguards Agreement.

The most elaborate grey-area-measure was the Multi-Fibre Agreement (MFA), in effect from 1974 (superseding agreements covering textiles begun in 1961), which allowed Member States to negotiate bilateral agreements to control imports of both natural and artificial-fibre textiles and clothing. This had a damaging impact on the NICs, and one of the few benefits they obtained from the Uruguay Round was the WTO Agreement on Textiles and Clothing, which aimed to control restraints in this sector, and phase them out within ten years.

Although the GATT aimed to be global, it accommodated regional organizations through the exception under article XXIV covering customs unions and free-trade areas, generally described as preferential trade agreements (PTAs). Economists have debated whether PTAs contribute to the broader goal of general multilateral liberalization, or hinder it since they are inherently preferential. This is usually evaluated by considering whether a particular PTA is on the whole trade creating or trade diverting, i.e. whether the increased internal trade is at the expense of trade with other countries. The legal conditions are laid down in article XXIV, which require that: (a) 'substantially all the trade' between the PTA members

---

10 The main target was Japan.

must be covered (the internal trade requirement); and (b) the tariffs and other external barriers after formation of the PTA shall not be 'higher or more restrictive' than before (the external trade requirement). The latter condition is especially hard to apply, particularly in relation to a Customs Union (which entails adoption of common external tariffs and trade regulations), and para. 5(a) of article XXIV states that it is the 'general incidence' of such barriers which should not increase.

The formation and growth of the European Community (EC)[11] caused the main difficulties in application of this exception during the GATT period. Indeed, periodic transatlantic trade wars erupted between the EC and the USA in the 1960s and 1970s. However, since this was a period of growth of international trade and of the global economy, and because US TNCs also benefited from the formation of the EC, these conflicts could be resolved by subsuming them into multilateral tariff negotiating rounds.

But the EC is not just a single trading bloc, it is at the centre of a web of PTAs which has become more extensive and complex. The countries with which the EC has PTAs can be categorized into three groups: (a) neighbouring European countries, usually potential future EC members (but also including Israel); (b) countries with historic ties with EC members, mainly Mediterranean countries and the African, Caribbean and Pacific (ACP) countries (mostly ex-colonies); and (c) other developing countries and transitional economies (ex-Soviet bloc). Indeed, by the time the WTO was established, the EC had a PTA with all but six of its trading partners,[12] although non-preferential imports from those six still accounted for 70 per cent of EC trade volume (Sapir 1998: 721).

Furthermore, in the early 1990s many other states also formed PTAs, some of which have been mentioned in Chapter 5: in the Americas, the NAFTA of 1992 bringing together Canada, Mexico and the USA; the Southern Common Market (MERCOSUR) founded in 1991 by Argentina, Brazil, Paraguay and Uruguay,[13] and CARICOM bringing together fourteen Caribbean states.[14] In Asia, the Association of Southeast Asian

---

11 This is the economic pillar of the EU, originally the EEC, it was renamed on the formation of the EU in 1992; for convenience, it will be referred to as the EC throughout this chapter.
12 Australia, Canada, Japan, New Zealand, Taiwan and the USA.
13 Bolivia, Chile, Colombia, Ecuador and Peru are now associate members, and a protocol of adhesion was signed with Venezuela in 2006, but its entry must be ratified by the parliaments of Paraguay and Brazil.
14 This has a long history, dating back to the Caribbean Free Trade Association (made up of Commonwealth Caribbean states) which established a Caribbean Community, including a Common Market, by the Treaty of Chaguaramas of 1973; although a decision was taken

Nations (ASEAN), which had existed since 1967 as a primarily political organization, agreed in 1992 to establish an Asian Free Trade Area.[15] In Africa, the Economic Community of West African States (ECOWAS), originally founded in 1975, extensively revised its charter in 1993, to include provisions for both economic cooperation and a customs union (to be established by 2000). ECOWAS has overlapping membership with the West African Economic and Monetary Union (known by its French acronym of UMOA, since its members are francophone), established in 1994 to succeed the previous monetary union. In east and southern Africa also, several organizations sprang up, with considerable overlapping membership: the Southern African Development Community (SADC) formed in 1992 by fourteen south and central African states, with objectives including 'policies aimed at the progressive elimination of obstacles to free movement of capital and labour, goods and services'; and the Common Market for Eastern and Southern Africa (COMESA) established in 1994 following an earlier PTA, extending to Egypt and other north African states; as well as smaller entities such as the Southern African Customs Union (SACU) and the East African Community (EAC).

Thus, of the WTO's 120 founding members only three (Hong Kong, Japan and Korea) were not parties to any of the sixty-two PTAs then in force (Sapir 1998: 718).

8.1.2 WTO: beyond trade

The creation of the WTO was by any measure a remarkable achievement. The Marrakesh Agreement establishing the WTO was opened for signature in April 1994, and a narrow vote in the US Congress helped ensure that it received sufficient ratifications to come into force on 1 January 1995. By the end of 2008 the WTO had 153 members, 25 of which had joined since its formation. The latter included China, which understandably had a particularly arduous, fourteen-year negotiation

---

in 1989 to transform this further into a single market, the Revised Treaty of Chaguaramas establishing the Caribbean Community, including the CARICOM Single Market and Economy, came into force only in 2001.

15 ASEAN was founded by a Declaration in 1967 by Indonesia, Malaysia, Singapore, Thailand and the Philippines; they were joined by Brunei Darussalam (1984), Vietnam (1995), Laos and Myanmar (1997) and finally Cambodia (1999). The Declaration of ASEAN Concord of 1976 envisaged measures for economic cooperation, including 'progress towards the establishment of preferential trading arrangements as a long term objective', but only in 1992 was it agreed to establish an Asian Free Trade Area, based on a Common Effective Preferential Tariff, by 2008, and in 1995 the target date was brought forward to 2003.

period before satisfactory terms were agreed with its main trading partners and it could accede in 2001. Russia remains the only major trading nation not yet admitted, although others such as Iran also remain excluded, sometimes for political reasons.

Although the WTO Agreement itself is relatively short, its Annexes comprise a comprehensive package of agreements, totalling some 500 pages, all of which (except for the four 'plurilateral' agreements in Annex 4) are binding on all members. The substantive agreements are grouped in Annex 1. Annex 1A comprises a dozen agreements dealing with trade in goods, plus GATT 1994, which in effect renews the original GATT 1947, together with subsequent decisions ('understandings') by the contracting parties relating to it. Thus, the Codes and other elaborations of GATT rules, which were considered optional, were replaced by treaties binding all members. Annex 1B is the General Agreement on Trade in Services (GATS), and Annex 1C the Agreement on Trade Related Aspects of Intellectual Property Rights (generally referred to as TRIPs). Annex 2 is the Dispute Settlement Understanding (DSU), establishing the WTO's powerful adjudicative mechanisms. Annex 3 establishes the Trade Policy Review Mechanism, which although it provides policy- rather than rules-based procedures, can be very influential. Also part of the WTO package are the large number of Decisions and Declarations adopted in the UR.

The most dramatic expansion in the scope of the WTO resulted from the inclusion of Services and Intellectual Property Rights (IPRs). Both resulted largely from determined campaigns by coalitions of corporate interests, business lobby groups, policy-makers and ideologists, mainly from the USA. The details of these campaigns have been recounted and analysed by several studies.[16] Undoubtedly, the outcome owed a great deal to corporate power and lobbying: for GATS by industries such as financial services, telecommunications, construction and professional services; and for TRIPs by the media, computing, pharmaceuticals and chemicals industries. It also owed much to policy entrepreneurship by some key individuals and groups, and to their ideas and strategies. This potent mix involved far more than either interest-group lobbying or an influential 'epistemic community' of experts. It produced a hegemonic policy perspective or vision which could command support and overcome opposition because it responded to, while also helping to shape, the changing socio-economic circumstances of the times.

16 For Services, see in particular Drake and Nicolaïdis 1992; Kelsey 2008; for IPRs, see Sell 1998, 2003; Drahos and Braithwaite 2002a.

More fundamentally, therefore, it was the transition to a post-Fordist knowledge-based economy, or 'cognitive capitalism', which gave impetus to, and was shaped by, the lobbying in favour of internationalization of services and of intellectual property.[17] Not only were these activities accounting for a rapidly growing proportion of output and employment, they also came to be seen as key underpinnings of the economy and society as a whole. Since the early 1970s, the US deficit in merchandise trade had become endemic, so attention became focused on the contribution of other receipts to the balance of payments. Indeed, employment in manufacturing production was generally declining in many developed countries, due to a combination of the introduction of digital technologies and relocation to lower-wage countries, counterbalanced since the 1980s by a secular growth in employment in a wide range of 'service' sectors.

Services had traditionally been regarded as ancillary to 'real' economic production, and even unproductive, but they now came to be considered as value-creating in their own right. International transactions in services had been recognized as 'invisibles', contributing to the balance of payments. The OECD countries had included provisions for liberalization of invisibles in a Code of 1961 (see Chapter 5, at 5.1.1), and in 1972 an OECD high-level group on the prospects for trade in the run-up to the Tokyo Round coined the concept of 'trade in services' (Drake and Nicolaïdis 1992: 40). In the USA in particular, access to foreign markets for services was placed on the trade agenda, leading to the enactment of a procedure encouraging firms to identify 'trade barriers', under s. 301 of the 1974 Trade Act. This statute gave the power to the US Trade Representative (USTR) to act on complaints by US firms about 'unreasonable or discriminatory' practices barring their access to foreign markets.[18] The annual Trade Barriers Report became a powerful weapon in the hands of those wishing to expand the GATT agenda, although it was criticized as consisting 'merely of a compilation of self-serving industry claims and

---

17 Pioneering academic analyses were produced both in Europe (Touraine 1971) and the USA (Bell 1973), both from unorthodox Marxist perspectives, and both based on work done in the 1960s. Touraine's contribution remained confined to academic sociology, but Bell's work was highly influential, as it was done in the context of a Commission on the Year 2000 established by the American Academy of Arts and Sciences (Bell and Graubard 1997), and helped to establish 'future studies'.

18 The USTR was established as an executive office in 1962, and elevated to a Cabinet-level agency in 1974; in 1988 it was given direct responsibility for trade negotiations, with a duty to report to Congress; this allowed Congress to interrogate the USTR, which it cannot do for an executive office under the President; thus providing an important avenue for business lobbies to put pressure on the USTR (Shaffer 2003: 38–40).

anecdotal hearsay'.[19] Countries were threatened with trade sanctions by being placed on a 'Watch List' if their internal regulations were deemed to constitute barriers, and in some cases sanctions were actually applied by the USA.[20]

These factors and pressures led policy-makers and trade negotiators of developed countries to argue for a further broadening of the negotiating agenda of GATT's Uruguay Round. However, neither services nor IPRs could properly be said to be 'trade' matters. Although they involved or affected cross-border transactions, they both raised much more extensive issues, which were relevant to investment and business regulation more generally. These went well beyond the scope of the GATT, and were the remit of other organizations, notably UNCTAD, and the OECD. In fact, the GATT's trade rules also had points of intersection with many other areas of regulation, and these 'linkages' became more salient during the 1980s, in relation to matters such as environmental protection, labour standards, competition rules and business taxation.[21] Yet those issues remained peripheral to the UR negotiations, although their inclusion was pressed by some advocates, especially for competition policy (Petersmann 1993a). The extension of the WTO to cover foreign investment as well as trade was also a step too far; however, the UR did result in an agreement on Trade-Related Investment Measures (TRIMs).[22] Also, as we will see below, the broad scope of the GATS meant that it covered international investment in services, so that in practice commitments in services would mean revision of investment regimes to make them WTO-compatible.

The concept of 'trade in services' was in many ways inappropriate, since most services are delivered face to face and are often personal. Nevertheless, the issue gained in momentum. Other OECD countries

---

19 The quote is from a Commentary by Claude Barfield, Jr. (in Bhagwati and Patrick 1990: 105), responding to a contribution by Geza Feketekuty, the chief US negotiator on services, sometimes regarded as the prime architect of the GATS (Kelsey 2008: 76); the book (Bhagwati and Patrick 1990) provides much helpful detail and analysis of s. 301.

20 In the key period when India and Brazil were leading resistance to the US agenda in the UR negotiations, in October 1988 sanctions were applied to Brazil over its IP law, and in May 1989 India was placed on the Watch List over financial services; these external pressures interacted with domestic political processes, leading to the replacement of the key negotiators (Shukla 2000: 21; Kelsey 2008: 72–3; interview information).

21 For a critique of the extensive 'trade and' or 'linkage' debates, see Lang 2007a.

22 This required members to phase out investment measures inconsistent with GATT arts. III and XI; the 'examples' in the Illustrative List which is annexed cites local-content or export-performance requirements, and trade- or foreign-investment balancing requirements (discussed in Chapter 5, at 5.1.2).

joined the USA in urging inclusion of services in the UR agenda, and developing countries' concerns were allayed by adopting a 'twin-track' negotiating procedure, albeit aiming for an agreement to be included in the 'single undertaking' of WTO. The result was the GATS, which extended the WTO umbrella to every possible kind of commercial activity.[23] It also defined 'trade' in services extremely broadly, applied by article 1.2 to four 'modes of delivery' of a service:

(a) from the territory of one Member into the territory of any other Member;
(b) in the territory of one Member to the service consumer of any other Member;
(c) by a service supplier of one Member, through commercial presence in the territory of any other Member;
(d) by a service supplier of one Member, through presence of natural persons of a Member in the territory of any other Member.

Only (a) strictly entails cross-border supply of services; (b) includes not only services explicitly aimed at foreign consumers (such as tourism) but could extend to any service provided to such consumers; (c) includes any kind of FDI, and envisages a right of establishment; while (d) would give service suppliers a right to send staff to deliver the service, important in sectors ranging from construction to software, and to professional services such as law or accounting.

Where services had led, the media and pharmaceuticals industries followed on behind. The 1984 revisions of the US Trade Act extended s. 301 to intellectual property rights; it was strengthened by the 'super-301' provisions added in 1988, and as mentioned above these were selectively activated against key countries during the UR negotiations. A range of mainly US-based high-tech industries (chemical and pharmaceutical, computer software, film and music, electrical and auto) organized and lobbied to secure the inclusion of IPRs in trade negotiations, and were highly influential in the actual drafting of the resulting Agreement on Trade Related Property Rights (TRIPs) (Ryan 1998; Drahos and Braithwaite 2002a, 2002b). This established for the first time as an international standard a relatively high level of IPR protection. It targeted issues regarded as key by these business lobbies, notably copyright protection

---

23 GATS does not define the term 'services', so it applies to any transaction not primarily consisting of a sale of goods. The two also overlap, as was seen when the USA brought a complaint against the EU's banana regime, which fell under both GATT and GATS, since it also involved distribution and wholesaling services for bananas.

for software, patent protection for all technical processes and products, a minimum twenty-year period for patents, limitations on exclusions from IPRs and on compulsory licensing, and extensive provisions for enforcement of IPRs (see Chapter 9). These were all issues on which agreement could not easily be reached in the relevant forum, the World Intellectual Property Organization (WIPO).[24] This was, therefore, not a case of inventing a new paradigm, as with 'trade in services', but of strategic forum-shifting.

Thus, the linkages between the trade regime and related areas of economic regulation were used in a strategic way by powerful firms and states to provide a basis for the grand bargain of the UR which created the WTO. The linkages were not artificial, but had a real basis. However, the extension of the GATT to these issues took it into areas far beyond its remit. They were unfamiliar and in many ways inappropriate to be dealt with in the language and context of trade bargaining developed under the GATT. The forum-shifting had the effect of sidestepping or sidelining the international organizations with direct responsibility for the issues in question: WIPO for IPRs, and organizations dealing with specific service areas, such as ITU for telecommunications. The UR negotiators succeeded in taking advantage of the possibilities for trade-offs created by these linkages (Ryan 1998). However, it left a very difficult legacy for the WTO.

8.1.3 The power and weakness of the WTO

The new organization was faced with a wide spectrum of issues. Some resulted from the 'unfinished business' of the UR, and others were built into the new WTO agreements, which envisaged a continuing agenda of work.

The developing countries considered that the focus should remain on the existing agenda, especially as they had not received benefits they had been promised, which were supposed to be the quid pro quo for accepting TRIPs and GATS. The AoA had failed to deliver, since the rich countries'

---

24 Under the GATT, IPRs were treated as matters for national regulation, and hence the exceptions in art. XX included measures necessary to protect patents, trademarks and copyrights; but there had been disputes about alleged discriminatory effects of IPRs: a 1987 EC complaint against US procedures for seizing IP-infringing goods (renewing a Canadian complaint of 1981), which a GATT Panel did find unnecessarily discriminatory, and a 1988 complaint by Brazil against US s. 301 trade measures attacking Brazil's local working requirements for patents (which surfaced again in the WTO).

agricultural subsidies had been little reduced, but had been converted into other forms of support which claimed dubious validity under the 'green' and 'blue box' exceptions, although they were in effect indirect subsidies. Hence, agricultural liberalization, far from benefiting exports from developing countries, was damaging their own food self-sufficiency, due to dumping of cheap food such as milk powder, corn and frozen chicken pieces. The phasing out of the MFA actually damaged some developing countries especially in Africa, which had used preferential quotas to establish textiles-exporting industries, and would find it hard to compete with bigger producers as these quotas were removed.

The major developed countries for their part wanted to forge ahead, especially with monitoring IP standards under TRIPs, and negotiations for liberalization of services under GATS. The GATS opened up a potentially enormous field for negotiation, as 'services' is an open-ended term, not defined in the agreement, which could include any kind of economic activity, even services regarded as public.[25] The actual GATS commitments made as part of the UR varied: developed countries made commitments in two-thirds of service sectors, transition economies in about half and developing countries in only 16 per cent. They were subject to significant limitations: most commitments were for cross-border delivery; only six percent accepted delivery by movement of natural persons, and although commercial presence was accepted especially by developed countries, it was subject to limitations in 70 per cent of cases (Altinger and Enders 1996). No conclusions had been reached for some key sectors, and these were left to be dealt with by sector-specific negotiations, which produced deals on financial services and basic telecommunications (both in 1997), although no agreement could be reached on maritime services. The GATS itself (article XIX) mandated successive rounds of negotiations to achieve progressive liberalization, beginning within five years. Although these duly began in 2000, it became clear that significant further progress would require the linkage-bargaining of a new general negotiating round. But

---

25 Article 3(b) says that services 'includes any service in any sector except services supplied in the exercise of government authority'; the latter term is narrowly defined in 3(c) as 'any service which is supplied neither on a commercial basis nor in competition with one or more service suppliers'. This essentially excludes only activities carried out on a non-commercial basis by a state-authorized monopolist; hence, even services hitherto regarded as 'public' may be subject to international liberalization if either competition or commercial principles have been introduced (Krajewski 2003; Kelsey 2008: 123–8). The ambiguity of these provisions 'may have far reaching consequences' in the many sectors often regarded as public which have some private provision, such as health care (Mashayekhi *et al.* 2006: 47).

the sectoral negotiations, as well as the work of the GATS Council and Committees, showed that market opening raised important and complex issues of regulation (see further below).

The developed states also continued to press to add 'new issues', and the EC in particular tabled proposals for the first Ministerial meeting in Singapore in 1996 in relation to investment, competition, government procurement[26] and 'trade facilitation' (the reduction of burdensome customs and other procedures). They succeeded in establishing working groups to consider these, although another proposal to consider the linkage between trade and labour standards was firmly rejected.

At the same time, the increased centrality of the WTO brought it new prominence, while its emphasis on market opening was widely seen as favouring the corporate interests of TNCs, and undermining the ability of states and public bodies to ensure that economic regulation responded to social needs especially of the poor and disadvantaged (Raghavan 1990). The criticisms of the organization led to pressures to reconsider its role and structure, notably in President Clinton's speech to the GATT fiftieth anniversary meeting in May 1998, calling for the WTO to listen to ordinary citizens, consult representatives of the broad public, and bring openness and accountability to its operations.

Other international bodies also responded to the concerns about the social impact of economic liberalization. The ILO had already established a working party on the social dimensions of the liberalization of international trade following the UR debates on the trade–labour linkage, and its 1994 report had called for cooperation with the WTO. This stimulated fraught negotiations which led to the 1998 ILO Declaration on Fundamental Principles and Rights at Work, stating that membership of the organization carried the obligation to 'respect, promote and realize' four fundamental rights, embodied in ILO Conventions, on freedom of association, elimination of forced labour, effective abolition of child labour and elimination of discrimination in relation to work. It included a follow-up mechanism to encourage members to ratify and implement the relevant conventions, but even this mild measure was objected to by some developing-country representatives. UN human rights bodies initiated investigations on the impact on human rights of globalization and

26 The Agreement on Government Procurement (based on one negotiated in the Tokyo Round) remains a plurilateral agreement in the WTO, and only the EC (on behalf of its twenty-seven Member States) and a dozen other states have accepted it. However, it applies only to specified governmental authorities, and for contracts above specified value thresholds, and subject to a broad exception for national security and defence.

specifically of some of the WTO agreements, in particular agriculture, GATS and TRIPs (see further below, and Chapter 5, at 5.2.2.1).

Despite the many evident linkages between the WTO's concerns and those of other organizations, positive cooperation has been slow to develop, for a number of reasons. The most obvious linkages are with the IMF and World Bank, and this was recognized by the provision in article III of the WTO Agreement mandating cooperation 'as appropriate' with those bodies. A note of caution was struck in the Declaration, adopted as part of the UR, on the 'Contribution of the WTO to Achieving Greater Coherence in Global Economic Policymaking', which stressed the need to respect the 'necessary autonomy in decision-making of each institution',[27] and specifically to avoid the 'imposition on governments of cross-conditionality'.[28] This indicates the reluctance of governments to see stronger inter-organizational cooperation which they consider might further weaken national sovereignty. Thus, although formal agreements were concluded by the WTO with the IMF and World Bank, they mainly provide for participation of observers in relevant bodies and meetings, and arrangements for consultation on issues of mutual concern, which are specifically defined (Ahn 2003). Similar, although less formal, agreements have also been established with a wide range of other organizations. Although the WTO is not a UN specialized agency, it participates in the Administrative Committee on Coordination, through which the UN Economic and Social Council (ECOSOC) tries to ensure inter-agency cooperation (Tietje 2002).

There is certainly a great need for such cooperation, and no shortage of examples of when it could be beneficial. In practice, cooperation has been half-hearted: small states are jealous of their sovereignty, while large states prefer to use their capacity for forum-selection and forum-shifting, and secretariats tend to protect their turf. Certainly, the breadth of the WTO agreements is such that it could, as one commentator has suggested, operate 'as an open rather than a self-contained regime' and aspire to become the World Economic Organization (Bronckers 2001: 41). In practice, any such ambitions would be viewed with suspicion and indeed hostility on all sides. Many of the WTO's strongest advocates consider that it should

---

27 Reinforced by the opinion of the Appellate Body (in *Argentina – Footwear* (1998): para. 72), that these agreements are of an administrative nature, and do not 'modify, add to or diminish the rights and obligations of Members' under the respective agreements.

28 Many developing countries have been made to reduce tariffs due to World Bank or IMF conditions, but if these go beyond their GATT/WTO commitments they are not formally binding.

stick to its essential focus on trade liberalization, and some of these such as Jagdish Bhagwati regret its expansion, especially to include TRIPs (Bhagwati 2005). On the other hand, critics of liberalization, who regard the WTO as the embodiment of economic globalization, are divided on its role.

Some consider that the WTO should be modified to counterbalance the thrust of trade liberalization by taking account of the different imperatives of other regulatory regimes with which it comes into collision. Thus, environmentalists, who were energized by the saga of the Tuna–Dolphin dispute in the GATT (discussed below; see Kingsbury 1994), pressed for 'greening the GATT' (Esty 1994), and in response a previous working group became the WTO Committee on Trade and Environment. Similarly, international trade union organizations have argued for a 'social clause', linking market-access rights to compliance with basic international labour standards (ILO 1994; Leary 1996; Evans 1998).

However, such suggestions have met with suspicion and even hostility from both governments and NGOs in developing countries. From their viewpoint, links between trade and either environmental protection or labour standards would create additional barriers to developing country exports, although the concern to ensure that trade results in employment growth and improvement of labour and social standards has a long history (Charnovitz 1995). The opposition has been strengthened by the fact that it has been developed country governments, especially the USA, which have proposed the extension of the WTO agenda to both environmental and labour issues, in response to domestic political pressures. The EU, for its own reasons,[29] has tended to advocate other 'new issues', especially competition and investment rules. Thus, a rare point of agreement among developing-country governments has been their general opposition to all suggestions to extend the scope of the WTO. For their part, many civil society critics of the WTO consider that the organization is so deeply flawed that what is needed is not only its radical reform, but a fundamental reorientation of the trading system (Jawara and Kwa 2004: ch. 10).

The enormous and contradictory pressures on the WTO climaxed in the dying days of the millennium with the debacle of the ministerial meeting in Seattle in December 1999. As police battled demonstrators in the streets, the beleaguered negotiators in the conference rooms failed to agree on the launch of a new negotiating round, for which developed countries

---

29 Perhaps because the European Commission, which leads the EU's trade negotiations, would expand its role if the scope of the WTO were extended in these directions.

had pressed, hoping indeed to have it concluded by 2003. Nevertheless, some progress was made, and by holding the next Ministerial in closed and secretive Doha, agreement was reached on a basis for a new round. However, at Cancun in 2003 a new grouping of developing countries led by Brazil, India and South Africa (the G20) made an effective input which, linked with pleas from the poorest countries for an end to unfair practices by the rich, especially in commodities such as cotton, forced a reformulation of the programme, which came to be called the Doha Development Agenda. Despite determined efforts at Hong Kong in 2005 only moderate progress was made,[30] and the negotiations were then in effect put on hold, although some work on details continued, pending a new political impetus. Despite the election of a new US President little changed, indeed efforts were needed to deflect threats of a new turn to protectionism due to the economic crisis.

The events at Seattle and Cancun led to some re-evaluation of the WTO's profile, procedures and structure. A Report by a panel of eminent supporters produced recommendations for improvements, aimed essentially at enabling the organization to pursue its agenda more effectively (WTO Consultative Board 2004), but they were largely ignored. There was indeed frustration on all sides with the decision-making procedures of the organization, which envisage over 150 members taking decisions by 'consensus' but as a fall-back one-state-one-vote,[31] which in practice has evolved semi-formalized methods of negotiation through various overlapping groupings (Jawara and Kwa 2004: 22–4). The difficulty of reaching agreement in this way led Pascal Lamy, the EC trade negotiator who became WTO Director-General in 2005, to describe the procedures as 'medieval'. While this was meant to be derogatory, one commentator

---

30 An interesting exception was fisheries, where concern for the global crisis of fish stocks, and cooperation between a range of bodies including NGOs, resulted in proposals which commanded broad support, focusing on the elimination of fishing subsidies, and exemptions for artisanal and local fisheries, and hence entailing close cooperation between WTO and other bodies, such as regional fisheries organizations (Schorr 2004). The continuing negotiations revealed important points of dispute, such as the scope of exceptions to the ban on subsidies, and the role of fishery organizations in supervising national fishery management. Nevertheless, the interactions between WTO subsidy rules and international standards (set by e.g. the Food and Agriculture Organization), does seem to have opened up space for information-sharing and inter-regime scrutiny, as well as contestation, and several different mechanisms have been proposed in the negotiations for managing the regulatory interactions (Young 2009).

31 The GATT practice was formalized in art. IX of the WTO Agreement, which defines 'consensus' as the lack of objection by a state when a decision is taken.

responded that if 'the WTO evokes the characteristics of flexible, plural-istic medieval political organization', perhaps 'the untidiness of the WTO is a reflection of our plural world' (Wolfe 2005a: 632, 642).

The problems of the WTO run far deeper than its formal decision-making procedures. The issues with which it deals are now highly detailed and complex, involving a mixture of technical and political–economic aspects (Howse 2002). They are generally beyond the understanding of most transient elected politicians, although some who remain in post for some years do manage at least to master their briefs. The formation of the WTO has helped to create a significant cluster of aficionados, including officials, lobbyists, academics and activists, many of them very knowledge-able, and capable of debating the issues in both technical and political terms, sometimes passionately. They converge on the biannual Ministe-rial meetings,[32] which create an arena for both debate and negotiation which is in many ways deeply flawed, yet surprisingly open, for a diplo-matic body. In between, the organization pursues its purposes through its bureaucratic structures, interspersed with higher-level meetings, its activities under continuing scrutiny by the wider circles of specialists. Despite its extensive responsibilities, the organization itself is compar-atively under-resourced;[33] and poor countries are able to devote only derisory resources to WTO matters, while even the richest and biggest have great difficulty in formulating and implementing coherent policies in the face of the extent and complexity of the issues involved.

In the meantime, the central role of the WTO as a multilateral organi-zation is being threatened by the rapid growth of PTAs, mainly bilateral. As they have continued to proliferate, their validity under WTO rules has become more dubious, but they have become tacitly accepted, much as the grey-area measures of the 1970s.[34] A provisional 'transparency mechanism' was agreed late in 2006 to try to improve notification and

---

32 Formally, the WTO's main decision-making body is the Ministerial Conference, which must meet at least every two years; between such times its functions are fulfilled by the General Council (WTO Agreement, art. IV).

33 In 2008 its secretariat numbered 629 staff, and its annual consolidated budget was SwF185m. ($158m.); by comparison, the IMF's 2009 budget had gross administrative expenditures of $967m., and at end April 2008 it had 1950 professional and 636 other staff, while the World Bank had over 10,000 employees, with a net administrative budget of $1,637m. (figures taken from their respective Annual Reports).

34 Although GATT, art. XXIV requires prior notification, this has often been disregarded. Combined with the need for a decision on compatibility to be by consensus (which effectively gives the participants in the agreement a veto), it has meant that preferential agreements have been tolerated regardless of formal validity.

evaluation, based on a 'factual examination' by the WTO Secretariat. By 2010 over 450 notifications had been made to the GATT or WTO, while some 219 actual agreements were in force, virtually every member was party to at least one, and some to twenty or more.[35] A substantial proportion of world trade now takes place under such arrangements,[36] and they increasingly cover many issues other than tariffs, including services, investment, competition, labour mobility, labour standards and intellectual property (World Bank 2005: 35, 97–118). Indeed, they are often highly complex treaties, which governments may agree to on the basis of broad geopolitical considerations rather than any accurate calculation of overall economic advantage. The traditional regional free-trade areas or customs unions between geographically contiguous countries have now been greatly overtaken in number by such bilateral agreements, often between distant partners (Crawford and Fiorentino 2005). Although there is some trend to regional clustering, the overall pattern has been a 'spaghetti bowl' of intersecting arrangements (World Bank 2005: 39).

From a free-trade perspective, these developments could, optimistically, be viewed as a stage towards a new level of greater multilateral economic integration, or more pessimistically as a fragmentation of the multilateral system. Critics considered themselves engaged in a fight on many fronts against the drive for opening of markets on behalf of corporate interests.

8.2 The role of law and the problem of democracy

A central issue for the WTO is how to accommodate its functions and powers to those of other public bodies in the complex system of multilevel governance of the contemporary global economy. This issue lies behind the conflicting views which portray the WTO as either a tool of the powerful trading blocs or a bulwark for smaller states, a protector of the consumer or of corporations.

This institutional question has been debated through the concept of the 'constitutionalization' of the WTO. However, as will be shown below (at 8.3), the idea has been pressed most strongly from a particular, ultraliberal perspective. This seeks to build on the attempts to legitimize the

---

35 Data from the WTO website: an agreement which covers both goods and services is counted as two notifications (see also www.bilaterals.org).

36 According to World Bank estimates, by 2002 one-third of world trade took place between PTA members, although only 21% was actually preferential trade, and only 15% benefited from an 'economically meaningful tariff preference' (World Bank 2005: 41).

WTO purely in terms of the rule of law, which relies on a formalist conception of law, and emphasizes enforcement through the WTO's Dispute-Settlement system. In this optic, the importance of the WTO agreements is precisely that they constrain national policy choices.

Proponents of this view of the WTO argue that national state regulation tends to be protectionist because it is the product of the 'capture' of states by special interests. For example:

> Free trade and democratic government face a common obstacle – the influence of concentrated interest groups... The WTO and the trade agreements it administers act to restrain protectionist interest groups, thereby promoting free trade and democracy.
>
> (McGinnis and Movesian 2000: 515)

This reflects a 'public choice' theory of political economy, which advocates a view that constitutions should confine state power in order to safeguard the rights and liberties of individuals (Brennan and Buchanan 1985).

However, this perspective conveniently overlooks the converse process: the deployment of the economic power of some sections of big business to secure the capture of international arenas such as the WTO by sectional interests, and thus to restrict the regulatory powers of states, which generally have at least some form of accountability.[37] An alternative view stresses the need for sensitivity in the application of WTO obligations to its own proper limits as a trade organization, and to the specific competences and roles of other public bodies, especially national states and international organizations (Helfer 1998; Howse 2000).

Certainly, the legitimacy of the WTO is seen to derive from law, demonstrated by the great stress placed on the WTO as embodying the rule of law in world trade. Thus, after the organization was shaken by the debacle at Seattle, the then Secretary-General Mike Moore delivering a speech entitled 'The Backlash against Globalization?' concluded as follows:

> The WTO is a powerful force for good in the world. Yet we are too often misunderstood, sometimes genuinely, often wilfully. We are not a world government in any shape or form. People do not want a world government, and we do not aspire to be one. At the WTO, governments decide, not us.
>
> But people do want global rules. If the WTO did not exist, people would be crying out for a forum where governments could negotiate rules, ratified by

---

37 This pattern originated in US trade policy, with the establishment of the office of US Trade Representative (USTR), and the development of its powers and duties to open foreign markets for US firms under the provisions of the Trade Act, s. 301, discussed at 8.1.2 above.

national parliaments, that promote freer trade and provide a transparent and predictable framework for business. And they would be crying out for a mechanism that helps governments avoid coming to blows over trade disputes. That is what the WTO is. We do not lay down the law. We uphold the rule of law. The alternative is the law of the jungle, where might makes right and the little guy doesn't get a look in.

(2000)

A subsequent Director-General, Pascal Lamy, more subtly stressed the 'integrated and distinctive' nature of the WTO's legal order, and considered its relationship to the legal systems of other organizations with sensitivity to accusations of being hegemonic (2006: 977). However, he was forthright in stating that the WTO's basic philosophy is that 'trade opening obligations are good, and even necessary, to increase people's standards of living and well-being' (Lamy 2006: 978), and although he pointed to various means by which the WTO legal system contributes to an overall coherence of international law, he accepted that there are 'cracks' in that coherence (2006: 982).

Not only is legality central to the legitimation of the WTO, the organization itself is a major embodiment of the trend towards legalization in the governance of international economic affairs, and indeed of world politics (Goldstein *et al.* 2001). Here, again, views differ on the nature and role of the legality involved. Some put forward a view of legalization as being based on rules which are regarded as binding, which are precise, and the interpretation of which has been delegated to a third-party adjudicator (Abbott *et al.* 2000: 404–6). However, this has been criticized as taking a narrow view of law (Finnemore and Toope 2001), indeed a formalist one (Picciotto 2005; see further Chapter 10, at 10.1.1).

From a broader perspective, WTO rules can be seen to operate as an interface between legalities (Arup 2000: 8–9), and their interpretation can serve as a means of managing the complex economic and political interactions characteristic of the current phase of globalization. All these issues will be discussed in the remainder of this chapter.

8.2.1 Deregulation and re-regulation: product standards

The primary impact of WTO rules is deregulatory, since they are concerned with setting limits or 'disciplines' on national state regulation. These constraints have given rise to the debate about how far WTO obligations limit national states' 'right to regulate'. This is partially expressed in the tension between free trade and fair trade, which has preoccupied economists and lawyers (Bhagwati and Hudec 1996). The free-trade perspective rests on the assumption that optimal economic welfare will result from exchange under conditions of equality in competition, usually with the corollary that this is best achieved by a minimal level of government action. Competitive equality is expressed in the principles of non-discrimination and market access which, as we have seen, are the foundation of the GATT, and permeate the many complex provisions of the WTO agreements.

The issue of 'fair trade' began to emerge in the 1970s, as the attention of GATT negotiators began to shift to the 'behind the border' barriers posed by domestic regulations, which were termed 'non-tariff barriers' (NTBs). As negotiation rounds reduced tariffs, exporters became more aware of the ways in which differences in national regulatory requirements act as market barriers. At the same time, the greater sophistication and complexity of manufactured goods and their production methods generated increased concerns about potential harms, leading to a growth of regulatory measures to protect consumers and the environment. Unsurprisingly, such measures could be shaped by governments and legislatures to suit local conditions and local firms, and foreign producers might regard the resulting standards as inappropriate and protectionist.[38]

---

38 The very term 'non-tariff barrier' carries the assumption that the real motivation for a regulatory requirement is protectionism, which is commonly assumed in writings on trade rules. To take two examples from many: 'As tariff barriers have been reduced under regional and multilateral trade agreements, recourse has increasingly been made to non-tariff measures to protect local business from foreign competition' (T. Weiler 2000: 74); also: 'Consider, for example, the issue of product-standards, which was often used as a convenient mechanism through which to implement a protectionist policy under the pretext of safeguarding consumer safety and product quality' (Reich 1996–97: 787). Evidence is rarely provided to support these assertions. More persuasively, Jackson (1997: 214) argues: 'The temptation of legislators and other government officials to shape regulatory or tax measures to favor domestic products seems to be very great, and proposals to do this are constantly suggested.' Jackson's examples (1997: 222 and fn. 28) show that standards result from public concerns, which become formulated in regulations appropriate to the socio-economic conditions of the country concerned, and that national legislative procedures make it easier for domestic industry lobbies to ensure that regulations suit local conditions. It is hardly surprising if the resulting standards are sometimes inappropriate for foreign producers. This does not bear out assertions that standards are adopted for protectionist reasons. A pertinent example is the EU ban on hormone-treated beef, which has been cited to illustrate the way in which protectionist groups resort to spurious safety concerns due to the GATT's success at reducing tariffs and overt discrimination (McGinnis and Movesian 2000: 549). This appears to ignore the facts that European concerns about meat safety are long-standing, that the hormone

The WTO's non-discrimination rules inevitably cut across a wide range of national state regulations. In the abstract, the principle of non-discrimination is neutral, and does not interfere with the national state's 'right to regulate'. In practice, the equal treatment test cannot easily be applied to regulatory requirements without having regard to their purposes or objectives. Issues of equal treatment are inseparable from fair treatment, which requires the evaluation of public policies establishing regulatory standards, such as those for the protection of consumers, producers, and the natural environment (Cottier and Mavroidis 2000; Picciotto 2003a).

The broad non-discrimination rules of the WTO continually raise questions about the validity of many economic regulations. In practice, rules which are facially neutral may be said to be discriminatory de facto. For example, the USA complained in 1995 against Korea's consumer protection rules, which laid down specified shelf-lives for food products such as long-life milk and frozen food. Even though they applied equally to all manufacturers, from the US perspective they acted as a barrier, preventing foreign suppliers from using superior preservation technology; following consultations, Korea agreed to change its regulations to allow manufacturer-determined shelf lives (*Korea – Shelf-Life* (1995)).

Conversely, differences in treatment may be justified by relevant distinctions between different products or services, depending on the purposes of the rules. This may include how goods and services are produced (in WTO terminology, processes and production methods, or PPMs).[39] Is tuna caught by methods which restrict the by-catch of dolphins 'like' tuna caught without such restrictions? Should a tomato which has traits introduced by genetic modification (GM) be treated 'like' other tomatoes (some of which may have been bred by traditional selection techniques)? Is beef or milk from cows which have been fed growth-promoting

---

ban was introduced in response to consumer concerns dating from the 1970s (Kramer 1989), and was imposed on local production and only consequentially to imported beef. Certainly, in the context of European overproduction of beef, the restriction seemed a small price to pay to avert what is by any judgement a small risk; while to north American producers it seems an unreasonable requirement acting as a market barrier to them, this hardly substantiates accusations of covert protectionism. For a knowledgeable and subtle evaluation (which nevertheless favours free trade), see Vogel 1995.

39 The issue of PPMs came to the fore in the GATT Panel report on Mexico's complaint against the US prohibition of tuna caught by methods which did not have restrictions on by-catch of dolphins equivalent to those adopted by the USA. The USA argued that this was non-discriminatory under GATT, art. III (and the Note to that article), but the Panel decided that art. III.4 only applied to regulations affecting 'products as such' (*US – Restrictions on Imports of Tuna* (1991): paras. 5.10–5.15).

hormones 'like' the beef or milk from other cows? Are building products made from asbestos fibre 'like' those made from other fibres? Thus, whether it is justifiable to apply special restrictions to GM tomatoes, beef from hormone-treated cows, or building products made from asbestos, depends on whether there are valid reasons to identify those features of the product as problematic. Little wonder that the issue of 'likeness' is considered one of the thorniest in WTO law. Indeed, the WTO's highest adjudicator, the Appellate Body (AB) has described the concept as an elastic one 'that evokes the image of an accordion . . . [which] stresses and squeezes in different places as different provisions of the WTO Agreement are applied' (*Japan – Alcohol* (1996): sec. H 1(a), para. 4). Clearly, it is the interpreter of the provision who squeezes or stretches the accordion.

Yet the jurisprudence of the GATT and the WTO has been reluctant to accept that the issue of 'likeness' is a normative one. The problem has frequently arisen in the context of taxation of alcoholic beverages, since firms selling internationally recognized products such as whisky and vodka have long complained that they are treated as luxury products in many countries and more highly taxed than local alcoholic drinks. The predominant approach of adjudicators has been to emphasize two main criteria: physical characteristics, and economic substitutability. The determining factor, from the point of view of trade rules, has been whether there is, *or could be*, a competitive relationship between the products. This was the view taken in disputes involving the Japanese Liquor Tax Law, which applied much lower taxes on the traditional local *shochu* than on imported products such as vodka, whisky and brandy. This was considered discriminatory both by a Panel in 1987, and later under the WTO by the AB (*Japan – Alcohol* (1996)). The competitiveness test essentially ignores the law's aims: often the motivation for regulation is to help protect consumers, by differentiating between products which might otherwise *become* competitive (Marceau and Trachtman 2002: 819–20). Thus, a country may consider it desirable to use high taxes to discourage consumption of products damaging to health, such as alcohol or tobacco, which are backed by the marketing power of large TNCs; the same level of taxes might be inappropriate for traditional local alcoholic or tobacco products, due to their different social and cultural characteristics, both of production and consumption. However, in the 1996 *Japan – Alcohol* decision the AB ruled that it is 'irrelevant that protectionism was not an intended objective'.[40]

---

40 *Japan – Alcohol* (1996): 27; Marceau and Trachtman also point out that the AB in *EC – Asbestos* (2001) suggested a two-step analysis, so that not only must the complainant show

The conflicts between market access obligations and the right of states to set regulatory standards was first tackled in relation to technical product standards. A Code on Technical Barriers to Trade was negotiated in the 1970s,[41] a revised version of which was adopted as an Agreement in the Tokyo Round in 1979, but binding only on states accepting it. This obliged the participating GATT states to base their domestic technical standards on those developed by relevant international bodies, although there were significant exclusions especially for health and environmental protection standards.[42] This gap was filled, in relation to human, animal and plant health standards, by the negotiation of the agreement on Sanitary and Phytosanitary Measures (SPS) during the Uruguay Round.

that like products are treated differently, but also that this difference is applied 'so as to afford protection to domestic production', which may allow for an 'aims' test.

41 A draft for a proposed GATT Code of Conduct for Preventing Technical Barriers to Trade (document MTN/NTM/W/5, 21 April 1975, p. 9 Annex) included the following key provisions:

> Art. 2(b) Where mandatory standards are required and relevant international standards exist or their completion is imminent, adherents shall use them, or the relevant parts of them, as a basis for the mandatory standards, except where such international standards or relevant parts are inappropriate for the adherents concerned. (c) With a view to harmonizing their mandatory standards on as wide a basis as possible, adherents shall play a full part within the limits of their resources in the preparation by appropriate international standards bodies of international standards for products for which they either have adopted, or expect to adopt, mandatory standards.

42 Article 2.2 of the Tokyo Round TBT Agreement read:

> Where technical regulations or standards are required and relevant international standards exist or their completion is imminent, Parties shall use them, or the relevant parts of them, as a basis for the technical regulations or standards except where, as duly explained upon request, such international standards or relevant parts are inappropriate for the Parties concerned, for inter alia such reasons as national security requirements; the prevention of deceptive practices; protection for human health or safety, animal or plant life or health, or the environment; fundamental climatic or other geographical factors; fundamental technological problems.

This Code framed the battleground for disputes between the USA and the EC over European restrictions on meat imports. The stricter EC regulation of slaughterhouses from 1983 was badly received by the US meat industry, which asked for recognition of the equivalence of US standards; this conflict was resolved by a compromise, after US threats of retaliation under s. 301. The conflict over hormone-treated beef (see n. 38 above) proved more intractable; when the EC introduced its ban in 1985, the USA moved to establish a Codex committee in 1986 to examine the scientific basis for concerns about residues from veterinary medicines; the issue was raised at monthly meetings of the GATT Committee from 1987, but the EC blocked the US request for a Panel to consider the dispute under the Standards Code, on the grounds that the measures were to protect human health and hence not covered by the TBT Agreement (Kramer 1989).

The WTO's TBT and SPS Agreements now require states to ensure that national regulations comply with relevant international standards, where they exist or are imminent. Standards are defined broadly, to include PPMs, if they are 'related' to product characteristics.[43] Thus, in the area of product standards an interesting and novel form of legal and institutional linkage has been created between the GATT/WTO and the work of a number of international standard-setting organizations.[44] These international standards are not laid down by the WTO itself, but by the relevant international bodies. The SPS agreement specifies the three main organizations setting standards within its purview, in particular for food safety the Codex Alimentarius Commission (Codex); other bodies may be recognized by the SPS Committee. Under the TBT, standards may be set by any body or system whose membership is open to the relevant bodies of all Member States of the WTO. The main global body for technical standards is the International Standards Organization (ISO).

The TBT and SPS Agreements in effect convert those standards, which the organizations themselves consider voluntary,[45] into binding legal

---

43 TBT, art. 2(4), and SPS, art. 3(1). Under the Definition in Annex 1 of the TBT, a technical regulation is any mandatory requirement laying down 'product characteristics or their related processes and production methods', including packaging and labelling. The AB adopted a broad definition of 'technical regulations' in *EC – Asbestos* (2001), deciding that '"product characteristics" include, not only features and qualities intrinsic to the product itself, but also related "characteristics", such as the means of identification, the presentation and the appearance of a product' (para. 67), including terminology, packaging and labelling requirements; it therefore held that the French ban on products containing asbestos was a technical regulation.

44 The plurilateral Agreement on Government Procurement also provides (art. VI) that technical standards should be 'based on international standards, where such exist'.

45 A representative of the WTO is said to have surprised participants at a Codex meeting by explaining that WTO rules apply to all Codex measures, even those considered by Codex as non-binding (see Comments by Marsha Echols, in Cottier *et al.* 2005: 195). Standards are defined very broadly: the SPS Agreement refers to 'standards, guidelines and recommendations'. This led the Secretariat of the Codex Alimentarius Commission to write to the SPS Committee for clarification on whether any differentiation would be made regarding the status of Codex standards, guidelines or recommendations. The SPS Committee responded that 'how a Codex text was applied depended on its substantive content rather than the category of that text' and that this content 'might have some bearing on how a Member could show that its measure is based on an international standard, guideline or recommendation' (Document G/SPS/W/86/Rev.1, 13 March 1998). The definition in the TBT Agreement (Annex A) is also broad, but applies *only* to non-mandatory norms: 'Document approved by a recognized body, that provides, for common and repeated use, rules, guidelines or characteristics for products or related processes and production methods, with which compliance is not mandatory.'

obligations on WTO Member States. Formally, the obligation is to 'base' national regulations on the international standard, not necessarily to apply it as such. However, the leeway allowed by the term 'based on' is not a wide one.[46] Furthermore, this obligation is considered to apply regardless of whether the national regulations are discriminatory or protectionist in intent.[47] A national regulation which is 'in accordance with' (TBT 2.5) or 'conforms to' (SPS 2.4) an international standard provides a 'safe harbour', protecting the regulation from potential challenge under trade law. The SPS Agreement additionally allows a state to adopt a higher standard of protection than the international standard, but only if there is a scientific justification (article 3), according to a risk assessment following principles laid out in article 5. Thus, the addition of the TBT and SPS Agreements in the WTO went considerably beyond the GATT non-discrimination obligations in establishing 'disciplines' on national state regulation.[48]

Thus, an alternative to national deregulation to meet the demands of liberalization is re-regulation based on international standards. The question of how to deal with regulatory differences was highlighted by the growth of conflicts from the 1970s onwards. The bulk of GATT complaints concerned NTBs and other 'unfair trade practices', and the proportion increased as the overall number of complaints grew in the 1980s (see 8.3 below). These covered a diversity of issues, including not only consumer protection and food safety regulation, but matters such as corporate taxation, intellectual property rights (IPRs), and environmental protection rules (discussed in more detail below). Hence, the problem was far from confined to product standards.

---

46 The Appellate Body (AB), in *EC – Hormones* (1998), decided that the requirement in SPS 2.2 that national measures must be 'based on' international standards is less stringent than the criterion in SPS 2.4 that creates a presumption of conformity if they 'conform to' such standards, recognizing that international harmonization is a 'goal yet to be realized' (paras. 168–71). This allows a state for example to adopt part only of the standard or make appropriate variations for local conditions. However, in *EC – Sardines* (2002), the AB said that the similar term 'as a basis for' in the TBT means more than simply the existence of a 'rational relationship' between the two, and certainly the national measures cannot contradict the international standard; also the phrase 'or relevant parts of them' in TBT 2.2 means *all* the relevant parts, a state cannot select only some (paras. 247–50).

47 Thus, in *EC – Hormones*, the EU was obliged to justify its ban on hormone-treated beef under the SPS agreement, regardless of whether it could be justified as non-discriminatory under the GATT.

48 For a careful analysis of the two agreements in relation to the GATT and the WTO, see Marceau and Trachtman 2002.

8.2.2 WTO and international regulatory networking

Thus, the WTO agreements in effect established mechanisms aiming at the international harmonization of a wide range of economic regulation. Yet global harmonization of the entire range of regulatory standards affecting goods and services would be an immense task. At the regional level the European Community, with its more developed institutional structure, has struggled long and hard to develop a system of regulatory coordination, involving a combination of mutual recognition and harmonization of standards (Dehousse 1989, 1992; Bratton *et al.* 1996: 29–43; Nicolaïdis 2007), and the EU has been described as a 'regulatory state' (Majone 1993), or a 'network state' (Castells 1998: ch. 5). In contrast, the GATT was a trade organization. It was not equipped to harmonize product standards, let alone standards in areas such as intellectual property, environmental protection, professional and technical services, taxation, investment incentives, or employment conditions.

Instead, the WTO became a central node in a web of regulatory networks. There are various ways in which the links between WTO trade rules and other types of regulation articulate. Some are still nascent, such as the interaction with corporate taxation (Slemrod and Avi-Yonah 2002; Daly 2005). Others are firmly established, but still fluid, as with IPRs, environmental protection and the wide range of services, some of which will be examined below. The form of the links varies, but in general they do not establish any coherent coordination, rather they open up new avenues for strategic manoeuvring and forum-shifting.[49] The conflicts and frictions between WTO rules and regulatory arrangements for which other organizations are responsible have stimulated various processes of international re-regulation.

8.2.2.1 The politics and science of global standards

This can be seen even in the area of product standards, where as we have seen a clear link is established between trade rules and the norms

---

49 Joanne Scott (2004) cogently argues that the uncertainty about the position of the WTO as a global node, compared to the more institutionalized structure of the EU, makes it harder to identify the proper role of the WTO towards other organizations, especially those setting substantive regulatory standards. Indeed, some links are opportunistic: for example, the SCM agreement provides a 'safe harbour' for export credits which conform to any international undertaking to which at least twelve of its original members were party; this was intended and has been found to refer to the OECD Arrangement on Officially Supported Export Credits, which is considered a 'Gentlemen's Agreement', and is mainly between OECD countries, although others may be invited to join (Flett 2011).

developed by international standards organizations. This has given a greater importance and impetus to the standards organizations, significantly transforming the range and character of their work. For example, in response to the GATT's increased concern with international standards, the International Plant Protection Convention (IPPC) became formalized as an organization and began an ambitious programme of standard-setting from 1992.[50] The work of standard-setting is now done in cooperation with the WTO, the staff of the various organizations keep in close touch with those of the WTO, and they are present as observers in the meetings of the relevant WTO Committee, while WTO staff attend theirs. However, the standards bodies do not function merely as subsidiaries of the WTO: their participants are generally technical specialists, only some of whom also attend the related WTO Committee, and they do not always view the need to agree international standards with the same urgency as do the WTO bodies. There is also some overlap between the concerns of the SPS and TBT Committees and the work of the standards bodies, and there can be disagreement among Member States as to which body should take on a particular task.[51] At the same time, converting the soft-law standards into hard trade law has both politicized the standards-setting process to some extent, and made it more difficult to reach agreement, because of their ramifications for trade.

The politicization of the work of bodies such as Codex and the ISO has been counterpointed by an increased emphasis on 'sound science' as the justification for standards. This also reveals a tension between political accountability and scientific expertise. It has been argued indeed that the growth of standardization based on authoritative expert knowledge is itself a form of regulating 'in a situation where there is no legal centre of authority', but which if based on private organizations and market-driven may provide order but without responsibility (Brunsson et al. 2000: 48). Despite the hope that shared scientific perspectives or dominant paradigms could provide a basis for regulatory convergence, science itself is not a source of neutral and universal principles, but an arena for rivalry and contestation (Atik 1997). Hence, the resort to scientific

---

50 In 1992 the FAO established a separate Secretariat for the IPPC, followed by the formation of a Committee of Experts on Phytosanitary Measures, and negotiations for revision of the Convention which was achieved in 1997.
51 For example, there has been disagreement in the SPS Committee on whether it should develop procedures for recognition of disease- and pest-free areas of exporting countries, or leave this to the standards bodies (interview information).

justification may politicize scientific debate, rather than using science to resolve political conflict.[52]

The tensions between science and politico-economic interests have been played out in the legal and institutional interactions between the WTO and standards bodies. It is notable that the SPS, which strongly emphasizes that standards must be based on scientific principles and evidence, grants authority to Codex, which is an intergovernmental organization, although dominated by experts, many from business firms. Codex has sought to strengthen its authority by a stress on science, but it remains 'beleaguered by disagreements' about the relative role of scientific and other factors (Schepel 2005: 182). For example, it has supported the separation of risk assessment (based on science) from risk management (which can take account of economic, social and political factors); but the Codex 'working principles for risk analysis' of 2003 emphasize the need for an 'iterative process' of interaction between risk managers and risk assessors, which suggests a recognition that risk assessment itself is value laden.[53]

The TBT, which does not designate any specific organization, has created an arena for institutional rivalry and contestation. In particular there has been a 'heated transatlantic debate' between the EC and the USA, involving conflicts over the requirements for legitimacy of international standards-setting, regulatory philosophy and economic advantage (Schepel 2005: 185–93). The US standards bodies claim that they themselves have international standing justified by the quality of their standards, but the European Commission favours international organizations based on national representation, such as the ISO, in which of course European countries are very strongly represented. Nevertheless, the EC considers

---

52 For an interesting account of how scientific evidence was used in the *EC – Asbestos* case see Castleman 2002. An advocate in WTO disputes has opined that the excessive reliance on science has resulted in some scientists providing opinions which are so non-specific as to be unhelpful, while others 'appear not to appreciate the point at which their role as scientist ends and the role of risk manager begins' (Flett 2011).

53 Winnickoff *et al.* 2005: 96. Wynne (1992) analyses how a formal approach to risk assessment abstracted from the social contexts misrepresents the indeterminate nature of those social dimensions but treats them as deterministic and capable of resolution by statistical and other quantitative techniques; for an evaluation of the attractions and limits of risk assessment see Heyvaert 1999; Kleinman and Kinchy (2003) provide an interesting analysis of the divergent cultures of regulatory policymaking in the EU and the USA which have generated different views on food safety issues such as bovine growth hormones and biotechnology; Lindner (2008) argues that there is nevertheless a power of alignment with international standards generated by the interaction of Codex and the WTO.

that standards should be adopted by consensus rather than majority voting, although its argument that this is required under the TBT has been rejected by the AB.[54] This view is presumably influenced by its experience in the long-running Meat–Hormones dispute, in which a crucial step was the decision by Codex, which normally approves standards by consensus, to adopt standards permitting hormone-growth promoters 'in accordance with good animal husbandry practice' on a vote of 33:29 with seven abstentions.[55]

A different solution was found for dealing with the trade–IPR linkage by the inclusion of the TRIPs agreement in the WTO. As will be discussed in more detail in the next chapter, TRIPs adopts a two-pronged approach to international standards. First, it incorporates into the WTO obligations the main provisions of the principal existing multilateral IP treaties, in particular the Berne Copyright Convention and the Paris Industrial Property convention. This applies regardless of whether the WTO member is also a member of WIPO or has ratified those agreements. In effect, a large body of international law which states could previously choose whether to accept has now become binding on all states desiring to be part of the world trading system. Second, the TRIPs agreement itself contains a large number of minimum requirements for IP protection, in relation both to substantive IP laws but also, very importantly, their enforcement procedures. Thus, the effect is to require states to revise or review their internal IP legislation and regulation for compatibility with TRIPs standards.

8.2.2.2 Regulatory interactions: environmental protection

The relationship between trade rules and environmental standards, spotlighted by the Tuna–Dolphin dispute under the GATT, has remained controversial in the WTO. The most persuasive basis for the Panel's decision in the Tuna–Dolphin case was the unilateral nature of the US regulations aiming to protect dolphins. One aspect of this was that the US regulations aimed to protect dolphins anywhere, not just in US waters, so could be criticized as 'extraterritorial'. This is hardly convincing as, like

---

54 *EC – Sardines* (2002): para. 227, emphasizing that it is a matter for standards bodies themselves. As Schepel points out, the Principles for the Development of International Standards adopted by the TBT Committee in 2000, which elaborated the Code of Good Practice annexed to the TBT Agreement itself, do not resolve but restate the dilemmas, stating that bodies should operate with 'open, impartial and transparent procedures, that afford an opportunity for consensus among all interested parties' (2005: 188).

55 *EC – Meat Hormones* Panel report (1997): para. IV.77. Various aspects of this case will be discussed below; for an overview, see Princen 2002: ch. 4; Kleinman and Kinchy 2003.

other environmental issues, they concern a common global resource; and the US regulations actually applied to tinned tuna sold *within* the USA. More convincingly, the Panel pointed out that the US regulations were formulated in a way which made it very difficult for Mexico to comply, since they required other countries' regulations to result in no greater catches of dolphin than those actually produced by the US regulations, a threshold which could not be known in advance (para. 5.33).

The issue of unilateralism was addressed more directly when a very similar dispute arose under the WTO, *US – Shrimp* (1998), a complaint by India, Malaysia, Pakistan and Thailand, which provided an opportunity for some significant development of WTO rules. The AB took the view that the US measures aiming to protect sea turtles might be justifiable under GATT, article XX(g), as intended to conserve 'exhaustible natural resources', especially as all seven species of sea turtles are listed as endangered by the Convention on International Trade in Endangered Species (CITES). It also pointed to the new wording in the Preamble to the WTO Agreement referring to the objective of sustainable development and protection and preservation of the environment, which should 'add colour, texture and shading' to the interpretation of the Agreement. The AB declined to go so far as to say that XX(g) would justify national state measures protecting *any* global resource, but accepted that sea turtles are migratory and some occur in US waters, so that there was a 'sufficient nexus' with the US (para.133). However, it pointed to the wording of the introductory paragraph or *chapeau* of article XX, especially the requirement that state measures under that article should not be applied in a manner constituting 'unjustifiable discrimination between countries where the same conditions prevail'. It considered that the US measures established a 'rigid and unbending standard' requiring other states (if they wish to export to the USA) 'to adopt a regulatory programme that is not merely *comparable*, but rather *essentially the same*', as that being applied by the USA (para. 163, emphasis in the original). This amounted, in its view, to using an economic embargo to require other WTO members to adopt essentially the same regulatory programme.

This interpretation reads into WTO rules an obligation at least to engage other states in serious negotiations to reach agreement on international measures. The AB pointed to the US participation in the conclusion of an Inter-American Convention for protection of sea turtles in 1996 as evidence that this was possible. As a consequence of the decision, the USA modified its regulations so that the exporting country could demonstrate that it has a 'comparably effective' regulatory programme as the USA. It also engaged in discussions and negotiations with countries in South-East Asia for a sea-turtle conservation agreement. On a follow-up complaint, the adjudicators accepted that the record showed that the USA had engaged in 'serious, good faith efforts', even though such a treaty had not yet been concluded (*US – Shrimp: Recourse by Malaysia* (2001)). In these decisions the AB adroitly established strong incentives for states to agree international standards affecting products in international trade.

Both the TBT and SPS now may be relevant to environmental protection regulations, since as we have seen both now include at least some PPMs. However, the type of measures covered by the SPS is very precisely defined, to cover the protection of human, animal or plant life or health from risks arising from 'pests and diseases' or 'additives, contaminants, toxins, or disease-carrying organisms', and it does not refer to environmental protection, whereas the TBT includes 'the environment' among the (non-exhaustive) list of 'legitimate objectives' in its article 2.2. Nevertheless, the WTO Panel in the *EC – Biotech* (2008) dispute accepted that EC measures restricting entry of genetically modified organisms (GMOs) fell under the SPS, on the basis that they aimed to prevent potential dangers to biodiversity of cross-breeding if GM plants or seeds were released into the atmosphere, which fell within the concept of damage to plants or animals from pests or diseases. This could be distinguished from measures aimed at more general threats to the environment, such as air or water pollution, which would therefore come under the TBT (*EC – Biotech* (2008): para. 7.210).

Since the Panel ruled that the measures fell under the SPS, the EC could not argue that its measures are based on the provisions of the Cartagena Protocol on Biosafety (2000), which the USA was involved in negotiating but did not sign.[56] Indeed, the Panel went much further and took the view that there was no need even to take the Protocol into account in interpreting WTO rules, since the Protocol could not be regarded as

---

56 The SPS specifies the organizations whose standards fall within its remit; under the TBT an international standard may be produced by any 'recognized body' open to all WTO members; this might include the Cartagena protocol, although only some aspects of the EC regulations relate to its provisions. There was a major conflict during the negotiation of the Protocol, over its relationship both with WTO rules and standards which might be developed by Codex and other bodies, which resulted in ambiguous and conflicting recitals in the Preamble to the Protocol, stating both that it should not be interpreted as changing rights and obligations under existing treaties, and that it should not be subordinated to other international agreements. Close analysis shows that WTO law could be sufficiently flexible to accommodate the bio-safety requirements of the Protocol (Eggers and Mackenzie 2000), but the *EC – Biotech* decision suggests that WTO adjudicators are unwilling to adopt an overtly harmonious approach.

forming part of the corpus of public international law, as not all WTO members are parties to it (*EC – Biotech* (2008): para. 7.70). This view, if upheld, would make it difficult to develop any legal cross-fertilization between WTO rules and international environmental law.[57]

The WTO Committee on Trade and Environment has also explored, at some length but inconclusively, various issues of the interaction of WTO rules with environmental protection, especially after being given a renewed impetus by the Doha Ministerial. The long-standing concern about the relationship to Multilateral Environmental Agreements (MEAs) which contain trade restrictions (such as CITES), was taken up as part of the broader Doha negotiation round.[58] Meantime, various practical measures have been taken, especially the development of cooperation activities between the secretariats of the WTO and MEAs, especially UNEP. Other issues are under continuing discussion, notably the need for international standards for organic products.

This overlaps with the difficult issue of non-state and non-mandatory standards, often for certification and labelling of products based on their beneficial environmental or social qualities, which has been considered by various WTO Committees. Unless such standards can be argued to be de facto mandatory due to a link with requirements laid down or advantages conferred by the state, they are likely to escape the discipline of WTO rules altogether. This may raise questions about the legitimacy of such standards, unless they are developed by processes which are inclusive, transparent, accessible and open. Some have argued that, provided that such procedural conditions are met, WTO rules should be interpreted so as to provide 'regulatory space', since social and environmental labelling standards offer the possibility of re-embedding global markets (Bernstein and Hannah 2008).

8.2.3 Services liberalization and re-regulation

Regulation is perhaps even more important for services than for products. Services usually entail long-term *relationships* rather than discrete

---

57 For a study of the interaction of trade and biotechnology, see Meléndez-Ortiz and Sánchez 2005, and for a thorough analysis of the *Biotech* report focusing on the treatment of the relationship of WTO rules to international law, see Young 2007.

58 But the mandate was very narrow: the original EU proposal that GATT art. XX should be amended to permit trade measures taken under an MEA was sidelined, and the Doha mandate excluded the thorny problem of potential disputes between parties and non-parties to an MEA. Attention shifted to liberalization of trade in environmental goods, or perhaps a broader category of environmentally-friendly products (Harashima 2008).

one-off *transactions*. They usually involve relationships of trust, confidence, and reliance on the professional skills or knowledge of the service provider. Such social factors are sometimes dealt with from the economic perspective, although inadequately, by concepts such as 'information asymmetry'. Although services are in many ways personal, they have increasingly become commercialized with the growth of the services economy. The international liberalization of services takes this a step further, since it entails a significant shift away from local, or face-to-face service relationships.

Due to their characteristics, services are subject to often quite extensive and specific regulation. To protect the consumer, service providers are often required to have appropriate qualifications, not only for traditional professions such as lawyers, doctors, teachers and accountants, but a wider range of activities often involving specialized skills or knowledge. Regulation is also often necessary to protect more general public interests, for example banking supervision to ensure financial stability, and price controls and public service obligations for providers of essential basic utilities, such as water, energy or communications. Commercial relationships are also often complex and problematic for services, requiring refinements or adaptations of competition principles. For example, activities such as energy, transport and communications depend on an infrastructure (tracks, pipelines, airports), the terms of access to which by different service providers are crucial. These are also factors that economists try to grasp through inadequate concepts such as 'natural monopoly', or 'imperfect competition'. This may lead to sector-specific regulation, which often entails supervision of pricing and investment, obligations to provide access or interconnection, and specification of safety and service levels.

8.2.3.1 GATS and the right to regulate

Whereas liberalizing trade in goods began with border barriers, liberalization of services was seen from the start as a matter of dealing with domestic regulations which were considered to be barriers to market access (Brock 1982). As with goods, the free-trade perspective inevitably created an impetus for deregulation:

> The very act of defining services transactions as 'trade' established normative presumptions that 'free' trade was the yardstick for good policy against which regulations, redefined as nontariff barriers, should be measured and justified only exceptionally.
>
> (Drake and Nicolaïdis 1992: 40)

This was seen clearly in the UR Services negotiations, where they created inevitable difficulties in crafting an agreement:

> By beginning from the baseline of labelling as potential NTBs anything that restricted competition, the diverse social purposes of existing regulations were obscured. Negotiators thus encountered problems when considering measures that restricted trade but served important purposes. The GATT context channelled the process towards a trade agreement but complicated the search for a balance between trade and regulatory objectives.
>
> (Drake and Nicolaïdis 1992: 70; see also Mattoo 1997: 107)

The recognition of the need for such a balance led to the early rejection of the idea initially proposed by the USA that GATT itself could simply be extended by adding the two words 'and services', rather than a separate agreement for services.

Instead, the GATS is a 'positive-list' agreement, which combines a sweeping potential coverage with a complex 'opt-in' system for negotiation of actual commitments.[59] It has few general obligations: only MFN (to which states were allowed to list exceptions),[60] and 'transparency' (requiring that all regulatory measures affecting services be promptly published, and that the GATS Council be notified of any changes to regulation of services in which the member has made commitments). It also has fewer General Exceptions than the GATT, so that states can only preserve their right to regulate by explicitly limiting their commitments. Commitments once made are difficult to modify,[61] so the principle is 'list it or lose it'.

Commitments under the GATS, and hence its main obligations, apply only to those sectors and 'modes of delivery' listed by each state. GATS in principle recognizes states' 'right to regulate' by allowing each state to exclude both horizontal and sector-specific regulations which may conflict with its obligations. This is done by listing them as limitations on the commitments in relation to the obligations of Market Access

---

59 Under the GATT tariff cuts also resulted from negotiated commitments; but the GATT (esp. arts. I, III and XI) has much more extensive general obligations than the GATS.

60 Over 400 were listed, 78 of them applying to all sectors, and although these are supposed to be for 10 years only, many are listed as 'indefinite'.

61 GATS, art. XXI permits modification but only subject to 'compensatory adjustments', which must be on an MFN basis, and agreed by other states or referred to arbitration; a procedure was established in 1999, but it seems rarely used, except e.g. by the EC as a result of expansion of its membership.

(MA),[62] and National Treatment (NT),[63] either 'horizontally' in relation to all services,[64] or in relation to specific service sectors. Thus, each state's commitments under the GATS takes the form of a complex Table, showing first 'horizontal' limitations (MA and NT, in relation to each of the four modes of delivery), and then commitments by Sector and Sub-Sector, in relation to each of the four modes of delivery, with columns listing both horizontal and sector-specific MA and NT limitations.

The importance of the 'right to regulate' became more apparent after the mid-1990s, following the experience in a number of countries of crises in key service sectors following deregulation and privatization. These included dramatic failures of electricity supply (e.g. in California in 2000 to 2001), a deterioration of safety and reliability of transportation systems,[65] and financial failures and crises culminating in the 2007–8 financial crash(discussed in Chapter 8). In addition, there have been growing concerns about the inequality of the benefits from liberalization, and even its impact on basic human rights, especially when applied to basic services such as water, healthcare, and education (see 8.3 below).

However, retaining the right to regulate is very problematic in practice, because of the complexity of the process for making commitments. First, the scope of the commitments made may not be appreciated, due to the indeterminacy of defining service sectors.[66] As Kelsey points out,

62 Article XVI lists the type of limitations which are deemed to be incompatible with MA commitments unless specified in a schedule, covering licensing limits or quotas based on an economic needs test, and participation limits for FDI. The MA obligations include any quantitative limits, e.g. on the number of banks, or lawyers, even if non-discriminatory between foreign and local suppliers. A total prohibition is also considered to be a quantitative restriction, as amounting to a 'zero-quota': this was decided in the *US – Gambling* case (2005), regarding the US prohibition on internet gambling. Pauwelyn (2005) argues that this was a mistaken decision, as it failed to maintain the strict separation between MA limits and disciplines on domestic regulation, and entailed a further intrusion into state regulatory autonomy.

63 Article XVII is worded differently from GATT, art. III, and specifies that NT may mean either formally identical or formally different treatment, considered to be less favourable if it 'modifies the conditions of competition' in favour of domestic suppliers.

64 For example, to limit FDI ('mode 3' market access, in GATS terms) by retaining restrictions on the maximum participation by foreign investors in local subsidiaries or joint ventures; or to apply immigration controls on entry of natural persons to deliver services (e.g. construction workers, software engineers, accountants).

65 This caused a crisis of the UK system of rail regulation in 2001 to 2002 (see Moran 2003: 116–18).

66 A Services Classification List was developed based on the UN Central Product Classification (CPC), but its use is not mandatory; the Panel in *EC – Bananas* said that for those

the commodification involved in the sectoral classification process tends to produce surprises, by abstracting from the social nature of the activity: for example midwives, together with medicine and dentistry, come under 'business services' (Kelsey 2008: 128). This can lead to apparently unexpected outcomes for even the best-resourced trade negotiators, as was shown by the decision in the *US – Gambling* dispute. There, the USA was found to have made a commitment to allow cross-border gambling services (e.g. via the internet) under the heading 'Other Recreational Services', although the USA considered that gambling came within its exclusion of 'sporting' services (Kelsey 2008: 174–81). These ambiguities, and the arcane nature of the process, create space for strategic manoeuvres: for example, potentially troublesome domestic constituencies can be sidestepped by negotiators who make or accept commitments which are deliberately ambiguous.

Second, national negotiators need a thorough familiarity with all the regulations relating, even indirectly, to each sector in which commitments are contemplated, and must anticipate possible complaints that formally neutral regulations amount to de facto discrimination. In practice, trade negotiators are often unfamiliar with the regulatory arrangements in the many diverse service sectors, while sectoral specialists may not appreciate the implications of non-discrimination principles or prohibitions on quantitative restrictions.

Third, any potentially invalid regulations must be carefully listed, in relation to the relevant sector and mode of delivery in which a commitment is made. This includes not only formal laws, but all 'measures' of an official character, and covers all levels of government, including local and regional. But negotiating rounds generate pressures on those involved to minimize their MA and NT limitations, sometimes on the basis of assurances that they are unnecessary, which may be of doubtful validity.[67]

Furthermore, the GATS envisages further 'disciplines' on domestic regulation under article VI which, in a similar way to the TBT and SPS

states who do use it, the CPC descriptions of sectors apply. The US in particular does not use the CPC classification.

67 For example, the chair of the Group on Basic Telecommunications informed states which had entered MA limitations that their commitments were 'subject to availability of spectrum/frequency' that these were unnecessary and should be withdrawn; this was based on the dubious grounds that states had the right to exercise spectrum/frequency management, provided that this is done in accordance with the principles of art. 6 of the telecoms Reference Paper (WTO doc. S/GBT/4 1997).

agreements, apply to all internal measures,[68] regardless of whether they constitute quantitative restrictions (MA) or are discriminatory (NT). It establishes general procedural standards, requiring that measures affecting services should be 'administered in a reasonable, objective and impartial manner'; that there must be provisions for 'objective and impartial review' of administrative decisions applying such measures; and even that applications for authorization to supply a service must be decided 'within a reasonable period of time'. Article VI.4 goes even further, in mandating the GATS Council to develop substantive disciplines on national measures. These should *inter alia*: (a) be 'based on objective and transparent criteria, such as competence and the ability to supply the service'; (b) be 'not more burdensome than necessary to ensure the quality of the service'; and (c) in the case of licensing procedures, not in themselves restrict the supply of a service. These three criteria apply immediately, under article VI.5, in sectors where commitments are made, pending the development of more specific disciplines, as envisaged by VI.4.

These apparently innocuous provisions are unprecedented in establishing general international legal standards for national regulation, with potentially enormous impact when backed by the WTO's enforcement mechanisms. The criterion that regulations be 'not more burdensome than necessary to ensure the quality of the service' is particularly sweeping. Yet the GATS is much more tentative than the SPS and the TBT about re-regulation based on international standards. It does not provide a general 'safe harbour' presumption of validity for national regulations which are based on international standards. Article VI.5(b) suggests only that 'account shall be taken of international standards of relevant international organizations' in determining whether national measures comply with these broad and potentially stringent standards.

Implementing article VI, the GATS Council adopted in 1998 some Disciplines on Domestic Regulation in the Accountancy Sector.[69] Aside from a very widely worded general obligation that regulatory measures should not be more trade restrictive than necessary to fulfil a legitimate objective, it essentially established procedural standards (transparency, fairness in licensing procedures). Although it did include a linkage similar to those in the TBT/SPS to 'internationally recognized standards of relevant

---

68 Although this article is in the section of the agreement headed General Obligations and Disciplines, its terms are such that in practice they apply essentially to states' commitments.

69 S/L/63 14 December 1998.

international organizations', these are only a factor which should be 'taken into account' when deciding on conformity of national measures. Instead of continuing a sectoral approach, the work under Article VI has shifted to considering professional services in general, while the Working Party on Domestic Regulation has adopted an even more generic approach, which seemed likely to rely on elaboration of the necessity test (Delimatsis 2008).

8.2.3.2 Regulatory interactions: finance

Various strategies are possible under the GATS to develop internationally coordinated or harmonized regulatory arrangements. One is by recognition of other states' licences or certificates based on education, experience or qualifications, which may be unilaterally, or by agreement, or through harmonization (article VII). This clearly could conflict with the MFN obligation, so it is subject to conditions that it should not be done in a discriminatory manner, and should allow adequate opportunity for other interested members to join any such scheme. However, the provision falls far short of appreciating, let alone providing for, the forms of international regulatory cooperation that are likely to be necessary in many service sectors. Where such systems have been established, notably in the EU for many sectors, they generally include not only mutual recognition but also an allocation of regulatory rights between home and host country, as well as provisions for cooperation, such as information exchange. Some allocation of responsibility is common for most forms of cross-border services: often the home country is responsible for licensing and supervising service providers, while the host country deals with consumer protection and market impact aspects.

Another possibility is for sector-specific standards or requirements for regulation. Thus, the GATS Annex on Financial Services provided a general 'carve-out' allowing states to regulate 'for prudential reasons, including for the protection of investors, depositors, policy holders or . . . to ensure the integrity and stability of the financial system'. This is a very broad exclusion, and subject only to the condition that any such measures which do not conform with GATS provisions 'shall not be used as a means of avoiding the Member's commitments or obligations' under it. This is a much less stringent restriction than those imposed in the General Exceptions article XIV of GATS, which restate GATT's article XX, including the 'necessity test'.[70] The broad carve-out reflects the greater

---

70 GATS, art. XII also allows restrictions to be introduced in the event of 'serious balance-of-payments and external financial difficulties', subject to specified conditions.

sensitivity to the need for host states to retain powers both of prudential regulation of finance and macroeconomic management, to prevent
financial liberalization from leading to financial or monetary instability
or crisis.

Indeed, this danger was highlighted at the very time that the Agreement
on Financial Services was being negotiated in 1997, by the eruption of
the Asian financial crisis (Das 1998). It was generally acknowledged that
this crisis resulted from liberalization of capital flows, encouraged by the
IMF, combined with inadequate host-country prudential supervision of
finance (Stiglitz 2002: 99 ff.; IMF–IEO 2005). Even advocates of financial liberalization suggested that host states should retain some capital
controls, as well as ensuring strong prudential supervision (Williamson
1999). Although it is arguable that the carve-out in the Financial Services Annex makes it unnecessary to list such provisions as limitations
on commitments, and many states have not, Chile did list its deposit and
reserve requirements (Mattoo 1998), which were widely credited with
having sheltered that country from the worst of the 1997–8 crisis.

8.2.3.3 Regulatory interactions: telecoms

The formalization of regulation has also been very important in the second key service sector, telecommunications (telecoms), to mediate the
interplay of economic and political power in a period of rapid social
and technological change (Scott 1998). Like financial services, this sector
was regarded as important both in itself and as a means for facilitating
other cross-border services, so the GATS also included a specific Annex
on Telecoms. However, instead of a carve-out for sectoral regulation, this
Annex laid down broad principles as disciplines on national regulation.
It established general obligations on all members to provide access on
'reasonable and non-discriminatory terms and conditions' to their public
telecoms networks and services, for service suppliers from other states for
the supply of *any* service for which that member has made a commitment.
There are restrictions on the conditions which may be required, although
developing countries are given a bit more leeway. Thus, if a state has
made a 'mode 3' (commercial presence) commitment in any non-telecom
sector, a company would have the right to connect its intra-firm telecoms system to the public network on 'reasonable terms and conditions',
since intra-corporate communications are covered by the Annex. The
Annex also refers to the importance of international standards, and
of the relevant international bodies, mentioning the International
Telecommunications Union (ITU) and the International Organization for

Standardization (IOS), and says that members should consult in particular with the ITU on implementation of these obligations. The bland terms of the Annex conceal some fundamental conflicts of interest and perspective, which have been played out through complex transnational regulatory interactions.

A central issue has been the terms and conditions for access to telecoms infrastructure networks, in the transition to a more diverse pattern of telecoms based on new mobile and internet digital technologies. This required that the costs of maintenance, development and digital upgrading of the infrastructure networks, which had historically been established by public or private monopolies, should be taken into account when giving access to newcomers which might otherwise simply 'skim off the cream' of lucrative intra-urban and international traffic, and undermine the public benefits of a universal service. This transition had to be managed in each country according to local geographic, economic, social and historic circumstances. The more developed countries experimented with various combinations of liberalization and regulation, with different degrees of success. This has been more difficult for poorer countries, which had inferior infrastructure, and were generally dependent on foreign firms for both equipment and services supply.

The very great international disparities and inequalities in telecoms were reflected in the regime which had become established, under the ITU, for settlement rates for international traffic. This involved two main elements. First, an accounting rate was agreed bilaterally between countries for international calls between them; and second the revenue from such calls was divided between them by an agreed formula, usually half–half. This entailed a transfer payment, or settlement, from the country from which the higher volume of traffic originated, of the agreed proportion of the receipts from the net traffic volume. The system resulted in some very large transfer payments, especially from developed to developing countries, due to the huge imbalance of traffic between them. Thus, in 1996 the USA alone paid out some $5bn (almost 5 per cent of its trade deficit), and developing countries as a whole received an average of $10bn per year, which was an important source of hard currency and far exceeded total development bank lending for this sector (Braga et al. 1999; Guermazi 2004: 84–5, 96).

This system could be justified as helping to finance the high costs of telecoms infrastructure development in developing countries (Tyler 1998). Unfortunately, however, some of these funds were also diverted, either for other government purposes, or to private pockets. At the same time, the privatization of telecoms in many countries, and the rapid boom especially in mobile telephony, provided opportunities for enormous profits for those with the political connections to obtain a lucrative licence, and the business connections to exploit it. Thus, when Telmex in Mexico was privatized in 1990 to 1991, it was acquired by a consortium headed by local businessman Carlos Slim, with France Télécom and Southwestern Bell; Slim quickly built a fortune, which Forbes in 2010 estimated at over $50bn making him the world's richest person.

The conflict between the ITU-based state-managed regulation of telecoms and GATS liberalization obligations came to a head when sixty-nine governments in 1997 concluded the Agreement on Basic Telecoms (ABT).[71] This established further principles governing the form that national telecoms regulation should take, by the novel means of a so-called Reference Paper which was annexed to each state's schedule of commitments. This required the state to maintain 'appropriate measures' to prevent anti-competitive practices by dominant suppliers, and specifically to ensure that suppliers of infrastructure networks ensure interconnection, at any technically feasible point in the network, under non-discriminatory terms and conditions, in a timely fashion and on 'cost-oriented rates'. It specified procedural safeguards, in particular that there should be an independent and impartial regulator, to which there should be a right of appeal for disputes over interconnection terms. There was also a recognition of the right of states to define universal service obligations, but subject to the tests of transparency, non-discrimination, competitive neutrality and necessity.

The commitments made in the ABT involved potential conflicts with the international settlement rate system, which the ITU had begun to reform. In particular, the differences in settlement rates would probably fall foul of the MFN principle, and to safeguard against this five countries[72] listed MFN exemptions under GATS article II in respect of the application of differential settlement rates under ITU rules. To cover the remaining countries, a semi-formal 'understanding' was reached for a moratorium on complaints under WTO Dispute-Settlement procedures about the

---

71 At the end of the UR a number of states made commitments in value-added telecoms, but none in basic telecoms. This term has no agreed definition, but it is usually considered to be equivalent to 'public telecoms transport service' in s. 3(b) of the Annex on Telecoms, i.e. 'the real-time transmission of customer-supplied information between two or more points without any end-to-end change in the form or content of the customer's information'.

72 Bangladesh, India, Pakistan, Sri Lanka and Turkey.

application of the ITU accounting rates, at least for three years.[73] This was presumably aimed at creating pressure for reform of the accounting rate system through the ITU to bring it into line with GATS liberalization principles, and indeed the ITU Secretary-General initiated consultations to this end in 1996.[74] Further pressure was produced by unilateral regulatory actions taken by the USA in 1997. Price caps for accounting rates for international traffic with the USA were established under a 'Benchmark Order', which the USA declared was compatible with WTO rules (and was anyway protected by the moratorium). It was considered justified by the fear that carriers could take advantage of US commitments to lease lines for international calls with the USA. Since this could take their US-bound traffic out of the ITU accounting system, it could result in further large increases in the US transfer payments (Cowhey 2004: 58). Instead, this US move accelerated the sharp decline in both the accounting rates for international traffic, and the transfer payments.

The ending of the moratorium in 2000 was soon followed by a US complaint against Mexico's telecoms regulatory regime, on the grounds *inter alia* that it gave the dominant Mexican operator (Telmex) the right to negotiate the international accounting rates, which was discriminatory and anti-competitive. The decision of the Panel largely upheld the US complaint, rejecting Mexico's arguments that its regulatory regime was justified as based on the ITU Accounting Rate system. In the Panel's view Mexico's terms and conditions for interconnection did not comply with the Reference Paper, mainly on the grounds that the rates charged were not 'cost-oriented'.[75] Yet the Panel report has been heavily criticized for

---

73 Report of Group on Basic Telecommunications, WTO doc. S/GBT/4 15 February 1997: para. 7. The Panel report in *Mexico – Telecoms* (2004), (discussed below) took the view that this 'understanding' was non-binding, and at most could act as an aid to interpretation of the important point of whether international interconnection was intended to be excluded from the Reference Paper; if anything it had the opposite effect, since it showed that 'even though negotiators considered at length the issue of rates for international interconnection, they chose not to adopt wording that would have expressly excluded certain types of interconnection from the scope of the Reference Paper' (para. 7.137).

74 See Guermazi 2004: 85, who put forward more extensive proposals based on differential treatment to ensure a 'soft landing' for developing countries.

75 The Panel decided that the fact that rates are established under an accounting rate regime is not relevant in deciding whether they are 'cost-oriented', nor are factors such as the general state of the telecommunications industry or the coverage and quality of the network. Although it accepted that Mexico's use of an incremental-cost methodology, which was in line with ITU recommendations, could be cost oriented, it decided that Mexico's actual charges were not cost oriented; this was based on evidence and analyses submitted by the USA, since Mexico did not submit any calculations, nor did it comment on those

ignoring 'serious economic flaws' in the US complaint, which 'advanced the private interests of AT&T, Sprint and WorldCom while depriving US consumers of a more ubiquitous telecommunications network in North America' (Sidak and Singer 2004: 48).

The Panel's report also dealt a blow to sectoral telecom regulation, by emphasizing that the obligations to take measures to prevent anti-competitive practices in the Reference Paper referred to classic pro-competition rules, and that these cannot be overridden by other legal obligations, such as a pricing scheme laid down in telecoms regulation. It treated with scepticism Mexico's arguments that there may be different perceptions of competition, and that Mexico's uniform pricing and proportionate return scheme for telecoms encouraged competition for market share in Mexico rather than rewarding operators which had large shares of the traffic from the USA (para. 7.259). It also took the view that pricing schemes which involve cross-subsidization were inherently anti-competitive (para. 7.242), and stated that predatory pricing could be dealt with in general competition laws or by means other than uniform pricing (para. 7.261). This prioritization of competition law runs counter to studies of the experience of key countries, which show the importance of sector-specific regulation, including of pricing, and that competition policy should support and not override specific telecom regulation (Kerf *et al.* 2005). While the Panel claimed that its interpretation 'does not unduly limit the broad regulatory autonomy of WTO members' (para. 7.267), its decision was attacked as 'überregulation' for having overturned the informed judgments of an independent regulatory authority, consistent with WTO rules, and based on expertise and detailed local knowledge (Sidak and Singer 2004: 48). This decision, which Mexico did not appeal, helped to accelerate the decline in ITU accounting rates, which were also being undermined by the growth of internet telephony and digital networks based on satellite and mobile digital technology.

The liberalization of telecoms paved the way for a wide range of other services which could be delivered across telecoms networks, from various

of the USA (*Mexico – Telecoms* (2004): paras. 1.184–7). It has been suggested that the disjuncture between Mexico's internal regulations and its GATS commitments could have been due either to 'unfortunate drafting of Mexico's telecommunications commitments', or perhaps because 'certain Mexican authorities actually sought a significant liberalization of telecommunications ... but did not want to assume the political costs', although either explanation is 'inconvenient for the credibility of Mexican trade policy' (Mena and Rodriguez 2005: 439).

types of e-commerce to audio-visual and entertainment services. These raise a tangle of legal and regulatory issues, both under WTO law itself, and in its interaction with other types of regulation, which came to the fore in the renewed GATS negotiations from 2000 (Kelsey 2008: 167–73). These began with the fundamental question of whether electronic delivery of products should be considered trade in goods (and hence covered by the GATT), or services (and under the GATS); this might depend on whether the products were digital, but there could be further complications for products in both formats. Next was the question of whether commercial access to the internet should be considered basic or value-added telecoms. Then there are questions about the classification of internet-based services such as games, online shopping, website hosting, and various types of multi media: are these 'computer and related services' or 'audio-visual services'?

All such services also raise questions about the interaction of liberalization obligations with sectoral regulation. This is perhaps most acute for cultural content products, where the impact of liberalization on domestic cultural diversity policies creates a clash between the perspective of 'trade trumps culture' and that of 'cultural sovereignty'. This became articulated by the formation, on the initiative of Canada, of an International Network on Cultural Policy, and a parallel coalition of civil society organizations, which led to the negotiation under the auspices of UNESCO of a Convention for the protection of cultural diversity. As with the Cartagena Biosafety Protocol (discussed above), conflicts during the negotiation of this convention resulted in provisions about its relation to other treaties which are ambiguous and conflictual, and create new possibilities for strategic manoeuvring (Kelsey 2008: 248–54).

8.3 The constitution of the WTO

The power of the WTO derives not only from its importance as a node of intersection of regulatory networks, as examined in the previous section, but also from the character of its rules. These constitute what can be called global meta-regulation: rules governing how states should regulate (Morgan 2003). We have seen in the previous section that the WTO rules act as a substantive 'discipline' on national state regulation, while also encouraging international harmonization, in a variety of ways. The power of the WTO's rules also is backed by its procedural disciplines, and the institutions through which they are enforced. The WTO certainly has a highly legalized institutional form. However, as we have seen, this does not mean that its rules establish a clear or predictable basis for economic activity. Rather, they provide a fluid framework for managing the interactions of various networks and levels of regulation.

Debate about the form of this framework has revolved around the question of the 'constitutionalization' of the WTO. This concept was applied to the GATT by the doyen of trade lawyers, John Jackson, who coined the term the 'trade constitution' in the following terms:

> It is a very complex mix of economic and governmental policies, political constraints, and above all an intricate set of constraints imposed by a variety of 'rules' or legal norms in a particular institutional setting. This constitution imposes different levels of constraint on the policy options available to public or private leaders.
>
> (1997: 339)

From a political perspective, Stephen Gill has attacked the 'new constitutionalism' represented not only by the WTO but other institutions of global governance as a 'project of attempting to make transnational liberalism, and if possible liberal democratic capitalism, the sole model for future development' (2003: 132). Gill argues that the global constitutionalization project was a central element of the neo-liberalism which dominated the era in which it emerged. David Schneiderman points out that this is a particular vision of constitutionalism, a constraining version; he suggests that in contrast an enabling version could offer a positive view of collective action, which may be rights based, or more broadly democratized (2008). From that perspective, the new global constitutionalism projected by both the WTO and the investment regime of NAFTA and the IIAs (discussed in Chapter 5, at 5.2), offers only one alternative, 'intended to shield the market from vulgar democratic politics' (Schneiderman 2008: 222).

In relation to the WTO, a detailed study by Deborah Cass suggests that the trajectory of WTO constitutionalization is still fluid, and she identifies three models or 'visions' of WTO constitutionalization: (a) institutional managerialism ('management of policy diversity between states by institutions and rules'), (b) rights-based constitutionalization; and (c) judicial norm-generation (i.e. the development of a WTO constitutional system by the Appellate Body) (2005: 21–2).

This section will consider the legalized procedures of the WTO as they have emerged (which correspond to the first and third of Cass's models), and then discuss what the impact might be of a more fully-fledged, rights-based constitutionalization (Cass's second option), which some have propounded.

8.3.1 Administrative legalization

An important, but often overlooked, feature of the WTO as an institution is the role of its committees, which constitute a 'hidden world of WTO governance' (Lang and Scott 2009). The WTO agreements establish wide-ranging procedural obligations which require continuing legal–administrative processes of regulatory evaluation, accommodation and coordination. A key principle in the agreements is '*transparency*': this imposes the obligation on states to publish all their laws, administrative measures and court decisions, and even provide translations of relevant texts into English, French or Spanish, as well as requiring them to establish enquiry points to answer questions and receive comments from interested persons in other states.[76] This is linked to *notification and consultation* obligations towards other states, often channelled through the WTO. Generally states must report to the organization new laws or changes to their laws and regulations which may significantly affect access of foreign goods and services to its market.[77] The SPS agreement goes further and requires, where a state proposes to adopt regulations not based on an international standard, that the notification normally must be prior to adoption, to allow sufficient time for other states to comment, and for consultations to take place. The TRIPs agreement also has a broad requirement (art. 63), that states must report all new IP laws and legal rulings to the TRIPs Council for review, and meetings of the Council include regular evaluations of the IP laws of states.

As with substantive regulations, there are requirements that regulatory procedures must comply with international standards, or with standards laid down in the WTO agreements. Thus, the TBT lays down criteria for conformity assessment procedures (art. 5), including the requirement to base any procedures requiring positive conformity assessment on international standards where they exist (5.4).[78] Finally, the agreements include

---

76 For developed country members: see TBT, art. 10; SPS, art. 7 and Annex B; TRIPs, art. 63; GATS, art. 3.
77 SPS, Annex B; TBT, art. 2.9; GATS, art. 3.3.
78 The SPS is less stringent, for example in its criteria for Control, Inspection and Approval procedures (Annex C); in particular, where an importing country prohibits importation of foods with non-approved additives, it is merely urged to 'consider the use of a relevant international standard as the basis for access until a final determination is made'. Similarly,

some obligations for mutual recognition of procedures and standards, and encourage the negotiation of bilateral or plurilateral agreements to facilitate this, under the supervision of the relevant WTO Committee.[79] Based on and going beyond these formal obligations, many of the WTO Committees provide a forum for presentations and discussions about recent regulatory developments in their fields. These frequently also involve representatives from other organizations responsible for those fields, such as food safety, technical standards or IP.

Thus, the WTO has become a key focus of extensive processes of re-regulation of global economic activity, often referred to as 'regulatory reform' (OECD 1994b). No one who has any sort of direct experience of how public bodies operate can doubt that regulatory reform is very desirable. Many bureaucratic restrictions may be hard to justify, or could be greatly simplified. However, domination of this process by the WTO creates some serious risks. As we have seen, the tendency of the WTO's market-access obligations is to treat regulatory differences as undesirable obstacles. Thus, its 'disciplines' or regulatory reform obligations (Kawamoto 1999; Weiler 2000) tend to require the removal of existing national state regulations, and create significant constraints for states' national regulatory processes. This seemed desirable from the 1980s neo-liberal perspective, which preferred no regulation and 'free markets' to a world where national states retained the autonomy to set their own standards. It became much less so after the mid-1990s in the era of the post-Washington Consensus (Drache 2000), with the growing recognition that stable markets require firm normative foundations, to ensure the security, safety and trust on which economic production and exchange depend. The 2007–8 financial crash finally sounded the death knell of deregulated markets, but the question of how to reconcile highly integrated world markets with effective and internationally coordinated regulation is far from resolved.

As we have seen in the previous section, the reconciliation of WTO disciplines with the demands for regulation creates a pressure for states to adopt globally approved regulations. However, a one-size-fits-all approach is often undesirable and impossible. Developing countries have been particularly wary of the possibility that WTO rules could become a

---

scientific risk assessment procedures which a state must use under SPS, art. 5 are to be designed 'taking into account' risk assessment techniques adopted by the relevant international organizations (5.1).

79 SPS, art.4; TBT, art.6; GATS, art. VII.

Trojan horse requiring the importation of a wide range of global regulatory standards. Thus, the challenge for the WTO as a global governance node is to find a framework for re-regulation that can strike a balance between global minimum standards and those appropriate to the diversity of local needs, conditions and values.

The deliberations of the WTO Committees can provide a means of debating how such a balance can be struck. They may provide a forum for interchange and learning about approaches to regulation, increasing the understanding about the specificities of circumstances in different countries, and developing compatible or harmonious approaches rather than the straitjacket of uniformity. If so, they could help to prevent or defuse international economic disputes. There is some evidence that in practice they do so more successfully than the WTO's more highly visible and lauded system of adjudication.[80] However, they also have significant institutional limitations, especially the inherited predisposition of the WTO towards liberalization and deregulation. Also, like many institutions of global governance, their activities take place in a relatively closed and secretive space, with little public input or accountability, and dominated by technicist discourse. Even the activist civil society organizations which scrutinize and criticize much of the work of the WTO do not penetrate much into these secretive enclaves. Without such broader legitimacy, these processes of generation of normative consensus will rest on very shaky foundations.

8.3.2 Adjudication

Much of the power of the WTO derives from its exceptional, indeed unique, procedures for enforcement of its rules through adjudication of disputes between members. In addition, the political acceptability of compliance with the wide range of WTO obligations rests essentially on the legitimacy of the quasi-judicial form of the WTO's Dispute-Settlement procedure, and principally its Appellate Body (AB).

The AB hears appeals on points of law from decisions made by Panels on complaints by states under all the WTO agreements. Unlike the Panels, which are chosen ad hoc,[81] the AB is a standing institution composed of

---

80 This argument is convincingly made by Robert Wolfe, using the example of how import restrictions on beef from countries with 'mad cow' disease (BSE) have been removed quickly and consensually by such discussions rather than adjudication (2005b).

81 Citizens of the states party to the dispute may not serve as panellists unless those parties agree, so panellists have been mainly from smaller states, and their selection is inevitably

seven members appointed for a four-year term, renewable once.[82] The AB's decisions take the form of reports to the Dispute Settlement Body (DSB), which is composed of government representatives, and has the general responsibility for the Dispute-Settlement system. However, the major innovation under the WTO is that AB reports must automatically be adopted within thirty days, unless there is a consensus in the DSB against adoption (DSU, art. 17.14). Thus, the adjudications of the AB are regarded as binding unless there is a political consensus against, a reversal of the GATT rule which needed a positive decision to adopt DS reports by the state representatives (including the disputants), and hence gave governments a power to block adverse rulings. States are required to implement the decisions within a reasonable period, by bringing their domestic regulations into line. If they fail to do so, the complainant may request 'mutually acceptable compensation', in the absence of which it may request the authorization of the DSB for the suspension of concessions in relation to the recalcitrant state – in effect trade sanctions. This makes the AB unusual as an international body whose decisions are backed by significant powers to ensure implementation.

The WTO's system of adjudication in effect confers a power to review any national laws and regulations which another party complains are not compatible with the very extensive regulatory requirements of the WTO agreements. This raises important issues of both legitimacy and accountability. The AB's power to review the validity of national regulations allows it in effect to deny validity even to laws enacted by legislatures. The primary actors in international trade disputes are the executive branches of governments, who decide when to bring complaints against others and are responsible for defending those brought against

a politicized process, mainly centring on the nationality and background of the panellists and ensuring a geographic balance (Davey 2002); proposals for a permanent panel body were discussed in the March 2003 *Journal of International Economic Law*. Panel meetings are usually closed (although a few hearings have been open, with the agreement of the parties), and documents submitted to them are confidential. The names of the panellists are published when they are appointed but do not appear on the report itself, which is usually a joint one, minority opinions being very rare.

82 It is composed of seven 'persons of recognized authority, with demonstrated expertise in law [and] international trade . . . unaffiliated with any government', appointed by the DSB to ensure that it is 'broadly representative' of the WTO membership (DSU, art. 17). Each appeal is heard by a Division of three members, assigned by rote, so that a judge may be a national of a disputing party, indeed this often occurs, since the AB has always included nationals both of the USA and the EU, which have been parties to the majority of cases. See Steger 2002; Bacchus 2002.

themselves.[83] However, decisions of the AB are also indirectly addressed to the legislatures, since they must be persuaded to accept the overruling of national regulations found to be non-compliant, and to amend them as necessary.[84] The legitimacy of the adjudications is indeed crucial, since trade countermeasures are at best a blunt instrument, and certainly a last resort.[85] Beyond the legislatures, the AB's decisions need the legitimacy of acceptability to the various constituencies and the general public represented by the legislators.

83 In the WTO only states may bring complaints. This is significantly different from both EC law, which can directly be invoked in national courts by private persons, and investment treaties, which provide for arbitration of investor-state disputes (see Chapter 5).

84 The WTO Agreement, art. XVI.4, requires each Member State 'to ensure the conformity of its laws, regulations and administrative procedures with its [WTO] obligations'. However, WTO rules are not generally considered to be 'supranational', i.e. to have direct effect as national law. As a condition of US ratification, the Congress specifically provided in s. 102 of the Uruguay Agreements Act that 'no provision of any of the Uruguay Round Agreements, nor the application of any such provision to any person or circumstance, that is inconsistent with any law of the United States shall have effect'. This leaves it in the hands of the Congress to decide how, when, and indeed whether, to bring US law into line with WTO requirements, and this has proved problematic e.g. in relation to the tax treatment of Foreign Sales Corporations (see below). A similar approach has been taken in Europe and in Japan. The EU legislative process entails obtaining the agreement of the Member States through the Council, which proved difficult e.g. for the Bananas regime. This has led to a normative debate about whether a state is entitled to provide compensation rather than bring its laws into line: compare e.g. Sykes 2000 with Jackson 2004.

85 A strict timetable requires a Panel report to be made and adopted within a year, and an AB report within a further four months, although the complainant may agree to delay or suspension. Nevertheless, since remedies can be only prospective and do not compensate for lost trade, trade restrictions can be maintained with impunity while the disputes process runs its course, as seen e.g. with the measures introduced by the USA in March 2002 to protect its steel industry which were maintained for twenty months. Sanctions are also counter-productive in damaging trade, although governments try to ensure that the targets are carefully selected to ensure the direct damage is caused mainly to the other state's firms, this is often difficult given the extent of internationalization of business networks. The victims are likely to be sectors dominated by smaller firms, which may be less able to lobby legislatures to ensure repeal of the measures which resulted in the sanctions. An excellent historical account and analysis, with suggestions for reform, is provided by Charnovitz 2001. The DSU also allows cross-retaliation (i.e. sanctions against a different sector or even a different type of market) subject to specific conditions; developing countries have begun to use this by suspending rights under TRIPs in retaliation for violation of obligations under other agreements, since these could hurt developed countries more than trade sanctions. Such retaliation by Ecuador and Antigua was approved, but proposals made by Brazil in 2005 and renewed in 2008 to suspend TRIPs rights in retaliation for violations found in the US regime for cotton subsidies were more complex and controversial: see Abbott 2009: 9.

The legalism of the WTO interacts with a legalization of national trade policy. The USA led the way, by establishing procedures in the Trade Act of 1974 for US firms and industry associations to file petitions on which the USTR must act.[86] The European Commission followed the USA in introducing procedures encouraging EU business interests to bring complaints,[87] as part of the Market Access Strategy launched in 1996, aiming to take the offensive in response to the spate of WTO complaints launched by the USA. At the same time, this procedure gives the European Commission in handling complaints greater autonomy vis-à-vis the Member States, which otherwise must authorize Commission action through the 'article 133 Committee'.[88]

The shift to formalized adjudication in the WTO has further accelerated this trend in other leading trading countries, such as Japan (Pekkanen 2001; Iida 2006), and Brazil (Shaffer *et al.* 2008). The many millions of dollars at stake in WTO disputes has led to a boom in trade law expertise, which further feeds the legalization process. The dynamic varies in different national contexts, but generally legalization opens new avenues for trade interests and lobbies to influence trade policy, although they must do so by deploying arguments about rights to market access and couch complaints about unfair trade practices in the terms of WTO law. Even

---

86 Under s. 301(a), the USTR is *required* to take action if it finds a breach of a trade agreement or of 'the international legal rights of the US'; under s. 301(b) USTR has a *discretion* to act against acts or policies of a foreign state it finds to be 'unreasonable or discriminatory' and a burden or restriction on US commerce.

87 In 1984 the EC adopted its version of s. 301, the New Commercial Policy Instrument NCPI (Zoller 1985), which was replaced from 1995 by the Trade Barriers Regulation TBR (EC 3286/94) enacted as part of its UR implementation package. The European authorities point out that unlike s. 301, the TBR aims only at enforcing rights under international agreements, and does not allow actions which are unilateral or aimed at forcing new concessions (van Eeckhaute 1999: 200, fn. 4; see generally Shaffer 2003: 94–101).

88 Under art. 133 (formerly 113) of the EC Treaty, the Commission conducts international commercial negotiations under an authorization from the Council and in consultation with a special committee appointed by the Council; this now includes services and intellectual property, and the authority may be given by a qualified majority, except for topics in relation to which unanimity is required for the adoption of internal rules or where the Community has not yet adopted internal rules. The TBR procedure allows a firm (if supported by the Commission) to override political opposition by a blocking minority of Member States in the art. 133 Committee. Thus, a complaint by German aircraft manufacturer Dornier, against Brazil's export financing scheme as applied to aircraft, was brought under the TBR since after informal inquiries the Commission could see that there would be opposition in the art. 133 Committee from Member States with firms acting as suppliers to the Brazilian aircraft producers (van Eeckhaute 1999: 211). However, the Commission also channels through the art.133 procedure many of the cases resulting from representations made to it by firms or business associations.

the possibility of resort to WTO adjudication thus becomes a strategic move to be contested in the multilevel games of regulatory diplomacy.[89]

8.3.2.1 Emergence of adjudication

The establishment of the AB was the culmination of a long historical process. From provisions in the GATT to deal with disagreements about trade liberalization commitments, a procedure emerged for a form of resolution of issues that were considered best treated as technical or non-political matters of interpretation. When the GATT began to move beyond tariffs and quotas to dealing with market access problems caused by regulation (referred to as NTBs), the disputes became more complex but also potentially more politically contentious. This led to a further strengthening of autonomous adjudication as a means of resolving such conflicts, to deflect or disarm domestic constituencies hostile to liberalization.

The original GATT provisions for resolving disputes (which still remain part of the agreement within the WTO) grew from the trade negotiation context. They give a state the right to request consultations if it considers that there has been a 'nullification or impairment' of a benefit due to it under the agreement, or the attainment of an objective of the agreement is being impeded. This may result either from failure of another state to comply with an obligation, or even from adoption of a valid measure ('non-violation complaints').[90] If the parties concerned cannot resolve the matter, it may be referred to the organization, which should investigate it and make appropriate recommendations to them, or 'give a ruling'. If the

---

89 A good example is the conflict over the prohibition on imports of fur products from animals caught by leghold traps introduced by the EU in 1991, which affected several other states especially Canada; this did not result in a reference to the dispute-settlement procedure of either GATT or the WTO, although its legality was very much in question; for an account of the complex political moves and negotiations, which resulted in an international framework agreement linked to standards, see Princen 2002: ch. 3.

90 The origin of the Nullification and Impairment clause in the GATT, arts. XXII and XXIII appears to have been the Report of the London Monetary and Economic Conference of 1933, which recommended that trade agreements should include a general clause requiring consultation where a government action affects commerce; such clauses were backed in bilateral agreements by termination provisions. This made no real distinction between claims of breach of legal obligation and other claims; the view taken was that law was too blunt an instrument to deal with economic questions (Hudec 1975: 21). Although some delegates argued for a more legalistic procedure limited to violations of obligations, this was rejected, especially in the trade chapter of the Havana Charter, which was destined to become the GATT (Hudec 1975: 34–6). In practice all but a handful of complaints have concerned alleged violations, although the possibility of non-violation complaints is regarded as an important safeguard for parties' legitimate expectations and the general obligation of good faith compliance (Chua 1998; Cottier and Schefer 2000).

matter is considered sufficiently serious, the organization could authorize the suspension of concessions or obligations under the agreement.[91] These provisions could be seen as a formalization of the remedy in international law of countermeasures, available to any state if a treaty partner fails to comply with an obligation, to suspend or withdraw an equivalent benefit it had granted under that agreement. They can also be seen as necessary to maintain the balance of concessions and commitments made under a multilateral trade agreement, since such undertakings may have extensive and unpredictable effects.

The emergence of the GATT Panel procedure, as a quasi-legal form of adjudication, has been carefully chronicled by Robert Hudec (1975, 1993). In the very early Plenary sessions of the contracting parties, some complaints about trade restrictions took the form of a request for an interpretation of provisions in the agreement. Very quickly, matters unsuitable due to their complexity for a ruling by the chair or a plenary debate were referred to working parties. Following the practice of trade negotiators, the aim was an accommodation between the disputants, with the help of neutrals. Where an agreed solution could not be reached, the views of the neutral parties would obviously carry most weight with the plenary, and a key report as early as 1950 was written essentially as an adjudication by the neutrals (Hudec 1975: 70). At the seventh plenary in 1952 there were as many as a dozen complaints on the agenda. These were referred to a single working party, described as a Panel. Assisted by the secretariat, new procedures were developed, in which the disputants presented their arguments to the Panel, which then took its decisions and drafted its report in private; the report was then discussed separately with the disputants before being finalized, again in private.

In 1955 the procedure was formalized, on the basis of a Secretariat report, which distinguished between Panels and Working Parties, stressing in particular that Panel members were appointed as individual experts, since their role should be 'to prepare an objective analysis . . . in which the special interests of individual governments are subordinated to the basic objective of applying the Agreement impartially and for the benefit of the contracting parties in general'.[92] Nevertheless, it was decided to limit the Panel procedure to specific bilateral disputes, rejecting the Secretariat's

---

91 The party against which such action is taken is given the right to withdraw from the GATT, subject to sixty days' notice.

92 'Considerations Concerning Extended Use of Panels', Note by the Executive Secretary, GATT L/392/Rev1, 6 October 1955, at para. 5; reproduced in Hudec 1975: 297.

suggestion that more general matters, such as consultations with states over their use of balance-of-payments waivers also might benefit from an 'objective and technical consideration of the issues involved' before a plenary decision. Delegates produced various objections, notably the view expressed by the French representative that the Panel report procedure should be used only for 'technical' and not 'political' matters (Hudec 1975: 359, fn. 23).

Thus, although the emergence of the Panel procedure was clearly important, it was kept within limited bounds.[93] Hudec, a long-term enthusiast for legal adjudication in the GATT, sees these Panels as embryonic: 'Legal rulings were drafted with an elusive diplomatic vagueness. They often expressed an intuitive sort of law based on shared experiences and unspoken assumptions. Because of policy cohesion within this community, the rate of compliance with these rather vague legal rulings was rather high' (1993: 12). In only one case in that period was a Panel report effectively rejected by the Plenary.[94] Further, there was a clear reluctance to characterize these procedures as a legal adjudication. Although the head of the GATT Secretariat, Sir Eric Wyndham White, was himself a lawyer, it appears he strongly opposed the creation of a legal section.[95] Significantly, the Panel procedure was not used for several years following the initial phase, from 1963 to 1970.

A new impetus was created by the widening of the agenda for liberalization, especially as the USA needed to open up new foreign markets, and to deal with the political ramifications as congressional support for free trade became dependent on ending what were regarded as unfair trade practices. Even the EC, which had taken a strong anti-legalist stance in the 1960s, had in 1972 initiated a GATT complaint against the DISC (Domestic International Sales Corporation), a form of tax exemption for export sales introduced in 1971, which the EC attacked as an export subsidy. The dispute ran for twelve years, until the Congress replaced the DISC with the Foreign Sales Corporation (FSC) (Hudec 1993: ch. 5). This

---

93 Hudec's comprehensive survey identifies 53 matters raised in the GATT between 1948 and 1959 which he classifies as legal; of these, some 20 were dealt with by reference to adjudicative working parties or panels.

94 See Hudec's Synopsis of Complaints (1975: 417ff.), and the more detailed discussion of the early cases in 1975. The report which was rejected had found that Greece's new *ad valorem* tariff rate for LP records violated its bound tariff on phonograph records even though this had been a duty based on weight; others, especially developing countries, supported Greece, and an *ad valorem* tariff rate was eventually agreed (Hudec 1993: 439).

95 This did not occur until 1981, fourteen years after his retirement (Hudec 1993: 137–8).

dispute brought the Panel procedure to new legal–diplomatic heights, as the US case was managed by the Treasury Department's General Counsel's office, which brought a counter-claim against three European states, and insisted that the claims be heard by a single Panel, including a tax expert. These tactics partly succeeded, in that the GATT Panel balanced its finding against the USA with a rather elliptically worded ruling against the European measures also. Probably intended to secure adoption of the report by consensus, this backfired, since most governments supported the Europeans, and disagreed with the Panel on this point (Hudec 1993: 82–3). The stalemate was only eventually resolved by a compromise under which the reports were accepted subject to an ambiguous 'understanding' (Hudec 1993: 91–2), which simply sowed the seed for a subsequent renewal of the dispute.[96]

The new growth of complaints in the 1980s, which continued during the Uruguay Round negotiations, increasingly concerned NTBs and other 'unfair' trade practices.[97] These raised the issue of 'linkages' between the GATT trade regime and other regulatory arrangements, including intellectual property (IP) rights,[98] consumer protection and food safety regulation,[99] and most notoriously, environmental protection measures, which were threatened by the two Panel rulings in complaints initiated in 1990 and 1992 against the US prohibition of sales of tuna caught by methods which endangered dolphins. It became increasingly difficult to find solutions to such disputes within the GATT framework, especially as the Panels interpreted restrictively the provisions for exceptions in article XX. This was expressed in the conclusions of the Report of the Panel in

---

96 The FSC, as well as another revised version, were again successfully challenged by the EU in the WTO (Lubkin 2002), resulting eventually in an authorization to suspend an unprecedented $5bn worth of trade concessions; although the Congress could not promptly agree acceptable modifications of the corporate tax regime that would be WTO consistent, only in November 2003 did the EU begin to initiate countermeasures.

97 Twenty-seven were filed in 1980 to 1982 (Hudec 1993: 139). In 1981 the new DG, Arthur Dunkel, had appointed a Director of Legal Affairs, and by 1983 there was a three-person legal office. Hudec calculated that of the complaints brought under the GATT, about half concerned NTBs and a further quarter other kinds of 'unfair' trade practices (subsidies and antidumping measures), 75% in total; the combined proportion rose to 86% in the 1980s (1993: 338).

98 A 1987 EC complaint against US procedures for seizing IP-infringing goods (renewing a Canadian complaint of 1981), and a 1988 complaint by Brazil against US s. 301 trade measures attacking Brazil's local working requirements for patents.

99 Notably, the US complaints in 1987 against EC prohibitions of meat imports, in relation to slaughterhouse standards, and then against hormone-treated beef; and in 1989 against Thailand's taxation of cigarettes, discussed above.

the first Tuna–Dolphin dispute, although in typically coded language. It considered that permitting the USA to apply its regulations to imported tuna would mean that the GATT 'would then no longer constitute a multilateral framework for trade . . . but would provide legal security only in respect of trade between a limited number of [states] with identical internal regulations'.[100] The Panel suggested that if the GATT were to permit trade restrictions for the purposes of environmental protection, it would have to develop more detailed rules to that end.[101]

The special importance of a quasi-legal adjudicative procedure for dealing with the wide range of regulatory measures having a trade impact was shown by the outcome of the Tokyo Round. This resulted in a formalization of the adjudication procedures in an Understanding on Dispute Settlement, which made more palatable to the Congress the Codes governing specific aspects of trade regulation, presented as 'valuable *new rights* obtained in the negotiations' (Hudec 1993: 55). Yet the US policy was rather contradictory: while the US administration blocked the setting up of a Panel or adoption of the report in several complaints against the USA, it also became more active in threatening or applying trade sanctions under s. 301 of the Trade Act against others who showed a similar reluctance to respond to US complaints (Hudec 1993: 222ff.). Significantly, the 1988 legislation authorizing US participation in the Uruguay Round negotiations also greatly expanded s. 301, requiring the USTR to conduct systematic country reviews of market-access barriers, and to take action against those found to violate US 'rights'. Paradoxically, therefore, the growing concern in other countries about US unilateralism also generated support for the US negotiating position in the Uruguay Round pressing for a strengthening of adjudication. A key factor in persuading states to accept automaticity in the WTO's DS procedure was the concern of states to curb the use of s. 301,[102] which in turn rested on the ability of the US administration to convince the Congress that the Uruguay Round

---

100 *US – Tuna* (1991): para. 5.27. Note that this Panel was deliberating during the crucial period of the UR negotiations in 1991 (Stewart 1991: 2786–93).

101 *US – Tuna* (1991): para. 6.3. The failure to do so, except for a brief mention of the 'objective of sustainable development' and protection of the environment in the preamble to the WTO Agreement, meant that, not surprisingly, the issues raised in the Tuna–Dolphin dispute resurfaced under the WTO with slight differences in the Shrimp–Turtle case.

102 The provisions remain on the statute book, despite a complaint by the EC: the Panel decided that they do not of themselves violate WTO rules, accepting US undertakings that they would only be used in compliance with WTO procedures where appropriate (*US – Sections 301–310 of the Trade Act* (1999)).

agreements embodied principles of fairness, not only in their substantive market-access rules, but crucially also in their DS procedures. Hence, the two most important features, the creation of the AB and the requirement for automatic adoption of reports, were related, since governments were reluctant to agree automatic adoption without some form of appeal.

Despite the major changes to the DS system in the WTO, it still remains a hybrid of trade diplomacy and legal adjudication. In the WTO, governments decide which matters to refer to adjudication, although as pointed out above this may be influenced by private lobbying or institutionalized domestic procedures for identifying cases. Even so, the timing and handling of cases remains in the hands of governments, which may prefer diplomacy.[103] For example, the USA, Canada and Argentina did not make a formal WTO complaint about the EU regulation of genetically modified (GM) products until May 2003, although their concerns had been expressed both within the WTO and elsewhere for some years. Similarly, issues such as agricultural subsidies and bilateral PTAs have not been challenged, even though they are damaging to the WTO as an institution, which perhaps indicates the dangers of tolerating measures which fall into legal grey areas. Many matters are dealt with without any complaint being made, and many complaints are resolved by negotiation or not pursued to a Panel decision, so that WTO 'cases' are only the visible tip of a much larger iceberg (Yi 2004; Wolfe 2005b).

As with any system of adjudication, an important test of its efficacy is whether its rulings assist parties in resolving potential disputes without resort to adjudication, which is extremely difficult to evaluate (Iida 2006). Karen Alter has provided some anecdotal evidence that the availability of adjudication may have made it easier for states to persuade others to comply with their obligations simply by threatening recourse to the procedure (Alter 2003: 785–6), but she has also cogently argued that the creation of a formalized dispute-settlement system has in some ways exacerbated conflict by allowing conflictual cases to escalate (2003: 788–91). Equally, a government may withdraw a measure in the face of a complaint by a powerful trading partner regardless of its validity. However, the merit of

---

103 DSU, art. 3.7 urges that before bringing a case a member should 'exercise its judgment as to whether action under these procedures would be fruitful', and that the preference should be for 'a solution mutually acceptable to the parties to the dispute and consistent with the covered agreements'. Although there is provision for consultations as well as mediation after a complaint has been initiated, these depend on the complainant, which can insist that the procedure follow the timetable.

the rules-based system is said to be that it gives some protection to weaker parties.

8.3.2.2 Independence, accountability and formalism

The AB is widely considered to have been a great success, establishing a reputation for independence and integrity in its decision-making (Esserman and Howse 2003), cemented by its collegiality and consensual approach (Ehlermann 2002, 2003). The AB's decisions are adjudications, although also still rooted in GATT diplomacy. Thus, they are described as 'reports' not judgments, and most of them continue the GATT practice of summarizing at great length the arguments of the parties before reaching the key section giving the analysis and decisions of the AB itself. Their inordinate length and legalistic style makes them impenetrable except to the determined specialist. Their tone is juridical, especially in the approach adopted towards the central task of interpretation of the WTO agreements. The AB has been mindful that under the agreements its role is 'to provide security and predictability to the multilateral trading system' by clarifying the rules, and that only the WTO's political bodies are empowered to provide interpretations of them.[104] Thus, in an early decision the AB stressed that WTO adjudications are binding only in the particular case. However, it was also careful to state that adopted reports 'form part of the GATT *acquis*'[105] since they 'create legitimate expectations among WTO Members', and so should be 'taken into account' in other disputes where they are relevant.[106] In practice, the AB has set about establishing a coherent body of jurisprudence which lawyers have little difficulty recognizing as a system of precedent (Bhala 1999a, 1999b).

In fact, the power to adjudicate disputes about the meaning of the WTO agreements inevitably also entails the authority to interpret them, to the extent that the texts are indeterminate (Trachtman 1999). Most disputes that reach either a Panel or the AB, are likely to revolve around some textual indeterminacy, if only because there is little point pursuing a claim whose outcome is plain. In fact, although the WTO agreements are extensive and

---

104 DSU, art. 3.2 firmly states that 'rulings of the DSB cannot add to or diminish the rights and obligations provided in the covered agreements', while the WTO Agreement itself (art. IX.2) specifies that 'The Ministerial Conference and the General Council shall have the exclusive authority to adopt interpretations . . . of the . . . Agreements', which requires a 75 per cent majority of states; art. X provides for the adoption of amendments.

105 This is a term borrowed from EC law, meaning the accumulated rights and obligations of states under the agreements and their accepted interpretations.

106 *Japan – Alcohol* (1996): section E.

detailed, their provisions are endemically indeterminate. First, there is the inherent indeterminacy of liberal legal forms. Even as basic a matter as the allocation of a product to a tariff group may be debatable, as seen from an early decision in which the AB overturned a Panel's view that the EC was wrong to reclassify some types of computer equipment from 'automatic data processing' to 'telecommunications' equipment.[107] In addition to this, the WTO agreements also often express compromises adopted to paper over policy disagreements between the negotiators which remain to be resolved. It is significant that a substantial number of the early cases taken to the AB have involved issues dating back to the GATT and which were well known during the Uruguay Round negotiations, as mentioned in the previous section. Trade negotiators had every opportunity to resolve these long-running concerns in an unambiguous manner, and did not do so. Finally, the WTO rules embody abstract general principles for global meta-regulation, which must leave scope for interpretation to allow adaptation to specific issues and circumstances. Hence the great importance of basic concepts such as 'like products', and 'no more trade-restrictive than necessary'.

Indeed, the general structure of the WTO agreements often entails the evaluation of two or more interacting general rules. As we have seen, the structure of the GATT and the WTO agreements is that broad non-discrimination and market access principles are counterbalanced by various conditions and exceptions. The evaluation of the legality of a particular measure must consider whether it entails differential treatment of 'like' products or services, and if so whether it may be justified as no more trade restrictive than necessary to achieve a purpose accepted as valid in one of the exceptions. As Trachtman points out, 'Each step in this analysis has involved a good deal of creativity on the part of the dispute resolution panels and now the AB; in none of these cases is the language of the treaty regarded as determinate' (1999: 346). Further complexity and uncertainty is created by the interaction of WTO rules with those of other regimes, such as food safety or technical regulations established by international standards organizations. Hence, for example, the sharp conflict over the legality under trade law of regulation of GM foods has been said to be 'submerged in considerable ambiguity and . . . uncertainty' not only in the WTO agreements but also in the 'bewildering labyrinth of rules' which regulators must negotiate (Covelli and Hohots 2003: 774, 776).

---

107 *EC – Customs Classification* (1998); the AB's decision and its reasoning were in turn criticized by Trachtman (1998).

To avoid being accused of creative interpretation of the rules, the AB has stressed a literal approach to interpretation, while treading extremely carefully in this regulatory labyrinth. Basing itself on the rules of treaty interpretation in international law, it has emphasized that 'the words of the treaty form the foundation for the interpretive process'. It has relegated to a secondary factor any teleological interpretation by reference to the object and purpose of the treaties, which it says are to be considered only as part of the context 'also to be taken into account in determining the meaning'.[108] Emphasizing the importance of the words of the texts, it has frequently corrected the reasoning in Panel reports, although rarely altering the overall outcomes. This approach can be regarded as formalist, in that it seems to adopt an essentialist view of the meaning of words, and to assume that the law is a closed and self-referential system of rules. The AB prefers to avoid discussing the inevitable choices presented by the interpretation of texts in terms of their policy implications, although it does sometimes justify its interpretation in terms of the policy outcomes.

Nevertheless, the AB's decisions deploy this approach with some subtlety, supplementing its emphasis on the words of the texts with some reference to the more general objects and purposes of the agreements, which form the 'context'. This works best when there is a fairly clear textual basis for a preferred purposive interpretation. However, the suspicion that the textual analysis may in practice be used to justify a chosen policy outcome is supported by instances when a plain textual interpretation has been rejected. This can be illustrated by an examination of the reasoning in the AB's Report in the *EC – Hormones* case (1998). It first used a textual analysis to stress that the requirement in the SPS that national regulations should be 'based on' rather than 'conform to' international standards means that harmonization is 'a *goal* yet to be realised *in the future*'. But it went on to reject a textual analysis of SPS article 3.3, on the grounds of its 'involved and layered language', in order to decide that for regulations to have a 'scientific justification' they must be based on a proper risk assessment as laid down in article 5 (Picciotto 2005: 492–3). The outcome

---

108 *Japan – Alcohol* (1996): section D. Here, as in many other of its decisions, the AB has relied on the rules of treaty interpretation set out in arts. 31–32 of the Vienna Convention on the Law of Treaties (VCLT), following its mandate in art. 3.2 of the DSU to clarify the provisions of the WTO agreements 'in accordance with customary rules of interpretation of public international law'. This is nevertheless a restrictive view of the VCLT's provision that: 'A treaty shall be interpreted in good faith in accordance with the ordinary meaning to be given to the terms of the treaty in their context and in light of its object and purpose.'

was a politically astute decision, which found for the complainants, while giving the EC an opportunity to validate the measures by carrying out a scientific risk assessment.

This is a standard pattern: a violation has been found in some 85 per cent of decisions, but the AB often finds a way to suggest how the national measures might relatively easily be brought into line with WTO market-access obligations, to preserve some scope for the state's 'right to regulate'. Similarly, it has significantly relaxed the harshness of the 'necessity test' in interpreting GATT article XX (and GATS article XIV), stressing that it does not mean that measures must be 'indispensable' to their valid objectives, but there must be a 'weighing and balancing' of the relative importance of the objectives, against factors such as the contribution of the measures to achieving those objectives and their restrictive impact on trade.[109] These subtle and apparently textual interpretations have gone some way to introducing some 'policy space' for national regulation (Schloemann 2008).

Although the AB is clearly aware of the policy choices implicit in its interpretations, which have generally been very astute, it articulates its role as being to reveal and implement the intentions of the negotiators of the agreements through an analysis of the texts.[110] However, the policy implications are less easily concealed from insiders who have the ability to track the details and trends of decisions. Against the general approbation of the AB, it has also encountered some trenchant criticism. This has come especially from trade lawyers, particularly in the USA, who consider that the AB has been unduly restrictive in its interpretations of the 'trade remedies' permitted under WTO law (anti-dumping and countervailing duties and emergency safeguards). Indeed one went so far as to assert that 'the WTO dispute-settlement system has been far more an exercise in policy-making and far less an exercise in even-handed interpretation of the carefully negotiated language of WTO agreements' (Greenwald 2003:

---

109 In *Korea – Beef* (2000), *US – Gambling* (2005), and *Brazil – Tyres* (2007).
110 For an analysis which generally approves the AB's textual approach, see Lennard 2002. Its cautious view of interpretation has been reinforced by its procedural rulings aimed at guiding panels towards a more legalistic approach, on matters such as the burden of proof, the standing of parties and the principle of judicial economy (Steger 2002: 487). Its emphasis on this last principle has been explicitly justified by reference to its cautious view of the function of dispute settlement. In the AB's view, WTO adjudication is not meant to 'encourage either panels or the Appellate Body to "make law" by clarifying existing provisions of the WTO Agreement outside the context of resolving a particular dispute. A panel need only address those claims which must be addressed in order to resolve the matter in dispute' (*US – Wool shirts from India* (1997): 19).

113).[111] This critic suggests that the approval of the trade community for the AB derives from 'a sense that because the decisions, almost without exception, go against countries that maintain trade restraints, they make for good trade policy' (Greenwald 2003: 114).

A key policy issue is at stake here: the degree of leeway which can be given to governments in relation to their interpretations of what the WTO agreements allow, or in legal terms the 'standard of review' to be applied by the AB to national measures. The difficulty is that the DSU does not state any general standard of review; uniquely, however, the Anti-Dumping Agreement (article 17.6) does specify that a panel must uphold a decision by national authorities if it rests on a 'permissible' interpretation, even if that is not the panel's preferred one. This provision was included at the insistence of the US negotiators, but has effectively been neutralized by a refusal of Panels to find any interpretation other than their own to be 'permissible'. Thus, the trade remedy rules have been applied just as strictly as have other exceptions to the WTO's market-access obligations. This is an entirely understandable choice, as the main exponents of anti-dumping and safeguards measures are the large trading blocs, the EU and the USA, which resort to them in response to pressures from powerful domestic industry lobbies. Such measures are generally deprecated in the trade community, and even the government authorities responsible for defending them may not be sorry if the WTO takes the responsibility for invalidating them. Furthermore, if decisions of national authorities were accorded the degree of deference in anti-dumping cases suggested by article 17.6, there could be pressures to interpret the other exceptions equally broadly. Such a more deferential or permissive approach to national measures restricting trade would be politically damaging to the WTO's Dispute-Settlement procedures, at least in the trade community.

Nevertheless, the AB has to some extent been caught in its own trap, since its emphasis on formalist interpretation hinders it from justifying its strict approach to trade remedies explicitly in policy terms. Its dilemma illustrates a more general disadvantage to the adoption of a mechanistic and closed approach to the interpretation of legal provisions in international agreements. An important merit of delegating the interpretation of legal obligations on a case-by-case basis to an adjudicative body is to introduce a necessary flexibility which allows incremental adaptation. Otherwise, it has been pointed out that legalization which takes the form

---

111 See also Tarullo 2002; and contra see Davey 2001; Ehlermann 2003; Esserman and Howse 2003 offer a balanced view.

of locking states in to detailed and rigid obligations may have a range of negative effects, making it harder to manage the social and political impact of trade agreements, and facilitating mobilization by powerful domestic lobbies to deter liberalization concessions, secure favourable wording, and put pressure on governments to insist on a strict application (Goldstein and Martin 2000).

The AB's caution is also due to its uncertainty about its accountability, expressed as a concern to avoid accusations that it has exceeded its mandate through judicial activism. In this respect it has been contrasted with the jurisprudence of the European Court of Justice, which 'often show a confidence and a willingness to take an activist approach (often to deal with an impasse at the EU political level) [which] demonstrates the difference between the ECJ's broad "constitution" and the more narrowly confined one of the Appellate Body' (Lennard 2002: 44). The importance to the WTO as a whole that the decisions of the DS system should be widely accepted as legitimate suggests further moves towards its juridification. Certainly, commentators have suggested reforms which would turn it into a full-blown Court, with standing Panels acting essentially as courts of first instance, hearings in public, and open acceptance of submissions by non-governmental organizations.[112] Significantly, however, the proposals put forward by governments have been much more modest.[113]

A shift towards greater procedural juridification would extend the accountability of the DS system beyond governments, and could encourage the AB to address its decisions more overtly to a broader public. This would entail a much more explicit articulation of the values underlying the WTO, and in particular the interaction of its market-opening liberalization principles with regulations embodying socially constructed preferences such as health and environmental protection. This has certainly been advocated by some (Bronckers 2001; Alter 2003). Others have taken a different tack, and have advocated the 'constitutionalization' of the WTO based on individual human rights (discussed in the next section).

---

112 See e.g. Weiler 2001; Davey 2003. The AB has taken a cautious step towards this last, by stating that such *amicus curiae* briefs may be accepted if they are 'pertinent and useful' (*EC – Sardines* (2002): para. 160). This met with hostility from many governments, and it was stressed in the DSB that the AB should not adopt any changes to its working procedures without consulting the DSB (DSB Minutes of 24 July 2000, WT/DSB/M/84: para. 86). The AB has diplomatically said in most cases that it has not taken such briefs into account as they have not been helpful.
113 See Report by the DSB Chairman to the Trade Negotiations Committee 6 June 2003 (TN/DS/9).

Thus, the AB is caught on the horns of an institutional dilemma. It feels restrained from expressing in more open terms the policy considerations which underpin its interpretations, for fear of usurping the political legitimacy of the governments to which it is primarily accountable. They in turn are motivated by a reluctance not so much to concede power as to admit to their domestic constituencies how much power has already been transferred to supranational instances such as the AB. Until the political system faces up to this, it will be difficult for global governance institutions such as the AB to develop in ways that are more directly accountable to a global public, and hence to contribute to new forms of democratic deliberation appropriate for multilevel governance (Picciotto 2001; Joerges and Neyer 2003).

8.3.3 Constitutionalization and human rights

The very wide scope of the WTO agreements and the power of its DS system mean that the AB is indeed an international economic court in all but name (Weiler 2001). This opens the possibility that the AB might follow the trail blazed by the European Court of Justice, which played a transformative role by developing doctrines such as supremacy and direct effect of European law, to help to reconfigure the EU as more than merely an international organization (Stein 1981; Weiler 1991). There are nevertheless significant limitations on the role a judicial body can play in this respect. These limitations are even clearer for the AB, which has been kept on a very tight leash by the WTO's Member States, as well as lacking the channels for networking with national judiciaries which have been an important element of the ECJ's relative success (Helfer and Slaughter 1997).

Nevertheless, a basis exists for the AB to seek to enhance both its own and the WTO's legitimacy by the incorporation of human rights norms. This would enable it to respond to criticisms that economic liberalization, as embodied in WTO principles, undermines human rights. Institutional initiatives have come from the UN High Commissioner for Human Rights (UNHCHR) and the UN Commission on Human Rights, who have produced a series of reports both on the general theme of the impact on human rights of globalization and on the effects of specific aspects of the WTO agreements, notably of the agreements on agriculture, intellectual property (TRIPs) and services.[114] Although these exercises seem to have

---

114 See UN Commission on Human Rights 2000, 2004; UN High Commissioner for Human Rights 2001, 2002a, 2002b, 2003, 2004a, 2004b.

been viewed initially with some suspicion and concern by the trade community, it seems that, as they have proceeded, some fruitful interchange of views has developed between the human rights and trade perspectives.[115]

8.3.3.1 WTO and the coherence of international law

A legal route is available for the AB itself to assert that WTO obligations should be interpreted in line with obligations under international law, including human rights principles. Pauwelyn expresses the view of international lawyers, which he concedes may have come as a surprise to some trade negotiators, that the WTO agreements form part of international law which contains many other treaty obligations as well as general rules which are also binding on states, and that WTO rules must be accommodated in some way to that general body of law (2001). Indeed, the AB has often stressed that the direction in the DSU (article 3.2) to clarify the WTO agreements 'in accordance with the customary rules of interpretation of public international law' requires it to apply the principles of the Vienna Convention on the Law of Treaties (VCLT), which include 'any relevant rules of international law applicable in the relations between the parties' as relevant context for treaty interpretation; and in *US – Gasoline*

---

115 The preliminary report submitted to the UN Sub-Commission on the Promotion and Protection of Human Rights in June 2000 by J. Oloka-Onyango and Deepika Udagama provoked a letter of complaint from the WTO to the High Commissioner for Human Rights in August 2000 (reported in Singh 2000). The objection was in particular to a reference to the WTO as a 'nightmare' for human rights, in the following context:

> WTO has been described as the 'practical manifestation of globalization in its trade and commercial aspects'. A closer examination of the organization will reveal that while trade and commerce are indeed its principle focus, the organization has extended its purview to encompass additional areas beyond what could justifiably be described as within its mandate. Furthermore, even its purely trade and commerce activities have serious human rights implications. This is compounded by the fact that the founding instruments of WTO make scant (indeed only oblique) reference to the principles of human rights. The net result is that for certain sectors of humanity – particularly the developing countries of the South – the WTO is a veritable nightmare. The fact that women were largely excluded from the WTO decision-making structures, and that the rules evolved by WTO are largely gender-insensitive, means that women as a group stand to gain little from this organization.

> (UN Commission on Human Rights 2000: para. 15)

This document was referred to in the WTO as the 'nightmare' report (Marceau 2002). Subsequent reports used more diplomatic language, e.g. the report of the Mission to the WTO in July–August 2003 of the Special Rapporteur for the UN Commission on Human Rights on the right to health (UN Commission on Human Rights 2004: Addendum 1), refers to constructive, helpful and informative discussions (paras. 4–5).

(1996): sec. IIIB it said that this 'reflected a measure of recognition that the General Agreement is not to be read in clinical isolation from public international law'.

This seems to chime with the suggestion in the International Law Commission's report on the Fragmentation of International Law (ILC 2006), that the VCLT requires interpretation of treaty obligations such as WTO rules as far as possible in such a way as to further the 'objective of "systemic integration"' (2006: para. 17). Since many human rights principles are recognized as obligations in general international law, and WTO Member States are all parties to the UN Charter, and many of them to specific human rights conventions, the legal route lies open for the AB to assert that WTO obligations should be interpreted in line with obligations under international law, including human rights principles.

Nevertheless, WTO adjudicators have been selective and cautious in their consideration of other international legal rules. First, a complaint under the Dispute-Settlement procedure must be based on a breach of WTO rules and, under the formalist approach, other rules can be applied only if they are raised, which would normally be by the defendant state. It has therefore been argued that, since no state has yet invoked human rights obligations in a dispute under the WTO, there is no incompatibility (Lim 2001: 284). Even when a party does invoke non-WTO rules, there is considerable scope for an adjudicator to decide what weight to give them. The AB itself has referred to other international legal principles at least as an aid to interpretation, for example in *US – Shrimp* it referred to the UN Convention on the Law of the Sea, as well as the CITES, to help to interpret the term 'exhaustible natural resources'.

On the other hand, both the AB and Panels have been much more cautious about the relevance of other international legal obligations if they are seen as introducing a different perspective from, or might be conflicting with, WTO rules. There is an instructive contrast between the attitude of the Panel in *Mexico – Telecoms*, which was willing to use ITU regulations to 'give precision' to the term 'cost-oriented', since both parties to the dispute as well as most (but not all) WTO members are also members of the ITU, and the Panel in *EC – Biotech*, which took the restrictive view that a provision in a related international treaty need not be taken into account unless *all* WTO members are party to that treaty. The AB itself was notably cautious in responding to the argument by the EC in *EC – Hormones* (1998) for the application of the 'precautionary principle' to food safety rules, on the grounds that: (a) opinions differ as to whether the principle is accepted as binding in international law;

(b) that it would therefore be 'unnecessary, and probably imprudent . . . to take a position on this important, but abstract, question'; and that in any case (c) the principle is reflected in WTO rules.[116] Its preference is clearly for a strict approach which assumes that rules are compatible unless it is impossible to comply with both. Thus, it has defined a conflict as 'a situation where adherence to one provision will lead to a violation of the other provision'.[117]

Even if a conflict were to be found, there is considerable room for debate on how it should be resolved under the various accepted treaty interpretation principles. In particular, the principle *lex specialis derogat legi generali* (priority should be given to a specific rather than more general rules) is likely to lead to the view that WTO trade rules cannot be overridden by general human rights obligations (unless, of course, the latter are considered fundamental principles of *jus cogens*). Even authors who consider that the AB should apply non-WTO rules where relevant tend to accept that in case of a conflict the WTO rules should prevail (Bartels 2001).[118] Indeed, in *Brazil – Tyres* (2007), the AB found that the partial exemption for MERCOSUR countries from Brazil's ban on imports of retreaded tyres, which was introduced as a result of a ruling by the MERCOSUR Court, was in violation of WTO law.

Thus, the general approach has been to view the WTO legal system as a self-contained *lex specialis* (Marceau 2002: 32ff.). However, it is also pointed out that 'if the WTO system is self-contained, it is not entirely self-contained' (Palmeter and Mavroidis 1998: 413), in particular that WTO rules may themselves refer to or incorporate other international law rules (Trachtman 1999: 343). Such provisions in effect make the WTO's DSS an

---

116 *EC – Hormones* (1998): para 123, which focused mainly on the SPS agreement. Not surprisingly, the Panel report in *EC Biotech – Products* (2006) followed this view (para. 7.89).

117 *Guatemala – Cement* (1998): para. 65, cited by Pauwelyn (2001: 551), who points out that this approach means that a state may be unable to exercise a right created under international law subsequent to the WTO agreements.

118 Bartels bases this on treating arts. 3.2 and 19.2 of the DSU as a 'conflicts' rule, since they specify that DS decisions cannot add to or diminish rights or obligations of WTO members, Panels and the AB must apply the WTO rule in case of a conflict. Marceau (2002) does not agree with this reasoning but comes to the same conclusion. Pauwelyn (in my view rightly) says that these provisions actually aim at reining in the DSS from expansive or adventurous interpretations of WTO trade rules, but provides only a very egregious example of a situation in which a Panel might be obliged to find a WTO rule invalid, namely if the WTO were to conclude a slave-trading agreement (2001: 564).

enforcement mechanism also for these other areas of international law.[119] The 'partly self-contained' view of the WTO means that it is a matter for each state to ensure compatibility of WTO rules with its international obligations, such as human rights norms, which are not specifically incorporated into the WTO agreements. 'States, members of the WTO, remain fully bound and responsible for any violation of their international law obligations but they cannot use the WTO remedial machinery to enforce them' (Marceau 2002: 34). Furthermore, the WTO is considered to be no more than a forum for states, with no executive powers, unlike the IMF and World Bank, so that neither the organization itself nor its secretariat can have any direct obligations to ensure compatibility of its work with human rights obligations (Lim 2001: 280).

This approach suggests a modest role for WTO rules and their enforcement, but the effect is in fact quite the opposite. It reinforces the power of the WTO's unique compliance mechanisms, by comparison with which other systems, such as those of international human rights instruments, must be described as weak. They rely mainly on self-reporting by states and scrutiny by committees of experts. Some (notably the International Covenant on Civil and Political Rights) also provide options for states to allow complaints by other states, as well as individual petitions, and other mechanisms such as fact-finding missions have also been developed. Crucially, however, compliance depends on 'naming and shaming', and lacks the hard economic impact of the WTO's ultimate sanction of withdrawal of trade advantages. These are the potential attractions of a more formalized inclusion of human rights principles within the WTO framework, which are effectively denied by treating WTO law in an apparently modest way as a *lex specialis*.

8.3.3.2 Formalizing a rights-based constitution?

Some have, therefore, argued for the formal incorporation of human rights principles into WTO law. From the academic perspective the most fervent advocate of the complementarity of these two approaches has been Ernst-Ulrich Petersmann, who has for some years and in many repeated writings proposed a combination of trade and human rights from a

---

119 Thus the AB has ruled on whether food-labelling regulations complied with a Codex standard (*EC – Sardines* (2002)), and a Panel has ruled on the validity of copyright exceptions under the 'three-step test' of the Berne Copyright Convention (*US – Copyright* (2000); see Chapter 9, at 9.3.2).

social-market perspective based on ordo-liberal theory.[120] This led to a memorably vehement clash with Philip Alston in the pages and on the website of the *European Journal of International Law*, in which Alston described Petersmann's approach as an attempt to 'hijack . . . international human rights law in a way which would fundamentally redefine its contours'.[121]

Formal incorporation would have the merit of resolving some of the uncertainties and difficulties of the present situation of a 'not entirely self-contained' WTO legal system. In particular, the explicit inclusion of human rights principles within the WTO would overcome a problem that judicialization would face, that adjudicators would have to apply only universally applicable human rights norms, or else generate non-uniform interpretations of WTO rules dependent on which human rights obligations are applicable between the parties to a particular dispute.[122] As Petersmann (2004: 607) points out, this is especially problematic as over thirty WTO members, including the USA, are not parties to the 1966 UN Covenant on Economic, Social and Cultural Rights.

Hence, Petersmann's project is to effectuate a substantive rapprochement between traditional human rights norms and the economic rights and liberties that he sees as central to the WTO:

> Just as UN human rights conventions do not refer to international division of labour, 'market freedoms', and property rights as essential conditions for creating the economic resources needed for the enjoyment of human rights,[123] so WTO law does not explicitly refer to respect and protection of

---

120 E.g. Petersmann 1993b, 1998, 2000, 2002a, 2002b, 2003, 2004, 2005. For a discussion of ordo-liberalism and its relation to classical liberalism, from a neo-liberal perspective, see Sally 1998.

121 Alston 2002: 816; the journal carried a rejoinder by Petersmann, and a longer and more acerbic exchange on its website which now seems to have been removed, although a similar sharp controversy surfaced in the journal's blog in 2008. This clash was followed by a project organized by the American Society of International Law and others, which resulted in two edited books (Cottier *et al.* 2005; Abbott *et al.* 2006); although Petersmann made substantial contributions in both, Alston was in neither one. He has continued to research and publish on economic and social aspects of human rights, although not on the interaction between human rights and trade law, see e.g. Alston and Robinson 2005.

122 Pauwelyn opts for the latter, conceding that it 'may complicate the matrix of rights and obligations between WTO members. But this is an unavoidable consequence of not having a centralised legislator in international law' (2001: 567).

123 'It is only in the context of the right to work (Article 6) that the Covenant on Economic, Social and Cultural Rights of 1966 refers to the need for government policies promoting "development and full and productive employment under conditions safeguarding fundamental political and economic freedoms to the individual" (Article 6.2).' [Footnote in the original.]

human rights as necessary means for realizing the WTO objectives of 'raising standards of living, ensuring full employment and a large and steadily growing volume of real income and effective demand, and expanding the production of and trade in goods and services' (WTO Preamble).

(2004: 607–8)

This clearly raises the question of *which* economic human rights should be recognized by the WTO, and *in what form*.

Human rights, as they have developed historically, have been most strongly articulated in the 'first generation' civil and political rights, while the 'second generation' economic, social and cultural rights are considered by many to be aspirations or at best goals for states to achieve; and 'third generation' collective rights such as self-determination and sustainable development are hard to operationalize as enforceable rights. Alston, in his critique of Petersmann, distinguishes between the 'instrumental' nature of the guarantees of economic liberties recognized by the WTO and the fuller 'political' character of rights as seen from the human rights perspective:

> [A]ny such rights arising out of WTO agreements are not, and should not be considered to be, analogous to human rights. Their purpose is fundamentally different. Human rights are recognised for all on the basis of the inherent human dignity of all persons. Trade-related rights are granted to individuals for instrumentalist reasons. Individuals are seen as objects rather than as holders of rights. They are empowered as economic agents for particular purposes and in order to promote a specific approach to economic policy, but not as political actors in the full sense and nor as the holders of a comprehensive and balanced set of individual rights. There is nothing per se wrong with such instrumentalism but it should not be confused with a human rights approach.
>
> (2002: 826)

In response, Petersmann accepts that the market rules governing trade are 'only instruments for promoting individual freedom as the ultimate goal of economic life and the most efficient means of realising general welfare' (2005: 34), and that human rights are based on the fundamental principles of human dignity and liberty, which are very different from the 'macroeconomic, state-centred conceptions of national income and "efficiency" cherished by many economists and WTO governments' (2005: 34).

Quite clearly, however, his view is that human rights provide a moral underpinning for market economies. This entails 'legal protection of individual freedom to participate in markets (e.g. as dialogues about values, decentralized information, coordination and discovery mechanisms) and to exchange the fruits of one's labour for scarce goods and services needed for personal development' (2005: 30–1). For him the key right is the right to property, which is recognized in classic human rights instruments such as the Universal Declaration of Human Rights of 1948, and he points out that it is complemented by the protection of intellectual property rights in the TRIPs agreement (Petersmann 2000: 21). As he suggests, a moral justification has been provided by liberal philosophers for this right in various ways: by Locke as moral entitlements to the fruits of labour, by Hegel as expressions of the will and personality of their owner, and by Raz as constituent elements of an autonomous life. Petersmann argues that the right to property includes the right to dispose, so these moral justifications also support 'private rights to supply or demand one's goods in private markets'; hence, markets can be 'justified not only on grounds of economic efficiency but also as preconditions for individual autonomy and for a free, informed and accountable society' (Petersmann 2000: 48–9).

The key difference between Petersmann and Alston seems to hinge not so much on the distinction between economic rights and human rights, as on that between individual and social rights. Alston specifically doubts whether Petersmann properly includes in his schema 'social' rights such as the rights to education, health care and food, which are rejected by fundamentalist liberal theorists of whom Petersmann approves, such as Hayek. These are very much economic matters, the question is whether they should be viewed as individual rights or socio-economic policies, and hence obligations on the state. Liberalism's emphasis on individual rights aims to protect individual freedoms from the potentially autocratic power of the state. Hence, the traditional human rights were civil and political rights. Their extension to individual economic rights in the same form could entrench liberal economic principles which assume that the pursuit of individual self-interest, especially through economic exchange, is ultimately beneficial to all. This could limit and constrain collective action or regulation through the state or public bodies. Petersmann indeed asserts that he considers economic and social rights equally as important as civil and political rights, a view which he contrasts with that held in the USA or the Anglo-Saxon world (2005: 69).

In contrast, the dominant perspective on social and economic rights in the contemporary human rights discourse views them as obligations *for the state* to 'respect, protect and fulfil'. Petersmann appears to accept the view put forward by the UN High Commissioner that this means that states may have *duties* to take action, whereas the WTO rules generally only refer to *rights* of states to regulate (2004: 615), and he concedes that this may entail the collective supply of public goods, and action to limit 'market failure' (2005: 64). However, for him state action is a fallback, and in his view human rights tends to prioritize liberty rights over rights to redistribution of resources (2005: 66). State action is likely to intrude on individual autonomy, especially if it entails collective provision or redistribution of resources. The priority which Petersmann gives to individual liberty, and his preference for property-based 'market' rights, would clearly restrict such state action. He nevertheless considers that his is a 'bottom-up' view of rights, which he contrasts to the 'top-down' perspective for example of Robert Howse, who has put forward some detailed proposals for shaping the WTO towards advancing the 'right to development' (2004).

In an earlier and seminal piece on the right to food, Alston criticized international law dealing with food issues as having remained 'hermetically sealed' from human rights considerations; he attributed this to the restrictive approach to international economic law which saw it as constraining rules aimed at permitting the free flow of commerce, while an equally restrictive approach to human rights law had been preoccupied with post-hoc responses to violations (Alston and Tomasevski 1984: 14–15). The recasted human rights discourses, to which Alston has notably contributed, do now emphasize the positive obligations of the state, but these are necessarily seen in terms of developing social programmes for economic development, rather than providing rights or guarantees directly to individuals. On the other hand, international economic law continues to be dominated by negative obligations on states, requiring them to remove obstacles to 'free movement' of economic factors, and these are more easily cast as individual rights (although WTO law does not yet, directly, take this form).

Indeed, neo-liberal constitutionalism aims to entrench internationally agreed principles to secure the 'effective judicial protection of the transnational exercise of individual rights' (Petersmann 1998: 26). It would enshrine economic rights such as the 'freedom to trade' as fundamental rights of individuals, legally enforceable through national constitutions in national courts (Petersmann 1993b). While accepting that freedom of trade should also be accompanied by other human rights, which should all be enshrined in the WTO 'constitution', Petersmann's emphasis is on rights of private property and market freedoms. However, he goes further and argues that liberal traders should welcome the inclusions of human rights protecting individual freedom, non-discrimination and equal opportunities, and that the mercantilist bias of WTO in favour of producers could be corrected by the protection of competition and of the rights of 'the general consumer and citizen interest in liberal trade and . . . human rights' (2000: 22).

The stress is on equality of rights, which appears to protect the weak. However, as classic critiques of liberalism argue, it tends to overlook the realities of inequalities of power. In human rights discourses, the non-discrimination principle may take account of inequalities by permitting positive discrimination or affirmative action, but this is an exception which is often contested. A similar tension would be created by inclusion of human rights in the WTO.[124] In practice, the rights which would be most firmly implanted in a WTO 'constitution' would be the market-access and private-property rights, and their entrenchment in a global treaty would benefit international traders and investors, i.e. mainly TNCs. The traditional civil and political rights were conceived as the rights of human beings, hence 'human' rights. Even economic rights when cast as human rights are commonly perceived as personal individual rights; hence the right to property finds broad acceptability as a right to *personal* property. However, economic development has resulted in ever more complex forms of institutionalization of socio-economic activity. Yet from the perspective of liberal capitalism, these are also 'private' property rights. This extends to all sorts of fantastical and fictitious forms of 'intangible' property rights, from shares in a company to today's complex financial derivatives, and the contradictory concept of intellectual property rights. All these could come to be protected under the concept of the human right to the protection of property. Furthermore, corporations may also be recognized as bearers of human rights; although this may come as a surprise to some human rights specialists (Walker 2006: 177), it is the position in the most highly developed system of human rights protection, the European Convention on Human Rights.[125]

Already, as we have seen in this chapter, the effect of institutionalization of the WTO is to constrain national policy choices by embedding

---

124 WTO law already recognizes an equivalent, in the principle of Special and Differential Treatment for developing countries, discussed above.

125 In particular the right to protection of property explicitly applies to 'every natural and legal person' (art. 1 of Protocol 1 of 1952); the European Court of Human Rights has also accepted that some of the other Convention rights extend to corporations, although comparatively few cases have actually been brought directly by companies (3.8 per cent of cases between 1998 and 2003: Emberland 2006: 14).

broad and stringent international obligations to liberalize international economic flows. This would be further reinforced by the strong vision of constitutionalization of the WTO, put forward especially by Petersmann, who considers that both national states and the WTO's rules and discourse are producer biased, and sees his proposals for entrenching human rights as a means of counter balancing this by representing general consumer and citizen interests (2005: 87). However, giving individuals, including 'investors' and corporations, rights which they could enforce directly, in national courts or through the WTO's DSS or both, would further constrain the possibilities of collective action through the state or public bodies, and operate to exacerbate economic inequalities by handing a powerful weapon to those whose economic power can be defended in terms of morally underpinned economic rights.

Other forms of recognition of human rights within the WTO could, of course, be envisaged. Most easily compatible with the original structure of the GATT as a type of 'embedded liberalism' (Ruggie 1982) would be to allow exceptions from trade liberalization obligations in favour of actions to protect and promote human rights. Pascal Lamy pointed to the exceptions allowed in GATT article XX, and seemed to suggest that these could be interpreted broadly, to the extent of saying that '[a]bsent protectionism, a WTO restriction based on non-WTO norms will trump WTO norms on market access' (2006: 981). However, he accepts that 'it will be for the WTO judge to determine the balance, the "line of equilibrium" between trade norms and norms of other legal orders' (Lamy 2006: 983).

This approach has been most thoroughly explored in the debate about the linkage between trade and labour rights, discussed above. It has of course been strongly criticized from the viewpoint of developing countries as a protectionist move by the rich (TWIN–SAL 1999). Some of the arguments have largely echoed trade liberalization perspectives, by suggesting that the comparative advantage of countries with low labour costs should not be undermined. However, from the human rights perspective the issue is not comparative wage rates, but violations of rights such as freedom of association and free collective bargaining. A more cogent criticism is that the GATT approach of allowing exceptions for types of state action recognized as being in the public interest would legitimate unilateral state action, and allow selective targeting of states considered to have inadequate protection of human rights. Inevitably, of course, such action is generally taken by economically powerful states, wishing to deny or control access to their markets to economically weaker states, sometimes using human rights violations as a pretext. Accusations of human rights violations have been used to justify trade and economic boycotts in the US actions against Burma/Myanmar and Cuba, which might have been found in violation of WTO rules had not an accommodation been reached (McCrudden 1999). Other methods which have been considered, which might help reinforce international labour standards by strengthening the role of the ILO through a linkage with the WTO (ILO 1994; Charnovitz 1995), have not been pursued, largely due to the strength of feeling about comparative advantage.[126]

Human rights could be recognized within the WTO in ways which might maintain the view of them as requiring the pursuit of socio-economic policies to achieve universal basic economic standards, simply by adding them as aims of the organization. The WTO Agreement currently expresses its broad aims as follows:

> relations in the field of trade and economic endeavour should be conducted with a view to raising standards of living, ensuring full employment and a large and steadily growing volume of real income and effective demand, and expanding the production of and trade in goods and services, while allowing for the optimal use of the world's resources in accordance with the objective of sustainable development, seeking both to protect and preserve the environment and to enhance the means for doing so in a manner consistent with their respective needs and concerns at different levels of economic development.

Although there is some recognition of social objectives, such as the pursuit of full employment and sustainable development, the statement essentially reflects the neoclassical economic assumptions underpinning trade liberalization, generally that 'a rising tide lifts all boats'. Inclusion of the achievement of basic socio-economic human rights such as food, water, shelter, health and education could inject concerns to ensure that policies should aim to achieve basic economic standards for all, rather than assuming that overall economic growth will automatically 'trickle down'. This could be strengthened by various institutional reforms which could

---

126 A Joint staff study of research on the impact of liberalization on employment concluded that no simple generalizations are possible and further research is needed, but broadly that globalization 'can be good for most workers in both industrialized and developing countries, provided the appropriate economic policies are in place. But it may not be good for all workers, and its distributional implications should not be ignored' (ILO and WTO 2007: 87).

'mainstream' into the WTO consideration of the impact of trade measures on human development (Howse 2004). Such a move might create space to debate the directions of trade and economic policies, going beyond the assumptions underpinning liberalization.[127]

8.3.3.3 Grand visions and technical details

It seems hard to sustain the view that there is a fundamental conflict between human rights norms and principles of economic liberalization as reflected in the WTO. Human rights had their origins in the liberal impulse of the Enlightenment, to expand the realm of individual freedoms against the autocratic state. However, the guarantee and protection of individual freedom in the economic sphere often tends to exacerbate social inequalities and undermine collective action through public bodies and states. Recognizing this, ideas and principles of human rights have undergone considerable development in the past half-century. Their formulation has evolved to a considerable extent towards articulating the protection of individuals within a perspective of social, cultural and economic rights, expressed as policy obligations on states.

However, human rights norms are still open to alternative, competing and conflicting interpretations. Issues which would be central to a meaningful debate about their application to economic regulation remain open, such as whether their subjects are individuals or social groups, human beings or legal persons (including corporations). Thus, the debate about the relationship of trade and human rights rules is as much a battle over human rights discourse as one over the shape of the world trade system. As we have seen in this chapter, trade rules are a combination of broad principles and more detailed regulation. Many of the WTO's general principles are couched in universalistic terms which appear to have much in common with basic human rights principles, notably non-discrimination. In addition, the WTO agreements include some general principles recognizing the need to take account of the social impact of economic liberalization, notably 'special and differential treatment' for developing countries, and the public interest objectives in the TRIPs, mentioned above. However, the general principles are usually expressed in such a way that they cannot be used to override the more specific provisions, except when formulated as exceptions permitting national state action. However, the strength of

127 This assumes that such changes would be politically feasible, which is doubtful. For a discussion of such debates, in relation to access to medicines, and the right to food, see Picciotto 2007b.

the WTO system depends on limiting and constraining such exceptions, since experience shows that they can be abused especially by the more powerful states, leading to a fragmentation of the trading regime.

Greater interaction between the trade and human rights viewpoints could have a variety of effects. One might be the (re)assimilation of human rights into the neo-liberal perspective of individual freedoms. As we have seen, that is the thrust of Petersmann's proposals for the integration of human rights into a 'constitutionalized' WTO. At the opposite pole, human rights discourses could be counterposed to the liberalization principles of the WTO, to challenge its underlying assumptions, and help provide a basis for radical alternative policies. A middle outcome might be that the introduction of human rights concerns could help temper the negative effects of liberalization by encouraging measures aimed at achieving basic standards of socio-economic provision. The outcomes of such interactions would also depend on the institutional form it takes. As shown above, the dominant view of the WTO's rule-based system is that it is and should remain largely self-contained from other areas of international law, including human rights. Paradoxically, however, this reinforces the power of the WTO as a node of global regulatory networks. On the other hand, inclusion of human rights norms within the WTO system might serve to strengthen the WTO's institutional legitimacy.

A major problem with many discussions of global economic governance is the wide gap between the clash of rhetoric and the cogency and constructiveness of detailed policy proposals and arguments. A significant drawback of the debates about economic liberalization and human rights is that they serve mainly to turn up the rhetorical decibel level, and contribute little to debates about specific issues of global economic governance. As Andrew Lang has argued, when trade rules are analysed from a human rights perspective, human rights norms do not provide either any new policy ideas or any means of choosing between existing policies, so that it is 'essentially illusory to think that we can derive or arbitrate, at least in any simple or direct way, alternative visions of the global trading order from human rights norms' (2007b: 87). More modestly, Lang suggests that injecting human rights arguments into trade policy discourse would help initiate reflection on its broader goals, which tend to become taken for granted within closed policy communities (2007b: 87), and indeed this has already occurred to some extent. It is less clear, however, given the widely disparate nature of alternative human rights visions, that the space this opens up would lead to advances in the evaluation of trade policies. In view of the strong correlations that exist between some versions of human rights and liberal trade policies in particular, the interaction could result in simply repeating the same debates in different language. The bigger threat, from the perspective of advocates of socio-economic human rights, is that any rapprochement of human rights and trade law would integrate the classical liberal antecedents of the former with the neo-liberal preoccupations of the latter.

9

Intellectual property rights

IPRs are a very peculiar institution. They are a grant by the state of exclusive rights over creations and inventions of the human mind, providing a monopoly to exploit intangible assets. The artificial scarcity created by state-enforced IPRs is in many ways inappropriate for knowledge-based assets, since they do not deplete when shared.[1] Indeed, both new technology and artistic and literary works provide the greatest social benefits by being used as widely as possible. Wide availability enhances both pleasure and profit, since diffusion also reduces the costs of further innovation. This is also true from the viewpoint of originators, who only rarely have an interest in concealing their creations. Originators also have other concerns, which can be protected in various ways, in particular in obtaining recognition for their contribution, and safeguarding the integrity of their works (sometimes referred to as 'moral' rights).

---

1 In economists' terms, they are non-rival. Private-property gives the right to exclude others from using an asset, commonly justified by the scarcity of natural resources. This is supported by a fetishized conception, based on the 'natural' characteristics of physical objects of property, which considers property as a thing, rather than a bundle of rights and obligations between people. This was starkly brought home to me when, in the course of an online debate on patents and biotechnology, an IP lawyer who had worked for a corporation engaged in genetic patenting said: 'Pharmaceutical companies do indeed wish to retain patent protection because of the control that it gives them. *It is their molecule* and they have the right to that control' (my emphasis). Property is better understood as a social institution, in particular because the right to exclude, which creates scarcity and hence rivalry, requires state action and support. This is especially so for IPRs, since they concern intangible objects; nevertheless, the fetishized conception carries over, reinforced by romantic notions of authorship (Boyle 1996). These romantic notions were most strongly embedded in the civil law systems of IP, especially the *droit d'auteur*, rooted in the natural rights perspectives originating in the Enlightenment. However, even in the more pragmatic common law systems the owner is considered to have an absolute right of dominion, while the rights of others are regarded as intrusive exceptions (Picciotto and Campbell 2003). Despite ideological differences, in instrumental terms systems have converged.

Economists have therefore always had difficulty finding adequate justifications for this state grant of monopoly rights.[2] The common rationale refers to the need for an economic incentive to encourage innovation. However, closer examination of the social and scientific, as well as economic, processes of innovation and creativity shows that many of the justifications for IPRs are weak at best (Macdonald 2002; Hope 2008: ch. 3). Human creativity has many and varied wellsprings, and is mainly a social rather than a solitary activity. But the main economic spur to innovation is the 'first-mover' advantage, which ensures a higher rate of profit for leading-edge firms until an innovation becomes generalized. This does not require the artificial creation of monopoly rights. Furthermore, successful innovation depends on collective interactions, often publicly funded or supported, taking place through an open circulation of ideas.

In fact, IPRs are generally exploited not by authors or inventors, whose creativity they are supposed to reward, but by large corporations. Such firms justify IPRs as necessary to allow them to recoup their investment in commercializing knowledge-based products which otherwise could be easily imitated by competitors. It is generally considered that IPRs should strike a balance between the rights of owners and limitations or exceptions to ensure the optimum social benefit from diffusion, to be determined by public welfare criteria. However, this perspective tends to overlook the primary question of the definition of the scope of the rights. The economic issue of the appropriate level of remuneration for investment in innovation is immediately biased when the rights are cast in terms of private property and the right to exclude. The private-property paradigm of IPRs is exacerbated by ideologies based on a romantic vision of individual authorship (Woodmansee 1984; Boyle 1996). The combination of potential economic rents and fervent defences of the 'natural' rights of creators and inventors have long made the process of legislating on IPRs subject to intensive lobbying by private interests. It is even more difficult to consider these issues in terms of global public welfare, given the very big differences in socio-economic conditions between countries.

These problems have become even more acute and more central in today's knowledge economy, which has further heightened the stark

---

2 Among the many discussions, see Plant 1934; Boyle 1996: ch. 4; Drahos 1999a; Boldrin and Levine 2002; Campbell and Picciotto 2006; Hope 2008: 68–74; and for an excellent critical history, May and Sell 2006.

paradox of IPRs. On the one hand, pressures from key industries of the new economy have resulted in an unprecedented strengthening of the private-property, exclusive-rights paradigm of IPRs, in particular with the establishment of a global minimum standard in the WTO's TRIPs agreement. At the same time, the centrality of IPRs in the knowledge economy has sparked conflicts over proprietary rights, and different models have emerged offering alternative possibilities, coalescing around forms of shared or common property. Although usually described as 'open source', they also often interact with forms of remuneration and benefit sharing through licensing. These have gathered momentum, posing their sharpest challenge to the private-property paradigm in some of the most advanced fields of the knowledge economy: biotechnology, computer software and the digital economy. Thus, IPRs have become a battleground of contending models for some of the key business sectors of the twenty-first century.

9.1 International development of IPRs

A frequent response to criticisms that IPRs are inappropriate for today's knowledge economy is that the problems posed are not new. Certainly, the argument that private property in intellectual products is incompatible with the interdependent and interactive nature of creative and intellectual work, was also central to the debates which accompanied the birth of IPRs in their modern form over two centuries ago.[3] Also, although IPRs were created by states which provided protection within their territory, the concepts and legal forms were spread internationally through emulation, and arrangements for their international protection were constructed by a relatively early date.

However, the early debates took place in a context where technological and social change had broken apart the pre-existing forms of property. Patents originated in the late Middle Ages, as a means of circumventing guild control of innovation, and encouraging its publication and dissemination; while copyright was initially a form of state control of printing

---

3 Sherman and Bently 1999: e.g. p 38. While these authors are undoubtedly correct to point out that the contemporary confrontations of IP law with cyberspace and biotechnology do not necessarily herald its death throes, but can be seen as a continuation of a long history (Sherman and Bently 1999: 1–2), the very flexibility offered by IP concepts suggests that the future could be very different from the past.

by granting licences to publishers, until reborn in the late-eighteenth-century Enlightenment as an automatic right for authors to the fruits of their labour (Prager 1944). The modern system of IPRs originated in the transition to industrial capitalism during the late-eighteenth and first part of the nineteenth century, when the infant private-property paradigm was created to break down old monopolistic privileges.[4] Now it is accused of being a lusty monopolistic giant sprawled across the pathways of development of today's technologies.

9.1.1 Birth of the modern international framework

The emergence of the modern systems of IPRs during the early nineteenth century in the main capitalist countries was accompanied by considerable controversy (May and Sell 2006: 111–15). At first, they usually required only national novelty (Ladas 1930: 26–7; Seville 2006: 23–36), which permitted and indeed encouraged the free importation or local manufacture of foreign inventions and cultural works such as books, which today is denounced as piracy.[5] Soon, however, as states (especially in Europe) established their IP protection laws, they also began to agree reciprocal recognition through a network of bilateral treaties, culminating in the multilateral agreements establishing the Paris Industrial Property Union of 1883, and the Berne Copyright Union of 1886.[6]

---

4 The famous Statute of Anne of 1710 aimed to limit the monopoly of the London Stationers Company by confining copyright protection to fourteen years (renewable once for a living author), the same term was chosen in the first US Copyright Act of 1790; attempts by publishers to extend this by relying on common law to give perpetual protection were rejected by the House of Lords in the famous case of *Donaldson* v. *Becket* (1774); the term has become greatly extended since then (see below). The French revolutionary law of 1791 gave any citizen the right to establish a theatre and perform plays, as well as granting authors of works the right to authorize their performance (Davies 1994: 78, 185).

5 Chang 2002: 84; indeed, in 1886 a US publisher was happy to be called a pirate (Seville 2006: 17). The term piracy is much misused in relation to IPRs.

6 On the Paris Convention, see Ladas 1930; Plasseraud and Savignon 1983; and for critical views, Kronstein and Till 1947; Penrose 1951; on Berne, Ricketson 1987; Ricketson and Ginsburg 2006a; and critical views in Goldstein 1994; May and Sell 2006. Both Paris and Berne operated as organizations, with secretariats, which merged in 1893 to create the United International Bureaux for the Protection of IP (known by its French acronym as BIRPI). It was reborn in 1970, with responsibility for all types of IPRs, as the World Intellectual Property Organization (WIPO), which became a UN specialized agency in 1974, although unique in being well resourced, due to its income from managing patent applications.

However, states took a mercantilist view of the international arrangements. Notably, the USA refused to give copyright protection for foreign works until 1891, and even after that required simultaneous local publication, to protect local low-cost publishing.[7] It did not join the Berne Convention until 1987, after it had become a strong advocate for international IPR protection, and had placed the issue on the agenda of the Uruguay Round. On the other hand, the USA was a strong advocate of international protection of patents as private rights in the Paris Convention, which was opposed especially by Germany, until the large German firms changed their strategy and began to use patents to form cartels, leading to Germany's accession to the Paris Union in 1901 (Kronstein and Till 1947).

Although these were formally treaties between states, both their initial negotiation and the gradual extension of protection in subsequent revision conferences were mainly due to the role of experts who became IP ideologists. In the words of one such:

> Decisive for the success of these conferences was the fact that most of the proposals for the improvement of international protection did not originate with the governments of the Member States, but were developed primarily by the interested circles of industry, their professional representatives and expert advisers.[8]

Indeed, during the twentieth century, in the main capitalist countries, there was a steady extension and strengthening of the private-property paradigm in IPRs, which was reflected and embodied in revisions of the Paris and Berne Conventions, and the negotiation of additional agreements covering other types of IPRs.

---

7 US copyright law historically has given less protection to authors (e.g. it does not recognize moral rights, and has a broad 'fair use' doctrine); throughout the nineteenth century, US publishers opposed international copyright, to preserve their freedom to reprint foreign works, and although some changed their position and joined in pressures for the USA to join Berne, the compromise law of 1891 retained the requirement that foreign works would only be protected if printed in the USA (Barnes 1974; Seville 2006). US law also required works to be registered and a copy sent to the Library of Congress. Hence, the USA relied on bilateral treaties until UNESCO drew up the Universal Copyright Convention in 1952, to draw the USA and some Latin American countries into the copyright system.

8 Beier 1984: 13. In the field of copyright they have been organized in the ALAI (Association Littéraire et Artistique Internationale), founded in 1878 with Victor Hugo as its honorary president, and for both copyright and industrial property the AIPPI (Association Internationale pour la Protection de la Propriété Intéllectuelle), founded in 1897 (see AIPPI 1997).

9.1.2 Post-colonial conflicts

By the 1960s, however, the international system came under increasing strain, as discourses which were more critical of IPRs once again gained political support. The international system was based on reciprocal benefits, and developing countries, whose IP laws and adherence to treaties had been decided while they were colonial dependencies, began to challenge whether they derived any benefit from giving protected access to their markets to foreign owners of IPRs. The long-standing economic critique of IPRs as enabling monopolistic control of technology and markets had particular salience in the context of nationalistic concerns about the role of TNCs in underdevelopment.[9] The Andean Community's Decision 24 of 1970 establishing a Common Regime for the treatment of foreign capital (discussed in Chapter 5, at 5.2.1.1) focused especially on the transfer and licensing of technology. Also in 1970, India amended its Patent Act of 1911 (based on British law), to exclude patent protection for food, pharmaceutical drugs and other chemical-based products, allowing protection only for processes.[10]

As colonies gained independence, the proportion of developing country members of the Paris and Berne Unions grew, and they pressed for modifications to suit their circumstances. These pressures, backed by the real possibility that many countries might leave the Union, led to the negotiation of a Protocol to the Berne Convention in Stockholm in 1967, with some relatively modest provisions to meet the needs of developing countries. However, strong opposition from publishers blocked

---

9 In the immediate post-war period, Western writers had already voiced concerns about the role of patents in the international cartels which had dominated the world economy from 1880 to 1940 (Kronstein and Till 1947; Penrose 1951; Kronstein 1973). Following a request by Brazil in 1961, the UN Department of Economic and Social Affairs (ECOSOC) produced a study in 1964 entitled *The Role of Patents in the Transfer of Technology to Developing Countries*. These concerns became formulated through theories of economic dependence, which became influential especially in Latin America, contributing to IPR policies through the work of researchers and officials such as Constantine Vaitsos and Pedro Roffe. This resulted in a highly influential study published by the UN in 1974 entitled *The Role of the Patent System in the Transfer of Technology to Developing Countries*, in which WIPO (then aspiring to the status of a UN agency) wrote the account of the existing system and UNCTAD the critique and reform proposals; this led to the Paris Convention review conference (Sell 1998: 70ff.; interview information).

10 It also reduced the term of protection for these from fourteen to a maximum of seven years, and introduced provisions for licences of right, and compulsory and state licences: see Chaudhuri 2005: esp. 37–8, who discusses in detail the effects of the various changes in the patent system at different periods on India's pharmaceuticals industry.

ratification by developed countries of these revisions, and a special conference was convened in 1971, at which the protocol was watered down even further.[11] Inevitably, some developing countries abandoned Berne, while others turned a blind eye to the rapid growth of low-cost local reproduction of foreign works, which was quickly denounced by the publishing and media industries of the rich countries as 'piracy'.

The developing-country viewpoint on control of technology became part of the broader call for a new international economic order (NIEO), and was articulated mainly through UNCTAD (see Chapter 2, at 2.2.3). It led to the formulation of a draft International Code of Conduct for the Transfer of Technology, based on the Andean Community instruments. Although the Code failed to be finalized in 1985, the outstanding issues were eventually resolved in the competition provisions of the TRIPs agreement.[12] Developing-country representatives also mounted a determined attempt to revise the Paris Convention, focusing especially on revisions to article 5 to permit 'local working' requirements and compulsory licensing. However, the drawn-out diplomatic negotiations between 1978 and 1981 resulted only in hardening the divergent perspectives.[13] TNCs with interests in stronger international IP protection, such as Pfizer and IBM, switched their focus to trade, and to the US political arena. An important success came in 1984 when they succeeded in obtaining the extension to IPRs of the sanctions provisions of s. 301 of the US Trade Act, furthering strengthening it in 1988 (Ryan 1998: ch. 4; Drahos and Braithwaite 2002a: 68–73; Sell 2003: 83–95). As discussed in the previous chapter, driven by these industry pressures, and using threats and trade sanctions against countries it considered had low IP

11 The Stockholm Protocol allowed developing countries to reduce the term of copyright protection, grant non-exclusive translation and reproduction licences, allow broadcasting of works for non-profit purposes, and grant compulsory licences for educational uses. The Paris Act of 1971 was limited to translation and reproduction rights (excluding broadcasting and public communication rights, which were quickly becoming crucial with the advent of the audiovisual and then the internet age), and was subject to strict criteria and procedural requirements, as a result of which few countries took advantage of it (Drahos and Braithwaite 2002a: 76–9; Ricketson and Ginsburg 2006a: 129–32, 924–60).

12 Roffe 1998: 265–70; Patel *et al.* 2001. TRIPs, art. 30 formulated a general limit on exceptions to patent protection, and art. 31 spelled out in detail the conditions for compulsory licensing; art. 31(b) became the focus of contention in the access to medicines dispute, leading to its modification (see below).

13 Interview information. Sell 1998: ch. 4 provides a detailed account especially of the two diplomatic conferences, in Geneva (1978–9) and Nairobi (1980–1).

standards, the USA eventually secured the inclusion of the Agreement on Trade-Related Intellectual Property Rights (TRIPs) in the package of WTO agreements.[14]

9.1.3 TRIPs and beyond

The TRIPs agreement effected a 'revolution in the history of IP protection' (Deere 2009: 1) by replacing the patchwork of existing treaties with a comprehensive multilateral legally binding framework. It did so by the unique mechanism of incorporating the main provisions of the Paris and Berne Conventions,[15] while adding many new obligations. Some of these amplify and go well beyond the existing conventions, notably by extending copyright protection to computer programs and databases (art. 10). Article 27 established a sweeping requirement that:

> patents shall be available for any inventions, whether products or processes, in all fields of technology, provided that they are new, involve an inventive step and are capable of industrial application . . . patents shall be available and patent rights enjoyable without discrimination as to the place of invention, the field of technology and whether products are imported or locally produced.[16]

14 For its drafting history and a commentary, see Gervais 2008; and a commentary and analysis from a development perspective is UNCTAD–ICTSD 2005.

15 WTO members are required to 'comply with' arts. 1–12 and 19 of Paris (TRIPs, art. 2) and 1–12 (except for 6b) and the Appendix of Berne (TRIPs, art. 9); also art. 35 requires members to provide protection to the layout designs (topographies) of integrated circuits 'in accordance with' specified articles of the Treaty on Intellectual Property in Integrated Circuits (IPIC). Article 2.2 also provides that nothing in TRIPs 'shall derogate from' any provisions of those conventions. The provisions not incorporated are mainly institutional and procedural; but 6b of Berne, which provides for moral rights of authors, was excluded because the USA does not accept the concept. Comments on the relationship between TRIPs and the WIPO treaties have been made by a Panel in *US – Copyright Act* (2000): paras. 6.63–6, and by the AB (overruling a Panel) in *US – Havana Club* (2002): paras. 333–41.

16 TRIPs does not directly prohibit local working requirements, and although arts. 30–31 establish limits, they could be argued to leave some room for such requirements (UNCTAD–ICTSD 2005: 482). In May 2000 the USA initiated a complaint against Brazil's law which provides for compulsory licensing for failure to work a patent which could be applied to require manufacture in Brazil. Supported by NGOs such as Médecins sans Frontières, Brazil, argued that the availability of compulsory licensing has played a great part in ensuring affordable access to medicines especially for HIV–AIDS, and the US complaint was withdrawn on the basis of an undertaking by Brazil to consult the USA if it proposes to apply the provision to a patent held by a US company (Sell 2002).

The exceptions were tightly drawn, especially the controversial article 27(3)(b), which requires patentability for microbiology.[17] The narrowness of the exceptions, combined with the broad sweep of the requirement of patentability 'in all fields of technology' made it harder to restrict the scope of patenting. Thus, as US court decisions extended patentability, notably to computer programs and business methods, competitive pressures created what Lord Justice Jacobs described as 'an arms race in which the weapons are patents' (*Macrossan* (2006): para. 18).

Extensive new provisions in TRIPs, Part III lay down detailed requirements for administrative, civil and criminal procedures for enforcement of IPRs. To ensure that states comply with these new high IPR standards, they are required to publish all their IP laws, regulations and administrative and judicial rulings, and to notify them to the TRIPs Council (art. 63). This Council is given powers to monitor compliance (art. 68), and regularly debates national IP laws in its meetings.[18] Finally, the WTO's powerful adjudicative mechanism applies (after a five-year transition period) to TRIPs, and hence to the provisions of Paris and Berne which it incorporates (art. 64).

Nevertheless, far from creating uniformity, TRIPs has resulted in 'an increasingly complex global IP system' (Deere 2009: 16). Indeed, as Carolyn Deere's detailed study shows, the contestations from the negotiations continued, and were further heightened as new participants joined the debates about the interpretation and legitimacy of the TRIPs provisions, and whether they should constitute a floor or a ceiling for national laws. On the one hand, as both its defenders and some of its critics pointed

17 The convoluted language allows Member States to exclude from patent protection animals and plants (although if non-patentable these must be given *sui generis* protection), but not micro-organisms; and states may also exclude 'essentially biological processes for the production of plants or animals other than non-biological and microbiological processes'; hence, micro-organisms and processes for production of plants and animals which are non-biological or microbiological must be patentable. Article 27(3)(a) is worded more simply in allowing exclusion of 'diagnostic, therapeutic and surgical methods for the treatment of humans or animals'; but this is only permissive, and leaves room for interpretation, so that e.g. genetic diagnostic techniques may still be patentable. These issues are discussed in more detail below.

18 The IP laws of China have been a particular focus for debate, and the USA followed up its concerns by bringing a complaint in 2007; the Panel report (*China – IP Measures* (2009)) was mixed: it held that the USA had not shown that China's limitation of criminal penalties to 'serious' or 'especially serious' cases failed to provide criminal penalties as required by art. 61 'at least in cases of wilful trademark counterfeiting or copyright piracy on a commercial scale'; but it upheld other complaints, in particular that refusal of IP protection for prohibited works (e.g. censored films or books) was a breach of art. 41.1.

out, its provisions did provide some flexibility for national laws (Picciotto 2003a). On the other hand, however, developing-country governments found themselves under continuing pressure not only to implement TRIPs stringently, but to go beyond it.[19]

The efforts of developed countries to extend the WTO framework by negotiating bilateral agreements (discussed in the previous chapter) included adding 'TRIPs-Plus' chapters in bilateral trade and investment treaties, which governments sometimes accepted due to much wider motivations, and these have entailed significant restrictions on domestic regulation, for example of health care.[20] There were also renewed efforts to conclude new multilateral IP harmonization conventions, which achieved some success with the conclusion of two new copyright treaties through WIPO in 1996.[21] By contrast, an initiative to negotiate a treaty harmonizing substantive patent law, renewing an attempt which had failed in the early 1990s,[22] ran into greater difficulties. Urged by developing countries and NGOs, WIPO opened up a wider WIPO development agenda, and in the face of lack of consensus specialists argued that harmonization would be premature and counter-productive (Reichman and Dreyfuss 2007). A more modest Patent Law Treaty agreed in 2000 did standardize some

19 In practice, there has been great variation in implementation, and national laws have often enacted standards of IP protection both stronger and weaker than, as well as in line with TRIPs; surprisingly, over one-third of the 106 developing countries (half of which were least-developed) included some TRIPs-plus provisions in their national laws (Deere 2009: 14). Administrative practice has also tended to give higher protection than TRIPs requires: national laws include compulsory licensing provisions, but these have been rarely used (only by fifteen governments to the end of 2007 according to Deere 2009: 14), and the use of competition laws to regulate licensing, permitted by TRIPs, arts. 8 and 40, seems infrequent.

20 See e.g. Kuanpoth 2006 for an evaluation of the potential impact on pricing and availability of medicines in Thailand of its proposed FTA with the USA, negotiations for which were suspended in 2006 after widespread protests. The US–Australia FTA, agreed largely out of geopolitical motives, required the establishment of a Medicines Working Group, providing a channel for US influence over Australia's medicine reference pricing scheme, which is disliked by pharmaceutical companies (Faunce 2007; interview information).

21 Both came into force in 2002. The WIPO Copyright Treaty mainly added a new right of 'communication to the public' (to cover internet transmissions), and required states to prevent circumvention of technological protection and rights management measures. The Performances and Phonograms Treaty extended the Rome Convention, also to cover digital technologies and the internet.

22 A draft was produced by a group of governmental and private experts in 1989, but it encountered opposition in the ensuing diplomatic negotiations, not only from developing countries – indeed a main stumbling block was the inability of the USA to persuade some elements of its domestic constituency to abandon its 'first-to-invent' rule for priority (Wegner 1993; see below).

important practical procedures. A much more controversial initiative for an Anti-Counterfeiting Trade Agreement was launched in 2007 by a group of OECD countries led by the USA, to establish a new, high standard for collaborative IP enforcement, generating considerable hostility from a range of critics (Fink and Correa 2009).

Difficulties with the attempt to impose a 'one-size-fits-all' approach to IP protection through the TRIPs agreement quickly became apparent, unsurprisingly in relation to pharmaceutical drugs. Even during the grace period given to developing countries for implementation, the USA brought a successful complaint against India, to enforce the transitional obligation to provide a registration system, aimed at enabling drugs companies to preserve their patent priority. However, another legal move by the pharmaceutical industry badly boomeranged. Opposing new legislation introduced in South Africa in 1997 aimed at ensuring availability of affordable medicines, a group of pharmaceutical firms, supported by the US government, challenged the law as unconstitutional, mainly on the grounds that it constituted deprivation of property without compensation.[23] This was backed by arguments that it was in breach of South Africa's international obligations under TRIPs, as well as trade pressures and sanctions by the USA under s. 301 (Klug 2008: 221). However, it generated legal counter-moves (Heywood 2001) and strong political opposition by a coalition of activists, and both the legal case and the US threats were dropped.

Furthermore, this drew global attention to the issue of access to medicines, and the ensuing campaign was able to build international support, especially around the issue of drugs for HIV–AIDS (Drahos and Mayne 2002: 248–50; Klug 2008). This achieved a compromise in a Ministerial Declaration on the TRIPs Agreement and Public Health at the WTO's Doha conference in 2001, subsequently formalized by the WTO Council.[24] Although this was portrayed by some as a victory for developing countries, it was a modest modification establishing a cumbersome procedure. After five years it had been used only once, to send two shipments of AIDS medicines to Rwanda by Canadian drug firm

23 *Pharmaceutical Companies' Notice of Motion* (1998).
24 A General Council Decision of 6 December 2005 agreed a Protocol amending the TRIPs Agreement (WT/L/641 8 December 2005), which would formally enact the decision of 30 August 2003 on the Implementation of Paragraph 6 of the Doha Declaration on the TRIPs Agreement and Public Health. Although not yet in force, this would be the first amendment of a core WTO agreement.

Apotex, which said it would not repeat the complicated process. However, the campaign focused attention on the problem of public health in developing countries and the impact of IPRs, and prompted new mechanisms for financing and pricing essential drugs (WHO–CIPIH 2006). As Peter Drahos has argued, the minor success achieved by the access to medicines campaign showed that even weak actors can achieve victories through skilful strategies exploiting the possibilities of networked governance (2007).

Exclusivity has come to be defined differently in the two main pillars of IP which emerged historically: industrial property (patents and related rights, and trade marks) and copyright (Reichman 1992: 329). These will be considered in the next two sections.

9.2 Patents, science and business strategies

9.2.1 Conditions and scope of patent protection

For industrially useful technologies, patents[25] provide a relatively short period of protection[26] under conditions which can be more or less stringent. The key conditions for patentability are that the product or process must not only be new, but entail a technological advance,[27] as well as industrial utility. However, once a patent is granted, the protection against imitation, for example by reverse engineering, is absolute: a rival product may be found to be infringing if it is adjudged to come within the terms of the patent claims even if no copying was involved. An independent inventor can be prevented from commercializing a product, unless her invention is distinctly different. The position is similar for other types of industrial property, such as trade marks. Hence, it may give valuable additional protection to obtain a patent for some functional works, such as computer programs, even if they are also covered by copyright, with its much longer period of protection.[28]

---

25 Referred to in the USA as utility patents, to distinguish them from patents on designs and plant varieties, which elsewhere have a distinct form of protection. For a thorough and practical account aimed at non-lawyers and focusing especially on the key area of chemical and biosciences, see Cockbain 2007.

26 Now extended to a minimum of twenty years from date of filing by art. 33 of the TRIPs agreement.

27 Referred to as 'inventive step', or in the USA as 'non-obviousness'.

28 Copyright protects the form of a program, while a patent covers what it does, so protects against other programs which function in the same way. The European Patent Convention art. 52 excludes from patentability 'schemes, rules and methods for performing mental

The economic justification for patent protection, on careful analysis, is limited at most to the need to reinforce the normal lead time gained by an inventor, by enabling and encouraging inventions with commercial prospects to be developed cooperatively without the need for secrecy, which may be hard to preserve for some inventions.[29] Today, applying for a patent is like putting in an initial stake in a poker game: the player may have a weak hand (an unsound claim), and as the stakes are raised may be unlikely to continue (applying for international protection, paying annual renewal fees), but the initial stake may pay off (e.g. leading to technological collaborations by cross-licensing).

Far from simply encouraging innovation, as is usually asserted, the effects of patents can be very negative:

> Nonsensical as it may sound, the patent system is essentially anti-innovative. This is not just because it assists a very specialized sort of innovation and discourages other sorts. Much more important is that the patent system satisfies the requirements of those who need to feel that innovation is controlled and contained, that innovation is in its place, part of process. Most innovation is not like this at all.[30]

acts, playing games or doing business, and programs for computers' if the application refers to these activities 'as such'; but the increasing pressure to match the USA in extending patentability especially to business methods and computer programs has led to a stricter interpretation of the phrase 'as such', and patents for programs in hardware or 'on a carrier' have been allowed under various justifications (*Macrossan* (2006)). The issue has proved too controversial to be resolved by EU legislation; and the Enlarged Board of Appeal of the EPO rejected a referral inviting it to lay down a general principle on the grounds that existing decisions while divergent were not conflicting (Opinion G-3/08, 12 May 2010).

29 Kitch 1977; Merges and Nelson (1990) analyse in detail how this shows the importance of definition of the scope of the patent (the degree of precision required in the description, and the breadth of the technology protected), which is generally the work of patent agents and examiners, subject to possible court decisions. They give as one example the breadth of the famous Harvard patent awarded in the USA in 1988 for a transgenic mouse sensitive to carcinogens (the 'oncomouse'), the claim for which extended to all 'non-human transgenic mammals' produced by this technique; this very wide scope was rejected by the EPO, although it granted a patent (Merges and Nelson (1990): 847). Applied research has focused on the role of patents in managing commercial interactions between innovators, starting from a neo-Schumpeterian view of the dynamics of competition based on innovation, and exploring the difficulty of exploiting scientific innovation if the only alternatives are secrecy or openness (McKelvey 1996). Although patent protection creates a market for some technologies, it greatly reinforces monopolization, and weak protection has facilitated rapid technological development in industries such as microelectronics and computing (Mowery and Rosenberg 1998: 43), and the German chemicals industry (Dutfield 2009).

30 Macdonald 2002: 34. Lack of patent protection seems to have assisted industrialization based on new technologies at the end of the nineteenth century, especially in small

Patent protection is not automatic, and both obtaining and defending a patent is a complex and expensive business. The claim must be drawn up by a technical specialist, and even if it is granted following examination by the patent office it provides no guarantee, the holder must be ready to sue anyone marketing products which may infringe the patent. This raises important issues about how rigorous patent examination should be. Its expense, the need for expertise, the delays especially due to large numbers of applications, and the difficulty of deciding increasingly thorny issues of patentability, provide arguments for nominal or cursory examination, leaving it to an 'opposition' process and the courts to resolve disagreements. On the other hand, a patent gives monopoly rights, and even if it can be disregarded or challenged this involves expense and uncertainty, so light standards for granting patents entail significant costs for competitors and for society.[31]

9.2.2 International patent protection

Patents are national, but the Paris Convention provides a right of priority for one year from the filing date in other Member States, as well as the obligation to give NT to foreigners, which makes it possible to protect an invention internationally by filing applications to create a package of national patents. Since 1978 the Patent Cooperation Treaty (PCT) has provided a procedure for a single international application designating the countries in which protection is desired. Applicants can also request an international search and examination, which is helpful especially for countries which do not have an examination system of their own. But under both these conventions, it is still necessary to comply with national formalities (including payment of initial and renewal fees), and the protection depends on each national law. The Paris Convention leaves the content of the rights entirely for each state to decide. However, TRIPs, article 27 now requires patents to be available 'in all fields of technology'.

Europe has a regional system (not confined to EU Member States) under the European Patent Convention (EPC) of 1973, with a European Patent Office (EPO) since 1978, but the EPO also grants only a bundle of national patents, the details of which are subject to national law. Although

countries with large export markets such as the Netherlands and Switzerland (Schiff 1971).

31 Interestingly, this issue was little discussed even in the USA, until the big jump in applications, and grants which many regarded as dubious, for patents in business methods and biotechnology; discussed below (Merges 1999).

a Convention for a single European patent was signed in 1975, and pressure to bring it into effect has been periodically generated, this has not yet come into force, a major obstacle being the apparently minor but nevertheless serious question of the language of the patent specification, and hence the place and language of litigation (Pitkethly 1999; Cornish and Llewelyn 2007: 127–30). A new approach was adopted in 2007 with a proposal for a unified system of patent litigation, based on a European Patent Court, a proposal for which was adopted in December 2009.[32]

Thus, the international patent system remains very much a multilevel one. Nevertheless, there has been some significant convergence of national patent laws in Europe, resulting from increasingly close interactions of patent specialists, particularly patent examiners and even judges (Ranitz 1999). At the international level also, technical convergence has been fostered, notably through the Trilateral Offices, a semi-formal arrangement for patent coordination established in 1983 on the initiative of the USPTO with the other two major patent offices, the European and Japanese. The Trilateral began with projects aimed at automation of the claims filing process and improvement of search quality, followed in 1997 by a more ambitious Action Plan, justified as aiming to reduce costs for the offices and applicants, to enable electronic exchange of search and examination data and establish concurrent search and examination of claims.

These types of informal intergovernmental coordination form part of much wider networks of patent specialists (Cheek 2001; Davies 2002). Thus, the international patent system could be said to operate more or less coherently, despite its formal fragmentation, largely due to the common understandings based on the habitus of the expert community of technical professionals, much like the regime of competition law discussed in Chapter 4, at 4.3, and international business taxation as seen in Chapter 6. Similarly also, despite the convergence fostered by this strong 'epistemic community', efforts at formal harmonization have failed.[33]

In practice, the main economic impact of patents is their use by large corporations, to boost both their control of technology and their

---

32 This proposed a hybrid between an EU institution and an international organization (to accommodate non-EU members of the EPO); it was referred to the ECJ for an advisory opinion as to its legality.

33 A major obstacle to harmonization has been the US adherence to the first-inventor principle, as opposed to the first-inventor-to-file principle prevalent elsewhere. This is thought to favour small inventors (Wegner 1993), and creates a lucrative practice for US lawyers. In practice, the difference is not as great as it seems (Bagley 2008). The US procedures could be argued to breach the NT principle, as it is more difficult for a non-US person to prove they were the first inventor (Wegner 1993: 56).

competitive position. Indeed, the emergence of such corporations and their growth to dominate the world economy was due in no small part to their control of science and technology, based on enormous investments in research and development (R&D), allied to exploitation of the patent system (Noble 1977: esp. ch. 6; Drahos and Braithwaite 2002a). From the last part of the nineteenth century, large corporations began to establish control of technological fields such as electrical engineering and chemicals, their patent departments devising techniques such as filing multiple patent claims covering related inventions, extending patent life by protecting incremental innovations, filing defensive patents to close off rival technologies, and harassing potential competitors with patent litigation. Patent monopolies could be used to circumvent competition laws, to create monopolistic domination of industries, and to form cartels by using cross-licensing and patent pools. Many of the international cartels by which US and European TNCs allocated world markets among themselves in the 1920s and 1930s were based on agreements to cross-license or pool patents.[34]

The key architects of the patent system have been the professional patent experts, who have usually combined specialist legal and technical expertise, and developed the fine skills of drafting patent specifications, so that they conceal more than they reveal while staking out as wide a claim as permissible (Dutton 1984: ch. 5; Drahos and Braithwaite 2002b). They have also played an important part in mediating between corporations, for example by devising and propounding mechanisms such as cross-licensing and patent pools (Verbeure 2009), as well as between commercial interests on the one hand and scientists and engineers on the other. Perhaps their key role has been as 'creative ideologists', expounding and proselytizing the virtues of the patent system, and exploring and developing its potential by interpreting and adapting its concepts.

9.2.3 Extending appropriation: isolation from nature

This role has been most important in the expansion of the boundaries of patentability, especially by exploiting the grey areas between a discovery (which is not patentable) and an invention (which is). Interpreting this

---

34 See Chapter 4, at 4.3.1: a prominent example was the 'marriage' in 1929 of chemicals companies IG Farben, ICI and Du Pont; 35 out of the 52 proceedings against international cartels launched by the US Department of Justice between 1939 and 1944 involved patent exchange agreements (Stocking and Watkins 1948: 293).

distinction has been especially crucial for the life-science industries, from organic chemistry to biotechnology (Dutfield 2009), which operate at the interface between humankind and nature. Chemical patenting was always problematic,[35] since it is hard to classify a naturally occurring chemical compound as a new invention, and many pharmaceutical drugs have in any case been based on compounds discovered in nature, notably the twentieth-century's wonder drugs, aspirin,[36] and penicillin (Temin 1979: 434). Hence, even in countries which did not exclude patents on medicines, they were not frequent until the second half of the twentieth century. The situation changed in 1948 when Merck obtained a US patent for streptomycin, although it had been identified in soil samples, on the grounds that it had been isolated from nature and purified to enable it to be 'produced, distributed and administered in a practicable way'.[37]

The form of legal protection helped to shape and transform the industries. In the USA from the 1950s the pharmaceutical firms began to pour enormous investments into research for new drugs, which could obtain patent protection as products and thus generate economic rents, competing for market share through advertising prescription drugs to doctors, rather than on price (Temin 1979). At the same time obtaining marketing approval for such drugs became more expensive and drawn out, as systems for prior approval were established and gradually strengthened, especially after dramatic failures such as thalidomide. So in the USA and some other countries, 'big pharma' firms emerged, pouring enormous sums into R&D and testing,[38] aiming to achieve super-profits if they could find a patentable wonder drug. Hence, while the pharma firms and their defenders consider that patent protection is justified by the high investments and long lead times due to testing, the effect has been to lock the pharmaceutical industry into a pattern of seeking pills for rich peoples'

---

35 It is sometimes said that patents were accepted quite early even for living organisms, citing the patents obtained by Louis Pasteur in the USA in 1873, then in France and the UK; however, these were process patents, for a superior method of manufacturing yeast (Federico 1937).

36 The German firm Bayer could not obtain a patent for aspirin in Germany, which only allowed process patents; a UK application in 1898 was granted, but it was invalidated in an infringement suit in 1905, on the grounds that the claim showed 'no element of invention or discovery beyond what was common knowledge' (Jeffreys 2004: 88).

37 Temin 1979: 436. In fact this built on earlier case law, notably the decision in *Kuehmsted* v. *Farbenfabriken of Elberfeld Co* (1910) upholding the US patent for aspirin (Drahos and Braithwaite 2002b: 463).

38 Although the need to invest in research is the usual argument for patent protection for pharmaceuticals, firms spend far more on testing and marketing.

ailments. Other countries did not permit patents for pharmaceuticals, for example Italy,[39] or they provided patent protection only for processes and not products. This encouraged manufacturers which produced low-cost 'generic' drugs based on traditional or familiar knowledge, or imitating others' inventions. Such firms became especially important in some middle-income developing countries, such as India, Thailand and Brazil.

The 'isolation' principle was later used, initially in Germany, to justify the patentability of a micro-organism, rejecting arguments that natural and living matter could not be patented (Winter 1992). This was most famously decided by the US Supreme Court when it overturned a US patent office (USPTO) policy decision and granted protection to a genetically modified micro-organism able to absorb marine oil pollution in *Diamond* v. *Chakrabarty* (1980); see Daus 1981. The court's decision was backed by the sweeping statement that 'anything under the sun that is made by man' is patentable. This opened the floodgates for patent protection, especially for biotechnology products, most notoriously with the Harvard 'oncomouse', and the method for animal cloning which was used to 'create' Dolly the sheep.

The decision chimed with US policies in the 1980s to foster knowledge-based business, resulting in moves to provide easier and stronger patent protection. The specialist patent Court of Appeal for the Federal Circuit (CAFC) established in 1982 adopted a more accommodating approach to patentability, especially the non-obviousness criterion. This relaxation affected a number of fields, in particular allowing patent protection for software and for business methods, as well as biotechnology. It was reinforced by other measures, including the Bayh–Dole Act of 1980, which enabled and encouraged recipients of public research funds such as universities to patent and exploit innovations commercially (Coriat and Orsini 2002).

Biotechnology patenting in particular has become highly contested, on both technical patent law and ethical grounds, since these technologies involve human interventions in nature (Drahos 1999b; Sterckx 2000). Criticism of biotechnology patenting resulting from genetic engineering charged it with contributing to the commodification of life forms and the 'appropriation of life', driven by amoral science allied to big business

---

39 A successful challenge was brought by pharmaceutical companies in the constitutional court, on the grounds that the exclusion of medicines from patent protection was unfairly discriminatory (Grubb 1999: 67); the consequence seems to have been an increased propensity to use patents but not an increase in R&D (Scherer and Weisburst 1995).

(Bowring 2003). The emergence of the new genetic sciences has sparked off a host of conflicts and debates, rooted in concerns about scientists interfering with nature, evoking Frankenstein. These have resulted in many new regulatory provisions and arenas, interacting in various ways, not least in the realm of ethics.[40] These contests have become mediated through complex and interacting networks of different regimes of regulation (Black 1998; Landfried 1999; Amani and Coombe 2005), intersecting also with trade rules for example on GM foods (see previous chapter).

A particular area of contestation has been the impact of products containing genetically modified organisms (GMOs) on the environment and biodiversity, and on traditional farming practices. The owner of a patent on a transgenic plant or animal may be able to claim rights in the progeny of that organism, if it contains the patented gene;[41] and hence use of the plant, seed or animal can be governed by a licence rather than outright sale. A stark example of the power this provides is the way that agribusiness giant Monsanto aimed to dominate farming especially in north America, even after the patent for its Roundup herbicide expired in 2000, by developing 'Roundup Ready' seeds for herbicide-resistant

40 TRIPs, art. 27(2) allows states to exclude from patentability 'inventions, the prevention within their territory of the commercial exploitation of which is necessary to protect *ordre public* or morality, including to protect human, animal or plant life or health or to avoid serious prejudice to the environment, provided that such exclusion is not made merely because the exploitation is prohibited by their law'. This permission is based on the EPC art. 53(a) (with the addition of the word 'commercial'), and is very tightly drawn, aiming as far as possible to insulate the issue of patentability from ethical or other concerns, so that they should be dealt with by separate regulatory regimes. However, given the commercial incentive which the patent system aims to provide, it is hard to detach ethical concerns, particularly in relation to biotechnology. There were considerable contests over the EU's Biotechnology Directive of 1998 (98/44/EC). In addition to a provision similar to TRIPs 27(2), it excluded '(a) processes for cloning human beings; (b) processes for modifying the germ line genetic identity of human beings; (c) uses of human embryos for industrial or commercial purposes; (d) processes for modifying the genetic identity of animals which are likely to cause them suffering without any substantial medical benefit to man or animal, and also animals resulting from such processes'. It also excluded '[t]he human body, at the various stages of its formation and development, and the simple discovery of one of its elements, including the sequence or partial sequence of a gene', but permitted patenting of an 'element isolated from the human body or otherwise produced by means of a technical process, including the sequence or partial sequence of a gene . . . even if the structure of that element is identical to that of a natural element'. It also established a European Group on Ethics in Science and New Technologies to evaluate ethical issues. See Romeo Casabona (1999) for a comparative survey of the regulation of the ethical issues.
41 Strictly speaking, these are rights to control the exploitation of the genetic fragment, which is not (formally) the same as ownership of the progeny itself, hence the dissent by Arbour, J. discussed in the next note.

crops such as cotton, corn and soybeans. Farmers had to acquire these seeds under 'technology user agreements', requiring them to use Roundup herbicide, forbidding the replanting of seeds from the plants, and giving Monsanto rights to inspect the farmer's fields to monitor compliance (Bowring 2003: 69–70).

Attempting to maintain such control involves enormous legal resources: by 2005 Monsanto had investigated thousands of farmers, filed 90 lawsuits involving 147 farmers and 39 small businesses or farm companies, and had a staff of 75 engaged on this task (Centre for Food Safety 2005). A celebrated conflict with Canadian farmer Percy Schmeiser resulted in a majority decision in the Supreme Court of Canada, upholding Monsanto's claim for patent infringement due to the presence of 'Roundup Ready' canola on Schmeiser's land. Although Schmeiser had never bought the seeds, and claimed that they must have blown onto his land from nearby farms, a majority of the judges found that he knew or ought to have known that he had saved and planted seed containing the patented gene, and that in any case he sold the resulting crop also containing the patented gene.[42] However, the court rejected Monsanto's claim that he must pay their licence fee of $15 per acre, and awarded no damages, since his crop made no additional profit due to the presence of the gene. Schmeiser countered with a lawsuit against Monsanto for contaminating his land with unwanted plants, which was settled in 2008, with Monsanto agreeing to pay the costs of clearing his land.[43]

9.2.4 Biotechnology battles

The issue of biotechnology patenting came to a head with the controversy over patent applications for partially encoded gene sequences, known as expressed sequence tags (ESTs), resulting from the human genome project (HGP) funded by the National Institutes of Health (NIH), filed in the names of J. Craig Venter and others in 1991 and 1992. This produced opposition, most strongly expressed by Jim Watson, one of the pioneers of microbiology who was by then the NIH's head of genome research, who described the applications as 'sheer lunacy'. The view of Watson and many other scientists was that the identification of specific

---

42 *Monsanto* v. *Schmeiser* (2004). The interpretation that ownership of the gene also entitled Monsanto to any plant containing it was described as an 'expansive doctrine' by Prof. Vaver (cited in *Monsanto* v. *Schmeiser* (2004): para. 80), and rejected in the dissenting judgment by Arbour, J.

43 See http://percyschmeiser.com.

gene sequences involved no genuine novelty, since it had been done by an automated, computerized process; and no industrial utility could be shown, since the functions of the sequences were unknown; furthermore, patenting could damage international scientific collaboration (Sulston and Ferry 2002: 104–6). The applications also met with objections from the USPTO, and were withdrawn in 1994. The controversy continued, as Venter resigned from the NIH to pursue genomics research with private funding, and by 1998 he headed the privately funded Celera Genomics, using an industrialized process for sequencing to compete with the HGP. The scientists urging that the HGP should remain a public project received support from Merck and other large pharmaceutical companies, funding from the Wellcome Trust, and high-profile political support from President Clinton and Prime Minister Blair. Nevertheless, Celera continued on its competing commercial track, claiming rights in its data.[44]

However, biotechnological knowledge posed significant problems for patentability, also because it increasingly took the form of information about nature, which would seem to come within the categories excluded from patentable subject matter: laws of nature, natural phenomena and abstract ideas. An attempt to establish an internationally agreed standard for patentability of biotechnology inventions was made through the Trilateral Offices. They were wary of engaging in any substantive harmonization of standards, and in 1990 suspended work on biotechnology during the negotiations at WIPO and the WTO (discussed above). This was resumed after 1995, when each of the three offices was wrestling with the problem of ESTs, and in 1998 to 1999 they conducted a joint 'technical study' on the patentability of DNA fragments.[45]

This Trilateral study helped the USPTO, also following a domestic consultation process, to issue a revised standard for the industrial utility requirement of patentability, which required applications to show 'a specific and substantial utility that is credible'.[46] Subject to this somewhat stricter criterion, the USPTO began granting patents for ESTs, and the patent offices in Europe and Japan have also done so, but even more cautiously. Nevertheless, many thousands of gene patents have been granted, although their validity remains contested, as is the case with the equally contested patents for business methods. In the USA an important

44 Sulston and Ferry 2002: 292; Dutfield 2009: 165ff. For a detailed study of how conflicts over patenting moulded business competition and science in the emergence of biotechnology, see McKelvey 1996.
45 This account is based on Davies 2002: esp. 156–61.
46 The EPO issued clarification of its regulation at about the same time (Davies 2002: 160).

counterweight to the USPTO has been the CAFC, which has continued to relax patentability standards, in particular overturning the USPTO's attempts to maintain or strengthen the novelty and utility requirements, justifying itself by the need to make the patent system 'responsive to the needs of the modern world'.[47] An opportunity for clarification by the US Supreme Court was turned down, when a majority of the Court declined to consider a case about patentability of a diagnostic method (*Metabolite* (2006)). The continuing uncertainty created even greater problems for science (Huys *et al.* 2009: 908–9), though perhaps not for lawyers.

These debates about patentability have reflected and mediated the tensions generated by the corporate competition to control commercialization of biotechnology, as well as affecting scientific interaction. For the biotechnology industry, patents became an important signal for financial market valuations of company share prices; but contests over patent grants and validity led to considerably volatility in these prices (Coriat and Orsini 2002: 1501). At the same time, some researchers argued that proliferation of patents ('patent thickets') was leading to an 'anti-commons', as owners of proprietary rights over upstream research tools could hinder, block or control downstream research and product development (Heller and Eisenberg 1998; OECD 2002a).

Various means have been explored to overcome this problem. A major result has been a process of corporate concentration, notably in plant biotechnology, mainly by the acquisition of research-intensive start-ups by large chemicals firms such as Dow and DuPont (Hope 2008: 64). A radical alternative, termed the 'biobazaar' by Janet Hope (2008), is to use the 'open source' approach developed in the context of copyright for software (see below), aiming to take advantage of the virtues of peer-production or 'democratized' innovation (von Hippel 2005). A more limited solution is to provide an exception, for example for research or experimental use, which is done in many patent systems, although the scope for such exceptions can be unclear, and is narrow under the TRIPs agreement.[48]

---

47 *AT&T* v. *Excel* (1999), cited in Merrill and Mazza 2006: 77.
48 van Overwalle *et al.* 2006: 143. The conditions in TRIPs, art. 30 are referred to as the 'three-step test': exceptions must be limited, must 'not unreasonably conflict with a normal exploitation of the patent', and 'not unreasonably prejudice the legitimate interests of the patent owner'. A WTO Panel upheld as consistent with TRIPs a Canadian provision allowing use for 'purposes reasonably related to the submission of information required' for regulatory purposes; but it found inconsistent the exception permitting manufacture of articles intended for sale after the expiry of the patent (stockpiling): *Canada – Pharmaceuticals* (2000).

The middle ground, which builds on the existing patent system while significantly transforming it, entails moving from exclusivity of rights to compensation systems, using complex contracting or licensing (van Overwalle *et al.* 2006; van Overwalle 2009). This involves techniques such as patent pools,[49] technology clearing houses, and collective or compulsory licensing systems. In effect, such techniques allow use without the need for seeking prior permission and agreement on the price and terms. Each of the mechanisms within this approach has its own advantages and difficulties. Some only postpone the problem of valuation, but royalty rates should be easier to agree after a commercial use has been developed than beforehand. Some forms of licensing overlap with open source, if they permit free use for non-commercial, research or humanitarian purposes, or in developing countries.[50]

9.2.5 Contesting commodification, property rights and access

Thus, the biotechnology revolution has sparked conflicts and debates, going well beyond the realm of patents, but also intersecting with it. The advances in biotechnology that accelerated rapidly from the 1970s enabled the isolation of genetic fragments, their cryogenic storage, and new forms of genetic manipulation. This has transformed the capacity to produce and reproduce plant, animal and human life forms, notably the ability to transfer traits between very different species. The drive of the biosciences firms to dominate the exploitation of these new possibilities has created complex new interactions between the appropriation and diffusion of knowledge, mediated by various regulatory arrangements and proposals.

9.2.5.1 Bioprospecting and biopiracy

A particular international concern has been the controversial practice of 'bio-prospecting'. Bio-prospectors have become active in searching out genetic resources, especially of developing countries which have high biodiversity. These practices also take advantage of traditional knowledge,

---

49 Notably, a patent pool for AIDS drugs was set up in 2008 by UNITAID; this organization was founded in 2006 by Brazil, Chile, France, Norway and the UK (now supported by twenty-nine countries), to improve access to medicines in poor countries especially for HIV–AIDS, malaria and tuberculosis, financed by a tax on airline tickets; it has also received funding from the Gates Foundation; see www.unitaid.eu.

50 For a proposed open licensing approach to university innovations to help to solve the problems of access to medicines and the R&D gap with poor countries, see Kapczynski *et al.* 2005.

for example by aiming to identify the specific genes responsible for the beneficial properties of plants long known to particular communities or groups. This is in many ways a further stage in the longer history of scientific and cultural imperialism. The collection of exotic species has long been one of the aims of imperial expeditions, and as botany became a more formal science in the eighteenth century, exploitation of the rich biodiversity of the countries of the South by the collection of botanical specimens, and the appropriation of traditional knowledge especially of medicine, became a central feature of colonial enterprise, led by respected figures such as Sir Joseph Banks (Schiebinger 2004).

There is a qualitative shift with the new biosciences, which involve novel methods for collecting and using plant, animal and human tissue samples, dissociated from the whole organism. Such genetic materials can now be made available in biobanks or databases, for analysis to identify cell lines or genes with potentially useful traits, such as disease resistance. Such collections may be held by public bodies or private firms:

> The US National Cancer Institute (NCI), for example, instituted collecting programmes in over 40 countries in the years from 1985–95, amassing a collection of 50,000 tissue samples and in excess of 114,000 different bio-chemical extracts. This collection is now housed in a dedicated repository in Frederick, Maryland, in 28 double-decker walk-in cryogenic storage freezers. Other similar-sized libraries of tissue samples and extracts are held by large corporations, such as Merck, Smith Kline Beecham, Bristol Myers Squibb, and Pfizer, and by smaller pharmaceutical companies.
>
> (Parry 2004a: 34; see also Parry 2004b)

As Parry explains, the NCI's policy is to lend out its samples for a nominal charge, and to leave it to users to negotiate with the original suppliers of the sample if a commercial application results. However, the commercial biobanks provide access for research purposes under licences which retain the right to negotiate commercial terms for use in any application which may result.

New types of public–private interaction have clearly emerged, as well as controversial concepts of property rights and ownership, perhaps most starkly when the tissue samples come from a human person's body. This was dramatized in the US case of *Moore* (1990), concerning patent rights to cell lines deriving from the spleen taken from a leukaemia patient without consent. The Supreme Court of California held that, while the non-consensual removal was a breach of the patient's rights, he did not own either the body parts or tissue which had been removed from him, or the genetic information derived from it; paradoxically, however, it con-firmed the proprietary rights of the scientists, or rather of their university employer (Boyle 1996: 21–4; Gibson 2008: 95ff.).

The claim to an exclusive private-property right in such tissue samples obtained from nature rests, as we have seen, on the principle of 'isolation', as well as needing to satisfy the criteria for patentability discussed above: novelty, inventive step and industrial utility. Considerable conflicts have emerged in relation to claims to inventions deriving from traditional knowledge, such as the medicinal or agricultural properties of plants, denounced as 'biopiracy'.

These were especially dramatized by conflicts over patents for formu-lations based on extracts of oil from the neem tree, claiming various uses as pesticides and fungicides, even though the many beneficent uses of the neem have been known in India reputedly for some 2,000 years. Neverthe-less, the agribusiness firm W. R. Grace, together with the US Department of Agriculture, was granted several US patents in 1990, despite attempted objections by activists and the government of India (Bagley 2003: 680ff.; Moyer-Henry 2008). A related patent was also granted by the EPO in 1994, but a successful legal challenge was mounted by 'an international network of patent warriors', including the Indian campaigner Vandana Shiva (2007: 281), although it took ten years to bring to a final positive conclusion (Bullard 2005). The greater success in Europe was due partly to different views of the novelty requirement: the EPO's Board of Opposi-tion accepted that evidence of the use of neem extracts by Indian farmers as a fungicide constituted prior public use.[51] In contrast, US law's public use test requires either written publication or open use within the USA; this effectively excludes knowledge based on oral traditions outside the USA.[52] Probably equally important for the outcome was the vociferous public campaign in Europe, where the EPO office in Munich on the day of the hearing was the target of demonstrators with placards proclaiming 'No Patents for Theft', and handing in a petition signed by over 100,000 Indian citizens (Bullard 2005).

Significantly, however, the Opposition Board did not accept the argu-ment that since the neem patent would deprive the Indian people of their cultural heritage and natural resources it would be contrary to 'ordre

---

51 However, this did include a printed document published by Indian scientists in Australia, and the lawyer on behalf of the opponents to the patents has stressed that the EPO's evidence requirement for prior public use is strict (Dolder 2006: 588).

52 See Bagley 2003, who argues that this is contrary to the US Constitution's IP clause.

public and morality' (Dolder 2006: 586). Furthermore, the rejection by the EPO did not invalidate patents granted by national offices either in the EU or other countries, and one researcher found '360 published and/or granted patents based on neem' (Moyer-Henry 2008: 5). However, some 20 per cent of these listed at least one Indian claimant, including India's Council for Scientific and Industrial Research, indicating an attempt by the Indian state to pre-empt claims by others (Moyer-Henry 2008: 6).

At about the same time, a similar claim to the EPO was made for an appetite suppressant based on the hoodia plant, whose properties were part of the traditional knowledge of the San people of southern Africa. This claim was rejected by the examiner for lack of novelty, but a revised claim was accepted on appeal, although on dubious grounds (Dolder 2006). In this case, however, those representing the San people were persuaded to discontinue their opposition, largely by the offer of payments of $120,000 for clinical testing and a share in the profits of any eventual product of 6 per cent of the royalties (Moyer-Henry 2008).

Such cases revealed that there is no clear separation or opposition between the public domain and private-property rights (Boyle 1996: 27–8). Firms in fields such as pharmaceuticals and agribusiness are very adept at managing the interactions between these spheres, to take advantage of knowledge which is available free in the public domain (and which may indeed have resulted from considerable public expenditure), and extract from it something which they can claim as private property. However, following conflicts such as those over the neem patents, the interactions became more complex. Interventions by activist groups and developing country governments made patent offices examine more closely claims based on traditional knowledge, such as the use of turmeric powder for wound healing, extracts of the maca plant for sexual dysfunction, or the yellow Mexican 'enola' bean.[53]

9.2.5.2 Controlling access and benefit sharing

These different claims have also generated complex contestations over the nature and forms of property rights. The denunciation of biopiracy as a new extension of colonial plunder (Shiva 1997; Aoki 1998) resulted in moves to develop regimes for 'benefit sharing', especially by developing country governments. This principle was articulated in the Convention

---

53 See e.g. Dutfield 2003a: 31–2, and the website of the activist ETC Group www.etcgroup. org.

on Biological Diversity (CBD), agreed at the 1992 Rio Conference, with the stated purposes of:

> the conservation of biological diversity, the sustainable use of its components and the fair and equitable sharing of the benefits arising out of the utilization of genetic resources, including by appropriate access to genetic resources and by appropriate transfer of relevant technologies, taking into account all rights over those resources and to technologies, and by appropriate funding.

The CBD places states, and hence governments, firmly at the centre in managing these complex issues of fairness, rights, appropriate access and compensation. Indeed, it has been criticized as 'redrawing the commons in the shape of nation states' (Hayden 2004: 120). Traditional peoples and communities may have concerns quite different from those of governments, for example to preserve the secrets of sacred knowledge, rather than benefit economically from its commercialization.

Developing-country states have been quick to develop regimes for access and benefit sharing (ABS).[54] Such systems include the Andean Community's regional Common System on Access to Genetic Resources of 1996, which vested in the states the rights to all non-human genetic resources within the territory, making access dependent on permission and a benefit-sharing agreement with the government. The Organization for African Unity adopted a model law in 2000; a Framework Agreement drafted by ASEAN at that time did not enter into force, but ASEAN members adopted their own national regulations, and a Centre for Biodiversity was set up in 1999. Legislation passed by India in 2002 requires foreigners to obtain prior approval from India's National Biodiversity Authority, while access by Indian resident citizens and corporations is governed by state biodiversity boards; the Biodiversity Authority is required to seek benefit sharing, which may include benefits to individuals, groups or organizations from whom the material is obtained.

Attempts to use benefit-sharing arrangements to deal with potential conflicts between the commercialization of bioscience and traditional knowledge have not always been successful. For example, an early bioprospecting agreement in the Maya highlands of Chiapas in Mexico in 1998, one of a number developed under funding from the US government's International Cooperative Biodiversity Groups, invested considerable resources into negotiating benefit sharing with local

---

54 Safrin 2004. The CBD has a database of ABS measures at www.cbd.int/abs/measures.

communities, but was abandoned after strong opposition from a coalition of activist groups (Hayden 2003; Safrin 2004: 655–6). This and other conflicts demonstrated the difficulties of the idea of paying compensation to identifiable communities or groups in exchange for the grant of commercial rights. Indeed, the national ABS regimes have been criticized as disregarding the concerns and interests of communities, especially indigenous people, and exacerbating the problem of the 'anti-commons' for biotechnological innovations, while being in practice unenforceable (Safrin 2004). Bio-prospectors frustrated by access restrictions can simply resort to other 'public' spaces (Hayden 2004).

The issue has been debated in a number of international arenas and networks. Developing countries have favoured the CBD (which has been ratified by 193 states, though not the USA), since it firmly recognizes benefit sharing, expects states to encourage conservation and sustainable use of biodiversity components, and specifies that there should be transfer of technology, including IPRs, to states which are providers of genetic resources, on mutually agreed terms. The CBD parties in 2002 agreed the non-binding Bonn Guidelines, and embarked on negotiations for a Nagoya Protocol, which however have been fraught with conflicts. These concern especially whether benefit sharing should apply to resources acquired before the proposed treaty enters into force, and requirements for patent offices to verify the origins of genetic material in patent claims and monitor their use (IISD 2010).

WIPO conducted a 'fact-finding mission' in 1998 to 1999, with a report published in 2001, and then set up an Intergovernmental Committee on Intellectual Property and Genetic Resources, Traditional Knowledge and Folklore. Looking at the issue from an IPR perspective, this Committee produced proposals dealing separately with 'traditional cultural expressions (folklore)' and 'traditional knowledge', and after a lengthy period of comment and discussion, began to work on a possible treaty, which might combine the two. Its work on traditional cultural expressions engages with fraught issues, including works of particular cultural or spiritual value or significance, involving various procedures and modes of protection, including both registration to protect from misappropriation, and secrecy. This perspective raises some fundamental questions about the relationship of modern concepts of IP to traditional cultural forms, especially of indigenous people; made even more intriguing by the radical impact of the new digital environment (see e.g. von Lewinsky 2008; Graber and Burri-Nenova 2008). WIPO's work on traditional knowledge opened the opportunity for developing countries to propose methods by which patent law could both prevent appropriation of traditional knowledge and promote benefit sharing. In view of the overlap with TRIPs, these have mainly been pursued through the WTO.

Thus, the Doha negotiating mandate in 2001 asked the WTO's Council for TRIPs to consider its relationship to the CBD, as part of the required review of TRIPs, article 27. A developing-country group immediately put forward a proposal:

> that an applicant for a patent relating to biological materials or to traditional knowledge shall provide, as a condition to acquiring patent rights: (i) disclosure of the source and country of origin of the biological resource and of the traditional knowledge used in the invention; (ii) evidence of prior informed consent through approval of authorities under the relevant national regimes; and (iii) evidence of fair and equitable benefit sharing under the national regime of the country of origin.
>
> (Cited in Dutfield 2003b: 22)

Not surprisingly, this led to protracted discussions and negotiations, and developed countries have remained opposed to linking patent rules to an ABS regime, which would also greatly strengthen enforcement of such a regime through the WTO Dispute-Settlement process. Agreement has been difficult to reach even in the CBD, and although linking the issue to trade negotiations in the WTO offers the possibility of 'bargain-linkage', there seems to be no appetite for such a deal, even in the Doha Development Round.

However, some defensive measures are possible without formal international agreement. Some developing countries have established systems for registration and formal publication of traditional knowledge. Notably India has established a Traditional Knowledge Digital Library, a database of some 1,200 formulations based on 308 plants for treatments of 214 diseases, translated from ancient texts;[55] and a Traditional Chinese Medicine Patent Database was set up by the Chinese Patent Office, containing over 22,000 records of patent literature with over 40,000 formulas.[56] As the EPO announced in 2009, access to these databases will facilitate the task of examiners, and avoid expensive and lengthy opposition procedures such as those over the neem.[57] Nevertheless, this does not prevent patent applications derived from such traditional knowledge, if they can claim

---

55 www.tkdl.res.in.   56 http://chmp.cnipr.cn/englishversion.
57 News item ' Protecting traditional knowledge: India opens online database to EPO examiners', 11 February 2009, www.epo.org/topics/news/2009/20090211.html.

an inventive step, and in particular if they are based on biotechnological isolation of the active genetic material or purification of active ingredients.

9.2.6 The public domain, commons and private property

As we have seen, the extensions of private proprietary rights have entailed significant appropriations from the public domain, sometimes denounced as a new enclosure of the commons (Boyle 2003). However, as the processes we have examined have shown, both the nature of the public domain and its interaction with private-property claims are fluid and contested. Indeed, the modern concept of the public domain, as a sphere of free circulation and debate of ideas and knowledge, developed together and in interaction with that of IPRs (M. Rose 2003). However, its nature and even existence become contested if private rights can be appropriated on knowledge abstracted from the public domain. Hence, its recent weakening has led some commentators to call for a reconstitution or reimagining of the public domain (Arthurs 2001; Lange 2003).

First, however, it is important to clarify the nature of the public domain, and its relationship with systems of common or collective property. Indeed, there has been a paucity of debate on different ways of shaping property rights, and the term property itself is commonly used as if it were synonymous with private property. Although sometimes thought of as allowing unlimited access for all and use for any purpose, in fact unlike *terra nullius* commons have generally been subject to their own norms of access and use and protected from private appropriation. Roman law had several categories of public, common and collective property (C. M. Rose 2003), and various traditional systems of common property may confine access to persons with a special status, such as shamans or healers, or for specific purposes, such as pasturing animals. Carol Rose has pointed out that in the old Anglo-American common law doctrines of trust, prescription and custom safeguarded various categories of public use of resources that, although capable of private appropriation, were thought to be of greater economic benefit if more generally available.[58] Waldron has distinguished between regimes of collective property, in which use is governed by considerations of the collective social interest, and common property, to which all have access, but which require some

---

58 Rose 1988; her detailed analysis shows how the fluid principles distinguished between rights of a general public in e.g. a road, and those of a more limited group or community, protected by prescriptive or common rights.

method of allocation of use, though there is an overlap between these ideal types (1988: 40–1). Collective property has since the nineteenth century normally involved state ownership, which has generally disintegrated in the past few decades. This has put great pressure on other forms of public property such as commons, but instead of strengthening them they have been weakened. For example, under the traditional patent system, public knowledge is considered a commons, which cannot be privately appropriated. However, as we have seen many of the problems caused by bio-prospecting resulted from a ready acceptance of the principle of isolation from nature, and a weakening of that of prior art.

Hence, the regulation of the commons, and especially of its interface with private property are crucial and delicate. Natural resources, which were treated as common access because they were considered inexhaustible or incapable of private appropriation, have been allowed to be considered *terra nullius* rather than commons. As they became subject to intensification of competition for differing uses, ecological concerns grew. There have also been increased intrusions on resources governed by informal or traditional norms, such as those of indigenous peoples. Concerns about such pressures were articulated by Garrett Hardin's article 'The Tragedy of the Commons' (1968), which had strong resonance. The article focused especially on the impact of population growth on the planet's finite resources, and it has often mistakenly been used as an argument for stronger private-property rights. Ironically, however, Hardin's call was for stronger public regulation even if it intrudes on private freedoms.[59] However, out of the conflicts over private appropriation from the public domain, new concepts of public property and the commons have begun to emerge.[60]

9.2.6.1 Plant breeders, farmers and biodiversity

A significant battle fought at the interface between collective, common and private property has concerned the protection of plant varieties. For long, new varieties were developed by the time-honoured practices of experimental cross-breeding by farmers and botanists. In the early part of the twentieth century this became systematized and supported by systems of quality certification, and many countries established public

---

59 The article advocated 'the necessity of abandoning the commons in breeding' (i.e. population control), which of course has been effectively, if drastically, carried out only by the Peoples' Republic of China (Hardin 1968: 1248; see also Hardin 1998).

60 There have also been some attempts to theorize and investigate models of collective action to govern commons; see notably the work of Elinor Ostrom (1990).

collections both of growing plants (*in situ*) and plant matter (*ex situ*). 'Indeed, in the early days the private sector relied heavily on public lines for the development of new plant varieties... particularly... for field crops such as corn' (Smolders 2005: 7). However, the increasingly large investments in breeding led to pressures for some protection. In 1930, the USA created a plant patent, but only for asexually reproducing plants excluding tubers, while in 1938 Germany provided for a *sui generis* plant variety right (Winter 1992).

On the initiative of France, an international system was established in 1961 by a Union for the Protection of New Varieties of Plants (UPOV). This provided for a plant breeder's right (PBR), to protect any new variety which could be shown to be distinct, uniform and stable. The PBR covered any type of plant, but it was initially defined quite narrowly, covering only commercialization, hence allowing propagation by other breeders. This also meant that growers could save seeds for their own replanting and for exchange, which came to be called the 'farmers' privilege'. However, these exceptions have been narrowed by revisions of UPOV especially in 1991, which extended PBRs to production, reproduction and propagation, and extended protection to harvested material including plants and to essentially derived varieties.[61] States are allowed to retain the farmers' privilege, but only for farmers to propagate for themselves; thus, exchange between farmers or commercialization of a derivative variety require permission. In the meantime in the 1980s, following *Diamond v. Chakrabarty*, the USPTO began to grant ordinary utility patents to plants, and this was approved by a majority decision of the Supreme Court (*JEM Ag. Supply v. Pioneer Hi-Bred* (2001)). The EPC excludes patents for plant varieties and for 'essentially biological processes for the production of plants', but the extent of this limitation is subject to interpretation (Sterckx 2010).

This has created a highly complex situation, with a great variety of forms of protection in different countries, each with its own conditions and providing a different scope of protection (Ghijsen 2009). The US alone offers utility patents, plant patents and plant variety protection; other states are parties to different versions of UPOV, and their national laws can vary greatly (Helfer 2004). TRIPs, article 27 now requires WTO members to provide some 'effective' form of plant variety protection, and

---

61 Article 15 of the 1991 UPOV Act limits the exception to acts done for private and non-commercial purposes, experimental purposes, and for breeding other varieties; and it permits a limited exception for farmers to propagate only for themselves. Thus, exchange between farmers or commercialization of a derivative variety require permission.

developing countries have been urged to take advantage of the flexibilities offered by UPOV.[62] Indeed, this arena can be seen as a paradigmatic example of the strategic interactions through which conflicting and overlapping regulatory processes create 'regime complexes' (Raustiala and Victor 2004).

At the same time, the intensification of plant breeding, especially through biotechnology, raised issues about the legitimate uses of plant material or germplasm made available freely in public collections. There was particular concern about the use of material housed in the network of International Agricultural Research Centers (IARCs), loosely coordinated through the Consultative Group on International Agricultural Research (CGIAR), aimed particularly at food crops for developing countries. This had originated with a programme initiated by the Rockefeller Foundation with the Mexican government in 1943, which developed a high-yielding wheat variety, later transferred to India. In response to concern about the food crisis in poor countries, the network of IARCs grew, the Food and Agriculture Organization (FAO) played an increased role, and in 1971 the World Bank agreed to set up and host the CGIAR.[63]

From this perspective, there was greater concern for safeguarding biodiversity as collective or common property. Hence, the FAO in 1983 adopted a plan of action for a Global System for Conservation and Utilization of Plant Genetic Resources. Its centrepiece was a formally non-binding Undertaking, which firmly stated that it was 'based on the universally accepted principle that plant genetic resources are a heritage of mankind and consequently should be available without restriction'.[64] However,

---

62 Smolders 2005; Cullet (2001) evaluates the African model statute and the Indian legislation, shows the disadvantages of monopoly rights, and suggests an alternative which is TRIPs compatible.

63 See www.cgiar.org/who/history/origins.html. Its somewhat uncertain status was articulated in 2009 in a grand Joint Declaration, which states that it consists of the Consortium of fifteen IARCs 'with its funders, working with partners to implement an agreed strategy and results framework consistent with this Joint Declaration [which] is a non-binding statement of aspiration and intent'.

64 The term 'common heritage of mankind' is used in international law to denote areas regarded as beyond national sovereignty, in particular the moon, the resources of the deep seabed and Antarctica (Baslar 1998). However, the treaties governing these areas established regimes to govern them, whereas the 1983 Undertaking referred only to 'international cooperation' and 'arrangements' which should be developed. Safrin (2004: 645) argues that the lack of a regime indicates that the term was misused, and what was intended was to establish 'international common property'; however, in view of the provisional nature of the Undertaking, it seems likely that it was hoped to establish a regime, and it is not clear that international law distinguishes between collective and

the implications of this principle were contested. Agreed Interpretations adopted in 1989 declared that PBRs, especially as governed by the UPOV, were 'not incompatible' with the Undertaking, and that 'free access does not mean free of charge'. A separate resolution endorsed the general concept of farmers' rights 'vested in the International Community, as trustee for present and future generations of farmers';[65] and a later resolution in 1991 affirmed that the 'common heritage' principle was subject to state sovereignty over plant genetic resources. As we have seen, this was elaborated in the CBD in 1992.[66] However, regulation of the use of germplasm accessed from public collections was left for further discussion in the FAO. During the 1990s controversies arose about patenting of biotechnological innovations derived from matter acquired from IARCs. In one case, a disease-resistant gene was sequenced, cloned and patented in California, though derived from a wild rice variety from Mali, and identified by scientists in India and the Philippines; the California scientists consulted IP specialist John Barton, who devised a benefit-sharing arrangement for licensing the gene, to fund scholarships for students from Mali, though no income resulted (Gupta 2005: 81–102).

Following extensive negotiations, agreement was finally reached in 2001 on an International Treaty on Plant Genetic Resources for Food and Agriculture (IT–PGRFA), which entered into force in 2004.[67] It committed the parties to promote sustainable agriculture, within an international framework, and spelled out in more detail the principle of farmers' rights, including the right to seeds, although these depend on state regulation. Its most distinctive and innovative achievement was the establishment of a multilateral system which aims both to provide open source access to seeds and other germplasm for research, breeding and crop development, and to channel income from any commercial development into a global fund to promote conservation and sustainable

common property. Indeed, the character of the deep seabed regime is far from clear, it has been the target of bio-prospectors, and several hundred patents have been issued on organisms originating there (Prows 2006).

65 As noted above, this concept was implicit in the UPOV, but it emerged in FAO discussions (see www.farmersrights.org/about/fr_history.html).

66 An influential background role seems to have been played by an informal group known as the Keystone Dialogue, initiated by William Brown, then chair of the US National Board for Plant Genetic Resources, which issued a Final Consensus Report in 1991: see www.farmersrights.org/about/fr_history_part3.html, and Prieto-Acosta 2006: 64.

67 Mekouar 2002; see www.planttreaty.org; it now has 127 parties, not including China, Japan or the USA (which was a signatory), but including the EU and its Member States, as well as most developing countries.

use of plant genetic resources, particularly by farmers and indigenous communities.

However, the IT–PGRFA still retains some ambiguity as to whether private rights can be claimed on material derived from the resources accessed from the open-source system. Its key article 12.3(d) states:

> Recipients shall not claim any intellectual property or other rights that limit the facilitated access to plant genetic resources for food and agriculture, or their genetic parts or components, in the form received from the multilateral system.

This was the result of a compromise in the drafting negotiations (Mekouar 2002; Cooper 2002; Helfer 2004: 89), and the implications of the term 'in the form received' are far from clear. Nevertheless, the phrase is repeated in the Standard Material Transfer Agreement (SMTA), which has been adopted to provide uniform licensing terms for material accessed under this multilateral system.[68]

States party to the IT–PGRFA agreed to place under the multilateral system all plant genetic resources under their control and in the public domain for sixty-four crops listed in Annex 1, and invited others to do the same. The listed items were chosen for their importance for food and agriculture, but did not include important crops such as tomatoes, soybeans or peanuts. A major extension resulted in 2006 when agreements were signed with eleven of the IARCs, which hold *ex situ* collections of some 650,000 accessions of germplasm, including the world's most important crops. As the IARCs began using the SMTA in 2007, it has become a foundational instrument for managing the use of plant material in breeding and biotechnology.

The SMTA establishes a kind of regulated global commons for material made available within the system. Conditions are laid down on recipients of material, which they in turn must apply if they transfer the material to others. They are that: (a) use of the material is only for 'the purposes of research, breeding and training for food and agriculture' not including 'chemical, pharmaceutical and/or other non-food/feed industrial uses'; (b) recipients are required to make available all non-confidential information resulting from R&D on the material through the treaty's information-sharing system; and they are encouraged to share with others the non-monetary benefits of the system (transfer of technology and capacity-building to developing countries); (c) recipients cannot

---

68 Available from www.planttreaty.org/smta_en.htm.

claim IPRs on the material or its genetic components 'in the form received'; (d) if a recipient commercializes a PGRFA product that incorporates material, a defined royalty must be paid if such product is not available to others without restriction for further research and breeding;[69] if there is no such restriction, defined voluntary payments are encouraged; (e) if recipients transfer material to another person, or transfer to another person IPRs on any products derived from the material or its components, such transfers must be subject to the same conditions, including the benefit-sharing obligations.

The emphasis of the system is on ensuring use for the collective good, and sharing the results of research and development. However, it accepts that a commercialized product may result, and in that case expects monetary benefit sharing; this is compulsory if the product restricts further research and breeding. The basic royalty is specified as 1.1 per cent less 30 per cent of gross sales (in effect 0.68 per cent). This income will flow into a Benefit Sharing Fund, to be used to finance projects under a Global Plan of Action adopted in 1996. It is not yet clear how much income this will produce, and the strategic plan adopted in 2009 envisages that the Fund will mainly depend on other sources. There are obvious similarities with the kind of open-access systems that have been developed for software (to be discussed at 9.3), as some commentators have pointed out (Srinivas 2006; Hope 2008: 306; Aoki 2009).

At the same time, the debates about, and the introduction of concepts and systems for, benefit sharing have begun to provide a means for managing the contested interactions between different resource regimes and knowledge domains. As Anil Gupta, founder of the Honey Bee Network, has argued: '[a]chieving sustainability in resource use requires the fusion of sacred with secular, formal with informal, and reductionist with holistic views' (Gupta 2005: 31). He has proposed various ways to provide incentives and non-monetary benefits, as well as monetary remuneration, emphasizing that: '[i]ncentives for creating a sufficiently strong desire for experimentation will become embedded when modern institutions recognize, respect and reward the experiments done in the past' (Gupta 2005: 29). However, as his practical experience has shown, this requires

---

69 The FAO's website provides no guidance on what this means; however, one of the IARCs, the International Rice Research Institute, advises that 'Plant Breeder's Rights under UPOV type Plant Varietal Protection (PVP) laws do not restrict the further use of the variety for research and breeding. Commercialization of a new variety that is protected by this type of Plant Breeder's Rights developed from IRRI germplasm would not trigger mandatory payments under the Treaty' (see www.irri.org).

scientists to work closely with local communities, to encourage and support grassroots innovators.[70] The formal top-down systems for benefit sharing can only at best provide a framework for such bottom-up activity.

9.2.6.2 Geographical indications and ethical or cultural brands

Some forms of collective property have also, rather unexpectedly, come into increasing prominence. The TRIPs agreement itself provides international protection for geographical indications (GIs), which are a type of collective property in favour of producers of goods the quality or reputation of which is linked to a specific locality. They are defined in TRIPs, article 22 as:

> indications which identify a good as originating in the territory of a Member, or a region or locality in that territory, where a given quality, reputation or other characteristic of the good is essentially attributable to its geographical origin.

International protection of GIs has long been considered important, as a matter of consumer protection or fair competition.[71] Thus, article 10 of the Paris Convention requires states to provide protection against unfair competition, including in particular 'indications . . . the use of which in the course of trade is liable to mislead the public as to the nature, the manufacturing process [or] the characteristics . . . of the goods'. This is now specifically incorporated into TRIPs, which also requires states to:

> provide the legal means for interested parties to prevent the use of any means in the designation or presentation of a good that indicates or suggests that the good in question originates in a geographical area other than the true place of origin in a manner which misleads the public as to the geographical origin of the good.

Member states are also required to refuse or invalidate a trade mark which contains a GI if it would mislead the public. Much may depend on what may be regarded in each country as misleading to 'the public'. Thus, the Scotch Whisky Association successfully opposed registration in India of 'Highland Chief', together with an image of a man in tartan,

---

70 For more about this work, see www.sristi.org.
71 For an account of international agreements relating to GIs, their relation to TRIPs, and an analysis of the TRIPs provisions on GIs, see UNCTAD–ICTSD 2005: ch. 15.

as a trade mark for a 'malted whisky'.[72] Also, a GI need not be a place name, but can be any kind of mark indicating a link with a place. Thus, a US company patented a rice variety, claiming 'Basmati-like' properties, and also registered trade marks, Kasmati and Texmati, but both the patent and the trademarks were successfully challenged by the Indian government (Rangnekar 2010: 9). TRIPs, article 23 also includes more specific protection for wines and spirits: it requires states to prevent the use of GIs identifying wines or spirits not originating in the place indicated by the GI, without reference to the test of misleading the public. Included in the Doha Round negotiations are proposals, debated and contested for over a decade, to create a multilateral register for GIs for wines and spirits, and to extend the higher level of protection in article 23 to other GIs.

GIs are especially interesting because they are collective or 'club goods' (Rangnekar 2004). Those entitled to use the GI benefit from the reputational advantages given by the link between the product, its place of origin, and the characteristics and quality associated with the product. Others can have access to the knowledge involved, but cannot benefit from using the GI. Thus, the club's membership rules and their monitoring are very important, as are the often detailed rules governing the product's quality and its production methods. The geographic link may be used to require local production and therefore protect producers in a specific locality. The economic advantages of a GI may produce considerable tensions and conflicts, but GIs are also 'invested with social and cultural meaning' which underpins the norms. This can create a shared sense of commitment and interdependence that help to build trust, resulting in 'cooperative competition', while also linking producers and consumers (Rangnekar 2010: 16–19).

In many ways similar to GIs is the creation of brand names or trade marks which are collectively owned or licensed for use by persons or groups complying with membership rules and production requirements. Most prominent are the ethical brands, chief among them being the Fairtrade mark, with its distinctive symbol, created in 2002. This is owned by the Fairtrade Labelling Organization International (FLO), which has developed and maintains the standards, while the important system of certification is done by an independent company, FLO-CERT.

---

72 This and other examples are given in the excellent account in Rangnekar 2010. See also the Special Issue on the Law and Economics of GIs, edited by Rangnekar, in the *Journal of World Intellectual Property*, March 2010.

Similarly, collective trade marks have been used to protect and support traditional art forms. Some have a long history, for example the creation by the Canadian government in 1958 of the 'igloo' logo, to certify items such as soapstone carvings as handmade by an Inuit. A more recent initiative was made by Creative New Zealand, a governmental arts-funding organization, to establish the 'toi-iho' mark, based on a process of peer review and verification by Maori artists of cultural and artistic identity and continuing practice. However, this met with diverse criticisms, on the one hand of under-promotion, and on the other of cultural commodification, and a decision was taken in 2009 to 'divest' the brand. Indeed, it is as important to prevent use of trade marks in ways which are offensive or denigratory to traditional culture (Brown and Nicholas 2010). As with traditional knowledge, protection and promotion of cultural heritage raises ethical and political concerns as well as economic considerations, and now involves complex interactions of various regulatory regimes (Coombe 2010).

9.3 Copyright, creativity and communication

9.3.1 Nature and scope of protection

Copyright protection for creative works is automatic,[73] the length of the term of protection has been increasingly extended,[74] and the requirement of originality which establishes the threshold of protection is generally set very low.[75] However, protection is only against copying: copyright does

---

73 Since its 1908 revision, the Berne Convention has prohibited any formalities as a condition of protection, although registration is used in some countries to determine authorship or ownership; the USA was virtually alone during most of the twentieth century in conditioning protection on affixing a copyright notice, publishing and depositing a copy, and registering claims in the Copyright Office; since the USA joined Berne in 1988 these are no longer a condition of protection (Goldstein 2001: 191).

74 The internationally agreed standard is now generally the life of the author plus 50 years, although for collective works such as cine films it is normally 50 years from publication (Berne Convention, art. 7; TRIPs, art. 12). However, it was extended to life of the author plus 70 years in the EU from 1995, and in the USA by the Sonny Bono Copyright Term Extension Act 1998: for details of the progressive extensions of the copyright term in the USA, see Brief for the Petitioners in the Supreme Court in *Eldred* v. *Ashcroft* (2002) (available from http://cyber.law.harvard.edu/eldredvreno/legaldocs.html).

75 Even in countries in the *droit d'auteur* tradition, a work must simply have the stamp of a human author. A compilation can be treated as a work in its own right if some skill is involved in the selection or arrangement. This now applies to databases, and in the EU an additional and more limited *sui generis* database right applies even if no such skill is involved, but its creation entailed substantial investment.

not protect ideas but only the forms in which they are expressed.[76] This is now firmly stated in TRIPs, article 9(2): 'Copyright protection shall extend to expressions and not to ideas, procedures, methods of operation or mathematical concepts as such'. Hence, emulation by independent means is permitted in principle; in practice, however, there is usually a presumption that the later work must have been copied. What constitutes copying may be a matter of interpretation: a substantially similar work may be considered to constitute non-literal copying. This makes reverse engineering hazardous, requiring specific provisions if decompilation is to be permitted.[77]

9.3.1.1 Extensions of private rights

In most national laws the scope of protection was defined from quite early as the right to control 'reproduction' (Ricketson and Ginsburg 2006a: 622ff.). This elastic concept gave the flexibility to extend the author's exclusive rights of authorization to derivative works (translations and adaptations), and then to new technological forms of communication: a recording, a wire or wireless broadcast, and eventually communication over the internet.[78] However, this proceeded at a different pace and with variations in each country, so the initial extensions to include mechanical and cinematographic reproduction were covered by specific provisions in revisions of the Berne Convention, until the 1967 revision gave an owner the exclusive right to control reproduction 'in any manner or form'. Thus, there has been a steady expansion of the scope of rights protected, and of what is meant by 'copying'.

At the same time, copyright has also been greatly widened by its extension during the twentieth century to grant separate rights in essentially industrial products: first photographs and cine films; and then sound recordings, and sound and television broadcasts, although in many

---

76 Berne applies to 'every production in the literary, scientific and artistic domain, whatever may be the mode or form of its expression', leaving it to states to determine whether expression means that works must be 'fixed in a material form'; it also allows states to exclude from protection 'official texts of a legislative, administrative and legal nature', and 'news of the day' (which was apparently intended to mean the facts, rather than reportage).

77 Notably, in art. 6 of the EC Directive on Legal Protection of Computer Programs 91/250/EEC.

78 The WIPO Copyright Treaty 1996 extended the author's right to control communication to the public to include making available works by any means by which 'members of the public may access these works from a place and at a time individually chosen by them'.

countries these are treated as 'neighbouring rights'.[79] This leads to a multi-plicity of owners of private rights in relation to a single product or activity: while the composer of a song, and the author of its lyrics, must authorize a performance or recording of it, rights in the recording belong to its producer. Additional specific protections have been created, for example in the UK for the typographical arrangement of a book, and in the EU for databases which do not meet the minimum originality requirements for full copyright protection as compilations. Computer programs do not easily fit into copyright, as they also are essentially collaboratively produced functional products rather than literary works, but copyright protection was gradually conceded in the 1990s, and is now required by TRIPs, article 10.[80] On the other hand, performers, to whom it may seem hard to deny the status of creative artist, have experienced greater difficulty in obtaining a property right.[81]

Despite the frequent assertion that copyright is necessary to reward and encourage creativity, in practice an enormous number of creative works are disseminated free by their authors, while the remainder are mostly owned contractually by firms. Thus, the commercial exploitation of IPRs in practice is done not by the inventor or creator, but by a commercial developer or intermediary such as a publisher. Control of copyrights greatly contributed to the growth of media empires in the second half of the twentieth century.[82] Although the media industries have effectively lobbied for the continual extension and strengthening of copyright as essential to the growth of the information economy, one leading copyright specialist and judge has gone so far as to say that:

---

79 Internationally protected by the Rome Convention for the Protection of Performers, Producers of Phonograms and Broadcasting Organizations of 1961, and the Geneva Phonograms Convention 1971; now by specific provisions in the TRIPs agreement art. 14, and the WIPO Performances and Phonograms Treaty of 1996.
80 Cornish and Llewelyn 2007: 806ff.; for an analysis of the problem and a proposal for a more appropriate *sui generis* solution, see Samuelson *et al.* 1994.
81 As already mentioned, the first authors' right was to authorize public performances, and the extension of the Berne Convention to give performers a right to their performance was resisted on the grounds that their role is less creative and should not be allowed to reduce the remuneration for authors (Ricketson and Ginsburg 2006a: 508–9); only under the Rome Convention of 1961 were they given the more limited right to control fixation of their performances, although this has now been extended to a property right to control dissemination of those fixations as part of a general extension of rights over recordings (WIPO Performances and Phonograms Treaty 1996; EU Directive 2001/29/EEC, art. 3). Of course, these rights are normally owned by the recording and media companies.
82 For example, Robert Maxwell built Pergamon Press on his acquisition of rights in German technical publications.

the fact that our system of communication, teaching and entertainment does not grind to a standstill is in large part due to the fact that in most cases infringement of copyright has, historically, been ignored.

(Laddie 1996: 257)

9.3.1.2 Exceptions and the public domain

The breadth of private rights means that the existence and extent of a public domain depend essentially on limitations or exceptions to copyright protection. The prohibition on copying applies to the whole or a substantial part of a work, but it is generally considered that even a small fragment can be substantial, such as a phrase of a literary work. Nevertheless, the Berne Convention provides for only one mandatory exception or permitted use: to allow quotations from a published work in a way that is 'compatible with fair practice' and to an extent justifiable by the purpose (article 10.1). States are allowed to make further exceptions, and the Berne Convention specifies use 'by way of illustration' for teaching provided it is 'compatible with fair practice' (article 10.2), and some uses in connection with news reporting (article 10*bis*). In many cases, such permitted uses are subject to arrangements for remuneration (to be discussed below).[83]

Rather than specify lists of further permitted exceptions, the 1967 revision included a general provision in article 9(2) allowing states to permit reproduction 'in certain special cases, provided that such reproduction does not conflict with a normal exploitation of the work and does not unreasonably prejudice the legitimate interests of the author'. This is now described as the three-step test, and was transposed into article 13 of TRIPs, but with the significant replacement of 'author' by 'right-holder'. In effect this gives the WTO's Council for TRIPs, and its dispute-settlement institutions headed by the Appellate Body, the ultimate power to decide on the legitimacy of copyright exceptions which protect the public domain.

Not surprisingly, the extent of exceptions has been highly contested, especially with the emergence of digital technology. In particular, use for educational, scientific or research purposes, and private use, although long accepted in principle, have become controversial. From the viewpoint of right-owners, the new technologies that allow individuals to make their own copies, from the photocopier to the DVD writer, threaten their exclusive right to control commercialization (Ricketson and Ginsburg 2006a: 780). On the other hand, users generally consider that they should

---

83 For a helpful survey and analysis of the exceptions and their application in the digital environment, prepared for WIPO, see Ricketson 2003.

have the right to photocopy part of a book, record a broadcast programme, or copy music to use on a new device or share with friends.

Thus, the paradox of copyright is that its central justification was and remains the public interest in encouraging the production of literary and artistic works to ensure a vibrant public sphere (Davies 1994); yet the gradual but inexorable extension of the scope of exclusive rights has given private owners the means to try to control and police that public sphere, challenging activities popularly considered legitimate. Copyright law attempts to mediate the ensuing tensions and conflicts.

9.3.2 Collective licensing and the socialization of property rights

An important method for managing this interface has been various forms of collective licensing. Collective rights organizations (CROs) have in practice been the main means for securing remuneration from 'secondary' rights in the audio-visual industries which dominated the twentieth century. Indeed, the first CROs were founded in France soon after the initial creation of the right for authors to control performances of their work.[84] However, the new technologies created new commercial opportunities, but also threats. The extension of both the scope of the author's right, and of copyright protection itself, to new formats created arenas of contestation, for example between the composer and lyricist of a song and the recording and broadcasting companies which could exploit its mass-marketing. While the primary rights could be dealt with by individual contracts, this is impractical for secondary uses by a mass public. In effect, it is these secondary uses that defined the commons of open communication: broadcasting, performing in public spaces, lending by libraries, and use for education and research. It was from the conflicts between private property in IPRs and the public spheres of mass communication that CROs emerged.

The legal framework for CROs has varied both between and within different jurisdictions, depending on the relative economic, political and cultural pressures generated by the different creators and users of the

---

84 The French copyright law of 1791 resulted from pressures by an informal association instigated by the dramatist Beaumarchais, which was incorporated in 1829 as the SACD (Société des auteurs et compositeurs dramatiques); and the legal support for a right of composers over performances of their music in the famous legal action in 1847 against the café-concert Les Ambassadeurs (now famous from the Toulouse Lautrec painting) resulted in the creation in 1851 of SACEM (Société des auteurs, compositeurs et éditeurs de musique); for a legal study of these CROs, see Schmidt 1971; and for a legal account of CROs in different countries, see Gervais 2010.

works in question. For example, in the UK in the last part of the nineteenth century, publishers profited mainly from sales of sheet music. Hence, the attempt by one Harry Wall in 1875 to set up a Copyright and Performing Rights Protection Office, by acquiring rights and demanding £2 plus costs from 'penny readings' and charity concerts was widely resented, and resulted in legislation to protect the public from what was regarded as extortion. An attempt in 1902 to form a British branch of SACEM was abandoned, and it was only after protection was extended to mechanical reproduction that the Performing Rights Society was launched in 1914. The concerns that there would be public resentment of a 'tax on music' were borne out when it was denounced as an 'inquisitorial combine' and un-English, and its early history was decidedly chequered, the key to its survival being its ability to strike deals with the BBC (Ehrlich 1989).

In the USA the power of the recording industry ensured that music 'mechanical' (recording) rights were subject to a statutory licence, under which the royalty remained legislatively fixed at 2 cents from 1909 to 1978.[85] Although this has been criticized as rigid (Merges 1996: 1313–14), it certainly succeeded in stimulating the massive growth of a recorded music industry, without noticeably diminishing the enthusiasm of composers to write songs.[86] In contrast, music performances have been licensed by privately formed organizations, beginning with the establishment of the American Society of Composers, Authors and Publishers (ASCAP) in 1914. However, users were reluctant to pay unless coerced by litigation, which left the courts to decide how far the exclusive rights could validly extend and legitimately be enforced.[87] In fact, decades of legal battles entailed payment of enormous lawyers' fees which have sometimes rivalled the income generated for composers (Kernochan 1985: 398). Resort by users to the antitrust laws resulted in consent decrees, which made the performing-rights organizations in effect regulated bodies.[88]

---

85 They remain fixed by statute, with a slightly more complex formula (including a rate of 24c for ringtones); details are given on the website of the Harry Fox Agency, which administers them on behalf of owners.

86 Under the 1976 Copyright Act, this became assimilated to a compulsory licensing regime, supervised by a Copyright Royalty Tribunal, established for cable, jukebox and public broadcasting performances.

87 ASCAP was effectively empowered by the Supreme Court decision in *Herbert* v. *Shanley* (1917) which narrowly defined the 'for profit' limitation of the music performance right, to cover music played to entertain diners in a restaurant.

88 The broadcasters also formed their own rival body to compete with ASCAP, Broadcast Music Incorporated, which accepted a consent decree shortly before ASCAP did (Kernochan 1985: 395–9).

They are now well established, and distribute around $1.5bn per year to their members or beneficiaries (Merges 2008).

From the private-property perspective, licensing schemes merely offer a solution to the collective-action and transaction-costs problems for individual owners to control the use made of their property (Handtke and Towse 2007). From this angle, any element of compulsion to licence may be considered an intrusion on the private-property right, since it means that 'the exclusive right to authorise has been degraded to a mere right to remuneration' (Jehoram 2001: 136). However, this assumes that the specification of the property right adequately and clearly reflects the incentives–access balance; as we have seen, this balance has been tilted by the inexorable extension of private rights, generally in favour of ownership by media corporations. Also, new technologies create new forms of diffusion which require that balance to be reformulated (Gallagher 2001). A composer could hardly have expected to obtain the same royalty for airplays on the new-fangled wireless as might have been appropriate from music-hall performances. In practice, the levels of remuneration have been set by licensing schemes, which experience shows entail some compulsion on both sides, if only to set the parameters for negotiation.

Thus, with the advent of photocopying in the 1960s, publishers revived the familiar refrain of 'piracy', although the real issue was the appropriate return (if any) that print publishers should obtain from the secondary market created by this new technology, and the legal disputes focused on the extent of the exception for 'fair dealing for research and private study' (Picciotto 2002). The rapid spread of private-copying technologies, first audio and then video recorders, created further conflicts, around the private-copying exception. The response in many countries, especially in continental Europe, was to establish systems of levies, either on copying equipment such as photocopiers, or media such as tapes and CDs. The income is distributed through the CROs, which stoutly maintain that the levies are remuneration to rights-owners for permitted uses and not a tax (IFFRO 2008: 7). However, despite attempts to ensure that payments correspond to the use made of individual authors' rights, both the collection and distribution of income depend on survey methodologies, which are inevitably broad-brush, and sometimes biased. Some of the income from levies is generally used for 'social' purposes, such as supporting needy authors, which sometimes raises suspicions of patronage and even corruption. With the transition to the digital environment, the suitability of levy systems became a matter of debate and uncertainty, as computers are multi-purpose machines (Hugenholtz et al. 2003).

Much of the public sphere is now subject to regulation by collective licensing, since the insertion of the three-step test in article 9(2) of the TRIPs agreement had the effect of making the permitted uses conditional on remuneration if feasible. This was seen in the first complaint under these provisions, brought by the EU essentially on behalf of the CROs representing the European music industries, wishing to extend the coverage of their licensing schemes by reducing the scope of the public performance exceptions in US law. These exceptions were the result of a delicate political compromise in Congress reflecting the long-standing and widespread practice of playing radio broadcasts in small cafés and stores; hence, the law allowed radio broadcasting without payment in business premises below a specified size (the 'business' exception), and of any broadcast performance by means of a 'homestyle' receiver (the 'homestyle' exception).[89] The Panel decided that the 'business' exception was too broad to qualify as a 'special case', but the 'homestyle' exception could do so. On the second two criteria of the three-step test, the panel first rejected the EU's argument that the lack of remuneration necessarily conflicts with normal exploitation and prejudices legitimate interests. It took the view that a conflict with a normal exploitation arises 'if uses, that in principle are covered by that right but exempted under the exception or limitation, enter into economic competition with the ways that right holders normally extract economic value from ... the copyright ... and thereby deprive them of significant or tangible commercial gains' (*US – Copyright Act* (2000): para. 6.183). However, it also stressed that 'normal exploitation' should be viewed dynamically in relation to the potential markets, and not merely to the existing situation, so that the central consideration was whether licensing could reasonably be organized and become accepted. It found that licensing could reasonably be provided for many of the uses covered by the 'business' exception, but not for the 'homestyle' cases. As regards the 'legitimate interests' requirement, the Panel's view was that the test should be whether the exception 'causes or has the potential to cause an unreasonable loss of income to the copyright owner'. This essentially meant whether a licensing scheme would produce reasonable levels of income. This again depends on the willingness of users to pay rates acceptable to owners. However, there can be a big gap between the expectations of owners and the willingness to pay of users. The price will determine the allocation of the benefits resulting from new communications technology, and may significantly affect its

89 For an analysis of the dispute and its background, see Helfer 2000.

impact: if owners demand a high fee for reproduction rights, the use of new communications technology would be significantly inhibited.

Thus, the regimes of collective administration of rights are an arena for contending concepts of property, and of allocation of rights and remuneration. Private-property idealists see them as at best a necessary evil, and deplore the notion that licensing should be compulsory (Jehoram 2001), ignoring the fact that compulsion results from the initial definition of the property right. Others see them as powerful yet increasingly fragile, precisely due to the vain attempts to force them into a private-property paradigm, and argue for their reconceptualization as forms of regulation (Kretschmer 2002a). In practice, although there is a wide variety of CROs, they generally involve collective contracts operating under legal constraints, either through competition laws or specific statutory schemes.[90] They override the authors' exclusive rights, since the schemes are generally compulsory, though subject to some form of administrative or judicial supervision. Thus, they have been described as entailing a socialization of property rights (Strowel and Doutrelepont 1989; Kretschmer 2002b).

9.3.3 Digital dilemmas

The most dramatic conflicts, which have shaken the private-property paradigm of copyright to its core, have occurred in the arena of the new digital economy. Many discussions of its impact on IPRs limit themselves to the problem of ease of copying of products in digital form, but the issues go deeper than that.

The central elements of the digital economy are *decommodification* and *decentralization*. Both further exacerbate the characteristics which create such powerful contradictions at the heart of IPRs. In the analogue economy, intangible cultural or knowledge goods can generally be commercialized by sale in a physically embodied form, even if their value far exceeds that of the form (for example the pleasure or profit to be derived from a book compared to the paper on which it is printed). Indeed, as already explained, copyright protects works in a material form. In its digital form, the same work can be communicated in disembodied form as electrical impulses, which are reconstituted so that it can be enjoyed

90 A survey is provided by Sinacore-Guinn 1993, who nevertheless tries to maintain that the 'golden rule' is that 'Collective administration must be designed and operated in a manner supportive of the private rights nature of creative rights' (1993: 815). For a detailed analysis of the important role of regulatory contracts in France, see Schmidt 1971.

by means of devices controlled by the user (a computer, an audio or digital player, etc.). This is linked to the element of decentralization. In the digital age, the relationship between the producer and the consumer (or rather user) is transformed, since the user also controls the means of production/reproduction. This opens up the possibility of much more interactive relationships, and indeed of new forms of networked production (Benkler 2003). These possibilities have been made very real by the establishment and growth of the internet. Decommodification and decentralization, combined with instant global communication through the internet, pose fundamental challenges to both the viability and legitimacy of the private-property, exclusive-right paradigm of copyright.

9.3.3.1 Defending exclusivity

Not surprisingly, the reaction of industries based on that paradigm has been to defend themselves, by seeking to bolster up copyright protection. As already mentioned, courts, legislatures and eventually the TRIPs agreement negotiators have been persuaded to give (rather inappropriate) copyright protection to computer programs; and they have also been given patent protection.[91] To protect digital products, the media industries have invested heavily in technological protection measures (TPMs): digital watermarks, encryption and content-management systems. These are attacked by critics as crippling products to make them 'defective by design',[92] but justified by their defenders as digital locks on private property and described as 'self-help systems' (Dam 2001). However, in the face of user resistance and subversion by hackers state sanctions have been required, to criminalize circumvention of TPMs to try to ensure excludability.[93] This generated new concerns about restriction of the public domain, by overriding exceptions and limitations on copyright (Nimmer 2000; Sheets 2000; Therien 2001), as well as about intrusion on the privacy of consumers (Bygrave 2002). One critic described them as a 'privatization trend' taking away law's role in managing the interface

---

91 For a discussion and critique of the decision to grant patent protection to software in the USA, see Lessig 2001: 207ff. In 2007 Amazon paid an undisclosed sum to settle a claim that its site infringed patents held by IBM on aspects of networking and e-commerce; while Amazon had itself earlier defended patents on its 'one-click' procedure against claims by rival bookseller Barnes & Noble (Waters 2007).

92 www.defectivebydesign.org.

93 Agreed internationally in the WIPO Copyright Treaty 1996, and enacted by the US Digital Millennium Copyright Act 1998 (DMCA), and the EU's 'Information Society' Directive (2001/29/EEC, arts. 6 and 7).

between private rights and the public sphere, which is 'transforming the Internet from a two-way medium of active cultural participation among citizens into a one-way medium for content distribution to passive consumers' (Jackson 2001).

TPMs also enable DRM (digital rights management), by which rights-owners attempt to control commercialization. Although digital technology and the internet enable easy worldwide communication and copying, the same technology makes it possible to set up control and payment systems. However, multimedia products are far from simple items of private property: they involve not only rights in the creative works involved (lyrics, music, text, graphics, performances) but also in the technological processes (software), including the TPMs themselves. Such software products are usually licensed, under terms which may assert rights over derivative works resulting from their use, so they can create further complex problems of joint ownership (Field 2001). This greatly complicates the problems of allocation of revenue streams.

Even more important than the potential resources involved in attempting to enforce exclusive rights in a networked world, however, is the investment of legitimacy. A very powerful popular ideology has quickly taken root, which considers the internet as a realm of freedom which should facilitate global human interaction, without state or corporate control. This is accompanied by a great reluctance to pay toll charges on the information superhighway. Although decried as unrealistic by corporate interests, it could be seen as rooted in an instinctual understanding of the basic economics of digital communication: the virtually zero marginal costs of access, most of which are borne by the user. Even leaving aside the issue of managing payments, the deployment of TPMs to control the use of content can create extensive problems and widespread resentment.

Open warfare broke out over peer-to-peer file-sharing. On the side of rights-owners it was led by the Recording Industry Association of America, and its international arm the International Federation of the Phonographic Industry, which blamed digital downloading for the decline of the hitherto highly lucrative CD sales. Their first legal target was the Napster website, which provided facilities for free file-sharing. Napster relied mainly on the argument which had proved successful in cases in the earlier period, when Sony had defended its home video recorders, on the grounds that they could be, and mostly were, used for 'time-shifting' (recording a TV programme for later viewing), which courts accepted was within the permitted fair use exception. The US federal courts in California decided this did not apply to Napster, since its users were making their files publicly available, and Napster 'knew or had reason to know' that copyright infringement was involved (*Napster* (2000)). Nevertheless, the appeal court modified the injunction against Napster to require the record companies to supply it with notice of infringing files, and an opportunity to remove them. This only delayed the demise of Napster, which was acquired in bankruptcy by Roxio in 2002, but relaunched as a subscription service.

Quickly, however, similar facilities were offered based on newer, more decentralized technologies, in which files are not stored or indexed on a central server, although they do use intermediary sites to host linking files known as 'torrents'. Fresh litigation against the suppliers of this software, Grokster and StreamCast Networks, caused the lower courts more problems, but the US Supreme Court firmly found them liable, essentially on the grounds that they were 'actively inducing' copyright infringement (*Grokster* (2005)). A similar case in Australia against the software's author, KaZaa, also succeeded, on the slightly different legal grounds that it 'authorized' copyright infringement (Ricketson and Ginsburg 2006b). In 2009 a court case closed down the notorious website the Pirate Bay in Sweden (Edwards 2009: 78–80).

Despite these successful cases against relatively easy legal targets, peer-to-peer file-sharing continued unabated. Legal cases brought directly against file-sharers, often teenagers, brought unfavourable publicity, and strengthened campaigns to defend internet freedoms. Rights-owners were obliged to shift to more difficult opponents, the internet service providers (ISPs) which are key intermediary nodes providing access to the internet. Anticipating their vulnerability, not only for copyright infringement but for other problematic content distributed through their services, the ISPs lobbied around the world for a limited liability regime. They argued that they are mere conduits or 'common carriers' like postal services, and despite a counter-attack by the media industries, achieved some protection from liability, under both the DMCA in the USA, and the EU's Electronic Commerce Directive.[94] These provide that those ISPs which are no more than conduits are generally not liable for content sent by users; but if they host or store information they are exempt only if they have no actual or constructive knowledge of illegal activity or information. On this basis, hosting ISPs established procedures for 'Notice and Take Down', so that once notified of content claimed to be illegal, they will remove it. This was in turn criticized by civil liberties groups, which found evidence

---

94 Directive 2000/31/EC 8 June 2000.

that they often remove content alleged to be illegal without checking, thus infringing freedom of speech.

Rights-owners were however unsatisfied, and broadened their campaign. They targeted hosting sites, some of which had become successful by providing intermediary services, such as eBay, Facebook and YouTube. Thus, eBay was accused of facilitating the sale of counterfeit products, and a French court in a case brought by luxury brand-owner Louis Vuitton Moet Hennessy found serious faults in eBay's processes and levied a substantial fine. However, other courts have been reluctant to require proactive policing by ISPs,[95] though some have argued that filtering technology is available and should be used (Goldsmith and Wu 2006). This issue was brought to a head by the titanic conflict between media giant Viacom, and the firm now dominating the internet and the digital economy, Google, which also owns YouTube. The lawsuit initiated in 2007 by Viacom argued that YouTube's business model was based on selling advertising by building traffic generated by unlicensed infringing content, which could and should be prevented by proactive policing. Google countered by claiming that Viacom had itself often secretly released media clips on YouTube, for publicity. Underlying the dispute, however, was a conflict about allocation of remuneration and possible methods of handling rights management, which they had not been able to resolve by negotiation.[96] Rights-owners have continued to lobby governments and legislatures, and have succeeded in obtaining legislation in several countries requiring ISPs to adopt procedures of escalating pressure on customers accused of illegal downloading, popularly known as the 'three strikes' rule.[97]

Despite these rearguard actions, however, new markets were opening up for digital products. Napster itself, restarted as a subscription service, had some success. Innovations came not from the media industries, busy defending their monopoly rights, but from computer and communications firms. Apple scored a great success with its iPod and iPlayer, linked to the iTunes music subscription service, which others emulated, although without Apple's proprietary technology. The distribution giant

---

95 A case brought in the UK by L'Oréal against eBay was referred to the ECJ in May 2009.

96 Edwards 2009: 66–71; Viacom's claim was rejected in the New York District Court in June 2010, where Judge Stanton stressed the big differences between YouTube and Napster or Grokster, and approved YouTube's notify-and-take down policy, putting the burden for identifying specific infringements on copyright owners (*Viacom* v. *YouTube* (2010)).

97 Such 'graduated response' rules have been introduced by industry codes, in some countries backed by law, e.g. the UK's Digital Economy Bill 2010; the draft ACTA treaty released in April 2010 included a provision which would make them an international obligation.

Amazon began to popularize e-books, which finally started to take off with improved reading devices such as the Kindle. Studies cast doubt on the exaggerated claims by media industries of their losses from copyright infringement. While they generally counted every unlicensed copy as a lost sale, more nuanced approaches showed that free distribution whets the consumer's appetite and can generate sales, and digital distribution offers the possibility of diverse marketing channels (Andersen and Frenz 2007; Smith and Telang 2009). A decline in sales of old media such as CDs was inevitable, and it became clear that the media industries' difficulties were mostly due to their own slowness in adapting to the new technologies, hardly surprising when their existing markets are protected. Once digital distributors such as Apple and Amazon opened up these new markets, sales of digital products began to rise rapidly; but the response of the media industries was to bite the hands that began to feed them, by demanding a higher price for the rights they controlled.

9.3.3.2 Markets and commons: open source

In the meantime, an alternative approach had emerged for governing rights, generally described as open source. This originated in 1985 when Richard Stallman established the Free Software Foundation, to encourage the development and dissemination of computer software on the basis that its source code should be freely available. However, Stallman did not invent the concept: the computer operating system Unix had become a widely used standard because it had been made available on an open-source basis. This was the suggestion of the engineers who worked on it for AT&T, the telecommunications company, during the time when it was prevented by antitrust restrictions from moving into the computing business. When these restrictions were lifted in 1984, AT&T began to assert proprietary rights; but this offended Stallman and others who had been used to working with freedom to access, use and improve software (Lessig 2001: 52–4). Stallman and Linus Torvalds released their GNU-Linux operating system under a General Public Licence (GPL), which allowed it to be adopted, adapted and further developed by networks of programmers, enabling it quickly to become a mainstay of computer systems.

Their example was adopted by others, so that the open-source movement became a worldwide community, integrating software-engineering techniques with copyright-licensing expertise, and built on powerful collaborative cultural practices. Indeed, some software developers 'concurrently tinker with technology and the law using similar skills, which transform and consolidate ethical precepts among developers' as they engage in legal and political battles (Coleman 2009: 422). This arena has been characterized as a bazaar, with a great many contending and competing peddlers of ideas and products, although underpinned by semi-formal institutions and norms.

The central feature of open source is that it uses copyright protection to overturn the exclusive rights paradigm. Open-source software is not unprotected by property rights, but is a type of common property: authors assert rights over their work but license its use. It is also not anti-commercial: Lawrence Lessig in particular advocates the term FLOSS – free *libre* open-source software – to make it clear that it is *libre* rather than *gratis*, in the words of Stallman 'as in free speech not free beer' (Lessig 2001: 12). Indeed, one of the basic principles of FLOSS licences is non-discrimination as to purpose: they 'may not restrict the program from being used in a business, or from being used for genetic research', the aim being to encourage commercial users to join rather than feel excluded from the community.[98] The term open source itself was adopted because of the ambiguous connotations of the word 'free'.

However, there have been disagreements and there are differences about how to manage the interface between the commons and the commercial world. Indeed, a large number of FLOSS licence standards have emerged, with many hundreds of variants, although the GPL is used for some 50 per cent of such licences (Kemp 2009). The key point of contention is the so-called 'copyleft' principle: users are allowed to use and adapt the software, and to issue a modified version, but such modified versions must be subject to the same licence conditions. This was done in GPL v2 by clause 2(b): 'You must cause any work that you distribute or publish, that in whole or in part contains or is derived from the Program or any part thereof, to be licensed as a whole at no charge to all third parties under the terms of this License.' Although apparently straightforward, this involves considerable issues of interpretation, notably of what is meant by 'contains', about which there have been significant disagreements. Although GPL v3, released in 2007, has dropped the word and adopted a new legal approach, a large proportion of FLOSS software is subject to GPL v2 (Kemp 2009: 578), and no doubt new disagreements will arise in relation to v3.[99] The GNU website provides licence texts and listings of

98 The Open Source Initiative's Open Source Definition: www.opensource.org/osd.html.
99 GPL v3 also extended the definition of distribution to include provision of services to third parties, apparently to deal with the problem that Google and others were using and modifying FLOSS software without disclosure (Bentley 2007).

the various licences which the FSF considers do and do not comply with its standards, with copious information and advice about them.

A rival set of standards and system of authentication are provided by the Open Source Initiative, formed to provide a more business-friendly alternative to the FSF, and applying a weaker version of copyleft principles, which permits commercialization of modified versions of licensed software. The philosophy articulated by one of its founders, Eric Raymond, especially in his influential essay 'The Cathedral and the Bazaar' (2000), is more pragmatic, arguing for the superiority of decentralized collaboration as a form of innovation. These themes have been taken up by a number of others, each with their own variations on the social, political and economic implications of decentralized collaborative networks (notably Benkler 2003; Weber 2004; von Hippel 2005). Similar arguments have been put forward for a new economics of 'open science' (Dasgupta and David 1994).

Thus, much of the core of the digital economy consists of a commons, regulated in a decentralized way by norms structured by contractual licences and supervised by informal organizations. One of its foremost theorists, Lawrence Lessig, argues that commons principles are inscribed into the very computer code of cyberspace, creating an innovation commons, but he accepts that this is not inherent in the technology because it is constantly under threat (2001: 175, 2006: 96–102). Certainly, there is no clear dividing line between the commons of cyberspace and the sphere of private exclusive rights. Successful corporations have been spun out from FLOSS innovations, such as Red Hat with its own version of GNU-Linux. Corporate giants such as IBM, Sun and Google collaborate in FLOSS-based projects. Microsoft, whose dominant position was built on proprietary rights, and which has strongly criticized GNU-Linux, has sought to infiltrate the 'mixed environment', notably by entering into an agreement with Novell in 2006 to encourage customers to adopt Novell's SUSE-Linux by waiving its patent rights against them (Kemp 2009: 572). Microsoft, and other proprietary software companies, also greatly benefit from user groups, which they monitor and sometimes foster and support, which are essentially FLOSS-style open collaborative networks. At the same time, Microsoft is the continual target of visceral opposition, both rhetorical and damaging, notably in the form of software virus attacks.

It does seem nevertheless that the phenomenon of peer-to-peer networked production, and the wider threats to the private-property paradigm posed by decommodification and decentralization are manifestations of major challenges to corporate capitalism. They are posed to both the nature of the corporation as an institutionalized form of organizing socialized labour, and to its capacity to accumulate capital by realizing the value of its outputs commercially. Certainly Microsoft, and a few other firms, have shown that both can be done successfully, spectacularly so in the case of Microsoft. It has succeeded in holding together its teams of 'microserfs',[100] cementing their commitment to the firm with stock options, and managing the complex processes of producing its extensive software suites. These have produced enormous revenue flows, but the vast bulk comes from a variety of large-scale licensing models, either with equipment manufacturers, or institutional licensing, rather than unit sales to individual customers. Microsoft and a few other niche software firms are very much the exception, and a vast amount of software is either bundled in hardware, marketed as 'shareware', or available as open source. The new giant of the digital economy is Google, which has built its revenue model on advertising and paid links, exploiting its centrality in the internet; but there is and can be only one Google.

9.3.3.3 Open access to the world's knowledge?

Computer software is in some ways a special case, but wider moves have also been made to enable open access to scientific and cultural work. The principles of FLOSS licensing have been extended to literary and other cultural works, through the Creative Commons movement, which similarly offers a suite of licence models based on open-source principles. There have also been several initiatives to make academic and scientific work available on open-access principles, either in repositories, or open-access journals, notably the Public Library of Science. Various projects have been launched to create global digital libraries, starting with Project Gutenberg and the Internet Archive, and then the Open Content Alliance. However, these are limited by being confined to works which are out of copyright protection, or donated.

An immensely far-reaching initiative was taken by Google in 2004,[101] when it launched its ambitious project to digitize all the books in the world. This is based on agreements with a number of university and national libraries, which in return obtained digitized copies of their books. Such a project seems feasible only with Google's enormous resources.[102]

---

100 See the novel by Douglas Coupland (1995) with this title, which explores the geek culture.
101 The idea was apparently mooted when Google was still a private start-up (Brin 2009), but the project was launched shortly after it became public with an initial public offering which generated $1.67b.
102 The French Bibliothèque Nationale initially tried to go it alone, but in 2010 recommended a partnership with Google because its progress had been too slow (Gaillard 2010).

Google also offered a partnership arrangement for publishers. Within five years, Google had digitized over ten million books, some two million of which are out of copyright, six million in copyright but out of print, and two million in copyright and in print (Samuelson 2010). Google Books gives readers complete access to those books which are in the public domain. The rest it aims to make available for 'browsing': online viewing (but not downloading or printing) of 'snippets' (extracts, the length depending on agreements with publishers).

This was a direct challenge to the exclusive rights paradigm of copyright. Although Google argued it was doing no more than allowing potential book buyers to look inside books as they would in a bookshop, the copying involved would go well beyond what would be tolerated even under the relatively generous US doctrine of fair use.[103] Nevertheless, Google's unilateral action posed a major challenge to rights-owners, especially in relation to the millions of out-of-print books and 'orphan works'.[104] Not surprisingly, lawsuits were soon brought by the Authors' Guild and a group of publishers. At the same time, Google's claim that it was building the digital equivalent to the great Library of Alexandria was challenged by those who said it would be more like a shopping mall (Samuelson 2009).

A remarkable proposal emerged from the litigation, the Google Books Settlement. The Settlement in effect establishes a gigantic CRO. Google would be authorized to provide open access to up to 20 per cent of the content of out-of-print books, while the whole of these books would be available via licences for libraries, and for individual purchase. Sixty-three per cent of Google's revenues both from these sales and from advertising would be channelled to rights-owners through a new Book Rights Registry. The initial settlement proposed to cover all books in which there was 'a US copyright interest', which under Berne and TRIPs would include almost all books in the world. The lawsuit was a class action, covering all potential claimants, so the settlement would have sweeping effects in creating a regulatory scheme, and would be subject to approval by the courts. Not surprisingly, the scheme quickly became the focus of a storm of debate, and it was amended in November 2009 to take account of some 400 legal submissions, notably one from the Justice Department. Its scope was reduced to books published in the USA, the UK, Canada and

---

103 Digitized books not made available but retained on Google's servers for indexing would also be infringing copies, and for those also a fair use defence would be unlikely to succeed.
104 Those whose author or rights owner cannot easily be traced.

Australia, and a procedure established to protect the interests of rights-owners who do not register. To try to restrict Google's monopoly, it included regulation on pricing and revenue models; and it allowed others to launch their own services.[105] Many other issues remained contentious, such as the opt-in or opt-out procedures, management of the Registry, and above all Google's dominant position.

The Google Books project has already made a major impact, and will be central to the future of book publishing in the digital age. Its development will be moulded by the progress and outcomes of legal manoeuvres, which will be extensive and complex. In the USA alone the legal possibilities are intricate and indefinite.[106] In France, a copyright infringement claim resulted in an award by a Paris tribunal in December 2009 of €300,000, which the publishers involved aimed to use to strengthen their bargaining position with Google. The Chinese Writers' Association wrote to Google objecting to digitization without prior permission, and Google responded apologizing for bad communication, initiating discussions.[107] Although there are some risks for publishers, the Google initiative seems to have convinced many of them of the potential benefits. However, there are clearly great potential dangers in the domination of this initiative by a single private firm (Vaidhyanathan 2007; Samuelson 2010), however benevolently it may paint its motives (Brin 2009). It is nevertheless both ironical and instructive that such a great blow has been struck at the exclusive rights paradigm of IPRs by a private monopolist.

9.4 From exclusivity to remuneration rights

As we have seen in this chapter, the exclusive private-property paradigm of IPRs creates significant obstacles in the knowledge economy. Nevertheless, a variety of means have been found to overcome these, usually taking the form of licensing schemes: for example, patent pools and cross-licensing; the standard material transfer agreement developed by the PGRFA; collective licensing by CROs; the GPL and other open-source software licences; the Creative Commons licences; and the Google Books project. All of these involve creative ways of managing the interface between private rights and the public domain or commons, while aiming to defend and enlarge the

105 See www.googlebooksettlement.com; Samuelson 2010.
106 See the chart issued in March 2010 for the Library Copyright Alliance: www.librarycopyrightalliance.org.
107 News item on AFP: 'Google apologises to Chinese writers over book flap', www.google.com/hostednews/afp.

latter. These developments certainly demonstrate the flexibility offered by legal forms, in this case regulatory contracts.

However, it should also be emphasized that they have only been possible because the obstacle of exclusive private-property rights has been overcome by compulsion of some sort. In the case of the SMTA and CROs, licensing has in effect been made compulsory by states due to strong pressures to protect the public domain; the open-access movement was strongly powered by innovators often working within public sector institutions and also fired by a zeal to protect the innovation commons; while Google Books was initiated by the dominant monopolist firm of the knowledge economy. The effect of these counter-pressures has been to shift IPRs from a right to exclude to a right to remuneration.

Such a shift is consonant with some scholarship on the economics of IP which points out that a right to remuneration, based on a liability rule, can be in many ways superior to a private-property right in creating the best conditions for bargaining to determine commercial value. This line of analysis originated with Calabresi and Melamed, who argued that the definition of proprietary interests should take account of welfare effects: their argument was that property owners claiming pollution nuisance should have a remedy in damages rather than an injunction, which would amount to a 'blocking' right against industrial development (Calabresi and Melamed 1972). More recently, Kaplow and Shavell's comprehensive review (1996) suggested that the preference for a property remedy to protect an individual's ownership of things is most appropriate for personal possessions, since they are likely to have a unique value to an owner, which would not be adequately reflected in a damages award. From the different perspective of political philosophy, Margaret Radin developed a critique of conventional economic analysis of property rights in her 'liberal personality theory of property', arguing for the priority of rights in personal over what she describes as 'fungible' property (1993). This line of thought would suggest that for non-rival goods such as IPRs, a liability rule would be adequate.[108] There is plenty of evidence that the 'blocking right' that IPRs have given rights-owners has been deleterious to welfare-enhancing innovation.

---

108 Kaplow and Shavell consider that there may be an economic justification for property protection of IP when owners consider that the compensation they might receive would be too low, giving little incentive to commercialize the asset. It is true that owners who consider that they have a private-property right often have an exaggerated view of its value, but the evidence on the negative impact of IPRs on innovation is too strong to allow that view to prevail.

In the context of the knowledge economy, the merits of a compensatory liability regime have been urged by Jerome Reichman.[109] In Reichman's version, this would be limited to low-level or routine inventions, although this raises the question of where the line should be drawn between innovations that have full property protection and the lesser 'incremental' ones. If one can cast off the mystique of the private-property ideology, the simple solution would be to recast IPRs as rights to compensation rather than rights to exclude. This would mean essentially that users would have an automatic licence, although the innovator would be entitled to appropriate compensation, rather than a right to exclude backed by the potential of injunctions and swingeing damages. Automatic licensing would certainly alter the balance of power between users and originators, but as we have seen in this chapter, it would result in licensing schemes of various kinds, and hence produce reliable revenues and greater stability and certainty for innovation. It would also make it easier to define with much greater subtlety the relative rights of different kinds of user, as well as calibrating rewards according to the importance of the innovation, as Reichman suggests. Originators will always have the option of keeping their innovations or works private, unless users are willing to offer reasonable levels of reward via licensing.

This solution is conceptually simple, and practically would be easier to implement than the increasing variety and complexity of IPRs. Nevertheless, it faces the daunting obstacle of the treaties, culminating in the TRIPs, which have erected international IP rules which in many ways entrench the private-property paradigm. At the same time, this process has now focused unprecedented public attention on the unsuitability of existing IP regimes for economic development, especially of poorer countries.[110] Combined with the growing concerns in the advanced countries as to the effects of strong IP rights in restricting the diffusion of innovation and distorting culture, there may be a basis for a radical rethinking.[111]

---

109 Reichman 2001; he has also argued for a compensation regime for 'hybrids' (Reichman 1994).
110 For a powerful critique in relation to copyright, see CopySouth 2009.
111 See Strandburg 2009 for a proposal to exploit TRIPs flexibilities by shifting to an 'administrative law approach' to proposed exceptions, and giving a wider role to WIPO as a broader-based innovation policy organization. Like other calls for a new perspective on IPRs within a broader innovation paradigm (e.g. TIP Expert Group 2008), I fear it underestimates the power of the private-property paradigm.

10

Law and legitimacy in networked governance

As the previous chapters have shown, the law and lawyers have played a key part in creating the concepts and institutional forms of corporate capitalism in the past century and a half. Legalization has been playing an equally central role especially in the recent decades in forming the institutions of the new global governance. This chapter will evaluate some of the main theories and debates about this role of law, and put forward my own perspective, in the light of the accounts and analyses of the previous chapters of this book.

The general argument is that what has been constructed is a corporatist economy, in which highly socialized systems of economic activity are managed in forms which allow private control and appropriation, yet are very different from those of the 'market economy' envisaged by classical liberal philosophy and political economy. Although the state and the economy appear as separate spheres, they are intricately interrelated in many ways, especially in the definition and allocation of property rights, and in extensive state support and interventions determining investment and profit rates. Working at the interface of the public and private in mediating social action and conflict, lawyers have played a key role in constructing corporatist capitalism, and are central to its governance and legitimation. This is also due to lawyers' techniques and practices of formulating and interpreting concepts and norms which are inherently malleable and indeterminate, and provide the flexibility to manage the complex interactions of private and public. These techniques and the lawyers who deploy them have also been central both to the construction of the classical liberal system of interdependent states, and its gradual fragmentation and the transition to networked regulation and global governance.

10.1 Globalization and legalization

10.1.1 Perspectives on the role of law

The role of law and lawyers in global governance has been analysed in very different ways. One influential group of US commentators has discussed the legalization of world politics from an essentially Weberian perspective, which sees law as providing predictability and certainty through a framework of clear rules regarded as binding (Goldstein *et al.* 2001). They assess the extent of legalization along a spectrum according to three criteria: being based on rules which are regarded as binding, which are precise, and the interpretation of which has been delegated to a third-party adjudicator (Abbott *et al.* 2000: 404–6). This has been criticized as taking a narrow view of law (Finnemore and Toope 2001), and it has been pointed out that there is a need to take account of divergent views of the epistemic relevance of legalization, and to reframe the debate to include processes of 'complex legalization', involving a wider range of participants (Brütsch and Lehmkuhl 2007: 3, 21–7).

Interestingly, these three proposed characteristics of formal legality are rarely found in combination. In particular, rules which are considered binding are often not precise. Formal obligations, especially in international law, are usually expressed in abstract terms, establishing general principles for the long term, and aiming for wide acceptance. Hence, provisions in formally binding multilateral treaties are often indeterminate and open to interpretation. We have seen many such examples, in virtually every section of each chapter in this book. In particular, Chapter 8 showed in detail the extensive scope for interpretation inherent in the rules of the WTO treaties, although they are both formally binding and subject to third-party adjudication. Such indeterminacy is hard to square with the view that states enter into treaties to provide 'credible commitments' through clear rules ensuring predictable conduct.

Sometimes ambiguity is the result of compromises during negotiations, resulting in a text attempting to accommodate contending viewpoints. One example of this is the provision (discussed in Chapter 9, at 9.2.5.1) in the IT–PGRFA prohibiting the claiming of IPRs on material derived from plant genetic resources 'in the form received'. Equally, the WTO agreements, as we have seen in Chapter 8, include many provisions which raise issues of interpretation which were known to be highly contestable, and indeed were being contested, in the period when the texts were negotiated and agreed. A number of the key disputes pursued under the WTO were continuations or replays of disputes already raised under the GATT: for example concerning food safety, corporate taxation or compulsory licensing of patents. Far from taking the opportunity to resolve such issues in the political context of the Uruguay Round negotiations and embody agreed outcomes in an unambiguous text, the negotiators often settled for general formulations which they must have known would frame future battles.

In addition, very frequently indeterminacy comes from both the nature of liberal legality itself, and the inherent ambiguity of language (Picciotto 2007a). Liberal legal rules are normally expressed in general and abstract terms, aiming to encompass a range of future possibilities. Hence, they are inherently open to interpretation. For example, the non-discrimination principles of NT and MFN which are central in international economic law, and form the core obligations in both trade and investment treaties, do not establish clear bright-line obligations, but principles expressed in general terms. Furthermore, being normative in character, they invite contending teleological interpretation by protagonists seeking justification for their preferred version. Hence, rather than providing a clear and precise basis on which parties affected can plan their activities, they generally create a field in which such parties pursue their conflicting and competing strategies mediated by contending interpretations of the rules. Thus, to adapt Clausewitz's famous aphorism, legalization is a continuation of politics by other means.

Furthermore, the view that 'hard' law provides precise rules, while quasi-legal 'soft' law is more vague or imprecise, does not stand up to examination. For example, financial market regulations discussed in Chapter 7, whether developed by private bodies such as the ISDA or public ones such as the BCBS, are as detailed as any legislation, but they are formally 'soft' law. On the other hand, from the formalist viewpoint, the WTO agreements rate highly as exemplars of legalization, since they lay down an enormous quantity of formally binding rules, the interpretation of which has been delegated to the WTO's Appellate Body (AB) as an adjudicator. Yet as we have seen, the suggestion that WTO rules are precise and unambiguous is highly dubious. They rely on abstract principles which necessarily leave scope for interpretation, often involving a 'balancing' of the non-discrimination obligations against permitted exceptions. The WTO's Appellate Body has itself described the key term 'like products' as an elastic concept (Chapter 8, at 8.3.2.2).

Conversely, even in regimes which are considered formally non-binding, a wide range of enforcement and compliance monitoring arrangements may be established, including third-party adjudication.[1] Furthermore, soft and hard law interact in many ways, to form what has been described as a 'tangled web' (Webb and Morrison 2004). We have seen in Chapter 8, at 8.2.2 how WTO law in effect implements the voluntary norms of standards bodies, and in Chapter 5, at 5.2.2.2 the ways in which corporate and industry codes can be enforced. The formalist perspective overstates the effects of hard law and underestimates the role of soft law in the networked governance processes described and analysed in this book.

10.1.1.1 Law in heterarchy

Much more appropriate to the heterarchical character of regulatory networks are concepts of legal pluralism. These emerged from legal anthropology in the post-colonial period (see Chapter 2, at 2.1.2), and have become important in the sociology of law. A legal pluralist perspective is particularly apposite, because it decentres state law, and brings to the fore both the plurality and the many modes of interaction of normative systems (e.g. Snyder 2000). However, legal pluralism's interest in the norms of a great variety of communities and social groups also means that it tends to view state law as just another normative system. What tends to be lacking is a theory or understanding of the state, and the relationship of state law to other norms (Fitzpatrick 1984). Hence, while pluralism may help in drawing attention to the existence and interactions of multiple legal orders, it is prone to the criticism advanced by von Benda-Beckmann that 'talking of intertwining, interaction or mutual constitution presupposes distinguishing what is being intertwined' (cited in Melissaris 2004: 61), or more sharply that it leaves us 'with ambiguity and confusion' (Teubner 1992: 1444).

The most sophisticated and complex attempt to establish a conceptual analysis which incorporates a pluralist approach has been that of Boaventura de Sousa Santos (Santos 1987, 1995, 2002). He distinguishes his perspective from that of traditional legal anthropology which conceived different legal orders as 'separate entities coexisting in the same political space', and sees socio-legal activities as operating in three time–spaces, the local, the national and the global. For him, the loss of dominance of state law has ushered in a third period of postmodern legal plurality:

---

1 For example, even Nestlé established a Commission chaired by former US Secretary of State Edmund Muskie to hear complaints under its corporate code based on the WHO Baby-Milk Code, although it was dissolved, having found some violations (Chapter 5, at 5.2.2.1).

'whereas before, debate was on local, infrastate legal orders coexisting within the same national time–space, now it is on suprastate, global legal orders coexisting in the world system with both state and infrastate legal orders' (2002: 92).

Santos cogently argues that '[w]e live in a time of porous legality or legal porosity, of multiple networks of legal orders forcing us to constant transitions and trespassings. Our legal life is constituted by an intersection of different legal orders, that is by *interlegality*' (1995: 473). He uses the metaphor of cartography to suggest that different types of laws are based on different scales, projections and symbolizations, and that social groups become more adept in the types of action suited to the legal order within which they are predominantly socialized (1995: 465–6). However, his analysis tends to be structuralist: he conceives of different legal orders as overlapping but mutually exclusive and that 'each legal construction has an internal coherence' (1995: 473). For example, he argues that the new *lex mercatoria* and the proliferation of business and corporate codes constitute 'the emergence of new legal particularisms' which 'create a transnational legal space that often conflicts with national state legal space' (1995: 469). However, the concepts of porosity and interlegality suggest that legal orders are capable of interpenetration and accommodation, rather than being conflicting and exclusive.

Analysts of regulation have attempted to capture the characteristics of different layers of regulation and their interaction. This kind of approach to regulatory interactions deploys concepts of responsive or reflexive law. As part of the response to the crises of the welfare state, Nonet and Selznick put forward a new modernist paradigm of responsive law, as an evolution from the repressive and autonomous phases of law, and envisaging regulation as an interactive process of developing methods to realize purposes expressed through law and thereby clarifying the public interest ([1978] 2001). The concept was taken up in regulation theory notably by Ayres and Braithwaite (1992), seeking to reassert a civic republican tradition in which layers of social institutions, from the state through industry associations and down to individual corporations, play their different parts in social regulation, lubricated by a two-way flow of public discourse.[2] This can help to frame an understanding for example of

---

2 It was also linked to John Braithwaite's general notion of the 'regulatory pyramid', seeing regulation as an interactive process, in which enforcers can escalate their responses to encourage or coerce compliance; he has applied the concepts to all manner of contexts, which has also led him to refine it in response to criticism and recognition of some of its limitations, by introducing the concept of 'nodal governance' (2008: 87–108).

the relationship between state law and corporate and industry codes of conduct.

The interaction of public and private has been analysed within this perspective through the concept of 'meta-regulation', or the supervision by public bodies of the adequacy of private regulation. The approach is helpful in suggesting that the content of law and of what is meant by compliance are negotiable, although it perhaps too easily accepts that consensus can be reached, and underestimates the competitive and strategic behaviour of actors in legal fields. The concept of meta-regulation seems an appropriate lens through which to view, for example, the approach in the BCBS's Basel II framework for financial risk management, discussed in Chapter 7, which aimed to supervise the banks' own risk-monitoring systems. The concept of meta-regulation was applied initially to national state laws which lay down overarching requirements or standards (for example, for environmental protection) with which more specific industry or corporate codes are expected to comply (Gunningham and Grabosky 1998; Parker 2002). It has been extended to describe the 'disciplines' laid down by WTO law on national states by Bronwen Morgan (2003), who described WTO rules as 'global meta-regulation', or rules prescribing how states should regulate. This formulation helps to characterize the form of overarching regulatory frameworks such as Basel II and the WTO, and their interaction with national law; although it is perhaps less apt in relation to the interactions of WTO rules with other regulatory arrangements discussed in Chapter 7, such as those of the SPS with Codex standards, or the intricate interactions between the WTO and ITU regulatory systems for telecommunications.

A different analysis has been offered by Gunther Teubner, whose pioneering work argued that the emergence of reflexivity in modern law resulted from the 'trilemma' created by the increased legalization, or juridification of the social sphere (1983, 1987). For Teubner it is the autonomy of the legal field that generates its autopoeitic self-referentiality, but the politicization resulting from increased application of law into social fields creates expectations which require instrumentalization, perhaps through new forms of self-regulation. The pressure for legal regulation to go beyond the limits possible through the autonomous logics of self-reproduction means that it either lapses into irrelevance, or results in disintegration either of the social field to which it is applied or of the law itself. Hence, regulatory failure is the rule rather than the exception.

In his work on globalization Teubner welcomes the potential it offers for law to become more detached from the political sphere of states, and instead to institutionalize constitutions for autonomous social sectors and the norms which they generate, which he suggests could enable new forms of repoliticization (2004). He rightly criticizes the view of globalization as an economic process which reduces the prospects of regulation through law, and points to the many new normative forms underpinning globalization, which seek validation through law. However, this systems–theoretical perspective significantly overstates the autonomy of the ill-defined social subsystems, and the self-referential nature of 'neo-spontaneous' generation of 'global law without a state', of which *lex mercatoria* is given as an example (Teubner 1997).[3]

10.1.1.2 Lawyering practices

It is important to complement perspectives analysing law as part of social structure with others which consider social agency. A more actor-oriented approach is taken by Pierre Bourdieu, who criticizes the confusion in systems theory between the symbolic structures of the law and the objective orders of the legal and other professional fields, in which agents and institutions compete for the right to formulate the rules, 'le droit de dire le droit' (1986, 1987). This is especially valuable in providing a basis for empirical and sociological studies of the actual practices of lawyering (McCahery and Picciotto 1995).

The techniques and practices deployed by lawyers centre on the formulation and interpretation of legal texts. Bourdieu argues that this involves the appropriation of the 'symbolic power which is potentially contained within the text', in terms of competitive struggles to 'control' the legal text (1987: 818). He suggests that coherence emerges partly through the social organization of the field, which produces mutual understandings based on 'habitus'; and partly because, to succeed, competing interpretations must be presented 'as the necessary result of a principled interpretation of unanimously accepted texts' (1987: 818).

This explains the apparent paradox that, while lawyers spend much of their time disagreeing about the meaning of texts, they generally do so

---

3 Teubner follows Luhmann, who considers that 'law is a normatively closed but cognitively open system': closed in that normativity must be decided by its internal self-referential processes, but open because it is dependent on being able to determine whether certain factual conditions have been met (1987: 18–20). Many have doubted the applicability of the theory of 'autopoiesis' (derived from biology) to social systems, which produces a highly structuralist model of society; although others reject this criticism, arguing that the social subsystems are seen as constituting society through their different modes of communication.

from an objectivist perspective. They usually prefer to deny that indeterminacy is inherent in legal rules, and tend to attribute disagreements to
bad drafting and lack of clarity in the texts, which are said to create 'loopholes' in the logical fabric of the law. Bourdieu's perspective can also be
integrated with the 'interpretivist turn' in socio-legal studies, and critical
approaches to law. These study the ways in which the indeterminacy of
legal texts provides the space for the deployment of legal skills and techniques, the introduction of political preferences and social values, and
ultimately the ways in which law is deployed in and mediates struggles
over power.

Based on an approach from Bourdieu, the extensive sociological
research of Dezalay and Garth has provided a more convincing account
of *lex mercatoria* than either Santos or Teubner. They examine especially
how law as a social practice mediates transformations of both the 'private'
sphere of economic activity and the 'public' sphere of politics, and their
interaction. They argue that the concept of *lex mercatoria* was a strategic
move in the competitive struggles between arbitration centres, in which
lawyers mediated skilfully between the spheres of political and corporate
power to create the new arena of international commercial arbitration
(1995, 1996). They show how the learned doctrine of *lex mercatoria*,
backed by the neutral authority of the grand European professors which
validated it in the eyes of their disciples in the third world, helped to
provide a 'middle way' in the post-colonial clashes over the scope of state
sovereignty, especially concerning the control of oil; but in practice the
legal arbitrations were only one strand (and a minor one) in the broader
political negotiations (Dezalay and Garth, 1995: 83–91, 1996: 313). Rather
than creating a purely private legal sphere outside the realm of state law,
the two have been deeply entangled, and the authority of law, especially
legal concepts of private rights, has been used to counter political notions
of state sovereignty in the struggles to reconfigure economic and political
power. This perspective is very relevant also to understanding the opening
up of new legal fields, such as the rapid growth of investment arbitration
under the NAFTA and BITs, discussed in Chapter 5, at 5.2.1.3.

Dezalay and Garth emphasize the importance of studying how and
by whom law is produced, and their focus is on the legal elites and
the resources and strategies they employ to dominate the production
of law. Investment in legal expertise is seen as a means of building social
capital, and conflicting perspectives about the content of law as essentially
strategies in competitive struggles. For them, law's claims to neutrality
and universalist ideals are deployed simply to give legitimacy to the elite

lawyers' powerful clients, which are governments and large corporations. They consider that '[l]aw and lawyers have been central to what can be characterized as US "imperial strategies" throughout the twentieth century' (2008: 718), although their role and character have changed. In particular, the enormous new investments in professionalized law and the trends to legalization since the 1970s have replaced the old establishment of 'gentleman lawyers' and legal generalists with a 'multi-polar field of quasi-state power with a much more institutionalized division of roles' (2008: 752).

However, their emphasis on studying *who* and *how* tends to disregard or discount the questions of *what* and *why*. The content of political and economic changes and conflicts, which provide the essential motive forces for change, are exogenous to their perspective. They characterize the success of law as resting on 'the ability of lawyers to take external conflicts within and among the leading institutions of the state and manage them by translating them into law'. For them, the conflicts are between 'factions contending for the definition and control of the state' (2008: 756), but this does not explain the nature or content of those struggles. They do accept that 'the content that emerges from these battles is important' (2008: 719), but their general assumption is that lawyers are an elite group acting on behalf of the powerful. Hence, whether lawyers choose to 'invest in' corporate or commercial law or human rights makes a difference only in terms of the form of domination they help to construct. They rightly point out that lawyers do not always favour liberal legality, but often side with authoritarianism, while on the other hand, at a different phase of the political cycle, a lawyer may need to invest in legitimacy by acting as 'reformer, modernizer, or promoter of social welfare'. However, Dezalay and Garth see this as 'the preventive management of social inequalities and tensions' by 'providing channels for incremental political and social change' (2010: 251).

This is a valuable corrective to perspectives which perhaps too readily accept the emancipatory potential of some formulations or fields of law, such as human rights. At the same time, it is also important to guard against a pessimistic reductionism which implies that power is always hegemonic and self-reproducing, and that the forms of domination are epiphenomenal. To say that law mediates power does not mean that it is a mere fig leaf for the 'real' relationships of power which occur somewhere else; on the contrary, it means that the exercise of power takes specific legalized forms. This also entails a recognition that legal forms legitimize acquisition and dispossession, and hence both the accumulation of wealth and economic exclusion and inequality, and that law also of course governs the legitimate use of force, and hence authorizes both economic and physical retribution and punishment. But to engage in critique of the strong claims made for the neutrality, objectivity, rationality, certainty and predictability that the rule of law is supposed to provide does not mean that law-governed decision-making is necessarily arbitrary, or that legal reasoning is irrational or merely a justification of political or economic power.

10.1.2 Law and power, property and the state

Considering what lawyers do also helps us to understand how specific legal forms help to construct social institutions and relationships and hence how they affect the particular ways in which power is exercised. This also entails consideration of the *power of law itself* as a form of legitimation. In general terms the power of the 'rule of law' lies in the claims of classical liberal or bourgeois legality to provide justice based on universal principles granting equal rights for all legal subjects. The central critique of these claims to legal justice is that enforcing formal equality between those who are unequal in material terms (economically, physically, socially, politically) reproduces inequality: 'between equal rights, might prevails' (Miéville 2005). However, this again implies that inequality and power are somehow external to law, and that law's neutrality merely provides a cloak for extra-legal forms of power.

This is a serious mistake, especially in the realms of economic law. To focus on law only as a balancing of rights is to restrict attention to economic exchange, where indeed all that is needed is to ensure the enforcement of apparently equal rights. Certainly, the ideologies of both classical liberalism and contemporary neo-liberalism consider that the role of law is simply to enforce contracts and protect property rights. Against this, welfare liberalism argues that there is a need for greater intervention to correct market failures, remedy asymmetries between parties to contracts, and perhaps even some redistribution to correct excessive social inequalities. Thus, principles of equal treatment may sometimes be modified by permitting differential treatment, though usually without affecting the basic structures.

What is generally overlooked is the role of law in shaping and defining the property rights on which exchange depends, as well as the extensive state interventions affecting pricing and profit rates, which take place through legal regulation. Property is commonly thought of as a natural institution, usually fetishized as control over a thing. Most analyses fail to take a historical perspective, and too readily accept ahistorical concepts, particularly that of 'the market'. Hence, the approach adopted in this book has been to trace the historical development of the central institutions of corporate capitalism. This helps to illuminate the dramatic changes that have taken place in the character and content of property, and hence in both 'the market' and the role of the state.

Basic theory tells us of course that markets require property rights. Beyond that, academic theory has told us surprisingly little useful about property rights. This seems to be largely due to a fixation on the concept of private property, amounting to an identification of property with private property. Philosophical and political theories have focused on the justifications for private property, going back at least to C. B. Macpherson's seminal critique (1962), and have therefore been largely irrelevant to the complexity and malleability of property institutions, as Andrew Reeve has pointed out (1986: 108–11). Economic theory, not surprisingly, has been focused on particularly simplistic notions of private property. Thus, Barzel defines property in economic terms as an individual's ability to consume a good, directly or indirectly through exchange (1997: 3). In development economics, a common prescription is to ensure security of property rights; indeed, this notion has been turned into a creed by Hernando de Soto. Yet such prescriptions are based on a ready acceptance of the fetish of private property, which imagines for example that providing individual titles to slum shack dwellings to be used as security for loans could solve the problems of lack of urban services to *favelas*. Sociology has largely neglected the analysis of property (Carruthers and Ariovich 2004), and when it does consider the matter is concerned mainly with the implications of property rights rather than analysis of the forms they take. In legal theory, Hohfeld's insights showed that property consists of a bundle of rights regulating the relationships of persons, and Robert Hale also left a strong legacy, arguing that law defines the 'background' rules of property, so that contractual exchange consists of 'mutual coercion' (Ireland 2003a). However, more recent work has tended to adopt either a political philosophy perspective (e.g. Waldron 1988), or that of law and economics.[4]

---

4 There are some alternative and critical perspectives, notably Margaret Radin's critique of mainstream law and economics, which links in with some more radical economic analyses (Chapter 9, at 9.4).

In fact, the basic legal forms of property and contract are infinitely malleable. In particular, the concept of exclusive private-property rights has been extended to intangible or 'fictitious' property. Thus, a legal claim on assets such as a share in a company came to be treated as a private-property right, so that the corporation is conceived as a private legal person, governed by contract, and 'owned' by its shareholders. Not only shares, but all manner of financial instruments have been formulated in terms of increasingly ingenious combinations of property and contract. The concept of 'intellectual property' enabled the complex and contentious interactions of science with nature on the one hand and commerce and business on the other to be articulated in terms of proprietorial control over new technologies. Literature, the arts and cultural life generally have also become moulded by proprietorial principles, and hence dominated by the media industries. Similarly, contracts have been transformed from simple bargains between individuals, and adapted to serve all kinds of administrative and regulatory purposes, otherwise thought of as the domain of public law (Campbell 1999).

The skilful use and adaptation of these private law forms have enabled continued private appropriation, even though economic activity and its organization have become increasingly *socialized*. This is above all the case for the corporate form, which enables the coordination of labour and assets on an enormous social scale, but within a framework of private ownership and control. The oligopolistic corporations which came to dominate the key global industries of the twentieth century, first in oil, minerals, chemicals, engineering, automobiles, food and agribusiness and then in pharmaceuticals, computing, media and the internet, can generate extraordinary profits. At the same time, their dominant positions have depended in many ways on state support. Many require concessions or licences: natural resource firms such as oil, mining and logging; now also telecommunications and broadcasting; construction and property development; and a wide range of professional services. Others have depended on state construction of infrastructure, such as roads, railways, telecommunications and energy networks; and the terms of access to such networks remain crucial. For many, such as pharmaceuticals, aircraft and electronics, the state is their major customer. At the same time, the enormous growth of state expenditure has made the incidence of taxation, including subsidies and incentives, a major element in profitability, especially in sectors such as oil, mining, banking and finance. Hence, tax 'planning' has become routinized; and TNCs in particular can take advantage both of competition to offer incentives to attract investment, and opportunities for international avoidance. Increased regulation in fields such as consumer and environmental protection also has a direct impact on profitability. In basic infrastructure and utilities industries, such as telecommunications, broadcasting, gas, electricity and water, decisions on the often very high levels of fixed investment and its financing by charges to consumers or general taxation are of major social importance. It has been to a great extent the difficulty of managing these decisions through state bureaucracies and financing them by taxation that led to privatization, although generally under public supervision. This has resulted in experiments in many forms of regulation, and public–private partnerships. Finally, as we have seen only too starkly in the 2008–9 crisis, the entire financial system and hence the world economy depend very directly on state support.

None of this looks remotely like the market economy envisaged by Adam Smith or the other great liberal political economists or philosophers. Instead, the key feature of 'regulatory capitalism' is the close relationships and tight interactions between the public and private, the state and the economy, government and corporations. Paradoxically, however, we have seen a parallel process of the functional fragmentation of the state, as well as an increased decentralization of business, and hence the emergence of both corporate networks and multilevel governance.

10.1.3 From transnational corporatism to networked governance

The enduring ability of private law forms to be adapted and reformulated to provide the institutional forms of corporate capitalism perhaps helps to explain the enduring myths of the market economy. In fact, as outlined in Chapter 4, what emerged from the end of the nineteenth century was a corporatist economy. It is notable that the 1880–1930 period also saw sharp debates about the nature and the appropriate form of the corporation and of competition (discussed in Chapter 4, at 4.1.1), and the emergence of new forms of regulatory law. This was strongest in the USA, with its antitrust law and sectoral regulatory Commissions; while in Europe and elsewhere governments took a more direct role in economic management, at least at national level. The inter-state rivalries and conflicts of the first half of the twentieth century offered stony ground for international politics and public international law, so the first lawyer-diplomats began to fashion forms of international economic regulation based on private law. Major firms in key industries used cartels to manage international trade and pool knowledge of new technologies (Chapter 4, at 4.2.3); international shipping was registered under the privately managed system of 'flags of convenience' (Chapter 3, at 3.2.3); conflicts and overlaps of national claims to tax international business were eliminated by devising international tax-avoidance structures using the flexibilities offered by the corporate form and other legal entities such as trusts (Chapter 6, at 6.3.1).

In the second half of the twentieth century, regulatory law became transnationalized. To a great extent US lawyers took the lead, shaping the legal forms as agents of the increasingly powerful US corporations. Indeed, they invented the TNC, by exploiting the freedom of incorporation (overcoming some initial opposition) to create complex corporate group structures, exploiting jurisdictional regulatory differences. They extended the reach of US regulatory law itself through expansive doctrines of jurisdiction (Chapter 2, at 2.2); and theorized 'transnational law' as a mixture of national and international, public and private law, also drawing on older doctrines of the *jus gentium* such as comity (Chapter 2, at 2.3.1). US ideas, concepts and institutions were transplanted into other national legal fields, often with the help of local lawyers, some of whom had absorbed such perspectives by pursuing postgraduate study in the USA. However, such transplants were also in some cases adapted by local acolytes to their own ideas and conditions, influenced by different legal cultures, producing hybrids.

For example, the export of the US antitrust philosophy to Europe and Japan resulted in significant adaptations (Chapter 4, at 4.3.1); the European Commission indeed became an enthusiastic convert to the competition law gospel, although US lawyers have complained that Europe applies a perverted version of the doctrine. In some arenas, non-US lawyers made their own contributions. For example, techniques to avoid perceived regulatory burdens such as double taxation, by exploiting jurisdictional interactions and the legal personality of companies and trusts, were developed also in the UK, France and the Netherlands (which became the home of the influential International Bureau for Fiscal Documentation). The strengthening of banking secrecy to develop a financial entrepôt and a system of discreet private banking was pioneered in Switzerland from the early 1930s (Chapter 6, at 6.3.5). Lawyers and bankers in London took advantage of the Bank of England's relaxation of exchange controls to use dollar deposits for sterling–dollar swaps, and create the Eurodollar market (Chapter 7, at 7.1.2). The field of IPRs has been dominated by continental European lawyers, especially from Germany and France, who have been in the forefront in developing the international framework and expanding IP to ensure corporate control of new technologies. This has involved both developing interpretations of general principles such as the right of reproduction in copyright, and isolation from nature for patents, and devising new concepts such as plant variety protection (see Chapter 9).

A particular contribution of European lawyers has been forms of supranational constitutionalism. Indeed, Europeans going back to Vitoria and Grotius first devised the notion of the *jus gentium* to manage and legitimize the complexities of conquest and colonialism (Chapter 2, at 2.1.1). Liberal internationalism from the last part of the nineteenth century also created the first wave of international institutions, whether private (e.g. the International Chamber of Commerce), quasi-public (e.g. the International Committee of the Red Cross), or intergovernmental (though with a strong private input), e.g. the international Unions (Chapter 2, at 2.1.2). Europeans also originated and sustained the organizations for international legal harmonization (the Hague Conference and UNIDROIT: Chapter 2, at 2.2.2), launched in the early twentieth century, and which took on a new life in its second half. In the second half of the twentieth century came first the building of international human rights institutions (more recently strengthened by the Rome Statute for the International Criminal Court), the Council of Europe, and then the great project for an ever-wider European Union (Madsen and Vauchez 2004). As the EU became transformed from a proto-confederation to a system of multilevel governance using a variety of modes of coordination, its development interacted with the emerging networks of global economic governance, especially through the WTO.

Although the models of supranational constitutionalism and transnationalism appeared to be very different, there has been an increasing convergence. This suggests that the processes of their construction have shared a similar dynamic. Indeed, it seems that the actual practices of lawyers, acting both on behalf and sometimes as critics of corporate capital, have significant similarities, even if the contexts in which they operate involve different legal cultures. Lawyers are also influenced by their clients: the economic and military dominance of the USA since the mid-twentieth century has meant that US governments have veered between asserting unilateral power and supporting multilateral frameworks; since the USA would inevitably dominate these, they are more likely to be proposed by the friendly rivals of the USA, such as Canada, or Europe. With the formation of the EU as a major economic bloc, projects such as the WTO are increasingly multilateral, especially with the recent emergence of China and a wider group of important developing countries (Brazil, India, South Africa). This seems to make multilateralism more difficult, as seen with the stalling of the WTO's Doha Round (Chapter 8, at 8.1.3), and the response to the financial crisis (Chapter 7, at 7.3.2.1).

Hence, the emergence of global governance, although dominated by the USA as the major power, is not just a process of Americanization, but perhaps a new form of empire. It has involved contributions from not only characteristically US styles, but also European, Latin American and Asian 'ways of law' (Dezalay and Garth 2001, 2010; Kagan 2007; Gessner and Nelken 2007). This indeed is a central element in the power of law: the ability of its general principles, norms and institutions to offer universal prescriptions, while being capable of adaptation by interpretation to suit local circumstances and cultures.

Furthermore, contributions can be made to the construction of the legal edifice from many hands and in different styles. Legal principles can be sufficiently flexible both to allow and to absorb radical departures. For example, the 'open source' movement has overturned the exclusive private rights paradigm of IPRs, but by asserting authors' rights; and FLOSS licences provide the flexibility to explore a variety of methods of both organizing and commercializing creativity and innovation, based on a kind of commons (Chapter 9, at 9.3.3.2). The issues raised by transnational liability litigation, seen most dramatically in the Bhopal case, cannot be described simply as an imperialist attempt to export US law or legal culture; but they do put into question the 'uncertain promise' of law in managing both hazardous activities and compensating victims (Chapter 5, at 5.1.3.2). Law is not neutral, it shapes and legitimizes social relations of power; but the directions of change depend not only or even mainly on law but on more general social processes of which law is part.

10.2 Constructing global governance

10.2.1 Legal creativity, interpretations and interactions

The important role of law in the construction of institutions and arenas of governance is therefore due to the key position of lawyers acting as professionals working for private clients or public bodies, and often both, and hence operating at the interface of the private and public spheres, and moving between the two (Dezalay 1996). Thus, William Cromwell could facilitate the creation of Panama as a state, then act for US shipowners using his knowledge of and contacts in Panama to create a convenient ship registration system, to be managed by John Foster Dulles, who later became the US Secretary of State; this was taken a stage further by former oil industry lawyer and Roosevelt's Secretary of State Edward Stettinius, who set up Liberia's registry to be run by a company in Virginia (Chapter 3, at 3.2.3). Similarly, Mitchell Carroll worked first for the US Commerce Department as adviser and representative to international tax meetings, then chaired the Fiscal Committee of the League of Nations and carried out for it a twenty-six country study funded by the Rockefeller Foundation, while building a tax practice representing firms such as Esso and Unilever, helping to found the International Fiscal Association and proselytizing in the US mid-West and the US Congress in support of the proposed UN (Chapter 6, at 6.2.2; Carroll 1978). However, such figures are lawyer-diplomats, and do not necessarily advance the claims of law: for example Sir Eric Wyndham White as head of the GATT Secretariat opposed the creation of a legal section, which did not occur until some time after his retirement, when circumstances and the nature of trade conflicts had changed (Chapter 8, at 8.3.2.1).

Law's key role is also importantly due to the techniques that lawyers have developed as creative ideologists of the texts which define the institutions and terrains through which economic activity is conducted. The key element of these techniques is the ability to assert authoritative interpretations of texts which are nevertheless inherently indeterminate and highly malleable. These techniques provide great advantages in managing the interactions between the different sites of lawmaking, adjudication, application and enforcement; as well as between different jurisdictions and arenas. In that sense, law is what Carruthers and Halliday (2007) have described as a recursive process. Social changes and political pressures are mediated through the formulation of legislative or administrative measures, which create a new potential legal field. Such a field may be left neglected and barren, if there is little incentive to cultivate it; but if it offers opportunities to build legal capital or exploit lucrative possibilities of representation, the work of cultivation will be intensive. Thus, the inclusion of investor–state arbitration provisions in the new-wave BITs in the 1990s and especially the NAFTA drew the attention of lawyers who quickly stimulated the growth of corporate litigation against states and its accompanying doctrinal debates (Chapter 5, at 5.2.1.3). Sometimes, a new field can be constructed largely by legal creativity making use of existing provisions, as with the development of anti-corporate litigation in the 1990s: in the USA the rediscovery and reinterpretation of the ATCA by Peter Weiss and his team, and the creative use of tort liability to sue TNCs in the UK by Martin Day's firm (Chapter 5, at 5.1.3.2).

Lawyers are able to move not only between the private and the public, but also between different public or semi-public arenas: they lobby legislatures and help to draft statutes; then devise legal forms to comply with, adapt to, or evade the measures; they make representations to executive bodies and administrative agencies charged with implementation; and they represent their clients before courts and tribunals which deliver adjudicative interpretations of the texts. Such processes have created and shaped the key legal institutions of corporate capitalism. Notably, the debates over corporate concentration in the USA in the period 1880 to 1915 were mediated by lawyers devising legal forms (agreements, trusts, mergers), lobbying legislatures (New Jersey and Delaware as well as the US Congress), and debating interpretations of the Sherman Act with the executive and in the courts (Chapter 4, at 4.1.1.2). The outcome was the creation and legitimation of the oligopolistic firm, organized as a corporate group, able to spread its tentacles around the world as a TNC.

Indeed, it is the development of these strategies that has created multilevel networked governance. This can be seen notably in the long-term development of the international patent system, traced in Chapter 9: it was the professional patent experts who moulded national patent systems, then helped to negotiate the Paris Convention, and began to develop strategies for international protection. In relation to medicines in particular, they explored the limits and extended the boundaries of the 'isolation from nature' principle, which became legitimized as a means of enabling and justifying protection for the large investments of the big pharmaceutical firms in blockbuster drugs. Meeting strong opposition to strengthening the Paris Convention in the 1970s, they shifted to the trade arena and achieved the implantation of the TRIPs agreement in the WTO; then they moved back again to advance the extension of protection by national implementation measures and bilateral treaties (Deere 2009). The malleability of the concepts has also been shown by the ways in which counter-attacks by insurgent patent-warriors have been accommodated, by formulating norms for access and benefit sharing, and mediating conflicts over use of plant germplasm in biotechnology through the International Treaty on Plant Genetic Resources for Food and Agriculture (IT–PGRFA) and the Standard Material Transfer Agreement, although these still remain controversial and conflictual (see Chapter 9, at 9.2.5).

10.2.2 Legal legitimacy and its limits

Hence, the fragmentation of the classical liberal international system was to a significant extent the result of these strategies, and provided lawyers with boundless new opportunities. The past thirty years in particular has seen an enormous increase in transnational law and lawyers. Although the main fields are now largely dominated by large internationalized law firms, there is considerable scope for other players. Some 'grand old men', gentlemen lawyer-diplomats and professorial practitioners continue to play a part, notably as arbitrators. Niche firms are able to build specializations, and can grow by merger or expansion, as with those specializing in offshore law and tax avoidance such as Appleby, originating in Bermuda, Maples & Calder of Cayman, and Mourant du Feu & Jeune of Jersey, which are all now sizeable international law firms. At the same time, corporate critics and activists have also mobilized, and have had some impact on the emerging patterns of governance. The work of the WTO and its many tentacles has been closely monitored by a variety of groups and NGOs, some of whose experts such as Martin Khor are pre-eminently well connected and knowledgeable. The combination of activism and esoteric knowledge has also had an impact in areas such as taxation, especially since the formation of the Tax Justice Network. Campaigns, such as that against the MAI (Chapter 5, at 5.2.1.4), the intervention of the 'patent warriors' opposing the neem patent application (Chapter 9, at 9.2.5.1), and the access to medicines movement (Chapter 9, at 9.1.3), have been quite effective.

The fragmentation of governance has also placed great weight on law as a form of legitimation, and exposed its limits. The exploitation of jurisdictional arbitrage and creation of new arenas have led to accusations of privatization and commercialization of sovereignty. This can be seen for example in the debate over tax havens. Although a key role was played by private professionals in exploiting existing legal provisions in convenient jurisdictions, and then advising their governments on creating new ones, these strategies as well as the consequent development of the 'offshore' financial system, owed much to the tolerance, collusion and support of regulatory authorities in the leading countries. Yet when the political backlash has come, it has tended to focus on the commercialized sovereignties of the small haven jurisdictions, and to overlook the continued availability of facilities in London and New York for bank secrecy to attract finance (Chapter 6, at 6.3.3 and 6.4.2).

Indeed, the resort to law has often resulted from failure to achieve agreement or consensus by political means. In such situations, law can provide subtle combinations of public and private regulation, suited to particular issues or fields. As already mentioned, law's indeterminacy can provide a formulation which sufficiently accommodates contending viewpoints, deferring conflicts to be dealt with in the future on a case-by-case basis. For example, conflicts in Europe over the patentability of business methods and computer programs have prevented clarification of the EPC provision prohibiting their patentability 'as such', leading the issue to be pursued through the subtle formulation of patent applications and debate in opposition procedures and litigation (Chapter 9, at 9.2.1). It has also been argued that the main reason why the bulk of credit derivatives have remained bespoke contracts traded privately in the OTC market is due to continuing doubts about their uncertainty, despite efforts to give them a wider legitimacy through more formalized regulation (Huault and Rainelli-Le Montagner 2009; Chapter 7, at 7.2.3). This demonstrates the limits of the power of specific cognitive communities to create social institutions with a broader legitimacy.

It is in this context that we can consider the role of supranational adjudication. This entails a move to try to legitimize international regulation by deferring thorny political questions to be dealt with ad hoc in a formalized legal–diplomatic arena. The role of the ECJ in the 'transformation of Europe', aiming to achieve integration through law, demonstrates both the power and the limits of such an institution. Although similar tribunals have been established in other regions, and indeed seem to be proliferating, their rhetoric and decisions are much more respectful of state sovereignty, notably the Andean Court of Justice (Chapter 5, at 5.2.1.1). It is instructive that the adjudicative system of the WTO was formulated in a much more modest way, avoiding any suggestion of delegation of decision-making power through interpretation of the rules to the adjudicators; and they themselves have respectfully played the game by couching their decisions, although carefully attuned to the concerns of trade diplomacy, in formalistic terms (Chapter 8, at 8.3.2). Much more problematic has been the development of international investment arbitration, which is not only procedurally a system of private justice, but entails judgments on public policies from the perspective of private, or at least corporate, interests (Chapter 5, at 5.2.1.3). Other arenas, such as the arbitration of double taxation disputes have remained even more discreetly private, refusing even a basic obeisance to formal legal legitimacy such as publication of decisions.

There are dilemmas of partial judicialization. Once issues are brought more into the open by providing for arbitration, they become more visible and attract attention, and sometimes criticism. This is especially the case where they are seen to provide private procedures for dealing with matters of public concern. One option is to maintain the legalization momentum, with proposals for the 'constitutionalization' of supranational adjudication. At a minimum, this would entail a clearer judicialization of the tribunals: permanent independent judges instead of ad hoc arbitrators who continue to represent private clients; open hearings and publication of judgments; rights of intervention by third parties and public interest groups. Although these seem logical steps to lawyers, there is not always political support, perhaps because of the conflicting interests involved (e.g. investment arbitration, Chapter 5, at 5.2.1.3).

Some would go further, and constitutionalize the rules themselves by 'balancing' economic rights with human rights, and even entrench the rules as individual rights directly applicable in national law, with a right of complaint by individual legal persons (including of course corporations) to the supranational court (Chapter 8, at 8.3.3). This would amount to a kind of global ultra-liberal constitutionalism. Some political theorists have proposed neo-Kantian models, which accept the need for a strengthening of the international institutional framework to provide an underpinning for 'cosmopolitan democratic public law'. However, this seems little different from the ultra-liberal model, somewhat reinforced by improving the representativeness of regional and international organizations.[5] The concept of constitutionalization itself can be interpreted very differently: in particular as aiming to constrain collective action through states or public bodies, or in an enabling and democratized version (Schneiderman 2008: 8–17; Chapter 8, at 8.3.1). However, if Europe has been the leader in supranational constitutionalism, the failure of the project for a European Constitution, despite the many contradictions and legitimation problems of the 'market without a state', demonstrates the limits of constitutionalization of global governance. On the one hand, social action and interest representation remain firmly focused on national (or sub-national) states; while on the other the dominant elements in corporatist capitalism are confident in their ability to control networked governance, which indeed they helped to construct.

5 This appears to be the argument of David Held: see 1995, 1997, and its evaluation by Dryzek 1999.

More modest roles can be devised for law in global governance, though they are nevertheless ambitious. From the viewpoint of traditional public international law, the extraordinary expansion of international legalization is certainly to be welcomed, but the fragmented and unco-ordinated character of this growth, in the form of autonomous ad hoc rule-complexes, raise questions about the lack of coherence of interna-tional law. This was taken up by the UN's International Law Commission through a Study Group, whose conclusions were cautiously reassuring (ILC 2006). It took the view that such fragmentation is natural, and results from both the multiplicity of issues facing the world and the 'dif-fering pursuits and preferences of actors in a pluralistic (global) society'. It was content to find that 'international law was always relatively "frag-mented" due to the diversity of national legal systems that participated in it'; yet 'the vitality and synergy of the system and the pull for coherence in the law itself' are reflected in tools it has developed (ILC 2006: para. 11).

Singled out in particular were the rules of interpretation notably in the Vienna Convention on the Law of Treaties. These of course have been relied upon heavily by the WTO's AB, although as we have seen WTO decisions have been cautious and selective in interpreting WTO rules in ways which could be said to contribute to any global systemic coherence.[6] Nevertheless, adjudicators are in some ways becoming a specialist com-munity, and some have served in different forums, for example as WTO Panel or AB members and investment arbitrators. Some decisions have applied common principles or created links between related regimes: for example, the desirability of an independent regulatory agency was an important factor in both the WTO Panel report in *Mexico – Telecoms* (2004) (Chapter 8, at 8.2.3.3) and the arbitration in *Biwater* v. *Tanzania* (2008) (Chapter 5, at 5.2.1.3). There are certainly many common con-cepts such as non-discrimination principles in parallel regimes such as investment treaties and the WTO, although also differences in the way they are understood for example in tax or IP treaties. Hence, the ILC could assert that international law is after all still 'a legal system' and not just a random collection of norms (ILC 2006: 14). Public international lawyers continue to investigate the issues of 'regime interaction' (Young 2011).

Perhaps more promising than schemes for constitutionalization or even attempts at coherence is the quest for a global administrative law.[7] This

---

6 Perhaps more the Panels than the AB itself: see Chapter 8, at 8.3.3.1.
7 See www.iilj.org/GAL for materials; in particular special issues of *Law & Contemporary Problems* (2005), the *European Journal of International Law* (2006) and *Acta Juridica* (2009).

has been led in particular by the Global Administrative Law Project based at New York University. It began from a realization of the 'vast increase in the reach and forms of transgovernmental regulation and administration designed to address the consequences of globalized interdependence' but also an identification of the concomitant growth of a 'little-noticed but important and growing body of global administrative law' (Kingsbury *et al.* 2005: 15–16). This enabled a pragmatic approach, surveying the multiplicity of institutions and arenas to discover and analyse the practices and principles which have developed, while putting forward a schema for systematization and proposals for the development of a putative administrative law for heterarchical global governance. Although this approach may contribute towards establishing principles of good practice and procedure, the issue of legitimacy of the substantive decision-making is unavoidable, and here the pragmatic conclusion is pessimistic: 'no satisfactory democratic basis for global administration is available but . . . global administrative structures are nevertheless required to deal with problems national democracies are unable to solve on their own' (Kingsbury *et al.* 2005: 50).

The reassertion of a public law perspective can certainly be used to challenge the often highly privatized institutions and arenas of global governance, notably international investment arbitration (van Harten and Loughlin 2006; Chapter 5, at 5.2.1.3). Yet, as with models of constitutionalization, there are different perspectives on the role of public administration. Indeed, the investment treaty regime can also be seen as a classic form of public law, establishing at the international level a framework for managing the 'universal tension between property rights and the public interest', to provide a check on illegal and arbitrary state action (Montt 2009). From this perspective, while procedural reforms could be conceded, they would hardly resolve the issue of political legitimacy.

10.2.3 Technocratic governance and democratic dilemmas

These questions about the role of law are also part of a broader debate about technocratic governance. The moves to legalization represent not only a failure to resolve issues politically, but also a concern that they should not be left solely to a specialized technocracy. Many issues and

---

This was a significant reorientation from earlier (although itself also pioneering) work, which focused on the impact of globalization on national administrative law (e.g. Harlow 1999; Aman 2002).

areas of global concern are indeed now governed by delegation to experts. For example, although TRIPs, article 27 now establishes a global standard of patentability, it takes the form of a principle expressed in broad and general terms. This leaves open important specific decisions about patentability, in the forefront of which is biotechnology. No formal arena is available at the international level to consider this, and even in Europe adjudication remains at the national level. The gap has been filled by the creation of the informal network of the Trilateral patent offices, which conducted a technical study of the patentability of genetic fragments, enabling some convergence of their national standards (Chapter 9, at 9.2.2 and 9.2.4). Similarly, despite a global diffusion of laws to regulate competition and considerable convergence of approaches, no formal global framework has been established. Nevertheless, informal networks and an expert community supply a degree of coordination that is probably as effective as would be provided if a competition agreement along the lines of the TRIPs had been included in the WTO (Chapter 4, at 4.3.3–4).

Very many examples of this type could be given, indeed technocracy constitutes the main form of global governance. This results not only from the difficulties of reaching international agreement, but from the more fundamental social changes that have led to the transformations of the state, its functional fragmentation, and the emergence of regulatory governance (discussed in Chapter 1, at 1.2.2). This has raised fundamental questions about the legitimacy of technocratic decision-making. Within national states, these have been dealt with in liberal states mainly through Weberian models of bureaucracy, according to which specialist technocrats must take decisions on the basis of an objectivist and instrumental rationality, within a framework of values decided by political processes, to which they are accountable. However, these models have come under increasing pressure, as a variety of factors has led to a growing public mistrust of expertise and science (discussed in Chapter 1, at 1.3.3). Expertise is important and indeed necessary especially in today's complex world. However, it needs to operate within new structures to ensure that specialist knowledge is developed and deployed responsibly and accountably.

Taking a wider perspective, some political theorists have argued that the effects of liberalization and globalization have been to unleash socially destructive behaviour based on the competitive pursuit of self-interest, as existing normative and institutional restraints are undermined or dismantled. They argue that this necessitates the reconstitution of democracy based on principles adapted to the emerging forms of the new public sphere, but which explicitly aim to structure it to ensure the most effective forms of popular participation. Indeed, new forms of active citizenship and political action have been developing, often around the local and national impact of regional or global policies. Some have also been institutionalized, for example the system of participatory budgeting pioneered in Porto Alegre and other parts of Brazil, which have also spread worldwide, although too often in forms which reinforce existing systems of political patronage (van Zyl 2010; Chapter 6, at 6.1.2).

The recognition that the public sphere has become fragmented into multiple intersecting networks and overlapping jurisdictional spheres emphasizes the importance of building democratic participation through new political principles, institutions and practices. These should recognize the diversity of political sites in which public policies are developed and implemented, also involving processes of reflexive interaction between these sites.

Jürgen Habermas in particular has argued that such principles must attempt to transcend the two main traditional constitutional models, which are increasingly proving inadequate for the contemporary phase of globalization (1996, see also 2001). On the one hand, liberal conceptions, based on a view of society as composed of individuals pursuing their self-interest or pre-formed 'preferences', see the role of the polity as complementing the market, and as aiming to identify a collective interest either by authoritarian means, or via majoritarian representative democracy. Post-industrial capitalism, with its integrated global production and marketing networks, raises a wide range of social, environmental and moral issues, which cannot adequately be resolved by aggregating individual preferences, using either authoritarian or democratic methods. The alternative model of civic republicanism rejects the narrow view of citizenship based on weighing and balancing competing private interests. However, its stress on an ethical politics based on visions of the common good implies a communitarianism requiring shared values, which in today's culturally fractured world takes reactionary forms, and may generate conflict rather than consensus.

Habermas has suggested that, whereas both these views tend to see the state as the centre, deliberative politics can be adapted to a decentred society.

> This concept of democracy no longer needs to operate with the notion
> of a social whole centered in the state and imagined as a goal-oriented
> subject writ large. Just as little does it represent the whole in a system of

> constitutional norms mechanically regulating the interplay of powers and
> interests in accordance with the market model.
>
> (1996: 27)

Others also have stressed the attractiveness of a direct, deliberative form
of participatory democracy for solving problems in ways unavailable to
representative systems:

> collective decisions are made through public deliberation in arenas open
> to citizens who use public services, or who are otherwise regulated by
> public decisions. But in deciding, those citizens must examine their own
> choices in the light of the relevant deliberations and experiences of others
> facing similar problems in comparable jurisdictions or subdivisions of
> government.
>
> (Cohen and Sabel 1997: 313–14)

In this perspective, decision-making, especially by public bodies, should
result as far as possible from active democratic participation based on
discursive or deliberative rather than instrumental reasoning. Instead
of the pursuit of individual interests based on the assumption of fixed
preferences, the aim is to go beyond an objectivist rationality (in which
choices are considered to be made by reference to absolute and objective
standards), without falling into the trap of relativism (Dryzek 1990).
Thus, while accepting that there is no single objective standard of truth,
since perspectives are always subjective (and hence epistemology is to
that extent relativist), truth can be said to be an emergent property of the
deliberative interaction between perspectives (and hence its ontology is
objective). In other words, there is an objective truth, even if we can only
know it through subjective interactions; this is the most basic justification
for democracy.

Deliberative democracy accepts the existence of a diversity of perspectives, and aims to facilitate interactive deliberation about values through
which preferences may change, or may be accommodated to each other.
An emphasis on process may help to overcome the weaknesses of this
model if conceived as a political ideal, or as relying on the generation
of consensus purely through the public use of reason. Crucially, account
must also be taken of inequalities of power, which generate conflicting
interests as well as imbalances in capacities to participate in a politics
based on reasoning.

Thus, a key element is the fostering of informed participation in deliberative decision-making, rather than merely elite or expert deliberation.

There is a certain tension between the two, since the deliberative evaluation of specialized knowledge or data entails a degree of insulation or autonomy from private interests and other pressures.[8] However, this may result in an unjustified authority being claimed by or given to the judgements of specialists or experts. Thus a key element in democratic deliberation is to ensure a fruitful interaction between various sites of deliberation, and an awareness by specialists of the conditional or contingent nature of their expert knowledge and judgements (Wynne 1992). Thus, experts should be more explicit about the assumptions behind the abstract models underpinning their evaluations, and allow input into their deliberations from both other specialists and alternative perspectives and social values.

This has important implications for lawyers, since law generally structures regulatory arenas and interactions, as well as mediating social conflicts and interactions. As we have seen, a significant weakness of international legalization is that it has reinforced formalism and instrumental rationality. Notably, international adjudicators have tended to rely on a closed epistemology, based on an objectivism which treats the abstract concepts in the texts through an instrumental rationality, resulting in decisions expressed in legalistic terms. This closure tends to exclude debate about the values involved in the interpretive choices made by the adjudicator, which would entail acceptance of a more extended and direct accountability to a broader political constituency, rather than through national governments. It is also technicist (taking its specialist part for the whole), since its closed rationality excludes reflexive dialogue with those outside its specialist epistemological sphere. The reasoning shown in the decisions of the WTO's AB (discussed in Chapter 8) reflects its

---

8 Thus, the work of Joerges and Neyer on the role of expert and scientific committees in regulatory decision-making in the EU (Joerges and Neyer 1997; Joerges 1999) characterized them as 'deliberative', in the sense that the participants approach issues open-mindedly rather than from pre-formed positions (in particular in favour of national interests), seeking to reach consensus through evaluation of valid knowledge (Joerges 1999: 320). However, they had reservations, especially about the management of the interaction between various types of committee, so that it was still questionable whether the EC committee system 'gives proper expression to the plurality of practical and ethical views which should be included within risk assessment procedures'. The conclusion seemed to be that the system is certainly not a closed or homogeneous epistemic complex, but its openness is limited or haphazard, if not selective (Joerges 1999: 321). Others have been more explicitly critical of the ways in which the European Commission's restriction of public consultation and involvement, through its management of the committee system, has undermined the legitimacy of some decision-making in the EU regulatory networks (Landfried 1999; Vos 1999).

accountability dilemma, hence they are generally expressed in legalistic terms, but astutely tread a difficult political line aimed at ensuring their acceptability to its various constituencies.

It is clearly illusory to consider that law alone can provide adequate legitimacy for global governance. It is nevertheless equally clearly important that the law and lawyers should play their part. This includes helping to construct forms and arenas of governance which are insulated from undue influence from private interests, and which foster democratic participation and deliberation based on explicitly articulated values and aims. Lawyers play a crucial role in accommodating public concerns to private interests. Lawyering entails interpretive practices which mediate between the public standards and values expressed in the wide variety of norms, and the particular activities and operations of economic actors, offering the hope that economic power might be exercised ultimately for the general good. However, this aspiration is illusory unless law operates within a broader democratic framework, in which legal practices themselves are also subject to high standards of transparency, accountability and responsibility. This includes the responsibility of each individual to reflect on their own practice and methodology, and when putting forward either analyses or prescriptions to do so on the basis of clearly articulated assumptions, taking due account of the perspectives of others, even if within a critical evaluation.

BIBLIOGRAPHY

Aaron, H. J. and Slemrod, J. 2004. *The Crisis in Tax Administration*. Washington, DC: Brookings Institution Press.

Abbott, F. M. 2009. 'Cross-Retaliation in TRIPs: Options for Developing Countries', Geneva: ICSID.

Abbott, F. M., Breining-Kaufmann, C. and Cottier, T. 2006. *International Trade and Human Rights: Foundations and Conceptual Issues*. Ann Arbor: University of Michigan Press.

Abbott, K. W., Keohane, R. O., Moravcsik, A., Slaughter, A.-M. and Snidal, D. 2000. 'The Concept of Legalization', *International Organization*, 54: 401–19.

Abbott, K. W. and Snidal, D. 2000. 'Hard and Soft Law in International Governance', *International Organization*, 54: 421–56.

Aberbach, J. D. and Christensen, T. 2007. 'The Challenges of Modernizing Tax Administration. Putting Customers First in Coercive Public Organizations', *Public Policy and Administration*, 22: 155–82.

Abolafia, M. Y. 1985. 'Self-Regulation as Market Maintenance', in R. G. Noll (ed.), *Regulatory Policy and the Social Sciences*, 312–43. Berkeley: University of California Press.

Adam, N. 1992. *Regulating Global Financial Markets*. London: Economist Intelligence Unit.

Adler, E. and Bernstein, S. 2005. 'Knowledge in Power: The Epistemic Construction of Global Governance', in M. N. Barnett and R. Duvall (eds.), *Power in Global Governance*, 294–318. Cambridge University Press.

Adler-Karlsson, G. 1968. *Western Economic Warfare 1947–1967. A Case Study in Foreign Economic Policy*. Stockholm: Almqvist & Wiksell.

Aguesse, P. 2007. 'Is Rating an Efficient Response to the Challenges of the Structured Finance Market?', *Risk and Trend Mapping No. 2*, Paris: Autorité des Marchés Financiers.

Ahn, D. 2003. 'Linkages between International Financial and Trade Institutions: IMF, World Bank and WTO': School of Public Policy and Management, Korea Development Institute.

AIPPI 1997. *AIPPI and the Development of Industrial Property 1897–1997*. Paris: AIPPI (Association Internationale pour la Protection de la Propriété Intellectuelle).

Akehurst, M. 1972–3. 'Jurisdiction in International Law', *British Yearbook of International Law*, 46: 145–257.

Akinsanya, A. 1980. *The Expropriation of Multinational Property in the Third World*. New York: Praeger.

Akinsanya, A. 1987. 'International Protection of Direct Foreign Investments in the Third World', *International and Comparative Law Quarterly*, 36: 58–76.

Alderton, T. and Winchester, N. 2002. 'Globalisation and Deregulation in the Maritime Industry', *Marine Policy*, 26: 35–43.

Alexander, K., Dhumale, R. and Eatwell, J. 2006. *Global Governance of Financial Systems: The International Regulation of Systemic Risk*. Oxford University Press.

Alford, D. E. 1992. 'Basle Committee Minimum Standards: International Regulatory Response to the Failure of BCCI', *George Washington Journal of International Law and Economics*, 26: 241–91.

Alston, P. 2002. 'Resisting the Merger and Acquisition of Human Rights by Trade Law: A Reply to Petersmann', *European Journal of International Law*, 13: 815–44.

Alston, P. and Robinson, M. 2005. *Human rights and Development: Towards Mutual Reinforcement*. Oxford University Press.

Alston, P. and Tomasevski, K. 1984. *The Right to Food*. Utrecht: M. Nijhoff; SIM Netherlands Institute of Human Rights.

Alter, K. J. 2003. 'Resolving or Exacerbating Disputes? The WTO's New Dispute Resolution System', *International Affairs*, 79: 783–800.

Altinger, L. and Enders, A. 1996. 'The Scope and Depth of GATS Commitments', *World Economy*, 19: 307–32.

Altman, Z. D. 2005. *Dispute Resolution under Tax Treaties*. Amsterdam: IBFD.

Alvarez, J. E. 1989. 'Political Protectionism and United States International Investment Obligations in Conflict: The Hazards of Exon–Florio', *Virginia Journal of International Law*, 30: 1–187.

Aman, A. C. 2002. 'Globalization, Democracy, and the Need for a New Administrative Law. Symposium: New Forms of Governance: Ceding Public Power to Private Actors', *UCLA Law Review*, 49: 1687–716.

Amani, B. and Coombe, R. 2005. 'The Human Genome Diversity Project: The Politics of Patents at the Intersection of Race, Religion, and Research Ethics', *Law and Policy*, 27: 152–88.

ANAO 2008. *The Australian Taxation Office's Strategies to Address Tax Haven Compliance Risks*. ACT: Australian National Audit Office.

Andersen, B. and Frenz, M. 2007. *The Impact of Music Downloads and P2P File-Sharing on the Purchase of Music: A Study for Industry Canada* (www.ic.gc.ca).

Anderson, B. 1991. *Imagined Communities*. London: Verso.

Anderson, M. 1989. *Policing the World. Interpol and the Politics of International Police Cooperation*. Oxford: Clarendon Press.

Andersson, S. and Heywood, P. M. 2009. 'The Politics of Perception: Use and Abuse of Transparency International's Approach to Measuring Corruption', *Political Studies*, 57: 746–67.

Anghie, A. 1999. 'Finding the Peripheries: Sovereignty and Colonialism in Nineteenth-Century International Law', *Harvard International Law Journal*, 40: 1–80.

Ansell, C. and Vogel, D. (eds.) 2006. *What's the Beef? The Contested Governance of European Food Safety*. Cambridge, MA: MIT Press.

Antoine, R.-M. B. 1999. *Commonwealth Caribbean Law and Legal Systems*. London: Cavendish.

Aoki, K. 1998. 'Neocolonialism, Anti-commons Property, and Biopiracy in the (Not-So-Brave) New World Order of International Intellectual Property Protection', *Indiana Journal of Global Legal Studies*, 6: 11–58.

Aoki, K. 2009. 'Free Seeds, Not Free Beer', *Fordham Law Review*, 77: 2275–310.

Appelbaum, R. P. 1998. 'The Future of Law in a Global Economy', *Social and Legal Studies*, 7: 171–92.

Appelbaum, R. P., Felstiner, W. L. F. and Gessner, V. 2001. *Rules and Networks: The Legal Culture of Global Business Transactions*. Oxford: Hart.

Arrighi, G. 2007. *Adam Smith in Beijing: Lineages of the Twenty-First Century*. London Verso.

Arthurs, H. 2001. 'The Reconstitution of the Public Domain', in D. Drache (ed.), *The Market or the Public Domain? Global Governance and the Asymmetry of Power*, 85–109. London: Routledge.

Arup, C. 2000. *The New World Trade Organization Agreements: Globalizing Law through Services and Intellectual Property*. Cambridge University Press.

Atik, J. 1997. 'Science and International Regulatory Convergence', *Northwestern Journal of International Law and Business*, 17: 736–58.

Aust, A. 2008. *Modern Treaty Law and Practice*. Cambridge University Press.

Australia Treasury, 2004. *New International Tax Arrangements (Participation Exemption and Other Measures) Bill 2004. Explanatory Memoranda*, Canberra: Parliament of the Commonwealth of Australia, House of Representatives.

Avi-Yonah, R. S. 1996. 'The Structure of International Taxation: A Proposal for Simplification', *Texas Law Review*, 74: 1301–59.

Avi-Yonah, R. S. 2001. 'Globalization and Tax Competition: Implications for Developing Countries': Inter-American Development Bank.

Avi-Yonah, R. S. 2007. *International Tax as International Law*. Cambridge University Press.

Avi-Yonah, R. S. 2009. 'Closing the International Tax Gap Via Cooperation, Not Competition', *Worldwide Tax Daily*, 10 September.

Avi-Yonah and I. Benshalom 2010. 'Formulary Apportionment: Myths and Prospects – Promoting Better International Tax Policy and Utilizing the Misunderstood and Under-Theorized Formulary Alternative', SSRN eLibrary.

Ayres, I. and Braithwaite, J. 1992. *Responsive Regulation. Transcending the Deregulation Debate*. Oxford University Press.

Bacchus, J. 2002. 'Table Talk: Around the Table of the Appellate Body of the World Trade Organization', *Vanderbilt Journal of Transnational Law*, 35: 1021–39.

Badie, B. 2000. *The Imported State: The Westernization of the Political Order*. Stanford University Press.

Bagley, M. A. 2003. 'Patently Unconstitutional: The Geographical Limitation on Prior Art in a Small World', *Minnesota Law Review*, 87: 679–742.

Bagley, M. A. 2008. 'The Need for Speed (and Grace): Issues in a First-Inventor-to-File World', University of Virginia Public Law and Legal Theory Working Paper Series. Working Paper 100.

Baiocchi, G. 2001. 'Participation, Activism, and Politics: The Porto Alegre Experiment and Deliberative Democratic Theory', *Politics and Society*, 29: 43–72.

Bairoch, P. 1996. 'Globalization Myths and Realities. One Century of External Trade and Foreign Investment', in R. Boyer and D. Drache (eds.), *States Against Markets. The Limits of Globalization*, 173–92. London: Routledge.

Baistrocchi, E. A. 2008. 'The Use and Interpretation of Tax Treaties in the Emerging World: Theory and Implications', *British Tax Review*, 352–91.

Bakan, J. 2004. *The Corporation: The Pathological Pursuit of Profit and Power*. London: Constable.

Baker, D. and Ayer, D. B. 1993. 'Anti-Trust Imperialism', *European Competition Law Review*, 14: 3–5.

Baker, R. 2005. *Capitalism's Achilles Heel. Dirty Money and How to Renew the Free-Market System*. Hoboken, NJ: John Wiley.

Baldwin, D. A. (ed.) 1993. *Neorealism and Neoliberalism: The Contemporary Debate*. New York: Columbia University Press.

Ball, G. W. 1967. 'Cosmocorp – The Importance of Being Stateless', *Columbia Journal of World Business*, 2: 25–32.

Ball, G. W. (ed.) 1975. *Global Companies: The Political Economy of World Business*. Englewood Cliffs, NJ: Prentice-Hall.

Bantekas, I. 2006. 'Corruption as an International Crime and Crime Against Humanity', *Journal of International Criminal Justice*, 4: 466–84.

Bantekas, I. and Nash, S. 2003. *International Criminal Law*. London: Cavendish.

Bantekas, I. and Nash, S. 2010. *International Criminal Law*. Oxford: Hart.

Bardach, E. and Kagan, R. A. 1982. *Going by the Book: The Problem of Regulatory Unreasonableness*. Philadelphia: Temple University Press.

Barfield, C. E. (ed.) 1996. *International Financial Markets. Harmonization versus Competition*. Washington, DC: American Enterprise Institute.

Barnes, J. J. 1974. *Authors, Publishers and Politicians. The Quest for an Anglo-American Copyright Agreement 1815–1854*. London: RKP.

Bartels, L. 2001. 'Applicable Law in WTO Dispute Settlement Proceedings', *Journal of World Trade*, 35: 499–519.

Bartlett, C. A. and Ghoshal, S. 1989. *Managing Across Borders. The Transnational Solution*. Boston: Harvard Business School Press.

Barton, J. 2000. 'Reforming the Patent System', *Science*, 287: 1933–5.

Barzel, Y. 1997. *Economic Analysis of Property Rights*. Cambridge University Press.

Baslar, K. 1998. *The Concept of the Common Heritage of Mankind in International Law*. The Hague: Kluwer.

Bassiouni, M. C. 1974. *International Extradition and World Public Order*. Leiden: Sijthoff.

Bassiouni, M. C. 2001. 'Universal Jurisdiction for International Crimes: Historical Perspectives and Contemporary Practice', *Virginia Journal of International Law*, 42: 81–162.

Baughn, C., Bodie, N. L., Buchanan, M. A. and Bixby, M. B. 2010. 'Bribery in International Business Transactions', *Journal of Business Ethics*, 92: 15–32.

Baunsgaard, T. and Keen, M. 2005. 'Tax Revenue and (or?) Trade Liberalization', Working Paper 05/112: International Monetary Fund, Fiscal Affairs Dept.

Baxi, U. 1986. *Inconvenient Forum and Convenient Catastrophe: The Bhopal Case*. Bombay: Tripathi.

Baxi, U. 1999. 'Mass Torts, Multinational Enterprise Liability and Private International Law', *Recueil des Cours de l'Académie de Droit International*, 276: 301–427.

BBS 1995. *Report of the Board of Banking Supervision Inquiry into the Collapse of Barings*. London: Board of Banking Supervision.

BCBS 1999. *Banks' Interactions with Highly Leveraged Institutions*. Basel: Basel Committee on Banking Supervision.

BCBS 2009. *Strengthening the Resilience of the Banking Sector – Consultative Document*. Basel: Basel Committee on Banking Supervision.

BCG 2010. *Global Wealth. Regaining Lost Ground. Resurgent Markets and New Opportunities*. Boston Consulting Group.

Bebchuk, L. A. and Roe, M. J. 1999. 'A Theory of Path Dependence in Corporate Ownership and Governance', *Stanford Law Review*, 52: 127–70.

Beck, T., Coyle, D., Dewatripont, M., Freixas, X. and Seabright, P. 2010. *Bailing out the Banks: Reconciling Stability and Competition. An Analysis of State-Supported Schemes for Financial Institutions*. London: Centre for Economic Policy Research.

Becker, G. S. 1976. *The Economic Approach to Human Behavior.* University of Chicago Press.

Beier, F.-K. 1984. 'One Hundred Years of International Cooperation – The Role of the Paris Convention in the Past, Present and Future', *IIC*, 15: 1–20.

Bélanger, J., Björkman, T. and Köhler, C. (eds.) 1999. *Being Local Worldwide: ABB and the Challenge of Global Management.* Ithaca, NY: Cornell University Press.

Belchem, J. 1992. 'The Neglected "Unstamped": The Manx Pauper Press of the 1840s', *Albion*, 24: 605–16.

Bell, A. S. 2003. *Forum Shopping and Venue in Transnational Litigation.* Oxford University Press.

Bell, D. 1973. *The Coming of Post-Industrial Society. An Essay in Social Forecasting.* New York: Basic Books.

Bell, D. and Graubard, S. R. (eds.) 1997. *Toward the Year 2000.* Cambridge, MA: MIT Press.

Bell, S. and Quiggin, J. 2006. 'Asset Price Instability and Policy Responses: The Legacy of Liberalization', *Journal of Economic Issues*, 40: 629–49.

Bellis, M. de. 2006. 'Global Standards for Domestic Financial Regulations: Concourse, Competition and Mutual Reinforcement between Different Types of Global Administration', *Global Jurist Advances*, 6: 3 (art. 6).

Benhabib, S. (ed.) 1996. *Democracy and Difference. Contesting the Boundaries of the Political.* Princeton University Press.

Benkler, Y. 2003. 'Freedom in the Commons: Towards a Political Economy of Information', *Duke Law Journal*, 52: 1245–76.

Bentley, L. 2007. 'Rosen: GPL Is Good, but OSL Is Better', 21 June, *IT Business Edge.*

Benvenisti, E. and Downs, G. W. 2007. 'The Empire's New Clothes: Political Economy and the Fragmentation of International Law', *Stanford Law Review*, 60: 595–631.

Berle, A. A. and Means, G. C. 1932. *The Modern Corporation and Private Property.* New York: Macmillan.

Bernard, A. B., Jensen, J. B. and Schott, P. K. 2008. 'Transfer Pricing by US-Based Multinational Firms', Discussion Papers CES 08–29 Washington, DC: Center for Economic Studies, Bureau of the Census.

Bernstein, M. H. 1955. *Regulating Business by Independent Commission.* Princeton University Press.

Bernstein, S. and Hannah, E. 2008. 'Non-State Global Standard Setting and the WTO: Legitimacy and the Need for Regulatory Space', *Journal of International Economic Law*, 11: 575–608.

Bhagwati, J. 2005. 'From Seattle to Hong Kong', *Foreign Affairs*, 84 (art. 15).

Bhagwati, J. and Hudec, R. E. (eds.) 1996. *Fair Trade and Harmonization. Prerequisites for Free Trade? Vol. 2 Legal Analysis.* Cambridge, MA: MIT Press.

Bhagwati, J. and Patrick, H. T. (eds.) 1990. *Aggressive Unilateralism. America's 301 Trading Policy and the World Trading System.* Ann Arbor: University of Michigan Press.

Bhagwati, P. N. 1989. 'Travesty of justice', 15 March, *India Today.*

Bhala, R. 1999a. 'The Myth about *Stare Decisis* and International Trade Law (Part One of a Trilogy)', *American University International Law Review,* 14: 845–956.

Bhala, R. 1999b. 'The Precedent Setters: De Facto *Stare Decisis* in WTO Adjudication (Part Two of a Trilogy)', *Journal of Transnational Law and Policy,* 9: 1–151.

Bingham, L. J. 1992. *Report of the Inquiry into the Supervision of the Bank of Credit and Commerce International (BCCI). Chairman: The Right Honourable Lord Justice Bingham.* London: UK Treasury.

BIS 1998. *Annual Report.* Basel: Bank for International Settlements.

BIS 2007. *Triennial Central Bank Survey. Foreign Exchange and Derivatives Market Activity in 2007.* Basel: Bank for International Settlements.

BIS 2009. *Annual Report.* Basel: Bank for International Settlements.

Bittlingmayer, G. 1985. 'Did Antitrust Policy Cause the Great Merger Wave?', *Journal of Law and Economics,* 28: 77–118.

Black, J. 1998. 'Regulation as Facilitation: Negotiating the Genetic Revolution', *Modern Law Review,* 61: 621–60.

Blackburn, R. 2002. *Banking on Death: Or, Investing in Life: The History and Future of Pensions.* London: Verso.

Blanpain, R. 1979. *The OECD Guidelines for Multinational Enterprises and Labour Relations 1976–1979. Experience and Review.* Deventer: Kluwer.

Blanpain, R. 1983. *The OECD Guidelines for Multinational Enterprises and Labour Relations 1979–82: Experience and Mid-term Report.* Deventer: Kluwer.

Bloom, A. 2001. 'Taking on Goliath. Why Personal Injury Litigation May Represent the Future of Transnational Cause Lawyering', in A. Sarat and S. Scheingold (eds.), *Cause Lawyering and the State in a Global Era.* Oxford University Press.

Blouin, C., Drager, N. and Smith, R. 2006. *International Trade in Health Services and the GATS: Current Issues and Debates.* Washington, DC: World Bank.

Blum, J., Levi, M., Naylor, T. and Williams, P. 1998. *Financial Havens, Banking Secrecy and Money-Laundering.* Vienna: UN Office for Drug Control and Crime Prevention.

Blumberg, P. I. 1986. 'Limited Liability and Corporate Groups', *Journal of Corporation Law,* 11: 573–631.

Blumberg, P. I. 1993. *The Multinational Challenge to Corporation Law: The Search for a New Corporate Personality.* Oxford University Press.

Blunden, G. 1977. 'International Cooperation in Banking Supervision', *Bank of England Quarterly Bulletin,* 17: 325–9.

Bodansky, D. 1999. 'The Framework Convention/Protocol Approach', WHO/NCD/TFI/99.1 Geneva: World Health Organization.

Bodenhausen, G. H. C. 1968. *Guide to the Application of the Paris Convention for the Protection of Industrial Property. As revised at Stockholm in 1967*. Geneva: United International Bureaux for the Protection of Intellectual Property (BIRPI).

Bogle, J. C. 2008. 'A Question So Important that it Should Be Hard to Think about Anything Else', *Journal of Portfolio Management*, 34: 95–102.

Boldrin, M. and Levine, D. 2002. 'The Case Against Intellectual Property', *American Economic Review Papers and Proceedings*, 92: 209–12.

Boltanski, L. and Chiapello, E. 1999. *Le nouvel esprit du capitalisme*. Paris: Gallimard.

Bolton, D. 1985. *Nationalization – A Road to Socialism? The Lessons of Tanzania*. London: Zed Books.

Bonney, R. (ed.) 1999. *The Rise of the Fiscal State in Europe, c.1200–1815*. Oxford University Press.

Bonsignore, E. 2008. 'Defence, Trade and the Misuse of Justice', *Military Technology*, 32: 8–9.

Botzem, S. and Quack, S. 2006. 'Contested Rules and Shifting Boundaries: International Standard-Setting in Accounting', in M.-L. Djelic and K. Sahlin-Andersson (eds.), *Transnational Governance. Institutional Dynamics of Regulation*, 266–86. Cambridge University Press.

Bourdieu, P. 1986. 'La force du droit. Eléments pour une sociologie du champ juridique', *Actes de la Recherche en Science Sociales*, 64: 3–19.

Bourdieu, P. 1987. 'The Force of Law: Toward a Sociology of the Juridical Field', *Hastings Law Journal*, 38: 805–53.

Bowring, F. 2003. *Science, Seeds, and Cyborgs: Biotechnology and the Appropriation of Life*. London: Verso.

Boyle, J. 1996. *Shamans, Software and Spleens. Law and the Construction of the Information Society*. Cambridge, MA: Harvard University Press.

Boyle, J. 2003. 'The Second Enclosure Movement and the Construction of the Public Domain', *Law and Contemporary Problems*, 66: 33–74.

Boyrie, M. E., Pak, S. J. and Zdanowicz, J. S. 2004. 'Estimating the Magnitude of Capital Flight due to Abnormal Pricing in International Trade: The Russia–USA Case': CIBER Working Paper; Center for International Business and Education Research, Florida International University.

Braga, C. A. P., Forestier, E. and Stern, P. A. 1999. 'Developing Countries and Accounting Rates Reform – A Technological and Regulatory El Nino?', *Public Policy for the Private Sector*, Washington, DC: World Bank.

Braithwaite, J. 1993. 'Transnational Regulation of the Pharmaceutical Industry', *Annals of the American Academy of Political and Social Science*, 525: 12–30.

Braithwaite, J. 2000. 'The New Regulatory State and the Transformation of Criminology', *British Journal of Criminology*, 40: 222–38.

Braithwaite, J. 2002. 'Rules and Principles: A Theory of Legal Certainty', *Australian Journal of Legal Philosophy*, 27: 47–82.

Braithwaite, J. 2005. *Markets in Vice, Markets in Virtue*. Oxford University Press.

Braithwaite, J. 2008. *Regulatory Capitalism. How it Works, Ideas for Making it Work Better*. Cheltenham, UK: Edward Elgar.

Braithwaite, J. and Drahos, P. 2000. *Global Business Regulation*. Cambridge University Press.

Braithwaite, V. (ed.) 2003. *Taxing Democracy. Understanding Tax Avoidance and Evasion*. Aldershot: Ashgate.

Brandeis, L. D. 1914. *Other People's Money, and How the Bankers Use it*. New York: Frederick A. Stokes.

Bratton, W. W. 2003a. 'Enron and the Dark Side of Shareholder Value', *Tulane Law Review*, 76: 1275–361.

Bratton, W. W. 2003b. 'Enron, Sarbanes–Oxley and Accounting: Rules versus Principles versus Rents', *Villanova Law Review*, 48: 1023–56.

Bratton, W. W. and McCahery, J. 1999. 'Comparative Corporate Governance and the Theory of the Firm – The Case against Global Cross-Reference', *Columbia Journal of Transnational Law*, 38: 213–98.

Bratton, W. W., McCahery, J., Picciotto, S. and Scott, C. (eds.) 1996. *International Regulatory Competition and Coordination*. Oxford: Clarendon Press.

Bräutigam, D. 2002. 'Building Leviathan: Revenue, State Capacity and Governance', *IDS Bulletin*, 33: 1–17.

Bräutigam, D. 2004. 'The People's Budget? Politics, Participation and Pro-poor Policy', *Development Policy Review*, 22: 653–68.

Bräutigam, D., Fjeldstad, O.-H. and Moore, M. (eds.) 2008. *Taxation and State Building in Developing Countries. Capacity and Consent*. Cambridge University Press.

Brecher, J., Costello, T. and Smith, B. 2000. *Globalization from Below: The Power of Solidarity*. Cambridge, MA: South End Press.

Brennan, G. and Buchanan, J. M. 1985. *The Reason of Rules. Constitutional Political Economy*. Cambridge University Press.

Brenner, R. 2002. *The Boom and the Bubble: The US in the World Economy*. London: Verso.

Brenner, R. 2006. *The Economics of Global Turbulence: The Advanced Capitalist Economies from Long Boom to Long Downturn, 1945–2005*. London: Verso.

Bretschger, L. and Hettich, F. 2002. 'Globalisation, Capital Mobility and Tax Competition: Theory and Evidence for OECD Countries', *European Journal of Political Economy*, 18: 695–716.

Brett, E. A. 1985. *The World Economy since the War – The Politics of Uneven Development*. London: Macmillan.

Brilmayer, L. 1989 *Justifying International Acts*. Ithaca, NY: Cornell University Press.

Brin, S. 2009. 'A Library to Last Forever', 8 October, *New York Times*.

Brinkley, A. 1993. 'The Antimonopoly Ideal and the Liberal State: The Case of Thurman Arnold', *Journal of American History*, 80: 557–79.

Brock, W. 1982. 'A Simple Plan for Negotiating on Trade in Services', *World Economy*, 229–33.

Bronckers, M. 2001. 'More power to the WTO?', *Journal of International Economic Law*, 4: 41–65.

Brown, D. and Nicholas, G. 2010. 'Protecting Canadian First Nations and Maori Heritage through Conventional Legal Means', 'New Zealand and Canada: Connections, Comparisons and Challenges' (conference), Wellington, New Zealand, 9–10 February 2010.

Brunsson, N., Jacobsson, B. and Associates 2000. *A World of Standards*. Oxford University Press.

Brütsch, C. and Lehmkuhl, D. (eds.) 2007. *Law and Legalization in Transnational Relations*. London: Routledge.

Buchanan, J. and Tollison, R. D. 1984. *The Theory of Public Choice*. Ann Arbor: University of Michigan Press.

Buckley, P. J. and Roberts, B. R. 1982. *European Direct Investment in the USA Before World War I*. Basingstoke: Macmillan.

Budzinski, O. 2003. 'Toward an International Governance of Transborder Mergers? Competition Networks and Institutions between Centralism and Decentralism', *New York University Journal of International Law and Politics*, 36: 1–52.

Bull, H., Kingsbury, B. and Roberts, A. (eds.) 1990. *Hugo Grotius and International Relations*. Oxford: Clarendon Press.

Bullard, L. 2005. *Freeing the Free Tree*. Research Foundation for Science, Technology and Ecology, New Delhi, India; International Federation of Organic Agriculture Movements; the Greens/European Free Alliance in the European Parliament.

Búrca, G. de and Weiler, J. (eds.) 2001. *The European Court of Justice*. Oxford University Press.

Burley, A.-M. and Mattli, W. 1993. 'Europe Before the Court: A Political Theory of European Integration', *International Organization*, 47: 41–76.

Burnham, P. 1990. *The Political Economy of Postwar Reconstruction*. London: Macmillan.

Burrough, B. and Helyar, J. [1990] 2004. *Barbarians at the Gate: The Fall of RJR Nabisco*. London: Cape.

Burton, J. 1972. *World Society*. Cambridge University Press.

Busch, A. 2009. *Banking Regulation and Globalization*. Oxford University Press.

Buxbaum, R. M. 2000. 'Back to the Future? From "Centros" to the "Uberlagerungstheorie"', in K. P. Berger and O. Sandrock (eds.), *Festschrift für Otto Sandrock zum 70. Geburtstag*, 149–64. Heidelberg: Verlag Recht und Wirtschaft.

Buxbaum, R. M. and Hopt, K. J. (eds.) 1988. *Legal Harmonization and the Business Enterprise*. Berlin: Walter de Gruyter.

Bygrave, L. A. 2002. 'The Technologization of Copyright: Implications for Privacy and Related Interests', *European Intellectual Property Review*, 24: 51–7.

Cabin, M. A. 2009. 'Labor Rights in the Peru Agreement: Can Vague Principles Yield Concrete Change?', *Columbia Law Review*, 109: 1047–93.

Cabral, W. 1995. 'Bermuda', *Comparative Law Yearbook of International Business*, 23–8.

Cahill, K. 1986. *Trade Wars: The High-Technology Scandal of the 1980s*. London: W. H. Allen.

Calabresi, G. and Melamed, A. D. 1972. 'Property Rules, Liability Rules and Inalienability: One View of the Cathedral', *Harvard Law Review*, 85: 1089–98.

Calaby, C. A. 1989. 'The Basle Accord: An Opportunity for Expanding Bank Holding Company Securities Activities?', *George Washington Journal of International Law and Economics*, 23: 531–72.

Calderon, R., Alvarez-Arce, J. L. and Mayoral, S. 2009. 'Corporation as a Crucial Ally against Corruption', *Journal of Business Ethics*, 87: 319–32.

Callan, E. 2007. 'Global drive to recover stolen assets', 18 September, *Financial Times*.

Callon, M. (ed.) 1998. *The Laws of the Markets*. Oxford: Blackwell.

Campbell, D. I. 1990. 'Adam Smith, *Farrar on Company Law*, and the Economics of the Corporation', *Anglo-American Law Review*, 19: 185–208.

Campbell, D. I. 1993. 'Why Regulate the Modern Corporation? The Failure of "Market Failure"', in J. McCahery, S. Picciotto and C. Scott (eds.), *Corporate Control and Accountability. Changing Structures and the Dynamics of Regulation*, 103–31. Oxford: Clarendon Press.

Campbell, D. I. 1996. *The Failure of Marxism: The Concept of Inversion in Marx's Critique of Capitalism*. Aldershot: Dartmouth.

Campbell, D. I. 1999. 'The "Hybrid Contract" and the Merging of the Public and Private Law of the Allocation of Economic Goods', in N. D. Lewis and D. I. Campbell (eds.), *Promoting Participation: Law or Politics?*, 45–73. London: Cavendish.

Campbell, D. I. and Griffin, S. 2006. 'Enron and the End of Corporate Governance', in S. Macleod (ed.), *Global Governance and the Quest for Justice. Volume II Corporate Governance*, 47–72. Oxford: Hart.

Campbell, D. I. and Klaes, M. 2005. 'The Principle of Institutional Direction: Coase's Regulatory Critique of Intervention', *Cambridge Journal of Economics*, 29: 263–88.

Campbell, D. I. and Picciotto, S. 1998. 'Exploring the Interaction between Law and Economics: The Limits of Formalism', *Legal Studies*, 18: 249–78.

Campbell, D. I. and Picciotto, S. 2000. 'The Justification of Financial Futures Exchanges', in A. Hudson (ed.), *Modern Financial Techniques, Derivatives, and Law*, 121–33. The Hague: Kluwer Law International.

Campbell, D. I. and Picciotto, S. 2006. 'The Acceptable Face of Intervention: Intellectual Property in Posnerian Law and Economics', *Social and Legal Studies*, 15: 435–52.

Canan, P. and Reichman, N. 2002. *Ozone Connections. Expert Networks in Global Environmental Governance.* Sheffield, UK: Greenleaf.

Caprio, G. 1997. 'Safe and Sound Banking in Developing Countries. We're Not in Kansas Anymore', Washington, DC: World Bank Policy Research Working Paper 1739.

Carbonneau, T. (ed.) 1990. *Lex Mercatoria and Arbitration: A Discussion of the New Law Merchant.* Dobbs Ferry, NY: Transnational Juris Publications.

Carlisle, R. 1981. *Sovereignty for Sale.* Annapolis, MD: Naval Institute Press.

Carroll, M. B. 1978. *Global Perspectives of an International Tax Lawyer.* Hicksville, NY: Exposition Press.

Carruthers, B. G. and Ariovich, L. 2004. 'The Sociology of Property Rights', *Annual Review of Sociology,* 30: 23–46.

Carruthers, B. G. and Halliday, T. C. 1998. *Rescuing Business: The Making of Corporate Bankruptcy Law in England and the United States.* Oxford: Clarendon Press.

Cary, W. L. 1974. 'Federalism and Corporate Law: Reflections Upon Delaware', *Yale Law Journal,* 83: 663–705.

Cass, D. Z. 2005. *The Constitutionalization of the World Trade Organization: Legitimacy, Democracy, and Community in the International Trading System.* Oxford University Press.

Cassels, J. 1993. *The Uncertain Promise of Law. Lessons from Bhopal.* Toronto University Press.

Castells, M. 1996. *The Rise of the Network Society.* Malden, MA: Blackwell Publishers.

Castells, M. 1998. *End of Millennium.* Malden, MA: Blackwell Publishers.

Castleman, G. 2002. 'WTO Confidential: The Case of Asbestos', *International Journal of Health Services,* 32: 489–501.

Center for Food Safety 2005. *Monsanto v. US Farmers.* Washington, DC.

Champ, P. and Attaran, A. 2002. 'Patent Rights and Local Working under the WTO TRIPs Agreement: An Analysis of the US–Brazil Patent Dispute', *Yale Journal of International Law,* 27: 365–93.

Chandler, A. D. 1962. *Strategy and Structure: The History of American Industrial Enterprise.* Cambridge, MA: MIT Press.

Chandler, A. D. 1977. *The Visible Hand. The Managerial Revolution in American Business.* Cambridge, MA: Belknap Press of Harvard University.

Chandler, D. 2000. 'International Justice', *New Left Review,* 2nd series, 6: 55–66.

Chang, H.-J. 2002. *Kicking Away the Ladder – Development Strategy in Historical Perspective.* London: Anthem Press.

Charkham, J. P. 1994. *Keeping Good Company. A Study of Corporate Governance in Five Countries.* Oxford: Clarendon Press.

Charlton, A. 2003. 'Incentive Bidding for Mobile Investment: Economic Consequences and Potential Responses', DEV/DOC(2003)01 Paris: OECD.

Charnovitz, S. 1995. 'The World Trade Organization and Social Issues', *Journal of World Trade*, 29: 17–33.

Charnovitz, S. 2001. 'Rethinking Trade Sanctions', *American Journal of International Law*, 95: 792–832.

Charny, D. 1991. 'Competition among Jurisdictions in Formulating Corporate Law Rules: An American Perspective on the "Race to the Bottom" in the European Communities', *Harvard International Law Journal*, 32: 423–56.

Chaudhuri, S. 2005. *The WTO and India's Pharmaceutical Industry. Patent Protection, TRIPs and Developing Countries.* New Delhi: Oxford University Press.

Cheek, M. L. 2001. 'The Limits of Informal Regulatory Cooperation in International Affairs: A Review of the Global Intellectual Property Regime', *George Washington International Law Review*, 33: 277–323.

Cheng, I. 2002. 'Survivors who laughed all the way to the bank', 30 July, *Financial Times*.

Chetley, A. 1986. *The Politics of Baby Foods. Successful Challenges to an International Marketing Strategy.* London: Pinter.

Chimni, B. S. 2004. 'International Institutions Today: An Imperial Global State in the Making', *European Journal of International Law*, 15: 1–37.

Chinkin, C. 2000. 'Normative Development in the International Legal System', in D. Shelton (ed.), *Commitment and Compliance. The Role of Non-Binding Norms in the International Legal System*, 21–42. Oxford University Press.

Chua, A. T. L. 1998. 'Reasonable Expectations and Non-Violation Complaints in GATT/WTO Jurisprudence', *Journal of World Trade*, 32: 27–50.

CIMA 2008. *Investments Statistical Digest.* Cayman Islands Monetary Authority.

Claessens, S., Klingebiel, D. and Schmukler, S. L. 2002. 'Explaining the Migration of Stocks from Exchanges in Emerging Economies to International Centers': World Bank Development Economics Research Group.

Clarke, S. (ed.) 1991. *The State Debate.* Basingstoke: Macmillan.

Clarke, T. 2007. *International Corporate Governance. A Comparative Perspective.* London: Routledge.

Clausing, K. A. and Avi-Yonah, R. S. 2007. 'Reforming Corporate Taxation in a Global Economy: A Proposal to Adopt Formulary Apportionment', Hamilton Project Discussion Paper. Washington, DC: Brookings Institution Press.

Coase, R. H. 1988. *The Firm, the Market and the Law.* University of Chicago Press 1988.

Coase, R. H. 1993. 'Coase on Posner on Coase', *Journal of Institutional and Theoretical Economics*, 149: 96–8.

Cobham, A. 2005. 'Tax Evasion, Tax Avoidance and Development Finance', QEH Working Paper Series – QEHWPS129 Oxford.

Cockbain, J. 2007. 'Intellectual Property Rights and Patents', in P. D. Kennewell (ed.), *Comprehensive Medicinal Chemistry II.* London: Elsevier.

Coen, D. and Thatcher, M. 2005. 'The New Governance of Markets and Non-Majoritarian Regulators', *Governance*, 18: 329–46.

Coffee, J. C. 1995. 'Competition versus Consolidation: The Significance of Organizational Structure in Financial and Securities Regulation', *Business Lawyer*, 50: 447–84.

Coffee, J. C. 2001. 'The Rise of Dispersed Ownership: The Roles of Law and the State in the Separation of Ownership and Control', *Yale Law Journal*, 111: 1–82.

Coffee, J. C. 2002. 'Racing towards the top?: The Impact of Cross-Listings and Stock Market Competition on International Corporate Governance', *Columbia Law Review*, 102: 1757–831.

Cohen, J. and Sabel, C. 1997. 'Directly-Deliberative Polyarchy', *European Law Journal*, 3: 313–42.

Cohen, J. L. and Arato, A. 1992. *Civil Society and Political Theory.* Cambridge, MA: MIT Press.

Coleman, G. 2009. 'Code is Speech: Legal Tinkering, Expertise, and Protest among Free and Open Source Software Developers', *Cultural Anthropology*, 24: 420–54.

Collins, H. 1999. *Regulating Contracts.* Oxford University Press.

Collins, J. H., Hutchinson, D. S. and Wekstein, W. D. 1996. *A Financial Future for Nepal.* Boston, MA: Collins & Associates.

Cooke, C. A. 1950. *Corporation, Trust and Company.* Manchester University Press.

Coombe, R. 2010. 'The Expanding Purview of Cultural Properties and Their Politics', *Annual Review of Law and Social Science*, 5: 393–412.

Cooper, G. 2008. *The Origin of Financial Crises.* Petersfield: Harriman House Publishing.

Cooper, H. D. 2002. 'The International Treaty on Plant Genetic Resources for Food and Agriculture', *RECIEL: Review of European Community and International Environmental Law*, 11: 1–16.

Coornaert, E. L. J. 1967. 'European Economic Institutions and the New World: The Chartered Companies', in E. E. Rich and C. H. Wilson (eds.), *The Cambridge Economic History of Europe*, ch. 4. Cambridge University Press.

CopySouth 2009. *The Copy/South Dosier. Issues in the Economics, Politics, and Ideology of Copyright in the Global South* (www.copysouth.org).

Coriat, B. and Orsini, F. 2002. 'Establishing a New Intellectual Property Rights Regime in the United States: Origin, Content and Problems', *Research Policy*, 31: 1491–507.

Cornish, W. R. 1979. 'Legal Control over Cartels and Monopolization 1880–1914. A Comparison', in N. Horn and J. Kocka (eds.), *Law and the Formation of the Big Enterprises in the 19th and Early 20th Centuries* 280–303. Göttingen: Vandenhoeck & Ruprecht.

Cornish, W. R. and Llewelyn, D. 2007. *Intellectual Property: Patents, Copyright, Trade Marks and Allied Rights*. London: Sweet & Maxwell.

Costa, H. A. 2006. 'The Old and the New in the New Labor Internationalism', in B. d. S. Santos (ed.), *Another Production Is Possible*, 243–78. London: Verso.

Cottier, T. and Mavroidis, P. C. (eds.) 2000. *Regulatory Barriers and the Principle of Non-Discrimination in Trade Law*. Ann Arbor: University of Michigan Press.

Cottier, T., Paulwelyn, J. and Bürgi Bonanomi, E. 2005. *Human Rights and International Trade*. Oxford University Press.

Cottier, T. and Schefer, K. N. 2000. 'Good Faith and Protection of Legitimate Expectations in the WTO', in M. Bronckers and R. Quick (eds.), *New Directions in International Economic Law, Essays in Honour of John H. Jackson* 47. The Hague: Kluwer Law.

Couper, A. D., Walsh, C., Stanberry, B. and Boerne, G. L. 1999. *Voyages of Abuse. Seafarers, Human Rights and International Shipping*. London: Pluto Press.

Coupland, D. 1995. *Microserfs*. London: HarperCollins.

Court, J.-F. 1985. 'La France et les conventions fiscales', *Journal du Droit des Affaires Internationales*, 1: 31–90.

Covelli, N. and Hohots, V. 2003. 'The Health Regulation of Biotech Foods under the WTO Agreements', *Journal of International Economic Law*, 6: 773–95.

Cowhey, P. 2004. 'Accounting Rates, Cross-Border Services, and the Next WTO Round on Basic Telecommunications Services', in D. Geradin and D. Luff (eds.), *The WTO and Global Convergence in Telecommunications and Audio-Visual Services*, Cambridge University Press.

Crawford, J.-A. and Fiorentino, R. V. 2005. 'The Changing Landscape of Regional Trade Agreements', Discussion Paper 8 Geneva: WTO.

Cullet, P. 2001. 'Plant Variety Protection in Africa: Towards Compliance with the Trips Agreement', *Journal of African Law*, 45: 97–122.

Cuomo, A. M. 2009. *No Rhyme or Reason: The 'Heads I Win, Tails You Lose' Bank Bonus Culture*. New York: Attorney General of the State of New York.

Cutler, A. C. 1995. 'Global Capitalism and Liberal Myths: Dispute Settlement in Private International Trade Relations', *Millennium*, 24: 377–97.

Cutler, A. C. 2003. *Private Power and Global Authority: Transnational Merchant Law in the Global Political Economy*. Cambridge University Press.

Daintith, T. C. 1986. 'The Design and Performance of Long-Term Contracts', in T. C. Daintith and G. Teubner (eds.), *Contract and Organisation. Legal Analysis in the Light of Economic and Social Theory*, 164–89. Berlin: Walter de Gruyter.

Dale, R. 1996. *Risk and Regulation in Global Securities Markets*. Chichester: John Wiley.

Daly, M. 2005. 'The WTO and Direct Taxation', Discussion Papers 9 Geneva: WTO.

Dam, K. W. 2001. 'Self-Help in the Digital Jungle', in R. C. Dreyfuss, D. L. Zimmerman and H. First (eds.), *Expanding the Boundaries of Intellectual Property. Innovation Policy for the Information Society*, 103–22. Oxford University Press.

Das, D. K. 1998. 'Trade in Financial Services and the Role of the GATS, Against the Backdrop of the Asian Financial Crises', *Journal of World Trade*, 32: 80–114.

Dasgupta, P. and David, P. A. 1994. 'Towards a New Economics of Science', *Research Policy*, 23: 487–521.

Daunton, M. 2004. 'What is Income?', in J. Tiley (ed.), *Studies in the History of Tax Law*, 3–13. Oxford: Hart.

Daunton, M. J. 2001. *Trusting Leviathan: The Politics of Taxation in Britain, 1799–1914*. Cambridge University Press.

Daunton, M. J. 2002. *Just Taxes: The Politics of Taxation in Britain, 1914–1979*. Cambridge University Press.

Daus, D. G. 1981. 'New Life in US Patents. The Chakrabarty Case', *European Intellectual Property Review*, 7: 194–200.

Davey, W. J. 2001. 'Has the WTO Dispute Settlement System Exceeded Its Authority? A Consideration of Deference Shown by the System to Member Government Decisions and Its Use of Issue-Avoidance Techniques', *Journal of International Economic Law*, 4: 79–110.

Davey, W. J. 2002. 'A Permanent Panel Body for WTO Dispute Settlement: Desirable or Practical?', in D. L. M. Kennedy and J. D. Southwick (eds.), *The Political Economy of International Trade Law. Essays in Honor of Robert E. Hudec*, 496–527. Cambridge University Press.

Davey, W. J. 2003. 'The Case for a Permanent Panel Body', *Journal of International Economic Law*, 6: 177–86.

Davidow, J. 1981. 'International Antitrust Codes: The Post-Acceptance Phase', *Antitrust Bulletin*, 26: 567–91.

Davies, G. 1994. *Copyright and the Public Interest*. Weinheim: VCH Publishers.

Davies, H. and Green, D. 2008. *Global Financial Regulation*. Cambridge: Polity Press.

Davies, L. 2002. 'Technical Cooperation and the International Coordination of Patentability of Biotechnological Inventions', *Journal of Law and Society*, 29: 137–62.

Davies, W. 2009. *Reinventing the Firm*. London: Demos.

Davis, C. L. 2003. *Food Fights over Free Trade: How International Institutions Promote Agricultural Trade Liberalization*. Princeton University Press.

Deere, C. 2009. *The Implementation Game. The TRIPs Agreement and the Global Politics of Intellectual Policy Reform in Developing Countries*. Oxford University Press.

Dehousse, R. 1989. '1992 and Beyond: The Institutional Dimension of the Internal Market Programme', *Legal Issues of European Integration*, 1: 109–36.

Dehousse, R. 1992. 'Integration v. Regulation? On the Dynamics of Regulation in the European Community', *Journal of Common Market Studies*, 30: 383–402.

Delaume, G. 1989. 'The Myth of the *Lex Mercatoria*', *Tulane Law Review*, 63: 575–611.

Delimatsis, P. 2008. 'Determining the Necessity of Domestic Regulations in Services. The Best is Yet to Come', *European Journal of International Law*, 19: 365–408.

Dell, S. 1990. *The United Nations and International Business*. Durham, NC: Duke University Press, for UNITAR.

Dezalay, Y. 1996. 'Between the State, Law, and the Market: The Social and Professional Stakes in the Construction and Definition of a Regulatory Arena', in W. Bratton, J. McCahery, S. Picciotto and C. Scott (eds.), *International Regulatory Competition and Coordination*, 59–87. Oxford: Clarendon Press.

Dezalay, Y. and Garth, B. 1995. 'Merchants of Law as Moral Entrepreneurs: Constructing International Justice from the Competition for Transnational Business Disputes', *Law and Society Review*, 29: 27–64.

Dezalay, Y. and Garth, B. 1996. *Dealing in Virtue. International Commercial Arbitration and the Construction of a Transnational Legal Order*. Chicago University Press.

Dezalay, Y. and Garth, B. 1997. 'Law, Lawyers, and Social Capital: "Rule of Law" versus Relational Capitalism', *Social and Legal Studies*, 6: 109–41.

Dezalay, Y. and Garth, B. 1998. 'Le "Washington Consensus". Contribution à une sociologie de l'hégémonie du néolibéralisme', *Actes de la Recherche en sciences sociales*, 121–2: 3–22.

Dezalay, Y. and Garth, B. 2001. *The Internationalization of Palace Wars: Lawyers, Economists, and the Contest to Transform Latin American States*. University of Chicago Press.

Dezalay, Y. and Garth, B. (eds.) 2002. *Global Prescriptions. The Production, Exportation and Importation of a New Legal Orthodoxy*. Ann Arbor: University of Michigan Press.

Dezalay, Y. and Garth, B. G. 2008. 'Law, Lawyers, and Empire', in M. Grossberg and C. L. Tomlins (eds.), *The Cambridge History of Law in America. The Twentieth Century and After (1920–)*, 718–58. Cambridge University Press.

Dezalay, Y. and Garth, B. G. 2010. *Asian Legal Revivals: Lawyers in the Shadow of Empire*. University of Chicago Press.

DiMaggio, P. (ed.) 2001. *The Twenty-First-Century Firm. Changing Economic Organization in International Perspective*. Princeton University Press.

Djelic, M.-L. 1998. *Exporting the American Model: The Postwar Transformation of European Business*. Oxford University Press.

Djelic, M.-L. and Kleiner, T. 2006. 'The International Competition Network: Moving Towards Transnational Governance', in M.-L. Djelic and K. Sahlin-Anderson (eds.), *Transnational Governance: Institutional Dynamics of Regulation*, 287–307. Cambridge University Press.

Dolder, F. 2006. 'Traditional Knowledge and Patenting: The Experience of the Neemfungicide and the Hoodia Cases', *Biotechnology Law Report*, 26: 583–93.

Dolzer, R. 1981. 'New Foundations of the Law of Expropriation of Alien Property', *American Journal of International Law*, 75: 553–90.

Dolzer, R. and Stevens, M. 1995. *Bilateral Investment Treaties*. The Hague: Nijhoff.

dos Santos, P. L. 2009. 'On the Content of Banking in Contemporary Capitalism', *Historical Materialism*, 17: 180–213.

Dowd, K. 1998. *Beyond Value at Risk*. Chichester: Wiley.

Dowd, K. and Hutchinson, M. 2010. *Alchemists of Loss. How Modern Finance and Government Intervention Crashed the Financial System*. Chichester: Wiley.

Drache, D. 2000. 'The Short But Amazingly Significant Life of the ITO. Free Trade and Full Employment: Friends or Foes Forever?', Toronto (www.yorku.ca/drache/wto.php).

Drache, D. (ed.) 2001. *The Market or the Public Domain? Global Governance and the Asymmetry of Power*. London: Routledge.

Drahos, P. (ed.) 1999a. *Intellectual Property*. Aldershot: Ashgate.

Drahos, P. 1999b. 'Biotechnology Patents, Markets and Morality', *European Intellectual Property Review*, 21: 441–9.

Drahos, P. 2007. 'Four Lessons for Developing Countries from the Trade Negotiations over Access to Medicines', *Liverpool Law Review*, 28: 11–39.

Drahos, P. and Braithwaite, J. 2002a. *Information Feudalism. Who Owns the Knowledge Economy?* London: Earthscan.

Drahos, P. and Braithwaite, J. 2002b. 'Intellectual Property, Corporate Strategy, Globalisation: Trips in Context', *Wisconsin International Law Journal*, 20: 451–80.

Drahos, P. and Mayne, R. (eds.) 2002. *Global Intellectual Property Rights. Knowledge, Access and Development*. Basingstoke: Macmillan for Oxfam.

Drake, W. J. and Nicolaïdis, K. 1992. 'Ideas, Interests, and Institutionalization: "Trade in Services" and the Uruguay Round', *International Organization*, 46: 37–100.

Dryzek, J. S. 1990. *Discursive Democracy*. Cambridge University Press.

Dryzek, J. S. 1999. 'Transnational Democracy', *Journal of Political Philosophy*, 7: 30–51.

Duckworth, A. 1998. 'STAR Wars: The Colony Strikes Back', *Trust Law International*, 12: 16–25.

Duckworth, A. and Matthews, P. 1999. 'STAR Wars: Smiting the Bull', *Trust Law International*, 13: 158–68.

Dulin, A. 2007. 'Biens mal acquis ... profitent trop souvent', Paris: CCFD (Comité Catholique contre la Faim et pour le Développement).

Dunning, J. H. 1983. 'Changes in the Level and Structure of International Production: The Last One Hundred Years', in M. Casson (ed.), *The Growth of International Business*, 84–139. London: Allen & Unwin.

Dunning, J. H. 1988. *Explaining International Production*. London: Unwin Hyman.

Dunning, J. H. 2001a. 'The Eclectic (OLI) Paradigm of International Production: Past, Present and Future', *International Journal of the Economics of Business*, 8: 173–90.

Dunning, J. H. 2001b. 'The Key Literature on IB Activities: 1960–2000', in A. M. Rugman and T. L. Brewer (eds.), *The Oxford Handbook of International Business*, 36–68. Oxford University Press.

Dutfield, G. 2003a. *Intellectual Property Rights and the Life Science Industries: A Twentieth Century History*. Aldershot: Ashgate.

Dutfield, G. 2003b. *Protecting Traditional Knowledge and Folklore*. Geneva: ICTSD (International Center for Trade and Sustainable Development).

Dutfield, G. 2009. *Intellectual Property Rights and the Life Science Industries: A Twentieth Century History*. London: World Scientific.

Dutton, H. I. 1984. *The Patent System and Inventive Activity During the Industrial Revolution 1750–1852*. Manchester University Press.

Duxbury, N. 1990. 'Some Radicalism about Realism? Thurman Arnold and the Politics of Modern Jurisprudence', *Oxford Journal of Legal Studies*, 10: 11–41.

Dyer, A. 1999. 'International Recognition and Adaptation of Trusts: The Influence of the Hague Convention', *Vanderbilt Journal of Transnational Law*, 32: 989–1013.

Easson, A. J. 2004. *Tax Incentives for Foreign Direct Investment*. The Hague: Kluwer Law International.

Easterbrook, F. H. and Fischel, D. R. 1991. *The Economic Structure of Corporate Law*. Cambridge, MA: Harvard University Press.

Eatwell, J. and Taylor, L. 2000. *Global Finance at Risk: The Case for International Regulation*. New York: New Press.

Ebrill, L., Keen, M., Bodin, J.-P. and Summers, V. 2002. 'The Allure of the Value-Added Tax', *Finance and Development*, 39: 44–7.

Editorial 2008. 'The Moody's Blues', 15 February, *Wall Street Journal*.

Edwards, L. 2009. 'The Fall and Rise of Intermediary Liability Online', in L. Edwards and C. Waelde (eds.), *Law and the Internet*, 47–88. Oxford: Hart.

Effros, R. C. 1982. *Emerging Financial Centres*. Washington, DC: International Monetary Fund.

Eggers, B. and Mackenzie, R. 2000. 'The Cartagena Protocol on Biosafety', *Journal of International Economic Law*, 3: 525–43.

Egmont 2000. *FIUs in Action. 100 Cases from the Egmont Group*. Egmont Group (www.egmontgroup.org).

Ehlermann, C.-D. 2000. 'The Modernization of EC Antitrust Policy: A Legal and Cultural Revolution', *Common Market Law Review*, 37: 537–90.

Ehlermann, C.-D. 2002. 'Six Years on the Bench of the "World Trade Court". Some Personal Experiences as a Member of the Appellate Body of the WTO', *Journal of World Trade*, 36: 605–39.

Ehlermann, C.-D. 2003. 'Reflections on the Appellate Body of the WTO', *Journal of International Economic Law*, 6: 695–708.

Ehrlich, C. 1989. *Harmonious Alliance: A History of the Performing Right Society*. Oxford University Press.

Eisner, M. 1991. *Antitrust and the Triumph of Economics. Institutions, Expertise and Policy Change*. Chapel Hill, NC: University of North Carolina Press.

Emberland, M. 2006. *The Human Rights Of Companies: Exploring The Structure of ECHR Protection*. Oxford University Press.

Enron 2002. *Report of Investigation by the Special Investigative Committee of the Board of Directors of Enron Corp.*

Epstein, G. A. (ed.) 2005. *Financialization and the World Economy*. Cheltenham: Edward Elgar.

Epstein, R. 1985. *Takings. Private Property and the Power of Eminent Domain*. Cambridge, MA: Harvard University Press.

Erturk, I., Froud, J., Johal, S., Leaver, A. and Williams, K. (eds.) 2008. *Financialization at Work. Key Texts and Commentary*. London: Routledge.

Esanov, A., Raiser, M. and Buiter, W. H. 2001. 'Nature's Blessing or Nature's Curse: The Political Economy of Transition in Resource-based Economies', EBRD Working Paper No. 65.

Esserman, S. and Howse, R. 2003. 'The WTO on Trial', *Foreign Affairs*, 82: 130–40.

Esty, D. C. 1994. *Greening the GATT*. Washington, DC: Institute for International Economics.

European Commission 2001a. *Governance. A White Paper*. Brussels.

European Commission 2001b. *Towards an Internal Market without Tax Obstacles. A Strategy for Providing Companies with a Consolidated Corporate Tax Base for Their EU-Wide Activities*. Brussels.

European Commission 2003. *Modernising Company Law and Enhancing Corporate Governance in the European Union – A Plan to Move Forward*. COM (2003) 284 final.

Evans, G. A. 1999. 'The Human Genome Project and Public Policy', *Public Understanding of Science*, 8: 161–8.

Evans, P. 1998. *Trade, Labour, Global Competition and the Social Clause* Delhi: CUTS International.

Evenett, S. J., Lehmann, A. and Steil, B. (eds.) 2000. *Antitrust Goes Global: What Future for Transatlantic Cooperation?* London, Washington, DC: Royal Institute of International Affairs; Brookings Institution Press.

Fabian Society. Commission on Taxation and, C. 2000. *Paying for Progress: A New Politics of Tax for Public Spending*. London: Fabian Society.

Farrow, T. C. W. 2003. 'Globalization, International Human Rights, and Civil Procedure', *Alberta Law Review*, 41: 671–712.

Faunce, T. 2007. 'A dubious and secret influence on our public health policy', 13 June, Melbourne, *The Age*.

Faundez, J. (ed.) 1997. *Good Government and Law. Legal and Institutional Reform in Developing Countries.* Basingstoke: Macmillan.

Faundez, J., Footer, M. E. and Norton, J. J. 2000. *Governance, Development and Globalization: A Tribute to Lawrence Tshuma.* London: Blackstone.

Faundez, J. and Picciotto, S. (eds.) 1978. *The Nationalization of Multinationals in Peripheral Economies.* Basingstoke: Macmillan.

Featherstone, M. (ed.) 1990. *Global Culture. Nationalism, Globalization and Modernity.* London: Sage.

Federico, P. J. 1937. 'Louis Pasteur's Patents', *Science,* 86: 327–9.

Feigenbaum, H. B., Henig, J. R. and Hamnett, C. 1998. *Shrinking the State: The Political Underpinnings of Privatization.* Cambridge University Press.

Felstead, A. 1993. *The Corporate Paradox. Power and Control in the Business Franchise.* London: Routledge.

Ferguson, N. 2010. *High Financier: The Lives and Time of Siegmund Warburg.* London: Allen Lane.

Fidler, D. P., Correa, C. and Aginam, O. 2005. 'Draft Legal Review of the General Agreement on Trade in Services (GATS) from a Health Policy Perspective', Geneva: WHO.

Field, C. 2001. 'Copyright Co-ownership in Cyberspace: The Digital Merger of Content and Technology in Digital Rights Management and E-commerce', *Entertainment and Sports Lawyer,* 19: 3–8.

Fieldhouse, D. K. 1978. *Unilever Overseas: The Anatomy of a Multinational 1895–1965.* Stanford, CA: Hoover Institution.

Fieldhouse, D. K. 1986. 'The Multinational: Critique of a Concept', in A. Teichova, M. Levy-Leboyer and H. Nussbaum (eds.), *Multinational Enterprise in Historical Perspective,* 9–29. Cambridge University Press.

Fine, B. 1999. 'The Developmental State Is Dead: Long Live Social Capital?', *Development and Change,* 30: 1–19.

Fink, C. and Correa, C. M. 2009. 'The Global Debate on the Enforcement of Intellectual Property Rights and Developing Countries', Geneva: ICTSD (International Center for Trade and Sustainable Development).

Finnemore, M. and Toope, S. J. 2001. 'Alternatives to "Legalization": Richer Views of Law and Politics', *International Organization,* 55: 743–58.

Fischer-Lescano, A. and Teubner, G. 2004. 'Regime-Collisions: The Vain Search for Legal Unity in the Fragmentation of Global Law', *Michigan Journal of International Law,* 25: 999–1046.

Fisher, E. 2007. *Risk Regulation and Administrative Constitutionalism.* Oxford: Hart.

Fisher, W. F. and Ponniah, T. 2003. *Another World Is Possible: Popular Alternatives to Globalization at the World Social Forum.* Nova Scotia: Fernwood Pub. and London: Zed Press.

Fitzpatrick, P. 1984. 'Law and Societies', *Osgoode Hall Law Journal,* 22: 115–38.

Fjeldstad, O.-H. and Rakner, L. 2003. 'Taxation and Tax Reforms in Developing Countries: Illustrations from Sub-Saharan Africa', Bergen: Chr. Michelsen Institute Development Studies and Human Rights.

Fjeldstad, O.-H. and Therkildsen, O. 2008. 'Mass Taxation and State–Society Relations in East Africa', in D. Bräutigam, O.-H. Fjeldstad and M. Moore (eds.), *Taxation and State-Building in Developing Countries. Capacity and Consent*, 114–34. Cambridge University Press.

Fleming Jr., J. C., Peroni, R. J. and Shay, S. E. 2009. 'Worse than Exemption', *Emory Law Journal*, 59: 79–149.

Flett, J. 2011. 'Importing Other International Régimes into WTO Litigation', in M. Young (ed.), *Régime Interaction in International Law*. Cambridge University Press.

Fligstein, N. 1990. *The Transformation of Corporate Control*. Cambridge, MA: Harvard University Press.

Fligstein, N. 2001. *The Architecture of Markets. An Economic Sociology of Twenty-First-Century Capitalist Societies*. Princeton University Press.

Flood, J. and Skordaki, E. 1997. 'Normative Bricolage: Informal Rule-Making by Accountants and Lawyers in Mega-Insolvencies', in G. Teubner (ed.), *Global Law Without A State*, 109–31. Aldershot: Dartmouth.

Fox, E. M. 2003. 'International Antitrust and the Doha Dome', *Virginia Journal of International Law*, 43: 911–32.

Fox, H. 2002. *The Law of State Immunity*. Oxford University Press.

Franck, S. 2009. 'Developments and Outcomes of Investment Treaty Arbitration', *Harvard Journal of International Law*, 50: 435–89.

Franck, T. M. 1990. *The Power of Legitimacy Among Nations*. Oxford University Press.

Freedeman, C. E. 1979. *Joint-Stock Enterprise in France, 1807–1867: From Privileged Company to Modern Corporation*. Chapel Hill, NC: University of North Carolina Press.

Freedeman, C. E. 1993. *The Triumph of Corporate Capitalism in France 1867–1914*. University of Rochester Press.

Freeman, J. 2000. 'The Contracting State', *Florida State University Law Review*, 28: 155–214.

Freeman, J. 2003. 'Extending Public Law Norms Through Privatization', *Harvard Law Review*, 116: 1285–352.

French, K. R. 2008. 'Presidential Address: The Costs of Active Investing', *Journal of Finance*, 63: 1537–73.

Freyer, T. 1992. *Regulating Big Business. Antitrust in Great Britain and America 1880–1990*. Cambridge University Press.

Fridd, P. and Sainsbury, J. 1999. 'The Role of Voluntary Codes of Conduct and Regulation: A Retailers View', in S. Picciotto and R. Mayne (eds.),

Regulating International Business: Beyond Liberalization, 221–34. Basingstoke: Macmillan.

Froomkin, A. M. 2003. 'Habermas@Discourse.Net: Towards a Critical Theory of Cyberspace', *Harvard Law Review*, 116: 749–873.

Frynas, J. G. 2000. *Oil in Nigeria. Conflict and Litigation between Oil Companies and Village Communities*. Hamburg: LIT Verlag.

Fuest, C. 2008. 'The European Commission's Proposal for a Common Consolidated Corporate Tax Base', *Oxford Review of Economic Policy*, 24: 720–39.

Fuks, I. 2006. '*Sosa* v. *Alvarez-Machain* and the Future of ATCA Litigation: Examining Bonded Labor Claims and Corporate Liability', *Columbia Law Review*, 106: 112–43.

G30 2008. *The Structure of Financial Supervision. Approaches and Challenges in a Global Marketplace*. Group of Thirty.

Gaillard, Y. 2010. *La politique du livre face au défi du numérique*. Rapport d'information N° 338. Paris: French Senate, Commission des Finances.

Galanter, M. 2002. 'Law's Elusive Promise: Learning from Bhopal', in M. Likosky (ed.), *Transnational Legal Processes. Globalisation and Power Disparities*, 172–85. London: Butterworths.

Gallagher, K. P. and Birch, M. B. L. 2006. 'Do Investment Agreements Attract Investment? Evidence from Latin America', *Journal of World Investment and Trade*, 7: 961–74.

Gallagher, R. 1990. *Report of Mr Rodney Gallagher of Coopers and Lybrand on the Survey of Offshore Finance Sectors in the Caribbean Dependent Territories*, 1989–90, No. 121. London: House of Commons.

Gallagher, T. 2001. 'Copyright Compulsory Licensing and Incentives': Oxford Intellectual Property Research Centre Working Paper Series No. 2.

Ganghof, S. 2006. *The Politics of Income Taxation: A Comparative Analysis*. Colchester: ECPR Press.

Gapper, J. and Denton, N. 1996. *All That Glitters. The Fall of Barings*. London: Hamish Hamilton.

Gardner, R. N. [1956] 1980. *Sterling-Dollar Diplomacy in Current Perspective*. New York: Columbia University Press.

Genschel, P. 2002. 'Globalization, Tax Competition, and the Welfare State', *Politics and Society*, 30: 245–75.

George, S. 2004. *Another World Is Possible If . . .* London: Verso Books in association with TNI.

Gerber, D. 1998. *Law and Competition in Twentieth Century Europe*. Oxford University Press.

Gereffi, G. 2001. 'Shifting Governance Structures in Global Commodity Chains, with Special Reference to the Internet', *American Behavioral Scientist*, 44: 1616–37.

Gereffi, G. and Korzeniewicz, M. (eds.) 1994. *Commodity Chains and Global Capitalism.* Westport, CT: Praeger.

Gerstenberger, H. and Welke, U. (eds.) 2002. *Seefahrt im Zeichen der Globalisierung* Munster: Westfälisches Dampfboot.

Gervais, D. 2008. *The TRIPs Agreement.* London: Sweet & Maxwell.

Gervais, D. (ed.) 2010. *Collective Management of Copyright and Related Rights.* Alphen: Kluwer.

Gessner, V. and Nelken, D. (eds.) 2007. *European Ways of Law. Towards a European Sociology of Law.* Oxford: Hart.

Ghai, Y. and Choong, T. C. 1988. *Management Contracts and Public Enterprises in Developing Countries.* International Center for Public Enterprises in Developing Countries.

Ghijsen, H. 2009. 'Intellectual Property Rights and Access Rules for Germplasm: Benefit or Straitjacket?', *Euphytica*, 170: 229–34.

Gianviti, F. 1998. 'International Convergence and the Role of the IMF', in M. Andenas (ed.), *Transnational (Corporate) Finance and the Challenge to the Law*, London: Hart Legal Workshop.

Gibson, J. (ed.) 2008. *Patenting Lives. Life Patents, Culture and Development.* Aldershot: Ashgate-Dartmouth.

Gilbert, C. L. 1996. 'International Commodity Agreements: An Obituary Notice', *World Development*, 24: 1–19.

Gill, S. 2003. *Power and Resistance in the New World Order.* Basingstoke: Palgrave Macmillan.

Gilmore, W. C. 1995. *Dirty Money.* Strasbourg: Council of Europe.

Gilson, R. J. 2001. 'Globalizing Corporate Governance: Convergence of Form or Function', *American Journal of Comparative Law*, 49: 329–57.

Glasbeek, H. 2002. *Between the Lines.* Toronto: Between the Lines.

Glasson, J. and Thomas, G. (eds.) 2006. *The International Trust.* London: Jordans.

Glenn, H. P. 2000. *Legal Traditions of the World. Sustainable Diversity in Law.* Oxford University Press.

Glimstedt, H. 2001. 'Between National and International Governance: Geopolitics, Strategizing Actors, and Sector Coordination in Electrical Engineering in the Interwar Era', in G. Morgan, P. H. Kristensen and R. Whitley (eds.), *The Multinational Firm: Organizing across Institutional and National Divides*, 125–52. Oxford University Press.

Glinski, C. 2007. 'Corporate Codes of Conduct: Moral or Legal Obligation?', in D. McBarnet, A. Voiculescu and T. Campbell (eds.), *The New Corporate Accountability. Corporate Social Responsibility and the Law*, 119–47. Cambridge University Press.

Gold, P. H. 1981–3. 'Legal Problems in Expanding the Scope of GATT to Include Trade in Services', *International Trade Law Journal*, 7: 281–305.

Goldfrank, B. and Schneider, A. 2006. 'Competitive Institution Building: The PT and Participatory Budgeting in Rio Grande do Sul', *Latin American Politics and Society*, 48: 1–32.

Goldsmith, J. L. and Wu, T. 2006. *Who Controls the Internet?: Illusions of a Borderless World*. Oxford University Press.

Goldstein, J. 1993. 'Creating the GATT Rules: Politics, Institutions and American Policy', in J. G. Ruggie (ed.), *Multilateralism Matters: The Theory and Practice of an Institutional Form*, 201–32. New York: Columbia University Press.

Goldstein, J., Kahler, M., Keohane, R. O. and Slaughter, A.-M. (eds.) 2001. *Legalization and World Politics*. Cambridge, MA: MIT Press.

Goldstein, J. and Martin, L. L. 2000. 'Legalization, Trade Liberalization, and Domestic Politics: A Cautionary Note', *International Organization*, 54: 603–32.

Goldstein, M. and Turner, P. 1996. 'Banking Crises in Emerging Economies: Origins and Policy Options', Basel: BIS Economic Papers No. 46.

Goldstein, P. 1994. *Copyright's Highway. From Gutenberg to the Celestial Jukebox*. New York: Hill & Wang.

Goldstein, P. 2001. *International Copyright: Principles, Law, and Practice*. Oxford University Press.

Golob, S. R. 2003. 'Beyond the Policy Frontier: Canada, Mexico, and the Ideological Origins of NAFTA', *World Politics*, 55: 361–98.

Gordon, R. W. 1984. '"The Ideal and the Actual in the Law": Fantasies and Practices of New York City Lawyers, 1870–1910', in G. W. Gawalt (ed.), *The New High Priests: Lawyers in Post-Civil War America*, 53–74. Westport, CT: Greenwood.

Gough, I. 1979. *The Political Economy of the Welfare State*. London: Macmillan.

Governor of the Bank of England. 1973. 'Multinational Enterprises', *Bank of England Quarterly Bulletin*, 13: 184–92.

Graber, C. B. and Burri-Nenova, M. (eds.) 2008. *Intellectual Property and Traditional Cultural Expressions in a Digital Environment*. Cheltenham: E. Elgar.

Grandin, G. 2009. *Fordlandia: The Rise and Fall of Henry Ford's Forgotten Jungle City*. New York: Henry Holt.

Grandy, C. 1989. 'New Jersey Corporate Chartermongering, 1875–1929', *Journal of Economic History*, 49: 677–92.

Granovetter, M. and Swedberg, E. (eds.) 1992. *The Sociology of Economic Life*. Boulder, CO: Westview.

Graubart, J. 2008. *Legalizing Transnational Activism: The Struggle to Gain Social Change from NAFTA's Citizen Petitions*. Philadelphia: Pennsylvania State University Press.

Greenwald, J. 2003. 'WTO Dispute Settlement: An Exercise in Trade Law Legislation?', *Journal of International Economic Law*, 6: 113–24.

Groom, A. J. R. and Taylor, P. (eds.) 1990. *Frameworks for International Cooperation*. London: Pinter.

Grubb, P. W. 1999. *Patents for Chemicals, Pharmaceuticals and Biotechnology. Fundamentals of Global Law, Practice and Strategy.* Oxford University Press.

Guermazi, B. 2004. 'Reforming International Accounting Rates: A Developing Country Perspective', in D. Geradin and D. Luff (eds.), *The WTO and Global Convergence in Telecommunications and Audio-Visual Services.* Cambridge University Press.

Guex, S. 1999. 'Les origines du secret bancaire suisse et son rôle dans la politique de la Confédération au sortir de la Seconde Guerre mondiale', *Genèses*, 34: 4–27.

Guex, S. 2007. '1932: l'affaire des fraudes fiscales et le gouvernement Herriot', *L'Economie politique*, 89–103.

Gugl, E. and Zodrow, G. R. 2006. 'International Tax Competition and Tax Incentives for Developing Countries', in J. Alm, J. Martínez-Vázquez and M. Rider (eds.), *Challenges of Tax Reform in a Global Economy*, 167–82. New York: Springer.

Gugler, K., Mueller, D. C. and Yurtoglu, B. B. 2004. 'Corporate Governance and Globalization', *Oxford Review of Economic Policy*, 20: 129–56.

Guisinger, S. E. 1985. *Investment Incentives and Performance Requirements. Patterns of International Trade, Production and Investment.* New York: Praeger.

Gunningham, N. 1991. 'Private Ordering, Self-Regulation and Futures Markets: A Comparative Study of Informal Social Control', *Law and Policy*, 13: 297–326.

Gunningham, N. and Grabosky, P. 1998. *Smart Regulation: Designing Environmental Policy.* Oxford: Clarendon Press.

Gupta, A. K. 2005. *WIPO–UNEP Study on the Role of Intellectual Property Rights in the Sharing of Benefits Arising from the Use of Biological Resources and Associated Traditional Knowledge.* Study No. 4. Geneva: World Intellectual Property Organisation.

Gupta, A. S. 2007. 'Determinants of Tax Revenue Efforts in Developing Countries', Working Paper No. 07/184 Washington, DC: IMF.

Guzman, A. T. 1998. 'Why LDCs Sign Treaties that Hurt Them: Explaining the Popularity of Bilateral Investment Treaties', *Virginia Journal of International Law*, 38: 639–88.

Haas, E. B. 1964. *Beyond the Nation-State: Functionalism and International Organization.* Stanford University Press.

Haas, P. M. 1992. 'Introduction: Epistemic Communities and International Policy Coordination', *International Organization*, 46: 1–36.

Habermas, J. 1996. 'Three Normative Models of Democracy', in S. Benhabib (ed.), *Democracy and Difference. Contesting the Boundaries of the Political*, 21–30. Cambridge University Press.

Habermas, J. 2001. *The Postnational Constellation.* Cambridge: Polity.

Hadden, T. 1984. 'Inside Corporate Groups', *International Journal of the Sociology of Law*, 12: 271–86.

Hadden, T. 1993. 'Regulating Corporate Groups: An International Perspective', in J. McCahery, S. Picciotto and C. Scott (eds.), *Corporate Control and Accountability*, 343–69. Oxford: Clarendon Press.

Haley, J. O. 2001. *Antitrust in Germany and Japan, the First Fifty Years, 1947–1998.* University of Washington Press.

Hall, P. A. and Soskice, D. W. 2001. *Varieties of Capitalism: The Institutional Foundations of Comparative Advantage.* Oxford University Press.

Halliday, T. C. and Carruthers, B. G. 2009. *Bankrupt. Global Lawmaking and Systemic Financial Crisis.* Stanford University Press.

Halverson, J. T. 1991. 'Antitrust in a Global Environment: Conflicts and Resolutions: Harmonization and Coordination of International Merger Procedures', *Antitrust Law Journal*, 60: 531–42.

Hamilton, S. 2003. 'Putting the Client First: The Emerging Copernican Revolution of Tax Administration', *Tax Notes International Magazine*, 29: 569–76.

Hampton, M. P. 1996. *The Offshore Interface. Tax Havens in the Global Economy.* Basingstoke: Macmillan.

Handtke, C. and Towse, R. 2007. 'Economics of Copyright Collecting Societies', *International Review of Intellectual Property and Competition Law*, 38: 937–57.

Hansmann, H. and Kraakman, R. 2001. 'The End of History for Corporate Law', *Georgetown Law Journal*, 89: 439–68.

Harashima, Y. 2008. 'Trade and Environment Negotiations in the WTO: Asian Perspectives', *International Environmental Agreements*, 8: 17–34.

Hardin, G. 1968. 'The Tragedy of the Commons', *Science* (new series), 162: 1243–8.

Hardin, G. 1998. 'Extensions of "The Tragedy of the Commons"', *Science* (new series), 280: 682–83.

Hardt, M. and Negri, A. 2000. *Empire.* Cambridge, MA: Harvard University Press.

Hardt, M. and Negri, A. 2005. *Multitude.* London: Penguin Books.

Harlow, C. 1999. 'European Administrative Law and the Global Challenge', in P. Craig and G. de Búrca (eds.), *The Evolution of EU Law*, 261–85. Oxford University Press.

Harris, P. 2006. *Income Tax in Common Law Jurisdictions: From The Origins to 1820.* Cambridge University Press.

Harrison, B. 1994. *Lean and Mean: The Changing Landscape of Corporate Power in the Age of Flexibility.* New York: Basic Books.

Harvey, C. and Press, J. 1990 'The City and International Mining', *Business History*, 32: 98–119.

Haufler, V. 2001. *A Public Role for the Private Sector. Industry Self-Regulation in a Global Economy.* Washington, DC: Carnegie Endowment for International Peace.

Hawley, E. J. 1966. *The New Deal and the Problem of Monopoly. A Study in Economic Ambivalence.* Princeton University Press.

Hawley, J. P. 1984. 'Protecting Capital from Itself: US Attempts to Regulate the Eurocurrency System', *International Organization*, 38: 131–65.

Hawley, J. P. 1987. *Dollars and Borders: US Government Attempts to Restrict Capital Flows, 1960–1980*. Armonk, NY: M. E. Sharpe.

Hay, P. 1986. 'Refining Personal Jurisdiction in the United States', *International and Comparative Law Quarterly*, 35: 32–62.

Hay, R. J. 2006. 'OECD Level Playing Field Report: Consensus or Conflict?', *Tax Planning International Review*, 33: 3–10.

Hayden, C. 2003. 'From Market to Market: Bioprospecting's Idioms of Inclusion', *American Ethnologist*, 30: 359–71.

Hayden, C. 2004. 'Prospecting's Publics', in C. Humphrey and K. Verdery (eds.), *Property in Question. Value Transformation in the Global Economy*, 115–38. London: Berg.

Hayton, D. J. (ed.) 2002. *Extending the Boundaries of Trusts and Similar Ring-fenced Funds*. The Hague: Kluwer Law International.

Hedlund, G. 1986. 'The Hypermodern MNC – A Heterarchy?', *Human Resource Management*, 25: 9–35.

Heilbrunn, J. R. 2005. 'Oil and Water? Elite Politicians and Corruption in France', *Comparative Politics*, 37: 277–96.

Held, D. 1995. *Democracy and the Global Order. From the Modern State to Cosmopolitan Governance*. Cambridge: Polity Press.

Held, D. 1997. 'Cosmopolitan Democracy and the Global Order: A New Agenda', in J. Bohman and M. Lutz-Bachman (eds.), *Perpetual Peace*, 235–51. Cambridge, MA: MIT Press.

Held, D., McGrew, A., Goldblatt, D. and Perraton, J. 1999. *Global Transformations. Politics and Culture*. Cambridge: Polity Press.

Helfer, L. R. 1998. 'Adjudicating Copyright Claims under the TRIPs Agreement. The Case for a European Human Rights Analogy', *Harvard International Law Journal*, 39: 357.

Helfer, L. R. 2000. 'World Music on a US Stage: A Berne/TRIPs and Economic Analysis of the Fairness in Music Licensing Act', *Boston University Law Review*, 80: 93–204.

Helfer, L. R. 2004. *Intellectual Property Rights in Plant Varieties International Legal Regimes and Policy Options for National Governments*. Rome: FAO.

Helfer, L. R., Alter, K. J. and Guerzovich, M. F. 2009. 'Islands of Effective International Adjudication: Constructing an Intellectual Property Rule of Law in the Andean Community', *American Journal of International Law*, 103: 1–47.

Helfer, L. R. and Slaughter, A.-M. 1997. 'Toward a Theory of Effective Supranational Adjudication', *Yale Law Journal*, 107: 273–391.

Helleiner, E. 1995. 'Explaining the Globalization of Financial Markets: Bringing States Back In', *Review of International Political Economy*, 2: 315–41.

Heller, M. A. and Eisenberg, R. S. 1998. 'Can Patents Deter Innovation? The Anti-commons in Biomedical Research', *Science*, 280: 698–701.

Hellerstein, W. and McClure, C. 2004. 'The European Commission's Report on Company Income Taxation. What the EU Can Learn from the Experience of the United States', *International Tax and Public Finance*, 11: 199–220.

Henderson, A., Gentle, I. and Ball, E. 2005. 'WTO Principles and Telecommunications in Developing Nations: Challenges and Consequences of Accession', *Telecommunications Policy*, 29: 205–21.

Henderson, D. 1999. *The MAI Affair. A Story and Its Lessons*. London: Royal Institute of International Affairs.

Herring, R. J. and Litan, R. E. 1995. *Financial Regulation in the Global Economy*. Washington, DC: Brookings Institution Press.

Heyvaert, V. 1999. 'Reconceptualizing Risk Assessment', *Review of European Community and International Environmental Law*, 8: 135–43.

Heywood, M. 2001. 'Debunking Conglomo-talk: A Case Study of the Amicus Curiae as an Instrument for Advocacy, Investigation and Mobilisation', 'Health, Law and Human Rights: Exploring the Connections', an international cross-disciplinary conference honoring Jonathan M. Mann, Philadelphia, Pennsylvania.

Hildebrand, P. M. 2008. 'Is Basel II Enough? The Benefits of a Leverage Ratio', Financial Markets Group Lecture, London School of Economics, London, 15 December 2008. Speech by Mr Philipp M. Hildebrand, Vice-Chairman of the Governing Board of the Swiss National Bank.

Hilferding, R. [1910] 1981. *Finance Capital. A Study of the Latest Phase of Capitalist Development*. London: Routledge & Kegan Paul.

Hirsch, P., Michaels, S. and Friedman, R. 1990. 'Clean Models vs Dirty Hands: Why Economics is Different from Sociology', in S. Zukin and P. DiMaggio (eds.), *Structures of Capital: The Social Organization of the Economy*, 39–56. Cambridge University Press.

Hirst, P. and Thompson, G. 1996. *Globalization in Question. The International Economy and the Possibilities of Governance*. Cambridge: Polity Press.

Hobsbawm, E. J. 1990. *Nations and Nationalism since 1780. Programme, Myth, Reality*. Cambridge University Press.

Hobson, J. A. 1915. *Towards International Government*. London: Geo. Allen & Unwin.

Hobson, J. M. 2003. 'Disappearing Taxes or the "Race to the Middle"? Fiscal Policy in the OECD', in L. Weiss (ed.), *States in the Global Economy. Bringing Domestic Institutions Back In*, 37–57. Cambridge University Press.

Hodgkin, T. L. 1956. *Nationalism in colonial Africa*. London: Frederick Muller.

Hope, J. 2008. *Biobazaar: The Open Source Revolution and Biotechnology*. Cambridge, MA: Harvard University Press.

Horlick, G. N. and Meyer, M. A. 1995. 'The International Convergence of Antitrust Policy', *International Lawyer*, 29: 65–76.

Horn, N. and Kocka, J. (eds.) 1979. *Law and the Formation of the Big Enterprises in the 19th Century*. Göttingen: Vandenhoeck & Ruprecht.

Houlder, V. 2007. 'Offshore amnesty swells UK tax coffers by £400m', 6 December, *Financial Times*.

Hounshell, D. A. 1985. *From the American System to Mass Production 1800–1932. The Development of Manufacturing Technology in the United States*. Baltimore, MD: Johns Hopkins University Press.

Hovenkamp, H. 1991. *Enterprise and American Law 1836–1937*. Cambridge, MA: Harvard University Press.

Howse, R. 2000. 'Managing the Interface Between International Trade Law and the Regulatory State: What Lessons Should (and Should Not) be Drawn from the Jurisprudence of the US Dormant Commerce Clause', in T. Cottier and P. C. Mavroidis (eds.), *Regulatory Barriers and the Principle of Non-Discrimination in Trade Law*, 139–70. Ann Arbor: University of Michigan Press.

Howse, R. 2002. 'From Politics to Technocracy – And Back Again: The Fate of the Multilateral Trading Regime', *American Journal of International Law*, 96: 94–117.

Howse, R. 2004. *Mainstreaming the Right to Development into International Trade Law and Policy at the World Trade Organization*. E/CN.4/Sub.2/2004/17. UN Commission on Human Rights, Sub-Commission on the Promotion and Protection of Human Rights.

Hu, H. T. C. 1980. 'Compensation in Expropriations: A Preliminary Economic Analysis', *Virginia Journal of International Law*, 20: 61–95.

Huault, I. and Rainelli-Le Montagner, H. 2009. 'Market Shaping as an Answer to Ambiguities: The Case of Credit Derivatives', *Organization Studies*, 30: 549–75.

Hudec, R. E. 1975. *The GATT Legal System and World Trade Diplomacy*. New York: Praeger.

Hudec, R. E. 1987. *Developing Countries in the GATT Legal System*. Aldershot: Gower.

Hudec, R. E. 1993. *Enforcing International Trade Law. Evolution of the GATT Dispute-Settlement System*. London: Butterworths.

Hudson, A. 2009. *The Law of Finance*. London: Sweet & Maxwell.

Huertas, T. F. 1990. 'US Multinational Banking: History and Prospects', in G. Jones (ed.), *Banks as Multinationals*, 249–65. London: Routledge.

Hugenholtz, B., Guibault, L. and Geffen, S. v. 2003. *The Future of Levies in a Digital Environment*. Amsterdam: Institute for Information Law.

Human Genome Sciences. 2008. *Annual Report*.

Huxley, A. 2000. 'Rhodes, Arakan, Grand Cayman: Three Versions of Offshore', in I. Edge (ed.), *Comparative Law in Global Perspective: Essays in Celebration of the Fiftieth Anniversary of the Founding of the SOAS Law Department*, 145–70. Ardsley, NY: Transnational Publishers.

Huys, I., Berthels, N., Matthijs, G. and van Overwalle, G. 2009. 'Legal Uncertainty in the Area of Genetic Diagnostic Testing', *Nature Biotechnology*, 27: 903–9.

Hymer, S. [1960] 1976. *The International Operations of National Firms: A Study of Direct Investment*. Cambridge, MA: MIT Press.

Hymer, S. 1972. 'The Multinational Corporation and Uneven Development', in A. Kapoor and P. D. Grub (eds.), *The Multinational Enterprise in Transition*, 438–56. Princeton, NJ: Darwin.

IADB 2004. *Integration and Trade in the Americas. Fiscal Impact of Trade Liberalization in the Americas*. Washington, DC: Inter-American Development Bank.

IFRRO 2008. *Copyright Levies and Reprography*. International Federation of Reproduction Rights Organizations.

Iida, K. 2006. *Legalization and Japan: The Politics of WTO Dispute Settlement*. London: Cameron May.

IISD 2010. *Summary of the 9th Meeting of the Working Group on ABS of the CBD*. Earth Negotiations Bulletin 503. International Institute for Sustainable Development.

ILC 2006. *Fragmentation of International Law: Difficulties Arising from the Diversification and Expansion of International Law*. A/CN.4/L.702. New York: Study Group of the International Law Commission.

ILO 1994. *The Social Dimensions of the Liberalization of World Trade*. GB.261/WP/SLD/1. Geneva: ILO Working party on the Social Dimensions of the Liberalization of International Trade.

ILO 1998. *Overview of Global Developments and Office Activities Concerning Codes of Conduct, Social Labelling and Other Private Sector Initiatives Addressing Labour Issues*. GB.273/WP/SDL/1(Rev.1). Geneva: ILO Working Party on the Social Dimensions of the Liberalization of International Trade.

ILO 1999. *Further Examination of Questions Concerning Private Initiatives, Including Codes of Conduct*. GB.274/WP/SDL/1. Geneva: ILO Working Party on the Social Dimensions of the Liberalization of International Trade.

ILO 2003a. *Employment and Social Policy in Respect of Export Processing Zones (EPZs)*. GB.286/ESP/3, 286th Session. Geneva: International Labour Office.

ILO 2003b. *Information Note on Corporate Social Responsibility and International Labour Standards*. GB.286/WP/SDG/4. Geneva: ILO Working Party on the Social Dimension of Globalization.

ILO 2004. *A Fair Globalization: Creating Opportunities for All*. Geneva: World Commission on the Social Dimension of Globalization.

ILO 2008. *Declaration on Social Justice for a Fair Globalization*.

ILO and WTO 2007. *Trade and Employment: Challenges for Policy Research*. Geneva: International Labour Office and Secretariat of the World Trade Organization.

IMF 2009. *The State of Public Finances: Outlook and Medium-Term Policies After the 2008 Crisis.* Washington, DC: IMF Fiscal Affairs Department.

IMF–IEO 2005. *Report on the Evaluation of the IMF's Approach to Capital Account Liberalization.* Washington, DC: IMF Independent Evaluation Office.

Ingham, G. 1994. 'States and Markets in the Production of World Money', in S. Corbridge, N. Thrift and R. Martin (eds.), *Money, Power and Space*, 29–49. Oxford: Blackwell.

Ireland, P. 1996. 'Capitalism without the Capitalist: The Joint Stock Company Share and the Emergence of the Modern Doctrine of Separate Legal Personality', *Legal History*, 17: 40–72.

Ireland, P. 2003a. 'Property and Contract in Contemporary Corporate Theory', *Legal Studies*, 23: 453–509.

Ireland, P. 2003b. 'Property, Private Government and the Myth of Deregulation', in S. Worthington (ed.), *Commercial Law and Commercial Practice*, 85–113. Oxford: Hart.

Ireland, P. 2008. 'Limited Liability, Shareholder Rights and the Problem of Corporate Irresponsibility', *Cambridge Journal of Economics*. Advanced access online doi:10.1093/cje/ben040.

Ireland, P. 2009. 'Financialization and Corporate Governance', *Northern Ireland Legal Quarterly*, 60(1), 1.

ITF 2005. *Campaign against Flags of Convenience and Substandard Shipping. Annual Report 2004.* International Transport Workers' Federation.

Jackson, H. E. 1998. 'The Selective Incorporation of Foreign Legal Systems to Promote Nepal as an International Financial Services Centre', in C. McCrudden (ed.), *Regulation and Deregulation – Policy and Practice in the Utilities and Financial Services Industries*, 367–408. Oxford: Clarendon Press.

Jackson, J. H. 1997. *The World Trading System. Law and Policy of International Economic Relations.* Cambridge, MA: MIT Press.

Jackson, J. H. 2004. 'International Law Status of WTO Dispute Settlement Reports: Obligation to Comply or Option to "Buy Out"?', *American Journal of International Law*, 98: 109–25.

Jackson, M. 2001. 'Using Technology to Circumvent the Law: The DMCA's Push to Privatize Copyright', *Hastings Communications and Entertainment Law Journal*, 23: 607–46.

Jackson, P., Furfine, C., Groeneveld, H., Hancock, D., Jones, D., Perraudin, W., Radecki, L. and Yoneyama, M. 1999. 'Capital Requirements and Bank Behaviour: The Impact of the Basle Accord', Working Papers 1, Basel: Basel Committee on Banking Supervision.

Jackson, R. H. 1990. *Quasi-States: Sovereignty, International Relations and the Third World.* Cambridge University Press.

Jawara, F. and Kwa, A. 2004. *Behind the Scenes at the WTO. The Real World of Trade Negotiations. Lessons of Cancun*, updated edition. London: Zed Books.

Jayaprakash, N. D. 1990. 'Perilous Litigation: The Leak Disaster Case', *Economic and Political Weekly*, 22 December, 2761–66.

Jayaprakash, N. D. 1993. 'Plight of Bhopal Gas Victims', *Economic and Political Weekly*, 1 May, 838.

Jeffreys, D. 2004. *Aspirin. The Remarkable Story of a Wonder Drug.* London: Bloomsbury.

Jehoram, H. C. 2001. 'The Future of Copyright Collecting Societies', *European Intellectual Property Review*, 23: 134–9.

Jenkins, R. 1987. *Transnational Corporations and Uneven Development.* London: Methuen.

Jenkins, R. 2002. 'The Political Economy of Codes of Conduct', in R. Jenkins, R. Pearson and G. Seyfang (eds.), *Corporate Responsibility and Labour Rights.* London: Earthscan.

Jenkins, R., Pearson, R. and Seyfang, G. (eds.) 2002. *Corporate Responsibility and Labour Rights.* London: Earthscan.

Jenks, C. W. 1958. *The Common Law of Mankind.* London: Stevens.

Jensen, N. and Wantchekon, L. 2004. 'Resource Wealth and Political Regimes in Africa', *Comparative Political Studies*, 37: 816–41.

Jessop, B. 1982. *The Capitalist State: Marxist Theories and Methods.* Oxford: Robertson.

Jessup, P. C. 1956. *Transnational Law.* New Haven, CT: Yale University Press.

Joelson, M. R. 1976. 'The Proposed International Codes of Conduct as Related to Restrictive Business Practices', *Law and Policy in International Business*, 8: 837–45.

Joerges, C. 1990. 'Paradoxes of Deregulatory Strategies at Community Level: The Example of Product Safety Policy', in G. Majone (ed.), *Deregulation or Re-regulation? Regulatory Reform in Europe and the United States*, 176–97. London: Pinter.

Joerges, C. 1999. 'Bureaucratic Nightmare, Technocratic Regime and the Dream of Good Transnational Governance', in C. Joerges and E. Vos (eds.), *EU Committees: Social Regulation, Law and Politics*, 3–47. Oxford: Hart Publishing.

Joerges, C. 2001. 'Law, Science and the Management of Risks to Health at the National, European and International Level – Stories on Baby Dummies, Mad Cows and Hormones in Beef', *Columbia Journal of European Law*, 7: 1–19.

Joerges, C. 2007. *Conflict of Laws as Constitutional Form. Reflections on the International Trade Law and the Biotech Panel Report.* RECON Online Working Paper 2007/03.

Joerges, C. and Neyer, J. 1997. 'From Intergovernmental Bargaining to Deliberative Political Processes: The Constitutionalisation of Comitology', *European Law Journal*, 3: 273–99.

Joerges, C. and Neyer, J. 2003. 'Politics, Risk Management, World Trade Organization Governance and the Limits of Legalisation', *Science and Public Policy*, 30: 219–25.

Jones, C. A. 1987. *International Business in the Nineteenth Century: The Rise and Fall of a Cosmopolitan Bourgeoisie.* Brighton: Wheatsheaf.

Jones, G. (ed.) 1990. *Banks as Multinationals.* London: Routledge.

Jordan, R. S. (ed.) 1971. *International Administration. Its Evolution and Contemporary Applications.* Oxford University Press.

Joyner, D. H. 2004. 'Restructuring the Multilateral Export Control Regime System', *Journal of Conflict and Security Law*, 9: 181–211.

Jülich, R. and Falk, H. 1999. 'The Integration of Voluntary Approaches into Existing Legal Systems. Literature Survey': CAVA 99/09/4.

Justice, D. W. 2002. 'The International Trade Union Movement and the New Codes of Conduct', in R. Jenkins, R. Pearson and G. Seyfang (eds.), *Corporate Responsibility and Labour Rights.* London: Earthscan.

Kagan, R. A. (2007). 'Globalization and Legal Change: The "Americanization" of European Law?', *Regulation and Governance*, 1: 99–120.

Kahn-Freund, O. 1974. 'On Uses and Misuses of Comparative Law', *Modern Law Review*, 37: 1–27.

Kalderimis, D. 2004. 'IMF Conditionality as Investment Regulation: A Theoretical Analysis', *Social and Legal Studies*, 13: 103–31.

Kant, I. [1795] 1966. 'Toward Perpetual Peace', in M. J. Gregor (ed.), *Practical Philosophy*, 311–51. Cambridge University Press.

Kapczynski, A., Chaifetz, S., Katz, Z. and Benkler, Y. 2005. 'Addressing Global Health Inequities: An Open Licensing Approach For University Innovations', *Berkeley Technology Law Journal*, 20: 1031–114.

Kaplow, L. and Shavell, S. 1996. 'Property Rules versus Liability Rules: An Economic Analysis', *Harvard Law Review*, 109: 713–90.

Kapstein, E. B. 1994. *Governing the Global Economy. International Finance and the State.* Cambridge, MA: Harvard University Press.

Kar, D. and Cartwright-Smith, D. 2008. *Illicit Financial Flows From Developing Countries: 2002–2006.* Washington, DC: Global Financial Integrity (GFI).

Kar, D., Cartwright-Smith, D. and Hollingshead, A. 2010. *The Absorption of Illicit Financial Flows from Developing Countries: 2002–2006.* Washington, DC: GFI.

Kassim, H. and Wright, K. 2009. 'Bringing Regulatory Processes Back In: The Reform of EU Antitrust and Merger Control', *West European Politics*, 32: 738–55.

Kassoulides, G. C. 1993. *Port State Control and Jurisdiction. The Evolution of the Port State Regime.* Dordrecht: Nijhoff.

Kaufman, H. 2008. 'The principles of sound regulation', 5 August, *Financial Times*.

Kaufmann, D., Kraay, A. and Mastruzzi, M. 2005. *Measuring Governance Using Cross-Country Perceptions Data.* World Bank.

Kaul, I., Grunberg, I. and Stern, M. A. (eds.) 1999. *Global Public Goods. International Cooperation in the 21st Century*. www.undp.org/globalpublicgoods: Oxford University Press.

Kawamoto, A. 1999. 'How Can Regulatory Reform be Linked to the New Trade Round? Perspectives from the OECD Regulatory Reform Country Reviews', *International Trade Law Review*, (5) 124–30, (6) 58–63.

Kearney, N. 1999. 'Corporate Codes of Conduct: The Privatized Application of Labour Standards', in S. Picciotto and R. Mayne (eds.), *Regulating International Business. Beyond Liberalization*, 205–20. Basingstoke: Macmillan.

Keck, M. E. and Sikkink, K. 1998. *Activists Beyond Borders. Advocacy Networks in International Politics*. Ithaca, NY: Cornell University Press.

Keen, M., Kim, K. and Varsano, R. 2006. 'The "Flat Tax(es)": Principles and Evidence', Working Paper No. 06/218 IMF.

Kell, G. 2003. 'The Global Compact. Origins, Operations, Progress, Challenges', *Journal of Corporate Citizenship*, 11: 35–49.

Kellerman, C., Rixen, T. and Uhl, S. 2007. *Europeanizing Corporate Taxation to Regain National Tax Policy Autonomy*. www.fes.de: Friedrich Ebert Stiftung.

Kelsey, J. 1995. *Economic Fundamentalism*. London: Pluto Press.

Kelsey, J. 2008. *Serving Whose Interests? The Political Economy of Trade in Services Agreements*. Abingdon: Routledge-Cavendish.

Kemp, R. 2009. 'Open Source Software: An Introduction', *Computer Law and Security Report*, 24: 77–85.

Kennedy, D. 1986. 'Primitive Legal Scholarship', *Harvard International Law Journal*, 27: 1–98.

Kennedy, D. 2005. 'Challenging Expert Rule: The Politics of Global Governance', *Sydney Law Review*, 27: 5–28.

Kenyon, W. 2009. 'Companies need a culture change to escape bribery prosecutions', 19 November, *Financial Times*.

Kerf, M., Neto, I. and Géradin, D. 2005. 'Controlling Market Power: Balancing Antitrust and Sector Regulation in Telecoms', *Private Sector Development*, Washington, DC: World Bank.

Kernochan, J. M. 1985. 'Music Performance Rights Organizations in the United States of America: Special Characteristics, Restraints, and Public Attitudes', *Copyright*, 21: 389–410.

Kersting, C. 2002. 'Corporate Choice of Law – A Comparison of the United States and European Systems and a Proposal for a European Directive', *Brooklyn Journal of International Law*, 28: 1–75.

Kimenyi, M. S. 2005. 'Efficiency and Efficacy of Kenya's Constituency Development Fund: Theory and Evidence', Working Paper 2005–42 Storrs: University of Connecticut Department of Economics.

Kindleberger, C. P. 1969. *American Business Abroad. Six Lectures on Direct Investment*. New Haven: Yale University Press.

Kindleberger, C. P. 1980. *A GATT for Foreign Investment; Further Reflections.* Carnegie Center for Transnational Studies.

King, A. and Lenox, M. 2000. 'Industry Self-Regulation without Sanctions: The Chemical Industry's Responsible Care Program', *Academy of Management Journal*, 43: 698–716.

King, M. 2009. 'Speech at the Lord Mayor's Banquet', 17 June, London.

Kingsbury, B. 1994. 'The Tuna–Dolphin Controversy, The World Trade Organization, and the Liberal Project to Reconceptualize International Law', *Yearbook of International Environmental Law*, 5: 1–40.

Kingsbury, B., Krisch, N. and Stewart, R. B. 2005. 'The Emergence of Global Administrative Law', *Law and Contemporary Problems*, 68: 15–62.

Kingsbury, B. and Schill, S. 2009. 'Investor–State Arbitration as Governance: Fair and Equitable Treatment, Proportionality and the Emerging Global Administrative Law'. IILJ Working Paper 2009/6 (Global Administrative Law Series), New York University Law School.

Kitch, E. W. 1977. 'The Nature and Function of the Patent System', *Journal of Law and Economics*, 20: 265–90.

Kitching, G. 1989. *Development and Underdevelopment in Historical Perspective. Populism, Nationalism and Industrialization.* London: Routledge.

Klein, M. 2000. *No Logo. Taking Aim at the Brand Bullies.* London: Flamingo.

Kleinman, D. and Kinchy, A. J. 2003. 'Why Ban Bovine Growth Hormone? Science, Social Welfare, and the Divergent Biotech Policy Landscapes in Europe and the United States', *Science as Culture*, 12: 375–414.

Klug, H. 2008. 'Law, Politics, and Access to Essential Medicines in Developing Countries', *Politics and Society*, 36: 207–45.

Knightley, P. 1993. *The Rise and Fall of the House of Vestey.* London: Warner.

Kobrin, S. J. 1984. 'Expropriation as an Attempt to Control Foreign Firms in LDCs: Trends from 1960 to 1979', *International Studies Quarterly*, 28: 329–48.

Kohler-Koch, B. and Eising, R. (eds.) 1999. *The Transformation of Governance in the European Union.* London: Routledge.

Kolko, G. 1963. *The Triumph of Conservatism: A Reinterpretation of American History.* New York: Collier Macmillan.

Kongolo, T. 2008. *Unsettled International Intellectual Property Issues.* Alphen: Kluwer.

Kontorovich, E. 2004. 'The Piracy Analogy: Modern Universal Jurisdiction's Hollow Foundation', *Harvard International Law Journal*, 45: 183–237.

Kooiman, J. (ed.) 1993. *Modern Governance. New Government–Society Interactions.* London: Sage.

Kornai, J. 1992. *The Socialist System. The Political Economy of Communism.* Oxford: Clarendon Press.

Koskenniemi, M. 1988. *From Apology to Utopia. The Structure of International Legal Argument.* Helsinki: Finnish Lawyers' Publishing Company.

Koskenniemi, M. 1990. 'The Politics of International Law', *European Journal of International Law*, 1: 4–32.

Koskenniemi, M. 2002. *The Gentle Civilizer of Nations. The Rise and Fall of International Law 1870–1960*. Cambridge University Press.

Koskenniemi, M. 2007. 'The Fate of Public International Law: Between Technique and Politics', *Modern Law Review*, 70: 1–30.

Kotlikoff, L. J. 2010. *Jimmy Stewart is Dead: Ending the World's Ongoing Financial Plague with Limited Purpose Banking*. Hoboken, NJ: Wiley.

Kraakman, R. H. (ed.) 2004. *The Anatomy of Corporate Law: A Comparative and Functional Approach*. Oxford University Press.

Krajewski, M. 2003. *National Regulation and Trade Liberalisation in Services: The Legal Impact of the General Agreement on Trade in Services*. London: Kluwer Law International.

Kramer, A. E. 2010. 'Russia slow to pick up the lead in bribery cases', 29 April, *New York Times* (Global Edition).

Kramer, C. S. 1989. 'Food Safety and International Trade. The US–EC Meat and Hormone Controversies', in C. S. Kramer (ed.), *The Political Economy of US Agriculture. Challenges for the 1990s*, 203–33. Washington, DC: National Center for Food and Agricultural Policy. Resources for the Future.

Krasner, S. D. 2001. 'Sovereignty', Jan./Feb. *Foreign Policy*, 122: 20–7.

Kratochwil, F. V. 1989. *Rules, Norms and Decisions. On the Conditions of Practical and Legal Reasoning in International Relations and Domestic Affairs*. Cambridge University Press.

Kretschmer, M. 2002a. 'The Failure of Property Rules in Collective Administration: Rethinking Copyright Societies as Regulatory Instruments', *European Intellectual Property Review*, 24: 126–37.

Kretschmer, M. 2002b. 'Copyright Societies Do Not Administer Individual Property Rights: The Incoherence of Institutional Traditions in Germany and the UK', in R. Towse (ed.), *Copyright in the Cultural Industries*, 140–64. Cheltenham: Edward Elgar.

Krippner, G. R. 2005. 'The Financialization of the American Economy', *Socio-Economic Review*, 3: 173–208.

Krisch, N. and Kingsbury, B. 2006. 'Introduction: Global Governance and Global Administrative Law in the International Legal Order', *European Journal of International Law*, 17: 1–13.

Kristensen, P. H. and Zeitlin, J. 2005. *Local Players in Global Games: The Strategic Constitution of a Multinational Corporation*. Oxford University Press.

Kronke, H. 2005–6. 'The UN Sales Convention, The UNIDROIT Contract Principles and the Way Beyond', *Journal of Law and Commerce*, 25: 451–65.

Kronstein, H. 1973. *The Law of International Cartels (trans. from Das Recht der Internationalen Kartellen, 1967)*. Ithaca, NY: Cornell University Press.

Kronstein, H. and Till, I. 1947. 'A Reevaluation of the International Patent Convention', *Law and Contemporary Problems*, 12: 765–81.

Krueger, A. O. (ed.) 1998. *The WTO as an International Organization*. University of Chicago Press.

Krugman, P. R. 1994a. 'Competitiveness: A Dangerous Obsession', *Foreign Affairs*, 73: 28–44.

Krugman, P. R. 1994b. *Peddling Prosperity: Economic Sense and Nonsense in An Age of Diminished Expectations*. New York: W. W. Norton.

Kuanpoth, J. 2006. 'TRIPs-Plus Intellectual Property Rules: Impact on Thailand's Public Health', *Journal of World Intellectual Property*, 9: 573–91.

Kudo, A. and Hara, T. (eds.) 1992. *International Cartels in Business History*. University of Tokyo Press.

Kummer, K. 1995. *International Management of Hazardous Wastes: The Basel Convention and Related Legal Rules*. Oxford University Press.

Kuprianov, A. 1995. 'Derivatives Debacles. Case Studies of Large Losses in Derivatives Markets', *Federal Reserve Bank of Richmond Economic Quarterly*, 81: 1–39.

Kuritzkes, A., Schuermann, T. and Weiner, S. M. 2003. 'Risk Measurement, Risk Management, and Capital Adequacy in Financial Conglomerates', Brookings–Wharton Papers on Financial Services.

Ladas, S. B. 1930. *The International Protection of Industrial Property*. Cambridge, MA: Harvard University Press.

Laddie, J. 1996. 'Copyright: Over-strength, Over-regulated, Over-rated?', *European Intellectual Property Review*, 18: 253–60.

Lamoreaux, W. R. 1985. *The Great Merger Movement in American Business 1895–1904*. Cambridge University Press.

Lamy, P. 2006. 'The Place and Role of the WTO and its Law in the International Legal Order', *European Journal of International Law*, 17: 969–84.

Landfried, C. 1999. 'The European Regulation of Biotechnology by Polycratic Governance', in C. Joerges and E. Vos (eds.), *EU Committees: Social Regulation, Law and Politics*, 173–94. Oxford: Hart.

Lang, A. 2007a. 'Reflecting on 'Linkage': Cognitive and Institutional Change in the International Trading System', *Modern Law Review*, 70: 523–49.

Lang, A. 2007b. 'The Role of the Human Rights Movement in Trade Policy-Making: Human Rights as a Trigger for Social Learning', *New Zealand Journal of Public and International Law*, 5: 77–102.

Lang, A. and Scott, J. 2009. 'The Hidden World of WTO Governance', *European Journal of International Law*, 20: 575–614.

Lange, D. 2003. 'Reimagining the Public Domain', *Law and Contemporary Problems*, 66: 463–83.

Lapavitsas, C. 2009. 'Financialised Capitalism: Crisis and Financial Expropriation', *Historical Materialism*, 17: 114–48.

Larosière, J. de, Balcerowicz, L., Issing, O., Masera, R., Carthy, C. M., Nyberg, L., Pérez, J. and Ruding, O. 2009. *Report of the High-Level Group on Financial Supervision in the EU.* Brussels.

Lazonick, W. 1991. *Business Organization and the Myth of the Market Economy.* Cambridge University Press.

Leary, V. A. 1996. 'Workers' Rights and International Trade: The Social Clause (GATT, ILO, NAFTA, US Laws)', in J. Bhagwati and R. E. Hudec (eds.), *Fair Trade and Harmonization. Prerequisites for Free Trade? Vol. 2 Legal Analysis,* 177–230. Cambridge, MA: MIT Press.

Lee, R. 1998. *What is an exchange?: The Automation, Management, and Regulation of Financial Markets.* Oxford University Press.

Leigh Day & Co. 2009. *Memorandum to the Joint Committee on Human Rights Inquiry on Business and Human Rights.* Leigh, Day & Co. Solicitors.

Leigh, D. and Evans, R. 2007. 'BAE's secret $12m payout in African deal. Middleman reveals covert cash for "unnecessary" Tanzanian radar sale', 15 January, *Guardian.*

Leiner, B. M., Cerf, V. G., Clark, D. D., Kahn, R. E., Kleinrock, L., Lynch, D. C., Postel, J., Roberts, L. G. and Wolff, S. 2003. 'A Brief History of the Internet' (www.isoc.org/internet/history/brief.shtml: Internet Society).

Lennard, M. 2002. 'Navigating by the Stars: Interpreting the WTO Agreements', *Journal of International Economic Law,* 5: 17–89.

Lessig, L. 2001. *The Future of Ideas: The Fate of the Commons in a Connected World.* New York: Random House.

Lessig, L. 2006. '.commons', in J. N. Drobak (ed.), *Norms and the Law,* 88–104. Cambridge University Press.

Leubuscher, C. 1956. *Bulk Buying from the Colonies: A Study of the Bulk Purchase of Colonial Commodities by the United Kingdom Government.* Oxford University Press.

Levi-Faur, D. and Jordana, J. (eds.) 2005. *The Rise of Regulatory Capitalism: The Global Diffusion of a New Order.* London: Sage.

Levy, N. 2003. 'EU Merger Control: From Birth to Adolescence', *World Competition,* 26: 195–218.

LEWRG (London/Edinburgh Weekend Return Group) 1980. *In and Against the State.* London: Pluto.

Leyshon, A. and Thrift, N. 1995. 'Geographies of Financial Exclusion: Financial Abandonment in Britain and the United States', *Transactions of the Institute of British Geographers,* 20: 312–41.

Lichtenstein, C. C. 1997. 'The New Financial World of Cross-Border Capital Movements: The International Monetary Fund Agreement in the Light of the 1994 Mexico Peso Crisis', in A. Weber (ed.), *Währung und Wirtschaft. Das Geld im Recht. Festschrift für Prof. Dr. Hugo J. Hahn zum 70. Geburtstag.* Baden-Baden: Nomos.

Lillich, R. B. and Weston, B. H. 1975. *International Claims: Their Settlement by Lump-Sum Agreements.* Charlottesville: University Press of Virginia.

Lillich, R. B. and Weston, B. H. 1988. 'Lump-Sum Agreements: Their Continuing Contribution to the Law of International Claims', *American Journal of International Law*, 82: 69–80.

Lim, H. 2001. 'Trade and Human Rights What's at Issue?', *Journal of World Trade*, 35: 275–300.

Lindgren, C.-J., Garcia, G. and Saal, M. I. 1996. *Bank Soundness and Macro-Economic Policy.* Washington, DC: IMF.

Lindner, L. F. 2008. 'Regulating Food Safety: The Power of Alignment and Drive towards Convergence', *Innovation: The European Journal of Social Sciences*, 21: 133–43.

Lipson, C. 1985. *Standing Guard: Protecting Foreign Capital in the 19th and 20th Centuries.* Berkeley: California University Press.

Loughlin, M. and Scott, C. 1997. 'The Regulatory State', in P. Dunleavy, A. Gamble, I. Holliday and G. Peele (eds.), *Developments in British Politics 5*, 205–19. Basingstoke: Macmillan.

Lowe, A. V. 1983. *Extraterritorial Jurisdiction. An Annotated Collection of Legal Materials.* Cambridge: Grotius.

Lowenfeld, A. F. 1979. 'Public Law in the International Arena; Conflict of Laws, International Law and Some Suggestions for their Interaction', Academy of International Law, The Hague, *Recueil des Cours*, 163: 315–445.

Lowenfeld, A. F. 1990. 'United States Law Enforcement Abroad: The Constitution and International Law, Continued', *American Journal of International Law*, 84: 444–93.

Lowenfeld, A. F. 1996. *International Litigation and the Quest for Reasonableness.* Oxford: Clarendon Press.

Lowenfeld, A. F. 2002. *International Economic Law.* Oxford University Press.

Lubkin, G. 2002. 'The End of Extraterritorial Income Exclusion? The WTO Appellate Decision and Its Consequences', *Tax Management International Journal*, 31: 254–69.

Lugard, F. J. D. 1919/1970. *Political Memoranda: Revision of Instructions to Political Officers on Subjects Chiefly Political and Administrative, 1913–1918.* London: Cass.

Luhmann, N. 1987. 'The Unity of the Legal System', in G. Teubner (ed.), *Autopoietic Law: A New Approach to Law and Society*, 12–35. Berlin: de Gruyter.

Lutter, M. 1990. 'Enterprise Law Corp. vs Entity Law Inc. – Philip Blumberg's Book from the Point of View of an European Lawyer', *American Journal of Comparative Law* 38: 949–68.

Lyons, F. S. L. 1963. *Internationalism in Europe 1815–1914.* Leyden: Sythoff.

MacCormick, N. 1995. 'The Maastricht-Urteil: Sovereignty Now', *European Law Journal* 1: 259–66.

Macdonald, S. 2002. 'Exploring the Hidden Costs of Patents', in P. Drahos and R. Mayne (eds.), *Global Intellectual Property Rights. Knowledge, Access, Development*, 13–39. Basingstoke: Palgrave-Macmillan, Oxfam.

Macintosh, J. 2008. 'Board comes under fire', 17 September, *Financial Times*.

MacKenzie, D. 2003. 'An Equation and Its Worlds: Bricolage, Exemplars, Disunity and Performativity in Financial Economics', *Social Studies of Science*, 33: 831–68.

MacKenzie, D. 2006. *An Engine, Not a Camera: How Financial Models Shape Markets.* Cambridge, MA: MIT Press.

MacKenzie, D. 2009. 'All Those Arrows', *London Review of Books*, 31: 20–2.

MacKenzie, D. A., Muniesa, F. and Siu. L. (eds.) 2007. *Do Economists Make Markets?* Princeton University Press.

Macneil, I. R., Campbell, D., Feinman, J. M. and Vincent-Jones, P. 2001. *The Relational Theory of Contract: Selected Works of Ian Macneil.* London: Sweet & Maxwell.

Macpherson, C. B. 1962. *The Political Theory of Possessive Individualism: Hobbes to Locke.* Oxford University Press.

Madsen, M. R. and Vauchez, A. 2004. 'European Constitutionalism at the Cradle. Law and Lawyers in the Construction of a European Political Order (1920–1960)', in A. Jettinghoff and H. Schepel (eds.), *Recht der Werkelijkheid*, 15–34 (special issue on lawyers' circles, lawyers and European legal integration).

Maher, I. 2002. 'Competition Law in the International Domain: Networks as a New Form of Governance', *Journal of Law and Society*, 29: 111–36.

Maher, I. 2008. 'Regulation and Modes of Governance in EC Competition Law: What's New in Enforcement?', *Fordham International Law Journal*, 31: 1713–40.

Majone, G. (ed.) 1990. *Deregulation or Re-Regulation. Regulatory Reform in Europe and the United States.* London: Pinter.

Majone, G. 1993. 'The Rise of the Regulatory State in Europe', *West European Politics*, 17: 77–101.

Malkin, J. and Wildavsky, A. 1991. 'Why the Traditional Distinction between Public and Private Goods Should Be Abandoned', *Journal of Theoretical Politics*, 3: 355–78.

Mallaby, S. 2010. 'Wall Street owes its survival to the Fed', 2 December, *Financial Times*.

Manby, B. 1999. 'The Role and Responsibility of Oil Multinationals in Nigeria', *Journal of International Affairs*, 53: 281–301.

Manin, B. 1994. 'The Metamorphoses of Representative Government', *Economy and Society*, 23: 133–71.

Manin, B. 1997. *The Principles of Representative Government.* Cambridge University Press.

Mann, F. A. 1964. 'The Doctrine of Jurisdiction in International Law', Academy of International Law, The Hague, *Recueil des Cours*, 111: 1–162.

Mann, F. A. 1984. 'The Doctrine of International Jurisdiction Revisited after 20 Years', *Recueil des Cours de l'Académie de Droit International*, 186: 9–116.

Marceau, G. 2002. 'WTO Dispute Settlement and Human Rights', *European Journal of International Law*, 13: 753–814.

Marceau, G. and Trachtman, J. P. 2002. 'The Technical Barriers to Trade Agreement, the Sanitary and Phytosanitary Measures Agreement, and the General Agreement on Tariffs and Trade: A Map of the World Trade Organization Law of Domestic Regulation of Goods', *Journal of World Trade*, 36: 811–81.

Marcial, G. G. 1995. *Secrets of the Street. The Dark Side of Making Money*. New York: McGraw Hill.

Marcus, A. 1989. *The Middle East on the Eve of Modernity. Aleppo in the Eighteenth Century*. New York: Columbia University Press.

Marsh, D. 1992. *The Bundesbank: The Bank that Rules Europe*. London: Heinemann.

Marx, K. 1867/1976. *Capital: A Critique of Political Economy*. Harmondsworth: Penguin Books.

Mashayekhi, M., Julsaint, M. and Tuerk, E. 2006. 'Strategic Considerations for Developing Countries: The Case of GATS and Health Services', in C. Blouin, N. Drager and R. Smith (eds.), *International Trade in Health Services and The GATS: Current Issues and Debates*, 17–81. Washington, DC: World Bank.

Mason, J. R. and Rosner, J. 2007. 'Where Did the Risk Go? How Misapplied Bond Ratings Cause Mortgage Backed Securities and Collateralized Debt Obligation Market Disruptions': SSRN.

Mathews, D. 2002. *Globalizing Intellectual Property Rights: The TRIPs Agreement*. London: Routledge.

Matsushita, M. 1993. *International Trade and Competition Law in Japan*. Oxford University Press.

Mattli, W. and Büthe, T. 2005. 'Accountability in Accounting? The Politics of Private Rule-Making in the Public Interest', *Governance*, 18: 399–429.

Mattoo, A. 1997. 'National Treatment in the GATS: Corner-Stone or Pandora's Box', *Journal of World Trade*, 31: 107–35.

Mattoo, A. 1998. 'Financial Services and the WTO: Liberalization in the Developing and Transition Economies', WTO Staff Working Paper TISD–98–03.

May, C. and Sell, S. K. 2006. *Intellectual Property Rights: A Critical History*. Boulder, CO: Lynne Rienner.

Maycock, J. 1986. *Financial Conglomerates: The New Phenomenon*. Aldershot: Gower.

McBarnet, D. 2007. 'Corporate Social Responsibility beyond Law, through Law, for Law: The New Corporate Accountability', in D. McBarnet, A. Voiculescu and T. Campbell (eds.), *The New Corporate Accountability. Corporate Social Responsibility and the Law*, 9–56. Cambridge University Press.

McBarnet, D. and Kurkchiyan, M. 2007. 'Corporate Social Responsibility through Contractual Control? Global Supply Chains and "Other Regulation"', in D. McBarnet, A. Voiculescu and T. Campbell (eds.), *The New Corporate Accountability. Corporate Social Responsibility and the Law*, 59–92. Cambridge University Press.

McBarnet, D. and Schmidt, P. 2007. 'Corporate Accountability through Creative Enforcement: Human Rights, the Alien Torts Claims Act and the Limits of Legal Impunity', in D. McBarnet, A. Voiculescu and T. Campbell (eds.), *The New Corporate Accountability. Corporate Social Responsibility and the Law*, 148–76. Cambridge University Press.

McBarnet, D., Voiculescu, A. and Campbell, T. (eds.) 2007. *The New Corporate Accountability: Corporate Social Responsibility and the Law*. Cambridge University Press.

McBarnet, D. and Whelan, C. 1999. *Creative Accounting and the Cross-Eyed Javelin-Thrower*. Chichester: Wiley.

McCahery, J. and Picciotto, S. 1995. 'Creative Lawyering and the Dynamics of Business Regulation', in Y. Dezalay and D. Sugarman (eds.), *Professional Competition and Professional Power. Lawyers, Accountants and the Social Construction of Markets*, 238–74. London: Routledge.

McCahery, J., Picciotto, S. and Scott, C. (eds.) 1993. *Corporate Control and Accountability. Changing Structures and the Dynamics of Regulation*. Oxford: Clarendon Press.

McClean, J. D. 2002. *International Co-operation in Civil and Criminal Matters*. Oxford University Press.

McCrudden, C. 1999. 'International Economic Law and the Pursuit of Human Rights: A Framework for Discussion of the Legality of "Selective Purchasing" Laws Under the WTO Government Procurement Agreement', *Journal of International Economic Law*, 2: 1–48.

McGinnis, J. O. and Movesian, M. L. 2000. 'The World Trade Constitution', *Harvard Law Review*, 114: 512–605.

McGrath, J. 1994. 'The lawyers who rebuilt EuroDisney', *International Financial Law Review*, May, 10–12.

McKelvey, M. D. 1996. *Evolutionary Innovation. The Business of Biotechnology*. Oxford University Press.

McKinley, T. and Kyrili, K. 2009. 'Is Stagnation of Domestic Revenue in Low-Income Countries Inevitable?', CDPR Research Paper 27/09. London: School of Oriental and African Studies.

McMichael, P. 1996. 'Globalization: Myths and Realities', *Rural Sociology*, 61: 25–55.

McNair, L. 1961 *The Law of Treaties*. Oxford University Press.

McRae, D. M. 2000. 'The WTO in International Law: Tradition Continued or New Frontier?', *Journal of International Economic Law*, 3: 27–41.

Meeran, R. 1999. 'The Unveiling of Transnational Corporations: A Direct Approach', in M. K. Addo (ed.), *Human Rights Standards and the Responsibility of Transnational Corporations*. The Hague: Kluwer Law International, 161–70.

Meeran, R. 2009. Open Letter to UN Secretary-General's Special Representative on Business and Human Rights: The Genesis and Development of MNC Litigation in South Africa and a Possible Model for the Future.

Mehrotra, A. K. 2005. 'Envisioning the Modern American Fiscal State: Progressive-Era Economists and the Intellectual Foundations of the US Income Tax', *UCLA Law Review*, 52: 1793–866.

Meidinger, E. 2006. 'The Administrative Law of Global Private–Public Regulation: The Case of Forestry', *European Journal of International Law*, 17: 47–87.

Mekouar, M. A. 2000. 'Pesticides and Chemicals. The Requirement of Prior Informed Consent', in D. Shelton (ed.), *Commitment and Compliance. The Role of Non-Binding Norms in the International Legal System*, 146–63. Oxford University Press.

Mekouar, M. A. 2002. 'A Global Instrument on Agrodiversity: The International Treaty on Plant Genetic Resources for Food and Agriculture', FAO Legal Papers Online 24: Food and Agriculture Organization.

Meléndez-Ortiz, R. and Sánchez, V. (eds.) 2005. *Trading in Genes – Development Perspectives on Biotechnology, Trade and Sustainability*. London: Earthscan.

Melissaris, E. 2004. 'The More the Merrier? A New Take on Legal Pluralism', *Social and Legal Studies*, 13: 57–79.

Mena, L. N. A. O. and Rodriguez, R. 2005. 'Mexico's International Telecommunications Policy: Origins, the WTO Dispute, and Future Challenges', *Telecommunications Policy*, 29: 429–48.

Merges, R. P. 1996. 'Contracting into Liability Rules: Intellectual Property Rights and Collective Rights Organizations', *California Law Review*, 84: 1293–393.

Merges, R. P. 1999. 'As Many as Six Impossible Patents Before Breakfast: Property Rights for Business Concepts and Patent System Reform', *Berkeley Technology Law Journal*, 14: 577–615.

Merges, R. P. 2008. 'The continuing vitality of music performance rights organizations'. Law and Technology Scholarship 49: Berkeley Center for Law and Technology, Paper 37.

Merges, R. P. and Nelson, R. R. 1990. 'On the Complex Economics of Patent Scope', *Columbia Law Review*, 90: 839–916.

Merk, J. 2004. 'Regulating the Global Athletic Footwear Industry: The Collective Worker in the Product Chain', in L. Assassi, D. Wigan and K. v. d. Pijl (eds.), *Global Regulation. Managing Crises After the Imperial Turn*, 128–43. London: Palgrave Macmillan.

Merrill, S. A. and Mazza, A.-M. (eds.) 2006. *Reaping the Benefits of Genomic and Proteomic Research. Intellectual Property Rights, Innovation, and Public Health.*

Washington, DC: National Academies Press; for Committee on Intellectual Property Rights in Genomic and Protein Research of the National Research Council of the National Academies.

Merry, S. E. 1988. 'Legal Pluralism', *Law and Society Review*, 22: 869–96.

Mertes, T. and Bello, W. F. 2004. *A Movement of Movements: Is Another World Really Possible?* London: Verso.

Mestral, A. L. C. de and Gruchalla-Wesierski, T. 1990. *Extraterritorial Application of Export Control Legislation: Canada and the USA.* Dordrecht: Nijhoff.

Miéville, C. 2005. *Between Equal Rights: A Marxist Theory of International Law.* Leiden: Brill.

Mikulecky, D. 2001. 'The Emergence of Complexity: Science Coming of Age or Science Growing Old?', *Computers and Chemistry*, 25: 341–48.

Milward, A. S. 1992. *The European Rescue of the Nation-State.* London: Routledge.

Minsky, H. P. 1992. 'The Financial Instability Hypothesis', Jerome Levy Economics Institute Working Papers 74: Bard College, Levy Economics Institute.

Mitrany, D. 1943/1966. *A Working Peace System.* Chicago University Press.

Mommsen, W. J. and Moor, J. A. de (eds.) 1992. *European Expansion and Law. The Encounter of European and Indigenous Law in 19th and 20th Century Africa and Asia.* Oxford: Berg.

Monbiot, G. 2003. 'I was wrong about trade. Our aim should not be to abolish the World Trade Organisation, but to transform it', 24 June, *Guardian.*

Montagna, P. 1990. 'Accounting Rationality and Financial Legitimation', in S. Zukin and P. DiMaggio (eds.), *Structures of Capital. The Social Organization of the Economy*, 227–60. Cambridge University Press.

Montgomerie, J. 2008. 'Bridging the Critical Divide: Global Finance, Financialisation and Contemporary Capitalism', *Contemporary Politics*, 14: 233–52.

Montt, S. 2009. *State Liability in Investment Arbitration Global Constitutional and Administrative Law in the BIT Generation.* Oxford: Hart.

Moore, M. 2000. 'The backlash against globalization?', Speech to the Liberal International, Ottawa: WTO.

Moore, M. 2004. 'Taxation and the Political Agenda, North and South', Norwegian Institute for International Affairs.

Moore, M. 2007. 'How does taxation affect the quality of governance? Can dependency on taxation make governments accountable, capable and responsive?', Working Paper 280 Brighton, Institute for Development Studies.

Moran, M. 1984. *The Politics of Banking. The Strange Case of Competition and Credit Control.* Basingstoke: Macmillan.

Moran, M. 1991. *The Politics of the Financial Services Revolution. The USA, the UK, Japan.* Basingstoke: Macmillan.

Moran, M. 2003. *The British Regulatory State: High Modernism and Hyper-Innovation.* Oxford University Press.

Morgan, B. 2003. 'The Economization of Politics: Meta-Regulation as a Form of Nonjudicial Legality', *Social and Legal Studies*, 12: 489–523.

Morgan, G. 2006. 'Transnational Actors, Transnational Institutions, Transnational Spaces: The Role of Law Firms in the Internationalization of Competition Regulation', in M.-L. Djelic and K. Sahlin-Anderson (eds.), *Transnational Governance: Institutional Dynamics of Regulation*, 139–60. Cambridge University Press.

Morgan, G., Kristensen, P. H. and Whitley, R. 2001. *The Multinational Firm: Organizing Across Institutional and National Divides*. Oxford University Press.

Morris-Suzuki, T. 2000. 'For and Against NGOs. The Politics of the Lived World', *New Left Review* (second series), 2: 63–84.

Mosher, J. S. and Trubek, D. M. 2003. 'Alternative Approaches to Governance in the EU: EU Social Policy and the European Employment Strategy', *Journal of Common Market Studies*, 41: 63–88.

Mowery, D. C. and Rosenberg, N. 1998. *Paths of Innovation. Technological Change in 20th Century America*. Cambridge University Press.

Moyer-Henry, K. 2008. 'Patenting Neem and Hoodia: Conflicting Decisions Issued by the Opposition Board of the European Patent Office', *Biotechnology Law Report*, 27: 1–10.

Muchlinski, P. 1999. 'A Brief History of Regulation', in S. Picciotto and R. Mayne (eds.), *Regulating International Business. Beyond Liberalization*. Basingstoke: Macmillan.

Muchlinski, P. 2001. 'Corporations in International Litigation: Problems of Jurisdiction and the UK Asbestos Cases', *International and Comparative Law Quarterly*, 50: 1–25.

Muchlinski, P. 2007. *Multinational Enterprises and the Law*. Oxford University Press.

Munck, R. 1988. *The New International Labour Studies. An Introduction*. London: Zed Press.

Murphy, C. N. 1994. *International Organization and Industrial Change. Global Governance since 1850*. Cambridge: Polity Press.

Murphy, D. D. 2004. *The Structure of Regulatory Competition. Corporations and Public Policies in a Global Economy*. Oxford University Press.

Murphy, D. D. 2005. 'Interjurisdictional competition and regulatory advantage', *Journal of International Economic Law*, 8: 891–920.

Murray, D., Raynolds, L. T. and Taylor, P. L. 2003. *One Cup at a Time. Poverty Alleviation and Fair Trade Coffee in Latin America*. Boulder, CO: Fair Trade Research Group, Colorado University.

Murray, R. 1971. 'The Internationalization of Capital and the Nation State', *New Left Review* (first series), 67: 84–109.

Musgrave, R. A. 1992. 'Schumpeter's Crisis of the Tax State: An Essay in Fiscal Sociology', *Journal of Evolutionary Economics*, 2: 89–113.

Nadal, L. M. 2008. 'Why Is the Subpart F AFI Exception Temporary?', *Tax Notes International*, 50: 11–13.

Nadelmann, E. A. 1990. 'Global Prohibition Regimes: The Evolution of Norms in International Society', *International Organization*, 44: 479–526.

Nadelmann, E. A. 1993. *Cops Across Borders: The Internationalization of US Criminal Law Enforcement*. University Park, PA: Pennsylvania State University Press.

Naess, E. D. 1972. *The Great Panlibhon Controversy. The Fight over the Flags of Shipping*. London: Gower Press.

Naylor, R. T. 1994. *Hot Money and the Politics of Debt*. Montreal: Black Rose Books.

Neale, A. D. and Stephens, M. L. 1988. *International Business and National Jurisdiction*. Oxford: Clarendon.

Nesvetailova, A. 2007. *Fragile Finance: Debt, Speculation and Crisis in the Age of Global Credit*. Basingstoke: Palgrave Macmillan.

Neumann, F. 1942. *Behemoth* (Left Book Club edition). London: Gollancz.

Neumayer, E. and Spess, L. 2005. 'Do Bilateral Investment Treaties Increase Foreign Direct Investment to Developing Countries?', *World Development*, 33: 1567–85.

Nicholls, A. and Opal, C. 2005. *Fair Trade. Market-Driven Ethical Consumption*. London: Sage.

Nicolaïdis, K. 2007. 'Trusting the Poles? Constructing Europe through Mutual Recognition', *Journal of European Public Policy*, 14: 682–98.

Nicolaïdis, P. 1991. 'Investment Policies in an Integrated World Economy', *World Economy*, 14: 121–37.

Nicolaïdis, P. 1992. 'Competition Among Rules', *World Competition*, 16: 113–21.

Nimmer, D. 2000. 'A Riff on Fair Use in the Digital Millennium Copyright Act', *University of Pennsylvania Law Review*, 148: 673–742.

Noble, D. F. 1977 *America By Design. Science, Technology, and the Rise of Capitalism*. Oxford University Press.

Noll, R. G. (ed.) 1985. *Regulatory Policy and the Social Sciences*. Berkeley: University of California Press.

Nonet, P. and Selznick, P. 2001 (orig.1978). *Law and Society in Transition: Toward Responsive Law*. New Brunswick, NJ: Transaction Publishers.

Noonan, J. T. 1976. *Persons and Masks of the Law*. New York: Farrar, Strauss & Giroux.

Norr, M. 1962. 'Jurisdiction to Tax and National Income', *Tax Law Review*, 17 431–63.

North, D. C. 1990. *Institutions, Institutional Change and Economic Performance*. Cambridge University Press.

Northrup, H. R. and Rowan, R. 1979. *Multinational Collective Bargaining Attempts: The Record, the Cases and the Prospects*. Philadelphia: Industrial Relations Unit, Wharton School, University of Pennsylvania.

Nov, A. 2006. 'The "Bidding War" to Attract Foreign Direct Investment: The Need for a Global Solution', *Virginia Tax Review*, 25: 835–75.

Novy, A. and Leubolt, B. 2005. 'Participatory Budgeting in Porto Alegre: Social Innovation and the Dialectical Relationship of State and Civil Society', *Urban Studies*, 42: 2023–36.

Nussbaum, H. 1986. 'International Cartels and Multinational Enterprises', in A. Teichova, M. Levy-Leboyer and H. Nussbaum (eds.), *Multinational Enterprise in Historical Perspective*, 131–44. Cambridge University Press.

O'Connell, D. 2006. 'BAE cashes in on £40bn Arab jet deal', 20 August, *The Sunday Times*.

O'Rourke, D. 2002. 'Monitoring the Monitors: A Critique of Corporate, Third-Party Labor Monitoring', in R. Jenkins, R. Pearson and G. Seyfang (eds.), *Corporate Responsibility and Labour Rights*. London: Earthscan.

Odell, J. and Eichengreen, B. 1998. 'The United States, the ITO and the WTO: Exit Options, Agent Slack and Presidential Leadership', in A. O. Krueger (ed.), *The WTO as an International Organization*, 181–212. University of Chicago Press.

OECD 1977. *Restrictive Business Practices of Multinational Enterprises*. Paris: OECD, Committee of Experts on Restrictive Business Practices.

OECD 1979. *International Investment and Multinational Enterprises. Review of the 1976 Declaration and Decisions*. Paris: OECD–CIIME.

OECD 1987a. *Minimizing Conflicting Requirements*. Paris: OECD.

OECD 1987b. *Competition Policy and International Trade*. Paris: OECD.

OECD 1987c. *Introduction to the OECD Codes of Liberalisation*. Paris: OECD.

OECD 1987d. *International Tax Avoidance and Evasion. Four Related Studies*. Paris: OECD, Committee on Fiscal Affairs.

OECD 1994a. *Merger Cases in the Real World – A Study of Merger Control Procedures*. Paris: OECD.

OECD 1994b. *Regulatory Reform for an Interdependent World*. Paris: OECD.

OECD 1995. *Security Markets in OECD Countries. Organisation and Regulation*. Paris: OECD.

OECD 1996. *Controlled Foreign Company Legislation*. Paris: OECD, Committee on Fiscal Affairs.

OECD 1998. *Harmful Tax Competition. An Emerging Global Issue*. Paris: OECD.

OECD 2000a. *No Longer Business as Usual: Fighting Bribery and Corruption*. Paris: OECD.

OECD 2000b. *Codes of Corporate Conduct: An Expanded Review of their Contents*. TD/TC/WP(99)56/FINAL. Paris: OECD, Working Party of the Trade Committee.

OECD 2000c. *Tax Burdens. Alternative Measures*. Paris: OECD, Fiscal Affairs Secretariat.

OECD 2001a. *The OECD Guidelines for Multinational Enterprises. Text, Commentary and Clarifications.* DAFFE/IME/WPG(2000)15/FINAL. Paris: OECD, Directorate for Financial, Fiscal and Enterprise Affairs.

OECD 2001b. *Tax and the Economy. A Comparative Assessment of OECD Countries.* Paris: OECD.

OECD 2002a. *Genetic Inventions, Intellectual Property Rights and Licensing Practices. Evidences and Policies.* Paris: OECD.

OECD 2002b. *OECD Economic Surveys. United Kingdom.* Paris: OECD.

OECD 2002c. *Forty Years' Experience with the OECD Code of Liberalisation of Capital Movements* Paris: OECD.

OECD 2005a. *Revenue Statistics 1965–2004.* Paris: OECD.

OECD 2005b. *Measuring Globalisation: OECD Economic Globalisation Indicators.* Paris: OECD.

OECD 2006. *Tax Co-operation: Towards a Level Playing Field.* Paris: OECD.

OECD 2007a. *Measuring Globalisation: Activities of Multinationals – Volume I: Manufacturing, 2000–2004.* Paris: OECD.

OECD 2007b. *Tax Co-operation 2007: Towards a Level Playing Field: Assessment by the Global Forum on Taxation.* Paris: OECD.

OECD 2008. *Tax Co-operation 2008: Towards a Level Playing Field: Assessment by the Global Forum on Taxation.* Paris: OECD.

OECD 2009. *The Role of Stock Exchanges in Corporate Governance.* Paris: OECD.

OECD 2010a. *Promoting Transparency and Exchange of Information for Tax Purposes.* Paris: OECD–CFA.

OECD 2010b. *Addressing Tax Risks Involving Bank Losses.* Paris: OECD, Joint Report of the Forum on Tax Administration and Working Party No. 8 on Tax Avoidance and Evasion.

OECD–CFA 2002. *Reference Guide on Sources of Information from Abroad.* Paris: OECD, Committee on Fiscal Affairs.

OECD–CFA 2006. *Manual on Information Exchange.* Paris: OECD Committee on Fiscal Affairs.

OECD Watch 2005. *Five Years On. A Review of the OECD Guidelines and National Contact Points.* Amsterdam: SOMO.

Offe, C. and Keane, J. 1984. *Contradictions of the Welfare State.* London: Hutchinson.

Olson, M. 1965. *The Logic of Collective Action.* Cambridge, MA: Harvard University Press.

Ormrod, W. M., Bonney, M. and Bonney, R. 1999. *Crises, Revolutions and Self-Sustained Growth: Essays in European Fiscal History, 1130–1830.* Stamford: Shaun Tyas.

Osborne, D. and Gaebler, T. 1992. *Reinventing Government. How the Entrepreneurial Spirit is Transforming the Public Sector.* Reading, MA: Addison-Wesley.

Ostrom, E. 1990. *Governing the Commons: The Evolution of Institutions for Collective Action.* Cambridge University Press.

Owens, J. 2007. *Written Testimony of Jeffrey Owens, Director, OECD Center for Tax Policy and Administration, Hearings on Offshore Tax Evasion,* 3 May, Washington, DC: Senate Finance Committee.

Owens, J. 2009. 'Tax and Development', *Tax Justice Focus,* 4: 1–3.

Padoa-Schioppa, T. and Saccomanni, F. 1994. 'Managing a Market-Led Global Financial System', in P. B. Kenen (ed.), *Managing the World Economy. Fifty Years after Bretton Woods,* 235–68. Washington, DC: Institute for International Economics.

Palan, R. 1999. 'Offshore and the Structural Enablement of Sovereignty', in M. P. Hampton and J. P. Abbott (eds.), *Offshore Finance Centres and Tax Havens. The Rise of Global Capital.* Basingstoke: Macmillan.

Palan, R. 2002. 'Tax Havens and the Commercialization of State Sovereignty', *International Organization,* 56: 151–76.

Palan, R. 2003. *The Offshore World: Sovereign Markets, Virtual Places, and Nomad Millionaires.* Ithaca, NY: Cornell University Press.

Palmeter, D. and Mavroidis, P. C. 1998. 'The WTO Legal System: Sources of Law', *American Journal of International Law,* 92: 398–413.

Parker, C. 2002. *The Open Corporation. Effective Self-regulation and Democracy.* Cambridge University Press.

Parry, B. 2004a. 'Bodily Transactions: Regulating a New Space of Flows in "Bio-Information"', in K. Verderey and C. Humphrey (eds.), *Property in Question. Value Transformation in the Global Economy,* 29–48. Oxford: Berg.

Parry, B. 2004b. *Trading the Genome: Investigating the Commodification of Bio-Information.* New York: Columbia University Press.

Partnoy, F. 2002. 'ISDA, NASD, CFMA, and SDNY: The four horsemen of derivatives regulation?', Brookings–Wharton Papers on Financial Services.

Partnoy, F. 2006. 'How and why credit rating agencies are not like other gatekeepers', San Diego Legal Studies Papers 07–46: University of San Diego School of Law.

Partnoy, F. 2008. 'Hubris – is thy name Richard Fuld?', 12 September, *Financial Times.*

Patel, S. J., Roffe, P. and Yusuf, A. (eds.) 2001. *International Technology Transfer. The Origins and Aftermath of the United Nations Negotiations on a Draft Code of Conduct.* The Hague: Kluwer Law.

Paul, J. R. 1991. 'Comity in International Law', *Harvard International Law Journal,* 32: 1–79.

Pauly, L. W. 1997. *Who Elected the Bankers? Surveillance and Control in the World Economy.* Ithaca, NY: Cornell University Press.

Pauwelyn, J. 2001. 'The Role of Public International Law in the WTO: How Far Can We Go?', *American Journal of International Law,* 95: 535–78.

Pauwelyn, J. 2005. '*Rien ne va plus?* Distinguishing Domestic Regulation From Market Access in GATT and GATS', *World Trade Review*, 4: 131–70.

Payer, C. 1982. *The World Bank: A Critical Analysis.* New York: Monthly Review Press.

Payne, P. L. 1988. *British Entrepreneurship in the Nineteenth Century.* Basingstoke: Macmillan.

Pearce, J. H. N. 2007. 'The Rise and Development of the Concept of "Total Income" in United Kingdom Income Tax Law: 1842–1952', in J. Tiley (ed.), *Studies in the History of Tax Law. Vol. 2*, 87–118. Oxford: Hart.

Peckron, H. S. 2002. 'Watchdogs that Failed to Bark: Standards of Tax Review after Enron', *Florida Tax Review*, 5: 853–916.

Pekkanen, S. M. 2001. 'Aggressive Legalism: The Rules of the WTO and Japan's Emerging Trade Strategy', *World Economy*, 24: 707–37.

Pekkanen, S. M. 2003. 'International Law, Industry and the State: Explaining Japan's Complainant Activities at the WTO', *Pacific Review*, 16: 285–306.

Penaherrera, G. S. 1980. 'Viable Integration and the Economic Co-Operation Problems of the Developing World', *Journal of Common Market Studies*, 19: 65–76.

Penrose, E. T. 1951. *The Economics of the International Patent System.* Westport, CT: Greenwood Press.

Penrose, E. T., Joffe, G. and Stevens, P. 1992. 'Nationalisation of Foreign-Owned Property for a Public Purpose: An Economic Perspective on Appropriate Compensation', *Modern Law Review*, 55: 351–67.

Peredo, E., Lora, M. and Buxton, N. 2007. 'ICSID: Justice According to Transnationals', *Tunupa*, (34) (available from: www.funsolon. org/publicaciones/TUNUPA34CIADI.pdf; accessed 24/03/2010).

Perez, O. 2002. 'Using Private–Public Linkages to Regulate Environmental Conflicts: The Case of International Construction Contracts', *Journal of Law and Society*, 29: 77–110.

Perez, O. 2004. *Ecological Sensitivity and Global Legal Pluralism: Rethinking the Trade and Environment Conflict.* Oxford: Hart.

Perry, J. and Nölke, A. 2006. 'The Political Economy of International Accounting Standards', *Review of International Political Economy*, 13: 559–86.

Petersmann, E.-U. 1993a. 'International Competition Rules for the GATT–MTO World Trade and Legal System', *Journal of World Trade*, 27: 35–86.

Petersmann, E.-U. 1993b. 'National Constitutions and International Economic Law', in M. Hilf and E.-U. Petersmann (eds.), *National Constitutions and International Economic Law*, 3–53. Deventer: Kluwer.

Petersmann, E.-U. 1998. 'How to Constitutionalize International Law and Foreign Policy for the Benefit of Civil Society', *Michigan Journal of International Law*, 20: 1–30.

Petersmann, E.-U. 2000. 'The WTO Constitution and Human Rights', *Journal of International Economic Law* 3: 19–25.

Petersmann, E.-U. 2002a. 'Constitutionalism and WTO Law: From a State-Centered Approach Towards a Human Rights Approach in International Economic Law', in D. L. M. Kennedy and J. D. Southwick (eds.), *The Political Economy of International Trade Law. Essays in Honor of Robert E. Hudec*, 32–67. Cambridge University Press.

Petersmann, E.-U. 2002b. 'Time for a United Nations "Global Compact" for Integrating Human Rights into the Law of Worldwide Organizations: Lessons from European Integration', *European Journal of International Law*, 13: 621–50.

Petersmann, E.-U. 2003. 'Human Rights and the Law of the World Trade Organization', *Journal of World Trade*, 37: 241–81.

Petersmann, E.-U. 2004. 'The "Human Rights Approach" Advocated by the UN High Commissioner for Human Rights and by the International Labour Organization: Is It Relevant for WTO Law and Policy?', *Journal of International Economic Law*, 7: 605–27.

Petersmann, E.-U. 2005. 'Human Rights and International Trade Law: Defining and Connecting the Two Fields', in T. Cottier, J. Paulwelyn and E. Bürgi Bonanomi (eds.), *Human Rights and International Trade*, 29–94. Oxford University Press.

Peterson, L. E. 2006. 'More Spanish portfolio investors line up to sue Russia over Yukos', 13 October, *Investment Treaty News*.

Peterson, L. E. 2009. 'Argentine Crisis Arbitration Awards Pile Up, But Investors Still Wait for a Payout', *Focus Europe*: law.com.

Picciotto, S. 1983. 'Jurisdictional Conflicts, International Law and the International State System', *International Journal of the Sociology of Law*, 11: 11–40.

Picciotto, S. 1991. 'The Internationalization of the State', *Capital and Class*, 43: 43–63.

Picciotto, S. 1992. *International Business Taxation*. London: Weidenfeld & Nicolson.

Picciotto, S. 1995. 'The Construction of International Taxation', in Y. Dezalay and D. Sugarman (eds.), *Professional Competition and Professional Power*, 25–50. London: Routledge.

Picciotto, S. 1997a. 'Fragmented States and International Rules of Law', *Social and Legal Studies*, 6: 259–79.

Picciotto, S. 1997b. 'Networks in International Economic Integration: Fragmented States and the Dilemmas of Neo-Liberalism', *Northwestern Journal of International Law and Business*, 17: 1014–56.

Picciotto, S. 1998. 'Linkages in International Investment Regulation: The Antinomies of the Draft Multilateral Agreement on Investment', *University of Pennsylvania Journal of International Economic Law*, 19: 731–68.

Picciotto, S. 1999. 'Offshore: The State as Legal Fiction', in M. P. Hampton and J. P. Abbott (eds.), *Offshore Finance Centres and Tax Havens. The Rise of Global Capital*, 43–79. Basingstoke: Macmillan.

Picciotto, S. 2000. 'Lessons of the MAI: Towards a New Regulatory Framework for International Investment', *Law, Social Justice and Global Development* (www2.warwick.ac.uk/fac/soc/law/elj/lgd/2000_1/picciotto).

Picciotto, S. 2001. 'Democratizing Globalism', in D. Drache (ed.), *The Market or the Public Domain? Global Governance and the Asymmetry of Power*, 335–59. London: Routledge.

Picciotto, S. 2002. 'Copyright Licensing: The Case of Higher Education Photocopying in the UK', *European Intellectual Property Review*, 24: 438–47.

Picciotto, S. 2003a. 'Private Rights vs Public Standards in the WTO', *Review of International Political Economy*, 10: 377–405.

Picciotto, S. 2003b. 'Rights, Responsibilities and Regulation of International Business', *Columbia Journal of Transnational Law*, 42: 131–52.

Picciotto, S. 2005. 'The WTO's Appellate Body: Formalism as a Legitimation of Global Governance', *Governance*, 18: 477–503.

Picciotto, S. 2007a. 'Constructing Compliance: Game Playing, Tax Law, and the Regulatory State', *Law and Policy*, 29: 11–30.

Picciotto, S. 2007b. 'The WTO as a Node of Global Governance: Economic Regulation and Human Rights Discourses', *Law, Social Justice and Global Development*, paper 1.

Picciotto, S. and Campbell, D. I. 2003. 'Whose Molecule Is It Anyway? Private and Social Perspectives on Intellectual Property', in A. Hudson (ed.), *New Perspectives on Property Law, Obligations and Restitution*, 279–303. London: Cavendish.

Picciotto, S. and Haines, J. 1999. 'Regulating Global Financial Markets', *Journal of Law and Society*, 26: 351–68.

Picciotto, S. and Mayne, R. (eds.) 1999. *Regulating International Business. Beyond Liberalization*. Basingstoke: Macmillan.

Pierre, J. (ed.) 2000. *Debating Governance*. Oxford University Press.

Pinder, J. 1968. 'Positive and Negative Integration: Some Problems of Economic Union in the EEC', *World Today*, 24: 88–110.

Pitkethly, R. 1999. 'The European Patent System: Implementing Patent Law Harmonisation', Oxford: OIPRC.

Plant, A. 1934. 'The Economic Theory Concerning Patents for Inventions', *Economica* (new series), 1: 45.

Plasseraud, Y. and Savignon, F. 1983. *Paris 1883. Genèse du Droit Unioniste des Brevets*. Paris: Librairies techniques.

Porter, M. E. 1998. *The Competitive Advantage of Nations*. Basingstoke: Macmillan.

Porter, T. 1993. *States, Markets, and Regimes in Global Finance*. Basingstoke: Macmillan.

Power, M. 1997. *The Audit Society. Rituals of Verification*. Oxford University Press.

Prager, F. D. 1944. 'A History of Intellectual Property from 1545 to 1787', *Journal of the Patent Office Society*, 26: 711–59.

Prebble, J. 1998. 'Should Tax Legislation Be Written From a Principles and Purpose Point of View or a Precise and Detailed Point of View', *British Tax Review*, 112–23.

Preeg, E. H. 1970. *Traders and Diplomats. An Analysis of the Kennedy Round of Negotiations under the General Agreement on Tariffs and Trade*. Washington, DC: Brookings Institution Press.

Prieto-Acosta, M. G. 2006. 'Biodiversity versus Biotechnology: An economic and environmental struggle for life', in L. Williams (ed.), *International Poverty Law. An Emerging Discourse*, 48–86. London: Zed Books.

Princen, S. 2002. *EU Regulation and Transatlantic Trade*. The Hague: Kluwer Law International.

Prosser, T. 2000. 'Public Service Law: Privatization's Unexpected Offspring', *Law and Contemporary Problems*, 63: 63–82.

Prows, P. S. 2006. 'Tough Love: The Dramatic Birth and Looming Demise of UNCLOS Property Law', New York University Public Law and Legal Theory Working Papers 30.

PWC and WB 2006. *Paying Taxes. The Global Picture*. Washington, DC: World Bank and PriceWaterhouseCoopers.

Rabinowitz, V. 1978. 'The Cuban Nationalisations in the United States Courts: The Sabbatino Case and its Progeny', in J. Faundez and S. Picciotto (eds.), *The Nationalisation of Multinationals in Peripheral Economies*, 103–31. London: Macmillan.

Radaelli, C. M. 1997. *The Politics of Corporate Taxation in the European Union*. London: Routledge.

Radaelli, C. M. 2003. 'The Code of Conduct against Harmful Tax Competition. Open Method of Coordination in Disguise?', *Public Administration*, 81: 513–31.

Radice, H. 1975. *International Firms and Modern Imperialism: Selected Readings*. Harmondsworth: Penguin.

Radice, H. 1984. 'The National Economy: A Keynesian Myth?', *Capital and Class*, 22: 111–40.

Radin, M. J. 1993. *Reinterpreting Property*. Chicago University Press.

Raffaelli, M. 1995. *Rise and Demise of Commodity Agreements: An Investigation into the Breakdown of International Commodity Agreements*. Cambridge: Woodhead.

Raghavan, C. 1990. *Recolonization. GATT, the Uruguay Round and the Third World*. London: Zed Books.

Raikes, P., Larsen, M. F. and Ponte, S. 2000. 'Global Commodity Chain Analysis and the French Filière Approach: Comparison and Critique', *Economy and Society*, 29: 390–417.

Raiser, T. 1988. 'The Theory of Enterprise Law in the Federal Republic of Germany', *American Journal of Comparative Law*, 36: 111–29.

Randall, K. C. 1988. 'Universal Jurisdiction Under International Law', *Texas Law Review*, 66: 785–841.

Rangnekar, D. 2004. *The Socio-Economics of Geographical Indications*. Geneva: ICTSD–UNCTAD.

Rangnekar, D. 2010. *Geographical Indications and Localisation: A Case Study of Feni*. Warwick School of Law.

Ranitz, R. d. 1999. 'Jan Brinkhof in Conversation with Remco de Ranitz', *European Intellectual Property Reports*, 21: 142–46.

Raustiala, K. and Victor, D. G. 2004. 'The Regime Complex for Plant Genetic Resources', *International Organization*, 58: 277–309.

Raymond, E. S. 2000. 'The Cathedral and the Bazaar' (www.catb.org).

Raynalds, L. T., Murray, D. and Wilkinson, J. (eds.) 2007. *Fair Trade. The Challenges of Transforming Globalization*. Abingdon: Routledge.

Reader, W. J. 1975. *Imperial Chemicals Industries: A History. Vol. I: The First Quarter-Century*. Oxford University Press.

Rearden, W. 2006. '"A Delicate Inquiry": Foreign Policy Concerns Revive the Revenue Rule in the Second Circuit and Bar Foreign Governments from Suing Big Tobacco', *Saint Louis University Law Journal*, 51: 203–39.

Redfern, A. Hunter, M., Blackaby, N. and Partasides, C. 2004. *Law and Practice of International Commercial Arbitration*. London: Sweet & Maxwell.

Reed, M. 1999. 'From the "Cage" to the "Gaze"? The Dynamics of Organizational Control in Late Modernity', in G. Morgan and L. Engwall (eds.), *Regulation and Organizations. International Perspectives*, 17–49. London: Routledge.

Reeve, A. 1986. *Property*. London: Macmillan.

Reich, A. 1996–7. 'From Diplomacy to Law: The Juridicization of International Trade Relations', *Northwestern Journal of International Law and Business*, 17: 775–849.

Reichman, J. 1992. 'Legal Hybrids between the Patent and Copyright Paradigms', in W. F. Korthals Altes, E. J. Domenering, P. B. Hugenholtz and J. J. C. Kobel (eds.), *Information Law towards the 21st Century*, 325–61. Deventer: Kluwer Law.

Reichman, J. H. 1994. 'Legal Hybrids Between the Patent and Copyright Paradigms', *Columbia Law Review*, 94: 2432–558.

Reichman, J. H. 2001. 'Of Green Tulips and Legal Kudzu: Repackaging Rights in Subpatentable Innovation', in R. C. Dreyfuss, D. L. Zimmerman and H. First (eds.), *Expanding the Boundaries of Intellectual Property. Innovation Policy for the Information Society*, 23–53. Oxford University Press.

Reichman, J. H. and Dreyfuss, R. C. 2007. 'Harmonization without Consensus: Critical Reflections on Drafting a Substantive Patent Law Treaty', *Duke Law Journal*, 57: 85–130.

Reinhart, C. M. and Rogoff, K. S. 2008. 'Banking Crises: An Equal Opportunity Menace' (www.economics.harvard.edu/faculty/rogoff).

Reinhart, C. M. and Rogoff, K. S. 2009. *This Time is Different: Eight Centuries of Financial Folly.* Princeton University Press.

Reinicke, W. and Witte, J. M. 2000. 'Interdependence, Globalization and Sovereignty: The Role of Non-Binding International Legal Accords', in D. Shelton (ed.), *Commitment and Compliance. The Role of Non-Binding Norms in the International Legal System*, 75–100. Oxford University Press.

Reisman, W. M. 1992. *Systems of Control in International Adjudication.* Durham, NC: Duke University Press.

Renner, K. 1904. *The Institutions of Private Law and their Social Functions.* London: Routledge.

Revesz, R. 1992. 'Rehabilitating Interstate Competition: Rethinking the "Race to the Bottom" Rationale for Federal Environmental Regulation', *New York University Law Review*, 67: 1210–54.

Rhodes, R. A. W. (ed.) 1997. *Understanding Governance: Policy Networks, Governance, Reflexivity, Accountability.* Milton Keynes: Open University Press.

Ribstein, L. E. and O'Hara, E. A. 2009. *The Law Market.* Oxford University Press.

Richter, J. 1998. *Engineering of Consent. Uncovering Corporate PR Strategies.* The Cornerhouse.

Richter, J. 2001. *Holding Corporations Accountable. Corporate Conduct, International Codes and Citizen Action.* London: Zed Books.

Ricketson, S. 1987. *The Berne Convention for the Protection of Literary and Artistic Works.* Deventer: Kluwer.

Ricketson, S. 1995. 'The Future of Traditional Intellectual Property Conventions in the Brave New World of Trade-Related Intellectual Property Rights', *International Review of Industrial Property and Copyright Law*, 26: 872–99.

Ricketson, S. 2003. *WIPO Study on Limitations and Exceptions of Copyright and Related Rights in the Digital Environment.* WIPO Standing Committee on Copyright and Related Rights.

Ricketson, S. and Ginsburg, J. C. 2006a. *International Copyright and Neighbouring Rights: The Berne Convention and Beyond.* Oxford University Press.

Ricketson, S. and Ginsburg, J. C. 2006b. 'Inducers and Authorisers: A Comparison of the US Supreme Court's Grokster Decision and the Australian Federal Court's KaZaa Ruling', Columbia Public Law and Legal Theory Working Papers 0698: Columbia Law School.

Ridgeway, G. L. 1938. *Merchants of Peace: Twenty Years of Business Diplomacy Through the International Chamber of Commerce.* Boston: Little, Brown.

Rittberger, V. (ed.) 1993. *Regime Theory and International Relations.* Oxford: Clarendon Press.

Ritzer, G. 2008. *The McDonaldization of Society.* Thousand Oaks, CA: Pine Forge.

Roberts, S. 1994. 'Fictitious Capital, Fictitious Spaces: The Geography of Offshore Financial Flows', in S. Corbridge, N. Thrift and R. Martin (eds.), *Money, Power and Space*, 91–115. Oxford: Blackwell.

Rochet, J.-C. 2008. *Why Are There So Many Banking Crises?: The Politics and Policy of Bank Regulation.* Princeton University Press.

Rock, E. B. 2002. 'Coming to America?: Venture Capital, Corporate Identity and US Securities Law', Research Papers 02–07: University of Pennsylvania Law School.

Roffe, P. 1998. 'Control of Anti-Competitive Practices in Contractual Licences under the TRIPs Agreement', in C. Correa and A. A. Yusuf (eds.), *Intellectual Property and International Trade: The TRIPs Agreement* Deventer: Kluwer.

Rohatgi, R. 2007. *Basic International Taxation.* Delhi: Taxmann.

Roitman, J. L. 2005. *Fiscal Disobedience: An Anthropology of Economic Regulation in Central Africa.* Princeton University Press.

Romeo Casabona, C. M. 1999. *Biotechnology, Law, and Bioethics: Comparative Perspectives.* Brussels: Bruylant.

Rose, C. M. 1988. 'The Comedy of the Commons: Custom, Commerce, and Inherently Public Property', *University of Chicago Law Review*, 53: 711–81.

Rose, C. M. 1998. 'The Several Futures of Property: Of Cyberspace and Folk Tales, Emission Trades and Ecosystems', *Minnesota Law Review*, 83: 129–82.

Rose, C. M. 2003. 'Romans, Roads, and Romantic Creators: Traditions of Public Property in the Information Age', *Law and Contemporary Problems*, 66: 89–110.

Rose, M. 2003. 'Nine-Tenths of the Law: The English Copyright Debates and the Rhetoric of the Public Domain', *Law and Contemporary Problems*, 66: 75–87.

Rose, N. and Miller, P. 1992. 'Political Power Beyond the State: Problematics of Government', *British Journal of Sociology*, 43: 173–205.

Rose-Ackerman, S. 1997. 'The Role of the World Bank in Controlling Corruption', *Law and Policy in International Business*, 29: 93–115.

Rose-Ackerman, S. (ed.) 2006. *International Handbook on the Economics of Corruption.* Cheltenham: Edward Elgar.

Rosen, R. E. 2003. 'Risk Management and Corporate Governance: The Case of Enron', *Connecticut Law Review*, 35: 1157–84.

Rosenau, J. and Czempiel, E.-O. (eds.) 1992. *Governance without Government.* Cambridge University Press.

Rosenberg, J. 1994. *The Empire of Civil Society. A Critique of the Realist Theory of International Relations.* London: Verso.

Rosenberg, J. 2005. 'Globalization Theory: A Post-Mortem', *International Politics*, 42: 2–74.

Rosenthal, D. E., Knighton, W. M. and RIIA. 1982. *National Laws and International Commerce: The Problem of Extraterritoriality.* London: Routledge & Kegan Paul for Royal Institute of International Affairs

Roy, W. G. 1997. *Socializing Capital. The Rise of the Large Industrial Corporation in America.* Princeton University Press.

Rubin, G. 2008. 'Capital Windfall?', *ABA Banking Journal*, 100: 46–53.

Ruggie, J. G. 1982. 'International Regimes, Transactions and Change: Embedded Liberalism in the Postwar Economic Order', *International Organization*, 36: 379–415.

Ruggie, J. G. 2008. *Protect, Respect and Remedy: A Framework for Business and Human Rights.* United Nations Human Rights Council, Special Representative of the Secretary-General on the issue of Human Rights and Transnational Corporations and other business enterprises.

Ryan, M. P. 1998. *Knowledge Diplomacy. Global Competition and the Politics of Intellectual Property.* Washington, DC: Brookings Institution Press.

Safrin, S. 2002. 'Treaties in Collision? The Biosafety Protocol and the WTO Agreements', *American Journal of International Law*, 96: 606–28.

Safrin, S. 2004. 'Hyperownership in a Time of Biotechnological Promise: The International Conflict to Control the Building Blocks of Life', *American Journal of International Law*, 98: 641–85.

Sagafi-nejad, T. and Dunning, J. H. 2008. *The UN and Transnational Corporations: From Code of Conduct to Global Compact.* Bloomington: Indiana University Press.

Saint-Amans, P. and Russo, R. 2010. 'Amending Protocol Strengthens OECD Mutual Assistance Convention', *Tax Notes International*, 58: 1059–77.

Salacuse, J. 1990. 'BIT by BIT: The Growth of Bilateral Investment Treaties and their Impact on Foreign Investment in Developing Countries', *International Lawyer*, 24: 655–75.

Saldias, O. 2007. 'Supranational Courts as Engines of Disintegration – The Case of the Andean Community', Berlin Working Paper on European Integration No. 5 Free University of Berlin – Research College 'The Transformative Power of Europe'.

Sally, R. 1998. *Classical Liberalism and International Economic Order.* London: Routledge.

Samuelson, P. 2009. 'Google Books is Not a Library', 13 October, *Huffington Post.*

Samuelson, P. 2010. 'Google Book Search and the Future of Books in Cyberspace', UC Berkeley Public Law Research Paper No. 1535067.

Samuelson, P., Davis, R., Kapor, M. D. and Reichman, J. H. 1994. 'A Manifesto Concerning the Legal Protection of Computer Programs', *Columbia Law Review*, 94: 2308–431.

Sandel, M. 2009. 'A New Citizenship. The Reith Lectures' (available from www.bbc.co.uk/programmes/b00kt7rg).

Santos, B. d. S. 1987. 'Law, a Map of Misreading: Towards a Postmodern Conception of Law', *Journal of Law and Society*, 14: 279–302.

Santos, B. d. S. 1995. *Toward a New Common Sense. Law, Science and Politics in the Paradigmatic Transition.* Routledge: London.

Santos, B. d. S. 1998. 'Participatory Budgeting in Porto Alegre: Toward a Redistributive Democracy', *Politics and Society*, 26: 461–510.

Santos, B. d. S. 2002. *Toward a New Legal Common Sense*. London: Butterworths.

Santos, B. d. S. and Rodriguez Garavito, C. A. 2005. *Law and Globalization from below: Towards a Cosmopolitan Legality*. Cambridge University Press.

Sapir, A. 1998. 'The Political Economy of EC Regionalism', *European Economic Review*, 42: 717–32.

Sauvant, K. P. and Sachs, L. E. (eds.) 2009. *The Effect of Treaties on Foreign Direct Investment. Bilateral Investment Treaties, Double Taxation Treaties, and Investment Flows*. Oxford University Press.

Saville, J. 1956. 'Sleeping Partnership and Limited Liability, 1850–1856', *Economic History Review* (new series), 8: 418–33.

Sayers, R. S. 1976. *The Bank of England 1891–1944*. Cambridge University Press.

Schachter, O. 1984. 'Compensation for Expropriation', *American Journal of International Law*, 78: 121–30.

Schäfer, D. and Waters, R. 2010. 'HP raided in Moscow over €35m bribes probe', 15 April, *Financial Times*.

Schenk, C. R. 1998. 'The Origins of the Eurodollar Market in London: 1955–1963', *Explorations in Economic History*, 35: 221–38

Schepel, H. 2005. *The Constitution of Private Governance: Product Standards in the Regulation of Integrating Markets*. Oxford: Hart.

Scherer, F. M. and Weisburst, S. 1995. 'Economic Effects of Strengthening Pharmaceutical Patent Protection in Italy', *International Review of Intellectual Property and Copyright Law (IIC)*, 26: 1009–24.

Schiebinger, L. L. 2004. *Plants and Empire: Colonial Bioprospecting in the Atlantic World*. Cambridge, MA: Harvard University Press.

Schiff, E. 1971. *Industrialization without National Patents: The Netherlands, 1869–1912, Switzerland, 1850–1907*. Princeton University Press.

Schill, S. W. 2008. 'The Multilateralization of International Investment Law: The Emergence of a Multilateral System of Investment Protection on the Basis of Bilateral Treaties', Society of International Economic Law (SIEL) Inaugural Conference Paper.

Schill, S. W. 2009. *The Multilateralization of International Investment Law*. Cambridge University Press.

Schinasi, G. J. 2006. *Safeguarding Financial Stability. Theory and Practice*. Washington, DC: IMF.

Schloemann, H. 2008. 'Brazil Tyres: Policy Space Confirmed under GATT Article XX', *Bridges*, 12: 13–15.

Schloemer, E., Li, W., Ernst, K. and Keest, K. 2006. *Losing Ground: Foreclosures in the Subprime Market and Their Cost to Homeowners*. Center for Responsible Lending.

Schmidt, A. 1971. *Les Sociétés d'Auteurs SACEM–SACD: Contrats de Représentation*. Paris: Pichon & Durand-Audias.

Schmitter, P. 1996. 'The Influence of the International Context upon the Choice of National Institutions and Policies in Neo-Democracies', in L. Whitehead (ed.), *The International Dimensions of Democratization. Europe and the Americas*, 26–54. Oxford University Press.

Schmitter, P. C. and Streeck, W. 1991. 'From National Corporatism to Transnational Pluralism: Organized Interests in the Single European Market', *Politics and Society*, 19: 133–64.

Schneiderman, D. 2008. *Constitutionalizing Economic Globalization: Investment Rules and Democracy's Promise*. Cambridge University Press.

Schoenberger, E. 1997. *The Cultural Crisis of the Firm*. Oxford: Blackwell.

Schoenmaker, D. 2009. 'The Financial Trilemma in Europe', Vox.

Schorr, D. K. 2004. *Healthy Fisheries, Sustainable Trade. Crafting New Rules on Subsidies in the World Trade Organisation*. World Wildlife Fund.

Schroth, P. W. 2002. 'The United States and the International Bribery Conventions', *American Journal of Comparative Law*, 50: 593–622.

Schumpeter, J. A. 1918. 'The Crisis of the Tax State', in R. Swedberg (ed.), *The Economics and Sociology of Capitalism*. Princeton University Press.

Scott, C. 1998. 'The Proceduralization of Telecommunications Law', *Telecommunications Policy*, 22: 243–54.

Scott, C. 2002. 'Private Regulation of the Public Sector: A Neglected Facet of Contemporary Governance', *Journal of Law and Society*, 29: 56–76.

Scott, J. 1997. *Corporate Business and Capitalist Classes*. Oxford University Press.

Scott, J. 2004. 'International Trade and Environmental Governance: Relating Rules (and Standards) in the EU and the WTO', *European Journal of International Law*, 15: 307–54.

Scott, J. 2009. 'From Brussels with Love: The Transatlantic Travels of European Law and the Chemistry of Regulatory Attraction', *American Journal of Comparative Law*, 57: 897–942.

Seidl-Hohenveldern, I. 1979. 'International Economic "Soft Law"', Hague Academy of International Law, *Recueil des cours*, 163-II: 169–246.

Seidl-Hohenveldern, I. 1987. *Corporations in and under International Law*. Cambridge: Grotius Publications.

Sell, S. K. 1998. *Power and Ideas: North–South Politics of Intellectual Property and Antitrust*. Albany: State University of New York Press.

Sell, S. K. 2002. 'Trips And The Access To Medicines Campaign', *Wisconsin International Law Journal*, 20: 481–522.

Sell, S. K. 2003. *Private Power, Public Law: The Globalization of Intellectual Property Rights*. Cambridge University Press.

Servan-Schreiber, J.-J. 1967. *Le Défi Américain*. Paris: Denoël.

Seville, C. 2006. *The Internationalisation of Copyright Law: Books, Buccaneers, and the Black Flag in the Nineteenth Century*. Cambridge University Press.

Shafer, M. 1983. 'Capturing the Mineral Multinationals: Advantage or Disadvantage?', *International Organization*, 37: 93–119.

Shaffer, G. C. 2003. *Defending Interests: Public–Private Partnerships in WTO Litigation*. Washington, DC: Brookings Institution Press.

Shaffer, G. C., Ratton-Sanchez, M. and Rosenberg, B. 2008. 'The Trials of Winning at the WTO: What Lies Behind Brazil's Success', *Cornell International Law Journal*, 41: 383–502.

Shah, A. (ed.) 2007. *Participatory Budgeting*. Washington, DC: World Bank.

Shamir, R. 2004. 'Between Self-Regulation and the Alien Tort Claims Act: On the Contested Concept of Corporate Social Responsibility', *Law and Society Review*, 8: 635–64.

Shamir, R. 2008. 'The Age of Responsibilization: On Market-Embedded Morality', *Economy and Society*, 37: 1–19.

Shapren, A. J. 2003. 'Nafta Chapter 11: A Step Forward In International Trade Law Or A Step Backward For Democracy?', *Temple International and Comparative Law Journal*, 17: 323–50.

Sharman, J. C. 2006. *Havens in a Storm. The Struggle for Global Tax Regulation*. Ithaca, NY: Cornell University Press.

Sheets, J. 2000. 'Copyright Misused: The Impact of the DMCA Anti-Circumvention Measures on Fair and Innovative Markets', *Hastings Communications and Entertainment Law Journal*, 22: 1–27.

Shelton, D. (ed.) 2000. *Commitment and Compliance. The Role of Non-Binding Norms in the International Legal System*. Oxford University Press.

Sheppard, L. A. 2008. 'How Do US Holders of Swiss Accounts Come Clean? Part 2', *Tax Notes Document Service*, 26687.

Sheppard, L. A. and Sullivan, M. A. 2008. 'Offshore Explorations: Caribbean Hedge Funds, Part 1', *Tax Notes International*, 49: 108–18.

Sherman, B. and Bently, L. 1999. *The Making of Modern Intellectual Property Law. The British Experience, 1760–1911*. Cambridge University Press.

Shiller, R. J. 2000. *Irrational Exuberance*. Princeton University Press.

Shiva, V. 1997. *Biopiracy. The Plunder of Nature and Knowledge*. Boston South End Press.

Shiva, V. 2001. *Protect or Plunder? Understanding Intellectual Property Rights*. London: Zed Books.

Shiva, V. 2007. 'Biodiversity, Intellectual Property Rights, and Globalization', in B. d. S. Santos (ed.), *Another Knowledge is Possible. Beyond Northern Epistemologies*, 272–87. London: Verso.

Shivji, I. G. 1986. *Law, State and the Working Class in Tanzania*. London, Dar es Salaam: James Currey, Tanzania Publishing House.

Shukla, S. P. 2000. '*From GATT to WTO and Beyond*', WP 195 Helsinki: UNU/WIDER.

Sicular, D. R. 2007. 'The New Look-Through Rule: W(h)ither Subpart F?', *Tax Notes International*, 46: 589–623.

Sidak, J. G. 2003. 'The Failure of Good Intentions: The Worldcom Fraud and the Collapse of American Telecommunications after Deregulation', *Yale Journal on Regulation*, 20: 207–67.

Sidak, J. G. and Singer, H. J. 2004. 'Überregulation without Economics: The World Trade Organization's Decision in the US–Mexico Arbitration on Telecommunications Services', *Federal Communications Law Journal*, 57: 1–48.

Simon, H. A. 1982. *Models of Bounded Rationality*. Cambridge, MA: MIT Press.

Simon, H. A., Egidi, M. and Marris, R. 1992. *Economics, Bounded Rationality and the Cognitive Revolution*. Aldershot: Elgar.

Simpson, E. 2004. 'The Ramsay Principle: A Curious Incident of Judicial Reticence', *British Tax Review*, 358–74.

Sinacore-Guinn, D. 1993. *Collective Administration of Copyright and Neighbouring Rights*. Boston: Little, Brown.

Sinclair, T. J. 2005. *The New Masters of Capital: American Bond Rating Agencies and the Politics of Creditworthiness*. Ithaca, NY: Cornell University Press.

Singapore 1995. *Baring Futures (Singapore) Pte. Ltd: Investigation Pursuant to Section 231 of the Companies Act (Chapter 50) – The Report of the Inspectors appointed by the Minister for Finance*. Singapore: Ministry of Finance.

Singh, S. 2000. 'UN Human Rights Commissioner responds to the WTO. The UN Commissioner for Human Rights has responded to the complaints made to it by the WTO over an expert study on the human rights implications of globalization', 29 August. Geneva: SUNS.

Skeel, D. A., Jr. 2010. 'The New Financial Deal: Understanding the Dodd–Frank Act and Its (Unintended) Consequences', University of Pennsylvania Institute of Law and Economic Research Paper No. 10-21.

Sklar, M. J. 1988. *The Corporate Reconstruction of American Capitalism 1890–1916. The Market, Law and Politics*. Cambridge University Press.

Slaughter, A.-M. 1998. 'Court to Court', *American Journal of International Law*, 92: 708–12.

Slaughter-Burley, A.-M. 1993. 'International Law and International Relations Theory: A Dual Agenda', *American Journal of International Law*, 87: 205–39.

Slemrod, J. and Avi-Yonah, R. 2002. '(How) Should Trade Agreements Deal With Income Tax Issues?', *Tax Law Review*, 51: 533–54.

Smith, M. D. and Telang, R. 2009. 'Competing with Free: The Impact of Movie Broadcasts on DVD Sales and Internet Piracy', *MIS Quarterly*, 33: 321–38.

Smolders, W. 2005. 'Plant Genetic Resources for Food and Agriculture: Facilitated Access or Utility Patents on Plant Varieties?', *IP Strategy Today*, 13: 1–17.

Snyder, F. 1981. 'Anthropology, Dispute Processes, and Law: A Critical Introduction', *British Journal of Law and Society*, 8: 141–80.

Snyder, F. 2000. 'Global Economic Networks and Global Legal Pluralism', in G. A. Bermann, M. Herdegen and P. L. Lindseth (eds.), *Transatlantic Regulatory Cooperation*, 99–115. Oxford University Press.

Soederberg, S. 2009. *Corporate Power and Ownership in Contemporary Capitalism: The Politics of Resistance and Domination*. London: Routledge.

Sornarajah, M. 2004. *The International Law on Foreign Investment*. Cambridge University Press.

Soros, G. [1987] 2003. *The Alchemy of Finance: Reading the Mind of the Market*. New York: Wiley.

Spencer, D. 2007. 'International Tax Evasion', *Journal of International Taxation*, 18: (4) 44–64, (5) 36–48.

Spencer, D. 2010a. 'International Tax Cooperation. Centrifugal vs. Centripetal Forces', *Journal of International Taxation*, 21: (3) 38–51, (4) 46–60.

Spencer, D. 2010b. 'Climate Is Changing for Exchange of Information', *International Tax Review*, 21: (6) 1–3.

Spencer, D. and Sharman, J. C. 2006. 'OECD Proposals on Harmful Tax Practices. A Status Report', *Journal of International Taxation*, 17: (10) 3–20, (11) 32–39.

Spengel, C. and Wendt, C. 2007. 'A Common Consolidated Corporate Tax Base for Multinational Companies in the European Union, Some Issues and Options', WP 0717: Oxford University Centre for Business Taxation.

Srinivas, K. R. 2006. 'Intellectual Property Rights and Bio Commons: Open Source and Beyond', *International Social Science Journal*, 58: 319–34.

Steger, D. P. 2002. 'The Appellate Body and its Contribution to WTO Dispute Settlement', in D. L. M. Kennedy and J. D. Southwick (eds.), *The Political Economy of International Trade Law. Essays in Honor of Robert E. Hudec*, 482–95. Cambridge University Press.

Steil, B. (ed.) 1994. *International Financial Market Regulation*. Chichester: Wiley.

Stein, E. 1981. 'Lawyers, Judges, and the Making of a Transnational Constitution', *American Journal of International Law*, 75: 1–27.

Steiner, H. J. and Vagts, D. F. 1968. *Transnational Legal Problems: Materials and Text*. Mineola, NY: Foundation Press.

Steinmo, S. 1993. *Taxation and Democracy: Swedish, British, and American Approaches to Financing the Modern State*. New Haven, CT: Yale University Press.

STEP (ed.) 2006. *Beyond the Level Playing Field?*: Society of Trusts and Estates Practitioners.

Sterckx, S. 2000. *Biotechnology, Patents and Morality*. Aldershot: Ashgate.

Sterckx, S. 2010. 'Is the Non-Patentability of "Essentially Biological Processes" Under Threat?', *Journal of World Intellectual Property*, 13: 1–23.

Sterckx, S. and Cockbain, J. 2010. 'The Patentability of Computer Programs in Europe: An Improved Interpretation of Articles 52(2) and (3) of the European Patent Convention', *Journal of World Intellectual Property*, 13: 366–402.

Stevis, D. 2010. *International Framework Agreements and Global Social Dialogue: Parameters and Prospects*. Employment Working Paper No. 47. ILO Employment Sector.

Stewart, J. B. 1991. *Den of Thieves*. New York: Simon & Schuster.

Stewart, K. and Webb, M. 2006. 'International Competition in Corporate Taxation: Evidence from The OECD Time Series', *Economic Policy*, 21: 153–201.

Stewart, M. and Jogarajan, S. 2004. 'The International Monetary Fund and Tax Reform', *British Tax Review*, 146–74.

Stewart, T. P. (ed.) 1993. *The GATT Uruguay Round. A Negotiating History*. The Hague: Kluwer.

Stigler, G. J. 1971. 'The Theory of Economic Regulation', *Bell Journal of Economics*, 2: 3–21.

Stigler, J. E. 1998. 'More Instruments and Broader Goals: Moving Towards the Post-Washington Consensus'. The 1998 WIDER Annual Lecture, Helsinki, Finland.

Stiglitz, J. E. 2002. *Globalization and Its Discontents*. London: Allen Lane.

Stiglitz, J. E. 2008. 'Regulating Multinational Corporations: Towards Principles of Cross-Border Legal Frameworks in a Globalized World Balancing Rights with Responsibilities', *American University International Law Review*, 23: 451–558.

Stiglitz, J. E. and Chang, H.-J. 2001. *Joseph Stiglitz and the World Bank: The Rebel within: Selected Speeches*. London: Anthem Press.

Stocking, G. W. and Watkins, M. W. 1946. *Cartels in Action: Case Studies in International Business Diplomacy*. New York: Twentieth Century Fund.

Stocking, G. W. and Watkins, M. W. 1948. *Cartels or Competition?: The Economics of International Controls by Business and Government*. New York: Twentieth Century Fund.

Stone, K. 1996. 'Labour in the Global Economy. Four Approaches to Transnational Labour Regulation', in W. Bratton, J. McCahery, S. Picciotto and C. Scott (eds.), *International Regulatory Competition and Coordination*, 445–77. Oxford: Clarendon Press.

Story, J. 1997. 'Globalisation, the European Union, and German Financial Reform: The Political Economy of "Finanzplatz Deutschland"', in G. R. D. Underhill (ed.), *The New World Order in International Finance*, 245–73. Basingstoke: Macmillan.

Strandburg, K. J. 2009. 'Evolving Innovation Paradigms and the Global Intellectual Property Regime', *Connecticut Law Review*, 41: 861–920.

Strange, S. 1986. *Casino Capitalism*. Oxford: Basil Blackwell.

Strowel, A. and Doutrelepont, C. 1989. 'La socialisation du droit d'auteur a travers la généralisation des licences non volontaires: Un danger ou une nécessité?', *Revue Interdisciplinaire d'Etudes Juridiques*, 22: 133–48.

Sullivan, M. A. 2004a. 'With Billions at Stake, Glaxo puts US APA Program on Trial', *Tax Notes International Magazine*, 34: 456–63.

Sullivan, M. A. 2004b. 'Large Banks Keep More Profits in Tax Havens', *Tax Notes International*, 34: 1379–86.

Sullivan, M. A. 2007. 'Sex, Drugs and Tax Evasion', *Tax Notes International*, 46: 1291–4.

Sulston, J. and Ferry, G. 2002. *The Common Thread. Science, Politics, Ethics and the Human Genome*. London: Bantam.

Sumption, A. 1982 *Taxation of Overseas Income and Gains*. London: Butterworths.

Sutherland, P. F. 1979. 'The World Bank Convention on the Settlement of Investment Disputes', *International and Comparative Law Quarterly*, 28: 367–400.

Swank, D. and Steinmo, S. 2002. 'The New Political Economy of Taxation in Advanced Capitalist Democracies', *American Journal of Political Science*, 46: 642–55.

Switzerland–USA 2009. 'Agreement between the Swiss Confederation and the USA on the request from the Internal Revenue Service for information regarding UBS AG, a corporation established under the law of the Swiss Confederation' (www.ejpd.admin.ch).

Sykes, A. 2000. 'The Remedy for Breach of Obligations under the WTO DSU: Damages or Specific Performance?', in M. Bronckers and R. Quick (eds.), *New Directions in International Economic Law, Essays in Honour of John H. Jackson*, 347–57. The Hague: Kluwer Law.

Szeftel, M. 1998. 'Misunderstanding African Politics: Corruption and the Governance Agenda', *Review of African Political Economy*, 25: 221–40.

Tanzi, V. 1987. 'Quantitative Characteristics of the Tax Systems of Developing Countries', in D. Newbery and N. Stern (eds.), *The Theory of Taxation for Developing Countries*. Oxford University Press.

Tanzi, V. 1995. *Taxation in an Integrating World*. Washington, DC: Brookings Institution Press.

Tarbell, I. M. and Chalmers, D. M. [1904] 1966. *The History of the Standard Oil Company: Briefer Version*. New York: Harper & Row.

Tarschys, D. 2001. 'Wealth, Values, Institutions: Trends in Government and Governance', in OECD (ed.), *Governance in the 21st Century*, Paris: OECD, 27–41.

Tarullo, D. K. 2002. 'The Hidden Costs of International Dispute Settlement: WTO Review of Domestic Anti-Dumping Decisions', *Law and Policy in International Business*, 34: 109–81.

Taylor, W. 1991. 'The Logic of Global Business: An Interview with ABB's Percy Barnevik', *Harvard Business Review*, 69: 90–105.

Temin, P. 1979. 'Technology, Regulation and Market Structure in the Modern Pharmaceutical Industry', *Bell Journal of Economics*, 10: 429–46.

Tett, G. 2009. *Fool's Gold. How Unrestrained Greed Corrupted a Dream, Shattered Global Markets and Unleashed a Catastrophe*. London: Little, Brown.

Teubner, G. 1983. 'Substantive and Reflexive Elements in Modern Law', *Law and Society Review*, 17: 239–86.

Teubner, G. 1987. 'Juridification – Concepts, Aspects, Limits, Solutions', in G.
    Teubner (ed.), *Juridification of Social Spheres. A Comparative Analysis in the
    Areas of Labor, Corporate, Antitrust and Social Welfare Law*, 3–49. Berlin: de
    Gruyter.
Teubner, G. 1988. 'Enterprise Corporatism: New Industrial Policy and the 'Essence'
    of the Legal Person', *American Journal of Comparative Law*, 36: 130–
    55.
Teubner, G. 1992. 'The Two Faces of Janus: Rethinking Legal Pluralism', *Cardozo
    Law Review*, 13: 1443–62.
Teubner, G. (ed.) 1997. *Global Law without a State*. Aldershot: Dartmouth.
Teubner, G. 2002. 'Breaking Frames. Economic Globalization and the Emergence
    of *Lex Mercatoria*', *European Journal of Social Theory*, 5: 199–217.
Teubner, G. 2004. 'Global Private Regimes: Neo-Spontaneous Law and Dual Con-
    stitution of Autonomous Sectors?', in K.-H. Ladeur (ed.), *Public Governance
    in the Age of Globalization*, 71–88. Aldershot: Ashgate.
Therien, J. R. 2001. 'Exorcising the Specter of a "Pay-Per-Use" Society: Toward
    Preserving Fair Use and the Public Domain in the Digital Age', *Berkeley
    Technology Law Journal*, 16: 979–1043.
Thomson, J. E. and Krasner, S. D. 1989. 'Global Transactions and the Consolidation
    of Sovereignty', in E.-O. Czempiel and J. N. Rosenau (eds.), *Global Changes
    and Theoretical Challenges*. Lexington, MA: Lexington Books.
Tiebout, C. M. 1956. 'A Pure Theory of Local Expenditures', *Journal of Political
    Economy*, 64: 416–24.
Tietje, C. 2002. 'Global Governance and Inter-Agency Cooperation in International
    Economic Law', *Journal of World Trade*, 36: 501–15.
Timberg, S. 1955. 'Restrictive Business Practices as an Appropriate Subject for
    United Nations Action', *Antitrust Bulletin*, 1: 409–40.
TIP Expert Group 2008. *Toward a New Era of Intellectual Property: From Confronta-
    tion to Negotiation*. The Innovation Partnership, International Expert Group
    on Biotechnology, Innovation and Intellectual Property.
Tollefson, C. 2002. 'Games Without Frontiers: Investor Claims and Citizen Sub-
    missions Under the Nafta Regime', *Yale Journal of International Law*, 27:
    141–90.
Touraine, A. 1971. *The Post-Industrial Society. Tomorrow's Social History*. London:
    Wildwood House.
TRAC 2000. *Tangled Up in Blue. Corporate Partnerships at the United Nations*.
    Transnational Resource and Action Centre.
Trachtman, J. P. 1994. 'Conflict of Laws and Accuracy in the Allocation of
    Government Responsibility', *Vanderbilt Journal of Transnational Law*, 26:
    975–1057.
Trachtman, J. P. 1996. 'The International Economic Law Revolution', *University of
    Pennsylvania Journal of International Economic Law*, 17: 33–61.

Trachtman, J. P. 1998. 'Case-Note: EC – Customs Classification of Certain Computer Equipment', *European Journal of International Law*, 9: 551–2.

Trachtman, J. P. 1999. 'The Domain of WTO Dispute-Resolution', *Harvard International Law Journal*, 40: 333–77.

Treanor, J. and Tran, M. 1998. 'Markets in turmoil: rescued hedge fund was "leveraged 250 times"', 10 October, *Guardian*.

Tshuma, L. 1999. 'The Political Economy of the World Bank's Legal Framework for Development', *Social and Legal Studies*, 8: 75–96.

Turner, A. 2009. *A Regulatory Response to the Global Banking Crisis*. London: Financial Services Authority.

Turner, G. 2008. *The Credit Crunch: Housing Bubbles, Globalisation and the Worldwide Economic Crisis*. London: Pluto.

TWIN–SAL 1999. 'Enough is Enough', *Economiquity*, 2–4.

Tyler, M. 1998. *The Changing Role of Government in an Era of Telecommunications Deregulation*. Geneva: International Telecommunications Union, 7th Regulatory Colloquium.

UK Company Law Review Steering Group 2000. *Modern Company Law for a Competitive Economy: Developing the Framework*. Department for Business Innovation and Skills.

UK Inland Revenue 1967–77. *Review of Tax Havens 2*. Public Records Office File IR40/16744. London.

UK Law Commission 1997. *Legislating the Criminal Code: Corruption*. London: Law Commission.

UK Law Commission 2008. *Reforming Bribery*. LC 313.

UK Parliament 2009. *Draft Bribery Bill: Report of the Joint Committee, Oral and Written Evidence*. HL Paper 115-II, HC 430-II. London.

UK Treasury Committee 2008a. *Financial Stability and Transparency*. HC 371. London: House of Commons Treasury Committee.

UK Treasury Committee 2008b. *The Run on the Rock*. HC 56–I. London: House of Commons Treasury Committee.

UN 1974. *The Impact of Multinational Corporations on Development and on International Relations*. E/5500 rev.1. New York: United Nations.

UN 1983. *Draft Code of Conduct on TNCs*. Official Records of the Economic and Social Council, 1983, Supplement No. 7 (E/1983/17/Rev. 1), Annex II.

UN Commission on Human Rights 2000. *Globalization and its impact on the full enjoyment of human rights. Preliminary report submitted by J. Oloka-Onyango and Deepika Udagama, in accordance with Sub-Commission resolution 1999/8*. E/CN.4/Sub.2/2000/13. Sub-Commission on the Promotion and Protection of Human Rights.

UN Commission on Human Rights 2004. *The right of everyone to the enjoyment of the highest attainable standard of physical and mental health. Report of the Special Rapporteur, Paul Hunt*. E/CN.4/2004/49.

UN High Commissioner for Human Rights 2001. *The impact of the Agreement on Trade-Related Aspects of Intellectual Property Rights on human rights.* E/CN.4/Sub.2/2001/13.

UN High Commissioner for Human Rights 2002a. *Globalization and its impact on the full enjoyment of human rights.* E/CN.4/2002/54.

UN High Commissioner for Human Rights 2002b. *Liberalization of trade in services and human rights.* E/CN.4/Sub.2/2002/9.

UN High Commissioner for Human Rights 2003. *Human rights, trade and investment.* E/CN.4/Sub.2/2003/9.

UN High Commissioner for Human Rights 2004a. *Analytical study of the High Commissioner for Human Rights on the fundamental principle of participation and its application in the context of globalization.* E/CN.4/2005/41.

UN High Commissioner for Human Rights 2004b. *Analytical study of the High Commissioner for Human Rights on the fundamental principle of non-discrimination in the context of globalization.* E/CN.4/2004/40.

UN Security Council 2001. *Report of the Panel of Experts Pursuant to Security Council resolution 1343 (2001), paragraph 19, concerning Liberia.* S/2001/1015. New York.

UNCTAD (ed.) 1996a. *International Investment Instruments: A Compendium.* Geneva: United Nations.

UNCTAD 1996b. *Incentives and Foreign Direct Investment.* Geneva: United Nations.

UNCTAD 1997. *Transfer Pricing Regulations and Transnational Corporation Practices: Guidance for Developing Countries.* TD/B/ITNC/AC1(XIV)/CRP.2/Rev1. Geneva: Intergovernmental Working Group of Experts on International Standards of Accounting and Reporting.

UNCTAD 2000. *Tax Incentives and Foreign Direct Investment. A Global Survey.* ASIT Advisory Studies No. 16. Geneva.

UNCTAD 2004. *World Investment Report. The Shift Towards Services.* Geneva: UN.

UNCTAD 2005. *Investor–State Disputes Arising from Investment Treaties: A Review.* UNCTAD/ITE/IIT/2005/4. Geneva.

UNCTAD 2009. *Latest Developments in Investor–State Dispute Settlement.* UNCTAD/WEB/DIAE/IIA/2009/6.

UNCTAD–ICTSD 2005. *Resource Book on TRIPs and Development.* Cambridge University Press.

Underhill, G. R. D. (ed.) 1997. *The New World Order in International Finance.* Basingstoke: Macmillan.

US Congress 1975. *Covert Action in Chile 1963–73 (the Church Report).* US GPO 63–372. Staff Report of the Select Committee to Study Governmental Operations with Respect to Intelligence Activities.

US Congress 2003. *Staff Report of Investigation of Enron Corporation and Related Entities Regarding Federal Tax and Compensation Issues, and Policy Recommendations.* JCS-3–03. Joint Committee on Taxation.

US GAO 2006. *Company Formations. Minimal Ownership Information is Collected and Available.* GAO–06–376. Washington, DC: Government Accountability Office.

US GAO 2007. *Risk-Based Capital: Bank Regulators Need to Improve Transparency and Overcome Impediments to Finalizing the Proposed Basel II Framework.* GAO–07–253. Washington, DC: Government Accountability Office.

US GAO 2008. *Tax Administration. Comparison of Reported Tax Liabilities of Foreign – and US-Controlled Corporations, 1998–2005.* GAO–08–957. Washington, DC: Government Accountability Office.

US IRS 1984. *Sources of Information from Abroad.* Doc. 6743 (Rev.4–84) T22.2 IN 3. Washington, DC: Internal Revenue Service.

US Senate 1983 *Crime and Secrecy: The Use of Offshore Banks and Companies. Staff Study.* S. Print 98–21. Washington, DC: Senate Committee on Governmental Affairs, Permanent Subcommittee on Investigations.

US Senate 2006. *Tax Haven Abuses: The Enablers, the Tools and Secrecy.* Washington, DC: Permanent Subcommittee on Investigations of the Committee on Homeland and Security Affairs.

US Senate 2008. *Tax Haven Banks and US Tax Compliance.* Washington, DC: Permanent Subcommittee on Investigations.

US Treasury 1981. *Tax Havens and their Use by United States Taxpayers – An Overview (Gordon report).* A report by Richard A. Gordon, the Special Counsel for International Taxation, to the Commissioner of Internal Revenue, the Assistant Attorney General (Tax Division) and the Assistant Secretary of the Treasury (Tax Policy).

US Treasury 2008. *Blueprint for a Modernized Financial Regulatory Structure.* Washington, DC.

Vaidhyanathan, S. 2007. 'The Googlization of Everything and the Future of Copyright', *University of California Davis Law Review*, 40: 1207–31.

Vaitsos, C. 1970. 'Bargaining and the Distribution of Returns in the Purchase of Technology by Developing Countries', *Bulletin of the Institute of Development Studies*, 3: 16–30.

Vaitsos, C. V. 1974. *Intercountry Income Distribution and Transnational Enterprises.* Oxford: Clarendon Press.

van Der Pijl, K. 1998. *Transnational Classes and International Relations.* London: Routledge.

van Eeckhaute, J. C. 1999. 'Private Complaints against Unfair Trade Practices. The EC's Trade Barriers Regulation', *Journal of World Trade*, 33: 199–213.

van Harten, G. 2007. *Investment Treaty Arbitration and Public Law.* Oxford University Press.

van Harten, G. and Loughlin, M. 2006. 'Investment Treaty Arbitration as a Species of Global Administrative Law', *European Journal of International Law*, 17: 121–50.

van Overwalle, G. (ed.) 2009. *Gene Patents and Collaborative Licensing Models. Patent Pools, Clearinghouses, Open Source Models and Liability Regimes.* Cambridge University Press.

van Overwalle, G., Zimmeren, E. v., Verbeure, B. and Matthijs, G. 2006. 'Models for Facilitating Access to Patents on Genetic Inventions', *Nature Reviews Genetics*, 7: 143–8.

van Zyl, A. 2010. *What is Wrong with the Constituency Development Funds?* International Budget Partnership.

Vandevelde, K. J. 1998a. 'Investment Liberalization and Economic Development: The Role of Bilateral Investment Treaties', *Columbia Journal of Transnational Law*, 36: 501–27.

Vandevelde, K. J. 1998b. 'The Political Economy of a Bilateral Investment Treaty', *American Journal of International Law*, 92: 621–41.

Verbeure, B. 2009. 'Patent Pooling for Gene-Based Diagnostic Testing: Conceptual Framework', in G. van Overwalle (ed.), *Gene Patents and Collaborative Licensing Models. Patent Pools, Clearinghouses, Open Source Models and Liability Regimes*, 3–32. Cambridge University Press.

Vernon, R. 1971. *Sovereignty at Bay: The Multinational Spread of US Enterprises.* London: Penguin.

Vincent-Jones, P. 1999. 'The Regulation of Contractualisation in Quasi-Markets for Public Services', *Public Law*, 1–31.

Vitols, S. 2001. 'Varieties of Corporate Governance: Comparing Germany and the UK', in P. A. Hall and D. Soskice (eds.), *Varieties of Capitalism. The Institutional Foundations of Comparative Advantage.* Oxford University Press.

Vogel, D. 1995. *Trading Up. Consumer and Environmental Regulation in a Global Economy.* Cambridge, MA: Harvard University Press.

Vogel, D. 2005. *The Market for Virtue. the Potential and Limits of Corporate Social Responsibility.* Washington, DC: Brookings Institution Press.

Vogel, S. K. 1996. *Freer Markets, More Rules.* Ithaca, NY: Cornell University Press.

Volcker, P., Goldstone, R. and Pieth, M. 2005. *Manipulation of the Oil-for-Food Programme by the Iraqi Regime.* New York: Independent Inquiry Committee into the United Nations Oil-for-Food Programme (www.iic-offp.org).

von Hippel, E. 2005. *Democratizing Innovation.* Cambridge, MA: MIT Press.

von Lewinsky, S. (ed.) 2008. *Indigenous Heritage and Intellectual Property: Genetic Resources, Traditional Knowledge and Folklore.* London: Kluwer Law International.

Vos, E. 1999. *Institutional Frameworks of Community Health and Safety Legislation. Committees, Agencies and Private Bodies.* Oxford: Hart.

Wade, R. 1994. 'The East Asian Miracle: Why the Controversy Continues', in UNCTAD (ed.), *International Monetary and Financial Issues*, 65–79. Geneva: UNCTAD.

Wade, R. 1996. 'Japan, The World Bank, and the Art of Paradigm Maintenance: *The East Asian Miracle* in Political Perspective', *New Left Review*, 217: 3–36.

Wälde, T. W. (ed.) 1996. *The Energy Charter Treaty. An East–West Gateway for Investment and Trade.* London: Kluwer.

Waldron, J. 1988. *The Right to Private Property.* Oxford: Clarendon Press.

Walker, S. 2006. 'A Human Rights Approach to the TRIPs Agreement', in F. M. Abbott, C. Breining-Kaufmann and T. Cottier (eds.), *International Trade and Human Rights*, 171–9. Ann Arbor: University of Michigan Press.

Wall, J. F. 1990. *Alfred I. Du Pont. The Man and his Family.* Oxford University Press.

Warbrick, C. 2007. 'Recent Developments in UK Extradition Law', *International and Comparative Law Quarterly*, 56: 199–208.

Ward, H. and Lee, B. 2003. *Corporate Responsibility and the Future of the International Trade and Investment Agenda.* London: International Institute for Environment and Development.

Waris, A. 2009. 'Solving the fiscal crisis: legitimising taxation through realisation of human rights in Kenya', Ph.D. thesis in law: Lancaster University.

Waterman, P. 1988. *The Old Internationalism and the New.* The Hague: ILERI Foundation.

Waters, R. 2007. 'Amazon settles suit', 9 May, *Financial Times*.

Watson, A. 1974. *Legal Transplants: An Approach to Comparative Law.* Charlottesville: University Press of Virginia.

Watson, A. 1992. *The Evolution of International Society.* London: RKP.

Watson, A. 1993. *Legal Transplants: An Approach To Comparative Law.* Athens, GA: University of Georgia Press.

Webb, K. and Morrison, A. 2004. 'The Law and Voluntary Codes: Examining the "Tangled Web"', in K. Webb (ed.), *Voluntary Codes: Private Governance, the Public Interest and Innovation*, 97–174. Ottawa: Carleton Research Unit for Innovation Science and Environment Carleton University.

Webb, K. R. 2004. *Voluntary Codes: Private Governance, the Public Interest and Innovation.* Ottawa: Carleton Research Unit for Innovation Science and Environment Carleton University.

Weber, M., Roth, G. and Wittich, C. 1978. *Economy and Society: An Outline of Interpretive Sociology.* Berkeley: University of California Press.

Weber, S. 2004. *The Success of Open Source.* Cambridge, MA: Harvard University Press.

Weber-Fas, R. 1968 'Corporate Residence Rules for International Tax Jurisdiction: A Study of American and German Law', *Harvard Journal on Legislation*, 5: 175–251.

Wedderburn, K. W. 1985. 'The Legal Development of Corporate Responsibility', in K. J. Hopt and G. Teubner (eds.), *Corporate Governance and Directors' Liabilities. Legal, Economic, and Sociological Analyses on Corporate Social Responsibility*, 3–54. Berlin: Walter de Gruyter.

Wegner, H. C. 1993. *Patent Harmonization.* London: Sweet & Maxwell.

Weiler, J. H. H. 1991. 'The Transformation of Europe', *Yale Law Journal,* 100: 267–306.

Weiler, J. H. H. 1995. 'Does Europe Need a New Constitution? Demos, Telos and the German Maastricht Decision', *European Law Journal,* 1: 219–58.

Weiler, J. H. H. 2001. 'The Rule of Lawyers and the Ethos of Diplomats – Reflections on the Internal and External Legitimacy of WTO Dispute Settlement', *Journal of World Trade,* 35: 191–207.

Weiler, T. 2000. 'International Regulatory Reform Obligations', *Journal of World Trade,* 34: 71–94.

Weiner, J. M. 2008. 'Icelandic Bank Failure Reveals Tax Haven Links', *Tax Notes International,* 52: 443–55.

Weiner, J. M. 2009. 'Is Switzerland a Tax Haven?', *Tax Notes International,* 54: 356–60.

Weinstein, A. J. 1968. *The Corporate Ideal in the Liberal State 1900–1918.* Boston, MA: Beacon.

Weiss, L. (ed.) 2003. *States in the Global Economy. Bringing Domestic Institutions Back In.* Cambridge University Press.

Wellink, N. 2008. 'Recent market turmoil – implications for supervisors and risk managers', Remarks by Dr Nout Wellink, President of the Netherlands Bank and Chairman of the Basel Committee on Banking Supervision, at the GARP 2008 9th Annual Risk Management Convention and Exhibition, New York: BCBS.

Wells, W. 2003. *Antitrust and the Formation of the Postwar World.* New York: Columbia University Press.

Weston, B. H., Lillich, R. B. and Bederman, D. J. 1999. *International Claims: Their Settlement by Lump Sum Agreements, 1975–1995.* Ardsley, NY: Transnational Publishers.

Wheeler, D., Fabig, H. and Boele, R. 2002. 'Paradoxes and Dilemmas for Stakeholder Responsive Firms in the Extractive Sector: Lessons from the Case of Shell and the Ogoni', *Journal of Business Ethics,* 39: 297–318.

White, L. J. 2009. 'The Credit-Rating Agencies and the Subprime Debacle', *Critical Review: A Journal of Politics and Society,* 21: 389–99.

White, R. A. 2004. *Breaking Silence. The Case that Changed the Face of Human Rights.* Washington, DC: Georgetown University Press.

Whitehead, L. (ed.) 1996. *The International Dimensions of Democratization. Europe and the Americas.* Oxford University Press.

WHO–CIPIH 2006. *Public Health. Innovation and Intellectual Property Rights.* Geneva: World Health Organization, Commission on Intellectual Property Rights, Innovation and Public Health.

Wilkins, M. 1998. 'Multinational Enterprises and Economic Change', *Australian Economic History Review,* 38: 103–34.

Williams, B. 2000. 'Comment, Is Shell Report 2000's Sustainable Development Focus an Anomaly or Sign of the Future?', *Oil and Gas Journal*, 98: 74–6.

Williams, J. 1986. *The Economic Function of Futures Markets*. Cambridge University Press.

Williams, S. 2008. 'The BAE/Saudi Al-Yamamah Contracts: Implications in Law and Public Procurement', *International and Comparative Law Quarterly*, 57: 200–9.

Williamson, J. 1999. 'Whether and When to Liberalize Capital Account and Financial Services', Staff Working Papers ERAD 99–03 Geneva: WTO.

Williamson, O. 1985 *The Economic Institutions of Capitalism*. London: Collier-Macmillan.

Wilson Committee 1980. *Committee to Review the Functioning of Financial Institutions*. Cmnd 7937. London: UK Government.

Winickoff, D., Jasanoff, S., Busch, L., Grove-White, R. and Wynne, B. 2005. 'Adjudicating the GM Food Wars: Science, Risk, and Democracy in World Trade Law', *Yale Journal of International Law*, 30: 81–123.

Winter, G. 1992. 'Patent Law Policy in Biotechnology', *Journal of Environmental Law*, 4: 167–87.

Wolf, M. 2007. 'Why the credit squeeze is a turning point for the world', 11 December, *Financial Times*.

Wolfe, R. 2005a. 'Decision-Making and Transparency in the "Medieval" WTO: Does the Sutherland Report have the Right Prescription?', *Journal of International Economic Law*, 8: 631–45.

Wolfe, R. 2005b. 'See You in Geneva? Legal (Mis)Representations of the Trading System', *European Journal of International Relations*, 11: 339–65.

Woodmansee, M. 1984. 'The Genius and the Copyright: Economic and Legal Conditions of the Emergence of the "Author"', *Eighteenth-Century Studies*, 17: 425–48.

Woods, N. 2006. *The Globalizers: The IMF, the World Bank, and their Borrowers*. Ithaca, NY: Cornell University Press.

Woolcock, S. 1996. 'Competition Among Rules in the Single European Market', in W. Bratton, J. McCahery, S. Picciotto and C. Scott (eds.), *International Regulatory Competition and Coordination. Perspectives on Economic Regulation in Europe and the United States*, 289–321. Oxford University Press.

Woolf, L. S. 1916. *International government; two reports by L. S. Woolf prepared for the Fabian Research Department, together with a project by a Fabian Committee for a supernational authority that will prevent war*. London: Fabian Society.

World Bank 1983. *World Development Report*. Washington, DC.

World Bank 1988. *World Development Report*. Washington, DC.

World Bank 1993. *The East Asian Miracle*. Washington, DC.

World Bank 2005. *Global Economic Prospects 2005: Trade, Regionalism and Development*. Washington, DC.

WTO Consultative Board 2004. *The Future of the WTO*. Geneva: World Trade Organization.

Wuerth, I. 2009. 'Wiwa v. Shell: The $15.5 Million Settlement', *ASIL Insights*, 13 (14).

Wynne, B. 1992. 'Risk and Social Learning', in S. Krimsky and D. Golding (eds.), *Social Theories of Risk*, 275–97. Westport, CT: Praeger.

Xanthaki., H. 2001. 'Centros: Is This Really the End for the Theory of the Siège Réel', *Company Lawyer*, 22: 2–8.

Xiao, G. 1998. 'Reforming the Governance Structure of China's State-Owned Enterprises', *Public Administration and Development*, 18: 273–80.

Yeung, H. W.-C. 1998. *Transnational Corporations and Business Networks: Hong Kong Firms in the ASEAN Region*. London: Routledge.

Yi, Y.-J. 2004. 'Standards and science in trade regulation in the global age: a critique of the WTO SPS Agreement in relation to public health and safety concerns', Ph.D. thesis in law: Lancaster University.

Yntema, H. E. 1953. 'The Historic Bases of Private International Law', *American Journal of Comparative Law*, 2: 297–317.

Yntema, H. E. 1966. 'The Comity Doctrine', *Michigan Law Review*, 65: 9–30.

Young, A. K. 1979. *The Sogo Shosha: Japan's Multinational Trading Companies*. Boulder, CO: Westview Press.

Young, M. A. 2007. 'The WTO'S Use of Relevant Rules of International Law: An Analysis of the Biotech Case', *International and Comparative Law Quarterly*, 56: 907–30.

Young, M. A. 2009. 'Fragmentation or Interaction: The WTO, Fisheries Subsidies and International Law', *World Trade Review*, 8: 477–515.

Young, M. A. (ed.) 2011. *Regime Interaction in International Law*. Cambridge University Press.

Zaki, M. 2004. 'Face à Londres, la Suisse se positionne comme place "proper" pour les trusts', 22 November, Geneva, *Le Temps*.

Zammit, A. and Utting, P. 2006. *Beyond Pragmatism: Appraising UN – Business Partnerships*. Geneva: UN Research Institute for Social Development.

Zapatero, P. 2009. 'Legal Imagination in Vitoria: The Power of Ideas', *Journal of the History of International Law*, 11: 221–71.

Zee, H. H. 1996. 'Empirics of Cross-country Tax Revenue Comparisons', *World Development*, 24: 1659–71.

Zee, H. H., Stotsky, J. G. and Ley, E. 2002. 'Tax Incentives for Business Investment: A Primer for Policy Makers in Developing Countries', *World Development*, 30: 1497–516.

Zeile, W. J. 1997. 'US Intrafirm Trade in Goods', *Survey of Current Business*, February, 23–38.

Zhang, P. G. 1995. *Barings Bankruptcy and Financial Derivatives*. Singapore: World Scientific.

Zoller, E. 1985. 'Remedies for Unfair Trade: European and United States Views', *Cornell International Law Journal*, 18: 227–45.

Zukin, S. and DiMaggio, P. (eds.) 1990. *Structures of Capital. The Social Organization of the Economy*. Cambridge University Press.

INDEX